This is a volume in
THE UNIVERSITY OF MICHIGAN HISTORY OF THE MODERN WORLD
Upon completion, the series will consist of the following volumes:

The United States to 1865 *by Michael Kraus*

The United States since 1865 *by Foster Rhea Dulles*

Canada: A Modern History *by John Bartlet Brebner*

Latin America: A Modern History *by J. Fred Rippy*

Great Britain to 1688: A Modern History *by Maurice Ashley*

Great Britain since 1688: A Modern History *by K. B. Smellie*

France: A Modern History *by Albert Guérard*

Germany: A Modern History *by Marshall Dill, Jr.*

Italy: A Modern History *by Denis Mack Smith*

Russia and the Soviet Union: A Modern History *by Warren B. Walsh*

The Near East: A Modern History *by William Yale*

The Far East: A Modern History *by Nathaniel Peffer*

India: A Modern History *by Percival Spear*

The Southwest Pacific to 1900: A Modern History *by C. Hartley Grattan*

The Southwest Pacific since 1900: A Modern History *by C. Hartley Grattan*

Spain: A Modern History *by Rhea Marsh Smith*

Africa to 1875: A Modern History *by Robin Hallett*

Africa since 1875: A Modern History *by Robin Hallett*

INDIA

A Modern History

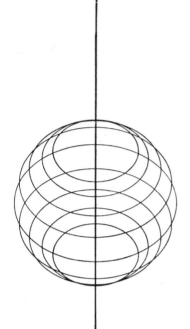

The University of Michigan History of the Modern World
Edited by Allan Nevins and Howard M. Ehrmann

INDIA

A Modern History

BY PERCIVAL SPEAR

NEW EDITION
REVISED AND ENLARGED

Ann Arbor: The University of Michigan Press

TO THE PEOPLE OF
INDIA IN DEEP GRATITUDE
FOR ALL THEY HAVE TAUGHT ME
*And specially
to the citizens of Delhi,
a much-loved city*

Preface

The purpose of this book is to portray the transformation of India under the impact of the West into a modern nation state. But India, as the seat of an ancient civilization, the creator of two world religions and the host of two cultures, has her roots deep in the past. The present cannot be understood without reference to these influences from the past, some still powerful as in the case of caste, and some still active and creative as in the case of certain aspects of Hindu thought. Mahatma Gandhi has reminded us that the world can still be moved by ancient creeds as well as by modern slogans. For this reason more space has been given to the early history of India than is usual in some works of this series. Indian society itself has its beginnings in the third millennium B.C. and reached full stature in the first millennium A.D. Down the centuries there have been successive developments which are still living influences today. The plan of this book has therefore been to give a general historical view of India's past, emphasizing those aspects which time has proved to have been creative agents in the formation of the present. Thus, the formation of Hindu society, Buddhism, the rise of the Rajputs, and the coming of Islam are treated as themes relevant to the present, while the details of wars and dynastic lists, chronological controversies, and changes of frontiers are omitted as irrelevant.

So we proceed until the period of the Mughal Empire (1526–1761). An effort has been made to give a picture of India at that time, as being the last period of Indian independence immediately preceding the British occupation. Much that was accomplished by them would have been impossible but for the previous achievements of the Mughals.

From the mid-eighteenth century the emphasis has been on the transformation of India under Western influences and the rise of the modern Indian nation.

The spelling in general follows the system adopted by Sir W. W. Hunter and used by him in his *Gazetteer of India*. Exceptions are words like Lucknow, which had already established themselves with an accepted spelling. Diacritical marks have been omitted.

The presentation of money values has posed a problem. Until the end of the nineteenth century the rupee was generally valued at about ten to the English pound. Since the twenties it has been about thirteen to the pound. Rupee values have been generally turned into dollars at the current exchange rate of a little less than three dollars to the pound. But such devices often fail to give an adequate sense of comparative values. Another method, which has been attempted in some instances, is to assess relative values in terms of purchasing power. For instance Akbar's revenue at the end of his reign in 1605 was about twenty times, in terms of real value, that of James I of England at the beginning of his reign in 1603.

This book owes much to many persons and sources. But chiefly I would like to mention the faculty and students of history at the Berkeley campus of the University of California: the faculty which by their generous invitation provided the occasion for the preparation of the lectures which were the basis of this book, and the students who by their interest and attention encouraged me to proceed from speech to paper. Nor can I forget those Indian friends who, during my twenty years' residence in India, gave me an insight into the country and its people, interested me in the subject and encouraged me to pursue it. And finally to my wife, whose insight and shrewd criticism improved the form and added wisdom to the book.

PREFACE TO THE SECOND EDITION

For the second edition of this book I have thought it best to leave the main body of the work unchanged. The aim has been to bring the record down to the end of 1971, thus including the Indo-Pakistan confrontation of December 1971 in the twelve days war. To this end Chapter XL, *Nehru's India,* has been revised and enlarged to cover the last eight years of his life to his death in 1964. A new chapter XLI has been added, entitled *Contemporary India,* which covers the Shastri and Indira Gandhi ministries to the end of 1971. *Concluding Reflections* now becomes Chapter XLII. The list of "Suggested Readings" has been revised throughout and a number of new titles added. An effort has been made to explain and assess the recent changes both in India's internal politics and economy and in her external relations and situation.

Contents

INDIA

A Modern History

Introduction

✿ PHYSICAL BACKGROUND

The history of India provides both an inspiration and a challenge to the historian. It inspires by its vast range and scope, its color, its variety, its rich cluster of personalities; it challenges with its complexities, its long periods of obscurity, its unfamiliar movements, and its stark contrasts between luxury and poverty, between gentleness and cruelty, creation and destruction. For the few with gorgeous processions and rainbow pageantry there were the many with mud huts and a handful of rice or millet a day, with the burning heaven for a canopy and the stifling dust for perfume.

In India everything seems strange at first sight to the foreign observer. The climate, the face of the country, the nature of the people, their habits, institutions, thoughts, and worship all present surprises and riddles. The Westerner considers the earth and his surroundings to be solid but the Indian regards them as *maya* or illusion; the healthy eater finds most advanced Indians to be vegetarian; the Western belief in force and power is matched by the Indian belief in thought and nonviolence. The introduction of Western ideas and customs has only increased the confusion. Here are operators on the Bombay Stock Exchange devoting their gains to the protection and veneration of the cow, and cotton-mill magnates subscribing funds for the encouragement of hand spinning and weaving. There are keen businessmen who do nothing without the advice of an astrologer and men of action who are at times unavailable because they have passed into meditation. If we seek to understand Indian people and things in terms of Western experience we shall certainly fall into many pitfalls, and it is therefore best that we should begin this work with a survey of the Indian scene and some consideration of relationships in general between India and the West.

Physically, India forms with Pakistan, Burma, and Ceylon a sub-continent well marked by geography. Ceylon is separated from India only by a shallow strait; Pakistan has no physical barrier between it and India save the Thar Desert adjacent to Sind. Only Burma is more remote, being cut off from India by a tangle of hills and tropical jungle. But she is more easily accessible by sea from India than by land from southeast Asia, and though her present form of Buddhism came from Siam, her trading connections and a significant element in her population come from India. The subcontinent itself is bounded on the north by the great Himalaya or Snowy Range, spreading in the northwest to the complex of mighty ranges known as the Karakoram and the Hindu Kush, rising toward the northeast to the peaks of Everest and Kinchinjanga, and though moderating its height to the east, retaining its impenetrability with dense hill-clad jungle. The reason for this impenetrability is not only the height of these mountains or the virulence of the mosquitoes which the jungles breed; it is the depth of the hill systems which stretch beyond. North of the Himalayas extends the lofty and desolate Tibetan Plateau, and north of that again the Gobi Desert, while the eastern jungles stretch across a series of parallel valleys with turbid rivers far into southeast Asia. To the northwest there is again a plateau—of Afghanistan leading into that of Iran and the plains of Turkestan. But here the heights are more moderate, the passes easier, and the hinterland beyond more prosperous and populated. It is therefore here, through the Khyber Pass and Khurram Valley in the north, and the Bolan and other passes in the south, that new arrivals have entered into India. For the rest, India is bounded by the sea, which has proved a highway for commerce, both east and west, but whose expanse has been too great to allow large-scale migrations, like the Anglo-Saxon move to England. We thus find in South India a meeting place of merchants and in the north a crucible of nations.

But Indian history has not only been determined by the existence of passes in the northwest or marine highways in the south. The configuration of India itself has been of great significance. We may first note the two great river systems of the Indus and the Ganges. Together these form two great level corridors running from the mountains southward to the Indian Ocean and southeastward from the upper Indus itself to the Bay of Bengal. You can travel from Peshawar to Karachi by train without passing through a tunnel, and do the same from Rawalpindi to Calcutta, distances of 900 and 1,663 miles by rail, respectively. The watershed between the river Jumna in the Ganges system and the Sutlej in the Indus system is so slight as to be imperceptible to the traveler.

With the exception of the middle sections of the Indus which are rainless and the Salt Range between Attock and Rawalpindi these great riverine plains are highly fertile, with a climate which in many places will grow two crops a year—wheat to the north and rice in Bengal.

We may next notice the Thar Desert and the barren lands of Rajasthan, which separate Sind from the rest of India no less effectively with their sand than the mountains divide India from China. South of the Ganges lies central India with its extensive pattern of hills and forests. The hills are not very high and the forests not very tropical, but their extent has formed a barrier which has hindered without quite forbidding intercourse beyond them. The river Chambal is usually regarded as marking the southern limit of Hindustan or northern India and the river Narbada as the boundary of the Deccan.

The Deccan is a great plateau in the center of the Indian peninsula. It is furrowed by great rivers like the Godavari and the Kistna, but they are not navigable like the northern streams. It is buttressed, as it were, by chains of hills or ghats on either side which catch most of the sea-borne monsoon rain. This feature together with the nature of the soil makes it less fertile than the northern plains. Toward the west the hills fall away to the valleys of the Narbada and the Tapti, leading to the fertile plains of Gujarat and Kathiawar, the modern and ancient Saurashtra. On either side of the Deccan Plateau the hills fall away to coastal plains, where typically tropic conditions prevail. That on the east, known as the Carnatic, is broader and more fertile, while that on the west, the country of Malabar, is narrow, picturesque, and indented until it broadens into the plain of Travancore. Here pepper, cardamon, and sandalwood grow and elephants are trapped in the teak forests.

We thus have tropical conditions along the plains of the east and west coasts, into Gujarat on the western side and through Orissa to Bengal on the eastern. The seasons are marked by the monsoon rains and the climate is generally damp, steamy, and enervating. Wherever a level space can be found the fruits of nature abound; the feeling is one of exuberant life welling up from within nature. Over the Deccan, central India, and the northern plain as far as Oudh, the climate is generally subtropical. Lack of moisture inhibits such tropical crops as rice and the same factor produces a perceptible alternation of hot and cold seasons. Subtropical crops like cotton, indigo, and sugar prosper wherever the soil is suitable. Over the northern plain from the Ganges to the Indus the climate may be called continental, while over Rajasthan desert or semidesert conditions prevail. In the Punjab and as far as Delhi great summer heats rising to 120° Fahrenheit are followed by bracing cold and chilling north winds producing frost. Here temperate crops such as wheat and pulses prevail, though the almost constant sun makes two crops possible in a year wherever water is available. Water is the desire of the north and dust the great enemy; salubrity is the quest of Bengal and the south, while over all the sun presides; monsoon rains and dust-laden clouds are but interludes to the enduring splendor of its rays. Finally, we must not forget the great hills of the north where all climates from the luxuriantly tropical to the arctic are to be found in ascending tiers. Perhaps the dominant impression of their southern slopes is the trees, beginning with the cactus and the prickly pear in the foothills, past the odoriferous and tuneful pines to the great deodars and other firs which add dignity and solemnity to the silence and the great spaces of the mountains.

These physical factors have exercised a very important influence upon the destiny of India. In the south and Bengal the tropic conditions have endowed these areas with natural products and made them marts of commerce while limiting the energies and physique of the people. In the north the more bracing air has nurtured hardier races, which the rich soil has maintained. It has thus been the northern races which have tended to aggression and the southern of whom we have the longest record of commerce.

But it is not only climate and soil which have affected the fortunes of India; the configuration of the country has been even more significant. We may first note the northwest passes to the Indus Valley. These passes derive their importance from the fact that they connect with the Iranian Plateau of Afghanistan and Iran, which again, through passes over the Hindu Kush Mountains or the strategic gap of Herat, leads into that great reservoir of the human race, the plains of Turkestan and the steppes of Central Asia. These passes have therefore been the main means of ingress into India, not only because they were passes but because there were peoples beyond them ready to pass through. Once descended to the Indus, the newcomers were guided by the shape of the country. Those who went south into Sind found themselves, as it were, in a blind alley which they could occupy but not leave. The sea blocked them to the south and the Thar Desert no less effectively barred them to the east.

The desert and the hills of Kashmir and the Panjab form a natural corridor down which invaders passed until they reached the upper Jumna River on the Ambala-Delhi-Agra axis. From here one route continued southeastward to the Bay of Bengal, while another led south, across the Chambal River through Malwa toward central India.

The former was the easier and more attractive route and was the usual first line of progress. But the latter was also practicable and without special difficulty. Having proceeded as far as Gujarat to the southwest and the Narbada to the south, however, the migrants found themselves faced with great semiarid hilly regions of east-central and central India. Here migration tended to stop, and so we find today that the south still retains its early racial characteristics and shows little sign of northern mixtures.

But while migration as such was difficult beyond the Narbada, intercourse was not impossible. In consequence we find that northern cultural influence spread to the south. India is today a land of a single culture, and one of the chief strongholds of traditional Hinduism, which developed in the north, is now to be found in the south. Nowhere are the Brahmins more influential or possessive than in the south. The "fundamental unity of India" is a cultural and not a racial phenomenon.

In the political sphere also the north expanded to the south but here another principle came into play. States require agents to maintain their authority and agents have to be transported. The physical obstacle of central India was not great enough to inhibit an army from moving into the south. But it was serious enough to make it difficult to reinforce that army and maintain political power. The long lines of communication across difficult country, the slow and vulnerable means of transport made supply and support precarious, so that any check to a northern power was apt to mean the isolation of its agents in the south. The south was prosperous enough to attract the north, and weak enough to be periodically conquered. But then central India, like a sluice over which an advancing wave has flowed, has interposed to cut off the southern dominion from its source of power. So we have, as in the case of the Mauryans, the Turks, and the Mughals, northern empires reaching out for southern rule only to break down in the moment of achievement because of the strain on their lines of supply.

Socially, the geography of India has also had very important consequences. It has few naturally separate areas which a group could occupy and there develop an individual consciousness or in which a number of people who had been thrown together could develop a common feeling of unity. Indian geography supplied no Iberian Peninsula as for the Spanish nation, no France bounded by the sea and the Pyrenees, no England hedged by the silver sea. Where such areas did exist, they have either been too small to withstand attack as with the Vale of Kashmir, or too broken up within themselves, as in the case of the subalpine Himalayan tracts. The great geographical areas of India shade off into one another without any clearly defined boundaries. In consequence, invading peoples, once they have overcome initial resistance, have tended to move *across* both peoples and country to the limit of their capacity for expansion. Instead of displacing the occupiers, as the Saxons did the Britons in England, they superimposed themselves. Thus arose that special feature of Indian society, the existence of races in social tiers, instead of side by side in contiguous groups. The racial as well as the social division of society was horizontal instead of vertical. This pattern of social life encouraged the caste system, which itself tended to preserve the racial distinctions by giving them a sacred character and inhibiting intermarriage.

Finally, we may note certain "pockets" which seem to lie outside the general pattern just described. One of these is Kashmir, whose fertile and picturesque vale lies to one side of the main route into India from the northwest. It has proved too small to develop a nationality of its own and too weak to withstand successive invaders. Historically, it has been a rock pool on the shore of Indian history, overrun by successive tides of foreign invasion and exposed again as each tide receded. The coast of Malabar was too indented to encourage Malayali unity; that factor and the foreign trade which was the chief occupation of the area promoted instead the growth of city-states, of which Calicut with its Zamorin was the most famous and long-lived. It is not so easy to see why Gujarat did not attain national consciousness, for it had geographical unity and separation, fertility, and a degree of racial homogeneity. In this case it would appear that the Rajput clan system with its organization of society into aristocrats and others, and its political patchwork system, was responsible.

The geopolitical position of India in relation to the neighboring land masses and the ocean may conveniently be considered at this point. We have seen that the north has been the main center of Indian power in historical times, because of its great expanses of fertile plain and its more vigorous inhabitants. It is only when the north is strong that invaders can be kept beyond the Indus. We are apt to remember the occasions when they marched through rather than when they were driven back. Yet these occasions did occur, as when Chandragupta Maurya drove back the Seleucid Greeks, Pushyamitra the Bactrian Greeks, and the sultans of Delhi kept at bay the Mongols. Yet this was not the only condition of Indian stability. The next westward seat of power has been historically the Iranian plateau, and much depended on the nature of its control. Beyond Iran lay Turkestan and Central Asia with their vast and incalculable reserves of nomadic man power.

A strong Iran was therefore necessary as well as a strong northern India. A strong Iran and weak India might mean incursions into India like that of Nadir Shah the Persian and Ahmad Shah the Afghan in the eighteenth century. A strong India with a weak Iran meant that India might still be exposed to attack from central Asia, as in the time of the Mongols in the thirteenth century.

From the Indian point of view, a strong Iran was desirable in order to control the dam containing the central Asian reservoir of man power. When a strong power existed in both areas a balance was formed which tended to promote stability. Examples of this state of affairs are the Mauryan and Seleucid regimes in the second century B.C., the Gupta and Sassanid empires in the fourth and fifth centuries A.D., and the Mughal and Safavid empires in the sixteenth and seventeenth centuries. One of the early mistakes of the British in India was to seek a balance of power *within* India. Historical experience has shown that such balances, whether attempted between the Deccan and the south, or between north and south, have been unstable and illusory; geography and the potentials of power, or in other words the geopolitical facts, work toward the domination of the subcontinent by a power centered in the north. The true balance of power is to be found *outside* India, that is to say, between centers in Iran and North India respectively. In parenthesis it may be remarked that the Indian position today is unstable, because the Iranian power is weak and divided (between Iran, Afghanistan, and Pakistan), while the central Asian power is formidable. Security from the latter can only be obtained by reliance on a transoceanic source of power, which means that the Indian destiny may be affected by many forces and accidents beyond the reach of the most skillful diplomacy.

But we must not lose sight of certain other factors in India's geopolitical position, which in modern times have become of greater significance than formerly. The first of these is the control of the East Indies, which constitute India's eastern gateway to the world. Not only are the East Indian products and markets important in themselves so that their removal or hostile manipulation would be a serious matter for India, but the East Indies also form the gateway to the farther East with its great centers of civilization, trade, and power. Hostile control of the East Indies could injure Indian trade and direct a threat to Indian integrity. Full security therefore requires Indian or friendly control of Indonesia. Until recent times the East Indies were less significant to India than the northwest passes, because the complex of power situated there was much less, and it was far less subject to incursions from the further East. But modern developments have underlined both these elements as factors in Indian security. The Dutch control of the East Indies in the nineteenth century tended to obscure the reality of the situation, for it was not then generally realized that the Dutch were, in a sense, agents of the British controlling power. The workings of the principles of sea power involved Dutch dependence on Britain in Asia during this period so that the East Indies were, in fact, a part of the British-Indian power system. But the Japanese incursion during World War II vividly exposed the underlying realities. Today no Indian government can be indifferent to what happens in the East Indies.

A final factor in Indian geopolitics is the sea in general. As a means of trade it has been important since classical times when Arab and Greek, Syrian and Jew braved its dangers for the rewards of the spice trade. It became of political importance when ships could sail direct from Europe around Africa. During the eighteenth century this fact altered the fate of India. But while India can never be indifferent to the sea, it should be remembered that sea power only became a vital factor in Indian affairs when her own center of land power had broken down. Had this remained intact, the contests of English and French in the eighteenth century would have been no more momentous for India than the rivalries of English and Portuguese in the early seventeenth century. While we can say, therefore, that the sea is a factor of importance in the Indian scene, we must add that it is not a vital one. The vital factors through Indian history have been the establishment of a strong land center within India itself, and the control of the Iranian Plateau or friendship or balance with the dominant powers there. Modern developments have added a third: control of, or friendship with, the East Indian powers.

✿ RACES, LANGUAGES, AND PEOPLES

India has no typical figure such as America's Uncle Sam, Britain's John Bull, or France's Marianne. The reason is not far to seek. Indian unity has so far been too fleeting and the sentiment of nationalism too recent to produce a symbolic figure. Or perhaps we should say that these two factors have not yet been able to overcome the basic obstacles to the emergence of such a figure. These are the immense diversity both of the peoples and the traditions of India. Typical figures of the south do not suit the north, nor do traditional figures like Rama and Sita fit in with modern conditions. The *sannyasi,* the rajah, the frontiersman, the beturbaned Rajput have all at times been put forward as typical figures but none has received general acceptance nor would be regarded as satisfactory by present-day India.

Indian diversity runs through the categories of the physical, the cultural, and the linguistic. The mixture of the basic physical types has produced the distinct races of India, which in turn have developed the various languages now spoken. In the first of these fields we rely upon the anthropologist, and in the second upon the philologist. It is only when we come to culture that the historian comes in with the sociologist.

Little is known of the earliest inhabitants of India as of primitive man everywhere, except that they must have been forest-dwellers, root gatherers, and hunters. It is surmised that these dwellers were possibly of the Australoid type, akin to the peoples now to be found in Australia, New Guinea, and parts of the East Indies. Relics of these people are still found in the forests of South India. But the main physical substructure of the Indian races today is the Dravidian type. With their dark skin, low stature, long heads, and broad noses people of this kind spread throughout the subcontinent in prehistoric times. They remain dominant in the south with only slight intermixtures from elsewhere. Their characteristic features are to be found today in the Santal people of Chota Nagpur. To this was added, around the northern and eastern edges of India, a tincture of the Mongolian racial type, the basis of the races of central and eastern Asia. In Bengal and Assam the mixture is considerable, but otherwise the Mongolian influence does not extend much beyond the foothills of the Himalayas.

The third main physical constituent of India is that of the Aryan-speaking peoples, or more properly the Caucasian physical type of tall, fair-haired, long-headed, and aquiline-featured people. These have moved into India during historic times as invaders and migrants, beginning with the early Aryan-speaking peoples of the second millennium B.C. down to the Turko-Iranians from the eleventh century A.D. onward. It is the mixture of these types in varied proportions and different localities which has produced the various physical strands in India today. Before enumerating them let us remember that a physical type is not the same thing as a race or a nation, which is held together by intangible cultural and spiritual strands as well as physical likeness. A race or nation, indeed, like the Bengali, may contain more than one physical type, while a type like the Dravidian may express itself in more than one racial form, such as the Tamils and the Andhras.

The simplest and most prominent physical type is the Dravidian, which extends from the Vindhya Mountains through the Deccan to

Cape Comorin. Apart from certain intrusions in the west, to be mentioned presently, the Dravidian type is dominant throughout this region. The only modifications are a certain Aryan intermixture in the upper castes of the south, some Australoid influence from the aboriginal tribes, and some Arab and other foreign blood on the west coast. In the west and north of India we find a Dravidian substructure, the racial types being produced by mixtures on a large scale of Dravidian and other races, Caucasian or Mongoloid. In the west of the peninsula is to be found the type known as the Scytho-Dravidian, produced by a mixture of invaders with the local inhabitants. They are fairer in complexion than the pure Dravidian, with finer noses; they have broad heads and are of medium stature. Examples of this type are the Maratha Brahmins and the Kunbis.

In the heart of Hindustan, in the modern state of Uttar Pradesh, is to be found the Aryo-Dravidian type, extending through Behar and to parts of Rajasthan. Their form is the result of fusion of the local Dravidians with the early Aryan-speaking tribes of the Vedic and Epic ages. Their stature is medium to short, often stocky, their color light to dark brown, the head long to medium and the nose medium to short. These are the people who have formed the core of the modern Indian Congress and can be said, in a sense, to be the present ruling race of India.

In the Panjab, Rajasthan, and Kashmir the Caucasian element is stronger, reinforced as it has been by a series of later invasions. Here is to be found the Indo-Aryan type, tall and fair, with dark eyes and long head and with narrow and prominent nose. Some of the Rajputs, the Khatris of the Panjab, and many of the Jats belong to this group. They are thought to be the nearest approach to the physical type of the original Aryan invaders of India. Further to the northwest the later arrivals have provided the dominant strain to produce the Turko-Iranian type. This group includes the frontier tribes and the Baluchis. They are generally tall and fair, with broad heads, dark eyes, and long aquiline noses. Sir William Jones in the late eighteenth century concluded from their looks that they were the Lost Ten Tribes. Though an important section of the Baluchis speaks the Dravidian tongue of Brahui it would seem that there is little Dravidian blood left in this region or trace of the early Aryan invaders. Turkish and Iranian strains dominate the area.

In the remaining corner of India we find another Dravidian mixture but this time compounded with Mongolian blood. The extensive mixture of Mongolian and Dravidian strains has produced the Mongolo-Dravidian type which prevails in lower Bengal and Orissa, except where pockets of pure Dravidians exist such as in the Santal parganas. The type includes the Bengal Brahmins and Kayasths and the Muslims of East Pakistan; its members are dark, with broad heads, medium stature, and medium to broad noses. Finally, there is the Mongoloid type, modified only by small infusions of Dravidian and "Aryan" blood. Of a small but sturdy physique, these people display marked Mongolian features. They are dark yellow in color, with flat faces and slanting eyes, with noses fine to broad and broad heads. They are to be found in the hills of Assam, in Bhutan, Sikkim, and Nepal, and along the Himalayas as far as Little Tibet in northern Kashmir.

The languages of India are as various as its races and peoples. Sir George Grierson, in his great Linguistic Survey, listed 225 distinct languages in addition to dialects, which in some parts of India, as the Himalayas, vary almost from valley to valley. But while this classification is scientifically justified, the position is not in fact as complicated as the statement suggests. Many of the languages are spoken by very few people, while others are closely related and can be understood by members of other language groups. The languages of India can, in fact, be reduced to three main families, two of which include the great majority of the inhabitants. The smallest of the groups is the Munda or Kolarian languages, which are those of primitive tribes unrelated either to the Dravidian or Aryan languages.

We are thus left with the two main families, the Dravidian and the Aryan. The Dravidian languages spread from the borders of Orissa through eastern and southern India to Cape Comorin. Tamil may be called the senior of the group, since it was the first to develop a literature of its own which was for some centuries unaffected by northern influences. Tamil is spoken along the Coromandel coast from Madras southward and inland on the coastal plain as far as Bangalore. Northward from Madras, Telugu is spoken along the coast to Orissa, and inland through much of the former Hyderabad state and the northern districts of the old Madras Presidency. Its limits are now sufficiently defined by the boundaries of the newly formed Andhra state. Kanarese, or Kannada, is spoken in the Mysore Plateau, its limits being defined by the newly enlarged Mysore state. The fourth Dravidian language is Malayali, which is spoken along the Malabar coast and through Travancore. Again, the new state of Kerala broadly indicates its area.

When we proceed to the Aryan group of languages we meet with more complication. Their areas of dominance are not so well defined, nor are the genealogies so simple. The early invaders of India spoke a language, or perhaps a group of dialects, which are described by philologists as belonging to the Aryan group of languages. To this group belong the Greek and Latin tongues, ancient Persian or Avestic, and the later Teutonic and Slavic languages. This connection was first noticed by Sir William Jones in the late eighteenth century and was amplified by the philologists of the nineteenth. It is thought that two groups of Aryans spread over the Middle East. The westerly one gave birth to the literary languages of Persia and Media. From Persia descends modern Persian through the medium of Pahlavi, or Avestic, with a liberal addition of Arabic influence. Avestic is the sacred language of the Zoroastrians and so of the Parsi community in western India today. From Medic are derived the frontier tongues of Pushtu and Baluchi. It was the eastern group of dialects which was carried to India by the Aryan invaders during the second millennium B.C.

One of these dialects achieved a literary form and a sacred prestige as the vehicle of the hymns of the *Rigveda*. This language was known as Sanskrit, and henceforward was the standard form of expression of the Indian genius. Sanskrit having early become fixed by its sacred character, spoken dialects or variations of it developed as the new invaders spread over the country. After 500 B.C. there is little internal development in the Sanskrit language. The various spoken dialects of the literary and fixed Sanskrit were called *prakrits*. It was one of these, that of Magadha or roughly the modern state of Behar, which was used by the Buddha in order that his teaching might be understood by the people without the intervention of the Brahmins. This dialect was called Pali, and the Buddhist works were written in it as the previous Brahminical books had been written in Sanskrit. Reverence for the written and sacred word was such that in course of time Pali also became a fixed literary language, too holy to change or develop. Pali thus became the sacred language of the Buddhists as Sanskrit was of the Brahmins and has so remained to this day. Its close relationship with Sanskrit can be seen by comparing the word *dhamma* ("moral duty") with Sanskrit *dharma*, or *pada* with *pala*. Pali was the principal dialect of Sanskrit spoken in north India in the sixth century B.C. As this in its turn congealed into holiness fresh spoken dialects appeared, but they never attained the status of literary languages because of the prestige of Sanskrit and Pali. Lacking the restraints of literary form or grammarian's logic, these dialects tended to break down in their turn under the influence of daily usage and the strain of meeting fresh languages imported by invading peoples as well as the local dialects of still unassimilated Dravidian tribes.

The great race movements in northern and western India in the sixth and seventh centuries and the social turmoil they involved were decisive in the history of Indian languages. The old dialects broke down altogether and in their place there began to appear from about 1000 A.D. the modern Indian languages in areas where the population had become fixed. The condition of such language formation was a stable population; the ingredients were classical Sanskrit and *desh* or local dialect words. Sanskrit continued to be the language of religion and literary expression, with an ever-growing prestige. As such it exercised a large influence on all the new languages and provided an unfailing quarry of words. *Desh* or dialect words came from the languages of such invaders as the Huns or the Gurjaras, or from local Dravidian dialects. The variety of these foreign and local tongues helps to explain the variety to be found in the various Indian Sanskritic languages.

The most important of these languages was Hindi, which developed from the *prakrit* spoken from the Jumna to Behar. From the same *prakrit,* though with other differing ingredients, developed Rajasthani, Gujarati, and Panjabi. From other *prakrits* developed Sindhi, Lahnda, and Kashmiri in the north and Marathi in the west. All these languages began as spoken dialects only. Their "breakthrough" into a literary form was usually the result of religious sentiment. The sacred language might be Sanskrit, but the people demanded something more intimate and familiar for their daily spiritual sustenance. So religious devotees composed religious lyrics in the new languages. Their popularity won them recognition, and in time versions of the great religious epics came to be composed in the new languages. In some parts, as in Rajasthan, bards extolled the deeds of heroes in ballads and so assisted the process of growth. They obtained a literary form which was ready for further expansion when prose writing developed in the nineteenth century. Thus it came about that India developed a number of distinct languages, each with a literary form, but none so far developed as to be able to provide a common language for the whole country. Sanskrit continued to be the language of learning, while Persian, after the coming of the Muslims, became the language of public business and of the polite.

The introduction of Persian, from the thirteenth century onward, led to the rise of the last of the modern Indian languages, Urdu, or the language of the camp. This is an amalgam of the Hindi spoken in north India and Persian, Hindi supplying common words and syntax, Persian the higher vocabulary and more high-flown forms. Hindus learned Persian for convenience of business and Muslim nobles the local language. The joint product passed to the court, to become first the court "patter" and then its accepted form of expression.

It is a union of race with language together with geographical and historical circumstances which has produced the peoples of India as we know them now. Thus there is no "Scytho-Dravidian" people in India today; there is a Maratha people who speak a common language and are largely but by no means wholly of that physical type. Bengalis, a very individualized people, include pure Dravidians, Mongoloid, and Mongolo-Dravidian types. In this case physical propinquity has produced a common language and historical circumstance a common group consciousness.

On this basis we can now characterize briefly the Indian peoples who together make up the modern Indian nation. Starting from the north, we have the Panjabi, divided almost equally between Hindus and bearded Sikhs. The Panjabi is a sturdy countryman, a keen farmer, and a ready fighter. With a cause and a leader he can be formidable. He is not noted for intellectualism; he is a keen sportsman and in his Sikh branch has shown great enterprise. In Rajasthan the Rajputs dominate, and they are to be found all across northern and central India. They are India's historic traditionalists. Romance and chivalry linger around them. In the modern world they are sport-loving, socially conservative, with high ideals of honor and etiquette, slow-moving in adapting themselves to modern conditions. They may be called modern India's problem people.

The people of Uttar Pradesh, from the Jumna to Behar, are the leading people of modern India. They guard the Hindu tradition at Banaras, they govern the country in the persons of Mr. Nehru, Pandit Pant, and others. The language of Hindi has been declared the national tongue. They are more stocky than the Panjabis and darker complexioned. They are more intellectual without being impractical; they are modern India's managers par excellence. The people of Behar share some of these qualities and also some of those of Bengal. Until recent years they have been an almost entirely rural people of landlords and peasants. In Bengal we come upon a people noted for their artistic achievement and sensibility, their intellectual brilliance, and their mercurial temperament. The modern Indian renaissance began among the active-minded Bengalis, giving to the country a long line of literary, philosophic, religious, and political figures. The best known in the West are Rabindranath Tagore and Vivekananda. The people of neighboring

Orissa and Assam are gentler and less brilliant and temperamental; their modern development has been quite recent.

Turning to the west, we come to the Gujarati and Maratha peoples. The Gujaratis, whose center is round the Gulf of Cambay, are noted for their enterprise and business capacity. They are prominent in the cotton industry of India, and they have flourishing commercial colonies in Kenya and elsewhere. The Gujarati is no mystic; rather he is the stuff from which millionaires are made. The Maratha is lean and wiry; he is hard-headed and as enduring as the stony hills of his home in the western Ghats, tenacious and purposeful. He has an intense local patriotism and pride and is a relentless fighter. The Brahmins are noted for their high intelligence; at one time two Poona Brahmins were simultaneously heads of the two factions of the National Congress. Their spiritual home is Poona, their capital Bombay; for nearly three hundred years they have dominated the life of western and central India.

In the south we come to the four Dravidian peoples, the Tamils, the Andhras or Telugus, the Kannadigas, and the Malayalis. Their areas are now sufficiently covered by the modern states of Madras, Andhra, Mysore, and Kerala respectively. The Tamils have the longest cultural tradition, stretching back prior to the Christian era, and the most highly developed language. The Tamilians are noted for their powers of intellect and memory, their combination of modern knowledge and orthodox ways, and their love of English. With his caste mark and turban, grave courtesy and dignified ways, the Tamil gentleman is a landmark in southern India. He regards English as his second language and does not see why he should learn Hindi as well. The Tamil has much business ability and enterprise. He has not hesitated to venture overseas and has important interests in Burma and southeast Asia. The Andhra to the north is less dominating than the Tamil of whom he has on occasion been jealous. Now that he has a state of his own, in whose creation this last feeling was one factor, he is free to develop on his own lines. Like all the Dravidian peoples, the Andhra is physically slighter, gentler, and less energetic than the people of the north in general. But he is just as intellectual and no less tenacious. The Kannadigas and the Malayalis do not vary greatly from the general Dravidian pattern. But they contain two groups, the Hindu Nairs and the Syrian Christians, which are noted for their energy and enterprise. We may conclude this survey by mentioning the Parsis of Bombay and the west coast. They are of Persian origin and not much more than 100,000 strong, but their ability and enterprise has been such that they hold a dominating position in the commercial and industrial life of modern India. Of pale complexion as befits their origin, they can always be identified by the curiously shaped peaked hats which they habitually wear. They are the Jews of modern India but without the handicap of any anti-Iranianism.

♬ EAST AND WEST—TWO-WAY TRAFFIC

We are all ready to think of India as a country different from our own, but we usually think of it as different in the wrong way. We concede to India an unfamiliar climate, gorgeous colors, the strange costumes and bizarre conduct of its people, but at the same time assume that their standards of conduct and modes of thought are similar to ours. We assume that Indian civilization is at bottom similar to ours, with the addition of a few strange customs and ideas. But in fact the opposite is true; resemblances to Western customs may be found but it is the basic conceptions which differ. It is a difference at the root which has produced a different flower.

A first and obvious difference is that of religion. Hinduism in all its forms is quite strange to the West. Yet it is easy to assume that the varieties of religious practice in India, and especially the differences between Hindu and Muslim worship, represent nothing more than those of the denominations with which we are familiar. Even if one cannot go from temple to mosque with the same facility that one can move from church to church with their notices of "welcome to all," the difference is perhaps no more than that between Roman Catholics and Protestants. Are not both groups Americans at heart, participating in the same American culture and loyal to the same way of life?

Proceeding from worship to daily life, we find further differences. The Hindu, for example, is in the main a vegetarian, and some are so strict as to abstain from eggs and even from red-colored vegetables like the beet. In particular he regards beef, that mainstay of so many millions in the West, with repulsion bordering on horror. The Muslim has no such feelings about meat in general and beef in particular, but for him pork is unclean and wine is forbidden. The Hindu observes frequent short fasts, and their vogue was utilized by Mahatma Gandhi in his long fasts for political or moral purposes. The Muslim has his month of fasting, whose observance is a point of honor. But these again, we may say, are curious customs indeed, but things which need not affect basic processes of thought or standards of value.

Proceeding further, we find that these habits are in fact set in differing patterns of life. The whole of traditional Hindu life is arranged according to the intricate socio-religious pattern known as caste. Caste determines the family structure and often the family occupation; caste determines marriage, status, and position in life. On the Muslim side there is a different pattern of family life, and the custom of female seclusion. If we are still inclined to dismiss these differences as superficial or as a kind of social eccentricity, we come next to Hindu ideas about life. It soon becomes clear that they are not only radically different from ours, but that they are closely related to the traditional pattern of society which claims to be their social expression.

Examples of these unique ideas, which pervade all Hindu thinking and form, as it were, the mental atmosphere which the traditional Hindu breathed, are the concepts of *karma, dharma* and *maya. Karma* is literally "action" and the concept may be described as the law of consequences. Every action, good or bad, has its consequence or fruit. The consequence comes back to the individual, the fruit must be plucked or the crop reaped, by a law from which there is no escape. This idea is closely linked with that of the transmigration of the soul, or reincarnation, since the fruits of one's actions clearly cannot all be experienced in a single physical existence. These two concepts are intimately interwoven into the texture of the Hindu mind, from the prince to the peasant, from the philosopher to the worldly wise merchant. They serve as a justification of the whole system of caste, justifying both the claims of the privileged and the disabilities of the lowly. The nearest English equivalent of *dharma* is moral duty. But *dharma* is a unique kind of moral duty. Every caste, every group in society, has in traditional Hinduism its own *dharma* or moral duty. These moral obligations vary widely, so that a man might conform to the standards of one caste and at the same time be held to be failing to perform the duties of his own. Thus the moral law was cut up, as it were, into a number of competing fragments; there was no single set of rules applicable to all. *Maya,* the last of our trio, means *illusion.* It expresses the deep conviction of the Hindu mind that the material world is illusory. It is mind alone that exists; man is but a thought in the mind of the Creator, and "the gorgeous palaces, the cloud capp'd towers" of his world but projections of his own imagination. The highest flights of Indian religion have pointed the way to release from this world of illusion; freedom's dream has not been liberation from earthly tyranny but escape from the wheel of life or the clogs of the world altogether.

This theme could be elaborated much further. But enough has been said to indicate that Hindu culture differs from that of the West, not only in its religious observances or in particular customs, but in the pattern and texture of its social life and in the basic ideas which underlie them. In other words, Indian traditional culture must be recognized as a culture in its own right, quite distinct from that of the West, before we can begin to understand it. A culture is a pattern of life based on ideas about its nature, and a civilization is the expression of this pattern and these ideas in outward forms. India differs from the West in these fundamental respects, and understanding of her outlook and her development and of her reaction to Western influence can only start from this basis.

Having established that India possesses a separate culture standing on its own ground and worthy of study in its own right, we come to a proposition which logically follows. It is that we cannot expect cultural influence between the West and India to be only a one-way traffic. We must expect India to influence the West as the West has surely influenced India in recent times. And this is, in fact, exactly what has happened through history. It is a process which has gone on from very early times and has continued to the present day. Nor has the process been confined to what may be thought the characteristic features of Hindu culture, such as philosophy; it has included fields usually thought of as Western preserves, such as economics. In this sphere India was one of the channels by which silk and the silkworm came from China to Europe. But much more important has been the Indian contribution of cotton textiles. From the classical days of Greece and Rome Indian cottons have been known and prized in Europe; it was not long after their advent in England in quantity at the hands of the East India Company in the seventeenth century that the woolen industry took alarm and sought a ban on their sale altogether. To this day technical cotton terms betray their Eastern origin. Thus calicoes are named after the port of Calicut in South India, muslins after Mosul in Iraq, and chintz from a Sanskrit word meaning speckled. In fact the advent of cotton has revolutionized dress in the Western world since the medieval days of woolens and linens and velvets. The spice trade, the one generally admitted gift of India and the East Indies to Europe, flourished long before the Christian era. Plutarch records that Aristion, the tyrant of Athens, used two quarts of pepper for a practical joke in 88 B.C. The Visigoth Alaric took 5000 pounds of pepper when he sacked Rome in 410 A.D. In more recent times India has supplied indigo, which displaced the old English woad and was used for naval uniforms, so adding the term "navy blue" to the language. More recently still, in the nineteenth century, tea was grown in India, first to supplement and then virtually to displace China tea on the English and American markets. Indian tea completed in Britain a social transformation begun by China tea, that of converting a beer-drinking people noted for its inebriety into a tea-drinking one noted for its temperance. Among drugs which India and Ceylon have supplied to Europe may be noted cinnamon and opium, that solace of Thomas De Quincey and inspirer of Coleridge's *Kubla Khan.*

In the social sphere Indian influence has been no less evident, and this too in recent rather than ancient times. The use of water for ablutions and the taste for baths were brought into Britain in the eighteenth century by the India-returned "nabobs" along with their Indian manners, their taste for curries, and their retinues of servants. Manners and servants disappeared, but India contributed to English life that most apparently English of all customs, the taste for the daily "tub." In the sphere of clothes, the turban came in as a fashion to be periodically revived. But the *shal* or shawl has become a permanent addition to a lady's wardrobe and was indispensable in the Victorian era. Pajamas are a direct loan from India, at first described in Indian inventories as "long drawers"; so are the type of riding breeches which fit tightly from ankle to knee and are baggy thereafter, known as "jodhpurs" from the Rajput state of that name. In the realm of amusement, the game of chess came from India via the Arabs. It had already reached the north by the tenth century, when one Norseman would upset the board of another rather than admit defeat. Polo or *chaugan,* which originated with the Turks and has been played in India for centuries, was another direct importation.

In the realm of speech, borrowing has been extensive. If the Greeks contributed to Sanskrit a few astrological and other terms, and English has contributed extensively to Indian colloquial speech in modern times, India has repaid the debt by her loans to the English language. A whole work of reference has been devoted to the anglicization of Indian terms for English use in India. But in addition to these terms, which may be described as a kind of Anglo-Indian patois, a large number of Indian words have become acclimatized into the spoken language of Britain itself. These are words like *durbar, bazaar,* and *pukka* which are of obvious Indian origin and which have retained substantially both their Indian form and meaning. There are others with the same characteristics whose Indian origin would not ordinarily be suspected, such as bangle, chutney, and loot (unknown in English before the late eighteenth century). Some have changed their form while retaining their meaning, as sepoy (*sipahi*) for soldier. The process of association has attached special meanings to particular words; thus *khak* ("dust") has given us khaki, the color of dust and so of uniforms devised for protection in the dust-covered veldt of South Africa, and *bangala* or *Bengali* was used successively for the light thatch-covered, single-storied houses of rural Bengal, and then for any single-storied building in Britain or anywhere else in the world. Bengal has added "bungalow" to the language. Then there are the words which have changed their meaning radically. *Panch,* the Hindustani word for five, gave its name to the well-known drink of punch, because, as originally constituted, it contained five ingredients. The word *diwan* was originally the couch or low seat upon which an eminent person sat and thence indicated the chamber containing the couch, and a high official who sat on it; in English it has become a type of low convertible bed-settee. The word *thag* in India described a ritual murderer who strangled his victims according to a set form both for private profit and in honor of a goddess. Today the thug is an armed gangster who enlivens the streets of our great cities. Then there are such words as pundit and mogul, whose meaning is twisted rather than wholly changed. The word pundit, the Indian title of the highest or Brahmin caste in India, is now used to describe any group of experts, with a slight suggestion of pedantry; the word mogul, taken from the name of the Indian dynasty which captured the imagination of Europe in the seventeenth century, now signifies any prominent figure in any walk of life. The mogul of the movies has succeeded the Great Mogul of India.

In the realm of religion India has certainly exercised a steady influence, both upon Islam and in the West. But its early details are too obscure for any confident assertions. In modern times, however, this influence has been more tangible. Vedantism was brought to the Western public with Swami Vivekananda's dramatic intervention in the World Congress of Religions at Chicago in 1893. Knowledge of it had been spreading in the world of scholarship earlier in the century. The Theosophical Society owes its inspiration to Indian thought and still has its headquarters at Adyar in South India. Nonviolence or *ahimsa* as a way of life as well as an ethical principle was given a new meaning for the West as well as the East by Mahatma Gandhi. Leo Tolstoy was one of its forerunners and Romain Rolland was its Western exponent.

In the intellectual world India not only made important progress in her own right, as did China, but also passed on her discoveries to the West via the Arab world. "Arabic" numerals, which replaced the clumsy Roman notation and made modern arithmetical calculations possible, were invented in India. So was the all-important zero, essential for the decimal system. This knowledge came to Europe via the Arab world in the early days of Islam. In philosophy the early story is again uncertain but it is certain that there was an exchange of ideas. Pythagoras and Plato both believed in the transmigration of souls. In modern times we can trace important currents of Western thought to Indian sources. After the discovery of Sanskrit literature by European scholars in the eighteenth century the monistic ideas of the Vedanta influenced a series of German thinkers from Fichte to Schopenhauer and Deussen. Albert Schweitzer, while himself critical of Indian thought, is perhaps indebted more than he suspects to the Indian principle of the oneness of all existence in his enunciation of the great doctrine of "reverence for all life." In England Carlyle found in the caste system a basis for his doctrine of superiority, which he idealized as hero worship. Friedrich Nietzsche went further and grew lyrical about the *Laws of Manu,* a legal treatise systematizing the caste system. *"The Laws of Manu,"* he wrote, "is a work which is spirited and superior beyond comparison." Thus India provided a basis for the doctrine of the superman. The study of Indian institutions provided much material for the ideas of the conservative English legal thinkers like Sir Henry Maine and James Stephens. Finally, India provided the material and the stimulus for the development of the new sciences of philology and comparative religion. The discovery of the connection between Sanskrit and the European languages led to the development of comparative philology as a regular discipline, and studies of early Indian religion through the same medium laid the foundation of the comparative study of religion.

In the literary field the Indian talent for the didactic animal story has greatly influenced the European imagination. While there is no need to dispute the Greek authorship of Aesop's fables, there is equally no doubt that the Indian nature story has largely enriched the European imaginative store. The collection of stories known as the *Panchatantra* passed, in one form or another, through the Arab to the Western world. Both Sinbad the Sailor and the Arabian Nights' Tales were influenced by it, and in various versions it has been translated into more languages than any book apart from the Bible. In recent times Indian literature was an important influence upon the development of the European romantic school of literature. Schlegel was immensely impressed by the *Bhagavad Gita,* while Goethe was equally impressed by Kalidasa's play *Sakuntala,* first translated into English by Sir William Jones. Today, while Indian scholars and writers take their place in all the modern sciences and the general stream of modern literature and art, their traditional and characteristic philosophy continues to influence the world through the polished and subtle writings of such men as Dr. Sarvepalli Radhakrishnan and the late Sri Arabindo Ghose. Not by wars and conquest has India influenced the outside world, but in the subtler and deeper realms of imagination and thought.

PART I
INDIA: ANCIENT AND MEDIEVAL

CHAPTER I

The Early Cultures

The traces of man in his primitive state are as yet few and confused in India. This is both on account of the size of the country and the restricted nature of the search. Archeologists are further hampered by lack of data with regard to climatic changes. In America and Europe the last geological age, the Pleistocene, from about 1,000,000 B.C., has been climatically charted by a series of ice ages, whose glaciers have left indelible marks. But in India something similar has only been discovered in the northwest corner (now West Pakistan), in the valley of the river Sohan. Even where we have traces of human occupation, nothing is known of the people themselves. We only have their tools, and the language of tools is limited. From the evidence that we possess it can be said that there are traces of human occupation from perhaps 400,000 B.C., when man everywhere was going through the long "kindergarten" stage of the race known as the Paleolithic or Old Stone Age. Tools found extending over a period of perhaps 300,000 years in the Sohan Valley have given their name to the pre-Sohan, Sohan, and evolved Sohan industries. Alongside the Sohan tools of flaked stones have been found shaped cores which are both more sightly and more efficient. Traces of both types have been found in Gujarat and south India. The users of these tools were hunters and food gatherers, moving about in small groups, in constant fear of the animal kingdom and the forces of nature.

At some date which is uncertain in India but is put after 10,000 B.C. in northern and western Europe, man passed into the Mesolithic stage, when implements of bone and flint supplemented those of stone, the dog was domesticated, and pottery appeared. There are traces of this stage in India in Mysore, the Vindhya Mountains, the Narbada Valley, and in Gujarat, but we cannot date them exactly or relate them to previous cultures. We do not know how one passed into the other.

The mesolithic passed into the neolithic or New Stone Age, whose characteristics are the use of nonmetal implements and a knowledge of agriculture. It was at this point that settled life became possible and villages were formed. Pottery developed and animals were domesticated. People collected in larger groups with domesticated animals and regular flocks. The family hunting groups became a tribe. Interchange commenced and here and there the village became a city. A refinement of the New Stone Age was chalcolithic culture, so called because stone implements were supplemented by those of copper or bronze. Things now become easier for the archeologist, for he has now not only flaked flints and worked bones to go on, but animal remains, pottery, and fixed sites of human habitation.

It is at this point that our knowledge of India passes from the confusing and anonymous traces of early man to something concrete and precise, to something that can be identified, described, and dated, and of the life of whose people we can form some sort of picture. From the fifth millennium the Iranian Plateau had been occupied by small communities of farmers and pastoralists. It is thought that during the fourth millennium some of these moved into the Tigris-Euphrates Valley, where they developed the riverine civilization of Mesopotamia. They were the forerunners of Sumeria, Chaldea, and Babylon. Eastward the movement was slower. On the Baluchi Hills the settlement mounds rise sometimes to a hundred feet of accumulated rubbish, suggesting long periods of occupation. But sometime in the third millennium B.C. these people descended into the valley of the Indus and its tributaries. We do not know what induced them to take this revolutionary step, what forces urged them from behind, or what incentive lured them in front. We do not know what perils they braved or what conditions they found. But it is certain that once they arrived in the plains of India progress was rapid. The archeologist's spade has revealed a fully developed civilization which is provisionally dated as flourishing from about 2500 B.C. to 1500 B.C. The exact nature of the change from small hill communities to city civilizations is unknown, because the lowest strata of the culture yet uncovered reveal it in an almost fully developed state. The whole of this exciting chapter of Indian history was in fact unknown before 1920. It was in the course of work on a Buddhist stupa at Mohenjo-daro in Sind that bricks of an unknown type were discovered which led to the identification of a new era in Indian history.

This civilization is known as the Indus Valley or Harappan civilization. Its sites cluster the middle reaches of the Indus and the banks of the dried-up Sarasvati River whose upper reaches survive as the

Ghaggar, issuing from the Himalayas near Kalka. Sites have been identified as far west as Rupar on the Sutlej and as far south as Gujarat bordering the Arabian Sea. The civilization seems to have two focal points, at Harappa some 150 miles southwest of Lahore and at Mohenjo-daro, not far from Rohri and Sukkur on the middle Indus. Both these sites have all the appearance of metropolitan cities. They were either the centers of two political unions or the twin centers of a single community. In any case their cultural content is identical.

It is this cultural contact which catches the imagination, emerging so suddenly and so completely from simple hill communities whose sites are rarely more than two acres in extent. Both cities measure three miles in circumference. In each there is a citadel on a mound containing traces of palaces, halls, granaries, and baths. Traces of places of worship are not so clear, but in the case of Mohenjo-daro at least, they may well be hidden under the Buddhist stupa later superimposed on what was probably already the most sacred portion of the site. Beyond the citadels we find a planned city laid out in squares or blocks with parallel lines of streets intersecting at right angles. The houses off these streets were built on the courtyard plan and are notable for their careful drainage systems running off into brick-lined sewers in the streets. Nothing like this was known again in an Indian city until the nineteenth century. This drainage system, the use of baked (instead of sun-dried) bricks, and the figures on seals to be mentioned later suggest damper conditions than the present arid climate of central Sind.

Not many human remains have been found, so that it is only possible to conjecture about the nature of the race which built the cities. But many objects of copper, bronze, and pottery, including a large collection of terra-cotta toys, have been discovered which tell us much about their life and art. Most intriguing of all are the seals engraved with animal designs and bearing the signs of an unknown script. A number of these have also been found in Mesopotamia in the remains of the Sargonid period from 2350 B.C. onward. Their use is unknown, but it has been suggested from their numbers (twelve hundred in Mohenjo-daro alone) and standardization that they had a commercial function, such as seals for cotton bales. Their craftsmanship is exquisite, and, apart from some small seals at the lower Harappan levels, they are uniform in quality. The writing on the seals is likely long to remain an archeologist's riddle in the absence of a bilingual tablet or an inscription of length with recurring features. The longest found so far has only seventeen characters. All that can be said at present is that the script

INDIA

Physical Features

0   100   200   300   400   500

Scale of Miles

Land above 6000 feet
 "   "   1000 "
Sea Level to "   "

is pictographic in character, would seem to be mature, and is not clearly related to any other known script.

Though much must remain in the shadows, there arises from all the evidence the picture of a sophisticated community whose life centered about two great metropolitan cities which were linked by water. There were agriculture and an active commerce which seems to have had connections with the contemporary civilization in Mesopotamia. There were well-developed arts and a high degree of public hygiene. We do not know how the people were ruled, and we can only guess at their worship. But citadel mounds and their appurtenances suggest that there may have been a regime of priest-kings on the Mesopotamian model. Perhaps most intriguing of all, traces can be found of later features of Indian life. On the material side, the bullock cart of modern Sind with its characteristic solid wheel is represented among the clay toys of Mohenjo-daro. On the religious side, we find the pipal tree represented as sacred, and traces of the cult of Shiva, god of fertility and strength of later Hinduism.

As the Indus civilization appeared in a developed form at a date estimated to be around 2500 B.C., it vanished about a thousand years later with but few traces of previous decline. During this long period it apparently maintained a high level of stationary prosperity. Its sites extend from Gujarat in western India to the banks of the Jumna on the borders of the Panjab; its influence may well have spread still further.

We do not know the cause of the Indus civilization's collapse, but it is now quite certain that the area of its influence lay athwart the route of the next invaders of India. These were the Aryans, one branch of whom is generally held to have entered northwestern India about 1500 B.C. or at the approximate period when the Indus Valley civilization is thought to have been overthrown. The suggestion that it was the Aryans who overthrew the Indus Valley dwellers is attractive and the arguments persuasive. It may serve as a provisional hypothesis with the caution that the case must be regarded as nonproven until more evidence of various kinds has come in. The early Aryan literature speaks of wars against dark-skinned aboriginals of repellent habits and glories in the storming of cities. In Harappa conclusive traces have now been found of a final conflagration. It may thus be assumed that the last traces of the Indus culture were extinguished in some such way. It should not be supposed, however, that there was a planned campaign like those of Taimur or Nadir Shah in later days leading to the shock of battle and the horrors of a sack. Rather the Aryans are likely to have infiltrated in groups which united on occasion to form waves of migration. The strength of the Indus dwellers was no doubt undermined before it was destroyed. As they fell into Aryan subjection their conquerors borrowed elements of the culture which they were destroying and despising.

When we pass to the age of the Aryans we find ourselves relying on literary rather than archeological evidence. Suggestive archeological work is proceeding, especially in the study of pottery and on sites like Hastinapura on the Ganges. In time this may complete the link between the two cultures, but for the present our knowledge of the Aryans comes from their own writings. Who were the Aryans? We do not in fact know who the original Aryans were, or what they called themselves. The word *Arya* signifies "kinsman" and by derivation "noble." The people thus called were apparently a group of tribes which emerged from the steppes of south Russia and central Asia during the second millennium B.C. One group entered Europe to become the ancestors of the Greeks; other tribes found their way into Asia Minor and others entered Iran. This eastern stream subdivided, one branch settling in Iran or Persia itself to found Persian civilization, and the other moving westward to enter India. All these tribes had the common physical characteristics of fair skins and blue eyes, common institutions in the elected chief or king, a council of nobles and a body of freemen, and a common religion of the worship of the powers of northern nature. They were pastoralists and agriculturalists, they had domesticated the horse, the sheep, and the cow, and they used implements of iron as well as of copper and bronze They shared a common language group which is known as the Aryan group of languages, and to which most of the languages of modern Europe belong. At one time it was thought that Sanskrit, the sacred language of India, was the parent tongue but it is now realized that, like ancient Avestan in Iran, it was an early offshoot from an unknown parent stem. As all we definitely know about the "Aryan" peoples is that they spoke a related group of languages or dialects, it is best to refer to them as the "Aryan-speaking" peoples.

The branch of these people who came to India may be called the Aryas par excellence, for this is the name which they gave to themselves. It was not a tribal title like Angle or Saxon; the word had perhaps something of the connotation which "the Noble," "the Band of Brothers," or "the Pilgrim Fathers" would have for us. They christened the lands in which they first settled Aryavarta, or land of the Aryans. They settled along the banks of the Indus and in the Panjab and have left a more vivid picture of themselves than any other Aryan group through their early literature, the Vedas. The Vedas have given their name to this first period of Aryan India which is known as Vedic India.

It can be dated in a general way from 1500 to 1000 B.C., a period which covers the destruction of Knossos in Crete, the era of the great monarchies in the Near East, the exodus of the Jews from Egypt, and the reign of King David. During this time the Aryas in India were moving across the Panjab, destroying the last relics of the Indus Valley civilization, making contact with the survivors, and settling in villages to tend their flocks and practice agriculture.

The Vedic Indians have left no concrete remains, for they used wood or mud for their dwellings and had no large cities. They were a people of the sky and the open spaces. Their monument is the Vedas, which were transmitted by oral tradition for centuries before being written down. There were originally four of these [1] but the most important is the *Rigveda,* which is also the oldest. In the course of time other works were added to the four Vedas and acquired their sacred status. There were the *Brahmanas* which were explanations of the Vedic hymns with some early philosophic treatises or "forest books." Then came the *Upanishads,* numbering over a hundred; they were of incalculable importance, for out of them grew the characteristic Indian philosophy of the *Vedanta* (that which comes after the Veda). Finally, to the Vedic corpus was added the *Sutras,* legal and ritual treatises out of which grew collections of customary law of which the *Laws of Manu* is one. Thus the original Veda grew in bulk with time to form a collection of literature held sacred by all orthodox Hindus. It may be called as a whole the first Bible of the Hindus, being collected in much the same way over the course of centuries and gradually acquiring its sacred status by a general consensus of opinion. There are still many Hindus today who believe that all knowledge and all truth are to be found in the Veda. This is the Hindu version of Fundamentalism.

But we must now return to the *Rigveda* composed in the second half of the second millennium B.C. Some of it may be still earlier. The word *Veda* means knowledge and *rig* rich or choice. The book is in essence a collection of 1,017 hymns arranged in ten books. They are nearly all religious in character, being addressed to the Aryan gods. It is from these and with the aid of hints from the other three Vedas that our picture of Vedic India is composed. A quotation may be made from one of them to illustrate their character.

To the Dawn (*Ushas*)

She hath shone brightly like a beautiful woman, stirring to motion every
    living creature.
Agni (god of fire) hath come to feed on mortals' fuel.
    She hath made light and chased away the darkness.

Turned to this all, far spreading, she has risen and shone in brightness with
    white robes about her.
She hath beamed forth lovely with golden colours, mother of kine, guide
    of the days she bringeth.

. . . .

Send thy most excellent beams to shine and light us; giving us lengthened
    days, O Dawn, O goddess,
Granting us food, thou who hast all things precious, and bounty rich in
    chariots, kine and horses.
O Ushas, nobly born, daughter of heaven, whom the Vasishthas with their
    hymns make mighty,
Bestow thou on us vast and glorious riches. Preserve us evermore, ye gods,
    with blessings.[2]

The picture we get from these hymns is of a typically Aryan community, which has, however, features of its own. There is the tribe with
its king or chief, its council of nobles, and its freemen. The emphasis is
on nobility, the feeling is intensely aristocratic. The scorn of the outsider is more intense than that of the Greek for the barbarian. The people love nature and they worship its powers in deified form. To Ushas,
the dawn goddess, we may add Indra, the storm, Agni the fire, and
Varuna the sky. They are virile and warlike, they love dancing, music,
and charioteering, they are addicted to gambling. One of the rare secular
poems in the *Rigveda* is a gambler's lament. They love fermented drink,
or the *soma* juice, a whole section being devoted to the praise of its deified form. What must soon strike the observer of these lovers of light
and air, however, is the scanty traces of the later Hinduism to be found
in the hymns. The gods and goddesses of the *Rigveda* are scarcely worshiped today; the great gods of later Hinduism are not to be found there.
Animal sacrifices are freely offered and the veneration of the cow is
absent. There is a radical difference in social custom and structure.
Intoxicating spirits, forbidden to the high-caste Hindu, were not only
freely consumed, but deified in the form of *soma*. The flesh of cows, bulls,
and horses, all of which was tabu in later ages, was freely eaten. There
were classes but no caste. Above all, the priests, instead of being at the
head of the social pyramid, were subordinate to the nobles. Though
some of the hymns reach toward monotheism and the idea of the in-
dwelling spirit, the doctrine of *karma* so characteristic of Hinduism was
absent. In fact, we may say that the society of Vedic India conformed
much more closely to parallel Aryan societies elsewhere than to the
later classical Hinduism. The Indo-Aryans were still strangers from the
northwest who had brought their customs and their gods with them. Their

minds were still attuned to the colder regions which their ancestors knew; fire was more important to them than water.

From Vedic India we pass to the India of the Epics, which may be broadly dated from 1000 B.C. to 500 B.C. or later. It is still a dark age so far as historical records or archeological remains are concerned. But our literary materials are more copious and the picture of life which can be constructed more detailed. There is evidence of much development and change, and we are clearly in a different world. The period is named from the two great epic poems whose cores were composed at this time and from which we get most of our information. These are the *Mahabharata* and the *Ramayana*. The *Mahabharata* describes the great war between the Pandavas or five sons of Pandu, who reigned at Indraprastha on the Jumna (traditionally stretching south from the old city of Delhi), and the Kauravas or hundred sons of Dhritarashtra, brother of Pandu, whose capital was at Hastinapura on the Ganges. The positive core of historic truth within the story is now so deeply embedded in later accretions as to be unidentifiable. The real value of the work from the historian's point of view lies in the picture of society which its earliest portions afford and the comparison offered with the previous picture painted in the *Rigveda*. It is thought that the original poem contained about 8,800 couplets or *slokas*. The epic portion later grew to 20,000 couplets, while the whole work swelled to more than 100,000 couplets with a further appendix. There are now northern and southern versions. The work has in fact become a kind of compendium of Hindu ideas in the hands of a long succession of Brahmin editors. Inset into the sixth book is the philosophical dialogue known as the *Bhagavad Gita* or the Lord's Song.[3] This work was in form a dialogue between the Lord Krishna as chariot driver and the warrior Arjuna who was reluctant to fight against his relations. The doctrine is that of action with detachment, the performance of duty without passion or desire. For many Hindus today it has something like the authority of the Sermon on the Mount for Christians.

The *Ramayana* is a shorter poem of 24,000 couplets arranged in seven books of which five are regarded as original. It is more properly called an epic, for it is by one author, Valmiki, and deals with one hero and heroine. It relates the expulsion of Prince Rama and his wife Sita from Ayodhya in northern India, their wanderings in the forest, Sita's abduction by Ravana, the demon King of Lanka (in Ceylon), the siege of Lanka and destruction of Ravana with the aid of Hanuman, the monkey king, and the triumphant return of the reunited couple to Ayodhya. The poem has no known historical foundation but it has become an intrinsic part of Hindu life. The ten-day siege of Lanka is still celebrated in the Dasehra festival, when great paper images of Ravana and his knights are stuffed with fireworks and burned at the end of a ten-day festival-fair. The return of Rama and Sita to Ayodhya (by air) is commemorated by the charming festival of Diwali which in northern India marks the onset of the cold weather.[4] Lights are placed to guide the travelers home; the people in holiday mood repair to the bazaars to buy sweets and toys and return to make a children's festival. In Hindu life the night of lights has something of the atmosphere of Christmas Day in the West. The *Ramayana* has become more than a charming and exciting poem and the occasion of merry festivals. In the course of time Brahmin editors converted a straightforward adventure story into a book of devotion. In India today it has for millions the authority of the New Testament for the West. Rama is presented as an incarnation of the great god Vishnu. He is the ideal Hindu man and Sita the perfect woman. The popular salutation of "Ram, Ram" comes from the reverence induced by this poem. Other versions, such as that of Tulsi Das in Hindi in the time of Akbar, have inspired and solaced the many who do not know Sanskrit.

The picture presented by these two poems differs greatly from that of Vedic India. Even the language has changed. Sanskrit has developed from a flexible spoken tongue into a complex and stylized language. As it ceased to be spoken it became fixed in syntax and style so that it is easy to date later works from internal evidence only within half a millennium. For example, opinions of the date of the *Arthasastra,* ascribed to Kautiliya, vary from 300 B.C. to 300 A.D. Next we find that the Indo-Aryan heart center, as it were, has moved. From Sind and the Panjab it has moved southeastward to the Jumna and upper Ganges basins. The two capitals in the Great War lay on the Jumna and Ganges respectively, while the scene of the conflict was at Kurukshetra (field of the Kauravas) near Thanesar about a hundred miles north of Delhi. By the time we reach recorded history in the late fourth and early third centuries B.C. the center has moved farther east still to the confines of Behar. The people who have moved so far are no longer the pure Indo-Aryan tribes with their loose organization of chiefs and nobles. Now there is clear evidence of racial intermixture. Color is a distinguishing feature within the Aryan fold and not merely outside it. The fact that the five Pandava brothers were all married to one wife, Draupadi, suggests affinity with the Mongolian races of Tibet and the Himalayan regions, which practice polyandry. It was certainly quite un-Aryan. There is good reason for thinking, in the opinion of many scholars, that the conflict represented a struggle between more and less mixed sections of the Indo-Aryan tribes, perhaps between early and later arrivals in India. The inclusion of allies from all over India shows that the old horror of any contact with the *dasyus* or aboriginals was disappearing. In fact, assimilation was proceeding. The Great War was perhaps an attempt to stop it, in which case its inconclusive ending is also significant.

There has been a radical change in Indian religion since Vedic times. The old Vedic gods, with the exception of Indra, have been superseded by the accepted "great gods" of Hinduism, Brahma the Creator, Vishnu the gracious Preserver, and Shiva the Mighty and the Destroyer. They are anthropomorphic with personalities of their own; they have consorts like Parvati and Lakshmi who are as important and significant as themselves. Other gods come crowding in, some in animal forms like the elephant-headed god of jollity, Ganesha, or Hanuman, the monkey god. These are no Aryan powers of nature; their arrival must represent give and take with the people of the land. Most significant of them, perhaps, is Shiva, whose emblems are identical with finds on the Indus Valley sites. With new gods came new ideas. The idea of the incarnation of a god in human form (known as an *avatar*), absent from the *Rigveda,* is current coin in the Epics. Thus both Rama and Krishna are represented as incarnations of Vishnu. The idea of reincarnation of the human soul in successive lives, fundamental to historic Hinduism and a living belief today, is now established. Along with it came the doctrine of *karma,* or the law of moral consequences. The two are linked together, the one justifying and explaining the other. The course can be seen of a development away from the idea of God as a capricious, unpredictable power, to be propitiated or "worked" by sacrifices, spells, and charms to the conception of Him as the embodiment of abstract law with moral qualities. The *Gita,* perhaps a late addition to the *Mahabharata,* teaches a religion of moral duty. The doctrine of ahimsa or nonviolence to living beings, which led to the disappearance of animal sacrifices, has made its appearance.

Socially and politically there had also been great changes. The institution of caste, one of the cornerstones of Hinduism, of which more will be said in the next chapter, has appeared. In the *Rigveda* there were only four orders of society; now there are a number of segregated groups. The *Laws of Manu,*[5] which are thought to have been compiled between 200 B.C. and 200 A.D., recognize some fifty as distinct from the four orders. The loose tribal divisions of the Vedic period have given way to numerous little kingdoms. The court life as described in both epics was not unlike that to be found in the more out-of-the-way Indian states down to the twentieth century. In short, while the *Rigveda* gives us a picture of vigorous foreign tribes settling down in a new country, carrying their ideals and customs and traditions with them, the Epics show us a people long settled in the country, who have joined in some degree with the people of the land to develop a characteristic culture of their own. Hinduism has been born.

A final word must be said about the dates of this picture. It is thought that the major part of the *Ramayana* may have been written sometime after 400 B.C. Then came the core of the *Mahabharata,* which finally attained its present form, with its immense accretions, around 200 A.D. But the early parts of both poems embodied earlier works too and dealt with traditions which must already have been ancient because they had become legendary. It is therefore fair to believe that the core of the poems gives us a picture of society in the centuries before 500 B.C. while the later portions trace the development of thought down to the Christian era. All processes must be thought of as overlapping and all change as gradual. We find the first traces of political history, which means larger political units, from the seventh century B.C. From the sixth century B.C., the age of the Buddha and Mahavira, we have two other religious sources of information.

CHAPTER II

Hinduism

Hinduism has traditionally been regarded as a religio-social system with complicated rules collected in such compilations as the *Laws of Manu*. Within the system were to be found patterns of thought and religious disciplines of great variety, but it was the system itself which was characteristic and fundamental. In the nineteenth century research revealed that Hindu society was a complex of systems rather than a single construction; the word Brahminism was used to distinguish the system of the priestly hierarchy from other and older modes. At the same time European criticism of some traditional features of Hinduism made its friends anxious to find some other criterion of judgment. The search for "essential Hinduism" began. Ram Mohan Roy thought it was essentially a system of thought, to be found in the philosophical treatises called the *Upanishads*. The sage Dayananda, like a Puritan pointing to the Bible and primitive Christianity, taught that the four Vedas were the essential Hinduism, containing all knowledge and all guidance. More recently, as the corroding effect of Western skepticism has been felt more strongly, the tendency has been to emphasize the absorptive and syncretistic features of Hinduism, thus making it possible to declare that all the characteristic social features are later accretions which can be discarded without injury to the genius of the cult. Dr. Sarvepalli Radhakrishnan, the philosophic vice-president of the Republic,[1] for example, considers that Hinduism consists of an early deposit with a talent for absorption from elsewhere. Sardar K. M. Panikkar, diplomatist, historian, and publicist of the Indian Union,[2] goes further and turns Hinduism into an assimilative magic. Its skill is to absorb ideas and customs from all quarters, to assimilate them into a harmonious whole, and to clothe them with local color. Hinduism is not like a sponge, to hold foreign matter for a time and then disgorge; like the Hindu cow it absorbs and assimilates foreign matter to produce the precious nectars of milk and cream.

The more Hinduism is considered, the more difficult it becomes to define it in a single phrase. It is a gargantuan, many-bodied thing, gross and subtle at the same time, reaching to the skies and falling to the depths. In fact it is much easier to say what it is not than what it is. Using the characteristic Hindu method of negation we may begin our analysis by noting some things which Hinduism is not. First we can say that it is not a church in any Western sense. It has no organization, no dogma or accepted creeds, no councils to define the truth or archbishops to guide the faithful. All these things are to be found within Hinduism but you can be a good Hindu without any of them. Next, it cannot be called a religion. Hinduism contains religion; in fact it contains many religions, some of which are quite contradictory. A Hindu may have any religious belief or none; he may be an atheist or an agnostic and still be an accepted Hindu. Is Hinduism then a mere ritual of ceremonies and catalogue of duties, trivial and grave? Here we may seem to be getting nearer the truth, for neglect of certain duties does prejudice a man's reputation for orthodoxy. But in fact there is no one duty binding on all or any one ritual. A man could neglect any one of the prescribed duties of his group and still be regarded as a good Hindu. The most we could say is that he could not so easily neglect them all at once. Nor can Hinduism be dismissed summarily as mere tradition. Though tradition plays an important part in Hindu life, you can be a Hindu while disregarding most of it. And there is an ideological element as well without which Hinduism would not be Hinduism.

In such a confused and illusive field we can perhaps find a clue by considering what the Hindu criterion of Hinduism may be. What is it that makes a man a Hindu in the eyes of his fellows? What is the sanction applied to those who transgress whatever code there be? Since there are no constituted authorities with recognized jurisdiction, the only ultimate sanction is public opinion. It is public opinion working through the caste system which determines whether someone shall or shall not be regarded as a Hindu. It is public opinion which determines at one time the rules essential for observance, again working by castes. The method of enforcement traditionally has been social ostracism. If, for example, members of a caste broke the rules for marriage within certain groups of the caste or married outside the caste altogether, social ostracism would ensue. The whole family would be cut off from the social amenities of Hindu society. There would be no intermarriage, no interdining, no social intercourse, no service from the priests on the numerous ritual occasions of life. A sense of social guilt would fall on the family and a feeling of social isolation would desolate them. Such a measure would usually be taken by a caste *panchayat* or council. Since the castes were strictly hereditary, exclusion from one would not imply admission to another. Such measures were commonest when ceremonial pollution had taken place, often unwittingly or under duress. For example, the eating of beef was regarded with such horror that in times of tumult forcible contact with it would often lead to large-scale outcastings. In the early British period going overseas was considered as polluting by some castes. Some of those who went were outcasted outright; others had to pay the Brahmins for purification ceremonies; in others there was a division which might result in the formation of a new subcaste. The rules thus enforced have not remained fixed or rigid; they have varied greatly from caste to caste, and have changed radically if slowly down the ages. They are changing today, perhaps faster than ever before. The only certain sanction for all rules and guide for all action was the opinion of the caste itself. We thus arrive at a definition which, through its very imprecision, seeks to convey the indefiniteness and infinite variety of Hinduism itself. Hinduism, we may say, is a body of customs and a body of ideas, the two having such pervasive power and defensive force as to absorb or resist passively for centuries any system which comes into contact with it.

The outstanding Hinduism institution is caste.[3] Hindu society is divided into a great number of these, which amount to some three thousand today. The process of forming and absorbing castes still goes on, as can be seen from those valuable sociological documents, the census reports. Each caste has its *dharma* or moral duty [4] which its members are enjoined to observe. The castes themselves were formed within the four orders or *varnas* of Hindu society. These are defined in a famous passage of the *Laws of Manu* and have often been confused with caste. But they were classes in the Western sense rather than castes in the Indian manner. They were the Brahmins or priests, the Kshatriyas or warriors, the Vaishyas or merchants, and the Sudras or cultivators. All those outside the four orders were *mlechchas* or barbarians. They were outcasts. The conquered aboriginals or forest tribes who came to associate themselves with the Hindus gradually adopted the same system of castes among themselves. So arose the fifth order of outcasts or untouchables, presenting the paradox of the rejected forming a recognized wing, as it were, of the elect themselves. Hinduism came to be regarded as a system embracing all the inhabitants of India, those not being recognized within the four orders still being included, as it were, in an external pen in outer darkness.[5]

The nature of the caste system is a social wonder and its origin a stand-

R. Oxus

BACTRIA
Hindu Kush
AFGHANISTAN

R. Indus

TIBET

Taxila

R. Indus

R. Beas

PUNJAB

H
i
m
a
l
a
y
a
s

Harappa

R. Sutlej

Kurukshetra

Indraprastha

Hardwar
Hastinapura
R. Kampila
R. Jumna
R. Ganges

Ayodhya
KOSALA
(Kashi)
Banares Videha

R. Brahmaputra

R. Brahmaputra

BALUCHISTAN

RAJPUTANA

Mohenjo-daro

Aravallis

Arbuda

Mt. Abu

SIND

Prayag
Pataliputra
Magadha
Nalanda

Gaya

BENGAL

MALWA

Ujjain
Vindh'yas

R. Narbada

R. Godavari

KALINGAS
ORISSA

Western Ghats

Karnata

Peninsula

GUJARAT

BAY OF BENGAL

0 50 100 200 300 400 500

Scale of Miles

SINHALA

Lanka

Approximate extent of
the Indus Valley culture

Ancient India — to 200 B.C.

ing sociological mystery. It is thought that it attained the hard outlines it presented in the early nineteenth century at the time of the Muslim invasions from the eleventh to the fourteenth centuries. But of its origin we know little. We know that it did not exist in Rigvedic times. We know that by 500 B.C. it was in recognizable working order. We believe that it has been in existence for perhaps three thousand years. Its origin has long been a subject of scholarly speculation. Thus the French scholar Senart [6] thought that caste grew up as an extension of the tribe seeking to maintain its purity. The key for him was the purity of the conqueror. Sir H. Risley [7] based caste on color feeling leading to marriage restrictions. The shortage of women, he thought, compelled the fair-skinned invaders to take dark brides. Aversion to color (still to be found in India) put a stop to the process as soon as the deficiency was made up. This would explain the unique marriage restrictions (exogamy, endogamy, etc.) which are the basis of caste. In more recent studies Hocart [8] has suggested that caste is a sacrificial organization and as such is not confined to India. More recently still Dr. J. H. Hutton [9] has argued, on the basis of a great knowledge of the primitive tribes of India, that an essential ingredient of caste is the primitive idea of tabu based on the belief that soul-stuff or mana can be conveyed by sympathetic magic through touch. For Hutton touch leading to pollution was a key, for this explains the aversion of the aboriginals for the invaders as well as of the invaders for the aboriginals. Caste restrictions are mutual, not merely imposed from the top downward. Without presuming to pronounce on the learned debate, one may suggest that Risley and Hutton emphasize two aspects of caste which go far to explain its chief characteristics and its almost unique character in the world.

The castes have grown up within the four orders of *varnas* of Hindu society. They are subdivided in a great variety of ways to form a bewildering pattern of society. It is often not easy to determine to which order a particular caste belongs and there are many disputed claims to membership of an order. The *Kayasths* of north India, for example, claim to belong to the *Kshatriya* or warrior order, but this is not admitted by many. Within an order castes may be tribally divided. A Rajput, for instance, belongs to the warrior order. The Rajputs are themselves subdivided on a tribal basis into many subsections. The agricultural Jats and the pastoral Ahirs of northern India are tribesmen who have been accepted whole within Hinduism as a separate caste. A second division is by occupation. Each caste traditionally has a special occupation and in some cases it is the occupation which has brought the group together rather than the group which has taken to the occupation. The most obvious example is that of the Brahmins whose calling is that of the priesthood. Many Brahmins have taken to other walks of life today, but in other cases the correspondence of calling and caste continues. In the upper ranks the members of the writer castes continue for the most part in the clerical, literary, and administrative professions. Down the scale among the exterior castes there are the Chamars or leatherworkers, the Goalas or milkmen, while in central India there is a caste of hail averters. Another and confusing type of caste is the sectarian. These people gather together in a group devoted to some new belief or way of salvation. Soon they become a new caste, their caste of origin providing the subdivisions for marriage purposes. Examples of this process are the Lingayat sect of South India and the Kabirpanthis or followers of the mystic Kabir in the north. Some castes are formed by crosses between a higher and a lower caste. This is the traditional Brahmin explanation of the growth of caste and there is evidence that it has actually happened in some cases. Some castes have affinities with the national concept, in the sense that they are held together not only by a blood relationship but by attachment to a particular region. The Marathas of western India are the leading example of this type. Then there are the castes formed by migration. When this occurred in the past neither the old caste fellows nor the new neighbors would intermarry, so that a new self-sufficing caste had to be formed. The Nambudri Brahmins of South India are an example of this. Change in customs, such as the practice or disuse of widow remarriage or the eating of meat, may cause a part of a caste to break away and found a new group.

The first outstanding feature of caste is that of occupation. Every caste is supposed to have a characteristic employment. In the upper and Westernized classes today these distinctions are considerably blurred. The new occupations brought in by modern conditions are considered eligible for all, and many are difficult to classify on traditional lines. But even so there remains a marked tendency for people to follow the general bent of their castes. A banker or merchant will usually be found to belong to the *vaishya* or merchant order. Brahmins are prominent among intellectuals and politicians (statecraft being their secondary traditional occupation after priesthood). The members of the Sen subcaste of Bengali Kayasths, who were hereditary doctors, are often to be found today as practitioners of Western medicine. The next and universal feature of caste is the hereditary principle, expressed in a series of marriage regulations and restrictions. Every caste is divided in subcastes or *gotras*. Into some of these (including his own) a person may not marry (exogamy or marrying out). Into one of the others he or she must marry (endogamy or marrying in). Since marriage is universally considered an essential caste duty, it can be seen that in a small or scattered caste the problems of matchmaking may be both complicated and anxious matters. A further feature of caste is the series of restrictions affecting not only marriage, but food, water, touch, and ceremonial purity. All the regular castes abstain from beef, but some (like Rajputs) eat other kinds of meat. Some are forbidden all meat but not fish. Among the numerous vegetarians there are also grades, some regarding eggs as meat and some rejecting all red-colored vegetables as suggestive of blood. Touch is also important, for one caste may not eat anything touched by a lower caste. The complication of these rules is such that the only remedy in a residential institution is the anomaly of the provision of Brahmin cooks. Being of the highest caste, they cannot pollute anyone by touch. The last feature of the caste system is the idea of duty. A duty is attached to each caste which constitutes its *dharma* or moral code. Thus the duty of the Rajput was to fight, of the Brahmin to perform religious ceremonies, of the Ahir to tend flocks. These obligations are still realities in the more traditional portions of Hindu society. In addition there were other duties which are still recognized by the great majority. One is the maintenance of the family unit, for which people will make great sacrifices. Another is the performance of prescribed ceremonies, particularly at birth, marriage, and death. Caste contained not only a negative series of "don'ts" but also a positive series of "do's."

It will naturally be asked: how much of this system survives today? The observer who makes the round of official parties in New Delhi or joins in the fashionable social life of Bombay or Calcutta will probably notice little sign of its existence. Until little more than a century and a quarter ago the system was virtually in full force. But there is no doubt that among a great part of the new middle class, which governs India today, and especially in the great centers of population, the outlines of the system have been blunted and blurred. There is equally little doubt that in rural India, which still comprises 80 per cent of the population, the system is still in good working order. When "untouchables" are admitted to village wells or temples, the caste folk are apt to leave them. Dr. Hutton recorded, in the census of 1931, the continued existence of a group of "unseeables" in South India. The marriage arrangements and diet restrictions continue in these quarters in virtually full force. It is very difficult to say how far the process of change has actually gone. Some of the rich and highborn, apart from the merest externals, remain very orthodox; it is the middle class in general which has been most influenced by Western education and which has proceeded the furthest.

The process may be described as one of mellowing and broadening rather than of revolutionary abandonment. Among the middle class the occupational bar has been generally discarded, though the occupational *bias,* as already mentioned, remains. Interdining (which defies the tabu of touch) is widespread in public places and parties, but much less so in the home itself. Many will now eat any food but beef. Intercaste marriage, permitted by law for many years, is practiced by a very small minority; but the disregard of the subcaste division in marriage arrangements is much more common. The seclusion of women, common in north though not south Indian society, is decreasing as women's education grows. But orthodox feelings about the seclusion of Hindu widows are still very prevalent. An index of the strength of orthodox feelings even in the middle class was the prolonged opposition in the 1950's to the reform of the Hindu code of personal law which sought to improve the position of the Hindu woman and so impinged on orthodox custom. The extent and limitation of that effort of reform by legislation is perhaps the best positive yardstick we have of the progress of modification in orthodox beliefs.

Caste is so pervasive and ubiquitous in Hindu society that one is apt to overlook other important features of Indian life. One of these is the joint family. In a traditional Indian household the married sons with their families live together under the parental roof and are subject to the parental authority. The groups may comprise several generations. The patriarch controls the finances of the group, giving the sons allowances from their earnings; the matriarch is the autocrat of the home to whom the daughters-in-law are subject. The system provided the members of the family with security and maintenance in times of unemployment. It tended to produce a few outstanding personalities, such as are constantly met throughout Indian history; it also encouraged dependence and lack of initiative in the majority. Many a Hindu girl has wept at the prospect of marriage, not because she objected to her little-known bridegroom but for fear of what her mother-in-law might be like. The joint family was a powerful social unit, whose pressure on the individual was greater than the Westerner can easily appreciate. It could incite much sacrifice and devotion and also timidity and lassitude. It is legally recognized today, with special rules for inheritance and income tax. But the fluid conditions of modern urban life have made inroads upon it in the middle classes; once a couple have broken away on transfer to a distant town they rarely go back to the family seat.

The position of women in Hindu society demands special mention. Hindu tradition regards marriage as a sacrament. It was lifelong and there was no remarriage. Indeed, according to the Brahmins, it continued into the next world. Today both divorce and remarriage are legal, but neither is extensively practiced. There was no general rule of monogamy, but in fact, apart from rajas and high nobles, and a few notorious Brahmin groups, it was generally observed. The socially recognized exception was that made on account of lack of children. In the Hindu scheme of things woman occupied a subordinate position. In fact, she had no status at all as a woman. According to the *Laws of Manu* her business was to tend her husband and to worship him as a god. From this attitude sprang such customs as the wife's walking behind her husband in public, never eating with her husband nor eating at all until he had finished, even in private, and secluding herself in widowhood. These facts are formidable, but they are not the whole of the picture. In various aspects of life she had significance and a life of her own. She was the head of the domestic establishment. As a mother she was worshiped by her children; as a wife she was (or should have been) venerated by her husband; as a sister she was often dearly loved. Her childhood was often happy; during married life she was important as wife and mother. But in widowhood she had no place. She was held to be in perpetual mourning for her husband; her head was shaven, her bright clothes removed, she became the family drudge, sometimes cared for by her children but often unwanted and neglected. Many drowned themselves by jumping into wells, others went to some holy place to spend their days in devotion to a god, where their white garments make a place like Brindaban on the Jumna look like a city of ghosts. Some sought more gaudy relief; many others again bore their lot with that wonderful resignation, accompanied often by religious devotion, which is a hallmark of Indian womanhood. It was the Brahminical attitude toward woman as the handmaid of man which led to the dreadful custom of suttee or the burning of widows on the funeral pyres of their husbands. Some few insisted on it; others were coerced with persuasions and drugs. The extent of the practice varied widely in different ages. It was certainly very ancient and was not prohibited in British India until 1829. In the Indian states it continued longer. There are no more pathetic memorials than the suttee stones to be found near Indian cities or the vermilion handprints imprinted on palace walls by victims on their way to their husbands' pyres.

It is difficult indeed to say how much of this Brahminical system survives today. So much that is vital goes on behind doors which the Westerner rarely enters. Suttee disappeared more than a century ago. The new Hindu Code bills enforce monogamy and give women property rights and a share in inheritance. Western education, the permeation of Western ideas, and the efforts of reformers like Ram Mohan Roy and Swami Dayananda have done much to relax the traditional bonds. Many women of the middle classes now work alongside their husbands, many like Mrs. Pandit and Mrs. Sarojini Naidu have played notable parts in public life. But in rural India the old system with both its good and evil continues in large measure. Mrs. Pandit herself has recorded the shock she received on finding that her husband's relatives expected her, on his death, to retire into seclusion and dependence without property or occupation.

The "untouchables" or exterior castes number about a seventh of the Indian population. They vary greatly in character from the "unseeables" of the extreme south to the sturdy Mahars of western India who once supplied troops to the East India Company. Their disabilities have already been mentioned. Here we may note only two more points. Their disabilities were mental as well as physical, for the Brahmins taught that their present plight was due to sins in past lives. This could only be purged by dutiful performance of present duties. Their disabilities of touch and occupation, held to be unclean,[10] led to social segregation; every village had an "untouchable" hamlet some way from the main village with its separate wells and temples. In modern times a determined attack has been made upon their status. The missionaries began it, and Gandhi has been their greatest Hindu champion. Untouchability is now abolished by the constitution and great efforts are being made to raise them. The institution still prevails as a social custom in many parts, but it is being undermined by a number of forces. Education and ideas of brotherhood is one of these. Railroad travel has given practical aid by compelling relaxations of tabus in crowded compartments. City and industrial life, with its great aggregations of life and mass employment in factories, has helped. Much remains to be done, but it would seem that real changes are actually taking place.

The foregoing may be called a brief description of the Brahminical system as it was developed in the centuries after the close of the Vedic Age, with an attempt to note the relaxations and modifications of recent times. The Brahmin supremacy was essentially a rule of the mind. It was the acceptance by others of the mental concepts which gave them their power. Their ideas justified the hierarchical plan of Hindu society, and they provided a way of release for the soul on its journey toward union with the One. This is elaborated in the great systems of Hindu philosophy and the mystical and spiritual aspect of Hinduism. Let us glance at some of these. The doctrine of *karma*, or the law of moral consequences, is intertwined in Hindu thought with that of transmigration of the soul or rebirth in successive lives. No merit is unrewarded, no sin unatoned in the long run. We are what and where we are because of what we were and did. It follows that everyone's position, the Brahmin in his pride, the raja in his palace, the untouchable in his squalor, is the result of his own past actions. Linked with this is the doctrine of *dharma* or moral duty. There is a duty appropriate to every station in life or caste status. Only by fulfilling it can anyone hope to rise in a future life. These ideas of *karma,* rebirth, and *dharma* are still widely held even by the Westernized classes that may interpret them in a way quite different from that of orthodox Brahminism. Then come the inner Hindu doctrines which have attracted many Westerners. There is the doctrine of *maya* or illusion which sees the sensible world as a veil of illusion, hiding the perception of the one all-pervading Spirit. Spiritual life is a discipline of release from attachment to desire and the things of sense. The goal is *moksha* or freedom from illusion and attachment to the wheel of life and rebirth, of final union with the Supreme. There are the three *margas* or paths of discipline, the way of knowledge, the way of action or works, and the way of loving devotion. There are the four stages of life: of studentship; of householding or family life; of service to the community; and of retirement with contemplation.

Finally, we come to the religious cults of Hinduism, which are perhaps the first aspect to strike the external observer. Hinduism is polytheistic in the sense that there are many gods and goddesses. Yet at the same time there is an overriding sense of a Supreme Spirit behind all of them. Monism in philosophy and polytheism in religion are linked by the idea of incarnation. All divine beings are incarnations of the Supreme Spirit to some extent, whether as aspects of the divine nature in the case of the major deities, or as limited expressions of divine power like the village godlings or hill and river spirits. The Brahmins have included all cults from the pre-Hindu animistic awe of the powers of nature to the veneration of moral values in human form into a comprehensive expression of the divine. Hindu popular religion is protean in its forms and infinite in the diversity of its content.

Little trace survives today of the Vedic deities. Instead there is the Trinity of Brahma the creator, Vishnu the gracious or preserver, and Shiva the destroyer and the powerful. Vishnu and Shiva, in one or another of their forms, between them divide the allegiance of most Hindus. Each has his consort, again in many forms, with his particular cults. The best-known form of Shiva's consort Parvati is Kali, the goddess of destruction widely worshiped in Bengal. The Vishnu cult is distinguished by the belief that Vishnu has incarnated as an *avatar* or sent messenger. Krishna, Rama, and Buddha are three of his previous nine incarnations and there is one yet to come. Below these deities, who preside at the temples which cover the land, are to be found the village spirits, often only identified by a daub of red paint on a rock, a white flag on a tree, or a cairn on a hilltop. These are really survivals from the days of pre-Hindu animism and are usually in some way linked with one of the greater gods.

Hindu worship is ritualistic but not congregational, so we do not find the great assemblies of the faithful to be seen in Islam and Christianity. On a mass scale it expresses itself in popular festivals which mark the seasons or are identified with particular holy spots. The spring is marked by Holi, playful among the upper classes and apt to be bacchanalian in the villages. It is really a spring fertility festival. In the autumn come the two festivals of Dasehra and Diwali, already mentioned, the one commemorating the great epic war, the other the return of Rama to his home. Examples of festivals at holy sites are the Magh festival at Allahabad where the Ganges and Jumna join and the fair at Gurmukhteswar on the upper Ganges. For centuries thousands have traveled great distances to these occasions on foot or by cart; today with the help of the railroad and the automobile the number may run into millions.

There is no end to the study of Hinduism and no statement about it which cannot be contradicted. No one can be sure that he has fully penetrated its mystery. Veil screens veil, and when, drawing all aside, we believe we have penetrated to the innermost sanctuary, we are uncertain whether we have reached the All, or nothing.

CHAPTER III

The Dawn of Recorded History: Alexander and Asoka

The dawn of recorded Indian history can be placed around 600 B.C. Though no exact dates can be supplied for the next two centuries, we are able to obtain a general, if rather vague, picture from a variety of sources. The information mainly concerns the northern parts, it is true, but this was the scene of most vital change. There are inferences to be drawn from the epics; there are dynastic lists to be studied in the Puranas; [1] there are Buddhist and Jain writings and there is the Ceylonese historical chronicle, the *Mahavamsa*. From these sources it can be seen that the center of political gravity has moved still further eastward. As the Panjab in Vedic times gave place to Indraprastha (Delhi) and Hastinapura on the upper Jumna and Ganges in Epic days, so these places have yielded in importance to the modern region of Oudh in western Uttar Pradesh and Behar south of the Ganges. Ayodhya, Rama's city, was the capital of Kosala in Oudh. Banaras appears in history as the sacred city of Kashi, while near the modern Patna was the city of Pataliputra, the capital af Magadha in modern Behar. It can be loosely said that Ayodhya and Pataliputra have taken the place of Indraprastha and Hastinapura. In the south there is evidence of the process of the peaceful penetration of Hindu culture and of kingdoms formed along the eastern coastal plain or the Coromandel coast of South India. The kingdoms mentioned were larger than those of Epic days but none as yet approached the dimensions of an empire. Magadha, of whose kings in two dynasties to 322 B.C. we have some information, was probably the leading state. In the sphere of culture, both Jainism and Buddhism took their rise.

In the northwest the position was obscure, but it is here that we have the first evidence in Indian history of foreign political intervention as distinct from tribal migrations. It came from the first Persian empire whose leader Cyrus took Babylon from the successors of Nebuchadnezzar of Bible fame in 536 B.C. and allowed a "remnant" of the Jews to return to Jerusalem. The Persian empire stretched for two centuries from Egypt and the borders of Greece in the west across Asia Minor and the Iranian Plateau to the Asian Steppes in the north and India in the east. Darius I (521–485 B.C.) invaded northwest India about 518 B.C., conquering the Indus Valley and the west Panjab. These regions became the twentieth satrapy of the Persian empire. According to Herodotus this paid more tribute than any other in the empire. However that may be, it is certain that this connection provided the opportunity for the first Greek reports of India which the same historian included in his early fifth century B.C. *History*. Here began the European legend of the marvels of India with gold-digging ants, people with no mouths, and others who used ears as sunshades. Indians made their first appearance in Europe also, for a contingent accompanied Xerxes on his invasion of Greece and fought at Plataea in 479 B.C. In the fourth century B.C. Persian control relaxed, leaving behind a medley of small states. But Persian influence remained. We can see it, in art, in the lion capitals of the Asoka pillars; we can see it in the solar cults which appeared in India, in the idea of divine monarchy, and in the Mauryan imperial organization.

Thus Indian history proceeds in the half-light of inference and surmise for nearly three centuries. It passes suddenly into the full light of fact with the advent of Alexander the Great in 326 B.C. Having overthrown the Persian King Darius III (Indian elephants were present at the battle of the Issus in 331 B.C.), Alexander conquered Bactria (modern Turkestan) as far as the river Oxus. From there he crossed the Hindu Kush in the spring of 327 B.C. and spent the year subduing the turbulent tribes from a base at or near the modern Kabul so effectively that they never hindered his communications. The next year he crossed the Indus and was welcomed by the ruler of Taxila,[2] who was at odds with neighboring chiefs. Thus another tradition of Indian political life, the calling in of outsiders to tip the scale in an internal struggle, found its first example. Three thousand oxen, besides sheep, were killed to provide a feast for Alexander's army, suggesting that Vedic customs persisted in this corner of India when they had disappeared farther east and south. There followed the defeat of Porus or Puru, the ruler of the tract between the Jhelum and the Chenab, and a fighting advance to the banks of the Beas. Here his troops refused to advance farther into unknown lands and uncalculated opposition. In fact India, so often overrun by foreign invaders in times of disunity, was the only country in the ancient world to bring the world conqueror to a halt. It is also clear that this was achieved by persistent and courageous resistance. Having set up twelve altars on the north bank of the river where it flows east to west (long since swept away by changes in the river's course), Alexander retreated, characteristically making it the occasion of fresh discovery. He proceeded downriver to the Indus' mouth, defeating ruthlessly all who stood in his way. In late 325 B.C. he set out along the unknown coast route of Baluchistan, the fleet coasting along in conjunction. He reached Susa in Persia in May 324 B.C. and died the next year. By 317 B.C. the last trace of Greek authority in the Panjab had disappeared.

From the Greek point of view the Indian expedition was Alexander's Moscow campaign. He was too great to allow the sun and the desert to destroy his army as the snow destroyed Napoleon's. But he reaped nothing but loss from it, including the legend of his own invincibility. Another casualty was his health, which the hardships of the retreat, as well as his own excesses, may well have undermined. Perhaps he died of vexation at finding that the whole world could not be conquered after all. For Westerners his movements, which occupied three of the thirteen years of his reign, have been of absorbing interest, with the result that they have tended to exaggerate their effect upon India as a whole. From the Indian angle his importance was much less. For the chieftains of the northwest he was like a comet which blazes in the sky and vanishes. He became a subject of legend and folklore; eight chiefs today claim descent from him. But in the Gangetic plain where the larger kingdoms were rising he made so little impression that there is no reference to him in Indian literature. What, then, was the real significance of Alexander for India? The first permanent consequence was the opening of practicable routes between India and the West. The feasibility of the sea route was proved by Alexander's fleet, of the land routes by Kabul, the Mulla Pass and Baluchistan by his troops. The Hellenistic Age which followed Alexander kept them open for about two centuries. The next consequence followed from the former: it was an infusion of Persian influence into India whose traces have already been mentioned. A third consequence was the information obtained of the state of northwest India in the late fourth century. We learn not only that Vedic customs persisted in Taxila but that already diverse cultural influences were present. We also learn from the size of the Mallava army and the nature of its gifts that parts of the Panjab were prosperous, and know that politically a state of chronic warfare and near anarchy prevailed.

Immediately after the withdrawal of Alexander there commenced the rise of the first great Indian empire. Little is known of the origin of the founder or of any relationship with Alexander, but it is certain that the type of regime set up resembled Persian rather than Greek models. In 322 B.C., two years after Alexander left Sind, Chandragupta Maurya seized the throne of Magadha and thence steadily extended his power northwestward. When Seleucus Nikator became king of Babylon or West Asia in 312 B.C. he thought of recovering Alexander's Indian provinces. But his attempted invasion in 306 B.C. was defeated outright by Chandragupta. The next year a treaty gave to Chandragupta Kabul, Kandahar, Herat, and modern Baluchistan in return for five hundred elephants. The East had successfully counterattacked the West. About 302 B.C. Seleucus sent the Greek Megasthenes as ambassador to the Mauryan court; he wrote an account of the empire in his leisure moments. Chandragupta's empire extended from Herat to the Bay of Bengal. His son Bindusara (c.298–273 B.C.) probably conquered the Deccan. His grandson Asoka (273–232 B.C.) conquered Kalinga or eastern India in 261 B.C. His realm extended to the modern Mysore. About the year 185 B.C. the dynasty was overthrown and the empire broke up.

This is the bare record of the Mauryan empire. But the contrast with the previous ages is striking. For the first time we have a precise record based on ascertained dates. For about a hundred years there is a flood of direct historic knowledge instead of the inferences and guesses of the past. Then obscurity descends again and half knowledge reigns until the time of the Guptas. The sources of light begin with the writings of Greek observers preserved in later histories, of whom Megasthenes, the Greek ambassador already mentioned, is the most copious. Then come the pillar and rock edicts of the emperor Asoka, a unique series of monuments. There is thirdly a treatise on politics ascribed to Kautiliya, the minister of Chandragupta, called the *Arthasastra*. Classical Sanskrit being difficult to date, it can only be said for certain that it was composed after the time of Chandragupta but before the time of the Guptas (300–450 A.D.). Nevertheless, much of the contents of the book, which is a description of political institutions with advice on statecraft on Machiavellian lines, must go back to Mauryan times. Finally, there are inferences to be drawn from the religious literature of the time and some archeological evidence, such as the discovery of the remains of the city walls of Pataliputra.

The nature of this evidence involves a reversal of the usual order of historical evidence. Instead of a political outline with a vague social and institutional background, we have a description of political, social, and religious conditions with little political history. It is a picture rather than a narrative, the illumination of one period of ancient India with the clarity of a flashlight photograph. The impression we receive is of a highly organized and centralized bureaucracy. Its center was the monarch, who was treated as semidivine and lived in seclusion in his palace. His condition inevitably recalls Persian practice, a notion which is strengthened by other features such as the reverence of fire, the form of the Asokan inscriptions, and the relationship of the Kharoshthi script to Aramaic rather than Greek. Once again, and finally, it should be stressed that the traceable foreign influences of Mauryan days were Persian rather than Greek. Life in the capital itself was controlled by six boards, regulating respectively the industrial arts, foreigners, births and deaths, retail trade and barter, supervision of manufacture, and the collection of a sales or purchase tax. Provinces and towns were administered by centrally appointed officers who may be compared with the French prefects and German burgomasters. Similar authoritarian officers were to be found when the British rose to power some two thousand years later. The land administration was severe. All land was held to belong to the state, cultivators being movable if the officials were dissatisfied with their methods. The demand of the state was one-fourth of the gross produce as against a sixth laid down in the law books. Though the demand in later ages sometimes rose to a third, there is little doubt that the limit of a quarter, with additional imposts which invariably existed, left the peasant little more than a bare subsistence. The law was severe. In the cities it achieved security of property at the price of terror. Torture (eighteen kinds are enumerated in the *Arthasastra,* one of which, it is suggested, might be applied each day) was regularly used to extort confessions and also as a variety of punishment. The death penalty was administered in many forms. On the other hand irrigation was promoted and carefully regulated, while roads were maintained. Rather surprisingly, in view of later orthodox feelings, the drinking of liquor was recognized and regulated to the profit of the state. The whole system was held together by two further institutions. One was the army. It was organized on a regular basis and was thought to have numbered about 700,000 men. It included 9,000 elephants and probably up to 10,000 chariots. It was administered by a commission divided into six boards or committees. The other was the secret police, who were efficient and ubiquitous throughout the empire, operating through the most intimate channels.

Parts of this picture are not pleasant. It may be described as an efficient but severe bureaucracy. But there are other features as well. The bureaucracy was imposed on a rural economy of which we have an attractive picture in the Buddhist stories known as the *Jatakas.* The descriptions suggest an active trade and general prosperity. The harshness of the laws and the terror of the secret police were probably mainly felt by the inhabitants of the towns and the upper classes, amongst whom the struggle for power must have been intense. This severity and reliance on terror becomes intelligible when we remember the turbulence of north India as evidenced by Alexander's experience, the speed with which the empire was built up, and its immense extent. There must have been an ever-present danger of conspiracy and rebellion. The authorities of those days did not realize that they were providing a golden age for a remote future to look back upon.

Chandragupta founded the Mauryan empire, but his grandson Asoka adorned it. His is one of the great names of all ages. He was the first ruler of a great empire to preach the way of gentleness in preference to the way of force, to insist that the moral law was the key to public action. He ruled the empire without dispute for forty-one years. The crisis in Asoka's life came with the conquest of Kalinga. Remorse for the suffering then inflicted provoked a spiritual revolution. He thus describes it in Rock Edict XIII.

"Kalinga was conquered by his Sacred and Gracious Majesty when he had been consecrated eight years. 150,000 persons were thence carried away captive, 100,000 were slain and many times that number died. . . . Thus arose his Sacred Majesty's remorse for having conquered the Kalingas because the conquest of a country previously unconquered involves the slaughter, death and carrying away captive of the people."

From this moment Asoka spent the rest of his life promoting the law of duty or piety throughout his great empire. His inspiration was the teaching of the Buddha who had already been dead for some two centuries and whose doctrine must have been widespread. Asoka chose the novel form of publicity of inscribing his edicts on stone. These edicts are often more in the nature of moral discourses than laws and remind one rather of Chinese inscriptions containing the sayings of Confucius than the legal publications posted in modern public places. They were, in fact, state sermons rather than commands. Their number and wide spread suggest a deliberate intention of publicity while the latter feature helps to fix the limit of Asoka's empire. They appear on rocks, in caves, and on specially built pillars ranging from the northwest of modern Pakistan to the borders of Mysore.[3] This method further suggests that there must have been a literate class to read them.

The virtues which are proclaimed are broadly those of the Buddhist way of life. The individual is to cultivate simplicity, gentleness, and compassion; these feelings are to extend to all living beings, with the corollary of kindness to animals and vegetarianism in diet. Asoka himself gave up hunting, the traditional sport of kings, and is said to have been initiated as a Buddhist monk. The doctrine of ahimsa or nonviolence is perhaps the most prominent of all in the edicts. In personal relations the golden rule of doing as one would be done by was inculcated, while the moral duties of the subjects are matched by those of the sovereign, who is pictured as the servant of the people, laboring night and day for their welfare.

The edicts were a way of spreading Asoka's ideas within the empire. But he was not content with this; he carried the message abroad. In about 250 B.C. his brother Mahendra led a mission to King Tissa in Ceylon, which resulted in the king's conversion to Buddhism. Asoka's sister Sanghamitra founded a nunnery. Missions were despatched to the Hellenistic west where they reached Egypt, Cyrene in North Africa, and Epirus in northern Greece. Toward the end of his reign he summoned a religious convention at Pataliputra, reckoned as the first general council of the Buddhist Church. Monkish sources say it was called to repress heresy, but it was probably another stage in Asokan publicity.

It may well be asked whether a great empire, which had so recently seen so much violence, could be held together by such means. Could not these inscriptions, which have so stirred the world of scholarship, really be evidence of no more than an imperial whim, charming but irrelevant? Was not Asoka's ahimsa as fascinating but as ephemeral as Akbar's divine faith? The reference to Akbar perhaps affords a clue, for it will be seen later that it was not merely a private cult but rather an attempt to effect a moral integration of the nobility. The orthodox explanation of Asoka has been that he was converted to Buddhism following on his remorse for the slaughter in Kalinga and that his endeavor was to integrate his empire by turning Buddhism into a state church. A recent view [4] suggests that Asoka was, in fact, a greater Akbar. Conscious that his empire contained a great medley of races, full of independent spirit and with the most varied beliefs, and aware that force can never maintain empires for long, he attempted to promote an imperial ethic which might bind the governing classes in a common allegiance to an impersonal law. For this purpose he used what seemed to be the rising ideas of his day. In all probability he personally believed in those ideas, but he promoted them as the best way of permanently binding the empire together. His method was not the sectarian encouragement of the Buddhist Church, for that would have provoked division rather than unity. Buddhist aggression would involve Brahminical reaction. So he used concepts now associated with Buddhism and tried to secure their acceptance by attaching them to the prestige of the semidivine monarch. His efforts were in line with the solar cult of Akhnaton and the emperor worship of the Romans; it was more practical than the former and more noble than the latter. It was also more effective than Akbar's experiment, for it certainly promoted the spread of Buddhism in India.

CHAPTER IV

Jainism and Buddhism

Asoka's ideas lead naturally to the subject of Buddhism. Today it is known principally in its South Asian form in Ceylon, Burma, and Siam, in its unique Tibetan manifestation, and in Japan. It still exists in China but is much less in evidence. But it is hardly known in India which is the land of its birth. It is a recognized world religion: how then did it come to disappear from its own birthplace, the land of religions itself? The subject has been bypassed so far in order to maintain the continuity of the political narrative from 600 B.C. But it is an essential part of the Indian story, for India would not be what it is without it and it is therefore time to examine it.

Buddhism was one of several movements which arose in a period of unrest and ferment from about the year 600 B.C. Three causes may be hazarded for this ferment, one material, one moral, and one racial. On the material side there was the transition from a pastoral to an agricultural economy. The Indo-Aryan tribes were settling down, becoming tillers of the soil instead of shepherds of flocks. They were developing cities and becoming attached to the soil. Tribal groups were becoming territorial kingdoms. With crop-raising there began to be a surplus production which led to the development of arts and crafts, to exchange in the form of trade and commerce. Such a transition inevitably meant social tension. The merchant or *vaishya* class rose in importance and resented the privileges claimed by the upper two orders. To put it in modern terms, here was a situation which provided material for middle-class discontent with aristocratic privilege and priestly domination. Bourgeois aggressiveness bred anticlerical feelings.

The second force at work (in what proportions the two combined we cannot say at this distance of time) was a religious and intellectual ferment comparable with that of contemporary Greece. There was a striving after spiritual truth in a ferment of minds and much dissatisfaction with the current Brahminical order. In the thousand years or so since the Indo-Aryans had arrived the Brahmins or hereditary priests (worshipers of Brahma the creator) had seized the leadership of society from the nobles and had already established the most subtle and powerful domination of all, that of the mind. They had progressed, it is true, from the Vedic religion of hymns to the powers of nature and spells to secure boons and ward off dangers. They had developed the doctrine of *karma* or the law of consequences and the complementary doctrine of transmigration of souls from life to life. But the conditions governing the working of these laws were nonmoral and ritualistic. Reliance was placed on *mantras* or spells, on sacrifice, and on priestly ritual. The law of consequences was not yet a law of *moral* consequences. The developing conscience of the age revolted against this mechanistic religiosity. There grew up a longing for *moksha* or freedom or release from rebirth, the conscience demanding something more than ritual and the mind something more than formulae. With these gropings schools of asceticism and moral discipline and schools of philosophy or intellectual apprehension developed. From the former came movements like Buddhism, and from the latter the great Hindu schools of philosophy, which found expression in philosophical treatises known as the Upanishads. Their message was monism, the identification of the self within with the Self in the universe. It was expressed in the aphorism *Tat tvam asi* ("That art thou").

Another element should be added to this ferment. It was the tension between the non-Aryans admitted to the Hindu fold, and the Brahmins. For example, the tribe in the Nepal hills from which the Buddha came is thought to have been of Mongolian stock. The nobles of such groups had little relish for the Brahmin superiority which they found established in the new society. To sum up, we may say that a period of heart-searching and change was introduced by class tension caused by the economic transition and the rise of a mercantile class, by intellectual and spiritual tension caused by the mechanistic character of the Brahmin ascendancy, and by race tension caused by the expansion of Hindu society to include non-Aryan groups.

Many movements appeared in the sixth and fifth centuries, for which evidence exists in Hindu literature. But only two have survived until today. They are Buddhism and Jainism. We will note the latter first although its founder probably was born a few years after the Buddha and died a few years after his death. The founder of Jainism was Mahavira, who was born to a non-Aryan noble family about 540 B.C. and died about 467 B.C.[1] (during the great age of Greece and the glory of Athens). When he was forty he started his own order and spent the rest of his life teaching his "way" and collecting disciples. He believed that all life was impregnated with spirit, that not only animals and insects but "stocks and stones and trees" had each a separate soul. Each soul was a distinct creation and passed from form to form in life after life according to its deserts. The object of endeavor was to become one with the impersonal universe by breaking the chain of birth and death. From these ideas arose the doctrine of ahimsa or nonviolence which has exercised a profound influence on Indian life. Since all creatures have souls as much as humans, their lives must be respected. So pious Jains today will feed ants as a religious act, place cloths over their noses to prevent insects being drawn up their nostrils, and eat only by day to avoid accidents to insect life in the dark. The best death a Jain can die is by self-starvation. In average daily life this may be taken as reading "be as kind as you can and do your re- ligious duty."

Jainism was essentially a way of life, or, as Westerners might say, a way of escape, rather than a separate religion. Although reckoned as a separate religion in India, it is rather a nonconformist type of Hinduism than something completely apart. The caste structure of Hindu society was untouched and Brahmins were used for domestic worship. Today the relationships of Jains and some Hindu castes are very close so that it is difficult to say where one ends and the other begins. The Jains were strong in western and northern India until about 600 A.D., founding kingdoms and building temples. They are still numerous in the new Gujarat state and number about a million souls today. Far greater, however, has been their influence on Indian society in general. They share with the Buddhists the responsibility for the acceptance of the doctrine of physical nonviolence within the general body of Hinduism. Without Mahavira there would have been no Gandhi. They were also perhaps influential in extending the working of the law of *karma* in Hindu eyes through all the kingdoms of nature. This has tended to produce the moral inertia so often remarked on by foreign observers and to put a stumbling block of fantasy in the way of Western understanding of the true meaning of *karma*. It is not easy for the matter-of-fact Westerner to think of the fly in the soup as possibly a deceased relation.

Siddhartha Gautama, the Buddha or Enlightened One, also known as Sakyamuni or Savior of the Sakyas, was born into a noble family of the Sakya tribe at Kapilavastu on the borders of Nepal. The date now most generally accepted is about 567 B.C., though the Buddhists of

R. Oxus

BACTRIA

Hindu Kush

AFGHANISTAN

Kabul

Peshawar
GANDHARA
Taxila
Gujrat
Sialkot

KASHMIR
Martand

TIBET

BALUCHISTAN

R. Indus

PUNJAB

H i m a l y a s

R. Sutlej

Thanesar

R. Jumna

PANCHALA

R. Brahmaputra

RAJPUTANA

Aravallis

Muttra

Ahichhatdra

Kampil
Kanauj
Ganges

KOSALA
Ajodhya

VIDEHA

R. Brahmaput

SIND

Kosam

Banares

Patna

MAGADHA

Gaur

ASSA

Khajuraho

Buddh Gaya

R. Brahmaput

BENGAL

MALWA
Sanchi

Bharhut

GUJARAT
Ujjain
Kathiawar
Junagarh
Broach
Bagh

V i n d h y a s

R. Narbada

Tamluk

ORISSA

Ajanta
Ellora

MAHARASHTRA

KALINGAS

ARABIAN SEA

Western Ghats

A N D H R A S

R. Kistna
Amaravati

Malabar Coast

BAY OF BENGAL

Conjeeveram

CHOLAS

Tanjore

KERALAS
Madura
PANDYAS

CEYLON

0   100   200   300   400   500

Scale of Miles

Ancient India | *200 B.C. to 1000 A.D.*

Ceylon put it as early as 623 B.C.[2] He died around 487 B.C. at the age of eighty. Around his life there has grown a tangle of pious legend, through which it is very difficult to penetrate to the flowers of historic truth. On the main outline of the story, however, there is general agreement. Gautama grew up in an atmosphere of ease and luxury, married within his class, and had a son. In some way he became aware of the sorrow and suffering of the world and of the transitoriness of life. In his twenty-ninth year he left his palace and family, donned the yellow robe, and commenced to wander, a homeless ascetic. For six years he wandered, seeking wisdom and the secret of sorrow. He trod the well-worn path of asceticism and austerities without achieving his goal. He then gave up these practices, so that his disciples deserted him saying "the ascetic Gautama has become luxurious; he has ceased from striving and turned to a life of comfort." It was then that, sitting under a *bodhi* tree under a full moon at Gaya, he attained enlightenment or Buddhahood. The meaning of sorrow, the arising of sorrow, and the conquest of sorrow became clear to him. From Gaya he went to Sarnath near Banaras where, sitting in a deer park, he gave his first sermon. From that time he moved up and down north India, preaching the Path and organizing his followers.

The Buddha's teaching concerned the nature of sorrow, which for him was the manifestation of evil in the world. Sorrow arose from desire, and desire from attachment to the transitory features of an illusive world. Desire or attachment was the cause of rebirth in successive lives. Desire in its turn was fostered by illusion, the belief that the material, changing world was real. For the Buddha it was a dancing fantasm, tempting men with its glitter and movement to bind themselves to the ever-revolving wheel of life. Desire meant sorrow in life after life. The way of escape was to conquer desire. This would bring freedom from rebirth and absorption into the All, a state called Nirvana. Whether, in the Buddha's mind, this meant extinction or conscious bliss is uncertain; what is certain is that he considered this enlightenment infinitely preferable to the only alternative of enduring sorrow. It can thus be said that the doctrine of the Buddha amounted to a spiritual and mental discipline for the attainment of right views about life. About ultimates he was agnostic. There was no personal God in the original system. It would be a mistake, however, to picture the Buddha as a late-nineteenth-century rationalist, founding an Ethical Society and lecturing in rationalist halls. The accounts of his enlightenment have in them the marks of universal mystical experience, the feeling of oneness with the universe. It was this experience toward which the Buddha's doctrine and discipline led, and it was this experience which attracted his followers and dispensed with the need for theistic worship. Meditation took the place of prayer and inner peace of divine worship.

For a time the Buddha thought that his doctrine was "too profound and subtle" for "this race of mankind, who only seek and revel in pleasure." [3] But he repented and persevered with his teaching. There developed during his life a double way. The first was the way of renunciation for those who aspired to Buddhahood and freedom or release from the wheel of life. These disciples were organized in the *Sangha* or order, containing both men and women. They renounced the world and donned the saffron robe, lived in communities of monks and nuns, and had no possessions but their robes, their staves, and begging bowls. The modern state name of Behar derives from the word *vihara,* a Buddhist monastery, for it was once famous for these establishments.

The second way was for the householder, who, while continuing to live in the world, sought, as it were, to improve his ultimate prospects by right living. This was the Middle Way of historic Buddhism, eschewing all extremes, whose code was the "noble eightfold path." This is the ethic of popular Buddhism, and consists of right views, right resolves, right speech, right action, right living, right effort, right recollectedness, and right meditation. Without going further into these rules we may note the spirit which underlay them. One thread was that of ahimsa or nonviolence. The spirit of life was in all creatures and all creatures were therefore akin. While the Christian prays for all men, the Buddhist prays for all sentient beings. There follow such practices as vegetarianism and the refusal to take life. Another thread was compassion, which may be called the characteristic and pervasive virtue of the original system.[4] It is this feeling, together with that of abstraction, which irradiates the countenance of the Buddha in his Indian statues. It marked a distinction from the Brahmins of the time, for whom knowledge was the supreme gift. In the personality and message of the Buddha there is a serenity and spiritual calm which charms and subdues the student after two and a half millennia. Like the silver rays of a full moon on a calm night, the Buddha's words still shed their gentle light on the face of troubled humanity. "Now monks, I have nothing more to tell you than this; decay is inherent in all compounded things. Work out your salvation energetically."

> Lord Buddha on thy lotos throne,
> With praying hands and eyes elate,
> What mystic rapture dost thou own,
> Immutable and ultimate?

What peace, unravished of our ken
Annihilate from the world of men? [5]

It will be seen from the foregoing that primitive Buddhism, while it could perhaps not be called a religion in the strict sense, was much more clearly divided from the Hinduism of its day than Jainism. Jainism offered a new philosophy and a separate way of release or freedom within the framework of the Hindu social system. It was a movement rather than a new religion whose "separateness" from Hinduism was due to Brahmin hostility rather than its unique qualities. It was a Hindu heresy which did not die out. The Buddha, on the other hand, while accepting some basic Hindu ideas such as *karma,* separated himself from current Hinduism in a number of ways. He discountenanced caste, the key-stone of the Hindu social arch. He had no place for Brahmins, replacing them in his system with monks. Agnostic in ultimate belief, he could not support the gods of the populace. Like a later Protestant, he believed that the scriptures should be understood by the people. He taught in the current speech of the Gangetic plain, a dialect akin to the Pali which later became the Buddhist sacred language. He was an opponent of the priesthood, of magic and sacrifice, of privileges, and of hiding truth in the mystery of a strange language and unintelligible books. His message was for all equally. The Middle Path provided a way of life for all, the Discourses of the Buddha a holy book for all, and the life of renunciation a way of release for all. In some aspects, Buddhism was a democratic protest against Brahmin supremacy. It had therefore to separate itself from Brahminism or perish. When and where it later reunited with Brahminism it did perish.

Thus, from an early period Buddhism came to be a movement separated from general Hinduism by its attitude toward caste and the Brahmins. It early developed special characteristics which have remained in some degree ever since. As Christianity had the Cross as its symbol, Buddhism had the Wheel of Life. For its first five hundred years the Buddha was never represented in human form. With Buddhahood he had passed into the All and his place in the sculptures was therefore taken by the Wheel. When the Buddha had been turned into a savior (like the Amida Buddha of Japan) the symbol was that of the Buddha sitting in meditation. Buddhism was strongly monastic in character, for the direct path to freedom lay through complete renunciation. But Buddhist monasticism was more flexible than Christian, since vows were not irrevocable; people could enter monasteries for periods as some Christians withdraw for "retreats." Buddhism soon developed a vast literature which is more intelligible to the Westerner than the

Hindu, since it has a historical anchor in the founder and an ethical one in the Law. The *Jataka* stories, for example, some six hundred in number, deal with the incarnations of the Buddha before he attained Buddahood. Buddhism also developed a characteristic art. Its temples were stupas or solid mounds which encased relics and around which the devout processed as a form of devotion. The stupa at Sanchi in Central India dates from Asoka's time; the bold sculpture and stonework of the surrounding railings may still be seen. The subjects of both sculpture and painting were incidents in the life of the Buddha, his enlightenment, his discourse in the deer park, or incidents from the *Jataka* stories of his previous lives.

We do not know for certain and shall probably never know whether Asoka became a full Buddhist and how far he went in patronizing the movement. But it is certain that it grew to great strength in his time and was henceforward for some eight or nine centuries a serious rival to Brahminism. It was, however, never dominant in India, and it would be a mistake to label any one period as a Buddhist age. Buddhism, though it was implicitly incompatible with Brahminism, never quite severed its connection from popular Hinduism. Its tolerance permitted what its teaching denied, a syncretistic respect for the spiritual powers in the land. About the first century A.D. Buddhism divided into two main streams. The Hinayana or Lesser Vehicle continued the early tradition, regarding the Buddha as a teacher and his Law as a guide for men. This form is found today in Ceylon, Burma, Thailand, and Cambodia.

But in northwest India there developed the Mahayana or Greater Vehicle. The Buddha came to be reverenced not only as a teacher but as the incarnation of the Deity and the savior of mankind. It followed that there must be a radical change in the doctrine and the whole content of Buddhism. The Mahayana was a theistic religion with a church and priesthood, a doctrine and an elaborate ritual. In some ways it resembled the Catholic form of Christianity, as the Jesuit Fathers Huc and Gabert noticed when they visited Lhasa in 1842. At first it was a missionary religion. From northwest India and Afghanistan it spread north of the Hindu Kush Mountains into Central Asia; thence it traveled along the trade routes to China, where it has had a lengthy history. Chinese Buddhist pilgrims journeying to India have provided historians with priceless information about India in the first ten Christian centuries. From China Buddhism spread to Tibet where it united with the local cults to form the unique type of Tibetan Buddhism. From China it also jumped the sea to Japan where it is still a vigorous cult. This form of Buddhism also had its characteristic art. The stupa remained, but it was now surrounded with votive chapels and shrines to Buddha and the Bodhisattvas. Bells, processions, incense, and prayer wheels were prominent. In northwest India and beyond it produced a characteristic art form known as the Gandhara style,[6] where Greek craftsmanship combined with Buddhist piety to mold classic figures of the Buddha sitting with statuesque poise and calm.

Down to about 600 A.D. Buddhism in its earlier form, and from the first century A.D. in its Mahayana form, remained a powerful religion in India, contending with Hinduism for her soul. From that time it declined until at the end of the twelfth century the invading Muslim Turks found it only surviving in a debased form in Behar and Bengal. This disappearance of a great moral and religious movement after a thousand years of vigor from the land of its birth is one of the great historical mysteries. We do not know enough to explain the process in detail or to assess accurately the relative importance of the various factors involved. All that can be done is to suggest the nature of some of the forces which were at work. A preliminary factor was the preference, in the long run, of the Indian aristocracy for Hinduism. They preferred it, in spite of the priestly Brahmin supremacy which it involved, on account of the Buddhists' emphasis on ahimsa or nonviolence. Brahminism sanctified fighting for the military castes. Krishna's exhorting Arjuna to fight as a moral duty was preferable to the Buddha's otherworldliness. The center of Buddhism was renunciation, while in Hinduism there was a place for all worldly activity. A physically destructive factor was the barbarian invasions of the fifth and sixth centuries. The Huns burned the last city of Taxila, the center of northern Buddhism, and obliterated the Way from the northwest. The Turks about 1200 A.D. destroyed the Behar monasteries. The guardians of later Buddhism were the monks; with their destruction the system collapsed.

But Hinduism suffered at the hands of the outer barbarians also and yet survived, even in the northwest. The reason for this is to be found in the process which had been going on ever since the rise of the Buddhist challenge, for the Hinduism which survived the Huns and the Turks was different from the Hinduism which the Buddha encountered in the fifth century B.C. The old reliance on magic, on spells, on ritual prayers, and on sacrifice, animal and otherwise, had retired into the background. Hinduism had developed its own higher philosophy in the Upanishads, its own spiritual disciplines and its own paths to freedom or release. The renouncers could abandon the world as part of Hinduism, the believers in gentleness could practice ahimsa. The ethics of the *Gita* and the *Ramayana* provided a moral code within the Hindu fold, while the existence of cults of *bhakti* or devotion supplied a religion of the heart for more ardent natures. In fact, Hinduism had been transformed and in transforming itself had added many of the features whose absence had encouraged the rise of Buddhism. It was a counterreformation which succeeded. Buddhism thus lost much of its *raison d'être* as a reforming movement. It was one religion in competition with another, and in this contest Hinduism proved more flexible and embracing. And here must be noted another point which was perhaps vital in deciding the issue. Buddhism had never completely emancipated itself from popular religion. With the coming of the Mahayana the tendencies to compound with local deities increased. The Buddha, now the supreme deity, came to preside over a pantheon of Hindu gods. In the latter days of Buddhism in India the two cults were hardly to be distinguished in principle and in practice except by the prominence of monks and monasteries in Buddhism. In further India this process reached its limit when great temples were built for the worship of the compound deity Shiv-Buddh.[7] From the desireless renunciation of the sage of the Sakyas to the power cult of Cambodia was a far cry. Gautama would not have recognized such disciples as these.

To sum up, it may be said broadly that in India Buddhism acted as the reagent to Hinduism. It acted as the stimulus for the development of the parent cult and passed away when it had done its work. Its significance for modern India is not in the few relics left behind of its separate existence but in the nature of the Hinduism which replaced it. The spirit of Shiv-Buddh is to be found not in the frowning deities of Angkor but in the body of later Hinduism itself. Buddhism can claim with Jainism a share in acclimatizing ahimsa or gentleness within Hinduism. It can also claim to have introduced a moral content into the concept of *dharma* or religious duty; and in particular the addition of compassion to the list of the Hindu virtues. What may be called the higher Hinduism with its spiritual and moral discipline and its doctrine of the absorption of the self in the One owes much to early Buddhism. It was Buddhist influence which ended the Vedic and post-Vedic phase of Hinduism, a religion of nature worship and sacrifice, of spells and power propitiation. The Brahmins triumphed but only at the price of taking Buddhist ideas into partnership. The recognition of the Buddha as the ninth incarnation of Vishnu the Hindu Preserver god had in it a deep symbolism. Rising from Hinduism's jungle of popular cults of crude beliefs and practices there grew a nobler tree of enlightenment and self-realization through spiritual discipline.

CHAPTER V

The Invaders

Mauryan India marked one of the twin peaks of Indian civilization. In the view of some, like Professor Toynbee, it was the climax of the original Indian civilization, the second flowering some centuries later being that of a separate "affiliated" civilization. Be that as it may, it is certain that the breakup of the Mauryan empire in the early second century B.C. was followed by a period of confusion and obscurity. India, as it were, was getting its second breath before the next outburst of creative activity.

But this was not all that happened in these obscure centuries. India was at the same time receiving a variety of influences from abroad which were to affect both the make-up of her culture and the composition of her population. This is the significance of the period for contemporary Indians. A modern Indian who returned to Mauryan India would find many familiar features. The social structure would be recognizable, though possessing unfamiliar traits. The great gods like Vishnu and Siva would be there, though their cults would vary widely. The Buddhist and other cults, though unfamiliar, would be readily assimilated. But language would present a real difficulty. No modern Indian language existed then, nor was Sanskrit still a spoken language. The appearance and habits of the people in large areas would also be a puzzle, because they would have customs unknown to him. He would miss familiar figures, such as the Rajput and the Jat. It is this period which fills some though not all of the gaps which exist between Mauryan India and contemporary experience. This period will therefore be treated in broad outline, disregarding for the most part dynastic lists and chronological controversies. Our concern is with what India received at this time.

The first of the foreign influences was that of the Greeks. Alexander's incursion, as we have seen, was brief. But the Greek invasions of the second century B.C. were a different story. The materials are scanty, but their lack of volume has been balanced by the brilliance of their interpretation by a British and an Indian scholar.[1] For the early portion there are references in Greek literature, as there are also for commercial intercourse. There are also references in Indian literature. There is a little archeological evidence. But the main source of information is hoards of Indo-Greek coins unearthed in Afghanistan and northwest India. They are often of exquisite workmanship, and their provenance and characteristics have enabled scholars to deduce the course of the rise and fall of Greek influence in India.

Who then were these Greeks in India a century and a half after Alexander's departure? Alexander had inaugurated the age of Hellenism throughout the Middle East, using as his agents not only the ubiquitous charm of Greek ideas but Greek colonies planted as cities at strategic points. One which he planted in India was called Bucephala. After Alexander's death the region now known as Persia passed to the Greek Seleucids, who, as has been noted, battled vainly with Chandragupta Maurya for the control of Afghanistan and the Panjab. But about 250 B.C. the Seleucid empire began to break up. The Parthians, hardy horsemen of the borders of modern Persia and Turkestan, revolted and gradually gained control of Persia, where they faced the later Roman power in Mesopotamia (Iraq). But in Bactria, the modern Badakshan, north of the Hindu Kush Mountains, there remained an isolated Greek kingdom. With the turn of the second and third centuries B.C. one of their kings crossed the mountains to occupy Afghanistan and pushed on into the Panjab. Soon Bactria became independent, but the Greek adventurers pushed undaunted farther into India. Their kingdoms can be traced in their coins all over the northwest and the Panjab, a region which was known as Gandhara. The Indo-Greeks reached their zenith when the legendary Menander took part in an expedition which reached the walls of Patna or Pataliputra, the capital of Magadha and the one-time Mauryan empire about 150 B.C. Perhaps Menander represented only one party in a coalition of Indian powers; perhaps he conceived the daring design, like Babur the Mughal in a later age, of seizing the capital of the largest state in India and reviving a north Indian empire. In any case it is clear that the Greeks of the dispersion had lost neither their daring nor their skill since Alexander's day.[2] After the death of Menander, whose capital is reputed to have been at Sialkot in the Panjab, the Indo-Greek power gradually waned. For perhaps a century and a half they enjoyed substantial power, but by the turn of the Christian era they had disappeared into the hills.

Such an extended stay by such an active and intelligent people as the Greeks might be expected to have left some mark on the country. That the Hindus were aware of Greek thought as well as Greek soldiers and adventurers is suggested by the eleventh-century Arab scholar Alberuni's quotation from Varahamihira, "the Greeks, though impure, must be honoured, since they were trained in sciences and therein excelled others." [3] But this admission is quite distinct from the acknowledgment of actual Greek influence. And here the Westerner must be on his guard against allowing desire to outrun discretion or interest the limits of our knowledge. Western pride in the Greeks is such that it is easy, in looking for traces of their influence, to overlook other forms of evidence or counterindications. It has already been suggested that some of the influence attributed to Alexander was really more Persian than Greek. The impress upon India of the later Greeks may now be briefly summarized. They minted quantities of coins of brilliant craftsmanship from which the broad outline of their history has been traced. These constitute, in effect, the beginning of the Indian coinage. They left a school of religious art, known as the Gandharan, which decorated the monasteries of the northwest in the next few centuries with classical Buddhas and Bodhisattvas. In literature there is the Buddhist text known as the *Questions of Milinda* (Menander) which may be taken as an introduction of the Greek dialogue form into Indian literature. In language the Sanskrit terms for the significant words horse-bit, pen and ink, book, and mine are borrowed from the Greek. In science the debt would seem to be larger, for both Indian astrology and Hindu medicine (the Ayurvedic system) contain Greek words among their technical terms.

When all these traces of influence are added up, it cannot seriously be said that they come to very much. There was, it seems, little interpenetration of the mind and little impact on the Indian social system. The Greeks were few in number and were more easily Indianized, as the inscription on the pillar of Heliodorus in central India [4] suggests, than Indians were Hellenized. Scholars looking for Greek influence in India have in fact too often looked in the wrong direction. More solid evidence is to be found in the mundane world of trade and commerce rather than in the realm of the mind. In this field we have much literary evidence, backed by recent archeological finds of an extensive commerce between East and West lasting up to the fifth century A.D. It was at this time that the pattern of trade was laid down which lasted until the Industrial Revolution began in the late eighteenth century A.D. During the Hellenistic Age there developed both land and sea routes. A land route ran from Babylon through Herat and Kabul to

India by the various passes. There were two sea routes. One ran along
the Persian and Baluchi coasts to Sind and Barygaza (modern Broach)
in the Gulf of Cambay. The other, making use of the monsoon winds,
crossed the Indian Ocean of southern Arabia to the neighborhood of
Calicut in modern Kerala. Thence traders coasted round south India
as far as Arikimedu near the modern Pondicherry. The discovery of this
route is attributed to a Greek Hippalus and the date is thought to have
been about the turn of the Christian era. The navigator was blown
out to sea by the onset of the monsoon to discover that after days of
tossing he had reached not only land but the spice ports of south India
themselves. The northern route provided the north Indian courts with
luxuries; the southern gave Europe articles she could not produce herself. From the outset India had more to give than to receive, another
characteristic which lasted until the eighteenth Christian century. Europe
made up the balance of payments with bullion, which began the traditional drain on the precious metals to India which has lasted, not to the
eighteenth century only, but to the present day. In item after item, such
as wine and bullion on the European side, spices and drugs on the
Indian, we see the evidence of an enduring tradition. The main articles
of import were wines, coral, arms, glass, and chinaware (from Italy),
lead and tin (possibly from Britain), and bullion or coins. The articles
of export were spices (some re-exported even then from the East
Indies), drugs, scented woods, cotton, silk, and gems. Roman unification led to an expansion of the trade in the first three Christian centuries. At its height it was said that a hundred and twenty ships sailed
from Egypt every year. Most of the Indian products, as well as those
of the East Indies, were available in south India, which at the same
time was cheaper and easier to reach from Egypt or Europe owing
to the direct sea transport. It is therefore probable that the bulk of
the trade went there. This is supported by the traces of two trading
stations, at Muziris near Cranganore in Kerala and at Arikimedu near
Pondicherry on the east coast, and by references in Tamil literature.
Tamil poets speak of "the abode of the Yavanas whose prosperity
seems never to wane," of Muziris, where "the Yavanas come, making
the water white with foam and return laden with pepper," of palace
lamps held in the hands of "metal statues made by the Yavanas," and
of "the cool and fragrant wines brought by the Yavanas in their good
ships." [5]

One more result of this contact was of an unexpected kind. It was
nothing less than the import of new religions into the land of religion.
One was Christianity, whose modern representatives are the people

known today as Syrian Christians in the state of Kerala. Into their checkered history and present-day ramifications there is no need to enter, nor need we discuss the probability of the local claim that the church was founded by the apostle Thomas in person. There is a northern and a southern version of this tradition. The historian may agree that either might be true and that the southern version is the more likely of the two. But he must also admit that for neither is there any contemporary evidence. There is, however, good reason to believe that Christians were established as a body by the third century A.D., and it is certain that they were there by the fifth.[6] The first minister of finance of independent India was a Syrian Christian. The second religious invasion was that of the Jews. There exist today at the port of Cochin in Kerala two communities of Jews that both claim to have sought refuge there after the destruction of Jerusalem by the Romans in 70 A.D. The "white" Jews kept their Semitic stock intact while the "black" Jews intermarried locally.

With the disappearance of the Indo-Greeks, northwestern India was beset by a period of confusion and obscurity. It was a time during which, so the shadowy outline of the evidence suggests, not ordered armies on the march but whole peoples seeking new homes moved across the scene. For it was one of those recurrent periods when central Asia was in ferment, bubbling with activity like some human volcano, and throwing off streams of human lava. The Aryan invasions of India, Iran, and Europe in the second millennium B.C. had been one of these; the Teutonic invasions of Europe and the Hun incursions into both Europe and India in the fourth, fifth, and sixth Christian centuries was another; and the movements of Turks and Mongols from the eleventh to the fourteenth centuries another. Only the most general outline of events can be determined, for we have little evidence beyond stray literary references, inscriptions, and coins. The little evidence we possess suggests that while the people first appeared as barbarians they were open to civilizing influences and rapidly acquired a veneer of Hellenistic culture and a respect for the Buddhist religion. Thus the period, though confused and productive of new racial strains, left Indian civilization relatively intact.

This movement of peoples began, as has been noticed, with the Parthians (known in India as the Pahlavas) who in the mid-third century B.C. revolted from the Greek Seleucids in their lands near the shore of the Caspian Sea and gradually gained control of modern Iran in the course of the next century. From about 140 B.C. their bands, which may be thought of as groups of adventurers led by chiefs, spread into northwest India where they came into contact with the Indo-Greeks. Menander, the most famous of the Greek kings, is thought to have died about 130 B.C. The Parthian or Pahlava bands pushed the Indo-Greeks northward and themselves occupied the lower Indus Valley. Perhaps this was the result of thrust and counterthrust. The contest was not lethal, for trade continued and the invaders had a veneer of Persian and Greek culture. They introduced the term "satrapy" in political usage, which lingered on for several centuries. Gondophernes, one of the legendary hosts of St. Thomas, was a Pahlava chief.

Behind the Parthians came the Scythians or Sakas as they were known in India.[7] The Sakas were nomad tribes of central Asia that were pressed by another horde known as the Yueh-chi, which will appear again a little later. As so often in the record of central Asia, it is the nomad tribe in retreat from a stronger that appears as a menace on the frontiers of settled society. The Pahlavas had bypassed the Greeks in Bactria or Badakshan by going south of the Hindu Kush range. But the Sakas came down on them from the north. They overwhelmed the Greeks there about 130 B.C. By 60 B.C. they were south of the Hindu Kush Mountains and fifty years later had reached southern Afghanistan and southeastern Persia. The region of Seistan is equated with Sakasthana. Thence they spread into the Panjab or Gandhara where they eliminated the last Greek princes and moved through south Sind and into Gujarat and the western Deccan. They pressed the Pahlavas before them or superimposed themselves upon them. By this time they too had acquired a veneer of Persian culture so that their inroads were not unduly destructive. Their movement seems to have been more in the nature of a migration than the activity of war bands. They settled in a body and added a new element to the racial composition of western India. This is their importance in the Indian story, for it is from this mixture in western India that the Maratha people and language eventually sprang.

About 100 B.C., as has been noticed, the Indo-Greeks seem to have been strong enough to deflect the Pahlavas from the Panjab toward the lower Indus. But they could not withstand the Sakas who established a kingdom of Taxila in the foothills of the Panjab. They were now to be replaced by the biggest nomad movement of all. This was that of the Kushans, the section of the Yueh-chi horde which eventually came to dominate the rest. The Yueh-chi were driven out of China in the early part of the second century B.C. They moved westward along the route to the north of the Gobi Desert. They displaced the nomad Sakas from their pasture grounds and so set in motion their incursion into the Hellenistic world and eventually India. In their turn they were moved on by the nomad Wu-sun, and they then settled in the valley of the Oxus. Here they divided into five lordships, replacing the Sakas in Bactria as the Sakas had replaced the Greeks.

The Kushan chief known as Kadphises I united the five Yueh-chi sections about 40 A.D. and then crossed the Hindu Kush Mountains. In a long reign he extended his dominion over western Afghanistan and the Panjab. Thus the Kushan empire arose. His successor is thought to have acceded in 78 A.D. and to be identified with the Indian era known as the Saka which began in that year. He gained control of northern India as far as Banaras, occupied the Indus Basin, and possibly established overlordship as far as the river Narbada, the traditional boundary between Hindustan and the Deccan. There followed the era of the Kushan Indian empire for over a century. The Kushans had become a ruling class, who achieved their position, like others after them, by superior prowess and organizing skill and by tolerant respect for local customs, and kept it as long as they retained their unity and vigor. Their most notable king was Kanishka, who is generally thought to have ruled from about 120 to 160 A.D. His capital was at Peshawar (Purushapura) and his realm included, besides the Panjab, Kashmir, the Indus and upper Ganges valleys, Afghanistan, and tracts in what is now Chinese Turkestan. For northern India the Kushan regime was a time of peace and prosperity. For Buddhism it was a time of enlargement. Kanishka became its patron; he called a general council to settle the Hinayana canon of holy books. It is probable that in his time the transformation of Buddhism from the Hinayana to the Mahayana version, from the concept of the Buddha as the agnostic teacher of a mental discipline to that of a savior-god, was in full swing. We know few details, but we do know that northwest India is dotted with Buddhist relics of this period and that mounds identified with the Kushans are numerous.

Like so many of the Asian nomads, the Kushans seem to have been of mixed Turko-Mongolian stock. They are described as being "big, pink-faced men, built on a large scale." "They dressed in long-skirted coats, wore soft leather boots, and sat on chairs." The Kushan empire broke up some time in the third century. Little is known of the process, but it is thought to be connected with the rise of the new Sassanian dynasty in Persia. Kushan principalities lived on in the northwest until the sixth century, but the next unifying hand was to come from India itself in the East instead of from the West.

The Kushans present a much clearer picture to posterity than the

Pahlavas or the Sakas, but it is difficult to define their legacy in concrete terms. The Sakas added a new element to the population of western India, but the Kushans seem to have been too dispersed to do likewise. They patronized Buddhism, but Buddhism also has disappeared. They gave security to northern India for a century and a half, and this cannot have been valueless. The real legacy of the Kushans to India was perhaps that they provided the conditions in which Indian culture could rise to its second peak of achievement under the succeeding Gupta dynasty.

CHAPTER VI

The Imperial Age

The fourth century of the Christian era, when the Roman empire became Christian under the emperor Constantine, is known in India as the imperial age of the Guptas. During this period ancient India achieved its second cultural peak. The invaders of the preceding centuries seem to have been assimilated, and a number of cultural developments seem to have come to completion. It was an age of fruition, like the fullness of late summer, and resembles in this respect the age of Shah Jahan in the story of Indo-Persian culture and the Augustan age in Europe. This does not mean that there were not hints of further developments, as there were in eighteenth-century Europe, but rather that completion of effort and rounding off of achievement were the keynotes of the period.

Very little is known of the rise of the Gupta dynasty, as very little is known of the fall of the Kushan empire, and between the two events lies about a century of almost total obscurity. We know that the Kushan empire dissolved sometime after 200 A.D. Kanishka introduced a new era, beginning, according to majority scholarly opinion, about 120 A.D. No coin of this era has been found with a date later than the year 99. We can only guess the exact causes of the Kushan collapse, but certain possibilities can be established by inference. It should first be remembered that the Kushan empire was really only semi-Indian. Its central core was Afghanistan and the Panjab, its capital at Peshawar on the borders of the modern Afghan and Pakistani states. Its control of central and northern India was more that of overlordship than direct rule. Saka "satrapies" continued to exist as subordinate states. As so often in north Indian history, the impulse of change seems to have come from outside India itself. In 226 A.D. the Arsacid dynasty of Persia was replaced by the more vigorous Sassanids. The new dynasty encroached on the Kushan hold of Afghanistan and perhaps blocked the supply of adventurer recruits to the Kushan dominions upon which foreign rulers in India have always relied for the retention of their vigor. Such a crisis in the affairs of an imperial power is the moment for dependent states to revolt. This is what may have happened to the Kushans and brought their empire to an end. But there was no replacement of Kushans by Persians in the imperial seat. The new Persian kings were occupied with periodic wars with the Romans until the eve of their overthrow by the Muslim Arabs in the seventh century. In these circumstances there was something of a power vacuum between the lower Ganges Valley and the borders of Persia. Kushan chiefdoms existed in the Afghan uplands until the coming of the Muslims, while in west-central India Saka "satrapies" became independent again.

This situation was the prelude to the rise of the Guptas. The new empire, like Chandragupta's, came from the east instead of the west. We know very little of how it came to power, but it would seem that its core was again the continuing state of Magadha. It had started its career some nine centuries earlier, about 600 B.C., and had already grown into an empire under the Mauryas. After the fall of the Mauryas, Magadha survived as an independent state, beating off the attack of the Greek Menander and his Indian allies and escaping the Kushan domination. At the end of the third century the Lichchhavi tribe, from a branch of which the Buddha sprung nearly a thousand years before, came again into prominence. The first Chandragupta married princess Kumara Devi of this tribe and was able to extend his dominions from Magadha or modern Behar as far west as modern Allahabad or Prayag. The importance of the alliance is suggested by the issue of coins in the joint names of Chandragupta, his queen, and the Lichchhavi people. Now the Lichchhavis were a people of the foothills with affiliations with Nepal and Tibet. It seems likely that they were a martial race, like the modern Gurkhas. They may have been Mongolian, but more probably perhaps, they were a mixture of Mongolian and Aryan elements. Everything is mixed in India, which is perhaps the reason that there is so much emphasis upon racial purity. In this Lichchhavi-Magadhan alliance we can see a union of Indian statecraft with hillmen's martial vigor. Thus the undoubtedly Aryan Guptas may have found the spearhead they needed to recover Magadha's one-time imperial sway.

The first Gupta king died about 330 A.D., having founded a new era in 320 A.D. His son and successor reigned for over forty years, adding Bengal, the upper Jumna-Ganges Valley, and parts of central India. In fact his empire, except for the Panjab, nearly embraced the traditional limits of Hindustan—from the Indus to the Bay of Bengal, from the river Narbada to the northern mountains. A vital addition was made by the next ruler in the series with the conquest of Malwa, Gujarat, and Saurashtra. This marked the end of the Saka chiefs of Ujjain who had lingered on for some five hundred years. Further, it gave the new empire access to the western sea, where it took control of Barygaza or Broach in the Gulf of Cambay. This gave the empire a window looking toward Europe, where the eastern half of the Roman empire still flourished. It is this ruler, Chandragupta Vikramaditya, whose exploits are thought to be commemorated on the Iron Pillar which stands in the Qutab mosque near New Delhi. The empire continued until the mid-fifth century, when it was beset by invading Huns. By the end of the century the Gupta empire had broken down like its Mauryan predecessor, though the Magadhan kingdom still lived on. The sixth century is dark in Indian annals, from which it can be presumed that there was much strife and probably further foreign invasions. The few inscriptions refer to kings and dynasties, but the real clues are to be found in the almost unknown movements of peoples. As the Lichchhavis afford a clue to the origin of the Gupta power, the Maukharis of Thanesar and Kanauj do of its fall and the subsequent interregnum. Early in the seventh century the fog of ignorance lifts while Harsha of Thanesar and Kanauj rule a revived empire for forty-one years. Then it falls thick again and one can but dimly perceive jostling dynasties and commingling peoples. The Indian Middle Ages had begun.

For the Gupta period and for King Harsha the sources again become comparatively copious. Taken together they form the second illuminated hall in the mansion of Indian history. Coins are now copious and reveal through the centuries a bewildering variety of dynasties. Inscriptions, both on stone and copper, are numerous. The copper plate is an essential ingredient of the corpus of Indian inscriptions and a tool of the specialist, though there is nothing so dramatic as the edicts of Asoka. Then there is architectural and archeological evidence in the shape of temples and sculptures and wall paintings. Some of the hand-hewn Buddhist caves of Ajanta and some of the work at Ellora can be ascribed to this period. Then there is a wealth of Sanskrit literature which now reached its peak of achievement. Much of it is literary and philosophic, its historical material being incidental, but there is also the historical romance of Bana, which deals with the events of Harsha's reign.

Most vivid of all the records, however, are the accounts of the Chinese Buddhist pilgrims, Fa-Hien and Hieuen Tsang. Both were Buddhist monks who braved the perils of a westward journey through central Asia and across the mountains into northwest India in order to study authentic Buddhist sacred texts. Both stayed for several years in India and traveled widely. Fa-Hien set out in 399 A.D. and spent the years 401–10 in India itself, moving from monastery to monastery. He was so absorbed in holy things that no ruler's name is mentioned, but his references to the conditions of life are all the more valuable for being incidental to his main interest and so disinterested. His visit took place at the height of the Gupta empire, during the reign of Chandragupta II. Hieuen Tsang set out in 629 A.D. and spent the years 635–43 in Harsha's empire. More observant of secular life than his predecessor, his account and the work of Bana are the main sources for Harsha's reign. The work of these two Chinese monks imparts flesh and blood to the bare bones of dates, dynastic names, and formal inscriptions which are the historian's stock in trade for so much of the early period.

Judged by modern standards, these sources are not copious. But they are enough to provide a clearer picture of the age than of any period since the Mauryan. We know little of the characters of the emperors, some of whose personalities may have rivaled or surpassed those of Asoka or Akbar, but we do get a picture of the state of the north Indian countryside and its people. The administration, as Fa-Hien describes it, was milder than in the Mauryan age. The police regulations were less severe. Capital punishment was rare, punishment usually taking the form of fines or mutilation. The land revenue collections, the backbone of Indian administration until the nineteenth century, were moderate. One-sixth was the government's share of the gross produce, as compared with a quarter in the Mauryan period and a third in the time of Akbar. The countryside was peaceful and prosperous, studded with wealthy towns. Travel was evidently reasonably safe. Pataliputra was still flourishing and Fa-Hien admired the still-standing halls which Asoka had erected. Manners were mild, with a general abstention from meat and liquor. Outcastes, however, were severely treated. In the matter of diet Fa-Hien may have been speaking mainly of Buddhists, but his evidence is good for another feature of the day, that of tolerance. The Gupta government was Hindu, but it is clear that Hindus and Buddhists were living peaceably side by side. Fa-Hien moved freely from monastery to monastery and speaks of the great monastic establishments in the Jumna Valley. There is no hint of persecution. Hieuen Tsang found Buddhism in the east even more flourishing, for Harsha was himself a patron. At his periodic religious assemblies the image of the Buddha received the highest honors, those of the sun and Siva coming second and third. The country was open to foreign influences in a way which was not to recur for centuries. There was contact with west China by the overland route, with Europe and the Near East by sea, with Persia and the Middle East, and with Indonesia.

Our literary sources show that the arts and sciences had reached a high state of cultivation. Sanskrit had now replaced Pali as the official and literary language. Asoka's inscriptions were in Prakrit, a dialect intermediate to Pali. The first Sanskrit inscriptions date from about 150 A.D. Sanskrit was not only used for sacred writing, but for secular literature as well. It was during this period (fifth century) that Kalidasa, "the Indian Shakespeare," flourished, along with Dandin and Bharavi in the sixth century. Kalidasa's drama *Sakuntala* was first translated into English by Sir William Jones in the late eighteenth century and has ever since been recognized as a masterpiece by the non-Indian world. That and his lyrical nature poem the *Cloud Messenger* captivated Goethe and the early European romantics. In the realm of science Indian achievement was striking. There was interchange of ideas with the Greeks. Varahamihira, who lived in the sixth century, was learned in Greek sciences and used Greek technical terms. But the Indians went beyond the Greeks. By the seventh century they had devised a sign for zero and worked out a decimal system. In algebra they were also ahead. This knowledge was taken up by the Arabs of the early caliphate, who themselves absorbed all the knowledge they could find, whether from Greek or Indian sources. From them it percolated into Europe in its Dark Age, leading to the replacement of the abacus for calculation and the beginning of modern mathematics. In the practical arts also the Indians were far advanced. The Iron Pillar near Delhi, whose date is about 400 A.D., is of a fineness unknown to iron smelters until recent times. In thought the majestic fabric of Indian philosophy, first developed in the treatises known as the Upanishads, was reaching its full stature. Sankara, "the chief of the Vedantic philosophers" who developed the full rigor of Indian monism, flourished about 800 A.D., but the Vedantic philosophy reached maturity under the Guptas. It was an achievement of the human mind in the realm of abstract thought with which only the thousand years of Greek philosophic thought to 500 A.D., culminating in the Neoplatonic system, is to be compared.

The arts had also attained a high degree of development. Most of the buildings of the Gupta period have disappeared. They were the victims of the many changes which affected the area of the empire for centuries after its fall, of the commotions of the barbarian invasions, and of Muslim-Turkish destruction on religious grounds. Only in out-of-the-way places have complete buildings survived. These show signs of vigor and bold conception. In addition, the rock-hewn temple was excavated which has given to posterity some of its finest treasures at such sites as Ajanta and Ellora. Construction remained simple, centering round the sanctuary of the god. The true arch was not used, so that size involved massive construction. The merit of these buildings is to be found in their proportions and elaborate decoration. In the case of Buddhism the need for monasteries provided an opportunity for picturesque grouping. Closely linked with architecture was the art of sculpture, for it was largely used by both Hinduism and Mahayana Buddhism to adorn their temples. At Sarnath and Mathura enough has been found to enable the Gupta style to be identified and appreciated. The figures have a dignity, a grace, and a restraint of their own which distinguish them from the more florid examples of later schools. The motif of sculpture was religious, but this did not prevent the intrusion of both secular and erotic subjects. In the case of Hinduism the stories of the gods were represented in the idiom of the time, while believers in the *shakti* cults saw in the sexual act and organs symbols of the divine creative energy. This led to the voluptuousness and "indecency" of much of later Hindu sculpture and provided a pretext for puritan Muslim iconoclasm. In the case of Buddhism there were the incidents of the Buddha's life and of his previous incarnations as told in the *Jataka* stories to draw upon. Until decadent Buddhism became mixed with *shakti* cults itself, it covered a larger area of life with more restraint.

There is evidence that painting was very widely practiced and used for the adornment of palaces as well as temples and Buddhist halls. Little remains, but there is enough to attest to its excellence and to place this period in the forefront of mural artistic excellence. The most famous are the wall paintings in the Buddhist caves at Ajanta in central India and at Sigiriya in Ceylon. The paintings are notable for their freshness and vigor, their naturalistic grace, and the variety of their subjects. Though the inspiration was religious, any scene connected with the Buddhist story was legitimate. We find not only scenes of the Buddha and his followers, as a Christian artist might depict scenes of Christ and his disciples, but episodes of the court and camp, of the home and of nature. Since all the figures are depicted in the fashions of the time, as the sixteenth-century Flemish glassworker depicted Christian sacred scenes in the churches of the day, they provide a pictorial record of contemporary life.

In social life the main outline of Hindu society had now developed (as already described). But the system was not yet so rigid as it later became nor had some of its later features become pronounced. Manners, perhaps under the influence of Buddhism, were milder than before or since. The untouchables were rigidly segregated, but there was probably still some intercaste marriage. The Brahmins dominated Hindu society, but they still had the Buddhists to compete with. Women were subordinate, but they had more freedom of movement and took more part in general society than was later the case. Education was more widely diffused, perhaps another sign of Buddhist influence.

It will be convenient here to notice the extension of cultural influence beyond the Indian borders. The first few Christian centuries formed the great age of Indian expansion. We have already noticed the spread of Buddhism into the northwest and thence along the central Asian trade routes into China. But there was another movement overseas eastward. During these centuries Indian influence spread into Burma, Malaya, Indonesia, and the areas of southeast Asia known today as Siam or Thailand, Cambodia, and south Viet-Nam. The contact at first was mainly with south India and it began, as such things so often do, with trade. It is known that a trading connection with the East Indies existed by the beginning of the Christian era; in the *Jataka* stories they are referred to as "the land of gold" or "the island of gold" (probably Java). Roman sources make it clear that there was an active commerce by the second century A.D. connected with the then flourishing European trade. It is easy to imagine that merchant voyages would lead to mercantile colonies, such as the Arabs and the Europeans established later on. Because religion was an inseparable part of the lives of these merchants, Brahmins followed to perform ceremonies and Buddhist monks to spread knowledge of the Way.

The Indonesians had a basic culture of their own, but it was not as developed as the Indian, and they were therefore susceptible to foreign influence. There is little evidence of large-scale migration, so it would seem that it was in this way that Indian influence spread. Local chiefs, as they did later on with Islam, adopted the foreign religion in order to increase their prestige. They took Indian titles and sent for Brahmins to perform the proper ceremonies and introduce Sanskrit. The Brahmins would discover that the rulers were really Kshatriyas, or of the warrior order, and would make judicious admissions of the leading families to the higher castes. There is little evidence that the Indian caste system was transported bodily to the East Indies; rather Hinduism and Buddhism were superimposed on the local animistic cults. In southeast Asia the concept of the god-king fitted easily into the Hindu conception of the raja as the upholder of religion, and it is this idea we find embalmed in stone in the great temple of Angkor Vat in Cambodia, said to be the largest religious building in the world.

In some such way Indian influence, both Hindu and Buddhist, spread over Indonesia and southeast Asia during the first ten centuries of the Christian era. The influence was real and profound, but it was the influence of the mind rather than of physical colonization. The Indians charmed by their example rather than commanded by their arms. Dynasties of rulers with Sanskrit titles are found, few of whom probably had much Indian blood in their veins. According to tradition this contact began in the first Christian century; inscriptions in tolerable Sanskrit are found from the fifth century A.D. Indian influence at first flowed mainly from the peninsula, but later Buddhist Bengal also took part. Kingdoms were founded in Java, Sumatra, Malaya, Borneo, Cambodia, and Laos. Some of them became famous, like the Cambodian kingdom or the maritime empire of Srivijaya. To match the Hindu Cambodian monuments of Angkor Vat and the Bayon was the great Buddhist stupa of Borobudur in Java. In Thailand, Cambodia, and Laos Buddhism of the older form has replaced Hinduism; in Java and the islands Islam is the successor. Only in the dream island of Bali does the Hinduism of this period live on, a living cultural fossil of Indian eastward expansion. But though forms have changed elsewhere, much Hindu influence remains behind a Muslim façade. It was the Indian expansion of this age which has given this part of the world its present picturesqueness and nostalgic charm.

CHAPTER VII

New Peoples : The Rajput World : South India

Beginning with the fall of the Guptas and becoming complete after the death of Harsha in 647 A.D., north Indian history is confused and obscure for some five or six hundred years. This long period of time is perhaps the most difficult of all for historians of India, for there is confusion as well as obscurity, a medley of new peoples and emergent groups as well as a lack of information. Nothing like a clear picture of the period as a whole has yet emerged. Here all that will be attempted will be to characterize the main features of the time, to clarify the processes that were involved, and to explain the significance of these centuries in relation to modern India.

As the Dark Ages divide the modern West from the classical age of the Greeks and Romans, so do these centuries divide modern from ancient India. Though Hinduism and Brahminism survived the years of change, they were so modified that in a real sense we can say that there is no living tradition going back beyond the sixth Christian century. The period was a watershed of peoples and cultures. It is from this time that the modern languages and peoples and many features of the modern cults of India date. No Rajputs or Marathas or Jats are to be found before the sixth century; none of the early peoples like the Lichchhavis, no cult of the sun, no Buddhism are to be found after its close. The marks of this period can be briefly summarized. There is first, with the death of Harsha of Kanauj, a disappearance of imposing bureaucratic empires with closely knit organizations. Empires existed like those of the Gurjaras and the Pratiharas, but they are shadowy compared with the Mauryas and the Guptas. There were notable personalities like Raja Bhoja of Kanauj, but they are figures of legend or folklore rather than of history. There is not so much a lack of information as a lack of precise information. There are ballads and folklore, there is a copious general literature, but historical fact depends upon fragmentary inscriptions. To a considerable degree political history is reduced to epigraphy.

A leading feature of the age is fresh invasions from the northwest—and not invasions only but popular migrations on a large scale. They were strong and numerous enough to replace or break up the existing tribes and to form new cultural and social groups. Thus the period sees not only the disappearance of old names like Magadha and Kosala, but the advent of new ones like Rajputs and Jats. And it is some of these new ones, like the Rajputs, which have provided modern India with its most striking features. In the religious sphere Buddhism steadily declined and Brahminism assumed its modern form. Finally, it was an age of isolation. Chinese influence stopped short at southeast Asia to the east. In the west Europe was in the grip of the Dark Ages; she was painfully assimilating her own barbarians. In the Middle East Islam arose in the seventh century but was too absorbed in westward expansion and in conflicts with the Byzantine empire of Constantinople (the successor of Rome in the East) to look eastward beyond Iran. It was the coming of Islam which ended this period of north Indian history, but when Islam arrived in force, it was brought not by its sophisticated Arab exponents, but by the newly won and militant Turks. What might have proved a creative cultural exchange became at first a destructive clash of arms.

The first phase in this period was the collapse of the old empires. We can count Harsha's empire, for this purpose, as a revival of the Gupta empire, for it was similar in outlook, in organization, and in the people who composed and controlled it. With Harsha's death in 647 A.D. the unity of north Indian history was lost until the Turks roughly restored it in the thirteenth century. It is not surprising that there is evidence of greater prosperity in central and south India during these years, for they largely escaped the barbarian invasions and the destruction suffered by the north. The second phase of the period is the invasions and migrations. They not only overthrew the old regimes, but continued long after in wave after wave until they produced a new political, social, and racial pattern all over north and northwest India. The first attack came from the Huns, whose first onslaught was repulsed by the last of the great Guptas about 460 A.D. Other waves followed which broke up the empire, though the Guptas themselves continued to rule in Magadha for some time longer.

The Huns were the spearhead of one of the great folk movements which in historic times have periodically burst forth from the immense open spaces of central Asia. Thence came the Aryans in the second millennium B.C., spreading east and west to found classical Indian, Iranian, and European civilizations. Thence came, more than a thousand years later, the Pahlavas, the Sakas, and the Kushans. Thence also came the Goths and the Teutons to overthrow the western Roman empire in the fourth and fifth centuries and to become the ancestors of the modern European nations. Hard on their heels came the Huns. They were Mongolian, not Aryan, in race; they were wilder than all previous nomadic invaders; they aroused repulsion and struck terror wherever they appeared. Their visitation, though more dreadful than that of the Teutons, was briefer. If we may compare the Teutonic invasions to a flood spreading over the face of the countryside, the Huns can be likened to a tornado which strikes, destroys, and passes. In Indian parlance the word Hun or Huna became a synonym for any barbarian, as the words Yavana and Saka had become for foreigners in general. In the fifth century the eastern branch of these people, the "White Huns," occupied the Oxus Valley, while the western branch advanced across the Russian steppes into Europe. In 484 the Persian king Firoz was killed and the way was opened for large-scale incursions into India. The Huns destroyed Buddhist culture in Afghanistan and northwest India; they ended the long history of Taxila as a seat of learning by burning it; they established a short-lived dynasty in Malwa. By the mid-sixth century they had been defeated in India and were overthrown in the Oxus Basin by Turkish tribes, who now gave to the region its modern name of Turkestan.

The work of the Huns was to destroy. But this was not the end, for in their wake came others both Turkish and a mixture of Turk and Mongol. We do not know exactly when and how they came, for we have no records. We only know that new peoples shortly appear on the Indian scene. Thus we have the Gurjaras and the Maitrakas, who are mentioned as separate entities, and new groups appearing like the Jats and the Ahirs, and above all the Rajputs.

After the breakup of Harsha's empire political confusion, into whose details we need not enter, again descended upon northern India. But in fact something much more important was happening. It was a time of breakdown in the old society. But above all it was a time of assimilation of new peoples into the Hindu system. It was the last creative achievement of the Brahmins. Apparently without directing authority by means of a series of compromises and *ad hoc* decisions independently arrived at, but unerring in their general direction, the Brahmins absorbed whole peoples into the Hindu fold. We have to guess at the processes involved from the nature of the new society which appeared in the eighth century. The new paladins of Hinduism were in fact the co-opted barbarians of a few generations back.

The outstanding example of this process was that of the Rajputs, who became the dominant actors on the north and central Indian stage for four centuries and remained prominent until the nineteenth century. They are still an important element in the body politic. The word Rajput literally signifies not a race or tribe, but royal kin or sons of a king. These people gave their name to Rajasthan or Rajputana but they are, and always have been, a military aristocracy. It would seem that the Brahmins, finding their own kings unable to resist the inroads of the barbarian hordes, relied on their superior culture and compounded with them by admitting them to Hindu society on terms. The barbarians themselves, having little culture of their own, were flattered by these suggestions and "charmed" by the attractions of an old and complicated civilization. The Brahmins admitted the barbarian chiefs as Kshatriya members of the warrior order. Their followers were classed as Sudras, or cultivators. Their priests, if influential enough, were recognized as Brahmins, but always placed in a separate subsection, so that the older Brahmins retained their standing. Thus the tribes were broken up into groups and reformed into castes. The identification of the old barbarians with the new castes has been the work of the sociologist. By their alien habits are they known. Thus the Rajputs eat all meats except beef. The rite of *jauhar,* the corporate burning of women and children at the fall of a fortress while the men rush to death at the point of the sword, comes from outside India. The Jats, who claim to be Kshatriyas but are usually rated as Sudras, permit widow remarriage in defiance of the *Laws of Manu.*

This process did not stop with the exterior tribes which had recently penetrated into India. It also included many indigenous peoples of central and western India. They were mostly of Dravidian stock, hitherto largely untouched by Hindu influence. Like the tribes living on the borders of the Roman Empire and taking a tincture of classical culture therefrom, they found in the collapse of north Indian authority an opportunity to enlarge their borders. The great accommodation with barbarism included these peoples also, and on much the same terms. Their chiefs and nobles became Kshatriyas and called themselves Rajputs, their chief priests became Brahmins and their followers Sudras or less. The status achieved by each class depended upon the conditions of the moment, the prestige of the tribe, and the amount of pressure they were prepared to exercise. It must be remembered that all these tribes were too isolated to develop a great civilization of their own, and that for them the Brahminic culture of the north *was* civilization. To join Hindu society was a step up in the cultural scale even though it involved new disabilities for some members of the group. It was by some such process as this that the transformation was accomplished. No doubt the Brahmins made use of local ideas in furthering the change. Ideas of soul stuff could lead on to the higher Hinduism, while ideas of tabu and pollution would pave the way for the ceremonial and social distinctions of Hindu society. The process can be further illustrated by citing some examples. Thus the Sisodias of Mewar, or the modern Udaipur, are of foreign descent, and so are the Parihars (the Pratiharas) and the Chauhans. But the Rashtra-kutas of the Deccan, the Rathors of Rajasthan, and the Bundelas of Bundelkhand are of home manufacture. The Chandel Rajputs are thought to be of Gond descent. Some of the accommodations within the Brahmin fold can also be traced. Thus the Nagar Brahmins are the de-scendants of foreign priests while the Maga Brahmins come from the Iranian *magi*.

This great process of change altered the whole shape of Indian society in north and central India and gave it the pattern it broadly retained down to modern times. The major caste distinctions as still known today can be traced back to this period. There have been additions and modi-fications, but until the nineteenth century, no major changes. The Brah-mins emerged as definitely the leading caste. They were now, like the Catholic Church in the Middle Ages, the repositories of the sacred lore and the sacred language. They were the accepted torchbearers of Indian civilization. Caste distinctions became more rigid while tribal divisions became blurred. They were recognized as special caste subdivisions of one of the social orders. Barriers of marriage and touch and food tabus roped them off, as it were, from other groups in the same area. So tribes did not develop into nations with a local habitat. They remained centers of particularist feeling in a multicellular society. In the new Indian so-ciety the principle of separation was as important as the underlying unity of religious cults. Among the Rajput aristocracy the clan spirit produced a personalized political structure with a semifeudal form and a tendency to split up into smaller units. The new social system was admirable for conservation and defense, but it made combination difficult. As Brahmin supremacy came in at the door, political unity flew out of the window. The age of the Rajputs was one of chivalry and tuneful bards; it was also one of political divisions and social inertia. That was why the Rajput kingdoms, for all their bravery, went down before the next wave of Turkish invaders.

In the five hundred years from 650–1150 A.D. Rajput kingdoms rose and fell. North India was a turbulent sea of political change. Some of the kingdoms attained the dignity of empires and some of the kings the status of legendary heroes. Such empires were those of the Gurjara-Pratiharas who arose in the eighth century and ruled in Kanauj in the ninth and tenth centuries; and the Pala kings of Bengal and Behar, who controlled Bengal and Behar in the ninth and tenth centuries and Behar till the coming of the Muslims. There were the Gond-descended Chandels of Bundelkhund with their stronghold at Kalanjar. Among legendary figures were the two Raja Bhojs (the Pratihara of the ninth and the Pawar of the eleventh century), who form the background of many a bardic tale. "In the time of Raja Bhoj . . . ." But these empires were empires with a difference. They were clan supremacies, kingdoms of personality rather than the elaborate bureaucratic structures of the Mauryas and the Guptas. The people were probably only aware of their immediate chief, who might or might not owe allegiance to a greater lord.

Before we leave North India, one more cultural development may be mentioned. Though Buddhism was steadily declining, in a final effort of expansion it entered Tibet. In the early eleventh century Atisa and others from Magadha carried the Mahayana form to Tibet, where it united with the local Lamaism to form the unique brand of Tibetan Buddhism.

During the preceding pages very little has been said of South India. This is not because it was unimportant or its people uncultivated, but rather because the main forces of political and social change were to be found in the north. From the north cultural influences spread to the south to cover the whole subcontinent (and Ceylon) with the blankets of Hinduism and Buddhism. The south or peninsula India in fact formed a world by itself. It was physically isolated, not only by the encompassing sea, but by the tangle of forest and hill country which separates the Deccan from Hindustan. It was divided within itself by its lack of a physical center. The tableland of the center ran down to fertile coastal plains, wide in the east and narrow in the west. The sources of wealth were in these coastal plains. In consequence, kingdoms tended to form on the periphery and work toward the center of the region. Therefore we find neither a conquest of the south by the north nor the establishment of a united southern empire. Only the Mauryas and Guptas from the north controlled parts of the south and those for short periods only.

The south is the world of the Dravidian peoples as the north is that of the Aryans and their successors. Perhaps the race that developed the Indus civilization and the first comers to India apart from some Australoid forest dwellers, the Dravidians remained relatively pure except for some Aryan admixture in the Brahmin caste. The substructure of the rest of the Indian nation, they are dominant in the south. Many possess great artistic sensitivity and intellectual capacity. Ramanuja, second only to Sankara among Indian philosophers, was a south Indian. The southern Dravidians were articulated in four groups. There are the Tamils, who extend from the neighborhood of Madras to Cape Comorin, occupying the fertile eastern coastal plain; the Telugus or Andhras, from Madras to the borders of Orissa, in the area of the modern state of Andhra; the Malayalis along the west coast in the modern state of Kerala; and the Kanaras of the central plateau in the area of the modern Mysore state. Each has its own language of great complexity and also its own script.

The evidence is not yet sufficient for the prehistoric period of the south to be traced with confidence. The only thing we can be certain of is that it was independent of the Aryans. It would seem that the first impulse of development may have come from the Indus culture, although sufficient evidence for any certainty is still lacking. Development occurred first, as might be expected, in the fertile coastal plains, which encouraged cultivation. Of this we have evidence in early Tamil literature. Two foreign influences then determined the course of Dravidian evolution. They were the commercial and cultural factors. The commercial included both the position of south India and the nature of its products. It was a halfway house on the sea route between the East Indies and the Middle East and Europe, and also for the conveyance of goods from the East Indies to north India along the coastal routes. Its own products of cotton, pepper, drugs, woods, elephants, ivory, gold, and precious stones made it a center of exchange in its own right as well as for re-export of foreign goods. The flourishing state of this trade in the early Christian centuries has already been mentioned. The cultural factor was the spread of Hindu ideas from the north. Exactly how this happened we do not know, but we may surmise that the first contacts were through trade, probably by sea. In Indian cultural expansion the Brahmin and Buddhist monk has followed the merchant. These influences were pervasive and persuasive, not compulsive, for they had no backing of physical force. In effect Brahminism was grafted on to the existing Dravidian culture. While the south today is a stronghold of orthodox Hinduism, that Hinduism itself differs markedly from that of the north. It has been modified by the Dravidian genius as the Dravidian culture has been affected by Hindu ideas. For instance, apart from the Nayars of Kerala the Kshatriya or warrior order is virtually nonexistent in the south. Next to the Brahmins rank the Sudras and after them the

"exterior" or "untouchable" castes are numerous. The south has its special religious sects, its characteristic forms of devotion, its peculiar
temple architecture.

In this process of cultural change, dates, as usual, are difficult. It can
perhaps be thought of as covering the middle and later parts of the first
millennium B.C. A gleam of light is provided by Asokan inscriptions in
Mysore about 250 B.C. and the record of the Buddhist evangelization of
Ceylon by Asoka's brother Mahendra. From the beginning of the Christian era there is evidence of flourishing Tamil kingdoms whose prosperity
was doubtless built on their possession of desirable products and a key
position in south Asian maritime trade. Tamil was the dominant language up to 500 A.D., and from the study of its literature some idea of
the progress of Hinduization may be obtained. Up to 300 A.D. the literature shows little Aryan influence; thereafter it grows steadily. The Pallava
dynasty, which arose in the fourth and dominated the peninsula from the
sixth to the eighth centuries, was Brahminic. The kings patronized Vish-
nuism and Saivism alternately, while Buddhism and Jainism also flourished. The progress of Hinduism in the peninsula is further marked by
the course of temple building. South Indian Hinduism expressed itself
in mighty temples thickly studded with sculpture, but their styles are
quite distinct from those of the north.

There is no need to delve into the details of dynastic history. But we
may note that the modern state of Kerala along the southern part of the
western coast of India or Malabar derived its name from this period. The
well-known term, the Coromandel Coast, derives from the long-lived
Chola dynasty, the word being a corruption of the Chola term for land
(*mandalam*). Accounts exist of the Chola administration in the eleventh
century, which demonstrate both the advanced state of society and administration and a great continuity of local forms. The administration
rested on unions of villages, several of which formed districts which in
turn were grouped into provinces. The unions had their own assemblies,
treasuries, and administrative committees that dealt with the royal officers. They conducted the public life of the country, and their officers
were able to uphold their position with wonderful tenacity for centuries.
The revenue demand, as with the Guptas, was one-sixth of the gross
produce. There was a metallic currency. Irrigation was skillfully conducted, the most characteristic forms being "tanks" or reservoirs and
"anicuts" or dams across rivers. Thus life in the peninsula continued
largely in a world by itself, though not without outside contacts, until
the Muslim Turks from the north burst in upon it in 1310. Marco Polo

reported on this world, in the last few years of its untroubled existence, at the end of the thirteenth century.

There remains something to be said of western and central India during these years. Much of this area is the Deccan, the central tableland of the peninsula. The whole area may broadly be defined as lying between the river Narbada on the north and the Kistna and Tunghabadra rivers on the south, and extending to the sea on both sides. We have already noted the incursions of the Pahlavas and Sakas into the west. There were further movements connected with the Huns and their associated tribes. From this crucible of peoples arose the usual caste structure and aristocratic society, articulating itself into a series of dynasties. The process continued as in the south, until the Muslim Turks burst in early in the fourteenth century. Of importance for posterity was the emergence of the composite Maratha people along the slopes of the western Ghats or mountains. The name of their homeland, Maharashtra, is derived from that of the Rashtrakuta dynasty. It was in the time of this dynasty (eighth to tenth centuries) that the celebrated temple of Kailash at Ellora was carved out of the living rock.

By 1000 it may be said that India, after the metamorphoses just indicated, was fairly covered with Hindu society, expressing itself in a network of Hindu kingdoms. In the third millennium B.C. urban society spread over the Indus basin, Gujarat, and perhaps the upper Jumna and Ganges valleys. In the second millennium this was replaced by the pastoral nature-worshiping Aryan tribes that spread across the Panjab and into the Ganges Valley. In the first millennium a number of cultural centers developed, finding expression in kingdoms and empires, in universal religions and schools of philosophy, in the arts and sciences. They were to be found along the northern rivers, in the coastal plains of the southeast and southwest, and in fertile corners like Gujarat. But they were separated by wide areas of forest and hill and desert; they were not yet integrated into a cultural whole. In the first millennium A.D. not only were new races absorbed into the Hindu fold, but the cultural centers themselves, for all their infinite variety of custom and belief, were knit into a single cultural pattern. Political disunity and even anarchy, military impotence in face of foreign invasion, must not obscure the basic achievement of this epoch, the fundamental cultural unity of India.

CHAPTER VIII

Islam in India

Before the consequences of the fifth- and sixth-century invasions had worked themselves out, Islam had appeared in the middle Eastern world. The Hegira, or flight of the prophet Muhammad from Mecca, from which the Muslim lunar era is dated, took place in 622 A.D. or almost in the middle of the reign of Harsha. Muhammad died in 632, three years after the Buddhist pilgrim Hieuen Tsang had set out from China for the holy land of India. While he was wandering from monastery to monastery and attending the emperor Harsha's great religious assembly the Muslim followers of the prophet were making their first dramatic conquests. In 636, soon after the pilgrim had entered Harsha's dominions, the Arabs captured Jerusalem, where the splendid Dome of the Rock was shortly to rise, from the Byzantine Greeks. Before he started on his homeward journey in 643 the Persian Sassanids had been overthrown and Egypt wrested from the Greeks. Within three years of Harsha's death the caliphate was established at Damascus. There would seem nothing to prevent the Arabs from invading India at any time during the next fifty years, apart from preoccupations elsewhere. The north was again in tumult, and it should not have been difficult to gain a foothold. But in fact the Arabs were busy elsewhere. They spread along the north coast of Africa to conquer Spain in 711, only to be halted in the heart of France at Tours in 732. In Asia they were at grips with the Byzantine Greeks. They overran Asia Minor but were finally repulsed from Constantinople in 717.[1] The energy expended in these campaigns may well have precluded a major effort further east. In Iran itself the nomads of the desert came into contact with the nomads of the steppe. Arab and Turk faced each other, setting up a lasting dichotomy of race in the Muslim world. It was the resistance of the Greeks which set limits to the first Islamic flood and which perhaps determined that neither India nor Europe should become provinces of the

Islamic world. Thus it was not until 712 that the Arabs appeared on the borders of India, and then not in great force. In that year the Amir Muhammad bin Kasim conquered Sind for the Caliphate. But he made no headway in the Panjab and was shortly recalled and disgraced. Sind remained Muslim but no further progress was made. The Caliphate, transferred to Baghdad in 762, had other work on its hands. The rest of India enjoyed a respite of three hundred years.

Most of the previous invaders of India had been on a more primitive cultural level than the Indians; in consequence they could be absorbed with more or less difficulty into the Hindu system. The Greeks were few in number and eclectic in mind. The Muslims presented to India a new and confident world religion in the setting of the matured culture of the Middle East. It was a clash of equals. Islam could not be brushed aside as a barbaric crudity. These equals were so different that the clash never produced synthesis or assimilation. There was mutual influence but no fusion. A foreign cultural body was inserted into Hindu society, with profound results for Indian development. It is worth noting first some of the features of Islam and wherein it contrasted with Hinduism.

The prophet Muhammad (570–632) was by profession a camel-dealer of Mecca. He lived in a polytheistic society and received a revelation in visions which he embodied in the holy book of Islam, the Koran. The new religion he called Islam, or resignation to the will of God. Its followers were Muslims, or resigned ones.[2] Islam starts with an intense conviction of the unity and greatness of God. From this starting point it is formulated in definite doctrines and precise rules. It is a religion of clear-cut lines, of strong light and shade. From God Islam proceeds to the *Kalama* or creed. "There is no God but God and Muhammad is the prophet of God." The revelation of God to Muhammad is contained in the Koran, which is supplemented by the sayings and traditions of the prophet. The Koran has absolute authority, making Islam a "fundamentalist" religion; all controversy centers round interpretation. From the schools of interpretation has arisen the Muslim law or Shariat. The followers of the religion form a brotherhood which places every man on an equality before God and which overrides distinctions of class, nationality, race, and color. In the mosque there are no reserved seats; prince and beggar pray side by side.

Muslim doctrine begins with God. He is indivisible and absolutely "other" than man. The first proposition rules out polytheism and the second idolatry or image worship, since God must not be represented in the form of a creature. Here Islam parts company with Christianity, for the Trinity to it is polytheism and the Incarnation blasphemy. From this emphasis on the greatness of God or Allah arises fatalism and a belief in destiny. All that cannot be controlled or understood is the will of the omnipotent and inscrutable Allah. The moral code is largely based on that of Judaism as practiced in Arabia in Muhammad's time. There are ceremonial prayers, with Friday taking the place of the Saturday Sabbath. There is a month of fasting (Ramadan). There are festivals including celebrations of Old Testament events like the sacrifice of Isaac. There is the Judaic conception of "unclean meats" with the prohibition of pork. Spirits are also forbidden and the use of music in worship.

The social system of Islam may be described as a reformist version of current seventh-century Arabian practice. There was equal inheritance of property, which has tended to cause the breaking up of Muslim estates. Slavery was recognized (it still exists in Arabia) though good treatment was enjoined. But the greatest contrast to modern ideas lay in the Muslim attitude toward the home. Polygamy was freely practiced in the Arabia of that time. Muhammad restricted it to the taking of four wives. Subordinate wives (concubines, or the "handmaids" of the Old Testament) were also allowed. Fair treatment and proper maintenance were stipulated; women could also hold property and obtain divorce. But their whole status, both before God and man, was an inferior one. They could not join in public worship in the mosque, or take part in public life. The orthodox Muslim, like the orthodox Jew, thanked God that he had not been born a woman. In practice women lived secluded lives, seeing no men save near relations, and only going outside veiled or shrouded in a shapeless garment called the *burqa*. Few had any education, so that the great majority were unable to exercise the rights allowed by Muslim law. For the lower classes conditions were easier, but a rise in status meant an increase in restrictions. Probably throughout Muslim history the majority of marriages were monogamous for economic reasons. But here again a rise in the social scale meant an increase in matrimony and it was the upper classes that set the tone of social life. In spite of all this, tribal customs sometimes mitigated the rigor of the law and there were many distinguished Muslim women.[3] Nevertheless the historic Muslim world was very much a man's world.

The political theory of Islam was that all Muslims formed one congregation of the faithful. They elected the khalifa, or caliph, as the Commander of the Faithful who attended to their temporal needs. He was the sword but not the oracle of Islam. He was no pope, being neither prophet nor priest. In practice neither election nor universality lasted very long. The caliph of the day was the ruler who received the widest allegiance or who could gain recognition in a particular area. Thus Muslim rulers in India often claimed to be caliphs within their own realms. The world was divided by the lawyers into *Dar-ul-Islam*—the house of peace where Islam prevailed—and *Dar-ul-Harb,* the house of war where infidels ruled. War to extend or defend the *Dar-ul-Islam* was holy and hence arose the concept of jehad or holy war. In spite of this belligerence, tolerance toward the unbeliever has been a historic feature of Muslim doctrine. Religious minorities exist in various countries today after thirteen centuries of Muslim rule. An unbeliever was a *dhimmi* who purchased protection by payment of a poll tax called *jizya.* He was certainly a second-class citizen, but he did continue to exist.

For all its simplicity and legalism Islam proliferated into many sects. The two main sects are the Sunnis, to which the Afghans and Turks in India adhered, and the Shias, who became dominant in Persia. The strain of mysticism and free thought specially associated with Persia found expression in the Sufi movement, which included poets and devotees, ascetics and evangelists of the faith.

From the foregoing it is clear that Islam and Hinduism stood in marked contrast to each other. At the top the best minds of both could join (like the Muslim poet-weaver Kabir) in a common adoration of the Supreme, but from thence they fell further and further apart. In doctrine Islam is all definition and clarity while Hinduism is vague and confused. Compared to the crisp outlines of Koranic law the niceties of *dharma* are a fog of obscurity. Islam stands for transcendence; the command of Allah is all. Hinduism stands for immanence; the divine without is an expression of the divine within. Its final wisdom is the aphorism "Thou art That." This leads to incarnations of the deity and his worship in many forms. Polytheism and idolatry, commonplace to the Hindu, arouse the strongest feelings of repulsion in the Muslim. Since so much art is religious, this difference involves a clash in the world of art as well. On the social plane we have the principle of equality (for men) contrasting with the graded and sanctified inequality of caste. Here also strong feelings are involved. The Hindu on the other hand, though his social system was by no means wholly monogamous, objected to the Muslim principle of polygamy. Finally, in the sphere of custom the tabus of each side clashed. The sacred Hindu cow was for the Muslim a prospective tasty dish. In the relations of the two communities there was nothing that harrowed Hindu feelings more than the Muslim attitude toward the cow. On the other hand Muslims objected to music in worship. Music before mosques was one of the easiest ways of provoking a Hindu-Muslim riot. The reader should note that these contrasts and clashes were not matters of ideology and opinion only, the disapproval, for example, which a Baptist might feel for a Roman Catholic, or a Christian Scientist for a Latter-day Saint. They ran through the warp and woof of the two societies, they touched their deepest feelings about their way of life; they could arouse their fiercest passions. Only if these considerations are borne in mind will the historic relations of the two communities in India be intelligible.

Before proceeding further it is necessary to make an important qualification. Islam, like Christianity, has not been the same everywhere. Again like Christianity, it has been modified by the nations which have accepted it and the cultures which pre-existed it. As Spanish Christianity differs from the American Middle Western or Greek forms, so Indian Islam differs from the Arabian, and Persian from the Moroccan form. Islam as a socioreligious driving force has been modified both by race and by culture. The Arabs gave the original revelation a legalistic and litigious twist. Their great contribution was the development of Islamic law or the *Shariat*. The Turks were a hardheaded, practical race. They modified the religion to suit their convenience, a recent edition of the process being carried out by Ataturk in modern Turkey. Persia or Iran, with its culture and imagination, its proneness to mysticism and sensuousness, became the home of Islamic heresies. The Shias, dominant in Persia since the sixteenth century, began as a dissenting sect. The Aga Khan is the head of a heretical sect going back to the Persian middle ages. A modern example is the Ba'hai sect. Its mystical sense found expression in the poets, of whom Hafiz and Rumi attained world rank. In the cultural sphere the Arabs of the early Caliphate borrowed heavily from the classical Greek heritage of the countries which they conquered. Plato and Aristotle became familiar names in their thought; indeed, the knowledge of Aristotle was returned to the West at the University of Paris through Arab channels. The Islamic light, after passing through the Persian cultural prism, showed a spectrum of elegance, grace, and toleration not evidenced elsewhere. Though the Arabs first brought Islam to northern India, they never got further than Sind. The real bearers of Islam to India were the Turks, who were in different ages more or less influenced by Persian culture. In following the story of Islam in India it should therefore be borne in mind that every act of a Muslim is not necessarily an Islamic act. In tracing any action to its source, whatever judgment may be made upon it, the racial and cultural as well as the religious factor must be taken into account. To take a simple illustration, the Afghan blood feud or the cutting off of noses for infidelity is not an Islamic, but a tribal characteristic.

The Muslims of India, beginning as traders on the Malabar Coast and a few thousand troops in Sind, became in course of time one-quarter of the whole population. Given the initial disharmony between the two religions, the traditional Indian antipathy to foreigners, and the Hindu genius for absorption, this fact demands some explanation. How did the Muslim community grow so large? The first means of recruitment to be mentioned was the popular traditional one, conversion by the sword. There is no doubt that this occurred in times of crisis such as foreign invasion or of civil commotion.[4] It is equally certain that it was the exception rather than the rule. The evidence of co-operation of Hindu officials with Muslim rulers from early days and of relations with Hindu chiefs is too strong to admit of the reign of terror which continuous forcible conversion would mean in a country like India. Forcible conversion happened, but exceptionally. The next factor was the natural one of political influence. One path to fame and power in a Muslim state led through conversion. Some ambitious men became Muslims and found themselves in leading positions in the state. But Hindus could also be influential without denying their faith; in fact, the flow of converts from this source was never more than a trickle.

The largest accretions to the community came from two other sources —migration and persuasion. Under migration can be counted the soldiers of the invading Turkish armies, who settled down in the country. They either sent for their families or intermarried locally. In addition to individual adventurers, of which the records show there was a steady flow, and the rank and file of the invading Turkish armies, whole clans or tribes on occasion moved in. The most recent example of this on a large scale was the case of the Rohilla Afghans, who, uprooted from their homeland in the eighteenth century by Nadir Shah the Persian, moved into India in a body and settled in the submontane tract of Uttar Pradesh between the upper Ganges and the hills. Migration accounted for many of the upper-class Muslims in India, but the largest source of recruitment was conversion through persuasion. It is this factor which made the Indian Muslims as a whole a body Indian in blood as well as in outlook and affection. The process was carried on only to a limited extent by the orthodox *maulvis* of the cities and courts. Their interest was the law and their preference coercion. The most persuasive and effective agents of Islamic conversion were the Sufis. These were dedicated men, some leading ascetic lives, and some maintaining their families, who devoted their lives to the study and spread of Islam. They were often unorthodox, and included in their ranks many mystics and near pantheists, but as a class they were loyal Muslims. Their religion was individual and their appeal was to personal experience; in general they matched precept with practice and so made themselves magnets for the deep religious urge of all classes of Indians. The *maulvi* appealed to the head; the Sufi spoke to the heart. Some would live in community houses called *khanqahs,* some belonged to religious orders; others went alone and set up religious centers to which the aspiring and enquiring of all creeds came. Many of these centers have become celebrated places of pilgrimage, retaining their status even after independence.[5]

The Sufis were the people who made Islam, for all its sharp contrasts to local religion, attractive in India. They were the agents, but we still need a motive for large-scale conversion. Mass conversion occurred in East Bengal (now East Pakistan) and a number of group conversions took place all over north India. In the case of Bengal there was a Brahmin regime overlaying a popular if corrupt Buddhism. It is thought that the Muslims were welcomed as bringing relief from the Brahmins, and since there were no longer any Buddhist monks to turn to, the whole countryside became Muslim. Others may well have passed straight from animism to Islam. In other places in the north many outcaste communities found release from Brahmin domination and social restriction in embracing Islam. In the northwest caste groups of Rajputs and Jats became Muslim. These were often cases of clan decision, the attractions being worldly advantage, Muslim militancy, and freedom from Brahminism. These were groups which were comparative newcomers in the Hindu fold and had not yet been thoroughly Hinduized.

In these ways a military aristocracy became, in the course of centuries, a distinct community within Indian society and a separate province of Islam. The Indian Muslims were essentially Indian and were also definitely Muslim. They provided a unique feature of Indian life, for never before had so large a body of foreign origin remained distinct from Hinduism for so long.[6] The new community was concentrated mainly in the northwest and northeast where, by the processes already described, it formed the majority of the population. In the Ganges Plain connecting the two there were pockets here and there. Elsewhere in India the Muslims were more scattered, centering round royal courts as in Hyderabad or clustering in mercantile communities as in Gujarat. In class structure it consisted of a strong aristocracy, holding the principal civil and military posts, a small middle class and a large proletariat of peasants and town-dwellers. The middle class was small because merit won promotion to the upper ranks of a Muslim administration, and there were many Hindus available to fill subordinate and technical posts.

Indian Islam expressed itself in a distinctive culture which may be called Indo-Persian. The Muslim religion, modified by its Turkish and Afghan race-bearers, was further modified by the Persian culture by which all the invaders were more or less influenced. Persian was the language of official business and of polite society (as French was in England in the early Middle Ages). Persian literature was studied and cultivated by Hindus as well as Muslims; Persian manners became the standard of all Indian society. All these tendencies reached their peak under the Mughals, in connection with whom they will be further explained. The political side of the culture was an imperial tradition. The Muslims of India, as the result of much gifted leadership, felt themselves to be an imperial as well as a chosen race.

The separateness of Hinduism and Islam has been emphasized. The two bodies remained distinct for nine centuries, yet with so much intimate contact there was bound to be some mutual influence. As in the case of the Greeks, desire as to what is thought ought to be is apt to outrun recognition of what was. There was certainly mutual influence. Some of it was important but on neither side was it fundamental. On the Hindu side we find during the Muslim centuries a greater emphasis on the unity of God. We also find in the *bhakti* movements emphasis on such things as sin and forgiveness, which have a distinctly Judaic ring. A number of reforming movements have attacked caste. There have been a number of movements, of which Sikhism is the best known, which started by trying to bridge the gulf between the two communities; their basis was usually monotheism, no caste, and personal devotion. On the Muslim side we may say that the Indian atmosphere softened the original Turkish intolerance. Many Muslims were influenced by Hindu philosophy. In daily life saint worship and other Hindu practices established themselves, and the caste system made itself felt in marriage arrangements.

There was much give and take, but no fusion or synthesis. In daily life there was much day-to-day tolerance and consideration, but behind it all was a permanent tension between the two ways of life. Indo-Persian culture spread a mantle of elegance over the whole of Indian aristocratic society, but Hinduism and Islam remained apart.

CHAPTER IX

Turks and Afghans

The main impact of Islam upon India was delivered by the Turks. The Arabs had sent traders to Malabar and soldiers to Sind, but there their influence stopped. It was as significant for India that Islam was introduced by Turks instead of Arabs as that later the West was introduced by the British instead of the French. In both cases there was a racial and a religio-cultural element involved; in both cases the content of the former was greatly modified by the nature of the latter. India would be a different place today if the French (or some other nation) had introduced the West instead of the British; so would it have been if there had been an Arab empire instead of a Turkish in India. We should always remember that the first two centuries of Muslim India was the period of the Turkish empire in India. Indeed, it could more appropriately be labeled the Indo-Turkish period than given the dynastic labels which are usual. In following this period with understanding, the Turkish element is as important as the Islamic.

Who then were the Turks and what were their characteristics? They were one more of the races which have periodically "swarmed" from the great racial hive of central Asia. Their origin is obscure, and so is their racial composition. There has been much intermixture with Mongolian types and their language and literature are influenced by the same source, but as a whole they were more Aryan than Mongol. They were grouped in tribes that roamed the steppes like others before them. Within the steppes themselves tribes constantly rose and fell without record or outside knowledge. Tribes would dissolve and coalesce, be overcome or subjugate others. It was in this process that the intermixture took place which puzzles ethnologists. The result was seen when the tribes impinged upon civilization, but the why or wherefore is unknown. So, for the most part, are the reasons for the swarming of the tribes themselves.

The Turkish tribes in their nomadic state were a restless, vigorous, and warlike people. They carried their hardihood and vigor with them but they also proved susceptible to religious and cultural influences. These they encountered in the region now known as Turkestan on the borders of modern Persia and Soviet Asia. Here Islam reached forth from Persia, and Persian culture (in its Islamic form) exercised its subtle sway. The Turks gave allegiance to both Islam and Persian culture. They brought to both their rough nomadic ways; they gave to Islam an intolerant and sometimes ferocious twist, and they seemed to the Persians uncouth barbarians. The Persian attitude was rather that of the Athenians to the semi-Hellenized Macedonians. So we find the Turks capable of ruthless destruction and also of creative achievement, of fierce intolerance and also of skillful patronage of the arts. They produced both the destroyer Timur (Tamerlane) and the philosopher king Akbar.

In the latter part of the first Christian millennium the Arab caliphate controlled Persia from Baghdad. But it came more and more under the influence of Turkish tribes that eventually dominated it. Kingdoms were carved out owning nominal allegiance to the caliph but which were in fact dynastic empires. Thus the caliphate, instead of providing a shield in Iran to protect India from the outer barbarians, became a filter through which they percolated. The Turkish tribes at this time may perhaps be described as semibarbaric, owing allegiance to Islam and accepting Persian culture, but being liable to strange aberrations of tyranny and savagery. In 1071 they burst into the West when they overthrew the Greek emperor and overran Asia Minor. Five years later they took Jerusalem, an act which set in motion the Crusades. Eastward they established themselves at Ghazni, between Kabul and Kandahar in modern Afghanistan. From this point their leader Mahmud led a series of raids on northwest India, culminating in the sack of Mathura (sacred to Krishna) and the destruction at the great temple of Somnath, on the coast of Kathiawar in 1024–25. It is typical of the Turks of that time that the ruthless destroyer of temples and slayer of idolaters was a patron of the arts at Ghazni. Alberuni, the Muslim savant who wrote a classical work on Hinduism, resided at his court. Mahmud's raids had two important results. The first was the conquest of the Panjab, which, with a few interludes, has been Muslim territory ever since. The gateway of India had been secured. The second was to set up in Indian minds a tradition of Muslim intolerance. After the early Turkish period the tradition was so deeply rooted that no policy of toleration, nor the general practice of the live-and-let-live principle which was the day-to-day custom of Indian life, could eradicate it. In the popular Hindu mind a Muslim was as intolerant as a *bania* was avaricious or a

Rajput brave. Perhaps the chance of the ultimate conversion of India to Islam was lost in the din of Mahmud's idol-breaking.

In the twelfth century the successors of Mahmud were replaced by another Turkish dynasty which fixed its headquarters at Ghur. In 1186 Lahore, the last Ghaznavid stronghold, was taken, and the way was clear to move against Hindu India. In 1191, while Richard I was besieging Acre during the third crusade against Saladin, Saladin's fellow Turk Muhammad of Ghor marched into Hindu India. In that year he was defeated by a coalition of chiefs led by Prithvi Raj, one of the heroes of Rajput legend. The next year he returned, overthrew and killed Prithvi Raj on the same field of Thanesar, and marched to Delhi which he made his capital. The Turkish empire in India had begun. Its hallmark, as it were, was the famous Qutab Minar near modern Delhi, which was designed as a tower of victory and still attracts thousands of visitors.

From this initial victory the empire spread rapidly over the confines of the traditional Hindustan. The year after the capture of Delhi Jai Chand Rathor of Kanauj, whose dominions roughly extended over the modern state of Uttar Pradesh, was defeated, Banaras sacked, and his kingdom annexed. The next year the fortress of Gwalior to the south of the river Chambal was taken. Two years later Behar, where a declining Buddhism with many monasteries persisted, was overrun. The massacre of the monks meant the virtual end of Indian Buddhism, and the burning of the monasteries and their records was a severe blow to Indian culture. The monkish remnant with some cherished manuscripts scattered to Nepal, Tibet, and the south. At the beginning of the new century came the turn of Bengal. Many of the ruling class fled to Nepal and the Himalayas where their descendants are to be found today. There, except for the addition of Sind from its local Muslim rulers a few years later, remained the Turkish empire in India through the thirteenth century.

The speed and completeness of the Turkish victory against opponents so brave and stubborn as the Rajput chiefs would seem to call for some explanation. One reason was the conservatism of Indian military practice. Indian tactics against Muhammad of Ghor did not differ very much from those used by Porus against Alexander a millennium and a half earlier. The mace was pitted against the arrow, masses of undisciplined infantry against well-mounted and controlled cavalry, adept at wheeling maneuvers. More important, however, were the jealousies of the Rajput clans. These jealousies survived down to recent years, and were one of the factors which prevented the Indian princes from making common cause on the eve of independence in the twentieth century.

Thus against the Turks no united front was lasting and each prince could be isolated and defeated. Jai Chand deserted Prithvi Raj at the second battle of Thanesar, only to be separately overthrown later. When the turn of the Deccan came a century later, similar jealousies paralyzed united Hindu action.

Perhaps the decisive factor which determined not only the Hindu defeat but the failure to stage any comeback was the social and religious tension which existed throughout the country. Socially, the Rajputs and their counterparts in the south were an agrarian aristocracy, separated from the middle classes and the peasants both by class and caste. To the peasants the then rulers were oppressive landlords rather than popular leaders. It might be supposed that Turkish destruction of temples and monasteries would excite general horror as well as terror. But the peasants found that Turkish horrors only occurred when their armies were on the march and were not in fact much worse than the behavior of other armies. Religious destruction occurred mainly in the cities, and again generally during campaigns. On the other hand they were saved from the oppression of their own people, such as Brahmin pressure on the Buddhists in Bengal. The peasants therefore remained inert and in some places even welcomed the invader. The middle classes acquiesced because they were employed to run the new administration. Local chiefs were largely left in possession and were not going to risk all for a displaced chief who had formerly oppressed them. In these circumstances religious horror was confined to the temple Brahmins and Buddhist monks, who were the chief sufferers. Clan jealousies and class resentments thus combined to prevent either united Indian action or the growth of a strong antiforeign sentiment.

The nature of the new empire which had united India for the first time since the fall of the Guptas in the fifth century A.D. also deserves some thought. The regime began as an army of occupation belonging to a ruler as interested in central Asia as India. It developed into a Turkish colonial empire recruited from émigrés fleeing from the Mongol flood which engulfed Turkestan, Iran, and Iraq. It broke up when that stream dried up through the revival of Turkish fortunes, and local leadership faltered. In their ability to survive when cut off from their home base these Turks resembled the Indo-Greeks. But they possessed the faculty of united action as well as of daring leadership. Because of the paucity of their numbers they resorted to terror tactics in dealing with Hindu rajas; because of their lack of sophistication they gave a fanatical twist to Islam and became idol breakers and temple destroyers. In essence their rule was a military occupation on a religious and racial foundation.

India — in the Turkish Period

It was severe because it was insecure. But the severity, as has been already explained, was limited generally to the Hindu leaders. Hindu cooperation was accepted in all branches of the state. Hindu rajas and landlords generally became tributaries instead of being displaced. Hindu officers and clerks were employed in the secretariats. Hindu auxiliaries accompanied the armies on their campaigns. It could be said that there was less social displacement at the time of the Turkish conquest of north India than in William I's conquest of England.

Another feature of the regime was the military slave system characteristic of Turks elsewhere.[1] The first Turkish dynasty (1206–90) is known as the Slave dynasty because it sprang from this class. By this system children were taken from their homes and educated as military slaves or servile soldiers. Many were of great ability, with no other allegiance but to the state and themselves. One could be a prime minister or commander in chief and still a slave. In India a military slave stepped on to the throne in 1206; hence the name of the dynasty. The system provided a body of servants devoted to the state; its political drawback was its tendency to promote periodic palace revolutions.

A final feature of the Turkish period in India was its artistic brilliance. The sultans patronized the humanities while often practicing inhumanity; they used Hindu artists and craftsmen and welcomed many refugees from the land overrun by the Mongols to the northwest. In three centuries north, central, and western India were covered with nobly conceived and brilliantly executed buildings. A new Indo-Muslim style was developed, both Indian and Muslim. In literature and learning India became a province of the Persian cultural empire with her own poets like Amir Khusrau and historians like Barani.

During the thirteenth and fourteenth centuries this severe yet remarkable minority government performed certain functions of lasting importance. On the destructive side it achieved the final obliteration of organized Buddhism. Indian Buddhism was already in deep decline; a religious body which could be extinguished by the massacre of its monks could not have had much vitality. This action was a hastening of the inevitable. The Turks overthrew Brahmin rule in Bengal and Rajput rule in north and central India. They turned Rajasthan into a desert citadel of Rajput clan freedom, and so created the legend of the romantic Rajput chief. More important was their breakup of the southern Indian dynasties, which had jostled each other with little outside interference for nearly a thousand years. They did not break up Hinduism itself, but they hindered it by depriving it of state patronage and they tended to drive it into itself. The caste system became more rigid, female seclusion more general.

But the most important function of these kings, which constitutes their main claim to Indian gratitude, since no one else could have performed it at the time, was that of warden of the marches. The era of Turkish expansion came to an abrupt end with the incursions of the Mongols under Genghis Khan in the early thirteenth century. These early Mongols had not even a thin veneer of Islam to cover their barbarism. They were dreaded as ferocious and repulsive destroyers. Genghis Khan died in 1227, having overrun Persia and become the master of an empire stretching from the Yellow Sea to the river Dnieper in South Russia. His grandson Hulugu extinguished the caliphate in Baghdad in 1258. The Turkish kings were thus isolated from their fellows and the rest of Islam by a flood of hostile barbarism. They stood firm, keeping the Mongols at bay until their dominion broke up. This vigil of more than a century was of the greatest value to India.[2]

The Turkish empire or Delhi sultanate lasted for just two centuries (1192–1398). Its history is divided into three phases. The Slave Kings (1206–90), whose greatest representatives were Iltutmish and Balban, established the empire, destroyed Buddhism, and kept out the Mongols. The Khiljis (1296–1320) pressed the independent Rajputs back into Rajasthan and carried Islam and the empire into the deep south in a series of daring expeditions. Under their successors, the Tughluqs, a breakup began and the divisive pattern which prevailed for the next two centuries began to emerge. Early in the reign of Muhammad Tughluq (1325–51) his rule was acknowledged even at Madura in the extreme south. Muhammad was brilliant but eccentric and ferocious; he was described by the Moorish traveler Ibn Batuta, who lived at his court for a time, as "of all men the fondest of making gifts and shedding blood." Most of his reign was spent trying to suppress revolts which his unwisdom had provoked. By his death the Hindu south had recovered its independence, the Deccan had broken away as a separate Muslim kingdom, and there were other Muslim splinter states. His successor, Firoz Shah (1351–88), restored stability to the north and let the rest go. Posterity owes him a debt for his careful restoration of historic buildings, including the Qutab Minar.

After the death of Firoz came the deluge of disintegration. Dynastic disputes opened the way for the second of the great medieval Asian destroyers, Timur.[3] Born in 1336, Timur was a Turk who profited by the dissensions of the descendants of Genghis to build an empire of his own. He reigned in Samarkand from 1369 to 1405, and built up an empire extending from the Mediterranean to the borders of China. Baghdad, Damascus, and Moscow were among his conquests, the Mongol Golden Horde and the Turks of Asia Minor among his victims. In 1398 he marched to Delhi, took and sacked it, and then marched back by a different route. He left two broad bands of destruction in his wake and general terror throughout the north. It was from this expedition that his successors, misnamed Mughals,[4] derived their claim to Indian rule. Babur, the first Mughal emperor, was a direct descendant of Timur.

The effects of this raid help us to understand better what India escaped as the result of the repulse of the Mongols. In the years following the raid there is evidence of economic as well as political collapse. The raid completed in the north the Balkanization of Muslim India which Muhammad Tughluq had already provoked in the south. During the fifteenth century India presented a bewildering array of political disunity. The country was divided among local dynasties whose courts often displayed much talent and taste as well as corruption and ferocity. The struggle for power among the minority rulers was intense, palace revolutions frequent, and violent deaths commonplace. In the north and center the energy of Turkish and Afghan chiefs was enough to maintain themselves against the Hindus but their sense of cohesion insufficient to revive the Delhi empire. In Delhi itself two kings contended for a time and the jingle was coined

> From Delhi to Palam
> Is the realm of Shah Alam.[5]

These dynasties are remembered today mainly by their striking buildings, which often exhibit a harmonious blending of Hindu and Islamic features. The mosques of Ahmadabad, Jaunpur, and Delhi are examples of these. In the north the Lodi Afghans eventually built up a power which exercised a loose control from the Panjab to the borders of Bengal. It was the third king of this dynasty who faced Babur at Panipat in 1526.

The most interesting part of India at this time was the south. We have noticed the revolt of the Muslim governor of the Deccan against Muhammad Shah in 1347. This was part of a twin movement of reassertion of the south against the north. The Muslim chiefs revolted against the control of Delhi, and Hindu chiefs rose against Muslim and Turkish domination. The first movement produced the brilliant and wayward Bahmini kingdom,[6] whose monuments still strew the Deccan and which lasted from 1347 to 1482. It then broke up into five fragments, to be gradually absorbed by the Mughals during the next two hundred years. The second movement produced the Hindu empire of Vijayanagar which came to control the whole of India south of the Kistna and Tungabhadra rivers, and flourished from about 1336 to 1565. During these years the Bahmini kingdom and its successors formed an uneasy balance of power with Vijayanagar. This was ended by the crushing Hindu defeat at Talikota in 1565 and the destruction of the capital city of Vijayanagar which followed. Thereafter, Muslim power again extended into the south until the Mughal Aurangzeb's writ stretched again for a time to Madura.

The Vijayanagar empire was founded by two brothers from Telingana (the modern state of Andhra) who had already resisted the Muslims in the service of the Raja of Warangal, been carried to Delhi, become converts in Muhammad Shah's service, revolted, and reverted to Hinduism. The new fortress capital on the south side of the Tungabhadra River soon became the nucleus of a powerful state which stretched from sea to sea across the peninsula, and eventually controlled the whole of the south except Calicut. Vijayanagar differed from earlier kingdoms of the south in that the ruling dynasty did not emerge from a local hinterland and then spread its authority over more distant regions. From the first the rulers were alien. They were Telugu speakers from the Andhra country and they established their realm in the Kanara country. They early lost their foothold in northern Andhra (at Warangal); their main expansion lay southward over the rest of the Kanara country (modern Mysore state) and southeastward over the Tamil country. Vijayanagar was an ideological state in the sense that it represented a revival of Hinduism against Islam. But it cannot be called a national state, for its government was a domination of a Telugu oligarchy over Kanaras, Tamils, and Malayalis.

The government seems to have had a central bureaucracy headed by the *raya* or king. This maintained the usual mercenary army including Muslim levies of mounted archers. Good horses were scarce in south India, and the Portuguese in the early sixteenth century found the import of horses through Goa a lucrative source of profit. This army not only resisted the Muslim powers but maintained the royal authority over the many local chiefs who were left undisturbed. The task was helped by the military colonies with fortresses at strategic points in the peninsula, rather in the Roman fashion. Chandragiri near Madras was one of these. It was the last refuge of the Vijayanagar kings, one of the last of whom in 1645 confirmed the grant of the site of Madras to the East India Company. As long as the center remained strong, a firm control could thus be exercised over the whole empire. In these circumstances for some two centuries the surplus wealth of the ever prosperous south, with its cottons, silks, spices, and perennial re-export trade, was canalized to Vijayanagar. This process made it one of the greatest cities of the world at the time; both European and Muslim visitors described its magnificence and luxury with awe. The system of control by an alien centralized oligarchy also explains why the sudden paralysis of that center proved irreparable. There was no reserve of national spirit, so that the subordinate chiefs flew apart to local independence.

Vijayanagar was a wonder city of the time. It was said to be as large as Rome, to have over half a million inhabitants, to extend over seven miles from the northern to the southern gate, and to have seven concentric city walls. Yet it was not a typically Hindu city. Vishnu and Shiva were worshiped and the Brahmins held a privileged position. Suttee, the burning of Hindu widows, was practiced on a large scale, and temple prostitution was widespread. But meat of all kinds except beef was consumed by princes and common people alike; animal sacrifices were carried out on a large scale in the manner of the Andhra country. It would seem that while orthodox Hinduism, both in its virtues and vices, was observed to an extent, in much of their daily lives, the people followed the local custom of the Andhras. Vijayanagar was a glittering city of pomp and power; politically it was the seat of an able but alien oligarchy and culturally the center of a hybrid Hinduism. Its function was to keep militant Muslims away from the deep south until they had lost most of their aggressive spirit and intolerance.

PART II
THE MUGHAL EMPIRE

CHAPTER X

Babur and the Mughals

With our arrival at the Mughal period we enter a more spacious field and breathe a fresher air. Instead of the general obscurity lit by occasional shafts of light, such as the Asokan inscriptions or Fa-Hien's travels, an obscurity only partly dissipated by the chroniclers of the Muslim centuries, India is bathed in a flood of light from a variety of sources. Instead of the occasional personality like Muhammad bin Tughluq which the earlier chroniclers revealed, we have a whole gallery of portraits of both men and women. Instead of the fissiparous tendencies of the preceding centuries, with their monotonous wars and often sickening tales of murders, massacre, and perfidy, we have a stable centripetal force steadily extending its influences throughout the subcontinent. Rulers become affable as well as capable; altogether the vagrant political and cultural winds of Hindustan blow with a more genial air.

The Mughal period in Indian history has certain distinguishing marks which had not been present in the same degree and in combination since the age of Harsha nearly a thousand years before. The first mark was its personalities. By coincidence or the working of some yet unfathomed historic law the sixteenth century was an age of greatness and creative endeavor nearly everywhere. Europe had its Renaissance and Reformation, its age of discovery, and its literary glories. France with its Francis I and Calvin, Germany with its Luther, Italy with its galaxy of artists and divines, Spain with its empire builders and Ignatius Loyola, England with its Queen Elizabeth and Shakespeare make an impressive array. In Russia there was the impressive if grim figure of Ivan the Terrible. In the Near East the Turkish Ottoman dynasty with Selim and Suleiman the Magnificent was in its heyday. Persia under Shah Abbas was renewing its political and artistic glories, while in the Far East the Chings in replacing the Mings were renewing the strength of China, and Japan had launched on a century of brilliance. In this galaxy the Indian constellation shone brightly, with Babur, Sher Shah, and Akbar in the political field, Abu'l Fazl in the world of scholarship and literature, the poets Faizi and Tulsi Das, and the artistic creators of Fatehpur-Sikri and the Mughal school of painting. In the seventeenth century the personalities become, if anything, more complex and diverse, so that the character of an Indian emperor and the vicissitudes of a succession struggle became part of the literary legend of western Europe.

The next note of the period was integration. Islam came into India as a divisive and destructive influence; under the Mughals its influence was toward unification. During this period we observe a tendency for the state to rise above religious animosities, for co-operation to take the place of rivalry, for harmony to replace bitterness and hate. There was more give and take between the communities, a greater tendency to work together for the common good than for centuries before and in large measure since. Along with this tendency to integration went a talent for organization, a regularization of life in all its departments. The Mughals found, as Babur forcefully explained, very little of either integration or organization. But they left a form and a name and a precedent for everything, as the British discovered when they began to examine the territories they had taken over. The state became more than a name in a distant city, occasionally descending in wrath on the countryside in military form, indifferent to suffering so long as the revenue was paid, and pitiless when it was not. Society at any rate in the north was covered with a sheath of form and regulation. The average man was more secure than before, and also felt that he lived in a society, framed to some extent at least by regulation and order. The state was no longer just a money-collecting, vengeance-dealing institution, but to a degree the support and canopy of daily life.

Finally, the Mughal period marked a general advance in refinement and elegance of life. Politics remained ruthless, it is true, at times of struggles for supreme power. But in the intervals, which were often prolonged, there was a noticeable mellowing of political rancor. Blinding and execution were largely replaced by exile or relegation to a distant province. Princes were proud to be cultured as well as awesome. The Mughal court became a center of Persian culture, whose rays were spread by its agents and its reputation throughout India from the fastnesses of Rajasthan to the temple courts of Madura. Persian elegance and Turkish vigor combined to infuse refinement and some degree of humanism into governmental authority and the aristocratic classes generally.

At the beginning of the sixteenth century, however, all this was yet in the future. India presented to the observer of that time a fragmented and unpromising appearance. The political confusion of a century past showed no signs of disappearing. In the north the Lodi regime at Delhi and Agra maintained a loose hold over the plains from the Indus to Behar. It was a confederacy of Afghan chiefs rather than an organized empire, held together by the personal qualities of Sikandar Lodi in succession to his father Bahlul. In Rajasthan the Rajput chiefs continued their long career of war, personal bravery, and political division. Mewar under Rana Sanga, it is true, was attaining considerable eminence, but its empire was of the same loose character as that of the Afghans. In both these cases the reputed pillars of empire turned out to be ropes of sand. In Bengal the Muslim kingdom which had separated from Delhi at the end of the thirteenth century continued. Animosities had cooled along with fighting vigor and the court presented an aspect of considerable syncretism. Perhaps encouraged by this and the comparative security of the country, a Vaishnavite revival headed by Chaitanya was appearing in the country.

In central India all was conflict and confusion. Malwa was threatened by the Rajputs and Gujarat. Gujarat itself waɔ prosperous under the famous Mahmud Begarha, whose beard descended to his waist and whose mustachios were tied behind his head, whose immunity to poison had become a legend thus described by the poet:

> The King of Cambay's daily food
> Is asp and basilisk and toad.

Under firm government for nearly a century, Gujarat was at this time something of a model state. Further south in the Deccan, however, the picture was very different. With the murder of Mahmud Gawan in 1481 the virtue departed from the brilliant Bahmini kingdom. Between 1482 and 1518 the realm was split into five successor states of Bidar, Golconda, Bijapur, Ahmadnagar, and Berar, each as ready to fight the other as the Hindu power to the south. The wealth accumulated during a century and a half of unified rule was being dissipated in internecine strife. Sandwiched in between the Bahmini kingdoms and Gujarat lay the little hill state of Khandesh, a relic of the revolts against Muhammad Tughluq and hitherto too remote and defensible to become the prey of one of the other competing Muslim kingdoms.

South of the Kistna lay the empire of Vijayanagar, the Hindu reply to the Muslim Turkish incursions in the south. Just beyond the Tungabhadra lay the great fortress capital of Vijayanagar itself, its splendor and wealth certified by both Muslim and European visitors. Vijayanagar presented a brilliant spectacle, but its strength was brittle. Along the Malabar

Coast lay a number of principalities sheltered from the interior by the belt of mountain and forest of the Western Ghats, and nourished by the spice trade, with its local production of pepper and re-export trade with the East Indies and the Islamic world. The ancient principality of Calicut was the principal of these, with Cochin as a second. Here a new influence had just appeared in the shape of the Portuguese, who came, in their own words, to seek Christians and spices. They also came to harry Muslims wherever they could find them, which led them into alliance with Hindu Cochin against the Muslim patron Calicut. Before long the Portuguese were to establish themselves at Goa and to control not only the spice trade from the East Indies but the whole commerce of the Arabian Sea. By the time that Babur appeared in India they held, in addition to Goa, Diu on the Kathiawar coast, Ormuz at the entrance of the Persian Gulf, and Socotra off the mouth of the Red Sea.

India was turbulent, restless, and divided. The political units were for the most part mere aggregations of power, held together by the ability of some individual or family and apt to change with the rapidity of the kaleidoscope. The position in fact was not unlike that which existed between 700 and 1000 A.D. when a contentious aristocracy struggled for power, never rising to the achievement of an integrated empire, or sinking from political confusion into actual barbarism. In this case the further complication of rival religions was added, but it seemed that they too had achieved an uneasy kind of balance, a sort of unity in conflict. Through all the political ferment the arts flourished wherever patrons were rich enough to support them. Trade flourished wherever there were centers of wealth, for it was in the interest even of rival rulers to protect a traffic from which they could get a handsome return and to foster foreign connections through which they could receive both welcome recruits and needed supplies for their campaigns. But if trade was brisk, it is equally clear that the countryside as a whole was miserable. It was over the country that the armies moved, destroying cultivation and uprooting villages; it was the peasants who had to supply food and labor for the forces, and the sinews of lordly politics in the form of revenue payments. The testimony on this score is as definite as that of the prosperity of the great cities. The misery of the people must be set in the balance against the magnificence of the towns.

India may thus be said to have been ready for some new development, though, as past precedent had shown, this did not mean that it would necessarily happen. It depended upon developments outside, and it is to these that we must now turn. India was as yet little concerned with what went on in China or Japan, or much with what happened in the East

Indies. Here Indian cultural influence still persisted, but it had long since lost any dynamic force. Instead, the East Indies had for some time been coming under the spell of Islam, through Arab traders and divines. Chief after chief adopted Islam in preference to the current corrupt Buddhism and Saivism, or else, as in Thailand and Cambodia, a revived Hinayana cult from Ceylon had purified religion but reduced Indian influence. Politically the sea empire of Mahapajit had dissolved, and the region had no sea power to match that of the Portuguese.

It was in the northwest that events were taking place that, as so often in the past, were to change the face of India. All through the fifteenth century the backwash, as it were, of the great tidal wave of Timur and his Turks had surged to and fro across Iran, Turkestan, and the steppes. Timur himself, after his Delhi raid, had crushed the rising Ottoman Turks in Asia Minor in 1402 and had died while on the march to China in 1405. Thereafter, his realm had rapidly dissolved in contests between his descendants. A number of Timurid dynasties divided Persia and Turkestan while the Ottoman Turks farther west recovered and went on to take Constantinople. The reintegration and expansion of the Ottomans was a signal for similar moves elsewhere. At the turn of the century the Safavid dynasty emerged in Persia which reunified the country under Shah Ismail (1501–24) and began to renew its ancient glories. In particular he elevated the characteristically Persian form of Islam, the Shia cult, as the state religion. In Turkestan the struggles of the Timurid chiefs for the possession of Samarkand were overshadowed at the turn of the century by the rise of the Uzbeg tribe in the region between the Ural Mountains and the Aral Sea. This mixed and warlike tribe found a leader of genius in Shaibani Khan, a descendant of Genghis himself.

It was while these contests were still undecided and indeed it looked as though an Uzbeg empire might be in the making that Babur was born in 1483 in Farghana, a little principality to the north of the Hindu Kush Mountains. His father was Umar Sheikh Mirza, fourth in descent from Timur in the direct line. His rule was troubled and in 1494 he died, leaving his precarious throne to his eleven-year-old son. Babur was fortunate in having faithful followers. For over ten years, as boy and young man, through immense hardships and hazards, he strove to recover the ancestral seat of Samarkand, only to be baffled at every turn by the terrible Shaibani Khan. In 1504 he secured Kabul to the south of the Hindu Kush range and from 1505 he settled down in a kingdom astride the range comprising the territories of Kabul, Kandahar, and Badakshan. In 1510 Shaibani Khan was defeated and killed by Shah Ismail of Persia. Encouraged by this, Babur obtained Persian aid to march once more on

Samarkand. But the Persian religion was so unpopular in Turkestan that Babur found his position as a Persian nominee untenable. In 1513 he abandoned his Central Asian ambitions and turned his face south and eastward. It is from this time that his interest in India dates, the area having been hitherto in his eyes an uninviting region of heat and dust. Had the Uzbegs been less formidable, or Shi-ism less repellent to Turkish taste, Babur's name might well have been but one of a long list of adventurers in Turkestan and Indian history might have taken a different course.

The establishment of Babur in Kabul and his abandonment of his Central Asian ambitions provided two of the conditions needed for a reunification of northern India—a man capable of the work, and his interest in the possible task. Babur paid his first visit to India, in the form of a reconnaissance raid, in 1517. Events in India now added a third—instability and unrest in the Lodi kingdom. Sikandar Lodi, who usually resided at Agra and gave his name to the suburb where Akbar was later buried, died in 1518. He had reigned in much the same loose style as his father, rather as the president of a confederation of Afghan nobles than a despotic monarch. His son Ibrahim had other views. He desired to increase the royal authority, which meant curbing the power of the nobles. While strong enough to retain his throne, he was not forceful enough to achieve his object without friction, and the result was a ground swell of discontent.

In this state of affairs Daulat Khan Lodi, governor of the Panjab, provided a fourth condition for a reintegration, an invitation to the eligible outsider. He invited Babur to India, no doubt hoping to profit himself in the process. Babur, who had raided India a second time in 1519, commenced a regular invasion of the Panjab on Daulat Khan's invitation in 1524. He was recalled, however, by an Uzbeg threat in the north, and it was not until the cold weather of 1525 that he set out on his fateful journey. The Panjab was secured, first, with Daulat Khan's connivance and then against his will.[1] In the spring of 1526 Babur moved on toward Delhi and met Ibrahim Lodi in the field of Panipat, fifty miles to the north, on April 21. Ibrahim's host numbered some hundred thousand men with one hundred elephants, while Babur had only some twelve thousand. But Ibrahim's host, if large, was disorderly, made up of contingents of chiefs who were in many cases halfhearted or disloyal. Many were there to see what would happen rather than to fight seriously. Babur's army, on the other hand, was a closely knit force of chiefs loyal to their leader and knit together by a common enterprise. Babur had, in addition, two other advantages. He possessed a train of artillery directed by Turkish officers from Constantinople, and horsemen trained in the Turkish tactics of wheeling and flank charges. With his front protected by breastworks and artillery, Babur used his cavalry at the critical moment with deadly effect. The result was a resounding victory; Ibrahim was killed in the rout. Afghan disunity prevented any possibility of a rally. Babur was able to occupy Delhi and Agra (where he immediately laid out a garden) without a blow.

But Babur was only at the beginning of his troubles. He had first to deal with the homesickness of his Turkish lieutenants, the Mughal *begs* who pined, in the heat and dust of Agra, for the cool airs and sparkling streams of the north. Babur himself felt acutely the discomforts and limitations of the north India of his day in the hot season, which he thus describes in his *Memoirs:* [2]

Hindustan is a country that has few pleasures to recommend it. The people are not handsome. They have no idea of the charms of friendly society, of frankly mixing together, or of familiar intercourse. They have no genius, no comprehension of mind, no politeness of manner, no kindness or fellow-feeling, no ingenuity or mechanical invention in planning or executing their handicraft works, no skill or knowledge in design or architecture; they have no horses, no good flesh, no grapes or musk-melons, no good fruits, no ice or cold water, no good food or bread in their bazars, no baths or colleges, no candles, no torches, not a candlestick.

Only a leader of exceptional powers could have retained such followers through the strain of north Indian hot weather. With the advent of cooler weather, however, Babur's anxieties did not diminish. While the Afghan chiefs to the east remained disunited and inert, Rana Sanga of Mewar prepared to dispute the empire of the plains with Babur. Rana Sanga himself enjoyed the supremacy of Rajasthan and great prestige throughout northern India. He hoped that Babur, like Timur before him, would retire to the hills with his gains, leaving him as the residuary legatee of empire. But he forgot that Timur was already the head of a great empire to which north India would only have been a small addition, and that while Delhi was rich in Timur's day it was poor in his own. Babur, on the other hand, had only a mountain kingdom to fall back upon. Hindustan was potentially rich, but owing to its divisions and commotions, immediately poor. Babur's gains were prospective, not immediate, and retreat would mean disaster, not the mere transfer of activity elsewhere. When the Rana realized that Babur intended to stay and had persuaded his *begs* to do likewise, he prepared for war. He received contingents from one hundred and twenty chiefs with eighty thousand horsemen and five hundred elephants and marched upon Agra. This army was more united than Ibrahim's and much stronger in cavalry, and it should have made short work of Babur's central Asian remnant and local levies. But it suffered from the usual defects of feudal levies with their jealousies and divided loyalties and also from the chronic Rajput reluctance to modify their traditional ideas of the mass charge and single combat. They had no artillery, though their numbers should have amply compensated for this defect. The small Mughal army was daunted by the Rajput reputation in a way it had not been by the Afghan host of Ibrahim; Babur made what may be described as a "backs-to-the-wall speech" and followed this up by publicly renouncing (not for the first time) his drinking of wine and by breaking up his drinking vessels. He then advanced to the attack on March 16, 1527, repeated the tactics of Panipat, and achieved another spectacular victory. Rana Sanga escaped and survived until 1529, but his power was broken. The Rajputs remained formidable in their own territory but their offensive power was crippled and their hopes of empire shattered.

Babur was now fairly established in India. But he still had to deal with the Afghan chiefs who had been trying to rally in Bengal and Behar. In 1529 he met and defeated them near Patna. Babur was now only forty-six years of age and seemed to have a long reign as emperor of Hindustan before him. But his early hardships and later exertions had worn him out and he died in December 1530. It is related that his eldest and favorite son was critically ill earlier in the year; Babur decided to follow the custom of offering the dearest thing in the world in exchange for his son's life. This was his own, and walking three times round his son's bed, he offered it up. Thereafter, Homayun began to mend and Babur's strength to leave him. We only have the chronicler's word for the story, but it is one which is eminently in character.

Babur must be rated as the founder of the Mughal empire in the sense that he gained control of most of Hindustan and defeated the two chief competitors for dominion, the Afghans and the Rajputs. But he was not the creator of the characteristic features of the empire. He was tolerant by habit and temperament, but he had no "Hindu policy." He administered firmly in the short space given him, but he had no special administrative policy. Land was parceled out to those *begs* who got control of it; his regime, so far as it went, was the semifeudalism of the Afghans and Rajputs, with a more loyal and united band of followers. He firmly controlled the *begs* but he had no imperial administrative service. All these things were to come later.

Babur is nevertheless one of the great figures of Indian history. His conquest and retention of India was in itself a triumph of personality. His resources were small, his enemies formidable, and his followers far from enthusiastic about settling down in the discomforts of contemporary India. His personality was not only vivid but many-sided; he was far more than an attractive soldier of fortune. His buoyant bearing of hardship and ill fortune, his geniality, his wit, his robust sense of humor endeared him to his followers and won over his opponents. To this he added the good manners and taste of Persia, an appreciation of art which was delicate and sincere, and a love of nature which was almost unique in his age. His first act on reaching Agra was to lay out a garden (still existing as the Ram Bagh). His artistic nature expressed itself in poetry, in which he ranks high among Turki poets, and in prose, of which his autobiography must rank as a masterpiece in any language. Literary ability united with sincerity to produce a self-portrait as attractive as it rings true, and a narrative as stirring as the events it describes. Babur's standard of honor was high and his chivalry extraordinary considering the nature of the men and scenes amid which he spent more than half his life. Even his faults were attractive, as readers will learn when they come upon his descriptions of his drinking parties and his periodical good resolutions to give up this un-Islamic practice. It was Babur's personality which made him the ruler of Hindustan and his personality which generated a fund of loyalty sufficient to sustain his wayward son through his vicissitudes of fortune and finally to seat his grandson firmly on the Indian throne. Babur's is a humane and gracious as well as an adventurous figure; it sheds a ray of welcome light upon the scenes of violence and perfidy, which make up so much of early sixteenth-century politics in this part of the world.

Babur's eldest son Homayun was twenty-three when he came to the throne. His age saved him from a war of succession because his brothers were too distant or too young to have large followings. Homayun had many attractive qualities. He was brave and a good general; he could inspire his followers and undergo great exertion. He was versed in the arts and may be described as a cultivated gentleman in the Persian style. His manners were polished, his bearing dignified; he was good-humored, openhanded, and affectionate. But with these qualities went certain traits which very nearly ruined all. His love of pleasure periodically got the better of his natural energy and good sense. When it extended to opium addiction it deprived him of the power of decision at critical moments. In addition his trusting and affectionate nature made it difficult for him to distinguish between friends and secret enemies and in particular to appreciate the ambitions and jealousies of his brothers. Homayun was one of those men who are born for trouble because one set of qualities wins them followers while another presents gifts to their enemies. Homayun was in essence a rather attractive dilettante who found himself playing the part of an empire builder in complicated and hazardous times.

Homayun had still to complete the conquest of Hindustan. There was Mahmud Lodi on the borders of Bengal. There were the Rajputs, sullen from their late defeat but biding their time for a favorable opportunity, and there was the brilliant Bahadur Shah of Gujarat, who saw in Rana Sanga's discomfiture an opportunity to secure control of Malwa. Within his own circle was his brother Kamran, who was to prove consistently faithless, and the younger brothers who though less malignant were always incalculable in their attitude. Kamran, who was at Kabul at the time of Babur's death, soon after acquired the Panjab, thus halving Homayun's resources. In 1535 Homayun, in a fit of energy worthy of his father, defeated Bahadur Shah in Gujarat and dazzled a warlike generation by his personal valor. Thereafter, he "took his pleasure" at Agra until events in the east compelled his attention. Here an Afghan chief, Sher Khan Sur, from modest beginnings had been steadily rising into prominence. Born in 1486, as a young man he ruled a district for eight years as his father's deputy. Dismissed in a fit of parental jealousy, he entered the service of Sultan Muhammad of Behar. In 1526 Sher Khan joined Babur and was made deputy of Behar for the young Sultan Jalal Khan. In 1533 the young Jalal was defeated by Sher Khan. This was the time for Homayun to act, but he waited until Sher Khan overran Bengal in 1537 and besieged Gaur with its accumulated treasures. From this point the contest assumed classic proportions; Homayun, brilliant, well meaning, and ill advised, stumbled from error to error, while Sher Khan, faultless in his strategy and diplomacy, made deft use of every blunder by his opponent. While Sher Khan was taking Gaur with its treasure, Homayun allowed himself to be delayed before Chunar. He then captured Gaur in his turn and took his ease there, while Sher Khan gathered strength on his flank at Rohtas and then cut his long line of communications. In 1539 Homayun was surprised and routed and fled to Agra. Sher Khan now openly claimed the empire of Hindustan as Sher Shah. The next year Homayun raised a fresh army but was still more decisively defeated at Bilgram, opposite Kanauj on the Ganges. In this moment of crisis Kamran closed the Panjab and Kabul to him. Homayun fled to Sind and after much wandering and misery and a narrow escape from his brother's forces at Kandahar, obtained shelter from Shah Tahmasp of Persia in 1544. It was while leading this dangerous and vagrant life that his son Akbar was born at Umarkot in Sind on November 23, 1542.

Sher Shah had a short and eventful reign of five years. Most of this time he was engaged in campaigns and he was incessantly on the move. Having chased Kamran from the Panjab, he proceeded to wrest Malwa from Raja Maldev of Marwar or Jodhpur. Sher Shah followed Maldev, the successor of Sanga to Rajput primacy, into Rajasthan and dictated peace in 1543. He then turned to the hilly area of Bundelkhand, adjacent to Malwa and the Ganges Valley. Here, while directing the siege of the great Rajput stronghold at Kalanjar, he was struck by a cannon ball and died of its effect.

Thus far Sher Shah added but one more to the long list of Indian soldier-adventurers. He ranks high as a general, had marked gifts of leadership and diplomacy, and the usual vein of Afghan ruthlessness. But Sher Shah was something more than this. He had a very uncharacteristic talent for organization and regularization which marks him as an outstanding figure in his own right, and made him an unconscious contributor to the real Mughal regime to be established by Akbar. During his ceaseless journeys he was as active an administrator as a soldier and he developed the outline of a system which may well be called the prelude or preface to Akbar's own. Remembering the limited time at his disposal and his other preoccupations, we must beware of assuming that every paper provision was transposed into concrete reality. The stone of evasion is highly polished in India, and it is not to be supposed that the detailed regulations of a king still threatened from abroad and not yet secure at home were obeyed further than it was thought his knowledge would reach or his writ would run. Nevertheless, when due allowance is made for these factors, it remains true that an impulse was given to imperial organization which had not been known since Timur's invasion. At the least a blueprint of empire was provided which another creative mind enjoying greater security could implement and develop. While omitting details of his measures, we should note the debt that Akbar and his ministers owed to his preliminary spadework.

Besides his administrative capacity Sher Shah possessed artistic taste more Persian than Afghan. His new city of Delhi contained a citadel of remarkable dignity (the Purana Qila) with a mosque which is a masterpiece of its type. His own tomb at Sasseram with its lake setting is an impressive monument and forms the climax of the Lodi or Pathan style of Indo-Muslim architecture. In these works strength and dignity were blended in proportions which carried them beyond the monolithic grandeur of the Tughluqs or the more sentimental fineness of the Khiljis and the Slave Kings.

Sher Shah was succeeded by his son Islam Shah. He conformed to the more general Afghan type. He was soon in conflict with his nobles, and died after a troubled reign of nine years. His only gift to posterity was the stronghold of Salimgarh on the banks of the Jumna at Delhi, which the Mughals turned into a state prison. At his death Afghan discord broke loose and Homayun saw another chance of empire. He had been received at the Persian court and had been given aid by Shah Tahmasp to recover Kandahar in 1545. Forgetting his promise to return this city to Persia, he went on to take Kabul from his brother Kamran, who was blinded at the nobles' insistence in 1553. Homayun was then free to look to India again at the precise moment when Afghan authority was breaking down. In 1555 he was able to reoccupy Delhi and Agra from the distracted Afghans, but before he was able to consolidate his power he died from the effects of a fall in Sher Shah's new palace in Delhi. He was nearly forty-eight years old, almost the same age as his father had been when he died.

CHAPTER XI

Akbar

When Akbar received the news of his father's death he was a boy just turned thirteen. He was at Kalanaur, in the Panjab, and his affairs were in the hands of the Turkoman chief Bairam Khan whose ability and loyalty fortunately equaled the roughness of his temper. His grandfather Babur had been eleven when he succeeded to the even less stable throne of Farghana. Ranjit Singh, who was to rule the Panjab in the early nineteenth century for nearly forty years, was ten when he succeeded to the chiefship of his clan. At this moment the Mughals seemed to have no greater chance of empire than either of the three contending Afghan factions. Their resources were less and their morale little higher. They owed their initial success to Bairam Khan. When he received the news of Homayun's death he was conducting a campaign against Sikandar, a relative of Sher Shah. At Chunar was another claimant, Muhammad Adil Shah, who compensated for his own ineffectiveness by the talent of his Hindu general Hemu. Hemu took Delhi before Bairam Khan could reach it and then proclaimed himself emperor under the style of Raja Vikramaditiya. The two armies met at Panipat, fifty miles north of Delhi, where the fate of India was decided for the second time within the space of thirty years. Hemu, blinded by an arrow early in the battle, was killed and his army dispersed. From this moment began the Mughal empire as a *raj* rather than as an adventure.

Bairam Khan continued to rule until 1560, and consolidated his young master's position. By that time the Mughals controlled north India from the Indus to the borders of Behar, and in the fortresses of Ajmer and Gwalior had secured the keys of Rajputana and the road to the south respectively. But Bairam was old and overbearing, Akbar young and masterful. The inevitable breach, reminiscent of Kaiser Wilhelm's with Bismarck, occurred, which ended with Bairam Khan's murder by a private enemy while on his way to Mecca. For two more years Akbar preferred sport to business; but the murder of his minister in his own palace by an unruly noble roused him to a fit of Mughal fury. He hurled the offender over the battlements with his own hands and henceforward was his own master.

Akbar is one of the most famous characters in Indian history and also one of the most complex. It is traditional even today, in the north Indian countryside, to attribute to him anything great or good, as anything unpopular tends to be attributed to Aurangzeb. He excelled in many fields. As a soldier he was noted for his lightning marches. In 1573 he covered six hundred miles in twenty-one days to surprise rebels who could not believe it was the emperor who was among them. He was an administrator of genius with the faculty of co-ordinating and inspiring the work of others. He was a leader of renown, who could inspire as well as command, and secure willing obedience from devotion as well as by fear. He was a statesman with large views who understood the art of conciliation. He was an intellectual who delighted in knowledge of all kinds, in theological argument and philosophical discussion. His inability to read, so often quoted, was no sign of the barbarism of the age, but a case of successful willfulness during a hazardous and vagrant youth. Authority came to him at the age of thirteen, when he was able to substitute readers and writers for the personal practice of these arts. He had a refined artistic taste which stamped itself on the arts of painting and architecture. He had, with occasional fits of Mongol rage, a generous disposition and a humane temper. Executions in his reign were few and he attempted to alleviate the miseries of famine. Above all, he possessed a personal magnetism which drew men unto him. His court became the center of a circle of public men and intellectuals whose ability and personal devotion have rarely been equaled. He himself was the center of a semiprivate cult within the court and of public worship from the populace. His name became a legend in his lifetime, not because of the length of his reign or the extent of his conquests nor even because he mixed humanity with his statecraft or generosity with his triumphs, but because of that something extra in the make-up, that flash of the eye or turn of the head, which marks the crossing of the gulf between ability and genius. Queen Elizabeth had it and so had Abraham Lincoln. It has been the hallmark of supreme gifts in all ages.

There were four major crises in Akbar's reign, which marked stages in his personal development. The first two were the fall of the protector Bairam Khan in 1560 and execution of Adham Khan in 1562; they jointly marked the ending of Akbar's youthful tutelage and indifference to government. For the next thirteen years we see him as a young, energetic, and large-minded youth, conquering and conciliating by turns. About 1575 Akbar went through a personal crisis of belief. Periods of solitary meditation and rounds of discussion in a hall built for the purpose marked this phase. Akbar emerged from this period about 1580 bereft of his faith in Islam and with a personal mysticism of his own which took formal shape in a religious cult known as the *Din Illahi* or Divine Faith. This religious crisis led to a political one. The forces of Muslim orthodoxy found a figurehead in his younger brother, Muhammad Hakim, the ruler of Kabul, and for a time he was threatened by subversive movements in the northwest and southeast ends of his realm. His triumph over his opponents left him the undisputed master of northern and central India for the next twenty-five years. He was free to pursue not only his personal religious ideas but the organization and integration of the empire he had acquired in the previous twenty years. In India authority grows with age on the snowball principle. Whereas in the West length of tenure tends to build up criticism and impatience, in India the mere passage of time will turn antagonism into respect, and supersede respect with reverence. Old age is sacred and the aged are revered. It was in this period that his name became the legend which lives in India today. Akbar the hunter grew into Akbar the general and statesman; Akbar the statesman passed through mental anguish into the mystic and sage, presenting to the world in his later years one of the few successful examples of Plato's philosopher-king.

It will be convenient to take Akbar's chief activities in turn, though of course many of them overlapped in time. First come his conquests. In this respect Akbar was a child of his age. Up to a point he was recovering the empire of his grandfather Babur, who in turn claimed the rule of north India as the descendant of Timur who captured Delhi in 1398. But Timur's expedition was no more than a raid with destructive results; he made no attempt to keep what he had won. In any case these claims did not go beyond the borders of Behar in the east and the river Chambal to the south. Akbar pushed his conquests further afield as his resources permitted. His aim was frankly the hegemony of India, and in this he followed the usual tradition of empire in India. As a politician, Akbar was an imperialist like most of his contemporaries; the interesting thing is to see what he did with the empire he won.

Bairam Khan had taken Jaunpur, which corresponds to the eastern portion of the present Indian state of Uttar Pradesh. In 1561 Malwa, that part of central India extending south of Agra between the rivers Chambal and Narbada, was occupied along with its rock-fortress capital of Gwalior. In this way the realm of Babur and the earlier empire of the

Lodis was restored. In the way of further progress lay the Rajput chieftains who occupied the semiarid region known as Rajputana which is the present state of Rajasthan. The Rajputs were formidable both for their valor and the strength of their fastnesses. They could not be bypassed with safety; and under capable leadership, like that of Rana Sanga in the early years of the century, they were capable of bidding for empire. Their weakness lay in their division into feudal chiefships, their pride which hindered co-operation, their conservatism which inhibited the adoption of new methods of warfare. Bairam Khan had seized Ajmer, the key to the Rajput country, but no move southward could safely be made until Rajput strength had been measured. Despite their defeat by Babur they continued to be rivals for the empire of Hindustan.

Akbar attacked the Rajputs in 1568, using their chronic dissensions as a pretext. The state nearest to Delhi, Jaipur, appealed for help against Mewar, the leading Rajput power. In successive campaigns Akbar took the great fortresses of Chitor and Ranthambor. On the first occasion the Rajputs marked their defeat by the *jauhar,* the dreadful ceremony of burning the wives of warriors who then sallied forth to their death in battle. Ranthambor surrendered after negotiations which were made the occasion by Akbar of a comprehensive settlement with the Rajput clans in general. By the grant of personal privileges implying equality of status even more than by political concessions Akbar bound the mass of Rajputs to himself and made them virtually partners in the empire. Only Mewar stood out in its arid fastnesses, not to be reconciled to the Mughals until 1616. Udai Singh was presently to build the lakebound fortress-palace of Udaipur as a substitute for the fallen Chitor, the most dreamlike, perhaps, of the Rajputs' creations, of marble set in water and brown hills beneath a canopy of blue. Akbar's Rajput success was sealed by the surrender of the great central-Indian fortress of Kalanjar, which had defied Sher Shah.

Akbar's Rajput war was the first great political turning point of his reign. Henceforth, he was no longer a foreigner imposing a foreign rule and an alien religion, but an accepted leader of a joint enterprise of empire-building. The foundation of an Indian empire ruled by Mughals, rather than a Mughal empire *in* India, had been laid. Akbar could go forward with no fear of popular revolt in his rear. His chief danger was treason among his own Muslim followers. The next conquest was that of the rich province of Gujarat, which borders on the Gulf of Cambay and includes the port of Surat, then the main outlet for Indian goods to the West as well as of the Muslim pilgrim traffic to Mecca. The province was occupied in 1572, but a revolt occurred the next year when it was thought that the summer rains would hinder rapid action. But Akbar equipped a striking force of three thousand horsemen, rode out of Fatehpur Sikri on August 23, and covering the six hundred miles between that city (near Agra) and Ahmadabad, defeated twenty thousand astonished insurgents on September 2. He was back again in his capital on October 4, having secured this rich prize for nearly two centuries. By securing Gujarat Akbar had acquired a rich province and an outlet for north Indian trade. His next step was to secure the still richer prize of Bengal. The fertility of its soil and the industry and skill of its inhabitants made it the richest province of India, while the rashness of its Afghan ruler made it an easy prey. Bengal was annexed in 1576, and its Mughal administration was still functioning when Clive defeated Siraj-ad-daula at Plassey.

There followed an interlude when Akbar's religious revolution led to revolts among his Muslim followers. The Afghan chiefs of Bengal rebelled while others rallied round his brother in Kabul. With their defeat the procession of conquest went on. In 1586 Kashmir, to become the summer vacation center for the emperors, was annexed; between 1590 and 1595 Sind and Baluchistan were added, while in the latter year Kandahar was taken from the Persians. In 1592 Orissa was added to Bengal. From 1590 began the last phase of Akbar's conquests, his invasion of the Deccan. By negotiation, by bribes, by war through deputies, and by his personal presence he added the states of Berar and Khandesh and part of Ahmadnagar to the empire. Progress was slower than elsewhere, partly because the resistance was more determined and partly because distance made reinforcement more difficult, while Akbar's age made his followers less enthusiastic. Too many were looking for the next reign. Akbar's Deccan difficulties were a warning that he had uncovered the Achilles' heel of all Indian empires—the thirst for dominion in the south and the difficulty, in the then prevailing conditions of transport and terrain, of holding what was taken. The Deccan drain proved as great a strain on Mughal strength as the "Spanish ulcer" on Napoleon's.

If Akbar had been only a conquerer he would deserve little space in a study of India. It was his work of integration and organization which made the Mughal empire something new in Indian experience and in many ways prepared the way (as will be noticed later) for the British rule in India. In Akbar's time the Muslims were probably less than the quarter of the total population which they later became. No empire could be secure which did not reconcile the Hindu population in some degree, and none could seriously influence the country which did not do more than discipline, more or less, a number of semifeudal chiefs. Akbar's

Hindu policy and administrative policy are thus crucial parts of his reign.

The Muslim rulers had early found it necessary to enlist Hindu support for their rule. Amid much profession of zeal for the Faith and occasional severities there was a large measure of tolerance in practice. But the Hindus were always subordinates rather than partners. In the administration they provided secretaries and agents, in the army auxiliaries. They could have careers which stopped short of power and fame, and they had to suffer spasmodic contempt for their religion and customs. The *raj* was an alien one whose Afghan and Turkish directors were mostly harsh and rude, and on occasions merciless. No true confidence could grow from this soil. Akbar early recognized that the Hindus could only be reconciled by equality of treatment and respect for their institutions; he also had the discernment to see that the Rajputs placed more stress on status than on power and had a capacity for loyalty which transcended religion and could be used in the imperial cause. Akbar's first step was in the intimate one of personal relations. In 1561 he married Jodh Bai, the daughter of the Raja of Amber or Jaipur, who became the mother of the emperor Jahangir. This custom of intermarriage, though frowned on by some of the chiefs, was in fact welcomed by others, because it raised their status and gave them influence at court. In the Mughal family it made for understanding and produced rulers like Jahangir and Shah Jahan who were of the country as well as in it. Some think that the glory of the dynasty departed when the custom was abandoned.

The essential pillar of this policy was the settlement with the Rajput chiefs and the policy of partnership which sprang from it. The chiefs on their side accepted Mughal suzerainty. On the Mughal side they were left in control of their territories as Mughal agents. Their religious feelings were soothed by exemption from the *jizya* tax on nonbelievers, and respect for their temples. Their dignity was flattered by the permission to beat their drums (a sign of royalty) in the capital and to enter the Hall of Public Audience fully armed. Finally, they were freely taken into the imperial service. Their rajas became *subadars* or governors of provinces and commanders of armies. Some, like Raja Bhagwan Das and Raja Man Singh, were high among Akbar's confidential advisers. The Rajput sense of dignity and capacity for loyalty were fully exploited, and they became one of the pillars of the empire.

The Rajputs were the military wing of the Hindus, but Akbar aimed at the community as a whole. The measures which had pressed most heavily upon these, as distinct from the peasant mass, which was oppressed impartially by both parties, were the *jizya* tax and contempt of religion in the form of temple destruction. The *jizya* was a poll tax levied on a non-

Muslim, in theory in lieu of military service, a sort of fee for protection. In India it was customarily collected from all Hindus except Brahmins. It was not always oppressively collected but was always resented as a symbol of servitude. Temple destruction was spasmodic, but keenly resented as sacrilege. Akbar completed abolition of the *jizya* throughout his dominions in 1579. Temples were safeguarded and the building of new ones permitted; indeed, after 1582 they were safer from interference than mosques. The emperor thus became the protector of all his people and the guardian of both religions. His court symbolized the neutrality of the state, where Brahmin and Jain ascetics, Jesuit fathers, and Muslim *maulvis* disputed before an agnostic emperor and a cynical court. Further, Akbar carried the principle of confidence to the ranks of non-Rajput Hindus. Raja Birbal, wit and courtier, was one of the emperor's confidants, while Raja Todar Mal of the *kayasth* or writer caste was responsible for the great revenue settlement of northern India.

Integration of the communities was the second feature of Akbar's reign; organization was the third. Akbar took over a feudal lordship and left a bureaucratic imperialism. He inherited a state depending upon personal prowess and loyalties and left a state built upon regulation and a graded imperial service. His first measure was that of an imperial service arranged in thirty-three grades. Though the titles were known before, such a service with regular ranks and fixed salaries had not been organized before. It provided an avenue of honor through which men could aspire to fame through service to the state and an instrument by which the state could make its will effective throughout the empire. Akbar paid these officers in cash. Though this was later changed to assignments on the revenue, the officer was still dependent on the state for his subsistence and could be deprived of both office and emolument at a stroke. These were the *mansabdars* or holders of imperial appointments. They performed both civil and military duties, and constituted in a single cadre a corps of civil and military officers.

Akbar's second administrative achievement was the organization of the local government. When communications depended upon horse transport, the chronic difficulty in large states was the control of distant areas. If left in the hands of junior officials there was no safeguard against external attack; if senior officers were given large powers there was constant danger of rebellion. Akbar continued Sher Shah's network of *sarkars,* not unlike the later British and modern Indian District. He then superimposed a province or *subah* of which there were fifteen at the end of his reign. Each province was ruled by a *subadar* or governor, a senior imperial officer who was responsible for security and order and commanded a body of troops. He was matched with a *diwan,* who was responsible for collecting the revenue and paying the troops. But the money he collected he remitted to Delhi and the money he disbursed he received from Delhi. Thus an ambitious governor had no ready money with which to pay a rebel force and an ambitious *diwan* no troops with which to revolt. There had to be a collusion and the danger of this was reduced by the practice of rotation in office. Both types of officer rarely stayed in one appointment for more than four years. Transfers were universal, which again provided another insurance against rebellion, the hope of promotion.

The third great administrative achievement was the land-revenue settlement. A tax on the produce of land, reckoned as a proportion of the gross produce, was the main source of Indian revenue until the industrial age. It was therefore one of the main concerns of any government and its collection one of the main sources of popular oppression. With the help of his minister Todar Mal, Akbar virtually remeasured and graded the whole of north India. Land was classified according to its soil and crop-bearing qualities. An average yield was estimated and a revenue assessment calculated according to prevailing arrangement. Records were kept in the villages and collections were made by imperial officers. There were of course many exceptions to all the rules, and much persisting extortion. But in general order was brought out of chaos, and rule substituted for battles of wit and of muscle between cultivators and government agents. Todar Mal's *bandobast* or "arrangement" became a legend in northern India and still formed the substratum of rural life when the British began to make enquiries at the end of the eighteenth century.

Akbar's loss of faith in Islam and the political upheaval which resulted have already been mentioned, and the subject may now be followed a little further. Akbar's religious views were probably far more important to observers who discussed them and courtiers who sought to take advantage of them than to the people at large. But they were of great importance to Akbar himself and were of some significance to India, if only by the process of negative reaction. The phase of doubt beginning about 1575 at first expressed itself in dissatisfaction with the orthodox divines of Islam. The so-called infallibility decree of 1579 claimed for Akbar the power to judge doctrinal disputes and to issue religious orders consonant with the Koran. He was to be *Khalifa* as well as emperor. But after the defeat of the rebellion of 1580 Akbar threw over Islam altogether and inaugurated a new cult. It was called the *Din Illahi* or Divine Faith, and from the first seemed to be mainly confined to the court. Its chief supporters were the scholar-statesman Abu'l Fazl and the Brahmin wit Raja Birbal, but

Akbar did not withdraw his confidence from men like the Rajput Man Singh, who declined to join.

The cult centered round Akbar himself, who was venerated as the prophet of the new faith and accorded the *sijdah* form of prostration previously reserved for worship in the mosque. The ideology of the cult was a simple monotheism, abjuring not only idolatry and polytheism but also the mission of the Prophet Muhammad and the Trinity of the Christians. This monotheism found moral expression in the four virtues of wisdom, courage, chastity, and justice. Full members took four vows, to devote property, life, honor, and belief to Akbar. There was an initiation ceremony, birthday and memorial feasts; vegetarianism was an ideal. In ceremonies the *hom* or fire sacrifice was borrowed from Hinduism, the worship of fire from the Parsis, prostration from Islam, and baptism from Christianity. The cult was in fact highly syncretistic as well as aristocratic. It can be loosely described as a royal theosophy. It faded away after Akbar's death, for though Jahangir had some leanings toward it, he could hardly be seriously regarded as a prophet.

Though the *Din Illahi* left behind hardly a ripple on the surface of Indian religious life, it was not without a wider significance. Many have regarded the whole episode as an eccentricity or aberration on Akbar's part and nothing more. But it is against the whole grain of Akbar's character that he should have gone to such public trouble for a purely private religious opinion. We may grant him sincerity of belief and genuine mysticism, but we cannot excuse him from the political sagacity which informed the rest of his life. The cult, apart from its philosophic aspect, was nicely calculated to provide a focus of loyalty for state officials over and above the two great religions of the country. The service of the emperor was to be something religious in itself and the person of the emperor to have a mystic quality calling for more than the obedience of expediency. Akbar separated the crown from religion and then gave it a halo of its own. In this way the empire could claim the equal allegiance of both communities as being something apart from them both. It is interesting to note that the halo or nimbus of ecclesiastical art, borrowed by Mughal painters from the Italian paintings introduced by the Portuguese to India, came to be attached to the heads of the later emperors, including that of the Muslim purist Aurangzeb himself. The *Din Illahi* passed away, but it did in fact help to surround the imperial authority with an aura of sanctity. Previous dynasties had been overthrown as soon as their strength decayed and had been forgotten in a generation. Respect for the Mughals lingered on after all reason for it had vanished and reverence for the office after all power had been lost. It still existed at the time of the Mutiny of 1857, though the effective empire had been dead nearly a hundred years. In some quarters it had not quite died by 1947.

A second effect of the cult was to outrage the right wing or orthodox party of the Muslims. We can see these feelings at work in the pages of the historian Badaoni, as we get the propagandist view of the cult from its supporter Abu'l Fazl. After the defeat of the rebels the orthodox party was helpless, and it got little encouragement from Jahangir. But the reaction of irritation did its work and the orthodox gathered strength to triumph with the victory of Aurangzeb.

Akbar's reign was also important in a cultural sense. It was he who gave to the empire an indelibly Persian character. Earlier sultans had used Persian as an official language, but outside the court and a learned circle it remained an administrative instrument only. Babur and his descendants were enthusiasts for things Persian, and Akbar had the time in which to impress the Persian cultural seal deeply upon Indian life. In the realm of language Persian became the polite language of all India, including the Rajput, the Maratha, and the south Indian chief. In the world of diplomacy and fashion, it was in India what French was in Europe. It was from this time that the hybrid tongue of Urdu, or the language of the camp, a mixture of Persian and Hindi, attained the status of a separate language. It is this form of Hindi, often spoken of as Hindustani, which Mr. Nehru spoke in his home at Allahabad, and which has now become an official language in Pakistan. Persian administrative forms and phrases and concepts are deeply imbedded in north Indian thought and practice. Persian manners, radiating from Delhi like French manners from Versailles, set the standard for the whole subcontinent and their influence lives on today. Persian painting was developed by Akbar with the help of Hindu artists to form the characteristic Mughal school of painting, whose miniatures are famous. Persian canons of architecture were similarly blended with Hindu traditions to form the beautiful and individual Mughal architectural style. The extent and success of this process can be seen by comparing Homayun's tomb in Delhi at the beginning of the reign with the city of Fatehpur Sikri in its middle. The style became so imbedded in the Indian consciousness that it is still practiced today in places. Many Hindu shrines are to be found in Mughal style. Persian gardens, introduced by Babur, became the norm of Indian ones.

It is given to few to stamp their personalities as well as their names upon an age. In the case of India it can certainly be said that the shape of things to come would have been different if Akbar had not reigned. On the whole India was fortunate in the conjunction of person and circumstance. In many ways the Mughal empire which Akbar established prepared the way for the British, who in turn laid the foundations of the new India. We can thus trace a direct connection between Akbar and his prototype today, Jawaharlal Nehru. This is his portrait as given by his son in his memoirs. "He was of the middle height, of a wheat colored complexion, with black eyes and eyebrows. His beauty was of form rather than of face, with a broad chest and long arms. On his left nostril was a fleshy mole, very becoming, of the size of a split pea which physiognomists understood to be an augury of great wealth and glory. His voice was extremely loud, and in discourse and narration he was witty and animated. His whole air and appearance had little of the worldly being, but exhibited rather divine majesty."

CHAPTER XII

The Great Mughals

The seventeenth century was the great age of the Mughal Empire. Akbar had reintegrated northern and central India and given it a Persian form. His successors maintained his work until the empire extended nearly to Cape Comorin and the Persian dress seemed the natural garb of India. India presented an impressive picture to the world and created the modern legend of wealth and power which lasted well into the nineteenth century. India was the land of the "Great Mogul." For the first time since classical days India was open to detailed and skilled European observation. She ceased to be a legend about which tales could be spun with little relation to the facts, as Marlowe did with Timur in his *Tamburlaine*. The image of India in the European mind, though no doubt seriously distorted in many respects, had some similitude to truth. India had become real to Europe.

The first point of interest in the century is that of personalities. Jahangir was a very different man from his father, but he was a striking personality in his own right. A demonic temper, a callous disregard for human suffering was mingled with a genial temperament, an acute sensibility for nature and art, a love of sport and good cheer, and a singular devotion to his wife Nur Jahan, the daughter of his prime minister and the sister of his son's. He could carouse with the sea captain Hawkins, joke about copies of Italian miniatures with the solemn ambassador of James I, direct with sensitive care the work of his painters, and in a moment of passion order the execution of a beater who had spoiled a shot at a hunt. The high-spirited Nur Jahan was the aunt of the lady of the Taj. In Shah Jahan we have a figure comparable to that of Louis XIV of France. Able, ambitious, and ruthless in his youth, he became a ruler noted for his magnificence and justice in middle years and for self-indulgence and affection in his age. He did for architecture what Jahangir did for painting, leaving to posterity the imperishable monuments of the Taj Mahal, the Jama Masjid of Delhi, and the Pearl Mosque of Agra. He spent his final years a prisoner in his Agra palace gazing at his wife's mausoleum, the Taj, because of the clash of two more personalities, his sons Dara Shekoh and Aurangzeb. Their conflict symbolized the age-old conflict between liberalism and conservatism, pride and calculation, openhandedness and dissimulation. The princesses Jahanara and Roshanara took sides in the conflict and have their names in monuments, in histories, and in folklore. The enigmatic Aurangzeb presents a double picture of ambition and dissimulation in middle age and benign devotion in old age. The Maratha leader Sivaji and Rajput chiefs like Jai Singh and Jaswant Singh complete a picture which is crowded with arresting and brilliant personalities.

It was well that the Mughal family was so well provided with talent, for personality, or the leadership principle, was the first of the four pillars which sustained the empire. A divinity did hedge the king, but only till a stronger man pulled him down. The power struggle was intense, as in modern Russia, with little mercy for "deviationists" or those not strong enough to maintain themselves. A Mughal ruler had to provide a dynamic for the Indian world and at the same time to hold a balance between Rajput and Muslim, Turk and Persian. His life was arduous with incessant business and public appearances, with the knowledge that one false step might lead to disaster. The second pillar of the empire was the Rajput alliance, which turned martial Hindus into imperial agents. The third was the policy of tolerance or secularism, which ensured the acquiescence of the Hindu community at large. The fourth was the balance of power which existed between the Safavid dynasty of Iran and the Mughals.

Jahangir reigned for twenty-two years. He was spared the usual fratricidal struggle for the succession because his two brothers died of drink before their father. But his eldest son Khusrau, an attractive but ill-advised youth, made an attempt to seize power. Jahangir took a fearful revenge on his followers and partially blinded his son. After years of hesitation and partial reconciliation he was handed over to the custody of his brother, in whose hands he soon disappeared. Jahangir soon dropped the *Din Illahi* as a measure of political caution, but he allowed the adulation of the emperor's person to continue, thus, with the help of the Indian readiness to venerate, turning him into a semidivine personage. But in spite of outward conformity with Islam he remained a free thinker and free liver, refusing to identify the state with a particular religion. During his reign Mughal expansion continued. Mewar, the surviving Rajput fastness in Rajasthan, capitulated in 1614. Kangra, a fortress in the foothills which had baffled Akbar, was taken in 1620, while in the Deccan Ahmadnagar was taken in 1616 and half of its kingdom annexed. In the northwest, however, the Persian ruler, Shah Abbas, retook Kandahar in

1622. Jahangir had dealings with both the Portuguese, who controlled the maritime pilgrim route to Mecca, and took heavy toll, and the British, whose East India Company had recently started operations at Surat. His decision to prefer the British to the Portuguese required insight in the circumstances of the times. It was based upon the Company's success against the Portuguese in the estuary of the Swally (near Surat) in 1612. From that time the Company became virtual naval auxiliaries to the Mughals in return for trading privileges within the empire. Captain Hawkins gave Jahangir much pleasure as a boon companion between 1607 and 1611, but it was Sir Thomas Roe, who drank little and spoke no Persian, who achieved a lasting settlement.

Shah Jahan, like his father, was rid of his brothers before his succession, but he stained his name by a wanton massacre of male collaterals. Shah Jahan united great executive ability with a taste for the magnificent and orthodox Islamic views. His reign is marked by a certain static splendor without and a certain slowing down of the pulse of government within. The appearance of the Mughal giant continued to be majestic, but the arteries were hardening within. We see it in art, where the vivacious nature drawings of Jahangir gave place to a formal though impressive vogue of portrait painting. In architecture after the supreme achievement of the Taj there is a tendency toward a certain frozen splendor, which can be detected in the new capital at Delhi. In government there was expansion without originality and activity without diversity. In policy habit tended to prevail over thought.

In religion it can be said that while Jahangir continued the secular state from conviction, Shah Jahan did so from habit. He was an orthodox Sunni Muslim who restored Islam as the state religion of the empire. In his time the Mughal empire was overtly a Muslim empire, but it remained a tolerant empire. Hindus and Rajputs were employed and trusted in high places as before; the outbreaks of fanaticism were few. Religion was subordinate to politics in statecraft. From this followed the continuance of the Rajput partnership, including its matrimonial aspect. Along with the pillars of personality, partnership, and tolerance, that of the balance of power was maintained if not strengthened. In 1638 Kandahar was recovered, only to be lost again in 1649. Three attempts were made to recover it without success, but the Persians were unable to advance any further.

Shah Jahan continued the traditional policy in the Deccan. The final absorption of Ahmadnagar in the Deccan left only the two Muslim kingdoms of Bijapur and Golconda between Shah Jahan and the lordship of all India. In 1653 the advance was renewed by Shah Jahan's third son Aurangzeb, and but for the war of succession both kingdoms would probably have succumbed at that time.

In 1656 Shah Jahan fell seriously ill and this led to the most famous war of succession in history. It was graphically described by the French doctor Bernier, through whom it became widely known in Europe; it remained until British times almost the only piece of Indian history known to the Western world. Shah Jahan's plight was regarded by his four sons as a signal for a struggle for supreme power, and they were not to be put off by the unwelcome news of their father's recovery. The eldest son, Dara Shekoh, was the chosen heir apparent with his father in Agra. He was a brilliant and artistic intellectual of liberal opinions, whose vanity led to overconfidence and the secret hostility of many followers. The second son, Shah Shuja, possessed ability but was poorly placed in distant Bengal. Murad Baksh, the youngest son, followed the Mughal drinking pattern. There remained Prince Aurangzeb, capable, calculating, and orthodox, without the riches of Bengal or the key position of Dara at Agra, but in command of an army experienced in the Deccan wars. By a series of bold and subtle moves he outmaneuvered and then overthrew Dara at Samugarh on a broiling June day in 1657. Having secured the central position, he made his father a prisoner in his own palace; he then arrested his deluded ally and brother Murad, and defeated in detail Shah Shuja in Bengal and an attempted comeback by Dara with Rajput help. The tragic drama ended with Dara's betrayal by an Afghan chief, his parade with ignominy through the streets of Delhi, and secret execution. The casualties were a father imprisoned, one brother killed, and two brothers, a son, and a nephew executed. It was indeed *takht ya takhta*—throne or coffin. From that time, except for a few days in 1680 when another son revolted, Aurangzeb was securely seated in power for nearly fifty years. His name became a legend for craft and dissimulation, for suspicion and ruthlessness. It was said that his eldest son never received a letter from him, to the end of his long life, without trembling.

Aurangzeb (whose regal name was Alamgir or World-Shaker) had in fact virtually two personalities and two reigns. In the first he was a less attractive edition of Shah Jahan, whose reign he really only extended. Toleration continued, though in a less friendly spirit, and the Rajputs were employed, though less confidence was shown. Wars, such as the Assam campaign of 1661–63, were continued on the periphery of the empire. The northwest frontier was guarded with a campaign in Balkh beyond the Pamirs in 1674–76. A new situation in the Deccan was dealt with along accustomed lines. This was the rise to prominence of the

Mughal India

Maratha chief Sivaji in the mountains of western India. His father Shahji had been an officer of Bijapur. Its weakness under Mughal attack encouraged him to add the possessions of others to his own, and his son Sivaji, with greater daring, defied the empire itself. He erupted into the Mughal orbit, as it were, with the sack of the great port of Surat. British merchants were present and described the scene, but escaped pillage themselves by stoutly defending their factory. Aurangzeb sent the Rajput Jai Singh, who reduced him to terms and brought him to Agra to become an imperial official or *mansabdar*. But then things went wrong. Suspicions were aroused on both sides, and Sivaji escaped from house arrest in a fruit basket and fled to the Deccan, where he raised the standard of revolt in 1670 and declared himself independent in 1675.

From about 1680, when Aurangzeb was about sixty-two, began his second phase and reign. The calculating statesman became a Muslim devotee, distributing benevolence and wise saws to the eventual detriment of his authority, passing his nights reading the Koran and retaining only his suspicions of his sons and alertness against intrigue. Aurangzeb came to regard himself as head of a Muslim state rather than as the president of all India. His relations with the Hindus deteriorated accordingly, undermining the foundations of the empire. He virtually transferred his capital to the Deccan where he spent the last twenty-six years of his life. Only one aspect of Mughal policy remained constant, that of expansion.

The most significant date in Aurangzeb's Hindu policy was the year 1679. He had already shown his disapproval of Hindu custom by prohibiting the playing of music in public. When the musicians staged a mock funeral of their instruments he advised them to bury them deep as they would never be wanted again. He had demolished the Visveswara temple at Banares in 1669—replacing it with a mosque—and the beautiful Keshava Deva temple at Mathura. These were isolated though impolitic acts, but in 1679 he reimposed the *jizya* tax on Hindus generally. This measure, along with the spasmodic destruction of temples wherever the Mughal armies were active, did a great deal to alienate Hindu support from the empire.

This policy in its turn led to a breach with the Rajputs. Their feelings were further irritated by Aurangzeb's attempt to seize a posthumous son of Raja Jaswant Singh of Jodhpur, one of the most faithful Rajput officers who died in 1678. A number of chiefs revolted and were joined by Aurangzeb's third son Akbar. For a moment Aurangzeb was in mortal peril, but craft and resolution extricated him as they had in 1656–57. Akbar fled to Persia and the Rajputs were defeated. But a breach had been made in their allegiance, and their support was no longer unquestioning or wholehearted.

The policy of expansion was so fixed a point in the Mughal firmament that it survived Aurangzeb's conception of himself as a Muslim monarch. The defender of the faith must still conquer Muslim Bijapur and Golconda. Both these crumbling kingdoms were overthrown in 1686 and 1687, and thereafter the empire extended down the east coast along the Carnatic as far as Trichinopoly and nearly to Madura. The overthrow of these kingdoms, however, made Aurangzeb's task harder than before. They had been centers of authority for two centuries and their disappearance meant the letting loose upon society of numbers of retainers and soldiers deprived of their means of livelihood. These roamed the Deccan, making it harder to maintain order and to cope with the intractable Marathas in their western hills. Close to Golconda the twin city of Hyderabad now became the center of the Mughal viceroyalty of the Deccan, its ruler receiving the title of Nizam-ul-Mulk or regulator of the kingdom. From about 1724 these provinces became gradually independent of Delhi and transmuted into the state of Hyderabad. But it preserved down to 1948 its Mughal forms and traditions, remaining for nearly two centuries a living fossil of the empire.

Aurangzeb's final preoccupation was the Marathas. Like Spain to Napoleon later, they became an ulcer which sapped his strength. Sivaji died in 1680, but the struggle was carried on by his son Sambaji. Sambaji was dissolute and careless; he was captured and executed in 1689. Aurangzeb thought the struggle was over, but it had long ceased to be dynastic and had become a popular crusade for freedom and the defense of religion. In Maharashtra every hilltop became a fortress requiring laborious efforts for its capture. The Marathas had seized the principality of Tanjore in the south and for eight years sustained a siege in the rock fortress of Gingi. Like a cancer which has been too forcibly removed, branches of the infection ran all over the Deccan and the south. Insecurity increased, and the royal camp was itself sometimes more like a beleaguered fortress than a base of operations. Still Aurangzeb toiled on. Fort after fort was taken and Marathas and the Deccan people alike were worn down. Only the approach of death induced him to retire to Ahmadnagar, where he died on February 21, 1707, at the age of eighty-eight. He is thus described by the Neapolitan doctor Gemelli-Carreri in 1695, when he was seventy-six:

"Soon after the King came in, leaning on a staff forked at the top, several *omrahs* and abundance of courtiers going before him. He had on a white vest tied under the right arm, according to the fashion of the Muhammedans, to distinguish them from the Gentiles, who tie it under the left. The *Cira* or turban of the same white stuff was tied with a gold web, on which an emerald of a vast bigness, appeared amidst four little ones. He had a silk sash, which covered the *catari* or Indian dagger hanging on the left. His shoes were after the Moorish fashion, and his legs naked without hose. Two servants put away the flies, with long, white horse-tails; another at the same time keeping off the sun, with a green umbrella. He was of a low stature, with a large nose, slender, and stooping with age. The whiteness of his round beard was more visible on his olive coloured skin. When he was seated they gave him his scimitar and buckler, which he laid down on his left side within the throne. Then he made a sign with his hand for those that had business to draw near; who being come up, two secretaries standing, took their petitions, which they delivered to the King, telling him the contents. I admired to see him indorse them with his own hand, without spectacles, and by his cheerful smiling countenance seem to be pleased with the employment." [1]

Aurangzeb left the empire weakened and undermined but not fatally injured. The supporting pillars had been shaken but not actually overthrown. The Rajputs and the Hindus generally thought of him as a deviationist rather than a destroyer, whose successor might restore the empire to its all-India status. Even the Marathas, as the sequel partly showed, felt the magic of empire and were not wholly irreconcilable. Fifty years passed before the empire finally crashed in chaos; it was the men and events of those years that finally determined a result which the policy of Aurangzeb only suggested.

CHAPTER XIII

India in the Seventeenth Century

During the seventeenth century India was more peaceful and prosperous, and presented a more impressive face to the world than had been the case for a thousand years and was to be for more than a hundred years to come. For the first time since the coming of the Muslims the imperial idea meant something more than the domination of one community over the other. It was accepted by both parties: India became all-India minded. Europeans visited the country in increasing numbers and all returned more or less impressed with what they saw. Despite disapproval of Hindu "heathenism" and traditional dislike of Islam, there was a general recognition that a great power existed in India embracing a developed civilization with great attainments in letters and the arts, with polished manners and a complicated social life. India occupied in the mind of seventeenth-century Europe something of the place taken in the eighteenth century by China. The picture of India derived from classical sources was at last replaced by a contemporary one. India was the land of the Great Mogul.

Our sources for this period are more copious and varied than for any previous age. They are in fact an extension of those available for Akbar's reign. For government and administration we have Abu'l Fazl's monumental *Ain-i-Akbari* or *Acts of Akbar*. This is really a political, administrative, and cultural encyclopedia of India, providing a detailed account of the whole Mughal administration. Then come a number of Muslim histories, which are both more detailed and more politically minded than the histories prior to Akbar's reign. Some of these are of high quality, like that of Khafi Khan, who could be fair to the Marathas, whom he detested, in their struggle against Aurangzeb. There are personal documents like Aurangzeb's letters, official correspondence, and reports. Besides these local sources we have a volume of evidence from European sources. A succession of travelers visited India and often resided for long periods; some settled down altogether. Some of them were men of great ability like Bernier; others like the Dutch and English made up for more humdrum minds by their diligence in detailed observation. Some, like Manucci, excused their slender attachment to fact by the sparkle of their anecdotes. The most famous was François Bernier, a French doctor who lived at the Mughal court for nine years; close to him come Tavernier, the French jeweler who valued the Peacock Throne, Sir Thomas Roe, James I's ambassador to Jahangir, Thevenot, and Carreri. In a class by himself is Niccolò Manucci who came to India as a boy of seventeen in 1653 and stayed till his death in about 1718. There were the Catholic missionaries of whom Father Sebastian Manrique is an example, the passing visitor like the Mecklenburger Mandelslo, and the merchants like the Dutchman Pelsaert. All these men traveled extensively; all saw different facets of Indian life, and most of them were reliable observers. They noticed and reported many things taken for granted by Indian writers, and those who mixed with the upper classes could report more objectively on the state of feeling around them than men personally involved in current political issues. Between these various sources we learn much, not only of the politics of the empire but also of its economic, social, and cultural conditions. For European knowledge of India the most important source of all was Bernier, not only because of the quality of his work but because he was the most widely read. His reports to the French minister Colbert provided a vivid picture of Aurangzeb's court in the early years of his reign, and of the war of succession by which he obtained the throne, an analysis of the administration and a description of Hindu society. To a large extent Europe's idea of India in the late seventeenth and eighteenth centuries was Bernier's.

The nerve center of seventeenth-century India was the Mughal court, whether in the palaces of Delhi or Agra, or on the move with Jahangir and Shah Jahan or in the wilderness in the Deccan with Aurangzeb. The whole apparatus of government moved with the emperor, and cities of tents were laid out with as much care and durbars held with as much decorum as in the permanent pavilions of the north. The emperor himself lived a laborious life in a setting of pomp, backed with the knowledge that any relaxation of effort and watchfulness might mean peril from revolt or death by conspiracy. Homayun relaxed and was driven out of India. Aurangzeb was oversuspicious and terrorized his family. Jahandar threw care aside and was overthrown within a year.

Soon after sunrise the emperor appeared at a public balcony where he gave a *darshan* or sight to the public. After reviewing cavalry or watching an animal fight he would proceed to the Hall of Public Audience where for two hours he would receive petitions, pass orders on appointments, and give audiences. The officials or nobles stood in serried rows according to their ranks; silence and strict decorum were maintained. It was at a durbar such as this that Sivaji fell out with Aurangzeb. He disliked the position allotted to him, and protested with such vigor as to create a disturbance. From the Public the emperor proceeded to the Private Hall of Audience (*Dewan-Khas*), where the principal ministers attended for confidential business. The privilege of entering the Red Curtain (*Lal Purdah*) to this hall was one of the most valued in the Mughal court. The entry of the *Lal Purdah* roughly corresponded with modern cabinet rank or a Privy councilorship in Great Britain. Even more confidential discussions took place in the *Shah Burj* or Royal Tower, or, if the court was in camp, in the emperor's private apartment. There followed a meal and a siesta. At 3 P.M. a second and shorter durbar was held if business called for it. In the evening an assembly was held of a less formal kind in the Private Hall with which pleasure, business, and social intercourse were mixed. It was then that Akbar listened to philosophic and religious discussion. With his son Jahangir there was a convivial bias; Sir Thomas Roe has vividly described the medley of business and gaiety which then obtained. It was a good time to put your point to the emperor while he was in the state to take it in. With Shah Jahan strict decorum reigned. He mixed business, music, dancing, and social intercourse in exact proportion. With Aurangzeb there was nothing but business. Only by continuous attention to business and alertness to every current of opinion could an emperor maintain his position.

Next to the emperor came his ministers. There was no formal cabinet but many informal councils. The chief minister was the wazir but he had to compete with others for the emperor's ear. Thus under a weak emperor the ministers were heads of rival factions whose moves obstructed rather than forwarded business. The ministers controlled the secretariat, which was elaborately organized and efficiently manned. Alas, nearly all the copious records they amassed have vanished, and we have to look for the fragments in the archives of subordinate governments like the Rajput states. Provided a steady impulse came from above, this machine worked smoothly and well.

The business of the government was to maintain order, to uphold the law of the various communities, and to encourage the cultural life of the country by means of court patronage. There was no idea of directing or shaping society; rather the object was to provide a dignified cover beneath which it could function safely and without interference. The state was an awning to shelter rather than a steel press to stamp some shape upon society. The ideal was expressed in the cry of an unknown person to Shah

Jahan as he was going out in procession: " 'Hail, O King! Thou owest a thanksgiving to God. The King is just, the ministers are able and the secretaries are honest. The coun̈try is prosperous and the people contented.' Shah Jahan raised his hands in prayer, bowed his head, offered thanksgiving to God and the nobles, and the people witnessed it." [1]

Private law was administered by the communities concerned; criminal law was dispensed by law officers according to the Islamic code. The protection of society and the honor of the state required the maintenance of the court, an army, and security forces. These in turn required money. The collection of revenue and the officers who collected it formed the hard core of Mughal administration. The actual collection was where the government touched the people, while the collectors formed the official aristocracy which ran the country. Let us look at collection first. The empire was divided between dependent states, whose rulers, like the Rajput chiefs, paid a fixed tribute while governing their own lands, and land directly subject to imperial rule. These lands were divided into *subas* or provinces (twelve in Akbar's time and eighteen in Aurangzeb's), *sarkars* or districts, and subdistricts leading down to the village. These units had government officers directly responsible to the center. The provincial governor or *subadar* [2] was a great personage and in distant locations it would seem might easily revolt. But the system was held together by two devices. The first was division of power. Each *suba* had two officers, a *subadar* and a *diwan,* who balanced each other as described in Chapter XI. The second was rotation of office.

The revenue itself largely depended upon the produce of the land. An elaborate system of measurement and assessment, devised by Todar Mal under Akbar, and backed by careful record-keeping, was in force. The officers dealt with the villagers directly, or with landlords who held hereditary estates or with fiefholders or *jagirdars* who held grants during the emperor's pleasure for service of various kinds. It is important to remember that the Indian system of landholding differed radically from modern Western notions of absolute individual possession. Many holdings were joint or collective. Occupancy was distinguished from possession, and failure to pay dues did not normally lead to ejection or forfeiture. Actual payments were largely a matter of bargaining between officers and taxpayers; it may be broadly said that the higher one went in the land scale the more precarious was his holding. There was thus a permanent state of negotiation between cultivators, landholders, and government officers for payments. In general some sort of balance was maintained, but it is easy to see how quickly relaxation of pressure from above would disturb the whole system and how any increase of that pressure would travel down the line to its terminus at the cultivator. The land revenue was the sinews of the state and its collection too often the scourge of the poor.

The instruments of the imperial will were the *mansabdars* or imperial service. In origin the title was a military one used by the horse-riding Mongols and Turks of Central Asia. It signified the command (*mansab*) of certain numbers of horsemen. The term and the idea of graded ranks was developed into a system by Akbar and survived in the state of Hyderabad down to 1948. In Mughal hands the term denoted a corps of officers directly dependent upon the emperor whose functions could be either military or civil. The service was scaled into thirty-three grades, from the command of five thousand (*panch-hazari*) to the command of ten. At first the figures were related to the number of horsemen an officer was expected to supply, but as resources dwindled ideas of dignity increased so that in the eighteenth century we come across commanders of fifty thousand, at a time when the whole empire might find it hard to pay so many men. The numbers must be regarded as indications of grades rather than troops employed. Within each rank there was a class (*zat*) determined by the number of extra horsemen (*sawar*) who were allowed and a further distinction in the number of months in the year for which the salary appropriate for the rank was payable. The *mansabdars* were arranged in three large divisions: commanders of from ten to four hundred were the *mansabdars* proper or plain officers. Commanders of from five hundred to twenty-five hundred were termed *Amirs* or lords; they may be equated to military officers from the rank of colonel. Officers with holdings from three thousand to five thousand were *Amir-i-Azam* or great lords; they are comparable to the higher ranks of general officers, or in the civilian sphere, men of state or federal cabinet level. The last two classes were the higher official nobility collectively known in seventeenth-century Europe as omrahs. (The Arabic plural of *Amir* is *Amrah*).

The omrahs may be compared with the British civil service which ruled India in the nineteenth century. In fact the British officials may be called their reincarnation in Anglo-Saxon form. They inherited their prestige and much of their power, their aloofness and some of their pride, their subordination and something of their wealth. There is even a curious correspondence in their numbers. According to the Dutchman de Laet, in Jahangir's time there were nearly nine hundred officers of the rank of two hundred and upward, while the *Padshahnamah* in the time of Shāh Jahān suggests a number of about one thousand.[3] The Indian Civil Service during the nineteenth century numbered upward of one thousand, the strength standing at about twelve hundred at independence in 1947. Like the Indian Civil Service in the nineteenth century again, the *mansabdars* were largely foreign. In Akbar's time 70 per cent of the *mansabdars* had come to India under Homayun or later; the remainder were equally divided between Indian Muslims and Indian Hindus.[4] "In fact," says Moreland, "the Imperial Service consisted in the higher ranks of foreigners, Muslims, Rajputs, Birbal, and Todar Mal." [5]

The mode of paying these officers was a vital one. Akbar insisted upon cash payments, which gave a very modern look to the service. Other rulers were not able to overcome the difficulties which this system involved, and the standard method became that of assignments on the land revenue. An officer would be assigned a tract of land from which he was entitled to collect the regular land revenue on his own behalf. The size of the tract would be so calculated that its revenue yield would approximately equal the cash salary attached to the office or *mansab*. Such a system was obviously open to abuse both from a powerful minister who might penalize an officer by allotting him barren land for his support and by a powerful officer who might get more than his share of land revenue. But so long as the center remained vigorous the omrah's position was far less imposing than appeared at first sight. In spite of his prestige and dignity, his magnificent household and his crowds of servants and armed retainers he was dependent upon the royal will for an income and position, which might at any moment be cut off. If the officer lost his office he lost his assignment of land as well; his assignment might be changed at any time, so that he had little chance of striking roots in any part of the country. He was not a hereditary noble landowner in the European sense, but an official drawing an income from a parcel of land temporarily allotted. He was not a hereditary but only a temporary landholder, at the most a life tenant.

The omrah suffered from a further liability. His receipts from his lands were usually in arrears, and in any case not easily realizable to meet the emergencies which constantly arose. Competition and emulation were as keen in Delhi as at Versailles. The government came to his rescue by allowing him advances from the treasury on the security of his revenue assignment. These advances were commonly large and were rarely liquidated. In consequence at the death of the omrah not only did the estate return to the state with the office, but the treasury officials sealed all his property as security for recovery of advances. In theory the balance would be returned to the heirs when the account was complete, but in practice it amounted to a death duty of 90 per cent. The next generation had virtually to make a new start. This could be done by means of fresh appointments to *mansabs*. But they were naturally lower in rank, and they might not be granted at all. There was thus little passing on of wealth from one generation to another. The whole system had certain peculiar consequences which gave to Mughal India some of its characteristic features. The omrah knew that his time was short and that he could pass on little to his children. At the same time his position demanded pomp and display as well as the maintenance of an armed force. He endeavored to provide for his family by marrying his daughters to rising officers and securing appointments for his sons. His current income was then expendable. It was spent upon his obligatory armed force, and upon maintaining as much personal pomp as possible. An omrah was judged by the number of his retainers in the streets and the crowd of clients and suppliants at his palace.

The fashion of the time went further, to competition in fine buildings. To this we owe the numerous architectural relics which strew the plains of Delhi and dot the whole of northern India. By building a mosque the omrah acquired religious as well as social prestige. The building of *sarais* or rest houses for travelers was esteemed a pious act, thus uniting usefulness with ambition. Large walled gardens provided with pavilions and water were popular and numerous. Above all the omrah would build his own tomb on a magnificent scale as something which might perpetuate his memory and defy confiscation. The quiet walled gardens and domed tombs which now provide the setting of foreigners' picnics are a legacy of unquiet lives and anxious days. These conditions help us to understand how the omrah, for all his proud face to the world, could be servile to his master. This side of the medal is sufficiently described by the Frenchman Bernier at the court of Aurangzeb.[6]

"What I have stated in the proceedings of the assembly of the *Am-Khas* appears sufficiently rational and even noble, but I must not conceal from you the base and disgusting adulation which is invariably witnessed there. Whenever a word escapes the lips of the King, if at all to the purpose, how trifling soever may be its import, it is immediately caught by the surrounding throng; and the chief Omrahs, extending their arms towards heaven, as if to receive some benediction, exclaim *Karamat! Karamat!* wonderful! wonderful! he has spoken wonders! Indeed there is no Mogul who does not know and does not glory in repeating this proverb in Persian verse:

> If the monarch says that day is night
> Reply:—'the moon and stars shine bright.'

The Mughal army was an elaborately organized machine. Its officers were the *mansabdars* and its main strength their contingents. There were in addition the levies of the dependent chiefs, which in the case of the Rajputs were valuable. In addition the emperor had his personal troops, which formed a standing army and kept in his hands the control of artillery. Communications were maintained by river from Delhi to Bengal and by a carefully maintained system of trunk roads, with *sarais* or rest houses and an organized government post. The Mughal army, except perhaps in its early days, was not so formidable in itself as by comparison with anything that could be brought against it. Shah Jahan's failure to retake Kandahar was warning that it was dropping behind the standards of the vigorous northerners. Nimble horsemen like the Marathas could baffle its clumsy technique and a determined general like Nadir Shah could shatter its array. Yet it could still withstand Ahmad Shah the Afghan in 1748. But the advent of European arms and tactics revealed the obsolescence of the Mughal military machine. Only an Akbar could then have refashioned it into an efficient instrument, and no Akbar was forthcoming.

During the seventeenth century India was probably more prosperous as a whole than at any time since the age of the Guptas in the fourth and fifth centuries A.D. The population was estimated by Moreland (a careful scholar) at about one hundred million in 1600, which was probably more than that of contemporary Europe. During the seventeenth century the revenue statistics suggest growth, and population may have reached one hundred fifty million by 1700. Thereafter, constant wars all over the country and periodic famines reduced it by 1800 to somewhere between the two figures. There were then large tracts of depopulated country.

The Indian economy was essentially a subsistence one. By and large the village lived on its own products and was to a large extent a self-sufficing unit. The chief inhabitants usually claimed kinship with a common ancestor, and the whole group was bound together by interweaving ties of caste, occupation, service, and relationship. The elders formed a directing group with a recognized council or *panchayat*. The headman (under various titles) represented rather than dominated the village, spoke with the enemy at the gate—or it might be with the revenue collector. The village had its own priest, banker, and shopkeeper (pundit and *bania*), its own artisans, its own police methods and methods of protecting itself. It showed extraordinary resilience in face of famine and pestilence, the shocks of nature, and the blows of war. It has been the most abiding social feature of Indian life, and in the words of Charles Metcalfe has "lasted where nothing else has survived."

The self-sufficing village was the basis of Indian economy. Its staple crops were wheat and corn and pulses in the north and rice in the east and south. Its surplus produce was skimmed off by the government agents to form the basis of the Mughal revenue. But India also possessed many products and industries which gave it a name for manufactures and for skill, a reputation for craftsmanship from China to Europe, and substantial purchasing power in west and south Asia. The finer industries were luxury trades it is true, for the poor communications made it impossible to distribute imports throughout the country. There were in fact two distinct types of industry. There were the local crafts, where villages spun their own cotton and wove their own coarse cloth (*khaddar*); there were local pottery, metal, and woodwork. Apart from these there were the bulk products and finer handicrafts. Sugar was grown in Bengal, the north, and in Malabar. Indigo was produced in quantity in Gujarat, making Indian dyes famous. Opium, later to become so important for the Chinese trade, was produced in Malwa, and shipped down the Ganges. Oil seeds (before the days of Deterding and kerosene) provided the fuel for lamps. Tobacco, despite Akbar's distaste and Jahangir's prohibition in 1617, was widely grown, the hookah, or hubble-bubble pipe, becoming one of the most characteristic sights and sounds of the country. Another bulk product was saltpeter, obtainable all down the Ganges Valley, which found a ready market in the belligerent Europe of the seventeenth century. Shipbuilding was carried on in Surat, but the Indian products par excellence were cotton and silk cloth. Silk was produced in Kashmir and Bengal. Cotton grew both in the north and on the western coastal plain, but its special home was the famous black soil of the Deccan. Cotton goods were exported both east and west, to Persia in return for carpets, horses, and luxuries, to the East Indies in exchange for spices and metals such as tin in Malaya. Along with spices, cotton goods became the staple of the trade with Europe. Indian spices were in fact secondary in her economy. The main Indian spice production was pepper along the Malabar Coast and in Travancore. The rest of her spice trade consisted of re-export of East Indian spices from the Malabar Coast, which had continued from classical times.

Beyond pepper from Malabar, indigo from Gujarat, sugar and rice from Bengal, pearls and diamonds from Golconda, the major Indian export was textiles, since weaving was the major industry. It was textiles which purchased Indian imports and gave India as a whole a favorable balance of trade. The chief necessary imports were raw silk, metals like copper, tin, zinc, and mercury, and materials for handicrafts like ivory, coral, and amber. Horses were imported to the south where they could not easily be bred, and specially when the Hindus of the south needed cavalry with which to withstand the northern Muslims. Then there were the luxuries to which each foreign customer contributed a quota. Africa provided slaves, besides ivory, amber, and ebony; Persia sent wines and fruits as well as carpets and horses; China, objects of art; and Europe wines and novelties as well as broadcloth. But when all had been paid for there was a large balance in India's favor, and this was made up by bullion, chiefly in the form of silver. There was a steady flow of the precious metals into India, a flow which has continued through historic times and was still measurable up to World War II. It has been reckoned that in the early years of this century the absorption of silver only amounted to between five and six million pounds sterling (fifteen to eighteen million dollars) a year.[7] Much of this money seemed simply to disappear. In fact, much was converted into ornaments which formed the working capital and movable banks of the villagers; much was used for the lavish display beloved by rulers, of which the Peacock Throne in Delhi was the supreme example; while the remainder disappeared into state and temple treasuries or the hoards of private people.

The bulk of this foreign trade was small by modern standards, but not so small as the figures might suggest when it is remembered that most of the goods exported were finished articles or items of small weight. The trade by sea outweighed that by land; early in the seventeenth century it was reckoned that about three thousand camels, carrying about five hundred tons, traversed the route to Kandahar,[8] whereas the sea-borne traffic was around thirty thousand tons a year. The profits of this trade, along with that of internal industry and commerce and the surplus of agricultural classes, formed a fund for consumption which could have been used for development such as irrigation, communications, and all those activities known as public works. We have to ask ourselves how this fund was actually divided and in answering we shall find the explanation of the traveler's description of the extremes of poverty and wealth. Men spoke of the riches of Ind, but when they actually arrived there the first person they met was a beggar. The surplus of agricultural production was mown, as it were, with a fine blade by the various landholders, who in turn passed on a portion to the government. A peasant might pay to a landholder or *zamindar,* a holder of land by government grant (*jagirdar*), a salaried official, or a plain revenue farmer. In any case little was left to him but subsistence. The Mughal principle was to take a third of the gross produce (or its value) for government; in the Deccan the amount claimed was usually a half. From this sum the landed classes were supported, with the balance going to government. The profits of commerce were skimmed off by a series of duties at ports of entry, at every provincial frontier, and at every large town. River crossings, markets, all had their tolls, provincial governors their "cesses," while local lords joined in so far as they dared. It was relief from these exactions which was a great object of European commercial negotiations with the authorities. No doubt some merchants were rich, but they were careful not to advertise it, as can be seen from the modest frontages of their houses in old Indian cities opening out into spacious courts within.

Thus the greater part of this surplus income, whether from agriculture or commerce, found its way into the imperial treasury. The first charge on this fund was the imperial service of *mansabdars*. A commander of five thousand had a net income of about Rs 18,000 or $4,000 a month after the force of his rank had been paid for.[9] When this service had been provided for, together with ancillaries like artillery and fortresses, there was the court to maintain. Even so there remained a surplus in government hands, while the figures given above show that there was also one in those of the *mansabdars*. Both court and nobles gave liberal patronage to the arts and learning. But apart from this there was not much productive spending. In the case of the *mansabdars* the precariousness of the wealth, the certainty that it would be seized at death, and the competitive conditions of their class led to the spending of most of this money on display, crowds of retainers, and unproductive building. In the case of the rulers the same thirst for display prevailed. It led to great artistic achievements like the Taj Mahal and the great mosque of Delhi.[10] But it also involved much pure waste. Productive spending was not absent altogether, but the total record is poor. Shah Jahan restored Firoz Shah's canal from the Jumna to Delhi, which ran till 1750, and was again restored by the British in 1820. Some roads and some *sarais* or travelers' enclosures were built, some wells were dug. But nothing was done to raise the condition of the peasants or protect them from the ravages of famine. In particular little irrigation was attempted. The canals which might have been an antidote to famine were neither built nor dreamt of. In many ways the Mughal regime in an economic sense may be described as a state capitalism. The state regulated production and took the profits. But it was a capitalism which thought only of itself and squandered the fruits of the industry of the people in luxury and display.

In between the lords and the cultivators came the members of the middle class. There were the merchants, who formed a world of their own, and the professionals, the doctors, the lawyers, the men of religion, of learning, and of literature, the "writers" or lower officials. Their position in general was lowly. They were divided by social and geographical barriers from one another, and they were all dependent in varying degrees upon patrons for their fortunes. They had little security beyond the pleasure of the monarch or the governor, and in times of tumult the men of commerce were the first to suffer. Like the early mammals they dodged warily between the legs of the lords of the earth, affecting to be too humble to be worth their notice.

The observer who landed in India in the seventeenth century would have found a few great cities whose thronging streets would have made them seem more populous than they really were. Such a one was Surat on the Swally or estuary of the Tapti, the port of entry and exit for trade and pilgrims for north and central India. Surat belonged to the commercial class of permanent cities. A second class was the religious center, which attracted pilgrims, devotees, and scholars with ancillary commercial activities. Holiness maintained these cities as love of gain maintained the others. Examples were Nasik in the west, Banares in the north, and Nadia in the east. The third class was the royal or administrative type which was the center of a court or government. Among such may be classed Delhi, Agra, Murshidabad, Hyderabad, and Poona. These waxed and waned according to political circumstances, as happened to Delhi during the years that Aurangzeb camped in the Deccan or Akbar preferred Agra as his residence. It was the less permanent "political" cities which were adorned with the finest buildings, for here prestige was the spur to expense. Cities tended to appear overcrowded, and so their numbers to be overestimated by observers, because all men of substance had followers in excess of their needs, who moved out with various caravans as easily as they moved in. Being no more than temporary sojourners, they roamed the streets to create an impression of congestion. In all the cities, but specially in the political ones, there were extremes of poverty and wealth, from the great ones in their palanquins with their armed followers to the beggars and lepers in numbers. There were extremes of magnificence and squalor, from marble halls and exquisite craftsmanship to the reed huts and crowds virtually without clothing or shelter. The decorum of the imperial durbars contrasted with the tumult and the dust and odors of the bazaars. These great cities were far between and were reinforced by small market towns which might be walled and contain the stronghold of some chief or official.

Between these urban centers stretched the great world of rural India. The countryside was far less populated than at present, having only about a quarter of the present inhabitants. Large areas were wilderness or jungle. Lions, now confined to Kathiawar, roamed Rajasthan as far as the Hariana tract. There were a few main routes or tracks, along some of which trees had been planted and *sarais* erected. There were large areas which were a law unto themselves or were virtually unknown, where tribes like the Bhils, the Gonds, or the Santhals carried on their forest and hunting craft untouched by Hinduism. Robbers or *dacoits* were a constant danger to travelers, who usually went in groups and sought some enclosure for the night. The rivers were mostly unbridged, to be forded in the dry weather and ferried in the rains. The pace of travel was that of the horse or the camel and the means of transport the bullock wagon or camel cart. It took up to three months to travel by this means from Delhi to Bengal. In the north, river transport down the Jumna and Ganges and through the Gangetic delta in Bengal was both quicker and easier for bulk transport, but elsewhere the carts groaned and creaked, while in central India nothing but the pack horse would serve.

In both town and country a contemporary traveler would notice an infinite variety of dress, race, and custom. The newcomers to India all tended to retain their customs and become hereditary groups while the fame of the Mughals attracted adventurers and hangers-on from all parts. Thus in a great city could be met representatives of all the Middle East— Arabs, Turks, Persians, Afghans, along with Negroes from Abyssinia and Mongols from central Asia. These mixed with Rajputs, Panjabis, Brahmins, and all the races of India, each with their characteristic dress, manners, and cuisine. The country scenes were less colorful but no less varied, for here were to be found not only a diversity of races, but every variety of Hindu sect. The devotees of Shiva, of Vishnu in his forms of Rama and Krishna, of the goddess Kali in her various forms, as well as of regional deities and village godlings each had their own worship, belief, and customs.

A second impression of our contemporary traveler would be that it was a predominantly male world. In the towns he would see no women of the upper or middle classes in the streets; all he would observe would be their closed and guarded litters and carriages proceeding from palace to garden pavilion or from palace to palace. For the Muslims seclusion was the rule, and in Muslim areas the higher class Hindus followed suit. In Muslim society, except in the highest circles the women had little education and few rights which they could exercise. Masterful ladies like the empress Nur Jahan and the princess Roshanara were the exceptions rather than the rule. Among Hindus they were freer to move in their own circles, but were bound by the Hindu concept of the widow as in perpetual mourning for her husband, by the practice of infanticide, which was widespread, and the custom of *suttee* or the burning of a widow on the funeral pyre of her husband, which was common in certain communities, especially among the Rajputs and the Brahmins of Bengal. In the villages the women were freer to move about than in the towns, but they would vanish at the appearance of a stranger. Hindus in general were monogamous, but there were many exceptions among certain classes of Brahmins, and the rajas were always a law unto themselves.

A third impression would be that of religion. Islam dominated the towns except in the religious centers and the extreme south. It set the tone, as it were, with its stately mosques and its colleges, its call to prayer, its devotees and its religious observances. Hindu worship went on but less flamboyantly and in more modest buildings. The traveler who visited cities only might think that he was in a Muslim land. In the country, on the other hand, the impression would be of Hindu devotion. Each village had its temple, its holy painted stones and trees. Wandering holy men were numerous, of all grades of sincerity. The temple bell matched the muezzin's cry, the Durga *puja* or Ramlila the rigors and excitement of *Ramzan,* the month of fasting. This impression of the dominance of religion was heightened by the fact of mutual participation in certain of the major festivals. Thus *Diwali* or the Hindu festival of lights in October–November was an occasion of common festivity; Holi, the saturnalian spring festival, was celebrated both in the Mughal palace and in a general rough-and-tumble in the towns and villages, while in areas where Muslim Shia influence was strong, the processions and ecstasies of sorrow of Muhurram were enjoyed by both parties.

This is the spectacle of seventeenth-century India. It was a country abounding in life and energy, and at the same time abounding in contrasts. As in the case of the Indian sun, with its strong rays and clear-cut shadows, there were no half shades or subdued tones. There were extremes of tragedy and comedy, of variety and monotony, of sentiment and cruelty. Magnificence went with dire poverty and feasting with famine. It repelled some observers like Bernier and Roe and dazzled others like Manucci. Taking it all in all, we can perhaps say that India was more peaceful, more prosperous, and perhaps happier than she had been for several centuries or was to be for more than another hundred years. Though less secure for all classes, material conditions compared not unfavorably with those of contemporary Europe.

CHAPTER XIV

Europeans in India in the Sixteenth and Seventeenth Centuries

The European connection with India, as has already been noted, goes back to the days of the Greeks. In the matter of trade and especially of spices, interchange never ceased. But direct contact lapsed sometime after 400 A.D. with the collapse of the Roman Empire in the fifth century and the rise of Islam in the seventh. From then on only occasional travelers reached India, such as Marco Polo in the south in 1300, and the Russian Nikitin in the fifteenth century. We learn more of India during these centuries from Muslims like the philosopher Albiruni and the Moroccan traveler Ibn Batuta than from Europeans.

During all this time the lucrative spice trade continued to be handled by go-betweens. The spices came mainly from the East Indies, and as far afield as the Moluccas (the home of cloves). They came by sea to south India, where they changed hands and pepper and some minor spices were added. Then they found their way by various routes and many jurisdictions to the West, to which they were distributed from Constantinople and Alexandria. Why was the European demand so urgent that the supply was attempted against such obstacles? The answer is to be found in the primitive conditions of life prevailing in medieval Europe. Not only were there no refrigerators and preserving plants, but there was a lack of agricultural knowledge to provide winter fodder for cattle. All fat stock had to be killed at Christmas when outdoor pasture failed; the cattle retained for breeding were often so weak that they had to be carried to the grass in the spring. Man subsisted on bacon smoked in chimneys, ham soaked in salt, and meat preserved with pepper. Here was the first need for spices. The second was to flavor the far-from-fresh meat when it came to be eaten. A third was to flavor sour wine, the art of mellowing having been lost with the fall of Rome. This was called "mulling," and the treatment of meat was called "powdering." English food remained as highly spiced as Indian food until late in the seventeenth century.

Faced with this steady and urgent demand, merchants found it worth their while to face many dangers and pay numerous tolls and bribes through Egypt, Iraq, and the Turkish lands to the distributing centers of Constantinople and Alexandria. Here the Italians (Venetians, Genoese, and Pisans) took over, incidentally providing with the profits the economic foundation for the Italian Renaissance. During the fourteenth and fifteenth centuries two developments affected and threatened this tenuous trade line. The first was the closing of the trade routes. The land route through Persia to the Caspian Sea and thence to Constantinople was overrun by Genghis Khan in the thirteenth and Timur in the late fourteenth centuries. The anarchy which they left was capped by the capture of Constantinople by the Turks in 1453. Thus only the Egyptian route remained open. The second development was the rivalries of the Italian cities. The Venetians defeated the Genoese decisively in 1380, and though ousted from Constantinople by the Turks, established themselves firmly in Alexandria. An idea of the growing difficulty of the trade is given by the following illustration.[1] Spices were brought from the East Indies to Calicut in south India and there sold to Arab merchants. They were carried to Jidda in the Red Sea where an ad valorem duty of one-third was paid to Egypt. Thence they went in smaller boats to Suez, then by camel to Cairo, by boats down the Nile, and by camel again to Alexandria. At each place an ad valorem duty was charged, with a special one at Cairo of one-third. A parting shot was a 5 per cent duty for permission to move the cargo oversea. After this must be added the Italian charges and the cost of distribution beyond the Alps. On top of this came the bribes and other inducements needed to clear each customs barrier.

The threat to the established trade routes provided one good reason for seeking a direct route to India, and the discontent of the Genoese another. To these may be added a third, crusading or anti-Muslim zeal, which hoped to undermine the prosperity of the Islamic Middle East by diverting the spice trade at its source. These motives coincided with developments in the arts of shipbuilding and navigation which made it possible to venture on long voyages on unknown seas. The knowledge and the motives found a focus in Spain and Portugal. The people of both were filled with crusading zeal because of their long and successful wars with the Moors, and both countries had access to the technical skill of the disgruntled Genoese. Spain went west to discover the New World. India, through her spice trade, can thus claim to be a founding mother of the American republic. The Portuguese, under the lead of Prince Henry the

Navigator, felt their way down the coast of Africa during the middle years of the fifteenth century. Bartholomew Diaz rounded the Cape of Good Hope in 1486 and Vasco da Gama arrived at Calicut in 1498.

When he landed at Calicut Vasco said that he came to seek "Christians and spices." The Christians belonged to the semimythical Prester John, a prince with whom the Portuguese hoped to join forces and take the Muslims in the rear. The evidence on which the Portuguese relied probably related to the kingdom of Abyssinia, precariously perched in the mountains of northeast Africa between Muslims and pagans. It was some time before the Portuguese realized that the Hindu temples were not Christian shrines and still longer before they discovered the actually existing Christians of south India, the Syrian Christians of Travancore. The Portuguese quickly found themselves involved in conflict. The Arabs controlled the spice trade in Malabar and brought pressure on the zamorin or ruler of Calicut to refuse them facilities. The first modern European contact therefore quickly became a hostile one, and the Portuguese found themselves committed to war against the Muslim traders and conducting their trade by the maintenance of sea supremacy and fortified bases. Their aims were the defeat of the Muslims and control of the spice trade, so injuring the powers of the Muslim homeland, and the spread of Christianity. To the Spaniards and Portuguese of this period Catholicism was a part of their cultural being and they carried it with them wherever they went. They could not be neutral like some of the Mughals or shed their religion when dealing with trade as could the Dutch and English.

The religious and cultural motives interacted upon each other to determine the shape of Portuguese activity in the East. Hostility to Muslims, who spread across south Asia to the East Indies, required that their trade should be backed by force and defended by strongholds. Geography decreed that the empire should be a maritime one and the nature of the trade to be controlled that it should be far flung. The explanation of the peculiarities of the Portuguese empire in the East is that the Portuguese were both crusaders and traders, and that they could not be one without being the other. The empire owed its enduring pattern to the genius of Affonso d'Albuquerque in his six years of rule (1509–15). He determined that the Portuguese should rely upon fortresses backed by sea power. They were to be so placed that they could control the seagoing trade of the whole of south Asia, taking toll of all trade they did not choose to divert to themselves. He spun, as it were, a spider's web to enmesh the trade of south Asia. The headquarters was fixed at Goa, on the west coast of India, rather than in the East Indies, because this was a convenient point from which the spice trade in Malabar and the trade with Egypt and the Persian Gulf could be controlled. Goa was seized in 1510. The net was completed by the capture of Malacca, which controlled the trade routes converging on the East Indies, in 1511; Ormuz in 1515, controlling the entrance to the Persian Gulf; and the setting up of posts in East Africa, on Socotra off the Red Sea, at Diu in Gujarat, and at Colombo in Ceylon. He failed to take Aden, but his zeal to injure Islam was so great that he planned to dig a canal from the upper Nile to the Red Sea, to ruin Egypt by the diversion of the river. Albuquerque sought to maintain the empire by providing a local population. He encouraged intermarriage with the Indian population, beginning at the final capture of Goa by arranging matches between his soldiers and the widows of the Muslim garrison. From this policy sprang the race Portuguese in name, dominantly Indian in characteristics, and Catholic in religion which is known as the Goanese.

The Portuguese dominion as it existed in the sixteenth century thus involved a commercial supremacy of the south Asia seas, an aggressive anti-Muslim attitude, and a resident population of mixed origin stiffened by periodical reinforcements from Europe. To this we must add a strongly Catholic tincture. Behind the soldier and the merchant came the priest. The saintly St. Francis Xavier converted the fisher folk of Malabar before proceeding to China and Japan. A bishop of Goa was appointed in 1520 and soon the city was filled with churches and monasteries. The Inquisition was introduced in 1560. Missionary orders appeared, Jesuit fathers proceeded to Akbar's court in 1579, and in 1595 a great effort was made at the Synod of Diamper to gather the Syrian Christians of Travancore into the Catholic fold. This crusading temper of the day created a wall of hostility with the surrounding peoples, which was increased by the doctrine (too often honored by practice) that no faith need be kept with an infidel. The Portuguese became proverbial for perfidy and cruelty, and in places like Bengal where they formed settlements beyond the limit of Portuguese authority, for lawlessness. Socially they were a slave-holding society, acquainted with the luxuries of the East.

It may well be asked how a dominion so clearly out of tune with the surrounding peoples could hold a dominant position for so long. The first answer is the inspired leadership in the early days by such men as Vasco da Gama, Almeida, and Albuquerque. Behind this came self-confidence and determination born of crusading success and devotion to the Catholic faith. The Portuguese were eminently fighting for a cause which they believed to be righteous and bound to prevail. The willing spirit was backed by the implements to give it effect. The Portuguese ships, built for the stormy seas of Europe and Africa, were much more than a match for the light Arab dhows and coasters of Indian waters. Unscathed themselves, they mounted cannons which could blow the local ships out of the water. The soldier's matchlock and crossbow outclassed the local bow and the disciplining of troops in groups was something unknown in Asia at the time. Portuguese maritime skill and superior armament accounted for their success by sea; the hostility they aroused explains their inability, for all their energy and courage, to found an empire by land.

The Portuguese ruled the south Asian seas for a century and were then replaced by the Dutch. Their fall was almost as rapid as their rise because their inner strength had decayed before the Dutch appeared. They suffered from a lack of home support, because the Portuguese resources were overstrained. A kingdom of less than a million people had to maintain empires in both the new and old worlds and its position in Europe as well. The absorption of Portugal by Spain in 1580 was a further blow. In the settlements the inhabitants were more concerned with preserving their homes and families than risking all in distant expeditions. They had more to lose than gain by adventure. Loss of home control meant loss of control over trade agents; corruption ate into the prosperity and morals of the settlements. Finally, the hostility of the surrounding peoples led them to take advantage of every sign of Portuguese weakness. The Portuguese could find no allies against the Dutch.

For a hundred years the Portuguese represented Europe in India and for another century they were prominent exponents. It was not, on the whole, a good start for the European connection. The word *farangi* or Frank, used by medieval Arabs for the crusading Frenchmen, acquired a rather contemptuous meaning through connection with the Portuguese. Those who adventured and pirated beyond the limits of the Portuguese empire earned much of this contempt, while in turn the peccadillos of the wandering Europeans who attached themselves to the Indian armies and courts were fathered on them. Apart from this they left a reputation for fanaticism, intolerance, and perfidy. There seems little doubt that in the south this record in these respects was worse than that of the local communities. On the whole the Deccan Muslims were tolerant and faith was observed as between the communities. The doctrine that no faith need be kept with unbelievers did the European name much harm. Even today the myth that modern Christians practice forcible conversion in western India can be traced back to the sixteenth-century Portuguese tradition. In the north, it is true, all these things could be found. Yet they were specially associated with northwestern invaders, who were foreigners to the Hindus, and at best "outsiders" to the north Indian Muslim.

Apart from these intangibles the Portuguese left some concrete traces.

One was a *lingua franca* of the ports, a corrupt Portuguese which held its own in maritime commerce down to the eighteenth century. Another was the race of Goans, or Luso-Indians as they used to be called, Portuguese in name, mainly Indian in blood, Catholic in religion, and often mercantile by profession. Apart from Goa itself, they are to be found as shopkeepers and businessmen all over India, especially in Bombay and on the west coast. To the traveling European they are often first known as stewards on liners. In commerce the Portuguese brought in tobacco, maize, and potatoes from the New World, all of which have become indigenous. In art they were exponents of the Renaissance and have left their mark in the churches of Goa and Indo-Catholic buildings generally. In nineteenth-century India a Protestant church was usually Gothic in style but a Catholic church was classical. Jesuits from Goa took Italian miniatures to Akbar's court, and their influence upon the Indian miniaturists was distinct and traceable. Artists like the Frenchman Austin of Bordeaux and the Italian Geronimo Verroneo, though not Portuguese, found their entry into India by this means. There is finally their religious influence. Though the great work of Catholic missions was carried on mainly by other hands than the Portuguese, it is fair to say that it was they, with St. Francis Xavier and the organization of the bishopric of Goa, who gave the impulse, and it was certainly they who retained control of the Catholic church in India. In the Goanese, the still independent Goa, the Catholic church in India, the lingering suspicion of Christians as proselytizers and forcible converters, Portuguese influence lives on in India today.

The second European arrivals in India were the Dutch. Their outlook was strictly commercial. Antwerp was the distributing center for spices in northern Europe, whence they were brought from Lisbon by sea. In 1580 Portugal was added to Philip II's Spanish empire, from which the Protestant Dutch were at that moment revolting. Their sea trade, through the stormy Channel and Bay of Biscay, made the Dutch some of the most skillful sailors of the day with some of the stoutest ships. The repulse of the Spaniards from what is modern Holland and the English defeat of the Armada in 1588 left the way open for maritime adventure in the East. There followed the rise of the Dutch East India Company. The Dutch, being untroubled with crusading scruples, made straight for the center of the spice trade in the East Indies. They fixed their base at Batavia or modern Jakarta, in Java, and set out to control the spice trade at the source of supply in Indonesia by means of their maritime skill. Under the direction of Coen, they devised the system extending from Persia to Japan, by means of which they monopolized the spice trade at the source of production and paid for its "investment" by means of a far-flung "country trade." Thus in the west, silk and carpets from Persia helped to pay for cotton goods in India, which bought spices or pepper in Ceylon or Travancore. To the east silk and porcelain in China obtained silver and copper from Japan, the silver being used to buy more cotton in India. The system was of course far more complicated than can be set out in a few words, but the principle is clear. It was to use the articles of the country trade to secure the goods needed to buy the spices and to help meet the overhead of the trade as a whole, for, though the spice trade in itself was highly profitable, and when under Dutch monopoly still more so, the cost of maintaining fleets and stations all over the East was also high.

The Dutch looked on the East with the eye of a merchant rather than a crusader who liked some profit on the side. They went straight to the source of the greatest profit, which was the East Indies. They ejected the Portuguese, whom they found in possession, from Malacca, and also from Ceylon and Malabar, from which they took cinnamon and pepper. But they never took Goa, although they besieged it. The reason that they did not persist was perhaps that they no longer feared the Portuguese ships and Goa was not important enough for their system to be worth a major effort for capture. They established fortified posts at Colombo in Ceylon, the Cape of Good Hope in South Africa, St. Helena in the Atlantic to provision their fleets for the East Indies. Colombo in addition supervised cinnamon production in Ceylon and pepper in Malabar. But India was for them a subordinate theater of activity. It played a supporting role only in the grand design of monopolizing the spice trade of the world. Their principal factories were at Surat, Cochin in Malabar for pepper, Negapatam and Masulipatam on the Coromandel Coast for cottons, Chinsura in Bengal for silk, saltpeter, and the up-country trade, and Agra. None attained the stature of the English settlements and all were subordinate to Batavia in the East Indies. Their influence in India was small, for they only cared for trade. In fact, as can be seen from their tombs at Surat, they were more orientalized themselves than Westernizers in the East. They carried on no religious propaganda in India and any cultural influence they exercised was in Ceylon and the East Indies. Their chief value for Indian posterity was in the records they kept, which form valuable economic material, and in their descriptive reports, which are valuable historical and social sources.[2]

The real importance of the Dutch to India was not their physical presence but the fact that their grip of the East Indies compelled the English to concentrate on India. It was the Dutch dog in the East Indian manger which turned the English horse to Indian pastures. The English at first were under much the same compulsions as the Dutch. They wanted a share of the new maritime spice trade from which they were excluded by the Latin powers on the ground of a papal ruling. Their allegiance to Protestantism reinforced their monopolistic exclusion with religious principle: The Dutch rebellion and the Spanish war not only excluded them from a share in the trade but endangered the supply of the goods themselves. The English, like the Dutch, sought alternative routes in the northwest and northeast passages, and alternative outlets in Russia and the Levant.[3] Spain's seizure of Portugal in 1580 removed one inhibition to direct action, because Portugal was an ancient ally of the English; the defeat of the Armada in 1588 removed another, the fear of Spanish power in Europe and on the sea. Reports by Drake of his visit to the Moluccas in 1579 on his voyage round the world, the capture of a galleon returning from the East, the reports of stray travelers such as Ralph Fitch, and the success of the first Dutch voyages,[4] were added incentives.

The first ships set sail on February 13, 1601, the East India Company having received its royal charter, granting it a monopoly of trade with the East, on the last day of the previous year. The Company's ships made straight for the East Indies, where spices were to be had. It was not until 1608 that the first Company's servant landed at Surat in India and went to the court of Jahangir. The English, like the Dutch, were commercially minded and they therefore concentrated their efforts upon the East Indies. But the Dutch were determined to establish a monopoly in the islands. They were not going to drive out the Portuguese in order to share the fruits of victory with the English. A struggle was inevitable, but it was also unequal because the new United East India Company of the Netherlands had eight times the capital of its English rival. The struggle culminated in what is known as the massacre of Amboyna in 1623, when the English on this East Indian island were seized and executed by the Dutch. Full redress was never obtained, and the event marks the virtual end of English efforts to obtain spices direct from the source.

From that time the English concentrated upon India, not because they wished to, but because they had no alternative. This diversion from the East Indies to India proper had important consequences. The pattern of trade was changed. Spices became of minor importance. At first indigo from Gujarat was important, then calicos and cotton piece-goods, and bulkier articles like saltpeter (for gunpowder), sugar, and yarn. These goods gave less profit than spices, but though the English did not know it, they were susceptible to a far greater expansion in quantity which was more than to make up for the smaller return per cent. A further consequence was that the English had to exercise great ingenuity in selling and in carefully studying their market. Their broadcloth had little attraction except in the north, while the silver, which was welcomed, brought them into bad odor with their countrymen, who considered its export as a drain on the real wealth of the country. They had to dispose of unsaleable goods and somehow find an alternative to silver for purchase. These needs led to the development of a country trade designed to provide the means of making up the "investment," and to a close study of markets and purchasers. By these processes the English merchants, for all their insular prejudice, came to know the official and mercantile Indians well. The knowledge thus painfully gained stood them in good stead when they plunged into politics in the eighteenth century. Without it they might easily have gone down in defeat or bankruptcy.

In India the English Company had to meet the opposition of the Portuguese, who controlled the Arabian Sea and the sea traffic from Surat. This was overcome by the sea action of 1615 off the river Swally and the siege of Ormuz, with the Persians as allies, in 1621. As soon as Jahangir realized that the English were stronger than the Portuguese at sea he was ready to grant trading privileges. In effect the Company became the naval auxiliary of the Mughals in return for trading privileges within the empire. It kept the seas clear from Portuguese ships and safeguarded the pilgrim traffic. It was under these conditions that the pattern of English settlements in India grew up. Surat was the headquarters of the Company from 1618 to 1687. Factories were established in the south, first at Masulipatam and then at Madras in 1641 in order to secure cotton piece-goods. From there a trade with Bengal was established on a rising demand for sugar, saltpeter, and raw silk, though it was not until 1691 that Calcutta was founded. Bombay was a Portuguese island which came to Britain as part of the dowry of Charles II's queen, Catherine of Braganza. It had little importance for commerce until the nineteenth century because of its unpromising hinterland. With the rise of the Marathas it became a valuable observation post and sally port.

Apart from a futile war between the English Company and Aurangzeb between 1687 and 1691, the European merchants lived peaceably in India, trading under license of the local authority and living for the most part in Indian cities. The Indian trade was profitable, though not dazzling. The success of the English led others to follow, such as the French, the Danes, and the Imperial Ostend Company. None could shake the Dutch monopoly of the East Indies or rival the English in India. Madras had its fort from the start, for conditions on the Coromandel Coast were unsettled following the breakup of the Vijayanagar empire. The merchants lived a corporate or collegiate type of life in a group of buildings which constituted the "factory." The factory was really a warehouse and office, described as a "godown" and counting house. The warehouse received the goods in preparation for dispatch to Europe, and it stored goods awaiting sale. There was no manufacture in our sense of the term. The senior merchants formed a council with one of their number as president or governor. There were corporate meals in a hall and a chapel served by a chaplain. In Surat the factory was bare of images, in order not to offend the Muslims. Bachelors were given joint quarters in the style of a college.

Apart from the Company's business the merchants busied themselves with their private trade within the country and across the Asian seas. In manners the merchants were more affected by Indian atmosphere than bearers of a Western cultural torch. They intermarried with the local Goans or Luso-Indians (a cause of some concern because the ladies were Roman Catholics). They wore Indian clothes in their houses and enjoyed Indian dishes at table. The midday dinners—gargantuan mixtures of Indian and European food—go far to explain the brevity of many of their lives. The amusements were shooting, gaming, the flying of kites, the letting off of cannons and fireworks (frowned on by the Company as a source of expense), and drinking in the Company's garden "with a collation." Processions were popular, with "music in the country style." In the matter of drinking, tastes were eclectic, Persian wine and country spirit or arrack mingling with madeira and port sent out from Europe. Manners were boisterous, and, as might be expected in a confined society, quarrels were frequent. In Bombay files of musketeers had to be brought into the hall to preserve order at dinner. Brawls among the younger members were common. "On the news of Farruksiyar's *farman* granting possession of five villages round Madras in 1717, two processions went round the town, one of all the civil authorities, a company of soldiers and 'all the English musick' which toured the port; and the other led by the Peddanaik on horseback, and consisting of Talliars and native music, a company of British soldiers, two trumpeters, the chief Dubash (Indian secretary) mounted, a palanquin with the *farman,* six sergeants and the Company's merchants. A salute of 101 guns was fired for the King, fifty-one for the Royal family and thirty-one of the company, and all the merchants of the town, English, Portuguese, Armenians and Mohommedans were entertained to dinner. 'The day concluded with feasting of the soldiers with tubs of Punch and bonfire at night; and the black merchants, to show their joy at the Hon. Company receiving so much favour from the Moghul, made abundance of fireworks in the Island.' " [5]

In general it can be said that the European merchants received more than they gave in the matter of manners. The garment known as "long drawers" was in fact the Indian pajama, and gave to the West its modern form of night attire. The custom of water ablutions was passed back to England by the "nabobs" of the eighteenth century. The factors smoked hookahs, the hubble-bubble pipes of the East, and when they became expensive [6] took to cigars and cheroots which again were passed back to Europe. These merchants had no regular vacations, and many in fact never returned home. Those who survived the early years settled down to a hybrid life and made themselves comfortable in the fashion of the country.

Apart from the established Portuguese and the resident merchants a considerable number of individual Europeans visited India in the seventeenth century. Some were men of means like Mandelslo, Thevenot, and Gemelli-Carreri, traveling out of curiosity; Pietro della Valle traveled to allay the pangs of frustrated love; some were professional men seeking their fortunes, some craftsmen and artisans, and some adventurers pure and simple. Among the professionals the figure of François Bernier is outstanding. He lived for nine years as the physician of Danishmand Khan at the Mughal court and sent to the French minister Colbert penetrating reports of the court and government and of the state of the country as a whole. Among the craftsmen were Geronimo Veroneo who worked on the Taj Mahal and Austin of Bordeaux who executed the *pietra dura* work of the throne in the Delhi palace. Below this level was a motley crowd who came to India to seek their fortunes and took any service which was offered. A favorite employment was that of artilleryman. It is recorded that in Shah Jahan's time these men were only required to aim the guns; many resigned in disgust when the stricter Aurangzeb insisted that they should load them as well. Outstanding in this group was the Venetian Niccolò Manucci. He arrived at Agra in 1656 at the age of seventeen in the train of an English ambassador and took service in the artillery of Dara Shekoh, the heir apparent. On the defeat of Dara, to whom he seems to have been sincerely attached, he set up as a physician without having medical knowledge. The rest of his life was spent wandering about India until his death, probably at Pondicherry in 1717 with a moderate fortune. His memoirs, the *Storia da Mogor,* are a highly entertaining and unreliable epitome of the age.

These varied vistants had little influence on the life of India as a whole. Those who were cultured like Bernier were too isolated and those who formed groups were not cultured enough. There was a meeting of mutual curiosity, but not a marriage of true minds. The Portuguese, who possessed both culture and belief in it, had put up barriers against themselves by their hostility to things Indian. In consequence their influence, as in the fine arts or in painting, was peripheral rather than central. Yet if the

Europeans gave little to India at this time, they at least brought back something to Europe. We have mentioned the subject of manners. In addition they provided modern Europe with its first serious reports of India. Hitherto men had relied on the classical authors like Herodotus and Megasthenes, with some seasoning of medieval legend like the works of Sir John Mandeville. They now had a series of factual reports, many of them reliable and some of high quality. It was from them that modern Europe drew its picture of India. It was a picture of a land of great wealth, of display and pomp, of a land of despotism and desperate struggles for power, and a land of strange religions and outlandish customs.

CHAPTER XV

India, 1700-1750

The dominant feature of India during the first half of the eighteenth century was the decline of the Mughal empire. This majestic institution fascinated the political imagination of both Indians and Europeans and its fate was naturally their first object of attention. But it must not be supposed that its collapse was obvious to the contemporary observer or clearly foreseen by many. Bernier in 1660 pointed out some of the weaknesses of the empire; the decline in its authority was noticed by merchants in the later years of the century. But the ignominious failure of Sir Josiah Child's war against Aurangzeb made men more cautious. Its collapse was freely prophesied but its continuance was assumed. The factors who journeyed to Delhi in 1714 for fresh privileges were highly respectful and delighted at their grant. The empire was in fact regarded as being a going concern until Nadir Shah's invasion in 1738–39, and its imminent collapse was not realized until the marches and countermarches of Maratha and Afghan which culminated at Panipat in 1761.

Apart from this long drawn-out political event there are certain other factors to be taken into account. The first was that while the Mughal power was declining that of the Marathas was rising. The Mughals were Muslims and the Marathas Hindus. It is easy to think of the Maratha movement as a renaissance of Hinduism, a revival of an ancient civilization by a simple and vigorous mountain people with a healthier outlook than the luxury-sodden Mughal nobles. But the Marathas, for all their energy, hardihood, and martial prowess, showed little sign of advanced culture. Their contributions to the India of their time were not philosophy or the fine arts, but the art of guerrilla warfare, the technique of plunder, and the exaction from peaceful inhabitants of the payment known as *chauth*. We must beware, therefore, of regarding the fall of the empire in terms of a Muslim decline and Hindu revival. The Marathas could be as ruthless to their fellow Hindus as to the Muslims. To the typical Maratha loot was more important than religion. The fact was that both the Hindu and Muslim cultures at that time seemed to be stagnant, with no fresh answer to the problem of the times.

A further factor was the state of thought and feeling in India and Europe. Thought and feeling are prior to action because it is the state of men's minds which determines their action. In India Hindu culture was dormant or withdrawn within the Sanskrit schools of Banaras and elsewhere and the retreats of contemplatives. The Muslim religion was also stagnant, receiving no impulse from outside and imparting none to the country. It could only point to tradition and appeal to the letter of the law. But the Muslim religion, as we have seen, was not the mainspring of the Mughal empire. The theocracy of Aurangzeb was a deviation from the norm of its Muslim secularism. Its inspiration was that of Persian culture, for which Islam provided the form rather than the essence. This being so, it was an important fact that Persian culture itself showed signs of exhaustion at this time. Not only did the Safavid empire collapse and the flow of Persian recruits to the imperial service gradually dry up, but Persians lost confidence in themselves and their way of life. The culture continued to be precious and delightful to its devotees, but its aggressive quality and infectious nature had passed away. Persia had nothing further to contribute in statecraft and administration, in literature and art. Its last creative achievement in India was the Urdu language and this may be said to have been accomplished when the emperor Muhammad Shah (1719–48) admitted Urdu poetry to the court.

While in India there seemed to be an absence of new ideas and a harking back to the past, in Europe just the opposite process was occurring. The end of the religious wars had ushered in a new age whose keynote was not merely indifference under the name of tolerance, but new philosophies based on reason and the study of nature. The Age of Reason or Enlightenment regarded reason as the new revelation, the instrument of man's moral and material progress, with the aid of which he could attain mastery of himself and of nature. Progress was not a fleeting achievement or a passing interlude, but was to be the normal condition of the new age. It was to mark Western civilization apart from all others, and steadily to advance it beyond them. The West began to think of itself as not only superior to other cultures but as destined to leave them ever further behind. A mood of boundless self-confidence set in, making every setback seem relative and every difficulty temporary. This new state of mind was matched by impressive material progress. The comparative peace of the eighteenth century saw a rapid expansion of commerce, and a corresponding accumulation of wealth. Even before the Industrial Revolution began around 1760, Europe was rapidly increasing her resources while India was dissipating hers in wasteful display and incessant internal struggles. A further feature was the technical progress of Europe associated with the development of applied science. The extent of these changes in altering the relationship between the two regions was seen as by a lightning flash on a dark night when the European companies fell to arms in the 1740's and brought their new military techniques to the East. If these facts are borne in mind the sudden rise of Europeans to supremacy in India in the later eighteenth century is easier to understand.

The first half of the century was dominated by the gradual breakup of the Mughal empire and the rise of the Marathas. A full understanding of this process has perhaps still to be achieved, but we can obtain some idea of its obvious causes. Reference has been made to the pillars of the empire as erected by the emperor Akbar. All these were cracked or undermined as the century proceeded. The pillar of personality, which had served the empire so well for nearly two centuries, failed after 1712. The pillar of toleration was badly shaken by Aurangzeb's theocratic Muslim views, his quarrel with the Rajputs, and his reimposition of the *jizya* or tax on unbelievers. The balance of power between Persia and India was upset by the fall of the Safavids followed by the meteoric rise of Nadir Shah, who thought more of plunder than civilized administration and relations between states. The Rajput alliance was strained by Aurangzeb's quarrel with the heirs of Jaswant Singh, and despite the efforts of Bahadur Shah was never completely restored. Some Rajputs, it is true, continued to cooperate until the final collapse, but the understanding which had once existed, and which had given the empire its organic character, was gone forever. Above all, the empire had ceased to exercise, in Professor Toynbee's phrase, that charm which draws men to causes and people by the infectious magic of its qualities. It was such "charm" that Akbar had exercised on the Rajputs, and the Mughals generally on the whole Indian princely order. Aurangzeb had attempted the spell on the Marathas, but had failed signally with Sivaji; with his grandson Shahu the spell was fitful and partial. With the Sikhs the magic failed altogether; with a great effort the empire crushed them by main force in 1717, but the very resort to force to crush an Indian community was a confession of a loss of creativeness. We may also note that the decline of Mughal power exposed, like a receding tide uncovering rocks, resistances to the whole regime which had been concealed in the flood tide of power. When power seems irresistible, those who may object to it on principle may feel flattered by some quite minor concession. But when the same power in a weakened condition makes an identical concession, the same recipient may reject it with scorn. The awe of power, or "the divinity that doth hedge a king," is something that affects every judgment and every situation. Without it hates and distastes long concealed resume their natural influence. Thus it was with the Mughals. As their power declined and with it the glamor of their authority, Hindus who had once been thankful for their tolerance and patronage became impatient of their alien religion and their assumption of authority. A stage was reached when concessions which fifty years earlier might have transformed the empire were treated as insults and hastened its dissolution. The British were to have something of the same experience two centuries later. In judging the fortunes of political powers, one has always to keep in mind not only their intrinsic resources, but the idea or reputation of their power in the minds of others, and the relationship of their power with that of external forces. The position of the British in India, for example, was radically affected by the change in their position as a world power as a result of World War I.

We can now glance at the main steps in the Mughal decline. After the death of Aurangzeb in 1707, his eldest surviving son, Bahadur Shah, made a not unsuccessful attempt to revive the imperial fortunes. He made peace with the Marathas, fomenting a civil war by releasing Sivaji's grandson Shahu from the court. He came to an understanding with the Rajputs and he defeated the Sikhs. But he was an old man when he came to power and died within five years. Then came two wars of succession which killed off the ablest princes and left a survivor in the hands of military adventurers. With Muhammad Shah (1719–48) there was an apparent revival, but it was really only a concealment of decline. He was one of those princes without the strength to dominate but with the craft to balance opposing forces and to play off rival factions against each other. The court continued in splendor while paralysis slowly spread from the center outward. In 1724 Nizam-ul-Mulk, a noble of the Aurangzeb school of duty and integrity, gave up the office of wazir or first minister and retired to the governorship of the Deccan provinces, where his descendants ruled until 1948. His departure was symbolic of the flight of loyalty and virtue from the empire. In 1738 came the first overt breach in the empire. The Mughals fared so badly in war with the Marathas that they had to cede the province of Malwa, thus cutting off their Deccan provinces from the north. Almost immediately the Persian adventurer Nadir Shah descended from the northwest. Divided counsels and jealousies led to defeat and capitulation. Delhi was plundered in 1739, the Peacock Throne removed, and enough spoil taken away to enable Persian taxes to be remitted for three years. It is an index of Mughal prestige that the empire appeared to recover from this stunning blow, and continued for another fifteen years in apparent splendor. Then civil war and faction descended on the court and the provinces rapidly dropped away. The Marathas had taken Malwa in 1738 and added Orissa in the forties. Nadir Shah took Kabul in 1739. Bengal was virtually independent from 1740. Gujarat and Sind followed in 1750. In 1754 the Panjab went to the Afghans and Oudh fell away as the result of civil war. With the assassination of Emperor Alamgir II in 1759 the empire ended as an effectual power. It revived for a time as a north Indian principality and it continued as a name until the turn of the century. The Mughals took little part in the struggle for power in north India around 1760, which cleared the way for the British.

The second dynamic force in eighteenth-century India, which was later to contend with the British for ascendancy, was that of the Marathas. The homeland of the Marathas, or Maharashtra, lies along the Western Ghats or mountains and extends across central India on the general lines of the eastern portion of the present Bombay State. The people are small and sturdy in physique with the hardiness which goes with residence in barren and stony hills. They were full of intelligence and possessed a toughness of fiber which could accomplish much with few resources. Once before, in the time of the Rashtrakutas, they had known something of dominion but for the most part the barrenness of their lands and their distance from the main sources of wealth had shaded them from the glare of empire.

The Marathas come into political history in the seventeenth century when the chief Shahji was a *jagirdar* or fiefholder of the Muslim kingdom of Bijapur in the western Deccan. His son Sivaji started to seize hill-forts on his own account. Bijapur was too distracted to deal with him and after his treacherous murder of the general Afzal Khan in 1659 [1] left him alone. Sivaji then turned his attention to the neighboring Mughal lands, his most dramatic achievement being the surprise and sack of the great port of Surat in 1664. The English merchants alone escaped damage on this occasion because they closed their factory gates and offered a bold front to all comers. A Mughal army led by the Rajput Jai Singh brought Sivaji to terms in 1665 and there followed the famous visit to Aurangzeb at Agra in 1666. Mutual suspicion led to an incident in the Durbar, to house arrest, and to Sivaji's escape in a *dhuli* or basket of fruit. From that time Sivaji was an open rebel. He underlined his independence by a coronation ceremony at Raigarh in 1674 and at his death in 1680 was the master of a vigorous and compact kingdom. Sivaji was assisted by a council of eight officers of state, which formed a cabinet in the American sense of the term. The organization was a skillful adaptation to the conditions of the country and people. For revenue purposes the country was divided into districts with an assessment system based on that of a neighboring Muslim state.[2] Justice was administered by village committees or *panchayats*. The three main communities of Brahmins, Marathas, and Prabhus were skillfully integrated in the army. Thus each hill-fort (of which there were two hundred and forty) had a Maratha *havildar* or commandant, a Brahmin *sabnis* or accountant, and a Prabhu *karkun* or storekeeper. Similarly the feudal fiefholders and the private adventurers were welded together into a mobile field force. We have a significant hint of the rebel and plundering nature of the state in the division of land into *swarajya* or homeland organized in sixteen districts and subject to regular administration and *mughlai* or alien Mughal land subject to raids and exactions. These exactions are worth noting, for they did much to give the Marathas their bad name in other parts of India and so prevent their attainment of empire. The principal one was *chauth* or an exaction of one-fourth of the revenue. In addition there was *sar-deshmukhi,* or an exaction of one-tenth. These levies may be compared to the Danegeld of Anglo-Saxon days. They were often levied by the Marathas as the price of their withdrawal from a province, which did not, of course, prevent them coming again next year. As a permanent impost they were supposed to guarantee a district from further raids, but this condition was often disregarded. They were levied on Hindu and Muslim alike and did much to make the Maratha name detested in the Indian countryside.

Sivaji used the unsettled conditions of his day to make war pay by plundering raids on neighboring lands. He also gave the Marathas a *mystique* or a dynamic which enabled them to meet the full force of Aurangzeb's attack when it came. He gave the various communities of Maharashtra a sense of common nationhood. He did this by combining them in a common cause of independence and defense of religion. He stirred their pride by his successes, he lined their pockets by his plunder, and he appealed to their consciences by his championship of religion. The symbol of plunder was *chauth,* of independence the hill-fort, and of religion the sacred cow. Sivaji's watchwords were the defense of the *desh* or homeland and of the cow. These measures gave the Marathas great power, but their limitations are easy to see. They were designed for a local, not all-Indian realm; they assumed an anti-Muslim crusade and the exploitation of all non-Marathas. No lasting empire in India could be built on this basis.

Sivaji might well have adapted his kingdom to imperial conditions if they had come his way. But his successors were of lesser clay. They had to withstand the full force of Aurangzeb's attack soon after Sivaji's death when his forces were released from their wars in the northwest. There followed an ordeal from which the Marathas emerged in 1707 undefeated but radically changed. It is usually said that the Mughals were the losers but in fact both sides lost. The military power of the Mughals was undermined, it is true, but at the same time the kingdom of Sivaji, with its careful balance of forces, was destroyed. The highly organized central executive and the recognized authority were gone. The Maratha power was reorganized on a looser system altogether which had in it from the beginning the seeds of dissolution. The chief steps were these. Sivaji's grandson Shahu, released from the Mughal court by Bahadur Shah in 1707, was at first in the hands of his fiefholders. In 1714 he appointed a man of genius in the person of Balaji Vishvanath Bhat to the office of peshwa or chief minister. The office became hereditary in the family, which maintained high ability for four generations. Shahu's second step was to decide that expansion should be to the north rather than the south. This meant that it was in the hands of the peshwa, and that the generals in command were his subordinates. Thus the peshwas became the effective directors of Maratha expansion. Shahu presided until his death in 1749, but thereafter his successors were pensionaries at Satara.

The first phase of the Maratha confederacy lasted from 1714–61. The peshwas directed expansion to the north and east from Poona, and by their energy and success overshadowed their equals in the south. Certain links were retained between the center and the expanding periphery which maintained some unity of control. All grants were in Shahu's name, and land grants were widely distributed as in William the Conqueror's England. The generals in particular were controlled by the grant of land in the homeland, where it could be easily confiscated. *Chauth* was divided between the peshwa and two other officers and finally audit officers went with the armies to represent the peshwa.

Under the auspices of the first three peshwas of the Bhat family, expansion went rapidly forward. Successful campaigns against the imperialists culminated in a raid to the suburbs of Delhi and the cession of Malwa in 1738. In the next decade Maratha power spread right across central India. Nagpur was taken, Orissa was occupied, and Bengal heavily attacked. We may note here the transition from the occupation of mainly Maratha country like that around Nagpur to attacks on non-Maratha Hindu land like Orissa and west Bengal. The Marathas behaved the same everywhere. Their bodies of light cavalry moved swiftly over the countryside spreading both terror and consternation. Their auxiliary light-armed bodies of adventurers who spread out round the main force like flies around a moving horse were prototypes of the later dreaded Pindaris [3] of the early nineteenth century. Gone were the days when even the Muslim historian Khafi Khan admitted the good behavior of the Marathas under

Sivaji. Aurangzeb's wars had soured Maratha behavior toward Hindus as well as Muslims.

It was in the next decade that the decisive moment came in the fortunes of Maratha expansion. They were invited to act as auxiliaries in the internal affairs of the empire in the north, first by the reigning wazir and then by his rival. The thoughts of empire thus stirred became a blinding vision when they were asked by the Delhi government to help in driving out Ahmad Shah the Afghan from the Panjab. A Maratha empire in north India, perhaps as a Maratha-run Mughal empire, seemed suddenly to become practical politics. Thus the Marathas became one of the parties concerned with the death throes of the empire.

The three parties concerned in the collapse of the empire were the Muslim chiefs of Delhi themselves, the Afghans, and the Marathas. We have noted that the empire seemed to revive after Nadir Shah the Persian's sack of Delhi in 1739. This revival lasted until Muhammad Shah's death in 1748. During this time Nadir Shah died, his empire broke up in disorder, and Ahmad Shah Abdali emerged as the ruler of an independent splinter kingdom. He is the virtual founder of modern Afghanistan. As soon as he was established in power he began to look, in the traditional manner, on the plains of Hindustan as objects of plunder and empire. His first attack was repulsed at Sirhind on the eve of Muhammad Shah's death. Twice, in 1749 and 1751–52, he was bought off, once with money and once by the cession of the Panjab. By 1756 the empire was weakened by civil war between rival prime ministers and the assassination of the emperor. This time Ahmad Shah took Delhi in 1757 and appointed a Rohilla Afghan as the guardian of the new emperor, Alamgir II. The Mughal minister now called in the Marathas to eject Ahmad Shah from the Panjab. The peshwa considered this invitation as a summons to empire. There was talk of "flying over the walls of Attock" on the Indus. Help was given on such a scale that, as so often happens in India, the auxiliary became the principal. The Maratha occupation of Lahore in 1758 was followed by the return of Ahmad Shah the next year and the dispatch of an imposing armament under the peshwa's uncle, the Bhao Sahib.

The field was thus set for a decisive encounter between two contenders for Indian empire. The event occurred on January 14, 1761, at Panipat, fifty miles north of Delhi, and already the scene of two great battles.[4] The result was the complete defeat of the Marathas. The Bhao Sahib, the peshwa's heir, and all the leading chiefs were killed and the Peshwa Balaji Baji Rao himself died within six months of vexation. By all the rules an

Afghan empire should have succeeded the Mughal and set about recovering the ground lost to the Marathas. But in fact this did not happen and it is worth while looking into the reasons a little more closely. The battle was decisive in the sense that its effects are still felt today. But the decision was negative. Panipat decided who should *not* rule India, and so left the stage open to the foreigner from overseas lurking in the wings, as it were, with at present no desire but to carry on trade in settled political conditions. Ahmad Shah remained in possession of the field and of Delhi. But the Afghan *khans* lacked the stamina of the Mughal *begs* who followed Babur. They would not face exile for the sake of empire or stay in the Indian heat in a country too exhausted by war to offer them rich rewards. Nor was Ahmad Shah's grip of Afghanistan so firm that he could afford to leave it for long. He therefore virtually abdicated the empire, leaving an Afghan chief to rule Delhi in the name of the fugitive emperor, who was in turn, in theory, his vassal. The Marathas were too weak to grasp the scepter thus thrown down. It was not until 1767 that their forces recrossed the river Chambal, the traditional boundary between the Deccan and Hindustan. It was not only exhaustion but dissension which had beset them. The shock of the defeat hastened the conversion of the centrally directed if loose confederacy into five virtually independent states. The young Peshwa Madhu Rao died in 1772 just as he was showing signs of his father's ability. Thereafter the Poona court was distracted by succession disputes, and its authority over the distant chiefs waned. Generals became heads of states and the struggle for supremacy within the Maratha confederacy became as important as the struggle for dominion without it. The peshwa retained his control of the Maratha lands in western India. But Berar and central India fell to the Bhonsla family with its capital at Nagpur. Most of Gujarat went to the Gaekwar family at Baroda, near Surat, while the Maratha power in west central and north India was divided between the Sindias and the Holkars. Their dominions became the states of Gwalior and Indore, which, along with Baroda, survived until independence in 1947. Madhu Rao Sindia, the ablest of these chiefs, dominated Delhi from 1785. He might have reunited the Marathas under his leadership but for his death at Poona in 1794. It was Holkar's defeat of the last peshwa which drove him into the arms of the British in 1802.

Hindustan was left without a master, a prey of marauding Sikhs, Rohilla chiefs, and rustic Jats. The emperor Shah Alam returned to Delhi in 1772 and for a time maintained a local kingdom of some vigor. With his brutal blinding by a Rohilla in 1788 the last flicker of empire went out. The time was known as the Great Anarchy or, in local parlance, the Time of Troubles. Villages fortified themselves, chiefs seized forts and set themselves up as kinglets; the strong man ruled and terrorized until a stronger came in his place. The appearance of Sindia and the rise of the Sikhs brought the beginnings of order, but it was not until the advent of the British that tranquility was really restored. It was in this way that the British proved to be the residuary legatees of the unclaimed estate of Hindustan.

PART III
THE BRITISH IN INDIA

CHAPTER XVI

British and French

We have noted the decline of the Mughal Empire, under whose aegis the British had been trading for nearly a century and a half. We have seen how their rivals, after undermining the Mughal power, proceeded to tear each other to pieces, finally falling out among themselves and splitting into contending factions. The stage of north India was thus left to such untutored bodies as the Sikhs and the Jats and any stray Persian and Afghan adventurers who attached themselves to the emperor at Delhi. What of the rest of India? Before the final collapse of the fifties the rest of northern India had become a number of virtually independent states. The Nawabs of Oudh, with the title of Wazir of the Empire, controlled what is now the core of the state of Uttar Pradesh. The three provinces of Bengal, Behar, and Orissa, the most productive part of India, were ruled with Mughal forms by a military adventurer, Alivardi Khan. In the center and west of India, from Orissa to Poona, the Marathas held sway. To the south a confused power struggle was taking place. The Mughal viceroy of the Deccan, the Nizam-ul-Mulk or Regulator of the Kingdom, had been a *de facto* independent ruler since 1724. His dominions formed a Mughal empire in little. With the capital at Hyderabad, it extended down the east coast from the borders of Orissa to the neighborhood of Tanjore. The northern portion of this coastline, as far south as Masulipatam, was called the northern Sarkars or districts; the southern portion was the coastal and fertile plain of the Carnatic where much fine weaving was done. It was also known as the coast of Coromandel, or the country of the Cholas, a Hindu dynasty which had disappeared nearly five hundred years before. To the northwest it approached Poona at Aurangabad and to the south its frontier ran along the river Tungabhadra, a tributary of the great Kistna. South of this river lay the Hindu kingdom of Mysore, destined to grow in strength under the direction of a Muslim adventurer, Haidar Ali. The tropical and hilly Malabar Coast on the west was divided between a number of Hindu principalities, as were the extreme south and southern shores of India. There was an uneasy balance among these powers. The only one with anything like a national dynamic was the Marathas, but they, as we have seen, were deeply committed in the north. Hyderabad was a dynastic state served by mercenaries in the interest of a minority (the Muslims and Mughal aristocracy). As in all such states, personality was a dominant factor in its vigor. For this reason the life of the aged Nizam was narrowly scrutinized and there was a general waiting on events which might follow his demise. Mysore was a state of the local people, but it had no serious popular backing and what vigor it displayed was due to its generals and rulers. The other states were mere satellites and opportunists.

In consequence of these conditions there was an air of expectancy in south India by 1740. The north could no longer control events in the south; the balance of power was known to be precarious, and there was no obvious empire-builder in sight. Apart from the plans of the rulers themselves, the country was filled with divisions and tensions. There was the Hindu-Muslim tension derived from Aurangzeb's attempt to control the south in the Muslim interest. There was the Maratha threat of domination, which cut across the former division because the southern Hindus disliked Maratha rule as much as Muslim. And there were the differences between the southern Hindus themselves, divided into the four Dravidian races of Tamils in the southeast, Telugus to the north and east, Kannadas in the center, and Malayalis along the west coast.

It was these conditions which made European intervention in the affairs of India possible and even welcome to some Indians themselves. But they did not in themselves cause that intervention. For this we must look to factors outside India altogether. It was the conjunction of causes making for conflict between Europeans in India with the fluid local situation which produced first European intervention and then European empire. For these causes we must look to the position of the European trading companies in India and the relations of their parent states in Europe. The English East India Company, as we have seen, had been trading for nearly a century and a half, and had been established at Madras since 1640. The factory or warehouse in an Indian city had developed into a fortified factory on a piece of leased land. The Company's western headquarters had been transferred from Surat to its own more defensible, though very unhealthy, island of Bombay. Calcutta had been founded in 1691, at the end of Child's war, in a marsh leased by the Mughals in some contempt. The fortified factory was called Fort William after William III. In Madras the factory was fortified from the first because the land was

leased from a Hindu chief. In the more religious period of its foundation, it received the name of Fort St. George, and its dependency near
Cuddalore that of Fort St. David. Around the settlements, partly on account of the commercial opportunities provided, and partly for security
as conditions grew more unsettled outside, grew Indian cities. In Madras
there was a Blacktown across the river from the Whitetown; in Calcutta
the Indian city stretched to the north of the fort while the garden-houses of
the merchants lined the river to the south. There are no very reliable figures among many estimates, but there were perhaps three hundred thousand Indians on the Company's territory in Madras, two hundred thousand in Calcutta, and seventy thousand in Bombay. The Company's
trade had steadily grown with indigo, saltpeter, cottons, and silk and
spices as the chief items. There was an extensive re-export trade in cotton
goods to Europe, and in addition there was a flourishing trade with
China. Moreover a considerable vested interest in the East had grown
up in England, not only on the part of the Company itself, but in shipping
needed for transport and the stores required by the settlements. In 1740
imports from India were valued at £1,795,000 or about $5,385,000 at
the present rate of exchange, which was more than 10 per cent of the
revenue of Great Britain at the time.

After the British came the Dutch. They had their Indian headquarters
at Negapatam, south of Madras, a factory at Chinsura in Bengal, and
stations in Malabar. But they were still subordinate to Batavia in Java,
and their activities were subsidiary to the main Dutch enterprise in the
East Indies. The Dutch company itself at this time was beginning to sink
under the weight of its overhead costs, and was in no position to rival the
English company. The Danes had stations at Tranquebar in the south,
where the first Protestant missionary activity was carried on, and at
Serampore in Bengal, but their scale of operations was small. The only
serious rivals of the English were the French. Louis XIV's minister Colbert founded the Compagnie des Indes Orientales in 1664 and in 1674
Pondicherry, south of Madras, was founded. The company languished
until it was reorganized in 1723. In the twelve years before 1740 the
value of its trade increased ten times; in that year, though still no more
than half that of the English company, it stood at the then substantial
total of £880,000 or $2,640,000. The company had posts at Chander-
nagore in Bengal, Masulipatam on the Nizam's coast, and on the Malabar
Coast. In addition it possessed in Mauritius and Réunion (then the Iles de
France and de Bourbon) posts near Madagascar which, though distant
from India, were convenient ports of call and places where military measures could be prepared unobserved. While the French company did not

Kabul
AFGHANISTAN
Peshawar
KASHMIR

P U N J A B
SIKH
Kangra
Lahore
Multan
BAHAWALPUR
KUMAUN

T I B E T

BHUTAN

S I N D
RAJPUT
Jodhpur
MUGHAL
Delhi
ROHILKHAND
Agra
Lucknow
Jaipur
OUDH
Gwalior
Allahabad
Buxar
Patna
Banares
BEHAR
Udanala

ASS

CUTCH

GUJARAT
Baroda
MALWA
BHOPAL
M A R A T H A
Plassey
Dacca
BENGAL
Chandernagore
Chinsura
Calcutta

Surat
KHANDESH
T E R R I T O R Y
Nagpur
B E R A R
Sambalpur
ORISSA
NORTHERN CIRCARS

Aurangabad
Bombay
Poona

KONKAN
Bijapur
N I Z A M
Hyderabad

Goa
Masulipatam

BAY OF BENGAL

MYSORE
C A R N A T I C
Mangalore
Mysore
Seringapatam
Arcot
Madras
Pondicherry
Ft. St. David

TRAVANCORE
Trichinopoly

CEYLON

INDIA
about 1765

0   100   200   300   400
Scale of Miles

Territory under
British Control

Hindu   Territory

Muhammadan ''

match the English in resources, it was well placed and widely spread. To the eyes of each side the other presented a substantial prize and a considerable danger. That is why the neutrality observed by the companies during the Anglo-French wars down to 1714 did not survive the next outbreak. Before 1725 the French position in India was negligible. By 1740 it was strong enough to alarm the English and excite French hopes of ousting them.

The actual clash of the two companies in India was the result of the conflict of their governments in Europe. Britain and France were keen commercial rivals. In addition the British, with their memories of Louis XIV, feared a fresh French bid for European supremacy. French resources were far greater than those of Britain, and Holland, which had borne the brunt of Louis XIV's attempt at supremacy, was now much weaker. Therefore, in the interests of the then paramount diplomatic doctrine of the balance of power, the British found themselves on the opposite side to France in every eighteenth-century war. The French, on their side, saw in the British the chief obstacle to world as well as continental power and took the initiative on their own, for instance in joining the United States in the War of Independence.

In 1740 the young Frederick the Great of Prussia seized the rich Austrian province of Silesia. The war of the Austrian Succession thus started dragged on until 1748, for Austria reacted with unexpected vigor. France supported Prussia against Austria and in 1742 Britain, already at war with Spain (the War of Jenkin's Ear), found herself at war with France. The Companies themselves had no arms, and the merchants would have preferred a peaceful coexistence. But the stakes were now too large and neither could control its government's ships and troops. In 1746 a French fleet under La Bourdonnais got the better of the British and there followed the capture of Madras on September 21. Quarrels prevented the capture of Fort St. David. In 1748 the British fleet returned and besieged Pondicherry unsuccessfully. The next year came the news of the Treaty of Aixla-Chapelle by which Madras was restored to the British in return for Cape Breton Island off the mouth of the St. Lawrence. If the Indian government had been vigorous, or the European merchants intent on their trade, the matter might have ended there for another generation. But neither was the case. Another conjunction of events during the next ten years converted European intervention in Indian affairs from, as it were, an eruption of the outer skin into a deep-seated internal malady.

It so happened that the control of the Nizam in the Carnatic relaxed just when it should have been tightened up. The Nizam ruled this province by a deputy governor known to the English as a nawab.[1] In 1740 the Mughal power was shaken by a Maratha invasion and succession disputes. In 1743 the Nizam installed a new governor, Anwar-ad-din, but the partisans of the old family remained, hoping for a change of fortune. In 1748 the Nizam himself died and there was rivalry between his sons for the succession. The second element in the conjunction was the character of the French governor Dupleix. He towered above his French mercantile contemporaries as much as Warren Hastings later overshadowed his colleagues. Dupleix was a merchant in the Company's employ who was promoted in 1742 from Chandernagore to Pondicherry. His commercial talents were already obvious but his political gifts were unknown. Dupleix was an admirable manager. But to this quality he added an imagination which could see far ahead of the immediate situation and a fertile resource in matching means to ends. He could inspire devotion and enthusiasm, as the memoirs of his *dubash* or secretary Pillai testify. His greatest gift was the power of penetrating beneath the surface appearance of affairs to the true realities of power. He was one of the select few who can detect changes of power potential at the time they are actually occurring. With these gifts he had the handicap of a too sanguine temperament and an oversensitive sense of dignity which led to quarrels with his colleagues.

It was Dupleix who dominated the second phase of the Anglo-French struggle. He determined to use his new-found force to secure an Indian power favorable to himself, who would then oust the English. In 1749, in the uncertainty after the Nizam's death he supported a rival claimant for the Carnatic governorship, Chanda Sahib. The ease with which Anwar-ad-din was overthrown with French help made clear the great advantage conferred by European arms and methods of warfare. The policy of using Indian alliances to ruin the English Company led Dupleix through a maze of diplomatic vicissitude until he found himself supporting the Nizam himself and enjoying the Mughal title of ruler of India south of the Kistna. Backing a successful candidate for the Carnatic led to backing a candidate for the nizamate at Hyderabad. Having installed Salabat Jang as Nizam in 1751, Dupleix found himself forced to proceed a step further. Salabat Jang would almost certainly lose his throne if French help were withdrawn. Dupleix was thus forced to keep an agent there with a French force. Thus the policy of Indian alliances grew into the policy of the Indian-sponsored state. For nearly seven years Dupleix's lieutenant, the Marquis de Bussy, maintained the Nizam's throne and French influence at Hyderabad through a whirl of conflict and intrigue, and it was only his recall to take part in the next Anglo-French war which brought the experiment to an end.

It is worth while looking at these measures a little closer, for these were the means by which Europeans gained so firm a foothold that they could not be afterward ejected. The policy of alliance with Indian powers was the device of acting as auxiliary to an Indian prince in his own concerns in return for measures on his part to ruin English trade. A friendly nawab of the Carnatic was desired for this reason, and a friendly nizam, because he was the overlord of the Carnatic. The idea of a sponsored Indian state went further. The principle was to sustain the ruler and influence his policy by providing sufficient force to maintain him against internal rivals and external foes. Its success required great diplomatic skill and restraint. Rulers ready to take such help were likely to be less rather than more vigorous than their rivals. Help once given was therefore likely to become permanent. It is difficult to see how in time the state could avoid falling into foreign hands unless the foreigner were ejected altogether. In this first instance the matter was not put to the test. Bussy conducted himself with great tact and skill and on his recall he left the state stronger than he found it. In addition, the case had few complications. There was little trade in Hyderabad and so there were no French merchants to make difficulties. The French mission to Hyderabad was political, not economic. When the experiment was repeated elsewhere this was one of the factors which contributed to its breakdown. After skilled leadership the next requirement was an adequate force for the purpose. This was supplied by a small number of French troops with a larger number of Indians officered by Europeans and trained in the European manner. It was the Anglo-French struggle which produced the "sepoy" [2] and it was Bussy who showed most clearly what could be done with them.

There remains the question of the superiority of European arms, on which the whole concept of allied and sponsored states rested. The first ingredient was the fact of discipline and *esprit de corps*. Men were drilled as a group; they were given uniforms which increased their sense of importance; they were given regular pay which ensured their loyalty. None of these things was common in India and regular discipline was unknown. The consequence was that these men acquired an *esprit de corps* quite unlike that of any other troops in India. The typical Indian soldier of the day was at best a mercenary; he was either the follower of some chief on whom he depended for employment or he was an adventurer with his own horse and arms who hired himself to one chief or another. Such people were apt to think more of their horses than their masters, since horses formed their working capital. The pay of all soldiers was usually in arrears. Loyalty was a calculated thing conditioned by the prospects of back pay and the fortunes of the patron of the moment. In addition to discipline there were tactics and arms. The habit of moving in concert gave the new troops a confidence which the old ones never possessed; the technique of firing volleys gave to a given number of shots a fire power unknown to the other side. The final advantage of the new methods was the ability to fire faster than the other side. The muskets could now be loaded in time for a second volley before cavalry could reach a line of infantry, and field artillery could do the same. This removed the terror of the cavalry charge, which had come down from the days of Timur and Genghis Khan. Few bodies of cavalry would stand two volleys before closing and no undisciplined ones could. In addition the infantry had bayonets which did not impede their firing, so that they were pikemen and musketeers in one. Their chief enemy was rain, which might dampen the gunpowder required for firing.

Perhaps to these technical advantages we might add one more. The European officers were professionals in a sense that few Indian officers were. They had a security of service and a national sentiment which made them loyal; their business in life was to obey orders and win victory, rather than make a name by serving now one chief and then another, and changing sides at convenience. All these circumstances added up to a force, which, compared with the current Indian ones, was like a steel knife compared with an ornamented silver one, or a machine gun compared with a rifle.

Dupleix was not alone in using the device of the allied state, but he was the man who showed its possibilities. For all his skill, however, it did not bring him the success he hoped for. Muhammad Ali, the successor of the Nawab defeated in 1749, retained Trichinopoly, where the English necessarily supported him. The tables were turned by the youthful Robert Clive, who seized and held Arcot for fifty days with 210 men. This diversion enabled help to be procured and led to a reversal of fortune by which the French with their Nawab were compelled to surrender. Dupleix was recalled and it seemed that the idea of Indian alliances had failed. Only Bussy was left in the sponsored state of Hyderabad. In 1756 the Seven Years' War broke out in Europe in which Austria attempted to turn the tables and recover Silesia. Again France and Britain were on different sides and again armaments were sent to India. This time the balance tilted decisively in favor of Britain. At Wandiwash in 1760 the French were defeated and Lally taken prisoner; in 1761 Pondicherry fell after an agonizing siege.

This was the end of the French contention for empire in India, though their influence long remained both in the person of adventurers at Indian courts and as a menace to be guarded against. It will be convenient to summarize their later history here. Many French officers preferred service with Indian princes to captivity with the British. Many after the wars preferred Indian service to return to France. These men formed the nucleus of the French who served Indian princes for the next half century, training disciplined forces and alarming the British. The most distinguished was General de Boigne, who trained the army with which Madhu Rao Sindia gained control of Delhi and northern India in the latter years of the century. In the south the French did not lose hope, but they never had another chance. Pondicherry was an open town and was easily occupied in 1778 when France joined the United States in the War of Independence. A French fleet went out and Bussy landed a force in 1783, but the effort ended with the Peace of Versailles. Thereafter France continued to be a distant menace. Fear of a revival of French influence in the south, after Napoleon's descent on Egypt, egged on the British to attack Tipu Sultan. After Napoleon's pact with the Russian Alexander at Tilsit there was much fear of French action from the northwest. The last Frenchmen in India were ex-Napoleonic officers like Allard and Court who helped to build up the Sikh army of Ranjit Singh.

CHAPTER XVII

Bengal

The Anglo-French struggle in south India was a kind of dress rehearsal for European intervention in Bengal. The incentives for action were there; the weakness of potential opposition, and the divisions which encouraged action were apparent. The methods of interference were tried out and developed. But European action in the South of India was indecisive because the south was both physically and economically separated from the north. The north of India was the reservoir of Indian wealth and manpower which was the vital part of the country. European action in Bengal was therefore the decisive phase of intervention. But for their experience at Madras the British action in Bengal might have taken quite a different form. Once launched upon action they had their southern experience to draw upon in dealing with Indian states. Why should not Clive do in Bengal what Bussy had done in Hyderabad?

Before going further we should notice certain broad differences between the situations in the north and south, which help to explain the different results which followed. In Bengal other Europeans had little influence. While Calcutta was the chief British station in India, Dutch Chinsura and French Chandernagar were both subordinate stations of their respective companies. Both were on the Hughli and helpless so long as the English company controlled the river. The Danish settlement at Serampore was too small to count. The East India Company dealt directly with the local power. There was, in fact, no European power to restrain its actions for fear of the consequences. A second difference lay in the power and personalities of the respective princes. Both areas were fragments of the Mughal empire, ruled by governors who had established themselves as hereditary princes. Both were imposing in size and enjoyed large resources. The ruler of Bengal governed Behar, higher up the Ganges Valley, as well, while the Nizam controlled the coastal plain of east India from Orissa to Tanjore. But the Nizams belonged to one of the leading official families of India, whose founder had come to India from Central Asia in the time of Aurangzeb. They had generations of experience of war and diplomacy and commanded forces that were formidable according to the standards of the day. Nizam Ali, who ruled from 1762 to 1802, was an able man who preserved his state intact against Marathas, Mysoreans, and the British. Even the subordinate Carnatic province survived until 1801.

In Bengal, on the other hand, the ruling family was of recent origin. Alivardi Khan was an adventurer who seized power in 1740. He and his family were "new men" who knew more about getting power than keeping it. His successors were feeble men until it was too late to retrieve the situation. A further difference lay in the wealth of the respective areas. Bengal on account both of the fertility of its soil and the industry of its inhabitants was the richest province in India. Apart from its plentiful rice crops it produced cotton, silk, and saltpeter in abundance. Its river system made transport easy and so facilitated commerce. Bengal annually paid an imperial levy of 53 lacs of rupees (about a million and a half dollars at the then existing rate of exchange) without seriously feeling the drain. In other words Bengal was a much bigger financial prize than the Carnatic. This brings us to the last important difference. In Bengal the merchants were a more numerous and important body than in Madras. This means that the power of private vested interest was stronger, and that they would be more difficult to control than in the south. When the merchants of Madras got out of hand they became creditors of the Nawab of the Carnatic; when the merchants of Bengal got out of hand they became direct exploiters of the people.

In the year 1756 Bengal had enjoyed a long period of internal peace. The chief calamity had been persistent Maratha invasions from Berar in central India. These had been repelled after years of fighting with the loss of Orissa. Calcutta bore the mark of this period in the Maratha ditch (now the Circular Road) which was begun in one of the scares of Maratha attack. So far Bengal and Behar had escaped the desolation which had overtaken upper India and the Deccan. The English company had been trading peacefully for more than fifty years and was proud of the commercial privileges obtained from the Mughal court by an embassy in 1717. The company enjoyed free trade in Bengal subject to an annual payment of Rs 3000. Settlement in the interior was allowed, and the company's servants could trade on their own account subject to the payment of the same dues as Indian merchants. The running disputes with the Nawab's government were part of the commercial game. The Bengal government itself seemed to be solidly based and the country as a whole was prosperous. But behind this façade of wealth and power the discerning eye could perceive much unrest. The imperial power was collapsing in Delhi, and this meant that Bengal was independent as well as autonomous and would have to fend for herself in a chaotic political world. Within Bengal itself there were serious tensions. The nawab was respected but he was also old. The chosen successor was a youth of barely twenty without experience and surrounded by jealousy within his family. In addition, the Hindu officers of the government chafed under Muslim control and were not likely to accept the new ruler as easily as Alivardi. In this they were supported by the Hindu banking house of Seth, which in effect financed government operations. There was therefore, in Bengal, in spite of its outward calm, an anxious waiting on events and an expectation of changes to come, as there had been in Hyderabad before the death of Nizam-ul-Mulk.

Alivardi Khan died in April 1756. His grandson Siraj was headstrong but fearful and vacillating. He first marched against his cousin and rival and then suddenly turned to attack the English company's settlements. For some time before Alivardi's death both English and French companies had begun to fortify their settlements (as distinct from their factories) in anticipation of war with each other (which in fact broke out in Europe in 1756). The French desisted on Alivardi's orders, but the English prevaricated. It was this which caused Siraj's sudden decision. Kasim-Bazar was seized and Warren Hastings taken prisoner and Calcutta then attacked. The slightness of its fortification was soon exposed. In four days resistance was overcome, the governor and the commandant having previously fled to the ships in the Hughli and left the garrison to its fate. There then followed the incident of the Black Hole. Little regarded at the time, this was later worked up into a major issue by imperialist historians. The interested reader is referred to a note at the end of the chapter.

Here was a head-on collision between a European company and an Indian prince. Fortunately for the British an armament had recently arrived in Madras in preparation for the expected French war, and an expedition was at that moment being planned against Bussy in Hyderabad. There were ships and there were men and there was also Robert Clive. By another chance Clive was given the command because the senior royal officer had scruples about a diversion to Bengal. The first steps were clear enough. Admiral Watson and Clive sailed with nine hundred Europeans and fifteen hundred Indians in October. Calcutta was recovered in January 1757 and the Nawab made peace in February. The company's privileges were renewed with permission to fortify Calcutta and coin money.

So far the matter was a local quarrel settled in the usual way, though on a larger scale than usual. But Clive, who took over the government of Calcutta from the discredited Drake, soon found that he could not rest there. Seraja feared that the Afghans, just arrived in Delhi, might march to Bengal. The peace treaty therefore included an alliance. For fear of the Afghans, Siraj sacrificed the French. Clive was able to seize their settlement of Chandernagar in March. He thus found himself repeating the French device in south India of alliances with country powers to defeat a European rival. The difference was that while Dupleix always just missed the mark Clive was completely successful. From alliance with a country power to sponsoring an Indian state as Bussy had done was but a step, and Clive found himself speedily pushed by circumstances. There was at this time no thought of annexation and conquest; these were the afterknowledge of imperialist writers wishing to make Clive appear more aggressive than he really was. What then did he want? He wished to safeguard the company's interest, which meant arranging for a friendly government in Bengal and Behar. He was also interested in money. The two ran together with consequences which will be noted shortly.

The situation in the spring of 1757 was highly unstable. Siraj, though at peace with the company and nominally its ally, had lost all credit and was the victim of active intrigue for replacement. The conspirators looked to Calcutta as the decisive factor in any revolution, and so Clive found himself not in the position of arranging a revolution himself but of choosing between rival promoters with competing offers. At the same time his own position was precarious because the French were still in strength in the Deccan, and Admiral Watson's ships and his own troops might at any time be withdrawn to meet a new French expedition. In these conditions the decision to intervene was natural, and it was no doubt encouraged by the belief that one hundred and twenty million dollars lay in the treasury at Murshidabad. The decision involved the support of the elderly brother-in-law of Alivardi, Mir Jafar Khan, one of Siraj's principal generals, and incidentally the deception of a Sikh banker who tried at the last moment to raise the terms of his treachery by threatening to betray the plot. The matter came to an issue at the cannonade of Plassey on June 26 when Mir Jafar held aloof until the issue was decided and Siraj fled in panic before any serious fighting had occurred.

Clive installed Mir Jafar as the governor of Bengal on June 28. From this moment private financial greed and public policy so intertwined themselves as to commit the British irrevocably to rule in India and to compass the ruin of Bengal. There was an immediate transition from the idea of an allied to that of a sponsored state, to be followed after years of maladministration and fighting by the decision to rule directly. It is important to notice that the steps were not planned or foreseen; they were taken one by one as circumstances seemed to dictate, following the pattern of French action in the south. They were due as much to the private shortcomings of the Company's servants as to their public acumen or their master's wisdom. Let us now follow each thread in turn. On the political side, Clive soon found that Mir Jafar required continuous support if he were to survive. The Murshidabad treasure turned out to amount to no more than four and one-half million dollars, which left Mir Jafar embarrassed to meet his commitments to the Company, let alone consolidate his rule. Efforts to raise more money embroiled him with his Hindu deputies and led to general discontent. Clive acted with energy. He put down revolts, kept Mir Jafar on terms with his deputy at Patna, and repulsed an invasion by the heir to the Mughal throne, the later Shah Alam. He also destroyed a Dutch expedition which hoped to take advantage of the Nawab's restiveness at his dependence. Clive left Calcutta in January 1760, having apparently more than restored the Company's position and successfully launched a sponsored Indian state.

From this moment the results of the financial and commercial settlements with Mir Jafar became visible. Their effect was to ruin the experiment of a sponsored Indian state, destroy the prosperity of Bengal, and bring the Company itself near to bankruptcy. This latter development brought the intervention of Parliament and the British government, so eventually leading the way to the British-Indian *raj* of the nineteenth century. The agreement with Mir Jafar stipulated that he should confirm the Company's privileges, pay three million dollars as compensation for the loss of Calcutta, one and one-half more millions to its European inhabitants, and $810,000 to the Indians and Armenians. But that was not all. A private agreement (unknown to the Company) gave $450,000 to the select committee of six (the directors of foreign policy in the Calcutta Council). The members of council received between $150,000 and $240,000 each. Clive himself received $700,000 in cash and in addition a *jagir* or estate worth about $90,000 a year on the plea that the title procured for him by Mir Jafar from the Delhi court required an estate to maintain it.[1] In addition to all this it was understood that the private and personal trade of the British merchants at Calcutta should be duty-free like the Company's goods. Private trade had long been a recognized perquisite of the East India Company's servant. Indeed he was expected to carry it on because he was only paid a nominal salary by the company. The internal trade of India and the overseas or "country" trade to Asia were considered to be his legitimate field, the trade with Europe being reserved for the company. Hitherto the British merchants in their private capacity had traded within Bengal on the same terms as Indian merchants, paying the same tolls and being subject to the same regulations. Now their goods were to go duty-free through the numerous *chaukies* or toll posts, armed with *dastaks* or passes like the Company's goods.

The combined effect of Clive's victory, of Mir Jafar's presents, and of free trade for British merchants was intoxicating on these peppery and contentious, but hitherto distinctly humdrum and unimaginative, Company's servants. In the past their horizons had been limited by the military power of the Nawab, by the necessity of competing with Indian merchants on equal terms, and by a belief that wealth could only come from normal trading. Now all three restraints were removed at once. They were made free of the wealthiest province of India, and it seemed that they had only to stretch out their hands to make fortunes and return to England. It is hardly surprising that this situation turned their heads and that they threw caution to the winds. The idea of an Indian state sponsored by the East India Company was wrecked by the folly and greed of the Company's own servants.

The intoxication of the Company's servants by their new-found power and the dazzling prospect of wealth was balanced by no external restraints. In the south the French had always to remember the British, to whom their allies would have turned if they took liberties with them. In Bengal both French and Dutch had been eliminated. In the south the princes were for the most part men of character, whereas in Bengal they were mostly feeble. In the south the Carnatic chiefs were backed by the powerful Nizam, and behind him were the Marathas; in the north Bengal was adjacent to the already defeated Oudh, beyond which the imperial power had dissolved among contending chiefs. The last restraining factor was removed by the departure of Clive, who, while largely responsible for opening the floodgates of corruption, did not permit others to go beyond certain limits.

The five years after Clive's departure may rightly be described as the period of open and unashamed plunder, which took twenty years of effort, both in Britain and on the spot, to correct. Present-taking spread throughout the Company's service. Private trade to the neglect of both Company business and the public service was the main concern. Just before Clive's return there were six abortive attempts to assemble a principal court of justice on account of the negligence of members. On his return he found "a youth of three years' standing" (about eighteen years old) "in charge of the Secretary's department . . . and a Writer [junior officer] held the post of Paymaster to the Army, at a period when near twenty lacks [two millions] of rupees had been deposited for months together in his hands." Residencies, or posts at Indian courts, were bought and sold like stocks and shares. Rennell, the first surveyor general of Bengal, reported in 1762 that in Madras the Company's servants lived if single at $16,000 and if married at $27,000 a year. The scale of values is indicated by his report in 1764 on his appointment to Bengal. He had an allowance of $2,700 and perquisites of $3,000 a year. "I can enjoy my Friends, my Bottle and all the Necessaries of Life for $1,200—Besides when I get acquainted with the Trade of this part of India I shall make much greater advantages, as I shall always be able to command a Capital." The beneficiaries of this system were the Company's servants and their Indian agents. A factor was known to make a fortune, spend it in England, make a second and lose it, and return for a third. The fortunes of many Indian entrepreneurs in Calcutta arose from the profits of their deals on behalf of Europeans. The losers were the merchants and people of Bengal and the Company. The merchants (unattached to the Company) were ruined by unfair competition of men exempt from duty and part of the government. The people, whether weavers or agriculturalists, were squeezed both by their Indian rulers and the agents of the Europeans, the one to make up for their payments to the Europeans and the other to swell their patrons' profits in the great rush to get rich. The Company suffered because its interests were subordinate to the private ambitions of its own servants, and the exhaustion of the countryside reduced the value of the "investment" for export to India.

We can now trace the steps in the collapse of Clive's sponsored Bengal state. Within a year of Clive's departure Mir Jafar was deposed in favor of Mir Kasim, who it was thought was more businesslike and more pliable. Mir Kasim gave presents to the council worth $600,000. He proved to be much abler than his predecessor and made a real attempt to reform the administration. The result was a head-on clash. The governor agreed that European merchants should pay an ad valorem duty of 9 per cent as against the Indian merchants' 40 per cent. At this the Calcutta Council overruled the governor, fixing the duty at 2.5 per cent. Mir Kasim then abolished all dues and the result was war. He was defeated in four pitched battles, executed his commander, his Indian bankers, and English prisoners in a frenzy of resentment and fear, and fled up-country. The next year he returned with the emperor Shah Alam and the Nawab of Oudh, but was defeated at the decisive battle of Baksar. Mir Jafar was restored as Nawab at the price of $1,300,000 to the army and navy. His successor, two years later, paid $420,000 to nine members of council.

The battle of Baksar marks the real end of the sponsored state. The

British had now made themselves the rulers of Bengal and Behar despite the Nawab; at the same time they had by their exactions and irregularities made clear their incompetence to rule. Something had clearly to be done if the Company's venture in Bengal was not to end in bankruptcy and anarchy. The behavior of the nabobs, or merchants who had returned since Plassey with fortunes of uncertain origin, had already caused disgust in English society. The news of the breach with Mir Kasim caused real alarm, for war is the surest road to bankruptcy for a commercial concern. Before the news of Baksar was known it was determined to send Clive back to Bengal to restore discipline in the Company and prosperity to Bengal. He sailed in June 1764 and arrived in Calcutta after an unusually long voyage on May 3, 1765. He intended to restore, but in fact carried out a new revolution.

From the moment when he seized Arcot in 1752 to his final return in 1767 Clive was a dominant figure in British-Indian affairs. He was, more than anyone else, responsible for the French defeat in the south, for the British supremacy in Bengal, for the period of license, and for beginning the restoration of discipline which followed. He stamped his character indelibly on the history of these years. He has been exalted as an imperialist hero, almost as a British-Indian solar myth, and denounced as a dangerous adventurer. The truth lies somewhere between the two. There is no doubt of his dynamic personality, which burst upon the world at Arcot, dominated the Bengal of Plassey, and cowed the mutinous officers and merchants of the Calcutta of 1765. In military affairs he was a guerrilla leader of genius, but never had an opportunity of showing whether he possessed gifts of larger strategy. In politics he possessed piercing insight, which divined the weakness of Siraj, saw clearly through the shifting forces of Bengal politics, and comprehended the reality of north Indian power politics in 1765. He had also the rare quality of restraint in victory which drew him back from north Indian empire in 1765 after proposing a march to Delhi some years before. With this impressive array of talents there went great faults. There was a certain recklessness in achieving his ends which led him both into conspiracy against Siraj and to chicanery in the episode of Amin Chand, the banker. His personal ambition prevailed over public policy. To build up his fortune for an English public career he started the lavish present-taking which sparked off the period of plunder in Bengal. Later in England itself the desire to retain his income of $90,000 a year from his *jagir* or estate led him into devious courses and unworthy compromises. He was vehement and superlative in all that he did; he lacked the sense of balance, the larger views, and the integrity which go to make the higher statesmanship. His virtues and his faults both had great consequences; both good and evil flowed from him. On the whole he ranks as the Conquistador of British India rather than a major Anglo-Indian statesman.

The Black Hole

The incident of the Black Hole was little regarded at the time and for many years after; the monument erected to commemorate it was neglected and eventually removed. We owe its later prominence to the efforts of the school of imperialist historians who treated it as a major atrocity. The incident has been given only passing mention in the text to accord with its significance at the time.

The story was started by J. Z. Holwell, the defender of Calcutta and himself a victim. His final version was that 146 prisoners were confined on a tropical June night in a room 18 feet by 14 feet, 10 inches (267 square feet), from which 23 emerged alive the next morning. The Black Hole was the current term for the local "lockup" in which European offenders were confined. Holwell has been shown to have been unscrupulous and unreliable, and this led to the suggestion (by J. H. Little in 1915) that he invented the whole incident. This raised two difficulties. How could the people who were known to have remained in Calcutta be otherwise accounted for, and how were the survivors persuaded to stick to the same story? By this time the theory of deliberate cruelty had been changed to one of negligence; the numbers involved and the details were now both subjected to doubt.

A new analysis of the evidence for the incident has recently been made to which the still interested reader is referred. It is by Brijen K. Gupta in the *Journal of Asian Studies,* XIX, no. 1 (November 1959), 53–63. His discussion is the most convincing the author has seen so far. His conclusion is that an incident occurred, but that the probable number of those who entered was 64 and of survivors 21.

CHAPTER XVIII

The Company Bahadur

The formation of the British Indian state, popularly known as the Company Bahadur, the valiant or exalted Company, may be said to have commenced with Clive's second governorship. Its main outlines were completed by the end of Cornwallis' tenure of power in 1793. This is not the place to trace in detail the clash of personality, the conflict of policies, and the colorful episodes which make this period the most lively of the whole Anglo-Indian era. Instead we shall try to draw out the main features of a state which seemed destined at one time to form a constituent unit of an Indian states system on the analogy of the European Concert of Powers, glancing in conclusion at some of the creative personalities of the period.

The two years of Clive's return saw a beginning of nearly every item of the new state. By his treaty with the emperor he delimited its frontiers and began the transfer of authority, by his internal measures he began the restoration of discipline and the organization of a separate administration, while the parliamentary enquiry which followed soon after began the process of enforcing responsibility for their acts upon the governors. It is true that after his departure the dismayed merchants closed their ranks and returned to exploitation. But its forms were more devious and their tone more subdued; they never recovered the boisterous buccaneering tones of the early sixties. It will now be profitable to pursue each thread of construction in turn.

The first theme is that of transfer of authority from Mughal and Nawab to the British. Until 1765 the Company had no sovereign status at all. The government was carried on by a governor acting formally under the emperor's authority. The Company was merely a trading organization. Its army was a private army which set up or pulled down nawabs according to its whim. The Company was like an overpowerful feudal baron of the Middle Ages, with a taste for kingmaking, a weakness for exploitation, and a knack of causing desolation. In 1765 Clive seized the opportunity of the defeat of the emperor Shah Alam to legalize the Company's position in Bengal. The Company was formally given the *diwani* of Bengal, or the authority, under the emperor, to collect the revenue. The other branch of Mughal government, the *nizamat* or police and judicial power, was left with the Nawab of Bengal. Since, however, the Company possessed the only effective army in Bengal, it practically controlled the whole administration, with imperial authority behind it. Clive left the judicial administration in the hands of the Nawab's officers. The revenue administration he confided to a deputy Nawab, who also controlled the judiciary as the Nawab of Bengal's deputy. This system was known as Clive's Double Government; a better name for it would perhaps have been the Divided Government. It was clumsy and it left the door wide open to abuses. There was too much power with too little responsibility. But it was a useful first step. The next step was taken by Warren Hastings in 1772 when the Company "stood forth as Dewan." Henceforward it collected the revenue through its own agents and forgot about the annual tribute due to the emperor. He reorganized the whole system of judicial courts, though he did not displace the phantom Nawabs from their nominal control. This step was taken by Cornwallis, from whose time British India virtually existed in its own right. But Mughal authority was never formally repudiated. When the British became the protectors of the now aged and blind Shah Alam in 1803 they accorded him imperial status, but no treaty was made defining the position on either side. He continued to be addressed as a superior and to be disregarded in practical affairs. One by one the honorifics of sovereignty were denied to his successors, but the position was never clarified, so that it was possible for him to claim during the Mutiny that he was reasserting his position against rebellious vassals. If the British had openly acted as his agents their position in the eyes of Indians in general might have been much stronger. On the other hand they did not fail to assert their own authority. In 1813 Parliament declared its sovereignty over the Company's dominions and in 1833 that the Company's Indian territories were British possessions.

The next feature of the Company state was direct administration by its own officials. When the Company took control in 1765 the whole government apart from the Calcutta Council was in Indian hands. The deputy Nawab had his judicial and revenue subordinates right down to the village level. Thirty years later all the higher posts were in British hands. This came about as the result of a desire to know the facts of revenue at first hand and a steady drive to control the Company's servants which will be described later. The Indian officials, from the deputy Nawab downward, were subject to pressure from the superintending British merchants. To find money for presents and favors they passed on the pressure down the line to the villages so that the Bengal cornucopia was being steadily squeezed to emptiness. The substitution of Company-controlled British officers was an attempted remedy for this. In 1769 the first attempt was made with the appointment of supervisors of the revenue, but they accomplished little. The first major step was taken by Warren Hastings in 1772 when he took over the revenue administration or "stood forth as Dewan." British collectors were then appointed to a number of districts, which became twenty-three in the time of Cornwallis. The collector's business was to collect revenue, mainly land tax, and he worked under a board of revenue. The collector came to represent government in his district, and has remained a powerful figure ever since. Cornwallis (1786–93) completed this work when he took over from the Nawab the whole judicial in addition to the revenue administration. He now appointed British judges for all courts, being assisted where necessary by learned Hindu and Muslim assessors. All these officials were known as covenanted servants because they had signed covenants with the Company on entering its service. There were thus separate revenue and judicial departments, both monopolized by British officials. In the light of what has already been said about the British merchants it might be thought that such arrangements would lead to wholesale corruption. In fact it was part of the drive against corruption. Cornwallis believed (and he turned out to be right) that he had the cure for corruption among the Company's servants.[1] He had no cure for the corresponding class of Indian officials and saw no prospect of it. He therefore excluded them from all offices worth more than fifteen hundred dollars a year. For the forty years from 1793 the whole administration of Bengal was in the hands of British officials, and the higher administration for much longer. This again had consequences which lasted through much of the British period. The Mughals had employed foreigners freely, but never so exclusively as this. Indians thought it natural for a large number of offices to go to the British, but they were irked by their own total exclusion. They actively resented the excuse later put forward that it was on grounds of inefficiency. This was a sore point in Indo-British relations into the twentieth century.

By the time of Cornwallis we thus find that the British had dispensed with Indian agency except in the lowest rungs of the ladder. The process of taking over the direct administration was completed by the establishment of a police service by Cornwallis, and the complete Europeanization of the army. From this time all commissioned officers were British, though the corps of European soldiers always remained small compared to the Indian troops. In the military as in the civil service there was something to be said for this process in the beginning. The Indians lacked the required technical knowledge in both fields. The British action was shortsighted in failing to realize that a remedy for Indian corruption and inefficiency, just as for European, could be found in education and proper conditions of service. There was no background of Western education in India, it is true, but special colleges could have been set up and a class of Western-trained officials established. The Indian gift for loyalty would have bound this class to the *raj* and formed a political pillar of empire as strong as Akbar's alliance with the Rajputs. The attachment and efficiency of the Indian part of the civil service in the twentieth century showed what might have been done had Cornwallis balanced his European work with the creation of a Western-trained Indian official class. As it was, the various services with their European monopoly built up a vested interest both in India and England which was interested in retaining places for families and friends. Along with much fine service by individuals there was a steady drag on Indian political progress imposed by those who were in effect defending their future prospects. This attitude did serious harm but fortunately never succeeded (as we shall see) in imposing an absolute bar to Indian official service. Had it done so, the parting between India and Britain would have been as bitter as that between Indonesia and the Netherlands. Had a policy of Indo-British co-operation in official service been adopted from the time of Cornwallis, the parting might never have taken place at all.

The policy of using direct European agency in the government succeeded because discipline was restored among the Company's service and a new spirit created. This achievement, like that of taking over the direct administration, was a gradual process. We may begin with the moment of maximum disorder, which may be placed in early 1763 when the Calcutta Council threw overboard Governor Vansittart's agreement with Mir Kasim and plunged Bengal into war for their private mercantile interests. Then present-taking was rampant, and trading without paying tolls, the intimidation of the Nawab's officers, and oppression of the peasantry were general. The governor was flouted by his own council. In 1776 the majority of the Madras Council arrested the governor, Lord Pigot, and kept him in confinement, where he died before orders from home for his release could arrive. The European officers of the Company's army staged a mutiny against Clive in his second term. At one time it was more important to be a creditor of the Nawab of the Carnatic then to be a member of the Madras government. The position was made still more difficult by the fact, of which we should here take note, that many of these malpractices were connived at, if not actually encouraged, from home. Many of the Company's servants were closely connected with the directors and other influential people at home. As soon as it was known that quick fortunes were to be made in the East there was a rush to secure nominations to Writerships. This patronage for plunder was a kind of aristocratic forerunner of the modern take-over bid. Lord Cornwallis complained of being pressed by influential men in Britain, including the Prince of Wales, to agree "to infamous and unjustifiable jobs." Those who had made fortunes, like Clive, could return to Britain, buy the Company's stock, and so influence elections to the Direction. Seats were bought in Parliament and the government's dealings with the Company influenced in that way. Every disciplinary action had its aftereffect, for it injured those at home as well as those abroad. No dismissed servant of the Company had need to despair, provided he had money and friends in Britain. The career of Sir John Macpherson (1745–1821) provides an interesting example, though it was by no means the most notorious. The son of a Presbyterian minister, he went to India in 1767 as the purser of a ship. He returned as the secret agent of Muhammad Ali, Nawab of the Carnatic. In 1770 he reappeared in Madras as a Writer of the Company, to be dismissed by Lord Pigot in his campaign against corruption, which led to Pigot's imprisonment by his own council. In 1779 Macpherson became a member of Parliament; he was reinstated by the directors and for four years was a member of Warren Hastings' Supreme Council in Calcutta. Here (we know from his letters) he posed as the friend of Warren Hastings in Calcutta and of Lord Macartney in Madras, whom he hoped to succeed. He lost their confidence but nevertheless acted as governor general for eighteen months between the departure of Hastings and the arrival of Lord Cornwallis. Cornwallis described his government as "a system of the dirtiest jobbing." But this did not hinder the award of a baronetcy and his return to Parliament. He died in 1821 full of years and wealth, if not honor. Sir Robert Fletcher, a military officer, was twice cashiered, once for leading a mutiny against Clive, and was thereafter twice commander in chief at Madras, where he was dismissed for causing a mutiny, to which he retaliated by arresting Governor Pigot. Reading between the lines, it is clear that Macpherson made a fortune through his relations with Muhammad Ali and illicit dealings as a Writer in Madras. Thereafter he had enough influence and "interest" never to be down for long. Fletcher could not have survived so many vicissitudes without strong support from home.

It is thus clear that it was not only the Company's servants who required disciplining; their "masters" at India House needed it as much. The work was accomplished by a mixture of strong action within the Company itself and the interference of Parliament from the outside. In the end Parliament both enforced discipline and the responsibility of the governors for the governed. First we may trace the process of converting a group of merchant buccaneers into a set of disciplined administrators. The starting point is again Clive in his second term. He saw, with that piercing clarity of his, that the vice of the situation lay in the fact that merchants held political power, that they had virtually no salaries since they were expected to earn their living by private trade. Clive compelled the Bengal officials to sign covenants against taking presents (as he had taken them himself), abolished the duty-free trade, and forbade private trade to holders of political posts. He provided for salaries by establishing a Society of Trade, with shares in the proceeds of the salt monopoly being given according to rank. The governor received $52,000, councilors and colonels $21,000 per annum. The directors disapproved, and instead of providing adequate salaries according to rank and office substituted commissions on the revenue to supplement them. This meant that rich districts did better than poor ones. The Resident of Banaras, for example, had a salary of $4,000 a year and a commission of $120,000 with, according to Cornwallis, other perquisites as well. After Clive's departure present-taking came back on a smaller scale and private trade was winked at. Warren Hastings kept these practices within limits. He was not able to abolish them and indeed, owing to the constant insecurity of his own position, he had to make use of them, in spite of a fresh interdict by the Regulating Act. It was not until the advent of Cornwallis in 1786, backed by the young William Pitt at the head of the strongest ministry of the second half of the eighteenth century, that a solution was found. A reluctant board of directors was forced to attach generous salaries to offices while fixing a higher age limit for holding them. This done, Cornwallis enforced the prohibition of private trade and ended illicit practices in general. The whole board of revenue was suspended, and most of its members subsequently dismissed; a regiment was found to have existed on paper only, salaries being regularly paid to nonexistent officers. Cornwallis then reorganized the Company's service into general and commercial branches. The former included the revenue and judicial departments, having nothing to do with trade, while the latter carried on the Company's trade with Europe. New arrivals opted for one branch or the other and stayed there for the term of their official lives.

This was the effective beginning of the civil service of British India. By 1800 the new security and encouragement of integrity had already thrown up names of distinction like those of Charles Grant, Sir John Shore, and Sir George Barlow. Members still commonly went to India as boys of fifteen. Two subsequent measures served to counteract the dangers of immaturity. Lord Wellesley started a college in 1801 (known as Fort William College) for the training of new arrivals before they were posted to the districts. He took a personal interest in its work and employed the Baptist missionary William Carey to teach Indian languages. The directors, in their characteristic way, disallowed this venture, but they were compelled to start a college of their own at Haileybury in England, where cadets received preliminary training before proceeding to India. There was a parallel institution at Addiscombe for the army. British India thus received a civil service which was disciplined, trained in some measure for its work, and given a sense of security and integrity. There were still misfits, and some corruption lingered for a generation; but in many ways it was in advance of the English civil service of the day.

The same principle operated in the next feature of the Company state, the responsibility of the government for the welfare of the governed. In the sixties of the eighteenth century the sense of responsibility of the new European governors of Bengal could hardly have been less. It was this very abandonment of self-interest and cupidity which led to reaction and the enforcement of control from Britain. The fact was that the directors and shareholders (or members of the Court of Proprietors) were only really concerned about malpractices when their profits seemed to be threatened. Thus alarm at the breach with Mir Kasim induced them to send out Clive on a reforming mission. Clive's success lulled them into a new sense of security until they were overtaken by a fresh and this time irremediable crisis. It was nothing less than the threat of bankruptcy. Clive believed that the revenues of Bengal could contribute a surplus of six million dollars toward the Company's commercial expenses and profits. On the strength of this the dividends were raised to 10 per cent in 1766 and 12.5 per cent in 1767. In 1767, in return for parliamentary recognition for the Company's Indian domain and in order to buy off a demand that the Crown should take it over, the Company agreed to pay four hundred thousand pounds a year to the state. If Clive had remained in Bengal the surplus he expected might have been produced. But greed and recklessness, with the help of a war in the south, now defeated themselves. In 1770 the Company found itself compelled to ask for a loan of three million dollars to avert bankruptcy. This was the death knell of the old easygoing piracy. The enemies of the Company, by no means all of them disinterested, sprang to the attack. Parliamentary enquiries, the first of a long and valuable series, were held; passionate debates took place. Clive, his nerves shattered by the struggle to retain his *jagir* and rebut parliamentary attacks, took his own life in 1774. Edmund Burke came to the fore at this time as a critic of the Company and its servants. The upshot was the

Regulating Act of 1773, passed on the eve of the outbreak of the War of Independence.

In return for a loan to liquidate its debts the Company had to submit to a measure of control by the British government. The great merit of the Regulating Act, a typical example of the British tendency never to do more than is absolutely necessary, was that it proved so defective that it had to be amended. A better act would have produced no such salutary aftermath as Pitt's India Act in 1784. The Regulating Act did much to stop the control of Indian policy by shareholders who bought and sold in order to influence the annual elections to the court of twenty-four directors. Elections were to be for four years for six directors at a time, and the financial qualification for a vote was doubled. In India a governor general was appointed with supervisory powers over the other presidencies and a Supreme Court set up in Calcutta to administer English law to Europeans. The measure said nothing about moral duty or the rights of the governed, but it did amount to an assertion of parliamentary authority over the Company and its servants. They were henceforth ultimately responsible to Parliament for their actions. The same doctrine of the supremacy of Parliament which was about to lose the Thirteen Colonies to Britain was to prove the instrument for transferring Anglo-Saxon values and institutions to the Indian subcontinent. Further, there was a clear inference that this new responsibility included attention to the welfare of the governed.

Having said so much, it remains to be noted that the defects of the act were so glaring that they compelled revision within ten years. The governor general was given power of supervision of the other presidencies without any means of enforcing his control. The insubordination of these presidencies entangled the Company in long wars with the Marathas, Haidar Ali of Mysore, and the Nizam. He was also given four councilors named in the act, two of them men from public life in Britain who looked down on a Company's servant like Warren Hastings and one a *condottiere* drawn from English politics and literature, Philip Francis. The result was prolonged wrangles within the council which paralyzed the executive at critical moments and, by souring the spirit of Warren Hastings under the strain, may be said to have been mainly responsible for his most questionable acts, the execution of Nand Kumar, the mulcting of Chait Singh of Banaras, and the treatment of the begums ("princesses") of Oudh. The powers of the Supreme Court were undefined, with the result that it administered English law to all comers, to the consternation and confusion of Bengal. Through this turbulence and trouble the Company's state was held together by the genius of Warren Hastings. However his more controversial acts may be judged, the talents and sagacity he displayed were superb; without them it is difficult to see how the Company could have survived during those years of storm without and stress within.

Talk of remedies began within a year or two of the passing of the act. But action was delayed by the crisis of the War of Independence. When the Company's charter ran out in 1780 Lord North's government, lurching toward the final disaster of Yorktown, tried to postpone the issue further. But the opposition was now gaining strength and was not to be put off. Parliamentary inquiries were begun and for a short time India became a first-class political issue. It was Fox's India Bill which led to the fall of the Fox-North coalition and the advent of the younger Pitt to power. His first measure was the India Act, which fixed the shape of British Indian government until the Mutiny of 1857. The achievement of Pitt's act was to complete the control of Indian policy by the British government without interfering with the Company's administration or exposing the rich patronage of the Company to the mercies of political wirepullers. The Company kept its appointments at the price of its political power. The responsibility of the rulers for the welfare of the governed was laid down and made enforcible. Section XXXIV of the act forbade the governor general to declare war on any Indian state without the express authority of the directors, and declared "to pursue schemes of conquest and extension of dominion in India are measures repugnant to the wish, the honor and the policy of this nation." The Company state was to cherish its Indian subjects, was to be responsible to Parliament for its behavior, and was to be an unaggressive and peaceable member of the Indian society of nations.

This control of Company policy by the Crown was achieved by Pitt's plan of double government. It was not the double government of Clive where two authorities, virtually responsible to no one, shared the proceeds of the country. The double principle was in London and was really a device by which the impetus of political decision was transmitted from the Crown through the India House to the local authorities in India. The Company continued to manage its trade and its local affairs. Policy was decided jointly by the British government and the Company, acting through a secret committee. The government acted through a board of control whose president was a member of the cabinet. The first president was Henry Dundas, a close friend of Pitt. The board had power to agree to all political dispatches, to modify or redraft them. It thus had the last word in all Indian policy. In India the governor general's powers were strengthened. He could take over the presidencies in time of war and override his own council. He became—and remained—the governor general *in* council and not the governor general *and* council. The act was good in itself, but it owed much of its immediate success to its inauguration by three of the ablest men of the day, two of whom were outstanding for their integrity and high-mindedness. These were William Pitt, the prime minister; Henry Dundas, the president of the Board of Control; and Lord Cornwallis, governor general from 1786 to 1793. The appointment of a man high in British public life raised the position above the stresses of local politics and made the task of enforcing authority in Bengal much easier. The enforcement of responsibility was completed by the impeachment of Warren Hastings. The procedure was the clumsy one of formal accusations made by the Commons to the House of Lords sitting as a high court of law. The proceedings began in 1787 in Westminster Hall amidst great excitement and ended eight years later with an acquittal on all the twenty-three counts. In the course of it Hastings lost most of his Indian fortune; he retired to his repurchased family house at Daylesford in Gloucestershire; he was debarred from honors or further employment and died in 1818 at the age of eighty-six. The motives of the promoters were mixed, from the open spite of Philip Francis to the crusading zeal mixed with personal feelings of Burke. In some ways Hastings was cruelly treated; there were many far more guilty than he. But behind the passion and rancor there was a deeper feeling that what was morally wrong in the West could not be right in the East. Though Hastings was acquitted, he suffered more than many much more guilty men. But he had come to typify the Bengal system and his fate was notice to lesser men that corruption and unbridled despotism would not be tolerated. With Hastings at the bar of the House of Lords and Cornwallis in Bengal the day of the money-maker and the oppressor was clearly over.

Thus by 1790 the Company state had taken a definite shape. It was one of the powers of Hindustan, recognized as such, and not yet aspiring to the hegemony of all India. Indeed, as we have seen, aggressive war and annexation were expressly forbidden by Parliament. Within the state the government was organized on authoritarian lines and in the hands of foreigners. Both these features were not unknown to Indians; the only novelty was the *degree* of strangeness and the effectiveness of the authority. The civil service was entirely foreign in its higher posts and so were the officers of the army. Once the governor general became the master of his council and had the backing of the home government, he became a great Mughal in miniature. He was circumscribed in his turn, it is true, by superiors in Britain and hedged round with regulations. Yet to the Indian eye and to that of his subordinates he was more formidable, because his authority, though less absolute in theory, was more effective in practice.

Below him the officials, though less corrupt and more public-spirited than before, kept up much state and were potentates in their districts. The aim of the government was much the same as before—that is, while collecting the revenue and guarding the frontiers, to allow the life of the various communities to continue untouched. There was little idea of reform of manners or the moulding of society. Practices like suttee or widow-burning, hook-swinging as an act of religious devotion, infanticide, Hindu widowhood, and Muslim polygamy were deplored as "heathenish" but regarded as customs of the country which could not be interfered with. Both religions were unmolested; officials presided at some religious festivals and collected pilgrim taxes for the upkeep of temples. This was the foundation of the later jibes at the "churchwardens of Jaganath." Along with religious recognition went patronage of learning and the arts. Warren Hastings led the way and in this was following an age-old Indian tradition. He and many of his contemporaries knew Persian, enjoyed its literature, and patronized its poets. In addition he knew Bengali and some Persian and Arabic. He founded an Arabic college in Calcutta, encouraged Sanskrit studies—which produced the first English translation of the *Bhagavad Gita* and *Sakuntala*—and helped Sir William Jones to found the Asiatic Society of Bengal in 1784.

The outstanding characters of this period of consolidation were Warren Hastings and Cornwallis. Hastings was probably the ablest British statesman in India throughout the British period. He has certainly been the most discussed. Mill and Macaulay attacked him, the imperialists glamorized him as a giant in bonds, and the liberals came to dim the glamor. To appreciate his achievement one must understand his difficulties, which is beyond the scope of a brief study such as this. In the first two years of unchallenged control he accomplished a major constructive work. In the next few years, when his every move was challenged in council, he was often overruled by a majority, and his position was constantly threatened in London, he defended Bengal and rescued Madras from a coalition of the strongest Indian powers—the Marathas, Haidar Ali of Mysore, and the Nizam. And he did all this when he was practically cut off from aid from Britain because of the American war and the European coalition which joined in. In the course of this work he committed some highhanded acts which it would be folly to deny, as it would be absurd to ignore his political achievements. In fact the opposition and frustration soured him, making him autocratic, relentless, self-righteous and suspicious. But he was still great. Without him British India could hardly have survived. Cornwallis was a man of quite different stamp. His leading qualities were integrity and common sense, both of which he had in such measure that his reputation survived the surrender of Yorktown which ended the American war. He could make big mistakes and yet achieve much. He was able rather than brilliant. He stumbled into war with Tipu Sultan through lack of diplomatic finesse; he created a landlord class and unwittingly depressed the peasantry of Bengal through insufficient understanding; he created a European monopoly of office which it took years to undo. Yet his constructive work was more important. He cleansed the administration so that it never went back to the old corruption. He laid the foundation of the great civil service tradition, he produced the first modern code of criminal law, and he established the rule of law. Without him, or someone like him, the British dominion in India could hardly have survived, any more than it could have without Warren Hastings.

CHAPTER XIX

The Road to Supremacy

It was fondly hoped in Britain, and not least by Pitt and Dundas, that the India Act of 1784 had established the Company's Indian state on a stable and unaggressive basis. The Company, it was hoped, would carry on its trade in peace, avoiding both expansion and entanglements in Indian wars. After all, trade was the object of its existence, and there could be no profits with constant war. But events both in Europe and in India soon ruled otherwise. Supremacy came within forty years of the passing of the act—so soon, indeed, that many have supposed that it was a deliberate design from the beginning. Here we shall try to explain the interplay of forces which made this result, at first reprobated by Parliament, inevitable in the circumstances of the day and finally welcomed as a great achievement.

The years from Clive's final return to Britain in 1767 to supremacy in 1818 may be divided into five phases. In the first, up to 1785, the Company Bahadur or Company state struggled to existence. In the second, from 1785 to 1798, there was a breathing space and the hoped-for stability. The third, from 1798 to 1805, saw Wellesley's forward move under the influence of a renewed French danger which passed into an abortive attempt at supremacy. The fourth phase, from 1805 to 1813, marked an interlude or standstill during the height of the struggle with Napoleon. These years saw such a deterioration in the conditions of Indian-controlled India that the final phase of planned supremacy, from 1813 to 1818, became inevitable. The decisive point in this development was Wellesley's attack on Mysore in 1798, and this, significantly enough, was the direct result of the revived French menace. The general factors we have to consider on the British side were the desire for trade and profits, and the fear of France. The desire for trade pointed to peace, and the better controlled the Company's servants were the more peaceful its policy was likely to be. Connected with this desire for trade was another factor, the desire of independent merchants in London to share or break the East India Company's monopoly. This accorded both with the new free-trade doctrine and the traders' natural inclinations. As more became known about India, the prospects of trade seemed brighter if the Company could be pushed aside and peaceful conditions established. This led to the argument that supremacy was necessary for peaceful trade. The commercial "outs" as well as the "ins" joined in the final pressure for completing control of India. The fear of France was dormant until Napoleon's descent on Egypt in 1798 with its implied threat to British India. From then on it was a potent political factor until Napoleon's downfall.

In 1767, after Clive's return, the political state of India was roughly as follows. The state of Oudh, ruled by Shuja-ad-daula, adjoined the Company's Bengal domain; it was rich and effete. From the Ganges to the Indus there was a practical political vacuum. For a few years the last of the Mughal Persian ministers revived the core of the empire at Delhi, but in 1785 it passed under Maratha control, together with the aging emperor Shah Alam. Beyond, local chiefs set up and pulled down robber states until the Sikh chief Ranjit Singh established himself in the Panjab at the end of the century. In Rajasthan a number of helpless and hapless Rajput chiefs were easy prey for the Marathas. The effective powers in India were three, the Marathas, Haidar Ali of Mysore, and the Nizam. The Marathas and Haidar were expansionist, the Nizam an opportunist. The Maratha power at this time stretched across India from the west coast like a returning tide after a recent ebb. It had spread to the Bay of Bengal in Orissa and touched the sea at Jaganath's temple at Puri. It lapped the frontiers of Shuja's dominion of Oudh, the remains of the Mughal empire (which may now be more fairly called the kingdom of Delhi), and touched the Rajput states of Rajasthan. Its frontiers on the southeast and south ran with those of the Nizam and Haidar Ali, and fluctuated with the chances of war and diplomacy. But this extensive power, united under the Peshwa Balaji Baji Rao before Panipat, was now divided. No sooner had it begun to gather strength again and to send its armies once more across the Chambal River to the north than the young Peshwa Madhu Rao died; thenceforward succession troubles and internal strife afflicted the Poona court and the confederation as a whole. The diplomatic skill of the minister Nana Fadnavis preserved a semblance of unity within a whirl of intrigue and conflict within the Regency Council. But his adroitness served to conceal the process of division which was now proceeding apace. The chiefs who had previously been generals of the peshwa fighting his northern campaigns became now in effect independent rulers. The lands they controlled became personal states. They were independent in their relations with others and competitors for the control of Poona. The Maratha power was now a loose confederacy of five powers which might occasionally unite on an issue of the Marathas versus the rest, but which usually sought to aggrandize themselves in the traditional Indian manner. An example of their relationship is to be seen in their dealings with the Nizam in 1795. In that year Nana Fadnavis united all factions in an attack on Hyderabad. The Nizam was routed so completely at Kharda that his capital lay defenseless, and he was compelled to cede half his dominions. Within a matter of weeks, however, the union had dissolved so entirely that the Nizam was able to threaten Poona in his turn and recover most of what he had lost. Amidst these divisions the Maratha dream of Indian empire vanished, for they could not decide the prior question as to who was to be their leader. Nevertheless they remained formidable, and, since their fundamental weakness was far from clear to most observers of the day, they appeared to be more formidable than they really were.

The five confederates are worth noting, for we cannot avoid some further reference to them. There was the peshwa at Poona who controlled western India and was the titular head of the Marathas. The peshwa as in theory the minister of the Raja of Satara, now a virtual prisoner; the peshwa himself was a minor and his power was exercised by his minister Nana Fadnavis. In Gujarat, the fertile province around the Gulf of Cambay, the Gaekwar family established itself at Baroda. It played a minor part in the struggles of the time, but survived as an Indian state until 1947. Across central India lay the lands of the Bhonsla, sometimes called Berar, but more generally the state of Nagpur after the raja's capital city. To the north the two most energetic chieftains, Sindia and Holkar, carved out synthetic states for themselves, named Gwalior and Indore after their respective capitals. These also survived until 1947. Madhu Rao Sindia was the ablest chieftain of his day. With a combination of Maratha cavalry and European-trained troops (the famous corps of the Frenchman De Boigne) he extended his dominions up the corridor between the Ganges and the Sutlej to the Himalayan foothills, taking the emperor Shah Alam under his protection. He died in 1794 at Poona, when he had defeated Holkar decisively and seemed about to control the whole confederacy. Holkar expanded principally at the expense of the Rajputs, and retained to the end the traditional Maratha tactics of cavalry war.

Across the Deccan, with its capital at Hyderabad, lay the country of Nizam Ali, the Nizam-ul-Mulk. It was in effect the surviving effective portion of the Mughal empire. It may be described as Aurangzeb's legacy to eighteenth-century India. Nizam Ali, who reigned from 1762 to 1802, was an able ruler, often misjudged by European writers because British contact with him was only close in his later years of timid and soured old age. Hyderabad lacked the vital force of Maratha tribalism. It was a Muslim aristocracy ruling a Hindu majority and depending on mercenary service and personal ambition for its support. It was weak in attack but surprisingly resilient in defense. Finally, we come to Haidar Ali of Mysore. He was a military adventurer who had risen from the ranks; he was often referred to as Haidar Ali *naik* or Corporal Haidar Ali. He rose by ability to command the army of the Hindu state of Mysore. In 1762 he retired the raja without actually occupying the throne himself. His position was rather like that of General Franco in modern Spain. He left it to his son Tipu to call himself Sultan. He controlled Mysore for twenty years and his ability was such that he overshadowed, in the eyes of the British of South India, both the Nizam and the Marathas.

It will be noticed that all these states were expansive, none recognizing any natural limits or frontiers. Only the Marathas had any backing from a particular people or trace of national spirit. Hyderabad and Mysore were mere power constructions, more or less vigorous according to the abilities of their rulers. In the case of the Marathas, community feeling was vitiated by their divisions, leading to civil war and internal struggles for power, and by their acquisitiveness, which gave them a name for imperialism and plunder over the rest of India. There was, in fact, no basis for an internal Indian balance of power. These states had no self-limitations, no restraints, no idea of live and let live. There was no conception of a Concert of Powers as in Europe, or of an international law imposing some degree of common code upon all. Perhaps we should rather say that the only law known to Indian tradition, contained in the *Arthasastra* of Kautiliya, assumed competition to the ultimate goal of supremacy. In thinking and hoping for a stable Indian states system, the British Parliament was applying concepts of the West to the totally differing conditions and ideas of the East.

This was the India which faced Warren Hastings when he became governor of Bengal in 1772. His desire, like that of the Company, was to live at peace, and his only personal military venture was to act as Shah Shuja's ally in a minor campaign against the Rohillas in 1773 for which he was later severely criticized. He declined all temptation to follow this up by marching to Delhi. But as governor general under the Regulating Act, Hastings was responsible for all the British possessions in India. The folly of the Bombay government embroiled him with the Marathas, while the culpable negligence of the Madras government provoked a coalition of the Nizam, Haidar Ali, and the Marathas just when the surrender of Saratoga had given a disastrous turn to the American war and Britain itself was threatened by a European coalition. Bombay interfered in a Maratha civil war on behalf of the unlucky prince Ragunath Rao. A series of misunderstandings among Calcutta, Bombay, and London saw an army from Bengal arrive on the west coast at the moment the Bombay army had capitulated while attempting to march to Poona. Hastings' diplomacy was able to divide the very divisible Marathas, but it was not until 1782 that peace was restored with all of them. The supreme test for Hastings came in 1780, when he was virtually cut off from Europe by the American and European wars. The Madras government, then in its lowest state of corruption, offended the Nizam by intrigues with his brother, who held the Guntur district, at a time when the Company was already at war with the Marathas. The result was a coalition of the Nizam, Haidar Ali, and the Marathas, which in 1780 devastated the Carnatic up to the walls of Madras. It is perhaps Hastings' highest claim to fame that he never despaired in this crisis or took refuge in recrimination. Instead he suspended the Madras governor, sent his best general to the south, and drained Bengal to support his forces. He detached the Nizam by removing his grievance and the Marathas in 1782. The advent of the French in 1782 might have turned the scale again but for the death of Haidar at the end of the year and the declaration of peace in Europe. Bussy himself had arrived with the main French force. The treaty of Mangalore with Tipu Sultan (Haidar's son) in 1784 restored peace to the Company and left its possessions intact. The Company had won its spurs as an Indian state. But it was no nearer to empire and was newly pledged to nonaggression by the India Act of 1784.

The second phase covers the years 1785–98. The Company's position was maintained by Cornwallis and Sir John Shore. Only one war occurred during this period, between the Company and Tipu Sultan of Mysore. It arose out of the rather clumsy handling by Cornwallis of a problem of conflicting obligations under separate treaties. The Company correctly claimed the district of Guntur from the Nizam. He claimed help under a treaty to recover a district confirmed to Tipu under the recent treaty with Tipu. Cornwallis offered to supply troops against any power not an ally of the Company, and omitted Tipu's name from the appended list. Tipu took this as a warning of impending attack and struck the first blow by attacking the Company's ally Travancore in the extreme south. After three campaigns Tipu was brought to terms and half his territories annexed. But he still retained formidable power. The administration of these areas was the virtual beginning of the Madras Presidency, now divided among the states of Madras, Andhra, and Mysore. Until 1801 the Carnatic remained in the hands of the Nawab's officers, or more correctly of his creditors. In default of trained civilians military officers were employed. It was in land-settlement work in this area that Sir Thomas Munro, later governor of Madras and generally regarded as the father of the Madras administration, made his reputation. If Cornwallis went too far in helping his allies Sir John Shore (1793–98) did something to restore the balance by not going far enough. When the Nizam was in straits from an attack by the united Marathas he was refused all help. The dividing line between aggressive action in the name of friendship, and desertion in the name of neutrality was becoming difficult to draw.

The third and decisive phase in the Company's rise to supremacy commenced with Lord Mornington's (we shall call him Lord Wellesley from his later title) term of office as governor general in 1798. There was a change of policy in Britain, and this was applied so vigorously by Wellesley that the final decision to establish supremacy became inevitable. In Britain, Pitt was still prime minister, but was now beset by France, revivified by revolutionary ardor and possessed of a heaven-born general in the person of the young Napoleon Bonaparte. In 1798 he conquered Egypt and marched into Syria. He was fascinated by the East and talked openly of marching to India. Even when he returned to France to become First Consul he dwelt much upon the East and thought a blow in that direction the best way of bringing Britain to her knees. The French danger to the Company in India therefore revived in an acute form, though at long range, as it were. The London government shared the fears of the Company, and this led to the appointment of the energetic and masterful young Wellesley, with a mandate to combat French influence in India. The second factor at work in Britain was a change of feeling among the merchants, which can be studied in the published correspondence of the director David Scott.[1] Briefly, an important section of mercantile opinion both within and without the Company was coming to think that the only way to secure satisfactory trading conditions in India was to control the whole country. People therefore no longer looked upon a forward policy with horror, and were ready to support one so long as it was successful. They were not yet for supremacy at all costs, and withdrew their support from Wellesley as soon as he met a setback.

To these forces at work in India we must add the factors operating in India. There were the continuing divisions and disorders of the Indian political scene. There were also traces of French influence in the persons of French officers who had remained in India after the fall of Pondicherry in 1761 and had built up corps of disciplined troops in various places. The most famous served Sindia in the north; another was the corps of Raymond at Hyderabad. Frenchmen in India were notably patriotic and the divisions of the revolution did not damp their ardor for long. The third factor was the personality of Lord Wellesley. He was an Anglo-Irishman, so often prominent in soldiering and empire-building, a brother of the great Duke of Wellington. He was young, ardent, masterful, and convinced of a mission to extend British power in India. He had a lofty disdain for "the cheesemongers of Leadenhall Street," as he described the directors. For him glory was much more important than investments and bank balances; all would come right, he thought, once he controlled India, and wars could cease. He sorely tried the directors, who could not recall him until he made a false step. He united great ability and the faculty of inspiring others with arrogance and highhandedness. After him there could be no going back.

Wellesley's first move was to deal with Tipu Sahib, the erratic but brilliant Sultan of Mysore. Tipu made no secret of his antipathy to the British, having his father's insight into and dislike of their probable progress to supremacy. His search for allies naturally led him to France. The governor of the Île de France incautiously revealed an accord with Tipu, while Tipu himself planted a tree of liberty at Seringapatam. This was enough for Wellesley and he prepared for war. His weapons were three: outright war against outright opponents, diplomacy leading to subsidiary alliance and practical subordination, diktats in the case of states judged to be effete. Wellesley never had any doubts about the morality of his policy because he felt that in a large view British rule was much better for India than Indian. He also had an exceptional talent for convincing himself on any particular issue that his opponent was not only wrong but culpably so. The case of Mysore gave a trial run to all three methods. As a preliminary to attacking Mysore he induced the now aged Nizam to accept a subsidiary treaty. This involved the disbandment of his French-officered force and the acceptance of a British one which the Nizam paid. In return the Nizam was guaranteed the integrity of his territories. The essence of a subsidiary treaty was security at the price of dependence on the British. The essence of dependence lay in the fact that the subsidiary force was paid by the prince though controlled by the Company. Princes always found it difficult to pay the force punctually and so were always at a disadvantage in bargaining. If they defaulted altogether or desired to resume their independence, the subsidiary force was at the heart of their dominions to enforce the Company's interests. Having thus secured his flank Wellesley proceeded with his campaign. Seringapatam was stormed in 1799, Tipu being killed fighting bravely in the breach. Wellesley annexed half the kingdom but returned the rest to the Hindu rajas of Mysore, whose present representative is now governor of the again enlarged state of Mysore in the Indian Union. The episode was completed by the pensioning of the Nawab of the Carnatic and the taking over of his coastal state. This gave the Madras presidency the shape it retained until after independence.

We may now notice the *diktats* or acts of the state which were the third feature of Wellesley's march to supremacy. The little state of Tanjore in south India was taken over on the occasion of a disputed succession. In 1799 the Nawab of Surat, descendant of the last Mughal governor, was pensioned and Surat taken over on the ground of its strategic importance. The Nawab of Oudh, in treaty relationship with the Company since 1765, was compelled to cede about half his state along the Ganges on the pretext of paying for a larger subsidiary force as protection against the Afghan power which was then breaking up. These formed the "ceded districts" of the new northwestern provinces, as distinct from the "conquered districts" shortly to be obtained by war.

Wellesley now faced the Maratha confederacy and believed that it was the sole obstacle to complete supremacy. In 1802 the peshwa was completely defeated by the brilliant Holkar and in despair accepted a subsidiary treaty at Bassein in December. The next year Sindia and the Bhonsla of Nagpur, who had united to oppose this arrangement, were defeated separately by Arthur Wellesley and Lord Lake. Cuttack was taken from Nagpur, thus joining Bengal with Madras in a continuous strip. Delhi and Agra, and the person of the old emperor Shah Alam, were secured in the north. Sindia and Nagpur admitted British residents. Supremacy seemed practically assured. But at this moment Holkar, who had stood sullenly aloof, dramatically intervened. Using traditional Maratha tactics, he defeated a British force under General Monson and advanced to the walls of Delhi. Bharatpur withstood five assaults by Lake's army. Though Holkar was later driven to the Panjab, it was clear that much greater efforts would be needed to complete the

Maratha defeat. But it happened that at that moment Britain's resources were strained to the limit. She was facing the threat of Napoleonic invasion and living through the months that led up to Trafalgar. In London Wellesley's spell was broken and his enemies moved in for the kill. Pitt, convinced that there must be a standstill, and that the Company had overstrained its resources, recalled Wellesley and persuaded Cornwallis to go out to restore the *status quo*.

The fourth phase of temporary withdrawal may rightly be called an interlude in the march to supremacy. It was impossible to undo all Wellesley's work. What in fact happened was a withdrawal from advanced positions and a watching of events. Sindia and Holkar were left virtually independent and the Rajput princes, who had sought protection, were left to their mercy. But the annexed lands were retained, and the treaty with the peshwa remained. The British were thus astride the Jumna and paramount in the south. Only the northwest, Rajasthan, and central India were beyond their control.

Such a situation could not last. To the northwest the British watched anxiously for a Russo-French move during the years of the Franco-Russian alliance from 1807–12. The most important result was the treaty of Amritsar in 1809 which recognized the Sutlej as the boundary between the Company and the rising Sikh ruler in the Panjab, Ranjit Singh. Within India another development was occurring. The former plundering auxiliaries of the Marathas, known as Pindaris, formed themselves into independent companies reminiscent of the "free companies" of medieval Italy. Their numbers were swollen by men of every class who had been uprooted by the troubles of the times. They had no creed or caste, no home or national pride. Their bases were in the hilly fastnesses of central India, their tactics were speed, their object plunder, their method terror. They were thus described by Sir John Malcolm, who knew them well.[2]

"The Pindaris were neither encumbered by tents or baggage; each horseman carried a few cakes of bread for his horse. The party which usually consisted of two to three thousand good horse with a proportion of mounted followers, advanced at the rapid rate of forty or fifty miles a day, neither turning to right or left until they arrived at their destination. They then divided, and made a sweep of all the property and cattle they could find; committing at the same time the most horrid atrocities, and destroying what they could not carry away . . . before a force could be brought against them they were on their return."

The depredations of the Pindaris increased from year to year. In

1812 they raided the Mirzapur district in British India bordering the Ganges; in 1814–15 they twice traversed the Nizam's dominions to plunder parts of the Madras Presidency.

The final phase was made possible by three developments. The first was the fall of Napoleon, beginning at Moscow in 1812 and completed at Waterloo in 1815. The second was the ending of the Company's commercial monopoly in 1813, which meant that the mercantile community as a whole was now behind the demand for stability. The third was the Pindari plague, which created a general desire among all classes, except a few major princes and adventurers, for the ending of the central Indian anarchy. As far as such a thing existed at that time in India, public opinion was behind the final British unification.

The new governor general was Lord Hastings.[3] A former boon companion of the prince regent, confessedly recruiting his crippled finances, he showed unsuspected talent and statesmanship and fully justified his military rank of general. He first dealt with a Gurkha incursion from Nepal. In the first and last Gurkha war the non-Gurkha land from the Kali River to the Sutlej and including the Simla hills was detached from Nepal. Mutual respect led from observance of the treaty to alliance and the use of Gurkhas in the Indian armies. By this stroke the northern frontier was made safe and the sites for the famous hill-stations secured. Hastings then planned a sweeping movement to entrap the Pindaris. When all was ready the Maratha princes were given the choice of co-operation or war. After agonies of indecision, Sindia agreed; in Nagpur and Indore there was resistance which was crushed. With parallel agonies the peshwa staged a campaign at the last moment. With his surrender on June 2, 1818, the British hegemony of India up to the Sutlej was complete. His territories were annexed to form the core of the Bombay Presidency, and to be administered with a tender regard for Maratha feelings and traditions by the ablest of all Indian civilians, Mountstuart Elphinstone. The Rajputs, relieved of the Marathas, hastened to accept British supremacy. Elphinstone settled Western India; Malcolm, Central India; and Metcalfe, Rajputana and the Sutlej-Ganges tract. The land had rest after some seventy years of almost perpetual strife.

CHAPTER XX

India in 1818

The year 1818 marks a watershed in the history of British India. In that year the British dominion *in* India became the British dominion *of* India. India was unified again in a way it had not been from at least 1750. Subsequent annexations were mere additions to a whole and did not radically alter the situation. India was a political entity once more. The unity, it is true, was external and political only. It was the events of the next hundred years which were to transform that external bond, by a process unique in the history of India, into an organic union of minds and cultures. This point in time is therefore a convenient moment to take stock of the situation, to note the position of India at the end of her "time of troubles" and the nature of the administration which now controlled her life.

The political settlement of 1818 was determined by the fortunes of the campaign against the Pindaris, which placed the peshwa's dominions in the Company's hands, by the Company's determination to secure effective control of all India up to the Sutlej, and by its equal anxiety to limit its administrative responsibilities as far as was compatible with safety. The subsidiary treaties had been a success in binding princes to the British side and their long-term defects were not realized. The same authority which eschewed Indian agency within its own territories therefore welcomed it in the form of dependent states. Effective control of land was recognized as conferring a title to rule. Not only Rajput chiefs with lineage of a thousand years, but the freebooter Amir Khan, partner till the last moment with the Pindaris, and robber chiefs who had established themselves in a locality and would be expensive to dislodge found themselves recognized as dependent Indian princes. It was in this way that the princely order of British India of some six hundred and fifty chiefs, large and small, was established. In effect the political fragmentation of 1818 was "put on ice," and there it remained until the heat of nationalism played upon it at the time of independence. The actual settlement took the following form. The heart of the Maratha power, in the form of the Peshwa's territories in western India with their capital at Poona, was removed to give form and body to the Bombay Presidency. Henceforth this presidency, containing the energetic and forceful Gujaratis and Marathas, rivaled in influence those of Bengal and Madras. Sindia retained his integrity as a neutral but was shorn of his influence in Rajputana. Indore or Holkar and Nagpur were restored with subsidiary forces. From the latter Saugor was detached to form the core of the later Central Provinces and Berar added to Hyderabad in reward for the Nizam's services. In Rajasthan the Rajput chiefs were accepted as dependent princes, their various subdivisions being refrigerated as effectively as those of lesser chiefs. Thus the patchwork map of British India was achieved. According to a gazetteer [1] published at the time the Company directly controlled 553,000 square miles with an estimated population of 87,000,000, and its allies and tributaries 590,000 square miles and 43,000,000 people; while 127,000 square miles with 6,000,000 people remained independent.

The mood of the country was one of relief that an intolerable situation had been brought to an end. There was resignation to rather than enthusiasm for the new empire. The English were not loved, but neither were they hated. They were disliked for their aloofness, their pride, and many of their habits; they were admired for their military skill, their discipline, and their tenacity which never admitted defeat. Their noninterference with religious and social customs earned them tolerance rather than affection. Little as they were liked, any possible alternative was liked still less. All classes, whether Hindu or Muslim, detested the Marathas. No one in the north wanted a return of the Afghans. The revival of the Mughal empire was beyond practical politics. The Rajputs lacked the art of combination and the south dreaded the revival of a Muslim power like that of Tipu or Haidar Ali. The only real alternative at that time was in the extent to which the principle of delegation of authority was applied. The British left as many local rulers as they dared and administered themselves rather less than half the country. The settlement was an *ad hoc* one and the question of the way in which the country should be treated had still to be decided. In sum we may say that the British *raj* at this time was regarded as a decree of destiny, which was the refuge of all Indian minds in perplexity; it was to be borne as long as things held sacred were not touched or until a stronger nation than the British arrived. There was little lament for the loss of independence (except amongst some Marathas) because there was no sense of national disgrace. There was, in fact, no sense of an Indian nation as yet; there could be no sense of loss for what had never yet been.

Among the British, especially the younger ones, there was exhilaration and a sense of achievement. Wellesley's young men had fulfilled their destiny. Many were intoxicated by the extent of the territories secured, by the fame of the princes overthrown, by the historical vistas revealed. They believed themselves to be entering a new age. It is from this time that people began to talk of India as a conquered country. But the seniors took a more sober view. They were astonished by the extent of their success, it is true, but their astonishment led to awe rather than exhilaration. They could see better than their juniors the forces which lay just below the surface of Indian life, which some turn of fortune might stir to united action. To them the new dominion was precarious, and they were preoccupied with the problem of right action in the new circumstances. Metcalfe spoke of the "power which giveth and taketh away dominion," and others were equally sober. The British are said to take their pleasures sadly; the conquest of India would seem to have been the saddest pleasure of all.

At this point it may be convenient to pause and consider briefly the reason for the British success. There was of course the preliminary political collapse of India with which the British had nothing to do. At the moment that they were taking control of Bengal the central Mughal authority in Delhi was collapsing for reasons which had nothing to do with Europeans. It was also an entirely internal struggle which decided that the Marathas should not succeed to the empty seat of authority. The initial causes of the British supremacy must therefore be attributed to local Indian forces. The failure of Mughal leadership, the Afghan invasions, and the stalemate which followed Panipat were all part of these. Perhaps the biggest single factor in this situation was the failure of the Marathas to rise above the level of plunder and extortion to that of empire-building. They never learned the art of sincere co-operation, of conciliating opponents, or of controlling dependents, whether they were Hindu or Muslim. The guerrilla warfare frame of mind was the result of Aurangzeb's destruction of Sivaji's compact and disciplined kingdom, but it deprived them of the hope of Indian leadership. The Mughals lost the confidence of the Hindus in Aurangzeb's later years, and their respect in the years which followed. The Maratha peshwas had the chance of leading a revived Hindu empire if they could have remained united among themselves and won the confidence of their fellow Hindus.

But the fact that the Mughal empire dissolved through internal stress does not explain why the British came to succeed it. Indian dissensions helped them in that one Indian prince was always ready to seek foreign help against another. Some sections of Indians preferred foreign rule to control by other sections of Indians. For instance, the Marathas preferred British rule to Muslim; the Rajputs, British suzerainty to Maratha; and the Muslims, British rule to Hindu. But we have still to find the qualities which enabled the British to make successful use of the opportunity presented to them. They were qualities and assets which enabled them to exclude their extra-Indian rivals in the first place and to defeat in detail their Indian opponents in the second.

The extra-Indian rivals were the Afghans and the French. The Afghans defeated themselves by their retirement from India after Panipat and by their later internal quarrels. The French, as we have seen, were a far more serious proposition. They possessed leaders of the highest quality in Dupleix, Bussy, and De Suffren, while in Europe they were the strongest power of the day. The essential cause of their failure was lack of sea power, which prevented their reinforcing their lieutenants on the spot. A subsidiary cause was lack of sustained interest by the French authorities. Between 1763 and 1778 all proposals for preparations were neglected, so that when the War of American Independence presented a golden opportunity for recovery, preparations had to be started *de novo* and forces only arrived in India when the war was nearly over. A further cause was the intense nationalism of the French, who saw in the ruin of the British Company an occasion for founding a French power in India rather than for the restoration of Indian freedom. Shrewd rulers like Haidar Ali had no mind to replace one European power in India by another, with the result that co-operation was lukewarm just when it might have been decisive.

On the British side we have first to admit some brilliant leadership. The names of Clive and Warren Hastings, of Wellesley and Cornwallis, of Elphinstone and Metcalfe would stand high in the annals of any country, and they were supported by men only slightly less in distinction like Sir Eyre Coote and Lord Lake, Sir John Shore and Lord Hastings. It is true that the Indians had brilliant leaders too, in the persons of men like Haidar Ali and Shuja-ad-daula, Madhu Rao Sindia and Jaswant Rao Holkar, Nana Fadnavis and Ranjit Singh. But they were working against each other as much as against the British, and in their subordinates they lacked a high standard of trained personnel. After leadership comes the military advantage of arms and discipline. This was a very real advantage but we must also remember that it was a diminishing one. The Indian princes, beginning with Mir Kasim, soon began to raise disciplined troops and organize parks of artillery themselves, and in this they had the French to help them. Sindia's French-trained corps under De Boigne could not have been much inferior to those of the Company, and the British themselves admitted that the Sikh army of Ranjit Singh was equal in quality to their own and their artillery possibly superior. It was not solely by superior arms or military discipline that the British won India.

A more solid advantage was the *civil* discipline of the Company's servants. This may seem a paradox in view of the quarrels and disregard for duty of so many in the late eighteenth century. Could the creditors of the Nawab of Arcot or the private traders of Bengal be seriously called disciplined? All things are relative, and it is a fact that in comparison to current Indian practice their standards of loyalty and public spirit were high. The absence of revolt, the faculty of standing together in danger, was commented upon by the Indians themselves. This was notable in the days of Warren Hastings when abuses were rife, and became more pronounced as morals improved from the time of Cornwallis onward. Every Indian chief was threatened by the revolt or desertion of his lieutenants at any moment. The desire to stand well with the *de facto* power and the absence of national feeling or corporate spirit beyond the tribe or the clan or personal group encouraged wholesale desertions when a leader's fortune seemed to waver. The Company's servants, on the other hand, were tied to the Company's interest in the long run, however much they might disregard it for their own profit in the short. They had a feeling of solidarity with their own nation and of being champions of its cause. A victory of an Indian leader was a victory for himself; a victory of an English general was a victory for England.

Such advantages might have sufficed to build up and maintain a dominion in India, but they could hardly have secured an enduring supremacy. The decisive factor in the British rise to power was their superior resources. At a time when the accumulated treasures of the Mughals had been scattered by Aurangzeb's Maratha campaigns, by the wars of succession, and by Nadir Shah's plunder of Delhi, when the resources of the whole countryside had been drained by incessant campaigns and raids, the British were entering into the Industrial Revolution. Their economy was rapidly expanding while India's was contracting. Akbar's revenue in 1605 was stated from official accounts to be about \$51,000,000 when the total revenue of James I was barely \$3,000,000. By the end of the eighteenth century the Company's gross revenue from an area smaller than that of Akbar's empire was about $25,000,000, while the revenue of the United Kingdom was around $43,000,000. At the same time the Company's import and export trade were each worth about $100,000,000, with an annual favorable balance of trade of $15,000,000. It was these resources, conveyed to India by sea power, which enabled the British to repair every reverse and replace every loss. While Indian leaders were marching hither and thither to extort revenue from the countryside to prevent their troops from mutinying from arrears of pay, Britain was sending a steady supply of money, stores, and men to India. It was not only a case of the best generals or best troops, but also of the best paymaster.

Before accepting British supremacy as inevitable, it is well to consider some possible alternatives. The Persians ruled themselves out by their divisions after the death of Nadir Shah. The Afghans ruled themselves out by Ahmad Shah's retreat from Delhi in 1761 and their own subsequent divisions. Within India itself there were the Marathas, the Nizam, and Haidar Ali of Mysore. We have already noted the dissensions of the Marathas. If the British had been removed entirely it is possible that some chief after many years' conflict might have established supremacy. But there is no evidence that it would have been either stable or popular. The Nizam was an astute diplomatist and opportunist, adept at dividing his opponents. But there is no sign that he or his successor possessed any Napoleonic or empire-building talents. In Haidar Ali we have a man of action of the first class. But for the British he might well have dominated India south of the Kistna and divided central India with the Marathas. But his rule was essentially a personal one; there is good reason to suppose that his state, being a Muslim military dictatorship imposed on a Hindu countryside, would have fallen to pieces on the death of his son Tipu Sultan. In any case he could not have controlled the north, the key to Indian empire, without first defeating the Marathas. There remain the Sikhs under Ranjit Singh. But he rose to significant power after the main crisis of Indian fate in 1798–1805. In the absence of the British the extension of his power southward would have been barred by Sindia, and it is profitless to speculate further. The political signs in India in the late eighteenth century suggested that India was entering upon one of those prolonged periods of confusion such as occurred in the fifteenth century after Timur's invasion or in the centuries previous to the Turkish invasion at the end of the twelfth century. All these powers had this in common; they were traditionalist in outlook. They had no interest in things European apart from weapons of war for the furtherance of their power. They were re-

volving within their traditional cultural orbits. They were mostly unaware of and certainly not interested in the ferments of ideas, the practical inventions, and the material progress of contemporary Europe.
No doubt such things would have penetrated into India in time, but it
would probably have required a shock like that administered by Admiral Perry to Japan in 1853 to cause them to be taken seriously. An
Indian empire at that time or the more probable medley of powers
would have meant a postponement of the integration of the Indian
peoples and culture with those of the West.

There remains to be considered a European competitor. The only
one in the field was France. If we suppose France to have defeated
Britain and then to have established an empire of its own, what kind
would it have been? If we take the instructions of the French government to Bussy in 1781 for his expedition to India as any kind of clue,[2]
it is likely to have taken the form of a controlling agency of a number
of feudatory states. For these states the model would have been that of
Morocco; for directly ruled territories that of Algeria. There would
have been free social intercourse, a pronounced cultural dichotomy,
and a concentration of all political power in French hands. It is hard
to see how, under such a regime, India could have developed as quickly
and extensively or moved to independence as smoothly as in fact proved
the case. A painful and embittered parting of the ways might well have
jeopardized the whole position of the West in India. For the British it
could be said that, though their motives were primarily commercial
and though in their early stages they were guilty of plunder and rapacity,
they were yet subject to a public opinion seething with ideas and ideals,
which before long was to produce a revolution in their rule.

What was the sort of India which met the gaze of the rather breath-
less soldiers and "politicals," still rather surprised at their own temerity
and success? The first thing that struck them was the exhaustion
of the countryside. The reports of Metcalfe from the Delhi territory,
Malcolm from central India, Elphinstone from the Maratha lands
of western India, of Briggs from Gujarat, Tod from Rajasthan, and
Munro from the south tell the same tale. Where famines had occurred,
as in the Delhi district in 1782, there had not been the tranquility or the
energy to repair the damage. Everywhere villages had been deserted to
avoid the plundering horseman, the tax collector, or the plague, while
those that remained were fortified for defense against all comers. The
state of insecurity was such that it was not safe to picnic amid the ruins
which strewed the plain of Delhi, for fear of lurking robbers or stray
marksmen. Between Delhi and Agra, on the imperial road, one could

only spend the night safely behind some fortification. The surplus wealth of the country had been swept into the financing of military operations, and these in turn had steadily reduced the capital which produced the surplus wealth. All cultural activities, such as the maintenance of mosques and temples, Hindu and Muslim seats of learning, canals, roads, and public inns, were crippled for lack of support. The countryside was dotted with the decaying remains of quite recent glory which no one could afford to keep up.[3]

A second feature of India at that time was a general stagnation of life. Politically, no one had anything to look forward to. The old and rival systems had crashed; there was no possibility of reviving them, and no sign of any alternative apart from the British. Culturally, both communities were living in the past. Hinduism had developed intellectually into a refinement of critical commentaries and socially into a multiplication and subdivision of caste. The original thought of the fourth and fifth centuries, the philosophic range and depth of a Ramanuja, was a thing of the past. As with many societies fearful of the future, Hindu society tended to cherish as precious things which a more vigorous age would have rejected as abuses. Thus suttee was held up as a Hindu virtue rather than a vice, the seclusion of women regarded as a mark of respectability, and Brahmin dominance as the mark of Hindu excellence. Sanskrit studies were carried on in the *tols* of Banaras, Nasik, and Nadia, but Hindu society at large drifted steadily from religion toward superstition. Those who wanted to play a part in the world learned Persian. Nor was Muslim society in a much better condition. In Islamic thought, politics and society are closely connected. The Mughal political eclipse was therefore specially depressing. Under Shah Wali-ullah of Delhi there was a return to the ideas of early Islam, but this did not affect the community as a whole. Their leader, the supposed sword of Islam, had failed them, and there only remained musing on the inscrutable decrees of fate and talk of a revival of the true faith in its primitive form. But since Islam had been established in India by military conquerors and had been maintained by the Mughals as a branch of the Caliphate, this gave little consolation. They had put their trust in princes and the princes had fallen. Materially, they were in an even worse plight than the Hindus. When in power they had monopolized high offices, leaving the daily work of administration to a Hindu middle class. When deprived of office they had no profession to fall back upon and hardly any group that could take a positive attitude toward the new order. The dispossessed gentry and reduced *maulvis* or clergy could only sigh for the past and hate the present. That is why the Mutiny, which began as a Hindu outbreak, came to be identified more with the Muslims in the end.

All the arts which depended on patronage were in decay. Architecture suffered most, because it was most expensive and depended much upon the good taste of the patron as well as the architect. In most of India there was no money, in Lucknow and Calcutta no taste. Buildings of significance in the Mughal style practically ceased with the turn of the century. The painters of the Mughal and Rajput schools, whose work had challenged the Italians two centuries before, dispersed to provincial centers and eked out a living by commercial art, and still-life and draftsmen's drawings for Englishmen. Only in the hills (especially Kangra) did real art linger on at the courts of some of the hill rajas. Music made no progress, and literature, with a notable exception, seemed to have lost its inspiration. The historians writing in Persian virtually ended with Sayyid Ghulam Husain, the author of the *Siyar-ul-Mutakherin,* compared by Macaulay with Burnet's *History of My Own Times.* The provincial literatures like Hindi and Marathi were still largely concerned with religious verse and ballads. The notable exception was Urdu, the hybrid Persian-Hindu language to which the emperor Muhammad Shah had given court recognition in the early eighteenth century. It flourished at Delhi and Lucknow and produced a line of poets and thinkers in the nineteenth century, with a poet of genius in Ghalib. Education, as surveys in the next few years revealed, was at a discount.[4] The gentry still learned Persian, the language of polite intercourse; the merchants learned to write their own commercial dialect but little else; the religious of both persuasions studied their classical languages for years at a stretch while the rest went without. Many colleges were in ruins and schools were few. The Indian mind, lacking an object for its meditations, or hope for its spirit, revolved more and more within itself.

Apart from this cultural stagnation, India was suffering at this time from a number of social diseases. All of them had been carried within the Indian body social for centuries, but with the disintegration of the late eighteenth century they had broken out with fresh vigor like boils on a diseased body. They were the products of fear, despair, and the uprooting of thousands from home and society. Together they cast a shadow over Indian society and helped to give Hinduism its early reputation in Europe for fantasy and barbarism. In the religious world the cults of fear, especially those connected with the goddess Kali, flourished. Devotion tended to take the form of self-inflicted injuries. Thus hook-swinging, in which the victim had hooks passed through his flesh behind the shoulders and was then swung to and fro at the end of a long pole, was very popular. So was the practice of casting oneself before the car of a god during processions at religious festivals. Both these were suppressed by the British. There was child sacrifice at Saugor Island, fortunately even then an isolated practice. Infanticide, always existent where (as with the Rajputs) girls' dowries were large and failure to arrange a marriage a disgrace, had greatly increased with the poverty of the times and the shortage of men. Then there were the thugs, robbers, and ritual murderers working in honor of Kali. They had been known since the thirteenth century. With the breakdown of society in central India numbers of uprooted, landless men joined them, as others had joined the Pindari plunderers. Posing as merchants, they would join a group of travelers; and, having won their confidence, would strangle them at a given signal with the *rumal* or ritual hand-kerchief. They were adept at concealing the traces of their crimes and disappearing. In the early years of the nineteenth century they operated as far north as the Ganges and as far south as the Kistna on the borders of Hyderabad and Madras.[5] The practice of suttee, reported by Megasthenes in the third century B.C., grew under the same influences. In theory it was a voluntary devotion of her life by the widow to her husband, who in orthodox Hindu doctrine was her god. She went to join him because by her sins in a former life she had caused his death. *Sati* means devoted. In practice many suttees were forced by relatives anxious to acquire the holy prestige of having a *sati* in the family or wishing to be rid of an unwanted family member. It was prevalent among the Brahmins in the Ganges Valley, especially Bengal, where several hundred burnings were recorded annually by British officials up to 1828. It was extensive among the Rajputs, particularly in Rajasthan, and also in the Panjab. It was common among rajas, where it was often frankly compulsory. It was prevalent in south India during the Vijayanagar regime, but had been largely suppressed by Muslim rulers there before the British took control.[6] Lastly, there was dacoity, or gang robbery. This practice, like brigandage in China, rises and falls in India with the general prosperity of the country. In the conditions of the times it was naturally rampant. In Delhi gangs of robbers in the country had divided the city into wards for convenient plunder by different groups.

CHAPTER XXI

The New Government

The time was thus ripe for a new start in India. But at first the new rulers had no such intention. They were awed by the magnitude of their achievement and could not believe that their dominion would be lasting. They had succeeded, they believed, because of a set of favorable circumstances which might change to their undoing. The wisest of them were the most diffident. They thought that they were sitting on a social and racial volcano, which was quiescent for the time being but might erupt at any moment. Thus Charles Metcalfe emphasized the "precariousness" of the Company's new dominion; Mountstuart Elphinstone considered that "the belief that our Indian empire will not be long-lived is reason and not prejudice"; while Sir John Malcolm wrote "in an empire like that of India we are always in danger." The ruler of Delhi, the opponent of the peshwa who organized his territories, and the pacifier of central India all concurred in this imperialist gloom. They had all in youth been ardent members of the forward school; in success they saw more of the danger than the opportunities.

The policy actually adopted will be described in Chapter XXIII. We will continue this one with a brief description of the administration as it actually stood about 1820. Everywhere the British found traces of the Mughal rule, and their respect increased with their knowledge. There was, in fact, more in common between the British and the Mughals than has been generally realized. Both took a paternalist view of society. Their object was to provide a frame of security within which the general business of life could proceed. Both therefore emphasized law and order while abstaining from cultural or social interference. But apart from this agreement on ends there was also a considerable community of spirit. Both groups, unlike the aristocrats of medieval Europe, were lovers of trade. High Mughal lords indulged in it almost as freely as the early Company officials. Shaista Khan, governor of Bengal for many years in the seventeenth century, was said to have amassed a fortune of $114,000,000 in this way. Both groups loved hunting and outdoor sports of various kinds and both were fond of good living. The typical Mughal feast was unhampered by Islamic disapproval of wine nor did the omrah mind trying prohibited meat under another name when visiting the Company's factories. In this they differed from the *maulvis* or Muslim clergy of the day and from the modern Indian Muslim or Pakistani. Again, both loved dignity and grand ceremonies. The Mughal court retained its strict decorum to the last and impressed its code of manners on the upper classes throughout India. The British, in their stiff way, were no less fond of etiquette and ceremony, and they also retained the habit almost to the end. The customs differed, but the love of the panoply of power informed both.

Supreme authority in India, subordinate of course to London, was exercised by the governor general and his council in Calcutta. There were two councilors and the commander in chief, but since Cornwallis' time the governor general had possessed the decisive voice in all essential matters. He was the real ruler, and on occasion would be absent from Calcutta for months at a time, governing India "from the stirrup," as one ruler described it, and sending his decrees to the capital by post runners. The governor general had full authority in the Bengal Presidency, which now stretched to the Sutlej, and powers of supervision over those of Bombay and Madras.

About half of British India, as we have seen, was governed by subordinate princes; it was with the other half that the governor general was directly concerned. Here he had three sets of agents to enforce his will. The first was the civil service, put on a firm basis by Cornwallis and developed in the time of Wellesley into an elite body. Its members were all British, were nominated by the Company's directors, and received preliminary education and training at Haileybury College before going out. The average age of arrival was about fifteen before the college was established and about eighteen thereafter. They had high salaries but no pensions or retiring age, which prevented some, who had fallen into debt in youth, from retiring when they should have. With some misfits, they numbered in their ranks many able men and developed a high level of integrity. The second agent of the governor general's will was the army, a minority being British and the majority Indian; the officer cadre was entirely British. Many officers were employed on political or administrative work and were known as "politicals." They were the object of much jealousy from their brother officers because of the higher emoluments and greater opportunities of civil employ. The third agent was the police force, again the creation of Cornwallis. The higher officers were also British. The reputation of this service was much below that of the other two. It was never free from corruption, but it was effective in restoring and maintaining order. The proceedings of the government were governed by a code of regulations promulgated by Cornwallis. A vital feature, as has already been mentioned, was the "Rule of Law" by which all officials, as in England, were answerable to the regular courts for breaches of official duty.

These agents established and maintained law and order. The second pillar of government was justice. This was administered through a network of the Company's civil and criminal courts. The judges were British, forming a separate branch of the civil service. Criminal law was based on the Muslim code shorn of its fiercer penalties, such as the loss of limbs. Since English law was as yet unreformed, the effect was to produce a penal system more humane than that of England at the time. Personal law was administered according to community practice, for which purpose Hindu and Muslim assessors sat with the British judges. It was the codification of these laws and their translation into English and the local languages which stimulated both translations from Indian classics and the development of prose writing in the local languages. Commercial law was based on British practice and so was the procedure in the courts, a very important innovation. For example, a Brahmin was liable to the same penalty as a non-Brahmin for the same offense.

The unit of administration was the district, of which Bengal had twenty-three in the time of Cornwallis. They corresponded roughly with the *sarkars* of the Mughals. Each district had at its head a collector (of revenue) who was also a magistrate, and a judge. Up-country the collector was called a deputy commissioner. The collector controlled the police under their superintendent. The district was divided into sub-districts under various names, and these again in subgroups down to the basic unit of the village. Apart from its headman, the village had a hereditary accountant and record-keeper. Certain variations did not affect the essential character of this structure, which has continued into the new India down to the present day. The district officer had to keep order, watch the local chiefs, and collect the revenue. He tended to be the countryman's friend, jealously watching encroachments from Calcutta and resisting strenuously the influence of outside townsmen. In general he stood for the *status quo,* and only later concerned himself with such things as local self-government, economic improvement, and social betterment.[1]

The collection of revenue was the main duty of the collector, and this was the third pillar of government as conceived at that time. The principal source of revenue was the land tax, collection of which involved the assessment of liability on crops. In northern India a great assessment had been carried out by Todar Mal in Akbar's time, after which the annual levy had been fixed by rule-of-thumb methods. The British found the wreck of this system and admired it even in decay. They owed much to these forgotten Mughal administrators, whose work formed the foundation on which they later built. By 1818 the British had settled Bengal, and made good progress in the south; elsewhere they were still enquiring and feeling their way. The work went steadily forward through the century, with refinements and improvements to form a monumental administrative achievement.[2] Without going into wearisome detail, it may be convenient to distinguish three district systems which involved three different approaches to the problem. In all systems there was the preliminary work of measurement of the land and classification of the soil. This was done by special settlement officers who worked for years at a time in remote places, sometimes cut off for long periods from their own society. This information was preserved in the district record office, while a complete record of holdings was kept by the village record-keepers. Then came an assessment of the value of the crop, the fixing of demand, and arrangements for revision. It is here that the systems diverged. In the earliest settlements in Bengal the British adopted what is known as the Permanent Settlement. It extended over Bengal proper, Behar, the Banaras district, Orissa, and the eastern coastal fringe down to the river Kistna. The special features of the Permanent Settlement were two. It was permanent in the sense that the demand was fixed once for all. It was a landlord settlement because the *zamindar* or landholder was the intermediary who collected the revenue from the peasant and paid it to the collector. It reflected British ideas about landed property in the eighteenth century, for the settlement turned what were really hereditary tax-collectors into landlords, the former cultivators becoming their tenants. The benefit of increased cultivation and rising prices went to the landlord, not the cultivator, since the landlord's payment to government was fixed, while he was free to demand the same proportion of the gross produce from new tenants. The social consequences of this will be noted in a later chapter.

The second system was that known as *ryotwari*, and was developed by Sir Thomas Munro in the Madras Presidency after the Cornwallis annexation of Mysore territory in 1792. Here the special features were its temporary nature and the elimination of the landlord. The settlement was made for thirty years (later changed to forty), after which a fresh measurement and assessment was made and the demand revised accordingly. By this means it was intended that the cultivator should benefit from his own improvements and from rising prices for a time, but that government should also share in the benefits of increased cultivation and enhanced money values. The settlement was made directly with the cultivator, whose holding was separately measured, recorded, and assessed, and the cash demand fixed by the settlement officer. Both the landlord or hereditary chief and the village elders were ignored. A variant of the *ryotwari* system was developed in western India. The principles of temporary settlement and elimination of the go-between were the same. But in Bombay the demand was fixed districtwise, the total sum being then divided among the individual holdings in due proportion according to the nature of the soil and the cash value of the crops. Here the village elders had more influence than in Madras but no more power. In both these systems the cultivator was protected from the landlord, as he was not in Bengal, but he was not protected against the government or against calamities such as crop failure.

The third system, known as the *mahalwari,*[3] was adopted with variations in the Panjab, the Delhi area, parts of the modern Uttar Pradesh and central India (now Madhya Pradesh). These settlements were again temporary, usually for thirty years. But in this case the demand was fixed not with landlords or directly with cultivators but with villages or estates. This was made possible because of the smaller number of landlords and the greater vigor of village institutions in these sections. The usual proceedings would take place, and then the demand would be assessed, in consultation with the village elders, on the village as a whole. The village authority, through its headman and *panchayat* ("council"), distributed the total demand among the individual cultivators. Later the demand was individually fixed with each cultivator out of the total demand for the village, but both were done in consultation with the village elders. They therefore retained significant influence and afforded some protection to the cultivator against injustice by the government.

The social consequences of these measures were very great. But they were not foreseen and were largely unintended, and may best be dealt with as part of the new policy to be described in Chapter XXIII. Here we are concerned with the administration as it stood when the British achieved control of India and stood forth, as it were, as the successors of the Mughals. A comparison which cannot fail to strike the observer is that with the Mughal system itself. In many ways the Company's rule may be described as a revived Mughal *raj* expressed in mercantile terms. There is the same pyramid of authority, the same elite to act as political cement, the same use of foreign agents and a foreign language, the same religious neutrality, and the same careful tending of the sinews of empire, the land revenue. The governor general in council can be compared with the emperor in his private audience chamber or *Khas durbar*. Though his legal powers were less, in many ways his authority was more effective. The civil and military services matched the Mughal *mansabdars* with their thirty-three grades. The Company's courts, administering a largely Muslim penal code and Hindu and Muslim personal law, can be seen as a more elaborate extension of the Mughal *Qazis, maulvis,* and *pandits*. For the foreign tongue of Persian we have its successor, English, while the British monopoly of high office was only an exaggeration of the Mughal practice by which 70 per cent of the higher *mansabdars* were foreign born. The policy of religious neutrality and the acknowledged British debt to Todar Mal's land system complete the picture. Where the British differed from the Mughals at this period was in their lack of identification with the country. They lived socially as a separate caste. They monopolized the government services and they professed a religion alien to nearly all in India. They were more respected than the Mughals because they were more powerful; they were less liked because they were more remote and more alien.

The officers who manned the new machine formed a fraternity which has been described as a "commonwealth of magistrates." Many of them were of high ability; all of them shouldered great responsibility; their work and their isolation promoted independence as well as, on occasion, eccentricity. They were subject to orders, but they had great individual discretion. They obeyed positive instructions, but they were very ready to explain just what the instructions should be. They had strong views and the vigor to express them. This they did through letters to each other, their superiors, and to Britain, and through the periodical press which grew up in all the main centers of British power. High officers, writing under well-known nom de plumes, would criticize the policies they were carrying out and tell the supreme government the way it should go. In this way the services developed a powerful public opinion of their own which exercised a potent influence on a government whose almost only nonservice member was the governor general himself. An example of this influence is to be seen in the proceedings of the first Afghan war and, at the end of the century, in the service attitude toward the admission of Indians to its higher ranks and to the introduction of self-government. This official forum of discussion and community of spirit combined with loyalty to the supreme government was something unknown to the Mughals, who could only be criticized in whispers and opposed in conspiracies. It was something peculiar to the British system which added purpose and flexibility to its strength.

CHAPTER XXII

The Completion of Dominion

From the year 1818 we can treat India as a political entity which has its own internal and external policies. But though the reintegration of India had been substantially achieved, it was not yet geographically complete. To the northwest was a region where geography did not provide clear frontiers, and which posed to each Indian empire questions of how much and how far. For these reasons British expansion did not end with the defeat of the Pindaris and the peshwa. During the next forty years a movement of rounding off of frontiers and determination of boundaries was going on which justifies the general term "completion of dominion."

The reader may well inquire, what was the motive behind these campaigns and annexations? Was it the fire of imperialism, only quenched by the snows of the Himalayas and the wastes of central Asia? The opinions of the administrators quoted in Chapter XXI hardly support this view, and in any case we should be faced with the difficult question of determining exactly what is meant by "imperialism." There were men like Lord Ellenborough and Sir Charles Napier who talked in terms of conquest, but the men in real control were for the most part sober realists. It must also be remembered that though the Company exercised less and less control over policy, those who did were no less subject to the pressures of commercial opinion. Dominion would not have been won nor would it have been retained if it had not been thought worth while. Wars cost money, and are rarely waged by commercially minded people for reasons other than profit. If, then, we put aside the mere desire to expand as a motive for the wars of the next forty years, we are left with two alternatives. One was the desire for trade and commercial profit. This may be thought to be second nature in a nation of shopkeepers. But in fact the circumstances of the day strengthened the force of this motive. Britain was in the van of the

Industrial Revolution, with a rapidly expanding economy. She sought markets for her manufactured goods as well as outlets for capital expenditure. The great populations of south and east Asia seemed to offer an unlimited market for cotton textiles, if only they could be reached; while the cold regions of central and northeast Asia promised the same for woolen goods. There was constant pressure on the British government to open up trade in China, Burma, Tibet, Nepal, and the northwest. Commercial expansionism was certainly one motive in British policy. The British government was not dominated by commercial pressure, but it was influenced by it. For example, on the one hand it resisted until the turn of the century traders' demands for the forcible opening of Tibet to British trade, while on the other hand it took action on what was essentially a traders' quarrel in Burma.

The other motive behind British policy was security. Many previous Indian empires had been overthrown by invasions, usually from the northwest. Believing their hold on India itself to be precarious, Indian policy-makers suffered from a nightmare of foreign invasion leading to internal revolt. This led to a morbid fear of attack upon the northwest which at times lost touch with reality and at times attracted the very dangers it feared so much. These two motives, together with some interference from London in the larger interests of British diplomacy, account for most of the moves before the Mutiny. A subsidiary motive, which was important on occasion, as in the case of the first Afghan war, was the desire of officials to gain distinction through new enterprises.

The situation on the borders of India in 1818 was as follows. To the north the Company's frontier ran with the snowy range, except where Nepal, Sikkim, and Bhutan ran down to the foothills. Only Nepal was important, while beyond lay the thinly peopled and desolate Tibetan Plateau. Nepal itself was controlled by the vigorous Gurkha dynasty which had established itself in Khatmandu in 1768. It had already tried conclusions with the Company in the war of 1814–15. Though the Gurkhas lost some districts in the plains and the hill states they had conquered as far as the Sutlej, they had deeply impressed the British by their prowess. Mutual respect and the prospect of little return kept the treaty of Khatmandu inviolate to 1947. The British resisted the temptation to interfere when civil dissensions led to the establishment of the Rana dynasty of hereditary prime ministers and the confinement of the king to his palace. Nepal later became a valuable auxiliary to British India by allowing its men to serve in the Indian army. Like Switzerland in the sixteenth century, its most profitable export was men, not goods. To the northeast of India lay the tangled hill districts of Assam, and beyond the Burman kingdom of Ava. This state, under a dynasty established in 1768, was then in an expansive mood and had won control of the whole Irrawaddy Valley.

To the northwest the position was far less simple. The Company's frontier ran along the Sutlej River, and then, as a result of the 1818 settlement with the Rajput states, through the great Indian Desert down to the sea at the Rann of Kutch. The Sutlej boundary was fixed by the treaty of Amritsar in 1809 with the Sikh chief Ranjit Singh. As with the Gurkhas, respect here was mutual, and the treaty endured as long as Ranjit lived. But the Sikhs were far more powerful than the Gurkhas, possessing an efficient Western-trained army and a powerful train of artillery. They could speak on equal terms with the British. Stretching down the Indus were the domains of the Amirs of Sind, once subject to the Mughal empire and later to the Afghan monarchy. Now five chiefs enjoyed a precarious independence, linked in the loosest of confederacies. Beyond the Indus lay Afghanistan, itself a splinter state from the old Persian empire. At this time it was undergoing convulsions whereby the ruling Abdali (also called Durrani) family was being replaced by the Barakzais. Beyond to the west lay Iran or Persia, elegant but decrepit. Beyond Persia in the great plains of Turkestan were the decaying states which had once been the terror of the whole Middle East. Beyond them again was Russia, little more than a shadow as yet, but already known for its successful campaigns against Persia.

In order to understand events in this region, it is necessary to consider shortly the geopolitics of the Indian region. It has already been explained that, from this point of view, India cannot be treated in isolation. There are no natural geopolitical divisions in India, which might promote the existence of a number of independent states and a balance of power between them as in Europe. There has never been a concert of Indian powers. The political orchestra has either played in unison or else dissolved in tumult. The balance of power lies between India and adjacent regions. India is open to the south to the sea. To the southeast she is closely concerned with Indonesia or the East Indies. A friendly power here has been historically vital for her export trade in textiles and imports of spices. A hostile power could gravely compromise Indian prosperity. It has been India's good fortune that in the historical period the rulers of Indonesia have been either weak or friendly. In the nineteenth century the Dutch rulers of Indonesia, because of their position in Europe and because of British sea supremacy, were virtually auxiliaries of the Indian empire. This did not deter them from characteristic hard bargaining, but it meant that India was secure from the East.

To the northwest Indian security has historically depended upon the existence of a strong power in the Iranian Plateau. If Iran was strong and India divided, there would clearly be danger of invasion. The ideal position was therefore a strong India balancing a strong Iran, as was the case with the Mughal and Safavid empires. A strong Iran was necessary to provide a defense from the incursions of the nomads of central Asia. Historically these incursions have been unpredictable events, arising from unknown causes within a vast area shielded from observation. Parthians, Scythians (Sakas), Kushans, Huns, Mongols, and Turks have issued forth, often bringing destruction to civilization and sometimes setting in motion creative movements in their turn. In this connection central Asia may be likened to a reservoir whose levels are unpredictable and subject to occasional rises and overflows. It has been the function of a strong Iran to provide a dam against these waters and so save India from barbarian floods. Every Indian statesman has therefore had to scan events in the northwest with care in order to take measures against brewing political storms before they have attained hurricane force.

In the story of British dealings with the northwest we see at work the two motives of trade and security. But of these security was the stronger, for not even a Manchester businessman could easily convince himself that there was a large market among Afghan tribesmen, nor could the most ingenious "political" in Simla easily convince the London government that wars in this region could be made to pay. In this area, however, a third motive must be added to the former two, that of high British policy in relation to Russia. The three together produced one of the most dreary and least profitable episodes in the history of British India.

In 1818 it seemed that there was little to fear in the northwest. Ranjit Singh's Panjab was strong but friendly; Sind suspicious but weak; Afghanistan distracted by civil war; Persia weak and Russia far distant. The first move was therefore for trade. Missions had already visited Kabul and Sind in Minto's time (1807–13). The sight of the Indus and James Burnes's account of Sind in 1825 kindled commercial imaginations; where there was a great navigable river there ought to be ships and trade. In 1831 a trial trip was made under cover of presenting Ranjit Singh with a gift of English cart horses. They were larger than any known breed in the Panjab, but unsuitable for riding, and they died of overfeeding. "Alas," said a Sindi, "Sind has now gone since the English have seen the river." So the event was to prove but for the moment Sind was protected from the designs of Ranjit Singh by the British governor general, Lord William Bentinck.

But it was not trade which dictated the next move. It was a mixture of security, fear, and European high politics. The French danger to India had gone with Napoleon, but in its place fear of Russia was beginning to grow. Russia had emerged from the Napoleonic wars, as she later did from World War II, as the strongest power in Europe. She had the prestige of the Moscow campaign and the defeat of Napoleon. She was the prop of the Holy Alliance, which was pledged to suppress democratic revolution wherever it showed its head. Russia was using then the tactic which she still practices today of advancing as far as possible short of a major war. Her main interest at this time was the Near East, where she hoped to oust Turkey from Constantinople and so obtain free access to the Mediterranean. Here she was helped by the presence within Turkey of suppressed Christian minorities, of whom one, the Greeks, was to rise in revolt in 1821. Her second interest was Persia, with the ultimate design of penetrating to the Persian Gulf. But the Caucasian frontier was mountainous, and beyond the Caspian the decaying Turkish Khanates still intervened between Russia, Persia, and Afghanistan. In 1821 the Greek revolt stirred Catholic and liberal sentiment against Turkey and at the same time the revolt of the governor of Egypt, Muhammad Ali (the founder of modern Egypt), threatened the dismemberment of the Turkish empire and the throne of the Sultan itself. Having posed as a friend of the Greeks and defeated Turkey in 1828–29, Russia then sided with Turkey against the revolting Egyptians. The climax came in 1833 when the treaty of Unkiar Skelessi gave to Russia something very like a protectorate over Turkey. This was the signal for a British diplomatic counteroffensive, directed by Palmerston, who may perhaps be described as the Dulles of the day. Palmerston was determined to thwart Russian designs on Constantinople, Russian control of the Dardanelles, and access to the Mediterranean, which would threaten both the overland route to India via Egypt and the whole British position in the Mediterranean. We may leave the diplomatic moves and countermoves in Europe to the diplomatic historians, noting the powerful motives provided for resisting and perhaps harassing Russia farther east.

Persia had been attacked by Russia in the days of the French alliance, and Russia had excluded Persian vessels from the Caspian Sea in 1813. The Persian comeback with British-trained troops failed signally and led to another humiliating peace in 1828. Persian policy now swung round, and Persia hoped to make gains in central Asia in return for subservience to Russia. In 1834 Persia conquered Khorasan on this plan and in 1837 laid siege to Herat in eastern Afghanistan. Herat was then the last stronghold of the old Afghan dynasty, while Kabul was controlled by its able supplanter, Dost Muhammad. This is the real beginning of the Russian problem in British Indian history, for in the eyes of London and Simla, Persia now meant Russia. The new governor general, Lord Auckland, found himself in a difficult position. Dost Muhammad was asking for help against Ranjit Singh, who had taken Peshawar, as well as for aid against the Persians and Russia. Ranjit Singh was an ally and a powerful one. And London had instructed him "to raise a timely barrier against the impending encroachments of Russian power." Auckland's decision seems to have been the worst possible one in the circumstances; in making it he seems to have been influenced both by London pressure (the exact nature of which is still unknown) and the zeal of his Simla advisers for expansion. The plan was to replace Dost Muhammad (thus placating Ranjit) by a member of the old dynasty, Shah Shuja. Ranjit skillfully avoided taking any action himself, so that the British found themselves marching to Kabul in 1839 and then virtually occupying the country, owing to Shah Shuja's unpopularity. They had left one vital factor out of their calculations, the feelings of the Afghans themselves. These proud, turbulent, and undaunted mountaineers cherished their independence above all else; the presence of the British united them as nothing else could. The occupation showed the Russian danger to be illusory. It was really a point scored in Palmerston's campaign of foiling the Russians in Europe. The end was an Afghan revolt in 1841, the destruction of the occupying army, and the British withdrawal from the country after certain retaliatory marches and battles. The attempt to counter a much-exaggerated Russian threat foundered on the rocks of Afghan love of independence and of lengthy communications. The war showed that at that time the Russian danger was largely imaginary and that British India was not strong enough to dominate the Iranian Plateau.

The occupation of Sind and the Panjab followed closely upon the Afghan war and was closely related to it. That of Sind was its direct consequence. When Auckland and his advisers realized that Ranjit Singh had no intention of marching himself to Kabul in the interest of Shah Shuja, they determined to carry out the whole project with British troops. But the direct route through the Panjab could not be used because of the danger of Sikh interference with the line of communications. So the route through Sind and up the Bolan Pass in Baluchistan was chosen. Bentinck's treaty of 1832 was thrust aside, a subsidiary force with payment was dictated, and the Amirs were compelled to pay arrears of tribute to Shah Shuja from which he himself had released them in 1833. At the end of the Afghan campaign the British could have withdrawn from Sind. But they were sore with the vexation of defeat. In Auckland's successor Ellenborough they had the governor general who most nearly fitted the description of "prancing proconsul," and in Sir Charles Napier a cheerful swashbuckling general. Before the civilian Outram could arrange evacuation he was superseded by Napier, who, having provoked the Amirs beyond endurance, then handsomely defeated them and annexed the country.[1]

The paradox of Sind is that while there is nothing to be said for the manner of its annexation, there is hardly anything more to be said for the Amirs themselves. They themselves had no legitimate claim to rule, being legally rebels against the Afghan authority as the successor of the Mughal. They were ignorant, obscurantist, rapacious, and suspicious. They understood little beyond hunting, and allowed a potentially fertile land to remain a desert. Trade was discouraged. The people were poor, life was at a standstill. Sind no more than the rest of India could escape the great Westernizing movement of the nineteenth century; the only question was the manner of its coming. It would have been better for such a movement to have come from within, but the Amirs themselves were quite incapable of initiating it. The coming of the West was inescapable; it was its manner which was inexcusable.

The case of the Panjab was very different. Though still largely unirrigated and but a shadow of what it later became,[2] it contained considerable resources, a vigorous population, a well-organized state, and an efficient army. In Ranjit Singh it had one of the ablest rulers of the nineteenth century. Any move against it would be a major operation, not to be lightly undertaken. The Panjab in history had been notable for conflict, for love of sport, and for the passage of armies. It was a land of tensions, and had rarely enjoyed an independent existence. Its prowess and reputation at this time therefore merit some enquiry. They are to be found in the nature of the government, which was essentially a dictatorship of the Sikh community with Hindus and Muslims in subordinate partnership. Ranjit Singh himself recognized this fact by preferring to call himself "general of the Khalsa" or Sikh community than to use his territorial title of Maharaja of Lahore. The Sikhs were the dominant force in the Lahore kingdom. They played a critical part in the Indo-Pakistan conflict of 1947, and they dominate today the Indian state of the East Panjab, which stretches from the Sutlej to the Jumna rivers. The development of the Panjab, and the whole question of Indo-Pakistan relations, cannot be understood without reference to the Sikhs, and it is therefore necessary to know something more about them.

The community of Sikhs, or "disciples," began with the preaching of the Hindu ascetic Nanak, who lived in the Panjab from about 1469 to 1539. Like many prophets of his day, he preached the realization of God through meditation and religious exercises. He denounced forms of worship whether Muslim or Hindu and the caste rules of Hinduism. He was one of the many who at that time tried to reconcile the two religious systems by promoting spiritual religion independent of outward forms. Nanak became the head of a set of quietist Hindus who acclaimed him a Guru or sage. He was followed by nine more Gurus who were regarded as inspired leaders of the group. Gradually the Sikhs built up a distinctive doctrine and characteristics, and gradually their minds turned from peace to war. The fourth Guru obtained from Akbar in 1577 the site in Amritsar where the Golden Temple, the Canterbury or Mecca of the later Sikhs, was to rise. The fifth Guru, Arjun, compiled the Adigranth, or first scripture of the community, containing many devotional poems which are now continuously recited by devotees in the Golden Temple. With him began the transformation of the sect from quiet retreat to active life. Arjun took to trade and politics and was executed by Jahangir for supporting his rebellious son. His successor "abandoned the rosary for the swordbelt." Before long the Sikhs were in active collusion with the Mughal authorities. The ninth Guru was executed by Aurangzeb in Delhi for refusing to become a Muslim. The tenth and last Guru, Gobind Singh, was a man of practical genius who gave the community its present form and its military prowess. The struggle with Mughal authority in his hands became an anti-Muslim crusade.

The hammer-blows of the Mughals and the statesmanship of Guru Gobind Singh completed the transformation of a sect into a community, one of the constituent elements of modern Indian society. Guru Gobind lost his sons in battle; after his death in 1708 the guruship lapsed and its place was taken by the Sikh scriptures or Granth Sahib as the sole object of worship. Under Gobind's guidance the Sikhs retained the basic Hindu philosophy with its belief in realization of the self, the law of karma, and reincarnation, but added so many other features as to make the Sikhs quite distinct from the rest of the Hindus. Their early hope of reconciliation with the Muslims led them to look kindly on Muslim practices, while their later crusade against them inclined them to borrow anything from their enemies which might be helpful to themselves. In fact, the later religion of the Sikhs can be described as an offshoot of Hinduism which borrowed heavily from Islam in order to give itself cohesion and fighting spirit.

While keeping the Hindu philosophy and a few vestigial Hindu customs, the Sikhs repudiated the polytheism of popular Hinduism. For them there was no intermediary between God and man save the Guru and later the Granth Sahib. In the social sphere, they attacked the basic Hindu institution of caste, a move in the age-old campaign against Brahmin supremacy. In this way they appealed to the low-caste and outcaste Hindus who joined them in large numbers and also to the sturdy Jats, who resented the pretensions of both Brahmins and Rajputs. The body was thus united into a brotherhood known as the *Khalsa* or pure. To their Vedantic philosophy, their book, and their brotherhood, the Sikhs added certain customs and rules which tended to bind them together and set them apart from others. The initiation and communion ceremonies, bearing a distinct resemblance to Christian rites, gave the new entrant a sense of "belonging" and of freedom from the shackles of caste. The title of "Singh," lion or champion, helped this process by dispensing with caste names. Once initiated, the Sikh from Gobind's time wore his hair unshaven, which gave him his characteristic beard and the turban necessary to cover the coils of his hair. This was one of the "five K's"; the others were the comb (*kungha*) in the hair, the shorts (*kuchcha*), the steel bangle (*kara*) on the wrist, and the sword or dagger (*kirpan*).[3] There were also rules of conduct, of which the prohibition of tobacco was the most important. Finally, war in defense of faith was a religious act and death in battle a martyrdom. A special group of armed devotees were known as *akalis*.[4] Most of these features were introduced by Gobind Singh and solidified during the eighteenth century. Their resemblance to corresponding features in Islam is unmistakable. Here we see the Granth Sahib matching the Koran; the initiation ceremonies, though different in character, have the same idea behind them. The wearing of long hair is related to the orthodox Muslim custom of wearing beards, while denunciation of caste and idolatry is a direct loan from Islam. Finally, the Sikh holy war resembles the Muslim *jehad* or fight for the faith, and their *akalis* the Muslim *ghazis* or champions. As so often happens in struggles for existence, in the course of them the weaker party borrowed heavily from the armory of the stronger.

We have noticed that the Sikhs were driven to the hills in the early eighteenth century in one of the last Mughal acts of vigor. There they remained until the times of Nadir Shah the Persian and Ahmad Shah the Afghan, dotting the foothills with forts and held together by the intensity of their faith. From about the middle of the century they reappeared in the plains, first as bands of marauders and then as ruling groups under robber chiefs. At the end of the century Ranjit Singh achieved supremacy over the other groups or *misls* and established himself at Lahore. From there he built up a compact kingdom which included Multan in the south, Peshawar to the northwest, and Kashmir to the north and was separated from British India to the east by the Sutlej. But Ranjit was not content with mere conquest. At the time of the British envoy Metcalfe's visit to Amritsar in 1809 Ranjit was profoundly impressed by the ease with which Metcalfe's disciplined guard repulsed an attack on his camp by the wild *akalis*. He determined to build a disciplined army equal to that of the British, and devoted to the project his own talents and the resources of the Panjab. At his death he had a regular army of forty thousand infantry and twelve thousand cavalry that claimed comparison with the Company's army and a park of artillery which was probably superior. Europeans were freely employed, but none were allowed any political influence.

Ranjit used the whole resources of the state to support the army, so that there was little left over for irrigation or commercial development. The most important places in the Sikh Panjab were military cantonments and the most important merchants the horse-dealers. Ranjit organized his army and his state on a skillful system of balance. In the army the Sikhs themselves were balanced by Hindu and Muslim contingents, and Panjabi officers by Europeans. In the state both Hindus and Muslims played an important though subordinate part, and representatives of both were among his close advisers. Ranjit himself bore a charmed life amid an unscrupulous and power-hungry court, because each chief knew that the consequences of his death were likely to be worse than the limit to ambition imposed by his continued life. Ranjit's only legitimate son was of feeble mind, which reinforced the uncertainty of the future. So great was the spell that in the nine months that Ranjit lay speechless from paralysis no one dared to touch him.

Such was the state of the surviving portion of independent India in 1839 when Ranjit died. As in south India in the 1740's and Bengal in 1756, there was tension in the air, and an expectation of great changes to come. In the next six years the most gloomy of anticipations was fulfilled. The struggle for power was intense, murderous, and reckless. Power passed from chief to chief and then to army committees or *punches,* which held the government to ransom. In 1845 the fourth successor of Ranjit was a boy of seven, with his mother as regent. The army was encouraged to attack the British in the hope that its spirit would be curbed by defeat. It actually did so in December and was defeated in four battles notable for bad generalship and gallantry on both sides. The state was not at once annexed. Instead the army was reduced, Kashmir detached and handed to the hill-raja Gulab Singh (who had changed sides), and a Resident posted in Lahore to advise a reorganized government. In this way the modern state of Jammu and Kashmir, the bone of contention between India and Pakistan, came into existence. It passed direct from Sikh to Hindu hands; British moderation in this respect exacted a heavy toll, both in human happiness and international relations. The Resident was Sir Henry Lawrence, who set about the work of reform with energy and insight. But many Sikhs did not consider that they had been fairly defeated. In Sir Henry's absence they rose in revolt against their own sponsored government, and were finally defeated in more bloody battles. The new governor general, Dalhousie, decided on annexation, partly because he thought that no one could govern better than the British, but also because he thought that no sponsored government could be stable in this tract of bitter rivalries and turbulent chiefs with a northwestern frontier exposed to tribal raids and foreign invasion. The prosperity of the modern Panjab, with the sextupling of the population, began from this moment. The measures that were taken and their consequences we shall note a little later, in Chapter XXIV.

British expansion into Burma remains to be mentioned. Burma differs from India in race, social conditions, religious tradition, and political history. Its racial types and languages are Mongoloid, it has no caste system, its religious tradition is Buddhist, and its political relations have been more with Indo-China and China than with India. In 1768, for instance, the Burmans sacked the capital of Siam, but they have never penetrated far into India. For these reasons we shall treat Burma as an external appendage of India, like Nepal or Afghanistan, only concerning ourselves with its internal affairs insofar as they affect Indian issues. The first Burman war arose from Burman expansionism. The Burmans were then an isolated people who imagined that "Ava was the centre of the universe, its arms invincible and its culture supreme." Acts of aggression in 1824 led to war, which resulted in the annexation of the two coastal strips of Arakan and Tenasserim. The heart of Burma was untouched. In the second and vital war of 1852 we see the commercial motive at work. The merchants were not strong enough to force the government into war, but strong enough to secure aid once they had got into trouble themselves. This time, after a model campaign, Rangoon and the rice country of lower Burma were annexed. This event was the real beginning of modern Burma, for it heralded the development of the export trade in rice and timber and the development of Rangoon as a great port. The final stage was in 1886 when Dufferin annexed upper Burma from the crazy king Theebaw. Here perhaps security and commerce were both motivations. It was fear of French influence from Indo-China (France was then seeking compensation in the Far East for defeat by Bismarck and was the second naval power in the world), as much as the grievances of the Bombay-Burma Trading Corporation, which precipitated action.

By about the middle of the nineteenth century the dominion of the East India Company had thus been rounded off. It extended everywhere to its natural frontiers except in Nepal, and to Burma where it exceeded them. Though the Company retained its name, it no longer dealt with trade and was in fact a subordinate agency of the British government in London. It administered India in somewhat the same manner as the British Broadcasting Company controls broadcasting in modern Britain, with the difference that a public inquest into its affairs took place on a grand scale every twenty years instead of an annual routine review.

CHAPTER XXIII

The New Policy

We have seen the East India Company establish its dominion in India and round off its possessions by the mid-nineteenth century. We have seen it organize its administration on what were largely traditional authoritarian lines. We have also noted that the main motive of all this activity was commercial. Security and tranquility for trade was the watchword. Even when the Company had to give up its trade monopoly and was deprived of its commercial functions altogether, the motive remained. It was, in fact, the strength of the commercial motive in Britain which thrust the Company aside in order that all might share in the profits of Indian enterprise. Thus far the merchant and the official were at one. Neither had any wish for innovation which might lead to dangerous thoughts in the Indian population and to Indian competition with British mercantile enterprises. Most members of both classes were content to regard the new Company as old Mughals writ large. There was, it is true, a liberal-minded group among the officials whose views were expressed by Sir John Malcolm's slogan, "Let us, therefore, proceed calmly on a course of gradual improvement," but it is likely that, if the services had been left to themselves, the improvements would have been gradual indeed.

But neither services nor merchants were left to themselves. Britain at this time was seething with new thoughts; it was the percolation of these among the more enlightened officials which was responsible for "improving" ideas. The clue to the change of policy in nineteenth-century India is to be found in the climate of intellectual opinion of the time. In the seventeenth century the civilization of India was regarded as alien and in many ways antipathetic to that of Europe; but it was not regarded as inferior. Descriptions of the great Mughals had in them respect and even something of awe. By 1800 all this had changed; Indian institutions were commonly considered to be effete, many customs odious, and Indian peoples barbarous. There was a new climate of opinion born of the great movement of European thought from the seventeenth century onward. The old deference to the classical world gave way under the impact of the Renaissance, the discovery of the New World, and the scientific revolution of the late seventeenth century, to a new confidence. In the eighteenth century, Europe, led by the French philosophers, believed that it had found the secret of progress and that this secret distinguished the West from all other civilizations. Not only was Europe already ahead of all others, but she would go on increasing her lead. That secret was the principle of reason which made possible both scientific progress undreamt of before and unknown to the ancients, and a remodeling of society on principles of justice. The Industrial Revolution, the child of applied science and the parent of unheard-of riches, gave an impetus to this process like the second stage of a space rocket. The former respect for the past gave way to a great pride in the present and an abounding confidence in the future. A symbol of this new spirit was Condorcet's *Essay on the Progress of the Human Spirit,* written under the shadow of the guillotine in 1794. It was minds breathing this intellectual air which now turned their attention to India.

The spirit began to affect India in the early nineteenth century. The criticisms of "nabobs" or returned Anglo-Indian officials in the 1760's had been concerned with the un-English behavior of returned Englishmen from the East, and the discussions of the Warren Hastings case with un-English behavior in India itself. It was generally agreed that Indian institutions, bad as well as good, should be left untouched. But from that time several new currents of thought gathered strength until they collectively achieved a change of policy which was responsible for the creation of modern India. The first of these may be called the radical and utilitarian stream. It consisted of those who accepted the French ideas of reason, humanity, and the rights of man, and those who followed the doctrine of utility of Jeremy Bentham. All Benthamites were radicals, but not all radicals were Benthamites. These men saw much to criticize when they looked at India. Their humanism was affronted by the collective injustice prevailing in the caste system and such features as suttee, the status of widows, infanticide, and the outcastes. Their sense of reason was outraged by the many superstitions prevailing in the India of the day. Several factors combined to make them specially potent in deciding the shape of the new India. Bentham's theory of legislation led them to believe that societies could be reformed by proper laws. Did not the Company's India afford a splendid field for such a process, with so much to reform and power in the hands of so few? Further, the Tory reaction of the Napoleonic period denied them the opportunity of putting their ideas into practice in Britain. Why not use India as a sociological guinea pig to demonstrate the virtues of the new philosophy? There was a decided element of authoritarianism in this left-wing stream of thought, so that they saw no difficulty in working through the East India Company. A further stroke was their penetration of India House in the person of Bentham's major disciple, James Mill. Mill, a self-made literary figure, published his *History of British India* (to 1805) in 1817, and was appointed the next year to an important position with the Company. The influence of this school was great when the reforming Whig government came into power in 1830 and began the great age of reform. Lord William Bentinck, on going to India in 1828, could write to Bentham "I shall govern in name, but it will be you who will govern in fact." Macaulay was a radical who helped to pilot the Charter Act of 1833 through Parliament and later helped to introduce English education into India. This school was all for introducing the West into India.

In this work they found unexpected allies in the religious evangelicals. These people abhorred the rationalist ideas of the radicals but found common ground in their views of India. There was a concord of disapproval. The evangelical was a humanist on Gospel grounds, as the utilitarian was on rational ones. The evangelicals were already leading a crusade against slavery within the British empire, and could they stop short of things as bad in India? Their Protestant theology condemned idolatry and their Protestant rationalism was shocked by non-Christian superstitions. In addition the evangelicals were filled with a thirst for winning souls for Christ; in India they saw, as they conceived, millions under British rule condemned to perdition. These motives were strong enough to bring evangelicals and utilitarians together for the reform of India. They had another trump card, that of influence in high places. The saintly William Wilberforce, the champion of slave emancipation and of Christian missions in India, was a close friend of the prime minister, William Pitt (1783–1801, 1804–6), and an influential member of Parliament. Charles Grant the elder was a chairman of the Company and his son a president of the Board of Control. Charles Simeon of Cambridge sent out chaplains who reformed Calcutta society.

A third current of opinion was that of the free-traders, which can be traced back to Adam Smith and his *Wealth of Nations,* published in 1776. The doctrine that trade grows with the removal of restraints found a ready target in the East India Company with its Indian and Chinese monopolies. It provided a rallying cry for the mercantile world, whose influence was steadily increasing. All these forces made for the introduction of Western ideas and institutions into India as the only way in which India could progress. They were opposed by the advocates of the *status quo*. One argument, that of the Oriental scholars, was that Indian institutions had a value of their own and should not be disturbed. But this went against the current of the time and was less and less regarded. A more effective plea was the danger of upheaval if innovations were too rapid or too sweeping. This was the administrators' argument and it carried respect in governing circles. The upshot was the inevitable British compromise. Certain customs which offended the moral sense should be rooted out. Beyond this, however, Indian institutions should be left undisturbed, but they should be matched by British or Western ones. The light of reason, it was firmly believed, once kindled in Indian minds, would lead them to reject the tradition of the East and accept the new truth from the West. This was expressed by Macaulay in his "Minute on Education" when he envisaged "a class of persons, Indian in blood and colour, but English in taste, in opinion, in morals and intellect." Indeed the whole outlook of the time was so well expressed by the same writer in a speech to the House of Commons that it is worth a rather lengthy quotation.[1] "The destinies of our Indian empire are covered with thick darkness. It is difficult to form any conjecture as to the fate reserved for a state which resembles no other in history, and which forms by itself a separate class of political phenomena. The laws which regulate its growth and its decay are still unknown to us. It may be that the public mind of India may expand under our system till it has outgrown that system; that by good government we may educate our subjects into a capacity for better government; that, having become instructed in European knowledge, they may, in some future age, demand European institutions. Whether such a day will ever come I know not. But never will I attempt to avert or to retard it. Whenever it comes, it will be the proudest day in English history. To have found a great people sunk in the lowest depths of slavery and superstition, to have so ruled them as to have made them desirous and capable of all the privileges of citizens, would indeed be a title to glory all our own. The sceptre may pass away from us. Unforeseen accidents may derange our most profound schemes of policy. Victory may be inconstant to our arms. But there are triumphs which are followed by no reverses. There is an empire exempt from all natural causes of decay. Those triumphs are the pacific triumphs of reason over barbarism; that empire is the imperishable empire of our arts and our morals, our literature and our laws."

We can now pass to the implementation of these ideas in India itself. Their progress can be gauged by noting developments at a number of points in time. In 1793, during the charter discussions of that year, Wilberforce proposed that Christian missions should operate in India with government support, but the proposal was rejected. Charles Grant's *Observations on the State of Society of the Asiatic Subjects of Great Britain,* which may be called the evangelical view of India, was privately printed as part of the campaign. In 1813 change began to break through. The Charter Act of that year, at Wilberforce's instigation, allowed Christian missions to operate within the Company's territories, though it withheld government support. The Company's commercial monopoly was abolished, thus allowing the private trader to operate freely. Further, thirty thousand dollars [2] were to be set aside annually for the promotion of learning among the people of India. This was done by a Tory House of Commons. In 1828 we find a Tory president of the Board of Control, a right-wing follower of the Duke of Wellington, writing to the governor general that "we have a great moral duty to perform in India." Clearly by this time reform was in the air. It was no accident that the new policy was introduced by the governor general to whom he wrote, Lord William Bentinck.

Bentinck was the radical son of the third Duke of Portland, the Whig prime minister and colleague of Fox and Burke in 1783. As a young man Bentinck was recalled in 1807 from the governorship of Madras for alleged misjudgment on the occasion of the Vellore Mutiny. For the next twenty years he sought vindication in the form of appointment to the governor generalship and eventually achieved his object in 1827 by a series of chances and circumstances which could only occur in a patronage-ridden society. He was far to the left of his father—as noted, he was an avowed follower of Bentham—and was determined to put his ideas into practice. He was regarded by the Duke of Wellington as hasty and unreliable; he "always feared that he would do some rash thing." They had clashed as soldiers in the Peninsular War. In fact, with the years a somewhat headstrong disposition was tempered by discretion and wisdom, so that he retained the vigor to reform while acquiring the tact to manage his opponents. Bentinck's first two years were difficult because the reactionary Duke of Wellington was in office and the president of the Board of Control was trying to unseat him. He had to endure much initial unpopularity through carrying out much-needed economies on the orders of the directors. He was nicknamed "the clipping Dutchman," and the legends of his cuts lingered in the services down to the twentieth century. The advent of the reforming Whigs to power in 1830 gave him his lead. By the time of his retirement in 1835 he was able to stamp the new policy indelibly on India with incalculable consequences for the future. His rule was a kind of New Deal for British India; it included a series of measures highly controversial, arousing strong passions, never wholly reversible, and permanently affecting the course of events. We have seen how the radical interventionism of the radicals and evangelicals was countered by the caution of the administrators as well as by the conservatism of the orientalists. In Bentinck in his maturity was found a man temperamentally fitted to combine reforming zeal with discretion. The result was neither an official mutiny (as at one time seemed possible) nor a revolution (as prophesied by critics) but a new era. The mutiny of 1857 can in some respects be regarded as a delayed-action response to his measures. But it would be unfair to father this explosion upon him, since there were clearly others who dropped matches around on the combustible material which is bound to accumulate in a period of social change. The first feature of the Indian New Deal was a frontal attack on practices which were considered to conflict with the universal moral law. With these practices, agreed the reformers, whether rationalists or clericals, there could be no compromise. Under this heading must be placed Bentinck's first measure, the suppression of suttee in 1829.[3] In orthodox theory this practice was a voluntary action by the widow impatient for reunion with her god-husband; in practice the decision was often induced by relatives who wanted the prestige of a holy sacrifice in the family or one less mouth to feed or the material possessions of the widow. For the fifteen years previous to suppression, recorded burnings in the Bengal Presidency had ranged from 500 to 850 a year. Governor generals for nearly thirty years had considered and shelved the problem. Bentinck acted, and met with no more opposition than a petition by the orthodox to Parliament. In the same class of measures came the suppression of the thugs or ritual murderers described in Chapter XX, the suppression of child-sacrifice at Saugor Island, and measures against infanticide. This latter was far more difficult to detect than suttee, and the success achieved far less easy to estimate. It was the first time, however, that a government in India had ever taken a stand on this matter and the results in the long run were impressive.

It was at this point that "root and branch" methods stopped short. There was no frontal attack on Hinduism or Islam as the missionaries and some radicals would have liked. No mosques or temples were demolished in the Akbar or Aurangzeb manner; the institution of caste was left intact. In 1833 all classes were declared eligible for public office, but this was in fact possible before at the will of the ruler. The only encroachment of substance was that change of religion should not debar an heir from lawful inheritance, thus impinging on Hindu and

Muslim personal law. This was regarded as a Christianizing measure but was defended as a measure of natural justice.

We now come to a series of measures which set up Western institutions, as it were, side by side with their Eastern counterparts and released Western ideas into the Indian intellectual mixture where they could ferment to produce their own results within the Indian mind. This Indian mental revolution was the most important result of all Bentinck's work. The first institution to note is the legal, for which Bentinck was only partly responsible. He inherited an elaborate system of law courts already observing English legal procedure, overburdened with arrears, and largely incomprehensible to the common people. His contributions were creation of two grades of Indian judges, which encouraged the process of percolating the Indian mind with Western legal principles; giving his confidence to Macaulay as the first law member of the government of India; and starting the process which eventually produced the Indian Civil and Criminal Codes of Procedure and the Indian Penal Code. While the legal process still seemed meaningless and often heartless to the Indian peasant, its spirit and ideas began to penetrate into the Indian mind. Such notions as human equality, the dignity of the person, the liberty of the subject were strange to orthodox Hindu thinking and in fact conflicted with orthodoxy at many points. The results of legal practice based upon Western assumptions were of immense importance both in shaping the outlook of the modern Indian and in undermining traditional Indian institutions.

The next measure concerned education. It is often thought to be the key measure of the whole, but it should in fact be regarded as one of a series of acts which collectively opened the doors of the West to the East. There had long been controversy as to the proper disposal of the annual grant of $30,000 made for the advancement of learning. Was it to be Western or Eastern learning or, as the Westernizers put it, useful or useless knowledge? With the support of Macaulay, who used the occasion to write his celebrated "Minute on Education" with its vehement and shallow attack on Sanskrit literature, Bentinck came down on the side of the West. In 1835 it was declared that the content of higher education should be Western learning, including science, and that the language of instruction should be English. A beginning was to be made with producing Macaulay's class of "Indians in blood and colour, but English in taste, in opinions, in morals and in intellect." The source of all knowledge had hitherto been supposed by all Hindus to reside in the Sanskrit classics, especially the Vedas. Persian was only a cultural and professional convenience. It was a challenge to orthodoxy to seek learning in Western knowledge through the medium of the English language. The addition of medical studies challenged the caste system, since dissection involved a breach of caste rule. The first orthodox students to attend the Calcutta Medical College went through the same kind of mental stress that a Westerner might experience who contemplated a change of religion which would involve social outlawry. When the first shock of innovation had been overcome, the Westernizing effect was more subtle. The student was free to practice his religion and observe the rules of his society. But new ideas were implanted in his mind by his studies, which, however carefully kept in separate mental compartments, had a habit of spilling over from the new to disturb the old. They entered through the textbooks of his study. The English poets; the Bible, portions of which were prescribed English reading in Calcutta for many years; prose writers like Burke, Macaulay, and John Stuart Mill were full of Western ideas and attitudes which were basically Christian and classical. Moral and spiritual ideas like the worth of the individual, the equality of all before God, and the primacy of conscience and reason entered into the Hindu consciousness. Political ideas like personal liberty and the rule of law, self-government and nationalism were implicit in all English literature from Shakespeare's Henry V downward and were reinforced by study of European liberal writers like Mazzini who were widely read in translation. The Bengali who loved to recite "This sceptred isle, . . . set in the silver sea, . . . this England" [4] could not fail before long to slip in "India" for "England." Similarly all scientific study, which was included in Western studies from the beginning, involved the acceptance of reason and experiment as the tests of truth and implied a challenge to the whole orthodox system of tradition and authority.

The next decision, taken by Bentinck at the same time for different reasons, was to substitute English for Persian as the official language of government business. In form it was the substitution of one foreign language for another. But in fact, owing to the position of the language chosen, it was a decision of incalculable importance. The Englishman's inability or reluctance to master foreign languages was an important factor in bringing about the affiliation of the ancient Indian civilization with the modern West. English was henceforth (from 1835) the language of diplomacy, of higher government business, and of the higher courts of law. The immediate consequence was that thousands of people all over the country, who would formerly have learned Persian as a means of livelihood, now took up English. The Persian cultural ethos which these classes had formerly acquired by these means was replaced by a British one. These people were subjected to Western influences in all the ways mentioned above. Scornful Englishmen made merry at the grammatical oddities of their subordinates. But behind mistakes of syntax and the often comic misuse of words lay dawning apprehension of a new mental world. "Babu" English was the baby-patter of the newborn cosmopolitan Indian. We can sum up the process by saying that with the English language came English letters; with English letters came English ideas, which were Western ideas in English dress; with the ideas came English customs, which were English expressions of the Western spirit. The study of English has produced such masters of the language as Rabindranath Tagore, Arabindo Ghose, and Sarvepalli Radhakrishuan, the philosopher and vice-president of the republic. The synthesis of East and West has been furthered by men like Ram Mohan Roy, Tagore, and Jawaharlal Nehru. Among British attitudes which have been accepted by Westernized Indians we may note the love of Shakespeare in the literary world, the reverence for Christ and the Sermon on the Mount in the religious and moral sphere, the acceptance of democracy in the world of politics, the enthusiasm for cricket and hockey in the sporting world, and the taste for tea parties in the social arena. None of these characteristics of the modern Indian comes from pre-British traditional India and they would all have taken a different form if some other nation than Britain had been the sponsor of Western culture.

Along with these government measures, we must note the activities of missionaries, at first mainly British, but later strongly reinforced by Americans with some Germans. Their primary concern was with souls, and some of their methods caused alarm among cautious officials. But they early embarked on two courses which made them important nation-builders. One we may call the "Good Samaritan" policy of hospitals, dispensaries, and orphanages, the other the policy of using education as a means of spreading knowledge of the Gospel. In the first aspect they presented practical Christianity in its most attractive form, while in the second their personalities as well as their teaching recommended the Christian ethic and Western outlook more effectively than they often knew. Missionaries sometimes in spite of themselves were allies in this process of Western innovation.

Apart from these deliberate innovations, a social revolution was taking place which fitted in with, though it was not intended to promote, a new Westernized class. This revolution was the result of government measures dealing with the land, which were part of its land revenue policy. We have seen that the settlement of the country involved a survey of existing holdings, an examination of past measures, and an attitude toward the future. The government's aim was greater revenue consistent with stability and contentment. While their land measures in general achieved this end, they also tended to depress the old landowning class that had formed the aristocracy and ruling classes of the past. An important agent in this process was the Sales Law, which ordained that if a landholder failed to pay his dues, he should not be fined or imprisoned as was done previously, but have his holding put up to auction. The early assessments, particularly in Bengal, were commonly too high; sales were numerous so that by 1815 the *zamindar* class was radically different from the class of 1750. The Sales Law operated everywhere and was reinforced by a new instrument invented by the land "settlers." This was the examination of rent-free tenures, which were numerous and arose as rewards for all kinds for political, administrative, and personal service, for literary and religious merit, or were given merely as personal favors. Many of these grants could not be proved, some were probably fraudulent, and others had been misused. The new authorities resumed all for which there was no documentary proof and thereby enhanced the revenue at the price of much individual hardship and a good deal of injustice. The net effect was to deal a further blow at the old landholding aristocracy, which was wedded to the old Indo-Persian culture and the old political regimes. The last and greatest example of this process was the proceedings of the Inam ("gift") Commission in Bombay. The European monopoly of high office, previously noted, had already pushed the old official class into the background; the land proceedings of the government drove many of them to poverty as well. In this way the social path was being cleared for the new and humbler men who were to ascend the hill of official success by the path of the English language. How these new men developed into a class will be the subject of a later chapter.

CHAPTER XXIV

Dalhousie and the Mutiny

The mutiny of the Indian army in 1857 was the most dramatic event in nineteenth-century India. There were much heroism, ferocity, and suffering on both sides. There was profound psychological shock which led to a fascination for the subject and mutual exaggeration. In this chapter an attempt will be made to place the event in proper perspective as an element in the development of modern India and a factor in the relations of India and Britain.

Before dealing with it more particularly, it is necessary to examine the few years previous, for it is in this period that the forces which clashed with the feelings and ideals of traditional India gathered full strength. They were directed by the confident hand of a man who himself embodied the progressive go-ahead spirit of the Victorian age. That man was the Marquess of Dalhousie, who with Wellesley, Bentinck, and Curzon stands as one of the four outstanding Englishmen of the century. Dalhousie was one of those proud and intelligent but impecunious Scotch lords who sought fame and fortune in official service. In Dalhousie's case his title did no more than give him a start in public life; his talents did the rest. He served as Gladstone's assistant when he was president of the Board of Trade in Peel's government. As vice-president (or undersecretary) he had to grapple with the railway boom of the 1840's. Each new railroad required parliamentary sanction, and in this way Dalhousie learned much about the needs and problems of a rapidly expanding and highly individualistic society. In 1848, at the age of thirty-five, he was chosen to succeed the Waterloo veteran Lord Hardinge, who had just defeated the Sikhs, as governor general. He was short and stocky in appearance. He had an oblong face, capped with a lofty brow and marked with the long nose and pursed lips of pride and determination. To his talents and character were added an abundant energy which wore out his body and left him a physical wreck on his return from India at the age of forty-four. He was generous to his colleagues and subordinates, but relentless to critics and opponents and hypersensitive to criticism. Dalhousie enjoyed the confidence of both the directors and the four governments which covered his eight-year term. The politicians in fact, in a period of confused politics, were glad to leave so able and confident a man to himself. Dalhousie thus became, in a way few others could claim to be, the government of India during his term of office.

Dalhousie considered himself "advanced," but this does not mean that he had what we would call leftish opinions. He prided himself in being abreast of the movements of the day; this meant that he believed in encouraging commerce and industry, in education, and in a certain amount of social welfare. It did not include democracy, but it did include an unbounded faith in Western civilization and its continued progress. Abroad, therefore, he appeared both as an aggressive Westernizer and as a reformer. He had no time for Eastern traditions because he considered Eastern culture to be effete. He wished to introduce Western ideas and institutions so far as possible. He was a paternalist who believed in steam engines. The Dalhousie period was one of change accelerated to a full throttle.

Within a few weeks of his arrival in Calcutta, Dalhousie was confronted by a Sikh revolt in the Panjab which led to the second Sikh war. After waiting through the hot weather on military advice he gave a taste of his quality when he announced "unwarned by precedent, uninfluenced by example, the Sikh nation has called for war, and on my words, Sirs, they shall have it with a vengeance." [1] On the Sikh defeat he annexed the Panjab on his own initiative and then proceeded to organize the new province with the utmost care. The Council of Regency was replaced by a Board of Administration with Henry Lawrence at its head and his brother John a member. When the two famous brothers fell out, Henry hoping to reform the sirdars or chiefs, John backing the peasants or cultivators, Dalhousie chose John as sole ruler. John's rugged ways and contempt for tradition appealed to Dalhousie, and John did not, as Henry did on occasion, contradict. The collaboration which followed was close and sincere. The two were the parents of what is known as the Panjab school of administration. It had a distinct ethos of its own. When John Lawrence became viceroy fifteen years later (1864) this school of thought entered the supreme government, and through various officers exerted an influence throughout northern India. It was the Panjab school which captivated Kipling's imagination and through him became identified with the whole civil service in India.

John Lawrence had to settle a wild country filled with pugnacious, sport-loving, ignorant, and passionate people. His lieutenants, the pick of the civil service of the north, became vigorous paternalists. They believed in rough-and-ready methods and distrusted rules, forms, and courts as devices invented in towns to cheat the sturdy countryman. They lived in an atmosphere of crisis, pistol on holster, ready to take horse to deal with rebels at a moment's notice. Sometimes they took horse when there were no rebels to deal with. They worked incessantly and they loved their charges so long as their superior wisdom was not challenged. The Panjab administrators solved the question of reform without interfering with local customs by developing a passion for public works. A bridge was prized as a connoisseur might prize a ruby; a road was a joy forever. The passion went further to jails, schools, railways, and canals. At the end of the century it found a new and creative outlet in organizing canal colonies on land newly reclaimed by irrigation. When the country was settled, forms of law and government had of course to come in. But the marks of the early days never quite left the Panjab.

Summing up, it may be said that the Panjab school of administrators were notable for their devotion to duty, which sometimes ran to tenseness and a permanent sense of crisis. Their brilliance had a slightly brittle quality; tenseness sometimes turned to harshness at critical moments. Amritsar and its aftermath in 1919 was a leading example of this trait. Its members were devoted to the welfare of the country people and generally distrustful of the urban classes. Their outlook was paternalist. Like most fathers convinced they are right, they disliked being answered back, and they found it difficult to appreciate the claims and attitudes of the new westernized class which arose in the twentieth century. They excelled in doing and making things; they fell short in understanding people. They found the Panjab a desert and left it the most prosperous province in India, with six times its former population. But they failed to integrate its three rival communities as Ranjit Singh had failed before. The penalties for this were division, massacre, and flight. The monument of the Panjab school is the roads and canals which intersect the region and give prosperity; its epitaph is the Partition of 1947. Lord Acton once said that the fault of British Indian statesmen was an undue belief in force. It was this which prevented the Panjab officials from achieving the creative act of uniting the Panjabis into one people.

Dalhousie's only other foreign war was the Burman in 1852, wherein lower Burma, along with Rangoon, was annexed, and the administration was organized with the same care, in conjunction with Sir Arthur Phayre. But the result was less striking because Indian models of administration were used in a country for which they were quite unsuited. Dalhousie's second major activity was the development of Western institutions and activities. Where Bentinck had planted, Dalhousie watered vigorously. He substituted, as it were, the hose for the watering can of his predecessors. He reorganized the Calcutta secretariat and obtained a lieutenant governor to relieve him in the overgrown province of Bengal. Then he launched out on a public works program, creating the department of that name. Irrigation canals, already begun in the north, were greatly extended. A great-roads program was carried out, including the Grand Trunk Road, from Calcutta to Peshawar. Above all, Dalhousie planned the system of Indian railways and started the first construction. He introduced the telegraph, which extended to Delhi by the end of his term. He founded an engineering college.[2] To all these projects he brought a planning genius which made him the most important figure in the introduction of the material aspect of the West into India in the nineteenth century. Bentinck made the first gestures; Dalhousie laid solid foundations upon which others like Curzon later built. But Dalhousie did not stop short at material projects. He was also responsible, along with Sir Charles Wood in Britain, for a large development in the newly introduced Western educational system. A grant-in-aid scheme enabled private colleges to multiply and the structure was crowned by the foundation of the first three universities.[3]

Dalhousie's third great work was his policy toward the Indian states. Hitherto they had been left largely to their own devices in a state of what was called "subordinate isolation." They provided a cheap way of keeping nearly half the country quiet, and they were largely left to their own devices. But rulers without fear of removal, opportunities for conquests, or prospects of all-India distinction (as under the Mughals) lost interest in their work and abuses developed. To Dalhousie the contrast between the standards of administration in British and Indian India seemed glaring. He was convinced that Western government was better in every way than Eastern. For him there was no thought of self-government being better than good government. His criterion was the Utilitarian one of what is useful and efficient. He therefore thought it right to extend direct British rule in India whenever a legitimate opportunity presented itself, and common sense to sweep away obsolete survivals of the past such as titles and pensions.

The opportunities presented themselves in the two guises of misgovernment and failure to have direct heirs. Under the former heading came the populous Muslim state of Oudh, a surviving province of the Mughal empire in what is now Uttar Pradesh.[4] There was no doubt of the effeteness of the dynasty or turbulence of the country, but the annexation, which deprived large numbers of their livelihood, caused grave discontent. The feelings of the people were expressed by the reply reported to Bishop Heber in 1824, when it was suggested that the remedy for their loud complaints might be annexation by the British. " 'Miserable as we are, of all miseries keep us from that,' . . . 'Are not our people better governed?' 'Yes,' was the answer, 'but the name of Oudh and the honour of our nation would be at an end.' " [5] Without actual annexation a province of the Nizam's state of Hyderabad was taken over to pay for his subsidiary force. The failure to have direct heirs involved Hindu law, and annexations in these cases touched closely upon Hindu sentiment. Hindu law allows adoption in the case of lack of direct heirs, the adopted having all the rights of natural ones. The custom, originating in the need for a son to perform funeral rites, was widely observed, and applied to states as well as individuals. Dalhousie's view was that the British government, as the paramount power, must approve all adoptions. In the absence of such approval any dependent state would "lapse" to the British. He applied this rule, among others, to the large Maratha state of Nagpur in central India in 1854,[6] the small but notable state of Satara, where Sivaji's descendants had ruled, in 1848, and the small Maratha state of Jhansi in central India in 1854, which possessed a high-spirited rani or queen.

Finally there came the pensions and titles of ex-sovereign families. These had long been an offense to the forward-looking and practical-minded school which thought that Indian sentiment was indifferent on the point, or if not that it did not matter. Dalhousie agreed. The Nawabs of the Carnatic and of Surat and the Raja of Tanjore lost their titles on the death of the holders. Nana Sahib, the adopted son of the ex-peshwa and the head of the Maratha Confederation, lost both title and pension on his adoptive father's death in 1853. Lastly the pensionary Mughal emperor, Bahadur Shah II, was informed that the imperial title would lapse at his death (he was eighty-one at the time) and the imperial family be removed from the Red Fort to a suburb twelve miles from Delhi.

Dalhousie left India in 1856 believing that his successor could look forward to a period of unruffled calm for constructive work. The statesman's work was done and the administrator could take over. He had taken everything into account except feeling. He forgot, as Disraeli said, that feeling rules mankind. Barely a year later India was convulsed by a military mutiny whose violence and unexpectedness, and the feelings which it aroused on both sides, have made of it the most enigmatic event of British Indian history. That there was a mutiny there is no doubt. But how much more was there? There are four main explanations. Some have seen in it only a military revolt caused by ignorance, negligence, and astonishing ineptitude on the part of the government and army. Many at the time suspected a conspiracy. Either the Brahmins were exploiting military caste grievances for orthodox purposes, or discontented Muslims were taking advantage of these same grievances to make a bid for empire against the infidel. Some nationalist writers have called it the first war of independence, seeing in it a first effort by the new India to shake off British rule. A fourth explanation is that the mutiny was an explosion touched off by military grievances against a background of social and political unrest. The social scene, with its tension between Eastern and Western influences, as it were, provided the gunpowder to which the military grievances provided the trail and the question of greased cartridges the match.

The first explanation, that of a purely military mutiny, does not explain why Muslim soldiers joined in a movement based on Hindu caste grievances. Nor does it account for the popular support which the mutineers received in some areas of Uttar Pradesh and Behar or the rising en masse of Sindia's army, which the British did not control. The doctrine of conspiracy was discounted at the time by John Lawrence, and no solid evidence has ever been produced to support it. The two leading figures, the Hindu Maratha, Nana Sahib, near Kanpur and the emperor Bahadur Shah at Delhi, were clearly taken by surprise, and so were their supporters. The view that the mutiny was a concerted movement against the British, a violent predecessor of Mahatma Gandhi's campaigns, overlooks the fact that there was then no Indian nation. The new classes with ideas of nationalism were then very few in number and they were wholly opposed to the movement. It was members of this class who were cut down at their posts in the telegraph office of Delhi; in all mutineer-controlled areas they went in fear of their lives as "friends of the English" and of the West. They had been created by the British and their fortunes were linked with them. The leaders of the revolt were backward-looking men whose aims were incompatible. Nana Sahib hoped to revive the peshwaship and the Delhi leaders the Mughal empire. Success would have meant a further war for supremacy between these two.

We are thus left with the broader view which sees in the mutiny neither a mere military *émeute* nor a preview of the future, but a military explosion which derived its force from the social forces out of which it arose. The preceding summary of Dalhousie's work provides us with a clue to this social unrest. We see an ardent and able ruler, filled with confidence in himself and his cause, driving forward regardless of tradition, which he despised, and of local opinion, which he underrated. His measures were the most radical of a series which seemed to threaten the old ways of life and the old established classes. A series of land settlements and of measures like the Sales Law had, as has been noted, ruined many landholders and made the rest fearful of their fate. The annexations had deprived many official and military families of their prospects and constricted the area remaining open to Indian talent. Rulers, whether Muslim or Hindu, wondered whose turn would be next, for if the doctrine of lapse applied only to Hindus, the charge of misgovernment might apply to all. Muslims in particular felt that in the case of the emperor, Oudh and Berar, the last vestiges of their old dominion, were being threatened. On top of this social unrest came the Western innovations which alienated the orthodox of both communities. English education was a threat to both Sanskrit and Arabic studies and exposed its votaries, in the eyes of both Hindu pundit and Muslim *maulvi,* to contamination by Christianity and infidelity. The telegraph was the work of the evil one, and railroads with their jostling of crowds in trains, a threat to caste. The government, these people thought, was secretly supporting Christian propaganda and was undermining caste as a first stage in the process. These were the thoughts and feelings which were running through north India in 1856 and of which the government, full of plans and self-confidence, was unaware or heedless. These feelings were communicated to the Bengal army, itself a close and largely hereditary corporation with a large Brahmin element, through the soldiers' families, who usually remained in their villages, to be visited at intervals of leave. They connected naturally with the particular military grievances which caused the actual outbreak.

To sum up, we can see the mutiny as the culmination of a period of unrest. That unrest was caused by the clash of old and new on the material, ideological, and religious planes. It was a last passionate protest of the conservative forces in India against the relentless penetration of the West. It is this which gave the mutiny its extreme emotional content, with soldiers professing loyalty one day and shooting their officers the next. They were torn to distraction between loyalty and affection on the one hand and belief that their religion and way of life were threatened on the other. The mutiny was the swan song of the old India.

We can now turn to the army. In 1857 the total strength of the Company's army was 238,000, of whom 38,000 were Europeans. It was organized in three divisions, the Bengal, Madras, and Bombay armies. The Bengal army contained about 128,000 Indians and 23,000 Europeans, the small numbers of Europeans being the result of withdrawals for the Crimean and Persian wars. It covered the area from Calcutta to the northwest frontier, and contained large numbers of Brahmins and Rajputs, the two proudest of the castes, of whom 40,000 alone came from the recently annexed state of Oudh. The Company had always been meticulous in observing caste rules, and this had had the effect of making the soldiers themselves more self-conscious about them. The same result occurred with the Sikhs after the mutiny, so that it was asserted that British recognition of traditional Sikh forms had much to do with the preservation of Sikh social cohesion and separateness from the Hindus. The men of the Bengal army were therefore particularly open to orthodox as well as to landholders' discontents with the Company's measures. There had been four minor mutinies in thirteen years and general discipline was lax. Military pride had been inflated by a series of successes over nearly twenty years. The army had some ground for thinking itself indispensable to the British.

But it was fear rather than pride that precipitated revolt, fear of the loss of caste, which would take away the basis of an ancient and cherished way of life. In 1856 the General Service Enlistment Act required the new recruit to serve overseas as well as in India, which some regarded as a breach of caste. Then greased cartridges were supplied for the new Enfield rifle and had to be bitten before insertion into the rifle. The grease was said to contain the fat of cows (sacred to the Hindu) and pigs (impure to the Muslim). In fact animal fat had been used in manufacture at Woolwich. The order to bite the cartridges was revoked and the men were allowed to use their own vegetable fat. Such prompt action would have disposed of an isolated grievance. But this grievance was not isolated. It appeared to many soldiers as the last straw to break the orthodox camel's back. Here was apparently the confirmatory fact of a series of rumors and taunts and suspicions that their military masters, in other respects the best in living memory, meant to destroy their caste. The spark was sufficient to set off an explosion, which in turn ignited the smoldering Muslim and agrarian discontent. So the revolt began as a series of frenzied outbreaks, gradually became more Muslim than Hindu in character, and ended with a number of agrarian risings.

The mutiny became a national event when the troops at Meerut rose, shot their officers, marched to Delhi forty miles away, and on May 11, 1857, compelled the aged emperor Bahadur Shah to become their leader. Soon after the Maratha leader Nana Sahib found himself the head of the mutiny in Oudh, with Lucknow as the center and British posts at Lucknow and Kanpur the objects of attack. It was round the two cities of Delhi and Lucknow that the fate of the movement was decided. A decisive factor was the fact that the Panjab remained quiet, owing both to the vigilance of John Lawrence and Sikh repugnance to the idea of a revived Mughal empire. Lawrence was able to sustain and reinforce the small British force before Delhi until it recaptured the city in September. The rising in Lucknow had been delayed by Henry Lawrence's skill until the end of June. His measures and the influence of his spirit [7] enabled the Residency to hold out until relieved first in September and finally in November. Set campaigns with troops sent out from Britain broke the rebel strength in the winter of 1857–58, and the final episode of Tantia Topi's marches ended with the Rani of Jhansi's death in action in June. The conflict during 1857 was fought under conditions of extreme emotional as well as physical strain on both sides. On the Indian side were the conflict of religious and military loyalties, the fear of disgrace, and the certainty of death with defeat; on the British, desperation and ferocity produced by the fear of treachery on all sides and the feeling of fighting with one's back to the wall. It was these explosive forces, reinforced by extreme climatic conditions, which led to the savage acts on both sides that gave to the mutiny its sinister reputation.

The British won out because, in a long view, they held all the cards in their hands. In a military sense, they had only to hold out until adequate reinforcements became available. After much initial ineptitude, they enjoyed distinguished and resolute leadership from men like the Lawrences and Governor General Canning. Beyond this, the moral factors were on their side. They believed in their right and mission to rule; the tide of Western self-confidence was still flowing strongly. National pride was at its height; death in battle meant a hero's crown; they were the martyrs of the secular religion of the age. But the rebels had no confidence in themselves or their cause. They feared losing something intangible but had no ideas of creating anything new. Their only positive aims were the restoration of vanished regimes, which would have clashed if they had been revived. In fear and confusion they rose and fought and died. But their deaths were not all in vain, for their failure convinced the quite formless but very real public opinion of India that the way of the old *rajs* could no longer be trodden and that in future terms must be made with the new forces from the West. Neither Mughal, Maratha, or the Company was the real victor of the struggle. It was the pervasive spirit of the West.

PART IV
MODERN INDIA

CHAPTER XXV

The New India

The end of the mutiny saw a series of measures designed to prevent its recurrence. Lord Canning, on whom the storm had burst, stayed on to carry out the first of these, and they were completed by his two successors. We may first summarize these briefly and then consider the deeper implications of the upheaval.

The first problem was to deal with the cries for vengeance which rose from panic-stricken commercials in Calcutta and soldiers and officials up-country, distraught by hardship and harrowing experience. Executions were summary and wholesale; the whole population of Delhi, mostly innocent victims of mutineer violence and cupidity, was turned out of the city to fend for itself. There were demands for the demolition of Shah Jahan's great mosque in Delhi as a retributory act. Canning, who earned the derisory title of "Clemency" in the process, with the help of the rugged John Lawrence and later powerful support from Britain, restrained this movement and restored the north to something like normality by the end of 1859. (The south, it should be noted, true to traditional pattern, had hardly been affected by the revolution in the north.) It was a task requiring courage and resolution, for the leaders had to work through agents many of whom were themselves infected with these feelings and themselves the victims of tragic personal loss.

We can now pass to specific measures. The East India Company was deprived of its governing powers in 1858, which were assumed by the Crown. It had long been little more than an administrative corporation working under government direction, and had even lost its right of patronage when entry to the services was thrown open to competition in 1853. The directors lingered on as a sort of political appendix in the form of an advisory body called the Council of India. Control in London was now exercised by a secretary of state for India, responsible to Parliament, who sat in the cabinet. In India the governor general became also the viceroy, or the queen's personal representative. Queen Victoria herself, through her Proclamation of 1858, was identified with the principles of religious toleration and racial justice. Her name soon became a myth as potent as that of the Company Bahadur, but one which was more personal and gracious. It supplied for the masses a maternalism to which the Indian mind is peculiarly susceptible. The central government was strengthened by the addition of extra members. Dalhousie's little legislative council of officials, which had become a little parliament in embryo, was remodeled with reduced powers and was permitted to include Indian members. The financial crisis caused by the mutiny was dealt with by experts sent from Britain,[1] who introduced annual budgets, an income tax, a revenue tariff of 10 per cent on all imports, and a paper currency. This was followed up in the '60's by permission for the government to borrow in the money market for productive purposes. These efforts ended the annual Indian deficits in 1864. The financial history of modern India really dates from this period.

The civil services were left much as before, but the army was remodeled. The Company's European army (in 1858 about 13,000 men) was disbanded and the European element supplied by regular British troops who went on an extended Indian tour. The proportion of Europeans to Indians was fixed at fifty-fifty in the Bengal army and one to two elsewhere. These figures were not strictly maintained, but the European proportions were always higher than before 1857.[2] The formidable Indian artillery was disbanded except for a few mountain batteries. The new Indian army left out the Brahmins and Rajputs of Oudh and brought in men from the Panjab, both Hindu and Muslim, the now reconciled Sikhs from the same quarter, Pathans from the frontier, and Gurkhas from Nepal. The regiments were communal, two Indian battalions being brigaded with one British. In the new army there was a far closer relationship between the British officers and their men than previously. In time this developed into a very high *esprit de corps* which has been carried over into both the new Indian and Pakistani armies. Finally, there were two declared changes of government policy. The princes, regarded by Dalhousie as obsolescent survivals of a past age, were hailed by Canning as "breakwaters in the storm." The general loyalty of their order was rewarded by the recognition of the right of adoption and the guarantee of their existing territories. While the supreme government claimed a right of interference as the paramount power, it also encouraged the princes to interest themselves in all-India matters. Subordinate isolation was transmuted into subordinate partnership. The second change was the attempt to rescue the peasant from his condition of dependence on the *zamindar* or landlord in the Permanent Settlement areas. This took the form of the Bengal Rent Act of 1859, which gave occupancy rights to all tenants of twelve years' proved standing. It was followed by the Panjab and Oudh Tenancy Acts of 1868. The idea of extending the Permanent Settlement to areas outside Bengal and Behar was finally dropped.

Much of the foregoing amounted to the familiar official exercise of shutting the stable door after the horse has escaped. We see much concentration on past errors and little attention to future policy. The declared official view was that the government had been seriously out of touch with Indian opinion, that it had underestimated the strength of traditional public feeling, and that it had particularly undervalued the princes. The army had been mismanaged, and called for a drastic overhaul. There had been undue strictness in land settlement operations. The implication was that when these mistakes had been rectified life could again proceed with a placid and static calm. There was no looking for new classes that could replace the discredited old ones in public esteem. There was little vision of an integrated India of the future. We have therefore to look deeper and consider the effects of these actions on India itself and the influence of the mutiny experience on the *tone* of the official British attitude toward India.

If we consider the implications of British action in the postmutiny period we shall notice a distinct change of attitude toward the country. The radical change of policy toward the princes, the more sympathetic attitude toward the big landholders such as the *taluqdars* of Oudh and also the smaller men implied a turning away from innovation and new respect for tradition and indigenous customs. The old India with its castes, its peculiar customs and survivals won no more approval. The reverse was probably the case. But the old was considered to be more incorrigible and more dangerous. The attitude that the extinction of the Mughal dynasty was not a matter of concern to Muslims had gone, to be replaced by one of caution and cynicism in all ideological matters. The Indian government's honeymoon with progress was over and was to be followed by the humdrum process of getting along with a traditionalist partner. As respect for the strength of Indian tradition had increased, so had faith in Indian regeneration on Western lines declined. The future seemed to portend an indefinite period of tutelage and trusteeship. In these circumstances the advocates of Western progress joined the gainfully occupied merchants and industrialists and the cautionary statesmen in advocating material progress along with noninterference in Indian life. This seemed the best compromise between reforming zeal and practical prudence. India must be left to reform herself in her own way. But she was too valuable to be left altogether. Therefore material development must go hand in hand with noninvolvement in Indian reform. This implied political tutelage until Indian reform took place from within. Time built up a large stock of skepticism that such a thing would ever happen, a stock so large that fifty years later many officials would not believe the evidence before their eyes.

This change of attitude was the cause of many of Britain's political troubles in India at a later date, for it produced a blind spot in her political vision which prevented her from perceiving the significance of the new Westernized class as it emerged. The directors of British policy had been accustomed to look to the traditional leaders of India for a response to the Western impact and to give a lead to the country as a whole. They did not realize that their various measures before the mutiny had undermined their position in the eyes of the people at large. Still less did they realize that the mutiny itself had completed their discomfiture in the eyes of their own people. The forms of deference and etiquette which are second nature in the Indian character effectively concealed this change in the Indian mind. The British looked to the old leaders to give a lead in the Westernizing process, believing that the rest of India would follow. No such lead came and the British looked no further. They could not bring themselves to take seriously the new class which was dependent upon their own institutions, the product of their own education. They were subordinates, it was thought, despised by their own leaders and so not of account in the country. For this political myopia heavy penalties were later to be exacted.

We now turn to the Indian side of the question. All the pent-up dislike of the old India for the West had been expressed in the mutiny. It was with this old India that the old governing classes were connected. They were its political expression. The collapse of the revolt meant for the Indian public the end of any reason for following these old classes further. Beneath the forms of tradition Indians are realistic people. The conclusion drawn from the events of 1857 was that the traditional forces were incapable of ousting the West by force. The leaders of those forces were therefore now mere ornamental survivals with no relevance for the future. The continuing genuflections to Raja Sahibs and Nawab Sahibs concealed an inner contempt for their pretensions. Following on this conclusion came the logical corollary that if India could not oust the West she must come to terms with it.

As the British felt that they must live with tradition in India, however little they liked it, Indians felt that they must tolerate the West, however distasteful it might be. If you cannot get rid of the monster, why not make terms with it? This change of attitude was not expressed in so many words by the people concerned; it was a silent process over the years for which the evidence is the behavior of the next two generations of publicly conscious Indians. To this fundamental change of attitude there was added a further consequence. The classes which stood for the old ways lost public esteem, while the classes identified with the new acquired a new authority. So the old aristocrats lost their grip of public opinion, while a new respect was accorded to the new educated and subordinate classes. Apparently cut off from the rest of the country by their foreign language and manners and thought to be incapable of leadership by their foreign rulers, these people came to be looked up to as the only ones who could strike a balance between East and West and restore self-respect to Mother India. Thus the psychological preparation was made for this class's leadership of the national movement to come as well as for the failure of the British to recognize their role.

A further consequence of the mutiny for Indian minds was a store of resentment at and bitter memories of the severe repression practiced by the British and the increased racial arrogance which followed it. This aspect has often been stressed rather than the one which has just been dealt with. But it was not, in this writer's belief, of nearly such great importance. Racial arrogance had existed in deplorable measure among many of the lesser Europeans long before the mutiny. What happened in this respect afterward was a mere extension of something already well known. It would have been an issue in any development of modern India, however peaceful. It cannot, therefore, be ascribed mainly to the mutiny. The memories of repression were certainly acute and often bitter, and in some families were handed down from generation to generation. But in their largest extent they were mainly confined to a few great population centers in northern India. Here the cherishing of wrongs was confined to the few, and widespread resentment tended to pass away with those in whom it had been implanted. Indians (except where the blood feud exists) do not readily brood upon wrongs; their postmutiny resentments would have faded even more quickly if the British had been readier to admit the ground for them. There remain to be considered the rural areas, which had their full share of repression in places where there were agrarian or religious uprisings, or where troops had passed. In the villagers' minds and in those of many town dwellers these excesses came under the heading of a *gardi* or calamity, one of those decrees of fate which was always liable to descend upon innocent cultivators when violence was abroad. In their apprehension the British avengers were in the line of marauding Turks, Marathas, and Pindaris, differing mainly in that their killings were preceded by curious ceremonies called trials and that they were less concerned with plunder, rapine, and torture.[3]

The government's gospel in the postmutiny years was public works. With the Panjab School it became a religion; the building of a bridge or completion of a road was a sacramental administrative act. John Lawrence, the apostle of the Panjab school (as Dalhousie was its patron saint), was viceroy from 1864–69. It was he who secured permission from London to borrow for productive public works like railways and canals. This technique was improved by his successor Mayo and became established practice.

The three main aspects of the public works program were roads, railways, and irrigation canals. The roads plan, already begun before the mutiny, was completed afterward, partly for strategical and partly for commercial reasons. The life to be found on them before the full development of railways has been immortalized by Kipling in his *Kim*. With the railway age roads fell into the background, to become mainly marching routes for troops changing their quarters. But with the advent of the automobile age they came into their own, providing the framework for the modern system of national highways. In this respect, as in many others, Dalhousie was a pioneer whose work has been largely forgotten because of the discredit attached to his doctrine of lapse, his annexations, and his connections with the mutiny.

The importance of the road program was obscured by the rapid development of railroads. We have noticed that 200 miles of track were in operation in 1857. These justified themselves in two ways. Their value in transporting troops seemed to provide the military key for dealing with any future military revolt. Secondly, the Indian public, whatever learned Brahmins might say or the devout orthodox feel, seized the new opportunities for speedy and cheap travel. Far from outraging religious feelings as had been feared, railroads came to encourage them by providing mass transportation to the *melas* or great religious festivals at places like Allahabad and Banaras. The former pilgrims walked for hundreds of miles, or, if well off, traveled in bullock or camel carts; the latter-day pilgrim goes by train. Within a generation of the cry that railroads would undermine orthodoxy, the popular cry was for more roads. After the mutiny, therefore, on strategical and commercial grounds backed by popular approval, railroad construction went ahead rapidly. By 1900 there were 25,000 miles of track and the main system was completed. By 1914, 10,000 more miles had been added. The system reached a peak, 43,000 miles, in the years before World War II. In proportion to its size India had the largest and best railroad system in Asia. The Indian railroads had another interesting aspect. They constituted a planned system in an age of individualism. In the absence of local investors either able or willing to take risks in railroad construction, the government planned the whole system and then let out sections to private companies for construction and operation. There was much controversy about the terms allowed these companies, which were charged to be unduly generous concerning guaranteed rates of interest and unduly expensive regarding construction. The essential points, however, were two: whatever the cost, the roads were solidly laid, so that they successfully bore great strains in both World Wars; and the grants to the companies were leases resumable every twenty-five years. Wasteful competing lines were avoided because the government controlled the railroad blueprint, and unification into a single system was made possible by easy stages from the beginning. In fact, before independence nearly the whole system was nationally controlled by a governmental railway board sitting in Delhi. It may be added that it was the strategical railroads in the northwest, admitted to be unremunerative, which have given Pakistan the core of its railroad system.

The effects of the building of railroads upon both Indian economic and social life were incalculable. Railroads were the great "enabling" measure of the modern Indian economy. They made possible both the development of major industries in India and the opening up of the interior to world markets. They did this by making possible the movement of raw materials in bulk, the supply of power at selected centers, and the distribution of the finished article to the ports or within the country itself. Railroads provided, as it were, the "nervous system" for the economic body of modern India. The government did not create the industries themselves, but in the construction of railroads made possible their development, which will be noted later. It was the railroad which overcame the obstacle of distance and the lack of water carriage all over the subcontinent except in Bengal and the Gangetic Valley.

Equally important were the social results. Rail travel did much, as has already been noted, to break down some of the less essential caste tabus. It brought thousands of all castes cheek by jowl in third-class carriages. It did not of course affect the main marriage and other social restrictions, but it encouraged social contact and exchange of ideas and so helped forward the adjustment of traditional India to the modern world. The pious Hindu traveled by train to worship at a holy site; in doing so he rubbed shoulders with men whose touch was supposed to pollute and heard in the unending talk how the new world was overtaking his world of the past. He could not be wholly unaware that the instrument of his piety was itself an engine of the menacing West. Further, the railroad encouraged travel and intercourse for commerce and public affairs all over India. Formerly journeys were long and arduous, to be undertaken only by the few; now they became relatively short and easy, available for the many. The all-India public conference was made possible by the railroad for people who at the same time were acquiring a common language through the vogue for English. It became commonplace for southerners to travel to the north and vice versa. Thus the railroads brought people from all parts of India together as had never happened before. The circulation of the new knowledge and exchange of ideas was correspondingly stimulated. The heavy, ungainly Indian trains,[4] with box-like compartments which seemed clumsy and comfortless to the Western eye, were in fact well adapted to the needs and habits of the average Indian traveler. The railroad was the circulating medium of the new English-speaking middle class. It was a principal agent in the development of India on Western lines. It is difficult to see how the National Congress could have started or the National movement have developed without them. A bullock-cart India would always be a divided India.

The third feature of the public works program was the digging of irrigation canals. Irrigation is an ancient and well-understood art in India, as visitors to Ceylon and south India soon learn. Its purpose was to provide water for land in areas where the monsoon rains were uncertain. It was developed by modern engineering skill to fertilize wholly rainless areas. When the British took control they found the Mughal system of canals in disarray in the north and many "tanks" or storage reservoirs in ruins in the south. Many reservoirs, however, were still in use, so that their first measures were those of restoration. In 1820 the Mughal canal to Delhi was reopened. The next phase was that of original works, which were first undertaken where water was plentiful. These included the great Ganges canal,[5] described by Dalhousie in 1856 as "unequalled in its class and character among the efforts of civilised nations," and the Grand Anicut (dam or barrage), two miles long across the bed of the river Cauvery in the south, built in 1835–36. The policy was thus well under way before the mutiny.

In the second half of the century it became a major concern for two reasons. The Panjab and Sind presented a challenge with their arid but potentially fertile tracts and a stimulus with their supplies of water from the Indus and the five rivers.[6] Secondly, it was now seen that irrigation, along with railway construction, provided the clue to the famine problem of India. Beginning in 1892 a series of rainless tracts were irrigated and peopled by canal colonies which became some of the most prosperous communities in India. In the Panjab a network of canals stemming from the five rivers and supporting such centers as Lyallpur sprang up. It is these canals which gave the Panjab its twentieth-century wealth and importance. The process was carried into Sind, where the great Sukkur barrage across the Indus in northern Sind was built in the 1920's. The Sukkur barrage is the largest single system of irrigation in the world, irrigating 5,000,000 acres. The system of the Godavari in the south extends over 2,500 miles. By 1947 the area of irrigated land in the Panjab was twice that of Egypt. By 1940 in British India some 50,000,000 to 60,000,000 acres, or one-fifth of the cultivated area of India, were irrigated land. This may be compared with about 20,000,000 acres under irrigation at the same time in the United States.

Irrigation has increased the productivity of land by enabling two crops to be sown where there was one before and making fertile wholly rainless regions, and also provided an insurance against famine by safeguarding large areas from failure due to the monsoon. Famine has been one of the great bugbears of Indian life. The great distances and lack of means of transport on a large scale, except in Bengal and up the Ganges, made it impossible to relieve scarcity in one area from abundance in another. European travelers gave harrowing accounts of famines in the Mughal period, when no one but Akbar had any pity for the victims. In 1769–70, in the early British period, Bengal itself, the most fertile part of India, was devastated by an estimated loss of one-third of its inhabitants. In 1782–83 the Delhi region suffered a similar visitation, from which it took over thirty years to recover. In 1837–38 famine overtook the upper-Ganges region. In 1866 Orissa was estimated to have lost one-fourth of its inhabitants from a famine which the Bengal government failed to foresee in time. Relief measures on both these last occasions were inadequate not only because of faulty organization but also for the old reason of lack of transport. In 1876–78, however, improved transport conditions enabled Lytton to attack the great famine in south India with success as well as with vigor. From this experience grew the great Famine Code of India. A regular procedure was devised for detecting the first signs of shortage, for declaring a state of scarcity and then of famine.

Places of assembly were then provided for the famine-stricken and work for those made idle by drought. Food was brought in by sea and by land and distributed according to plan. By these means the series of famines between 1896 and 1900 involved no serious loss of life. The people concerned changed their form of labor until the rains returned. Some were actually better off with the regular rations provided. Death from famine starvation became a thing of the past until the Bengal famine of 1943, when war conditions made the import of rice impossible and the transport of foodstuffs from other areas difficult. The ending of famines, with their toll of one-third or one-half of the population concerned, was a major achievement of British administration in the post-mutiny half century.

It was in this same half century that India's industrial development really got under way. It was not specially planned by the government, which was subject to economic pressures from Britain, but it was made possible by the railroads which the government provided. Private enterprise, both in Britain and India, did the rest. The railways brought capital to India and gave ideas to prospectors. We may begin with the coal and iron industries. Both items existed in quantity in Bengal and southern Behar, but until 1846 attempts to exploit them had produced an output of only 90,000 tons a year. The railroads provided both an easy means of access and a large market, taking one-third of the production. One million tons were produced by 1880 and 28,000,000 in 1938,[7] making India self-supporting in this respect. The availability of coal in turn helped other industries by providing their means of power. Along with coal went iron. Iron-smelting had reached a high degree of skill in ancient India, as the Iron Pillar at Delhi, cast in the fifth century A.D., bears witness. The use of coal made it possible to start a modern iron industry in 1875. The genius of the Parsi Tata family of Bombay developed the iron and steel industries at Jamshedpur in Behar. In 1913 the first steel was produced. At the outbreak of World War II in 1939 Tata's was producing 1,000,000 tons of steel a year and India ranked sixth in the order of world steel-producers. Tata's plant was the largest single steel-mill in the British Empire.

The new conditions enabled India to revive her age-old cotton industry on a mechanical basis. The hand cotton and spinning industry of India had been ruined partly by the East India Company's free-trade policy and partly by the competition of the new British power looms in the early nineteenth century. The one made the competition of the other deadly. Weavers of fine cloths lost their markets and returned to the land; only where railroads could not easily bring cheap foreign cloth did village weavers continue to produce rough homespun cloth, later made familiar to the world by Gandhi as *khaddar*. For a long time capital and confidence to set up machine cotton-mills were lacking among Indians. The American Civil War hindered matters by sending the price of raw cotton rocketing in Lancashire and so encouraging export instead of local manufacture. In 1887 Jamshed Tata opened his Empress Mill at Nagpur. Soon Bombay had eighty mills, and centers were established at Sholapur, Ahmedabad in Gujarat, Madras, and in the north. By 1914 India was reckoned fourth in the world list of cotton manufacturers.[8] Now India controls her own cotton market and exports to the Middle East, Africa, and southeast Asia.

The jute industry began in 1838 with the export of raw jute to Dundee in Scotland, the seat of burlap manufacture in Britain. At that time Dundee relied largely on raw materials from Russia. These were cut off in the Crimean War (1854–56), and Bengal supplied them in her place. Canny Scotsmen saw the advantage of manufacturing burlap on the spot in Calcutta. By 1908 Indian output exceeded that of Dundee. Jute made Calcutta an industrial city as well as a port and a center for entrepreneurs.

There remain to be mentioned the plantation industries. These did not need coal for power but did need railroads for transport. First comes tea. The tea of the Boston Tea Party came from China, for it was with China tea that the British tea-drinking habit was built up in the eighteenth century. An Indian plant was found in Assam which proved hardier in Indian conditions than the Chinese. From about 1850 the Indian tea gardens developed in Assam, Bengal, southern India, and the northern hills. Its growth was phenomenal. Indian tea virtually displaced China from the British market. In 1869 Britain took 100,000,000 pounds of tea from China and 10,000,000 from India. In 1900 she took 24,000,000 from China and 137,000,000 from India. In 1929–30 Indian tea exports were 377,000,000 pounds. Along with tea went coffee, tobacco, rubber, and cinchona, though on a smaller scale. These were all products of the tropical tracts or hilly regions of the south.

All this activity formed the blueprint for the industrial expansion of independent India. It should not be thought that the capital or the management was entirely in British hands. In fact both were about equally divided between British and Indians. Broadly speaking, Indian capital controlled the cotton and steel industries and shared the jute industry. British capital controlled the coal and plantation industries and provided the major portion of the investment in public works. British technicians were freely employed by Indians in cotton and steel mills, often turning out, on examination, to be Scotsmen. In her technical development India owes much to the barren hills of Scotland, which drove her sons to seek their fortunes abroad.

CHAPTER XXVI

The Mind of the New India

So far we have been observing the material measures whose execution was accelerated by the mutiny, and the important results which flowed from them. It is not too much to say that it was during this period that the body of modern India took shape and began to grow. We have now to consider the reaction of the Indian mind to pressures from the West. We have noted that one broad effect of the mutiny on Indians was to convince them that terms, intellectual as well as material, must be made with the new influences. But we have still to observe just what those terms were, just how the Indian mind reconciled the demands of the outside world with its own inner imperatives.

Before considering the Indian mental reaction further, certain pro-Western influences in this field should be noted. Although the government virtually abandoned the policy of social reform by legislation after 1857, it persevered in its policy of Western education. There was no compulsion to attend Western institutions, but a number of motives encouraged participation. Knowledge of English and Western qualifications opened the way to government employment, to the new professions of teaching, medicine, and the law, to the new technical services such as the railways, and to the higher reaches of commerce and industry. In consequence the pressure on the system was heavy, and its expansion did no more than meet a rapidly growing demand. The modern Indian educational system took shape with Sir Charles Wood's dispatch of 1854, which led to the opening of the first three universities in 1857 (Calcutta, Bombay, and Madras). Government colleges and schools in the main centers were now reinforced by private institutions by means of the grant-in-hand system, which enabled colleges and schools to be viable while charging low fees within the means of the new middle class. The universities, down to 1920, were organized on the model of then London University; that is to say, they were examining bodies, the teaching being provided in separate colleges recognized and affiliated for the purpose. In the interests of quick results the London standard was soon abandoned, with the result that there has never since been a fixed graduate standard in the Indian educational world. Many British teachers were engaged to give the new system a start. The defects of the system were many and attempts to improve it periodical.[1] The important aspect to notice from the present point of view is the existence and rapid expansion of a Westernizing agency on the intellectual level. The new India came to regard this baptism into Westernism as a necessary hazard in preparation for life in the Kali age.[2] The educational system was probably the largest single Westernizing agency in nineteenth-century India.

A further Westernizing influence was unofficial but of great importance. It was that of Christian missions. In the south, Roman Catholic influence had been continuous since the sixteenth century, but chiefly among the Syrian Christians of Travancore and the lower Hindu classes elsewhere. Protestant missions made a modest beginning in the eighteenth century, working from non-British centers like Danish Tranquebar. It was the evangelical movement in Britain which converted Protestant missions in India from the status of isolated efforts to large-scale enterprises. The efforts of pioneers like the Baptist William Carey and the Anglican Henry Martyn led to rapid development when the ban on missionary activity was raised in 1813. American Protestants joined the British, and the Roman Catholic effort was largely reinforced. The evangelistic effort of these missionaries still mainly impinged on the lower classes, and the Christian communities they built up lived lives rather apart from the rest of the community. But their other activities affected India at large. The medical work in hospital and dispensary touched all classes at a sensitive spot. Their schools and colleges were attended by non-Christians whose parents hoped that the effect of the Christian doctrines they were exposed to would be offset by the value of the moral teaching they received. Not many converts came from these institutions, but rays of Western influence were poured forth, made all the more attractive because of the personal contacts between foreign teacher and Indian pupil which were largely absent in the government system. In 1930 there were ten American, twenty-three British, three Union, one Indian, and one continental Protestant Christian colleges in India, as well as a number of large Roman Catholic ones. Christian missions were thus an important general Westernizing as well as a specifically Christian agency. Particularly significant was their part in carrying Western influence to the women's world, in the nineteenth century still behind the purdah or curtain. Devoted British and American women carried the gospel into Indian homes, while others started women's hospitals, schools, and colleges. These activities laid the foundation for the rapid progress of Indian women and their emergence to participate in the general life of the community in the twentieth century.

We have seen that the contact between Indian and Western culture in the Mughal age was superficial and disappointing in its results. The Mughal magnates loved European toys and wines but received no creative impulse. The larger contact of the eighteenth century was on the planes of war and commerce, and the Indian reaction was correspondingly mundane. The Indian prince saw a military threat supported by new techniques. The Brahmin saw another incursion of barbarians which he assumed would pass, as had so many previous ones. The princes tried to meet like with like, engaging European soldiers, drilling troops, and casting canon. They steadily improved until they produced the Sikh army of Ranjit Singh, but they failed to stem the military tide for reasons other than military already explained elsewhere. The first conclusion drawn from the British supremacy was that India must now endure a new set of Mughals in the seats of power while carrying on her own life as before. This was upset by the Company's new policy of the 1830's, by increasing interference in the life of the country under the name of "improvement," and by the inevitable pressures of a rapidly expanding Western society. Before these new influences the Brahmin felt like the Psalmist trying to flee from the Lord. India came to realize that she was faced with a full-scale challenge to her traditional life and values, and commenced to make that agonizing reappraisal which led the way to her modern transformation.

The first reaction was that of pure conservatism. The orthodox Brahmin shrank from Western innovations as he had done from the Islamic impact and from the Greeks many centuries before. The Brahminical system of exclusiveness was a good defense for any assault, ideological or otherwise, which was temporary. It was only as they saw the front of the attack widening, affecting one after another section of the national life, that dislike and disdain turned to alarm and hostility. We have noted how these feelings were played upon and aggravated by events and how they culminated in the emotional outburst which goes by the name of the Mutiny. In this context we can see the significance of charges that the government wanted to make India Christian and for that purpose was undermining caste. We can see why this charge came to be so widely believed though it was based upon such slender evidence. The conservative classes were content to live and let live, keeping their way of life to themselves. But circumstances and not government action only made this impossible. The result was emotional upheaval on the one hand and a series of attempts to come to terms with the new world on the other.

The second reaction was the move of a radical group in Calcutta to accept the West *in toto*. They accepted the Western claim to have found the secret of progress based on the principle of reason; they accepted Western humanist values. The only way to mend the abuses of Hinduism, they believed, was to end them. They were much influenced by the French and English rationalists, whose representative in Calcutta was David Hare the watchmaker. A section of them, influenced by Alexander Duff,[3] the Scots missionary, went further and accepted the religion as well as the philosophy and philanthropy of the West. Pains were taken to symbolize the break with tradition by ritual meals of beef, and one poet could boast of dreaming in English. The movement threw up a personality in the Anglo-Indian Derozio, whose meteoric career was cut short by an early death.

The movement for acceptance excited Calcutta in the thirties and then died away, though its tenets have been accepted by individuals ever since. It was in fact too radical for the essentially conservative mind of India. And it failed to satisfy one of the two principal needs felt by the average Indian when confronted with the West. They were the twin desires to draw level with the West in achievement and Western estimation and at the same time to be loyal to his Hindu past. The children of Mother India must meet the challenge of the modern world but at the same time remain loyal to their parent. It was not an easy task to reconcile conscience, reason, and traditional duty, and it is not surprising that several solutions were attempted before one was found which appealed to the mind and conscience of the new classes. India being a land of religion, it was natural that the first attempts should take the form of religious movements. The first of these was that known as the Brahmo Samaj or Divine Society, founded in 1828 by the Bengali intellectual and reformer, Ram Mohan Roy.[4] Ram Mohan Roy was the nearest approach to the universal scholar which nineteenth-century India produced. He knew ten languages, studied the religions of Hinduism, Buddism, Islam, and Christianity, and the philosophy and science of the West along with those of India. As a youth he wandered for six years in the time-honored manner seeking truth. A period of government service introduced him to the British and provided him with means. From 1814 he lived in Calcutta, promoting reforms of various kinds. He helped to found the Hindu College in Calcutta in 1816,[5] the first institution of higher Western education in India; he was a pioneer in journalism; he attacked the abuses of caste, suttee, and idolatry; he was an advocate of civil liberty, and he ended his life with a journey to England to plead the cause of the Mughal emperor and social reform. We shall return to his general attitude toward the West later, but here we are concerned with his foundation, the Brahmo Samaj.[6] The teaching of the Samaj combined an attempt to purify Hindu society by removing abuses and going back to first principles, and to revivify it by incorporating what was worthy from the West. It was a Protestant movement, but one with which Erasmus would have had more sympathy than Luther. Among abuses it numbered suttee, idolatry, and the extremes of caste; its first principle was reason as exemplified in the philosophic treatises called the *Upanishads*. Its loans from the West may be described as the principle of human dignity and as the ethical system expressed in the Sermon on the Mount. Ram Mohan Roy accepted Jesus as one of the religious Masters and advocated his teaching in a book called the *Precepts of Jesus*.

The Brahmo Samaj exists today with branches in several parts of India. Its members are enlightened and often distinguished, but the society did not capture the imagination of India as a whole. It was, perhaps, too intellectual and too precious, too much like the court cult of Akbar in the sixteenth century. There followed the more robust and militant cult of the Arya Samaj or Society of Aryas, founded by the Gujarati Brahmin ascetic Swami Dayananda in 1875.[7] The Arya Samaj was frankly Protestant in the Lutheran or Calvinist style. It attacked orthodox Hindu customs with vigor and bitterness. It carried its campaign against caste to the point of setting up a casteless society rather like the Sikhs and of welcoming in both outcastes and non-Hindus. It attacked idolatry to the point of devising an idol-free worship. It attacked Christianity and, more bitterly, Islam. More positively, it promoted social uplift and education. It placed its trust in the earliest Hindu scriptures, the Vedas, which it regarded as the inspired Word of God, containing all knowledge and wisdom. It was thus a religion of authority rather than of reason. But even the Arya Samaj found itself compromising with the West. It advocated education and found itself promoting it on Western lines. India was to be the land of the Aryas, but the Aryas were to be clothed and armed in the panoply of the West. The Arya Samaj took strong root in the Panjab, where it still flourishes. It became the spearhead of anti-Muslim feeling in the north and had much to do with the communal tensions there in the twentieth century. It did not, however, succeed in capturing the imagination of modern India as a whole. Its essential cry was to turn back to the age of the Vedas and the days of Aryan purity.

The modern Indian wished to be free to admire the Vedas, but not to go back to them. The Samaj failed through being too archaic.

A further movement was that of the seer Ramkrishna Paramhamsa.[8] He was a yogi or ascetic who sought self-realization along the classic lines of renunciation and devotion. His procedure was to identify himself with the methods and the ideals of each great religion in turn until he had attained what he believed to be the realization of the Divine Self within. The rest of his life he spent in the temple of Dakshineshwar near Calcutta discoursing with disciples and admirers. So far he was one more *rishi* or sage, and his message was withdrawal. But his disciple Vivekananda [9] added a gospel of action to that of contemplation. He taught that social service arose from contemplation and that self-reliance was its fellow. He founded a monastic order called the Ramkrishna Mission, which resembled in some ways Western missionary societies and which still carries on philanthropic work in many parts of India. Though this course was justified by the *Bhagavad Gita,* there is no doubt that the immediate inspiration came from Christian missions with their great network of schools, hospitals, and orphanages. It represented an incursion, or perhaps we should say a re-entry of the gospel of action, dominant in the West, into Hindu religion. Vivekananda took a further step in proclaiming the essential oneness of all religions. Westerners were inclined to see in this a denigration of Christianity from its unique position. But from the Indian point of view it was otherwise. Other religions had hitherto received no recognition from the orthodox; their adherents were *mlechchas* or outcastes in outer darkness. Now they were recognized as providing *margas* or ways to reality in their own right. It was a long step forward toward India's recognition of her place in the brotherhood of nations. Vivekananda's third work was his expedition to the West. Along with his talented Irish disciple, Sister Nivedita,[10] he attended the World Congress of Religions at Chicago in 1893. He made a profound impression, and put Hinduism on the map, as it were, of the Western world. The Vedanta missions to be found in California and elsewhere date from this time.

Still another influence was that of Theosophy. This time it was the West which was captivated by the East. The Theosophical Society was founded in 1875 by Madam Blavatsky, a Russian lady. Leadership fell to Mrs. Annie Besant, and the headquarters were established at Adyar in south India. Along with Pandit Malaviya she founded the Banaras Hindu University in 1910 and exercised important political influence with her Home Rule League. The importance of Theosophy to India was that it was a movement led by Westerners which put things Indian

on a level with things Western. It thus helped to bring the modern Indian into equal relations with the West, neither regarding himself as ex-
clusive and superior to others as did the old orthodox Brahmin, or as
inferior and behind the times as the ordinary Westerner implied. The
movement encouraged both self-respect and mutual respect, both essential ingredients for genuine fellowship with other nations.

All these movements tried to assure Indians that their past was respectable and worthy of their loyalty. In their attitude toward the West
they were divided between those who, like the Arya Samaj and Ramkrishna, taught that some things could be accepted because they fell
within the circle of old ideas, and those who, like the Brahmo Samaj
and Theosophy, were frankly syncretistic. But in general we may say
that they were all concerned with justifying the old ways to people facing a new world. This attitude sufficed for the mental needs of the new
Indians until the mutiny. But that event, as we have noted elsewhere,
proved to be even more a psychological than a political watershed.
From this time India as a whole, the old-timers passively and the new
generation actively, realized that she had to come to terms not merely
with the British Empire, nor with a few modern inventions, but with the
spirit of the West as a whole. There was a subtle change in the Indian
outlook, almost unperceived at the time. It was a change, one might say,
away from medieval theocracy and religious exclusiveness toward secularism and nationalism. Nationalism became a living force after the
mutiny among Westernized Indians, and nationalism is the natural religion of secularism. The new India decided to accept the West, not
merely tolerate it. The question for her now was no longer, how can
the old be shown to be still worth our loyalty, but how can the new be
accepted without loss of dignity or self-respect? It was in this predic-
ament that the ideas of Ram Mohan Roy, as distinct from the tenets of
his religious society, the Brahmo Samaj, came to have great significance.
Ram Mohan Roy provided not merely an excuse for accepting some
portion of the Western heritage, by claiming that this or that was really
to be found in Indian tradition or that various criticized portions of the
Hindu tradition were not an essential part of the Indian religion; he
provided a principle which linked the ideas of the East with those of the
West. He maintained that this tradition was firmly embedded in the
universally accepted *Upanishads* or early Hindu philosophic treatises.
By this means the new India was able to take the circle of Western ideas
to herself and to sort and classify them as she did her own. This principle was that of reason, which lies at the basis of the classical Indian
philosophy of the Vedanta set forth in the *Upanishads*. For our present

purpose the content of the Vedantic system does not matter. We are concerned with the concept of reason to be found therein, which could be used as a touchstone for testing all thought, whether Eastern or Western. In other words, Ram Mohan Roy abandoned the traditionally accepted bases of Hindu religion and Brahminic authority in favor of reason. Hinduism could be justified in its essentials on the ground that it provided a reasoned explanation of reality. Everything from the West could be considered in the same light. There could be assimilation and not merely borrowing at random. It was a case of one philosopher examining the system of another, not of a man adrift in a sea of new ideas clutching at the flotsam and jetsam of other worlds drifting by. Ram Mohan Roy's approach restored Indian intellectual and moral self-respect and gave Indians a sense of choosing rather than receiving the gifts of a new world.

It was in the fifty years from about 1830 to 1880 that the new Indian middle class became permeated with this outlook. One result of the new attitude was a reformist approach to traditional Hinduism. Some things could be safely discarded if the inner principle were inviolable. Thus the abolition of suttee came to be accepted. Certain Brahmin groups notable for their pride and polygamous practices lost credit. Infanticide came to be generally frowned upon. The next result was a willing acceptance of certain Western importations, what one might call an assimilation of them into Indian life. Such an acceptance occurred in the case of Western education, whose spread, in however unsatisfactory a form, was phenomenal from the 1850's. Sanskrit knowledge was traditionally sacred; the possession of Western knowledge carried with it something of the same aura. Another case was that of the Western professions of teaching, law, and medicine. Members of all three acquired something of the respect accorded to their traditional counterparts and something of the status given to all learning in India. The government official, right down to the bottom rung of the ladder, shared in the same process. He was a literatus glorified with the raja's or government's approval.

The same process went on in the world of ideas, which found their expression in institutions. An immediate result was the stemming of the tide which showed signs of moving toward Christianity in the twenties and thirties of the nineteenth century. Ram Mohan Roy provided the antidote, as it were, to the new spiritual virus introduced by William Carey and Alexander Duff. The symbols of this were his conversion of a Baptist missionary to Unitarianism, which was the result of his application of the principle of reason to traditional elements in the Christian faith, and his *Precepts of Jesus,* by which he introduced the moral precepts of Jesus into Hinduism on the ground of their innate reasonableness. This process was carried much further by Ram Mohan Roy himself, and his attitudes gradually permeated the new Indian class. He accepted the dignity and equal value and status of all individuals, with its corollaries of equality and social leveling. At one stroke in this way Brahminic privilege was discountenanced and the whole caste system undermined. The foundation was laid for social reform *within* the Hindu system, a foundation on which Mahatma Gandhi was later to build so imposing a structure. The acceptance of these ideas as modifying forces within Hindu society enabled Gandhi to claim the civil and political rights which went with them in the West. Thus Ram Mohan Roy provided a basis within Hindu thought for Indian democracy. Those who accepted the social implications of the new principles could claim the public and political rights which went with them. Ram Mohan Roy set an example in his own person, being an ardent supporter of the great Reform Bill of 1832, and holding a dinner to celebrate the French Revolution of 1830. Thus in the minds of the new Indians the new demands sprang from assumptions *within* their own society instead of being mere "foreign goods" imported for tactical reasons.

Two generations later a work similar to Ram Mohan Roy's for the Hindus was accomplished by Sayyid Ahmad Khan for the Muslims. In the early years of the century the Muslims sank into a mood of depression for which there seemed to be no remedy. They had lost their empire; they regarded the Hindus as idolaters and supplanters and the British as infidels. The first efforts at adaptation harked back to primitive Islam and led to a small militant movement mainly directed against the Sikhs. The mutiny deepened the mood of pessimism. It was Sayyid Ahmad Khan who roused the Muslims by providing an ideological link with the West, much as Roy had done for the Hindus. Again the link was reason, which in the Sayyid's mind connected the science of the West with the Aristotelian element in Islamic thought. His monument was the Anglo-Oriental College (Aligarh Muslim University in 1920) founded in 1875.[11]

CHAPTER XXVII

The New Class and the New Party

Who were the people who provided the physical envelope for the mind of the new India? They were for the most part, in the nineteenth century, men in modest positions in society though of good caste status. In India these two can often be wide apart. Modern India has not many examples of the log cabin to White House type.[1] But the bulk of the new class came from the subordinate strata of society and occupied, in the first generations, subordinate positions. There they would have remained in a purely Indian society. But the British, by measures and means already related, obligingly removed the classes above them, either by reducing them to poverty or by pushing them aside into a social backwater. As the class rose, it therefore found its only obstruction to be the alien governing class. It could evoke the new sentiment of nationalism for the officials' removal and so step into their place. Thus political change did not involve social displacement. This is one reason why the Indian revolution, if we may call the attainment of independence in 1947 by that term, did not involve a social revolution as well. The violence which accompanied it in the north had a racial-cultural rather than a social character.

This new class had the unique qualities in India of possessing characteristics which gave it homogeneity and of being spread in patches throughout the subcontinent. We may first inquire into its origins and make-up and then note the factors which brought the diverse elements together. The class owed its origin to the British, for it was their presence and activities which called it into existence and their deliberate measures which later expanded and solidified it. The first traces of the class were to be found in the Presidency towns among the people who ministered to the needs and wants of the Company's servants. So we can trace the origin of this class in Bombay to the Parsis, who controlled the Bombay dockyard for several generations, and in South India to men like Ananda

Ranga Pillai, who was the *dubash* or secretary of the French leader Dupleix. But it was in Calcutta with its superior wealth and greater activity, and, after 1756, its spreading hinterland, that the class first attained considerable proportions. It consisted of men who acted as go-betweens between the Company's servants and Indian society, and later provided the know-how of administration when the Company seized political power. They provided the finances for the private inland and the Asian overseas trade of the Company's servants, and naturally did not grow poor in the process. As the Company servants used their new political power to gather the wealth of Bengal into their hands, these men were their aiders and abettors, and received a corresponding "rake-off." For every "nabob" who returned to Britain in the 1760's to flaunt his ill-gotten wealth before an envious and critical society, there were several Indians who had become quietly affluent in Bengal.

There thus grew up a class of moneyed men who learned English for purposes of business, who later adopted some superficial British manners and customs, and who finally became interested in Western ideas. They belonged mostly to the Brahmin, Banya (mercantile), or Kayasth (ministerial) castes, which had a good position in the Hindu religious scale, but many were of humble origin. The notorious Amin Chand (Omichand) of Clive's day and Nand Kumar of Warren Hastings' time were early examples of the class. Warren Hastings' own secretary, Kantu Babu, became rich in his master's service and founded a Bengali house. Then there was Nawal Kishen (Nobkissen), whose father, after being secretary to Clive, was appointed by him political dewan or revenue officer to the Company in 1765. His son Radhakant Deva, though devoutly orthodox and a learned Sanskritist, supported English education and helped to found the Hindu College in Calcutta in 1816. Another example was the Tagore family. They were Brahmin *zamindars* or landholders, one of whose members, Dwarkenath, went into business in a large way. His son Devendranath, scholar and sage, was the leader of the Brahmo Samaj for many years and his son Rabindranath the poet, seer, and nationalist of the last generation. A relation, Abanindranath, founded the modern school of Indian painting. Ram Mohan Roy himself came from a landowning Brahmin family.

The order of class development was, first, money through service and finance, then the adoption of Western externals, and then the interchange of ideas. From this class in Bengal came the movement for Western education in the early nineteenth century and the Indian backing for Bentinck's measures. But its members could not of themselves have created the new India. They were only a small moneyed class in a corner of the country, who, if they could have gained control, would have been the old India dressed in frock coats. They started the Indian renaissance, but a far wider spread was needed if rebirth were to lead to the growth of a new nation.

So we turn next to merchants all over the country, who benefited by the improved trading conditions provided by the pax Britannica. Indeed, the British regime has often been described as a *banya raj* or merchant rule because it is held to have benefited this class. Merchants were conservative in their habits, and the cultural results of their connection with the British did not appear at once in the social sphere. But they had a custom of sending their sons to Western colleges with a view to their entering government service and so raising the family prestige. Later they sent their daughters to school also with a view to making better marital matches; and *they* in turn attended college because they wanted to go. This was why, along with Brahmins and Kayasths, Banyas were the most numerously represented in the schools and colleges of India. A special mention should here be made of the small Parsi community of Bombay and western India. By origin the Parsis were Persians who, from the seventh century onward, preferred exile to giving up their ancestral faith of Zoroastrianism, popularly called "fire worship." Ever since that time they had formed a commercial community in western India rather on the lines of those of the Jews in Europe. Numbering about one hundred thousand, they early associated themselves with the Company in Bombay, later took to Western education, and by the end of the century were the most Westernized group in the country. By that time also they largely controlled the cotton industry in Bombay, while the Tata family was beginning a new chapter in Indian development with its iron and steel projects.

A very important class was that of the subordinate official. In Indian tradition, government service was held next in esteem to Brahmin status and to literacy. A touch of the sacred hung about both literacy and government; literacy was the doorway to knowledge of the sacred Hindu scriptures, while government was held to be of divine origin. In Hindu thought the raja existed to maintain the *dharma* or moral law of the community. This feeling of sacredness, for it was not for the most part a reasoned thesis, was strong enough to attach itself to the Mughal and British governments as well as to the Hindu ones, to Persian and English literacy as well as to Sanskrit. The Indian servants of the Company, as we have seen, were excluded from all high office from the time of Cornwallis. But two factors steadily increased their importance. A succession of higher posts was gradually thrown open to them. The first great step was taken by Bentinck in the 1830's when he opened two grades of judgeships. By the second half of the century Indians were becoming high court judges.[2] Further, the "uncovenanted" [3] or subordinate civil service was increasingly manned by Indians, and these men often held posts of responsibility. The first Indian to enter the Indian civil service was Satyendranath Tagore. For many years entrants were few and far between, it is true, but by the end of the century one-fifth of the higher service was recruited from the subordinate service, and these men were nearly all Indians. The second factor was the increasing range of government activity. The old revenue, judicial, police, and military lines themselves increased in scope as governmental work increased. To these were added fresh departments. The rapidly growing canals called for irrigation officers. The railways had from the start the prestige of government service, and, though largely manned by Anglo-Indians at the outset, soon offered opportunities to Indians of all classes. A stationmaster was a man of consequence and a ticket-collector a person of respect. There were the customs, engineering, and forest services, and there was the ever-expanding Public Works Department. There came to be more government officials in more departments, with a small but increasing number holding responsible posts.

The fourth ingredient of the new middle class was the new professional group. First came the lawyers or pleaders. They were required by the new courts because the procedures were foreign and unfamiliar, a good deal of the law was also strange, and the judges were alien. From 1835 the proceedings of the higher courts were in English, which made a mastery of that language essential. The lawyers thus grew up as the first independent profession in India. They became the natural intermediaries between people and government and provided a pool for ultimate independent leadership of the new class. They were the first group of modern Indians to shatter the nineteenth-century myth of Indian incompetence. In every town down to the small country market town, the bar club became a social and intellectual center for the new Indians. Later it provided a natural political center. The influence of this class can be judged from the number of national leaders who received a legal training. The most eminent were Mahatma Gandhi, M. A. Jinnah, and the Nehrus. Others were the Patel brothers, Rajagopalachari, and C. R. Das.

After the lawyers came the journalists. They were a small group at first, owing to the natural difficulties of journalism in India. But in time journals of repute arose, such as the *Hindu* in Madras, the *Leader* in Allahabad, and the *Amrita Bazar Patrika* and the *Modern Review* in Calcutta. Journalists were independent and became men of influence. One of them became a minister in the first popular ministry of the old United Provinces in 1921. Another section of great importance was the teachers in schools and colleges. They enjoyed much respect because of their connection with learning, although their particular knowledge was secular and non-Indian. Some, of course, belonged to the government schools and colleges and so ranked as officials, but from 1850 onward the great majority were teachers in independent institutions. This profession grew rapidly as education expanded, and gathered prestige as universities sprang up. After the legal profession, that of the teacher or professor was the one most prominent in public life. Dadabhai Naoraji of Bombay, who sat in the British Parliament for many years; Gokhale, the moderate leader of the early twentieth century; and Tilak, his extremist counterpart, all began life as teachers. After the teachers came the doctors practicing Western medicine. Many of them came from the Hindu medical castes, but the study of Western medicine brought them into line with the new forward-looking groups. M. A. Ansari, a leading Muslim Nationalist in the twenties and friend of Gandhi, belonged to this class.

There were marginal groups such as cotton and jute technicians and retailers of European goods in the large towns, but the foregoing were the principal components of the new class. The significant thing about this class was not merely that it was evenly spread over India but that it possessed common characteristics which gave it a homogeneity never seen in India before. Granting that most of these people were in some way connected with the new administration, we can say that the essential reason for this unity of outlook and feature was the policy of using English both for the conduct of public business and also as the medium for instruction. To the latter must be added the Western slant of the content of that education itself. Both these measures dated from 1835. In the Presidency towns, of course, English had been studied for career purposes long before this, but it was the new policy which spread its knowledge throughout the country. The English language acted as a link connecting all these groups with a common instrument which gave them a common status in the community. It both united them among themselves and marked them off from the rest of society as "the English-knowing classes." Many thought this would be a bar to their further influence, but in fact it provided them with a platform of respect. India had been accustomed to a class literate in languages it could not understand. Sanskrit had been unintelligible to the masses for centuries and Persian was known only to the few.

With the link of language went the link of knowledge. All these people studied the same curriculum in the schools and colleges. They read
the same plays of Shakespeare, delighted in the same nature poetry,
read the same novels of Dickens and Thackeray, and studied the same
orations of Burke and essays of Macaulay. They all imbibed the scientific
atmosphere of the West and its democratic and liberal influences. This
tendency was increased by the English press, both British and Indian
managed, newspapers being their main reading matter after college.
Thus not only the English language but Western social values and ideas
of democracy and nationalism were the perquisites of this class. This
second link, like the first, both drew the new class together and helped
to set it apart from the rest of society. But the new group was not put
in a corner or out of view; rather it was placed on a pinnacle for all to
see. With this equipment the new class became the lighthouse of the
new age. The old middle classes had been divided by language and by
cultural and technical tradition as well as by caste and distance. They
had no common culture, no common status. The Muslim doctor (*hakim*)
would not share his knowledge with his Hindu colleague (*vaid*). The
teachers and lawyers had been equally cut off from each other. Now
all had common bonds in an alien language, body of knowledge, and
professional equipment.

Not only were they linked together by their education and common
language, but by the nature of their work. For it all involved, whether
in law, administration, teaching, medicine, or technical work, dealing
with Western sciences, concepts, and procedures. Thus the more the
class grew in size and prestige, the more enmeshed it became in the
world of the West. The more it might think of taking over power from
the foreigners, the less could it conceive of returning to the old ways.
If class members became political revolutionaries against the British
raj, they were also social revolutionaries on behalf of the new order.
This is why the take-over in 1947 resulted in an increase in the rate of
Westernization and not in a reversal of direction.

We have noted the mental, ideological, and occupational links binding this class together. Another link, the psychical, has now to be added
to complete the picture. The press has already been mentioned. The
English-language papers enabled each section of this class to learn of
the others and to know something of world events. Though these events
were bent, as it were, by a prism in an English direction, knowledge of
them helped to release the new class from the age-long self-centeredness
of traditional India. More than this, the press was a powerful factor in
creating an all-India consciousness. For the first time thinking people

learned what was going on in the country as a whole and found it habitually treated as a unity. The concept of "India" began to form in their minds and to displace or superimpose upon the previously dominant concepts of Bengal, Maharashtra, the Brahmins, the Rajputs and so on. People began to think of themselves as Indians as well as tribes or castes. The word "India" became for them a physical and psychical reality, embracing even non-Hindus, as well as a mystical one. The press not only helped to build up this new Indian consciousness, but provided a forum for discussion for the new ideas and customs. The smallness of the circulations did not matter, for each copy of a paper was read by groups rather than single individuals, and in turn provided material for larger groups.

The last link was that of the railways. From about 1870 onward they were binding the country together in a new network of communications, which was virtually complete by 1900. The railways made the postal system cheap, efficient, and relatively speedy. This was another asset for the new class, encouraging exchange of ideas. The railways promoted interchange of people. The habit of travel was easily acquired, and people came to think nothing of a night's journey for a meeting or a business engagement. Railways made the all-India society and conference possible. Without them there could have been no National Congress. Mahatma Gandhi preferred the bullock wagon to the train, but the Congress' pillar of victory was to be found at the end of a railroad.

These influences and physical aids helped to give the new class a common consciousness, a sense that it not only belonged to India but that India also belonged to it. Through the influences just noted, through the new literature, and through contact with the new ruling race they acquired a notion of nationalism distinct from Hinduism. "India," a secular concept with a geographical and physical content, replaced the sociotheological one of Aryavarta ("land of the Aryas"). The new nationalism was for all Indians, not only the pure Aryas. But the new nationalism was at first a dream or an ideal, a subject for poems, and the stirrer of pleasing emotions. It had to be embodied in a movement and a party before it could embrace the people as a whole. Before proceeding further it is necessary to relate this new Indian nationalism to the English liberalism of the nineteenth century with which it was so closely connected. English liberalism derived from the Whig revolutionaries of the seventeenth century, whose high priest was Locke, and the democratic French philosophers of the eighteenth, whose prophet was Rousseau. The emphasis of the former was on civil rights, and the liberty of the subject; of the latter on the more fundamental rights of man, on liberty, equality, and fraternity. These ideas crossed the Atlantic to find their place in the American Constitution and from thence returned to strengthen liberalism in an England distrustful of anything French during the Revolutionary War. They became the basis of the creed of the radicals or left wing of the English liberals. Periods of political progress in Britain up to 1914 were those in which the radicals were strong enough appreciably to influence the government of the day. The new policy introduced by Bentinck into India was a result of the radical-liberal ascendancy in the British reform era (1830–41). Introduce Western education and institutions, they believed, and India would transform herself in a generation. A radical weakness was over-optimism. India did not transform herself in a generation, and showed so little sign of doing it in the next that many people pronounced her incorrigible. The mutiny seemed the final proof to such people, who relegated Indian acceptance of the West and self-government to an indefinite future. They did not see the seed growing secretly, as has just been described. So we find a slowing down in positive government Westernizing measures to match the declining faith in Indian transformation. Between 1835 and 1880 the only measures of any importance that can be pointed to were the opening of the I.C.S. to competition in 1853 (enabling Indians to compete), Dalhousie's and Canning's legislative councils, the latter bringing in Indians, some self-government in the big cities, and the Queen's Proclamation in 1858.

But in the late sixties liberalism in Britain found fresh strength as it spread its roots among the broad masses of the new working classes. To do this was in accord with radical doctrine, and radical influence increased accordingly. It also found a champion in Gladstone, a late convert to the people's rights and a proclaimed believer in moral principles. Good government, he pronounced, was no substitute for self-government; what was morally wrong could not be politically right. "It is our weakness and our calamity," he said, "that we have not been able to give to India the blessings of free institutions." When returned to power in 1880 he sent out his disciple Ripon to begin the introduction of representative institutions into India. From his term of office (1880–84) dates the beginning of India-wide urban and rural self-government, which still follows in the main the original pattern. Ripon also freed the press from restrictions imposed by his predecessor and commenced industrial legislation by passing the first Factories Act. He then ran up against bureaucracy on a racial issue, and the controversy which ensued, as we shall see, was closely connected with the foundation of the National Congress.

It will thus be seen that the new class, increasingly informed by the press of events in Britain and India, could find in the acts of government and still more in the movements of British public opinion some grounds for optimism. There were those among their rulers, and still more among the rulers of their rulers, who thought that if there were as yet no Indian nation one ought to be created. Nor was this all. The new class derived much encouragement and gained much confidence from the work of European Oriental scholars. From the time of Sir William Jones in the days of Warren Hastings, who introduced Sanskrit to the learned European world as a language from which, or from a common parent of which, many European languages were derived, a succession of scholars revealed the range of Sanskrit literature and the depth of Hindu philosophy. Kalidasa influenced Goethe and the literary romantics, the Vedanta influenced Schopenhauer and the Western transcendentalists. Further, the richness of Indian historical tradition was revealed in works such as James Tod's *Annals and Antiquities of Rajasthan.*[4] Persian scholars did the same for Mughal India. Others revealed the Indian heritage in art and architecture. All this attention was to the new class as water in a thirsty land, avid as it was for respect. When it came from the new world of the West, the source at the same time of so much criticism and scorn, it was balm indeed.

The path of the new class was by no means strewn with the roses of approval grown in the gardens of European opinion. Opposition and criticism also played their part in heightening Indian self-consciousness. There was a body of criticism of Hindu or, more strictly, Brahminical institutions born of contact with Indian society when it was at its lowest ebb in the eighteenth century. This was reinforced by evangelical moralism which not only condemned suttee and infanticide but girded at idol-worship and polytheism as well. From these criticisms sprang notions that contemporary Indian society was not only corrupt but inferior, unprogressive, and semibarbaric. A president of the Ethnological Society could argue that Indians were inferior, as a race, to Europeans. Lord Northbrook complained in the seventies of the general official opinion that no one but an Englishman could do anything. Many of the new class agreed with some of these strictures in their hearts, but the harshness of the tone provoked a reaction and drew them together in self-defense. These thoughts of superiority were also expressed in the form of race feeling. The higher official might look on things Indian with wonder and disdain, but the lower order, especially the commercials or "box-wallahs" of Calcutta and the planters, translated their feelings into action. Indians were excluded from their society and were liable to insult in public places such as railroad stations. India was commonly regarded as a conquered country and its people as a subject race. Here again a common evil provoked a common resistance; the Brahmin and the Sudra felt a common grievance and were drawn together for its redress in a way which would never have happened otherwise.

The Indian middle class was created by British action. In emulation of British patriotism it created the image of Mother India and the myth of the Indian nation. The myth grew toward reality with the sunbeams of government measures and scholarly research and the snows of contempt and denigration. Some striking event or stimulus was needed to precipitate this highly charged solution of emotion into the crystals of political action. Such a development was bound to take place in the circumstances; the events of the late seventies and early eighties were merely the occasions for which the foregoing movements had provided the cause. The first body that could be seriously called political was the British Indian Association founded in 1851 which submitted the first proposals for Indian participation in government to Parliament in 1853. But it was during Lytton's viceroyalty (1876–80) that events began to take shape. Government policy provided a series of irritations to the new class and so heightened its self-consciousness. The Afghan war seemed to be a reckless adventure in which the lives of Indians were being used to further an imperialist cause. So did the dispatch of Indian troops to Cyprus during the Russian crisis of 1878. The Vernacular Press Act of 1878 seemed to be a gag for the Indian press from which the European press was exempt. The lowering of the age for competing in the I.C.S. examination in London was interpreted as an effort to go back on the policy of equal admission of Europeans and Indians.[5] Finally, there was the enforcement of complete free trade by the abolition, at the behest of the home government and over the heads of the Indian executive councilors, of the cotton duty of 5 per cent. This was felt to be a discrimination against India in favor of the Lancashire mill-owners and estranged the whole commercial class of western India. A young leader of fire and ability appeared in Bengal in the person of Surendranath Banerjea, whose critical faculties had been sharpened by his ejection from the civil service on what many considered to be insufficient grounds. His Indian Association, founded in 1876, grew rapidly as the result of these events.

Lord Ripon's measures allayed these discontents. The Afghan adventure was liquidated, the Press Act repealed, the salt tax reduced, and the Maharaja of Mysore restored to his state in 1881. Ripon then aroused enthusiasm and raised hopes by introducing representative institutions on the British model into local government. Surely this could only be a prelude to the application of the same principle to the national government? Then came the Ilbert Bill, so called after Sir Courtenay Ilbert, the law member who introduced it. It proposed to empower Indian sessions judges (of which there was now an increasing number) to try Europeans in the *mofussil* or districts, a power they already enjoyed in the Presidency towns. The nonofficial Europeans saw in this a threat to their position and affected to disbelieve in the impartiality of Indian judges. The pent-up racialism gathered by a series of measures found in this proposal what was thought to be a decisive issue, and a storm of tropic intensity burst upon the government. There were protest meetings, there was fevered agitation, and it was even proposed to kidnap the viceroy in Calcutta and hold him for ransom. Ripon found officials even within his own council covertly sympathizing with the opposition and received lukewarm support from London, where the government was under heavy fire. He bowed to the storm and agreed to a compromise by which Europeans could claim a jury half of whose members would be Europeans. One racial anomaly was thus removed at the cost of the creation of another. It was the turn of the new Indians to feel aggrieved.

From this episode sprang the formation of the Indian National Congress. When Ripon retired at the end of 1884 he was given an Indian send-off received by no viceroy before or since. He was a national hero, and long remained a sort of patron saint of the new movement. The new class perceived that the administration as a whole was against them, but they also felt that a strong tide of opinion in Britain was on their side. They were deeply impressed by the results of organized agitation. They were encouraged to act by a group of liberal-minded Englishmen which included A. O. Hume, a retired civil servant and son of the radical Joseph Hume, and Sir William Wedderburn. They received the guarded approval of the new liberal viceroy Lord Dufferin. In these circumstances the first meeting was held in Bombay in December 1885. It comprised only seventy members, who qualified by paying a small fee, and consisted mainly of lawyers, journalists, and schoolmasters. They were nervous and diffident. They seemed, in that first session, almost more concerned with insisting on their loyalty and the blessings of British rule than calling for progress and reform. But a start had been made, a call, if rather a muted one, had been sounded. It was from these modest beginnings that the Indian political giant of the twentieth century grew.

CHAPTER XXVIII

Nationalists and Government, 1885-1905

From the moment of the foundation of Congress in 1885 the issue of nationalism was a dominant one in the affairs of India. It was to grow steadily in conscious attention until it spread over the whole political and social firmament. But the actors of the time, even the nationalist ones, were far from being wholly aware of this. Most of the British placed self-government in a remote future; even twenty years later the founders of the Servants of India Society could refer to British rule as an inscrutable decree of providence, as though it were a permanent part of the political horizon.

In surveying this theme we shall notice successive breaches between the government and the nationalists, and successive *rapprochements*. Not only the conflicts such as the civil disobedience movements but also the settlements, including the final peaceful transition of authority, have to be explained. They fit in neither with the picture of a benevolent guardian busily preparing its ward for independent life, nor with that of a group of patriots rightly struggling to be free. The true picture was not only less idyllic and less tragic but also less simple. It is best, therefore, to begin with a brief analysis of the attitudes of both Indians and British to the idea of an Indian nation. On the Indian side we must recognize that the idea of an Indian nation, embracing all the inhabitants of the subcontinent, was a new and, from the point of orthodox Hinduism, a wrong one. Orthodoxy regarded India as Arya-varta, the land of the Aryas, which automatically excluded the Muslims, who numbered one-quarter of the total population, and by implication the outcastes, who numbered one-eighth. Even among Hindus, men had neither an equal value nor an equal place in society. There were the twice-born or higher castes and above all there were the Brahmins.

Apart from orthodox doctrine, there were strong particularist currents. In 1880 most Indians were still more conscious of their racial or local heritage than their Indian nature. A man was more aware of being a Maratha, a Bengali, or a Panjabi than of being an Indian. This latter consciousness was in fact the monopoly of the new Western-educated classes. Even today a Maratha biographer of Tilak [1] can see no inconsistency in condemning the imperialism of the British in India while looking back with pride and nostalgia on the Maratha empire in India, which he accuses the British of upsetting. Most Muslims looked similarly upon the Mughal empire, which they considered the Marathas had overturned. It does not matter that both were historically wrong; the important thing to note is that both were putting community or race before India as a whole. We must therefore recognize that nationalism was something that had to grow *within* India before it could settle accounts with the foreign possessors of power.

When we turn to the British we have also to recognize mixed motives and confused thinking. There was the element of vested interest, both economic and political, the last being especially strong in the services. But behind the Indian government and services was public opinion in Britain, which controlled the political masters of the Indian government in London. There were, of course, commercial circles which thought of India as a place for profit-making and hoped that the only subject of change was the law of supply and demand. But responsible leaders of both parties went beyond this. On the liberal side we have seen Gladstone, through his lieutenant Ripon, making genuine efforts to introduce the beginning of self-government on Western lines at a time when there could not possibly be said to have been any strong pressure for it from Indian opinion as a whole. This thread persisted right down to 1947; it advocated advances, it protested at highhanded acts like the Amritsar massacre; it was an important element in the final handover. There is no doubt, for instance, that if a conservative government had been in power in 1947, an attempt would have been made to postpone or modify it.

But from 1885 to 1945 liberalism was only in the ascendant during the period from 1905 to 1914. The conservative was the stronger influence. Responsible leaders agreed that India must move toward some form of self-government; they differed as to what form it should take. One wing, which from the time of Baldwin and Lord Halifax in the twenties became the majority, believed in Western self-government as the goal. They differed from the liberals in the pace at which they were prepared to proceed, which meant their estimate of Indian progress.

Another wing, influential before 1914, looked wistfully to an *Indian* form of self-government. India was to be governed by Indians on Indian lines. This meant paternalism united with Western education and techniques. It may be called the durbar or court system, as distinct from the parliamentary. The ruler would hear the views and plaints of his subjects and then act for their good with the advice of his ministers or close advisers. These people watched Indian princes being educated on Western lines and hoped that they would turn into enlightened despots in the eighteenth-century style. They looked for their counterparts in British India. Lytton founded the Statutory Civil Service for them; Minto proposed consultative assemblies for them. They looked but they did not find. These classes would not Westernize themselves in the prevailing conditions. Because they were looking so fixedly in traditional quarters, the British failed to see the new leaders arising in the new middle class. When these men knocked on the gates of government they at first received no answer because the tenants were scanning the horizon on the other side of the citadel for the traditional leaders who never arrived. There was thus at first a tragicomedy of cross purposes between Indians and British about the nature of political development and the identity of the developers. When this confusion was largely cleared up in the twentieth century, there arose a straight issue between India and Britain, not about self-government in itself, but about the pace of progress towards its realization.

For the first fifteen years of its existence, down to 1900, the young Congress was feeling its way. Mere payment of a fee for attendance gave way to election and the formation of representative bodies. But it remained, during this period, a cautious body of mainly middle-class gentlemen. Three Englishmen held the annual office of president during those first years, and the proceedings included loyal resolutions and remarks on the blessings of British rule. Indeed, few bodies appeared to be less revolutionary at this period, or less a menace to the established order. The resolutions dealt with matters of detail rather than principle, and it was not easy, even at that stage, to unite members from the various parts of India in equal enthusiasm for the different issues. The members from Bengal, being usually connected with the landlord class, attributed many evils to the government's failure to extend the Permanent Settlement throughout India, but the members from the west and south had little use for landlords. The commercially interested members from western India criticized the government for failing to prevent the decline in exchange value of the rupee, but this was not a burning issue in Bengal. In general, the main themes of discussion were the following. All were agreed on urging further progress in the Indianization of the services, specially the I.C.S. For this the holding of simultaneous examinations in Britain and India was urged, in order to eliminate the existing element of unfair competition produced by requiring examination in London only. All were agreed on the importance of extending representative institutions, though the tone of the demands was studiously moderate. There was also agreement about the economic discrimination of the government in the matter of cotton duties. A fresh edge was given to this grievance by the imposition of the cotton excise in 1892. As one of the measures for dealing with the currency crisis, an import duty of 5 per cent was imposed in that year. But as the result of an outcry from the Lancashire cotton interests a countervailing excise duty on cotton of the same amount was imposed at the same time. Both duties were reduced to 3.5 per cent in 1896,[2] but nationalists were not mollified. They had been given a clear example of the sacrifice of Indian interests for the sake of a foreign group, and they made full use of their case. Along with charges of discrimination went arguments about the "economic drain," the process by which it was alleged that the wealth of India was being steadily siphoned into British hands.[3] That a substantial sum went out of the country was undisputed; that much of it was a charge on capital productively employed in such projects as railway and canal construction was less often realized. The arguments were too involved to excite great indignation, but it was generally taken for granted that in the economic field the government was discriminating against Indian interests and that India was becoming poorer.

This was the most telling of the nationalist criticisms, for it undermined confidence in governmental integrity and excited emotion apart from merely forming opinions. But there were still broad areas of agreement between government and nationalists. One was the education policy, including the use of the English language. Another was the importance of law and order, for memories of the old anarchy had not quite died out. Another was such matters as the irrigation and famine policies. In general the new nationalists hoped to be accepted by the existing order rather than to supersede it.

Within the movement there were already signs of divisions which were later to become deep-seated. The first was the attitude of the Muslims. In Bombay many supported the Congress, but the Muslim Sir Sayyid Ahmad Khan, a prominent Westernizer and founder of the Aligarh Muslim College, held aloof. Democracy, he said, meant majority rule, and majority rule meant Hindu rule. His attitude was matched on the

Hindu side by the Maratha Tilak, who glorified Sivaji's exploits against Muslims and accused the Bombay government of partiality toward them. Congress was thus from the start a mainly Hindu body. A second problem was a fissure within the Congress itself. By a strange irony the two protagonists both belonged to the same Chitpavan Brahmin subcaste and both were domiciled in Poona, the citadel both of Maratha nationalism and of western Indian orthodoxy. They were Gopal Krishna Gokhale and Bal Gangadhar Tilak, later called by his admirers Lokamanya, or savior of the people. Both had the pride of high ancestry and both grew up in humble circumstances. Both experienced Western education. Both became teachers, joined the same self-sacrificing Deccan Education Society (1883), and both were professors in the Fergusson College which it opened in 1885. Both had great ability. But they reacted to these circumstances in opposite ways and became the leaders of rival schools of thought. Gokhale was the "moderate" whose views were dominant until his death in 1915; Tilak was the "extremist," the gadfly of both government and moderates until his imprisonment in 1908.

The split came on the double issue over the attitude toward the British government and the attitude toward social reform. Tilak coined the phrase *"swaraj* [self-rule] is our birthright"; he would tolerate no compromise with the foreigners, whom he would harry out of the land. In his own mind he drew the line at violence, but it is clear that this was a tactical decision rather than a moral conviction. Gokhale believed in reason, in liberal principles, in co-operation, and in gradual reform, and he used his great powers of persuasion to advocate these views. They also differed about social reform, a burning question for all nationalists. Gokhale and the moderates wished to press on with this and welcomed government co-operation, for they believed that only through social regeneration could the new Indian nation become strong enough to take over the reins of power. Tilak, on the other hand, would have no interference from outside the Hindu body. In his view it should be independence first and social reform afterward. To gain independence he was prepared to use orthodox sentiments and prejudices, such as anti-Muslim feeling, and feeling against such measures as antiplague precautions. He therefore appeared to many as a champion of Hindu orthodoxy whose triumph would put back the clock of both Indian nationalism and Hindu reform for many years. The two parted company in 1890 when Tilak resigned from the Deccan Education Society on a dispute over interpretation of rules. Tilak pursued a stormy career, using the editorship of the *Kesari* ("Lion") in Marathi and the *Maratha* in English to become the recognized leader of the left wing in Congress politics; Gokhale went through membership in the Imperial Legislative Council and the foundation of the Servants of India Society (1907) to the leadership of the dominant right wing. The rival ways of battle and irreconcilability versus reason and conciliation thus found at the outset two singularly able and redoubtable champions.

The government's attitude to the Congress was at first one of guarded approval. Lord Dufferin, a liberal of the diplomatic kind, encouraged its foundation and then assumed an attitude of Olympian detachment when government began to become conscious of Congress pinpricks. This detachment grew greater, and Dufferin described the new class as "a microscopic minority." At the same time the liberal current was still strong enough to promote some response from the official side. In 1892 there was passed the Indian Councils Act, which enlarged the imperial and provincial legislative councils and introduced the principle of election under cover of rules which provided for "recommendations for nomination" by corporate bodies such as municipal councils and chambers of commerce. In this way Gokhale entered the Legislative Council, where his persuasive oratory and grasp of political and financial questions won the respect of British officials, gained wide publicity for the Congress, and put it, as it were, on the official map.

Tilak fell out with the Bombay government at the time of the outbreak of bubonic plague in 1896–97. His attack on the methods adopted to fight it was followed by the murder of the chief antiplague officer and his own imprisonment for incitement to disaffection. But the main Congress body remained hopefully co-operative. It needed a Curzon to complete the breach between a slow-moving government and politically conscious Indians. At the time of his appointment in 1898 Lord Curzon was the rising hope of the imperialist wing of the Conservative party. He was able, eloquent, arrogant, and immensely industrious. He had traveled in the East and believed that he knew its secret. Imperialists of his day were full of the idea of trusteeship, which meant developing the estate of one's ward without any great expectation of handing it over. Curzon could not conceive that Indians could take over their own country in a foreseeable future, but he was convinced that he must work to the limit for their good. There followed a whirl of activity which can only be compared with Dalhousie's regime in scope and duration. Its broad effect, in the administrative sphere, was to build on the foundations which Dalhousie had laid; its result was to provide India with the framework of a modern state just at the time it was needed. India owes more to Curzon in this respect than she has yet cared to admit. His other great work was to transform nationalism from a set of individual opinions into a nationwide movement. He provided the hammer to the Congress anvil to make the sparks of the new patriotism fly upward.

Let us first summarize his achievements. Externally, the Indian empire had never been more imposing and apparently powerful. Curzon gloried in its pomp and panoply and did his best to display it convincingly to the world. He was tireless in visiting the Indian states, to the mingled pride and embarrassment of their rulers. He presided over the second great durbar in Delhi to announce Edward VII's coronation. He visited the Persian Gulf in what was very like a royal progress. His foreign policy was, however, cautious as well as splendid. He dealt cautiously with the Afghans, reconciling the new Amir Habibullah to the British connection with the title of "His Majesty." At the same time he settled the ever restive frontier on lines that lasted up to 1930. The semiforward policy of extending British authority up to the Durand line of 1893 demarking the Afghan and British spheres in the Pathan tribal territory had led to a great tribal revolt in 1897. Curzon found the army entangled in a system of strong posts subject to frequent sieges and deceptive withdrawals on the approach of reinforcements. He first withdrew the British troops from the advanced posts to form a mobile reserve. In this plan Chitral, the Khyber Pass, and the Khurran Valley were evacuated. Next, the bases to which the troops were withdrawn were linked by road and rail to facilitate quick lateral movement. Movable columns were stationed at the bases, while the vacated areas were policed by tribal levies known as *Khassadars*. In this way the tribesmen were given back their self-esteem, while the subsidy provided a powerful weapon for holding them to their duties. The essential features of Pathan tribal life were love of independence and poverty. It was poverty springing from the sterility of their stony hills which led the tribesmen to raid the plains so that Curzon's policy satisfied both their ruling passions in one measure. The new policy was completed by the creation of the North-West Frontier Province from the frontier tribal area and the five frontier districts of the Panjab.[4] The Panjab administration was vexed and sore, but the move enabled the supreme government to keep in much closer touch with frontier affairs and to confide frontier affairs to the frontier-minded.

Curzon's tour of the Persian Gulf reaffirmed British interest in these waters and was part of a wider British reply to French and German expansionism. In Tibet he was less happy. The bogey here was the possibility of Russian intervention, which the thirteenth Dalai Lama considered as a means of freeing himself from China. At that time imperial Russia was as much feared and suspected as Soviet Russia at a later date. The appearance of one Dorjieff in Lhasa led to the Younghusband expedition which eventually reached Lhasa in 1904. Nothing was gained from this expedition except cheap glory; it was the swan song of British imperialism in Asia.[5]

Internally Curzon undertook an overhaul of the bureaucratic machine. His descents on successive departments came to be dreaded; he was more feared than loved, but there is no doubt that it was his galvanic energy which enabled India to meet the crisis of World War I without breakdown. He then turned to a number of national questions. He carried out an important police reform in 1903. He devoted much time to the land question, stung partly by nationalist assertions that famines were due to overassessment, which left the peasant resourceless in an emergency. The Land Resolution of 1902 marked a further stage toward flexibility in assessment and the full realization that in India an expansion of revenue must be sought in other quarters than the land. The Panjab Land Alienation Act protected cultivators from eviction from their land for debt. Curzon started co-operative credit societies whose aim was to rescue the cultivator from the clutches of the moneylender, and set up at Pusa in Behar a research institute intended to promote improved methods of agriculture.[6] Curzon was equally active in promoting commercial and industrial life. During his time 6,000 miles of railroad were constructed, bringing the total mileage to 33,000. A railway board was set up for their management. His measures encouraged the growth of Indian industry, though he did not actively promote its development. He also planned the irrigation of six and one-half million acres of land. In cultural matters he was more active than any governor general since Warren Hastings. He ardently supported the Asiatic Society of Bengal which Warren Hastings had founded. He built the Victoria Memorial in Calcutta as a monument of British rule. Above all, he fostered the preservation of Indian artistic treasures and the discovery of the Indian past. He created the Archaeological Department which under Sir John Marshall was to unearth the cities of Taxila and to reveal, in 1925, the hitherto unsuspected Indus Valley civilization of the second and third millennia B.C. The last of Curzon's purely administrative reforms was that of the army. For this purpose he secured the appointment of Lord Kitchener, fresh from his laurels in the South African war, as commander in chief in 1902. For a time they worked together and achieved much. But in 1905 they fell out on the issue as to who should have the administrative control of the army. A London-devised compromise satisfied neither, and Curzon resigned in August 1905 in bitter disillusionment.

If the foregoing represented the sum of Curzon's activities, he would have gone down in history as a governor general as masterful as Dalhousie and nearly as successful. But this is not the whole story. Two further administrative acts trespassed into politics and precipitated developments which were the direct opposite of Curzon's intentions, for he was as politically blind as he was administratively clearheaded. The Congress had at first given him rather tepid support—support because of exertions against famine, his vigor in reform and development, his freedom from race feeling—tepid because of his Olympianism and self-confident imperialism. Curzon on his side thought little of the Congress. In 1900 he wrote, "In my belief Congress is tottering to its fall and one of my great ambitions while in India is to assist it to a peaceful demise." In 1904 his Universities Act sought to improve what had until then been merely examining bodies. Postgraduate studies were to be added to Calcutta and a residential system introduced. At the same time the governing bodies were to be strengthened by nominated members (usually government officials or educationists), which would enable them to exercise greater control over the affiliated colleges that actually imparted the instruction. Here he clashed with the members of the new middle class, for it was they who organized and staffed most of the colleges and they who were displaced from the governing bodies. Highei education was their special preserve, the means of their development, and the nursery of their hopes. Curzon looked to efficiency, but they saw in the Act an attempt to reduce their influence where they were strongest. Matters were not improved by a Curzonian speech which questioned the veracity of Bengalis.

While Bengali opinion was still disturbed by the Universities Act, Curzon announced the partition of Bengal into two provinces for reasons of administrative convenience. He called it "a mere readjustment of administrative boundaries." On the face of it there was much to be said for some change. The Presidency of Bengal had spread with the growth of British rule until it stretched to the river Sutlej in 1803. The North-West Province was detached in 1835, to become the United Provinces of Agra and Oudh in 1901. This in turn became the State of Uttar Pradesh in 1947. Assam was detached in 1874. But Bengal still retained the Mughal provinces of Bengal proper, Behar and Orissa, the realm of Alivardi Khan and Siraj-ad-daula, whom Clive overthrew. This area now contained 78,000,000 people; the lieutenant governor was so burdened that the region east of the Hughli suffered by serious neglect. Curzon's remedy was to create a new province of Eastern Bengal and Assam with a population of 31,000,000. This arrangement affronted the Bengali nationalists on two counts. The first was that the Bengali-speaking area was cut in half, and the second that this division ran neatly upon communal lines, Eastern Bengal becoming a Muslim province containing the bulk of the Muslim Bengalis. It was (except for Assam) a foreshadowing of Eastern Pakistan. The Hindu Bengalis, on the other hand, found themselves in a minority to Beharis and Oriyas in their own province of Bengal. For them "the adjustment of administrative boundaries" was a partition of the homeland. Speeches of protest and resolutions at public meetings provoked no response from Curzon. The Bengali leaders remembered the agitation of the British mercantile community in the eighties against the Ilbert Bill and the tactics of Parnell in Ireland. Led by the now mature Surendranath Bannerjee, they carried the agitation to the people. Monster mass meetings and protest marches were followed by the launching of the *swadeshi* movement which demanded "buying Indian" and a corresponding boycott of foreign goods, especially Lancashire goods. The backing of other Congress leaders and especially of Tilak in the west turned a Bengali popular grievance into an all-India question. Tilak improved the occasion by coining the word *swaraj* and looking forward to passive resistance. Through this whirlwind of emotion the viceroy remained unmoved, and the partition went through as planned. It was, however, a Pyrrhic victory. Not only was the partition reversed six years later, but the national movement received a fillip all over the country from which it never looked back. The Bengali populace, it is true, returned shortly to its traditional apathy. But the whole controversy drew the new middle class together as never before. Henceforth Congress was a definite party rather than a collection of groups, and the middle class a nascent nation instead of a collection of individuals. By his imperception Curzon put forward the nationalist clock some ten or twenty years. The breach between the government and the new intelligentsia was wide and deep.

CHAPTER XXIX

Portents of the New India

The year 1905 marks an era in the history of modern India. Before this time the influence of the national movement on public affairs had been peripheral, however important the developments which were going on beneath the surface. The British-Indian ship of state seemed to be pursuing a steady course, with stately deliberation, on a sunlit sea, untroubled by storms or more than a few ripples on the waters of opinion. The foreign captain pursued a charted course without hindrance, his foreign officers confident, his local crew obedient. Portents of trouble were no more than wisps of cloud upon the horizon. From 1905 all was changed. The National Congress came more and more into the center of the stage, and was more and more seen to be part of a national movement which was both transforming and reintegrating the Indian people under manifold influences from both East and West. The government had now to take it into account, and would soon find it its major preoccupation. From 1905 India was no longer something of a hermit kingdom, sealed off from almost all influences except those which came from the West through Britain. Through the nineteenth century the pervasive effect of British sea power made all other powers save Russia seem remote and unimportant. From this time the change in the international scene brought a clearer perception of the state of world affairs. The rise of Germany and the drawing together of the traditional opponents, Russia and Britain, to meet this danger, impressed India with a sense of new forces at work in the world. Above all, the meteoric rise of Japan, her acceptance into the circle of great powers as symbolized by the Anglo-Japanese alliance of 1902, and her sensational defeat of Russia in the war of 1904–5 caused Indian hearts to beat faster and youthful imaginations to kindle. As Lord Curzon himself remarked, "The reverberations of that victory have gone like a thunderclap through the whispering galleries of the east." It was followed shortly by the Young Turk and Persian movements in 1908 and 1909 and by the Chinese revolution of 1911. As in the 1740's in South India and the 1750's in Bengal, there was a feeling of change in the air, of great events impending. But this time it was not merely a change in power patterns, but in ideas and ways of living. For all these events, which stirred Indian minds and awoke them to the existence of an out-side world, were the result of the influence of the West upon old estab-lished Islamic and Oriental societies.

As world events began to impinge upon the Indian consciousness, there was a change of view both about Britain in India and about India in Britain. Britain still towered above other powers in Indian eyes. It was still commonly referred to as home [1] and considered to be the epitome of the Western world. But it was now realized that other giants were also walking the earth [2] whose existence had to be taken into ac-count; the British giant became less impressive by comparison; he was no longer unique in his genus. This change of emphasis in Indian minds proceeded much further in World War I and will be referred to again, but it had its origin at this time. In British eyes, too, India was ac-quiring a new perspective. It was ceasing to be merely a place of profita-ble service bringing honors at the price of discomfort and exile; it was beginning to be seen as a place where something was happening which must be understood and dealt with. The great Liberal victory in the general election of 1906 marked the end of the ascendancy of aristo-cratic opinions in Britain. New forces were appearing which were to transform Britain in a generation and break up the triumphant party itself within twenty years.

The immediate consequences of the Bengal partition were three. The first was the appearance of a terrorist movement in Bengal, western India, and the Panjab, almost for the first time in British Indian his-tory. Apart from the mutiny, the only specifically violent movement had been that of the Wahabis of Patna, a Muslim group which believed that war against an infidel government was a sacred duty. All three areas were stirred to life by the partition ferment. The connection was clearest in Bengal, where it assumed a religious form related to the cult of Kali, the goddess of destruction. Even bombs had to be hurled in the odor of sanctity. In western India it was linked with the embers of Maratha militancy, which the burning words and uncompromising at-titude of Tilak had stirred. In the Panjab, pacified only sixty years be-fore, violence was never far away. The grass roots of the movement were connected with the unprecedented price rise of the previous fifty years. The movement reached its peak with the murder of Sir Curzon

Wylie in London in 1909 and fired its parting shot, as it were, with the bomb thrown at Lord Hardinge when he entered Delhi in 1912. The groups concerned were small. They never captured the imagination of the masses and never infiltrated far into Congress. But they were significant because of their influence upon the actions of others. Anarchism and nihilism had become familiar; it was natural for an alien and despotic regime, imperfectly informed of local movements and mindful of a previous explosion, to be acutely nervous. Two acts were passed which made incitement to murder and the making of explosives felonious. They caused some real terrorists and many dabblers disliked by the executive to be severely treated, but they probably created more ill will in the middle class generally than they prevented violence among the real revolutionaries. Their chief achievement, perhaps, was to provide the means by which Tilak could be sentenced to six years imprisonment in 1909. When he returned to civil life he soon became a national hero and stepped easily from provincial to all-India leadership.

Terrorism and the government reaction were closely linked with the second consequence of partition. This was a split in the Congress party at the Surat Congress meeting of 1907. A division between two wings of Congress had long been clearly visible. The two groups were known as Moderates and Extremists. Tilak was the acknowledged leader of the Extremists, and it was equally clear that before the partition crisis he was in a minority. He was unable to dominate the Congress in the Bombay presidency in the face of the Moderate leaders Gokhale and Pherozeshah Mehta, let alone the Congress as a whole. It was partition which gave him his chance. He threw in his weight in the partition agitation and thus did much to make the question an all-India one. He supported the boycott and *swadeshi* movements. He and his followers then acted as a "ginger" or pressure group, taking advantage of the emotional pressure built up by the partition agitation to urge the Congress leaders to go further than they thought politic at the moment. He wanted to maintain the movement to boycott foreign goods and to extend it all over India. He went further and proposed to organize passive resistance to the government. Peace was kept with difficulty at the Calcutta Congress of 1906, over which the veteran Dadabhai Naoraji presided for the third time as a compromise gesture. The break came the next year at Surat, when the Moderates proposed a new constitution which did not include self-government on the lines of the British dominions as the ultimate goal of Congress. Tilak questioned the election of the president, Rashbehari Bose; his motion for delay was disallowed; a Maratha shoe was thrown and hit Mehta;[3] pandemonium broke loose and the meeting dissolved in confusion. A few months later, following the murder of a British official by a terrorist, Tilak was sentenced to six years' imprisonment for incitement to murder. That he was creating rather than directing the extremist movement was evidenced by the collapse of the group during the remaining pre-World War I years. On the other hand the terrorist movement went on, suggesting that Tilak was not, as was widely supposed at the time, its secret supporter.

What were the issues which brought the two groups to the point of schism? At the time Tilak's followers considered the Moderates to be little more than stooges of the British government. In the eyes of the Moderates, Tilak was a revolutionary who threatened to bring the whole movement down in ruins and who had to be stopped at any cost. Today it is rather the fashion to regard the Moderates as timid timeservers and Tilak as a fearless patriot and political seer. Indeed, there is something to be said for this view of Tilak; for it was his program, not the Moderate one, which achieved fulfillment in 1947, and it was his method of active resistance to government, rather than the Moderate one of remonstrance, which secured it. Nevertheless, regarding the break in circumstances, it is difficult not to feel that the Moderates were *right at the time,* as Tilak was partly right for the future.

The differences between the two groups were essentially tactical and procedural rather than of principle. How was the government to be treated, how was the Congress case to be pressed, and what were to be the professed objectives? Tilak believed that the British were susceptible only to pressure. This should therefore be relentlessly applied because they would not attend to anything else. Curzon's attitude about partition tallied with this view and played into his hands. It was the essence of his case for boycott and passive resistance. The Moderates, on the other hand, believed that, however adamantine the British-Indian government, there was a strong body of opinion in Britain ready to forward their views. They had high hopes of the new Liberal government and wished to do nothing to prejudice the forward move it was known to be considering. Tilak's line encouraged the terrorists who gave the government an excuse for repression. Tilak's policy, they believed, would lead to severe government action against Congress, which might drive the whole movement underground; this in turn would breed violence and revolutionary chaos. In the conditions of the time they were probably right, though they were perhaps overcautious in the expression of their views. There was another tactical gulf between them and Tilak—his use of orthodox sentiment and Maratha chauvinism as instruments for arousing popular feeling. Tilak protested that he was not a social reactionary and that he was an Indian patriot, but his critics felt that his policy was putting back the clock of social progress which was essential to a new India, and that the glorification of Maratha wars with the Muslims was divisive rather than unifying. In fact, it was Tilak's judgment that was at fault, not his heart or his principles. Fearless patriot and indefatigable worker that he was, he could never quite grasp the shades of circumstance which justified different types of action. That is why a man of better judgment with his ear more attuned to all-India opinion, such as Mahatma Gandhi, could later use many of the same methods with completely different results. When Tilak spoke many thought they heard Sivaji riding again; when Gandhi advocated the same passive resistance and called the government "satanic" he was hailed as an *avatar* or divine incarnation sent to liberate the country. In fact Tilak had three careers, each marked by a change of attitude. The first phase, in which he relied on Brahminical reaction and Maratha militancy, ended with his imprisonment in connection with the anti-plague measures. The second, in which he preached the all-India boycott and passive resistance, ended with his imprisonment for incitement to murder in 1908. In the third, which opened with his release in 1914, he became an all-India statesman who was able to unite Hindus and Muslims at least temporarily in the national cause in the Lucknow Pact of 1916.

We can now turn to the government's response to the nationalist protest. It is usual today to belittle the measures known as the Morley-Minto reforms. It is true that the degree of power which they transferred to Indians was trifling, but for their full assessment they must be seen in relation to other measures of the prewar period and their effect upon the opinion of the time. The importance of the Stamp Act in American history was not in the impost in itself but in its effect upon American opinion at the time. The Indian Councils Act of 1909 and associated measures made it possible for the Indian Moderates to control nationalist opinion and so prevent a sliding down the slippery slope to violence, which would have eventually engulfed India in a violent colonialist revolution. It is to the Morley-Minto reforms that India owed, at that moment in time, its orderly evolution to democratic freedom.

Lord Curzon left India in October 1905, feeling more bitter about Lord Kitchener than the Bengal demonstrators. His successor was Lord Minto, one of those imperial handymen who used to specialize in overseas governorships. His previous appointment was in Canada, where he was successful and popular. He was a shrewd and unostentatious Scot, an imperial administrator rather than a party politician. It was these antecedents and qualities which enabled him to work with the new Liberal secretary of state, instead of retiring like Lytton and Northbrook with a change in the London ministry. His levelheaded judgment and urbane temper provided a valuable foil to the sharp tongue and imperious manner of his colleague. The new secretary of state was John Morley, the radical and rationalist litterateur. He was an authority on Voltaire and Rousseau and the biographer of Gladstone. This authority on democracy and standard-bearer of liberty proved to have the traditional vanity of the author, to be nearly as nervous in execution as he was bold in enunciation of principles, and to relish power so much that he was loath to part with any portion of it. Many viceroys would have quarreled or retired in disgust. Minto provided the unflinching anvil on which the Morley hammer could shape the vessel of reform, accompanied by the sparks of epigram and eloquence.

The Liberals, who came into power early in 1906 with a great parliamentary majority, believed that the Act of 1892 was due for extension and that something must be done to meet the Bengal discontent. They were handicapped by their division into radical and imperialist wings, the latter of which in foreign and imperial affairs differed little from the Conservatives. Morley's first moves were cautious. The Bengal partition was maintained and Kitchener sustained in his controversy. In Tibet, Younghusband's harsh terms were relaxed. Morley then turned to a mingled policy of repression and reform. The two repressive acts sanctioned have already been mentioned, and of these it is sufficient to say that broadly they achieved their purpose. They have to be seen in the setting of Liberal policy as a whole rather than as an attempt to crush the nationalists in revenge for the partition agitation. On the constructive side, there was a steady refusal in public to admit that responsible parliamentary government could come to India in the foreseeable future. Morley specifically disavowed the idea when introducing the reforms, but there is some reason to believe that he, at least, was speaking with his tongue in his cheek. The alternatives were variations of the durbar plan, that is, paternal government assisted by the advice of notables and experts. Hitherto the notables and experts had been almost entirely British, and it was time to turn to the Indians. Minto leaned to the Indian idea of a durbar and proposed to associate Indian councilors and notables with the administration. It was the farewell song of the aristocratic school in the Indian services. Morley realized that the new middle class could not be disregarded, and that the now well-established tradition of Western education compelled the use of Western models for political institutions. Bentinck's and Macaulay's education policy and the Councils Act of 1892 between them had decided the course of political evolution. "Western institutions" meant in British eyes "representative institutions" and, ultimately, responsible parliamentary self-government. That is why, in spite of denials and disavowals, the Morley-Minto reforms committed India to democracy.

The durbar plan, in its frock-coated form, as we may now call it, had two aspects. One was the admission of Indians to executive office and the higher services, and the other the extension of Indian representation in the legislative councils. If the former course had been pursued earlier and more generously, the granting of responsible government might have been delayed, for a strong vested interest in the bureaucracy and paternalism would have grown up within the middle class, itself the center of the demand for self-government. As it was, just enough was given to prevent frustration from turning to despair and violence, but not enough to prevent insistent demands for more. Appetite grew with what it fed on. Morley secured the appointment in 1907 of two Indians to the India Council, the advisory body of the secretary of state, and the ghost of the old Court of Directors. When Minto first proposed the appointment of an Indian to the Executive Council, in Professor Dodwell's words "it startled some of them, like a pistol pointed suddenly at their heads." Sir Satyendra (later Lord) Sinha was appointed after the passage of the Morley-Minto Act in 1909. At the same time Indians were appointed to the provincial executive councils. A little later the Islington Commission (1912) was appointed to study ways of increasing the Indian element in the higher public services.

In the council sphere, the Imperial Legislative Council was enlarged from twenty-five to sixty members, of whom twenty-seven were elected by various indirect means. The advance here was not only in numbers, but in the open recognition of election. A nonelective majority was retained, which was to prove important a few years later, but actual officials were now in a minority. The powers of the council were also increased in two significant ways. The Act of 1892 allowed a discussion on the budget (in which Gokhale made his name) and the asking of questions, but not supplementaries. The Act of 1909 allowed supplementaries, a well-known device for prying information from reluctant ministers, and the tabling of general resolutions which enabled discussions on general policy. One of the first uses made of the latter facility was Gokhale's motion in favor of compulsory universal education. These things foreshadowed, though they did not embody, full parliamentary powers. The government was beginning to be accountable to the people for its actions. A final feature of the Act was less auspicious. Six constituencies were created for Muslim landholders on the plea that they were underrepresented on the various electoral bodies, and that on a general electoral roll based on a property franchise they would be under-represented on the score of property. These pleas (first made in 1906 by the new Muslim League) were true enough, but they opened the door to "communal representation," which eventually spread throughout Indian political life, often reducing it to questions of percentages and reserved seats. Behind the shadow of democracy had come the shadow of Pakistan.

The reforms, in general, were well received. The government had, in fact, been in close touch with Gokhale and the Moderate leaders. But much depended upon the manner of their implementation. This work fell to the lot of Minto's successor Lord Hardinge (grandson to the Hardinge of the Sikh-war days). Hardinge was the permanent head of the foreign office, so that the appointment looked like a surrender to bureaucracy. In fact he turned out to be as liberal as Lord Ripon and to have a far stronger character. With a rather chilly exterior and a dry manner of writing (his memoirs reveal little), he possessed the art of handling men and united determination with tact. In his hands a constitutional experiment thought by many to be a "leap in the dark" became something of a honeymoon between government and Congress. His government began with the visit of the new King George V and Queen Mary to attend the Delhi Durbar in 1911. This gorgeous event provided the occasion for three moves calculated to appeal to nationalist sentiment. Bengal was raised to the status of a governor's province,[4] alongside the presidencies of Bombay and Madras. The partition of Bengal was revoked, and Delhi was declared the capital of India. The first of these measures may sound like a mere administrative act. But in fact the Bengalis took great pride in their city and their province, and the raising of the provincial status, even in an alien political system, gave them great satisfaction. Under the second measure the two portions of Bengal were reunited in the new governor's province; Behar and Orissa were detached to form a new province with its capital at Patna, and Assam reverted to the status of a chief commissionship. The new arrangements, which were more like the old Mughal system, proved viable in practice, besides satisfying Bengali *amour-propre*. A few years later both Orissa and Assam became provinces and are now states in the Indian Union. The third measure was one of the few real secrets of Indian history. It was intended to appeal to

Indian sentiment but had practical advantages as well. Delhi was nearer the natural center of the north and on the borderland of the main strongholds of both communities. It would be free from European commercial pressure in Calcutta without being too dominated by Panjabi officialdom. It was nearer to both the frontier and the hills, thus making the annual exodus to Simla both shorter and cheaper. This could indeed, as was proved later, be dispensed with altogether, though the move gave British architects (Lutyens and Baker) the chance of designing an impressive monument to British rule to rival the Mughal creations, Indians saw in it from the first a symbol of the future, a foretaste of things to come. Delhi was to be, as it has since become, the center of the new India.

The psychological effect of these measures was perhaps even greater than the practical. They combined to give the new class the sense that it was being borne along into a new age. They provided the Morley-Minto reforms with an aura of meaning which obscured the smallness of their legal implications. During his remaining years before World War I, Hardinge developed the policy thus begun. In 1912 he enhanced his popularity by surviving a bomb thrown in the famous Chandni Chowk of Delhi on his ceremonial entry into the city as the new capital. The next year he took a public stand for the rights of Indians in the new Union of South Africa which electrified Indian opinion. It was at a time when Gandhi, then a lawyer practicing in South Africa, was leading a passive-resistance movement with skill and success against the Union government of Generals Botha and Smuts. He spoke of "the sympathy of India, deep and burning and not only of Indians, but of all lovers of India like myself, for their compatriots in South Africa in their resistance to invidious and unjust laws." A Liberal had spoken liberal things. The cabinet was alarmed but could not afford to recall him. His reward was the unanimity with which India, prince, congressman, Muslim and peasant supported Britain at the outbreak of World War I.

CHAPTER XXX

India in World Affairs, 1858-1914

Some factors affecting India's geopolitical position and the course of events up to 1857 have already been noted. A point for observation about India's position in the mid-nineteenth century was its insulation from world events and opinion. At this time India was (apart from the British) almost as isolated from the rest of the world as the Middle West of America. The Hindu princes and people had long been looking inward; they had, except in a restricted commercial sense, lost touch with their cultural children in the East Indies and still more with the offspring of Buddhism in China and Japan. Only the new Hindus looked to the West through British spectacles. The Muslims, through their Mughal rulers, had once been in close touch with developments in the Islamic world and affairs in central Asia. Most of this contact was now lost, except for some contacts in the northwest with the Afghans and the Persians. Even the cultural tie with Persia was wearing thin. The Islamic world itself, both in its original seat in Arabia and in its later political manifestations in Persia and Turkey, seemed to be in decay. The old Muslims could only see an eclipse of glory, a creeping paralysis of ruin, in their homelands; of new Muslims to match the new Hindus there were as yet hardly any.

In 1858 India's position in relation to the Iranian Plateau was still undefined. The attempt to dominate the Afghan portion of it had failed with the first Afghan war. Afghanistan remained firmly in the hands of Dost Muhammad Khan, but he showed no signs of emulating the conquerors of the past and restoring a reintegrated Persian empire. If the Iranian situation remained equivocal, the situation in the central Asian "reservoir" remained equally so. There was as yet no horde, nomad or modernized, to spill over into the plateau. The Turkish khanates were in decay. Whether on account of one of the periods of dessication in central Asia which inhibited growth of population or for lack of modern resources which caused these states to fall behind relative to others, they were increasingly decrepit. But Russia was not yet ready to move in. Despite her rebuff in Turkey at the hands of Palmerston's diplomacy in the late thirties, she continued to look southwestward toward the Balkans, Constantinople, and the warm waters of the Mediterranean. Here was a more rewarding prize than the barren steppes of the khanates, with subject Christian populations whose cause could be espoused for the subversion of the Turkish power. It was Czar Nicholas I who coined the description of Turkey as "the sick man of Europe." He endeavored to arrange a partition like that of Poland in the eighteenth century. But British and French concern for their position in the Mediterranean led to the Crimean War of 1854–56, which put back the clock of Russian expansion for another twenty years. The next czar, Alexander II the Liberator, was at first too interested in social matters such as the liberation of the serfs in 1861 to direct his eyes elsewhere.

In Europe itself the powers were too occupied with internal matters to pay much attention to the world beyond. The revolutions of 1848 had given a new impetus to national and democratic movements. The next twenty-two years were occupied with the unification of Germany and Italy. Only France under Napoleon III had the opportunity to look further afield. It was at this time that she made her abortive adventure into Mexico and her more lasting excursion into Indo-China. But here her activities were limited by British sea supremacy, an all-pervasive fact which not only kept Europe at arm's length from the American continent but also from the hinterland of Asia as well. Both Dutch and French possessions in the East existed essentially by permission of the British. There remained the Far East. Japan was still a hermit kingdom under the shoguns, about to be opened to the world by American action. The new or Meiji era dates from 1867. China lay inert and huge, like a disabled whale on the sea, apparently easy game for any roving bird of prey. Here again British sea power came in. Britain had already begun the opening process in the first opium war of 1839–40. The second in 1859–60 carried it further. Henceforth China was the victim of concession-hunting and pressure of all kinds. But it stopped short of annexation again because of British sea power. It was now British policy to prop up the Manchu dynasty in the east, as it was to sustain the Ottoman Turks in the west. The motive was the same—the fear of something worse if either state broke up.

The Indian government's reaction to this state of affairs was to let well enough alone. Dost Muhammad was friendly—he remained neutral during the mutiny—and so long as he lived there was no grave danger on the frontier. He would certainly resist Russian aggression, in which case he would certainly be helped. It was John Lawrence who described this policy with the phrase "masterly inactivity." In the late sixties, however, the situation began to change. Dost Muhammad died in 1863; his son Sher Ali was less able and was not firmly established until 1868. At the same time the Russians began to move forward in central Asia. Bokhara became a dependent ally in 1866. In 1868 Samarkand, the fabled capital of the great Timur and the coveted city of Babur, was occupied and in 1873 Khiva. Only the khanate of Merv then remained between the Russian empire and Afghanistan.[1] Alarm began to mount among political officers and publicists who did not, like Lord Salisbury, believe in the study of large-scale maps. Nevertheless, the policy of noninterference was persevered in by the viceroys Mayo and Northbrook until fresh Russian activity in Europe alarmed the London cabinet. Sher Ali was so impressed by Lord Mayo that he handed over to him the first letters from the Russian governor general Kauffmann. But Sher Ali became uneasy when Khiva fell in 1873, and started talking of an alliance which the Indian government could not offer.

In 1875 a revolt of the Christian subject peoples of European Turkey gave Russia the signal to move forward in the Balkans once more. In 1867 she declared war on Turkey and in 1878 was at the gates of Constantinople. Here she was stopped by the action of Britain under Disraeli. Bismarck acted as a mediator at the Congress of Berlin with the result that European peace was preserved. Bulgaria and an enlarged Serbia were created, while Russia stopped short of occupying Constantinople. Cyprus was occupied by the British as a guarantee of the treaty, an event which marks the beginning of the modern Cyprus question. From the time of the Russian intervention in the Balkans, the Afghan question became an aspect in the general Russian policy of Disraeli and Salisbury and must so be understood. Lord Northbrook retired in 1876 rather than carry it out, and its Indian end was then confided to the brilliant but wayward hands of Lord Lytton.[2] India was not only to be protected, but Afghanistan used as a means of bringing pressure to bear upon Russia in central Asia. There was no thought of annexing Afghanistan, but as in 1838 there was insufficient appreciation of the Afghan determination to be independent against all comers. The method adopted was to insist upon a British envoy in Kabul who would be a portent to the Russians and might be the forerunner of an army. As a beginning Quetta was secured in 1876 from the Khan of Kalat, thus threatening the southern flank of Afghanistan at Kandahar.

But Sher Ali, like Dost Muhammad before him, feared a British envoy above all else. It was generally supposed that the arrival of a British envoy was the signal for the end of a country's independence. The Russians on their side began to press, and Sher Ali found himself between two fires. At the height of the crisis in 1878 a Russian general, Stolietov, arrived in Kabul without resistance. With the triumphant conclusion of the Congress of Berlin the British government could have concluded the matter by obtaining Stolietov's withdrawal direct from St. Petersburg. Instead Lytton was allowed to send forward his own envoy. He was repulsed at the frontier and was then followed up by an army. Too late Sher Ali found that the Russians had no intention of providing any help. He fled from Kabul and died the next year. Peace was made with his son Yakub on terms of a British envoy at Kabul, the cession of two frontier districts, a subsidy of six lacs of rupees,[3] and British control of foreign relations. Sher Ali lost his throne because he gave too little; Yakub because he gave too much. Within six weeks of his arrival in Kabul the new British envoy was murdered, and the country blazed into a general revolt. Once more the British found themselves occupying a hostile country and faced with the problem of retiring without undue loss of face. Yakub retired to India, and Afghanistan was divided into three parts until there appeared another outstanding character in the person of a nephew of Sher Ali, Abdur Rahman. He was recognized as the ruler of Kabul in 1880. The British armies, after Roberts' famous march from Kabul to Kandahar to relieve the beleagured garrison there, retired, and Abdur Rahman thereupon reunited the country.

This phase of Afghan policy was adventurous, extravagant, and unnecessary. It was adventurous because it sought to use Sher Ali as a pawn with which to threaten Russia in Asia; it was unnecessary because the end of safeguarding India could have been achieved without forcing an envoy on the Amir; and it was extravagant because even success would have been financially ruinous. There was an aftermath to the crisis after the Russians drove the Afghans from Panjdeh in 1884. The Gladstone ministry supported Abdur Rahman, and the matter was settled by the bartering of Panjdeh for the vital Zulfiqar Pass.

At long last the British learned the lesson of the realities of the northwest regions. The first of these was that they did not possess the strength to dominate the whole Iranian Plateau or even the Afghan portion of it against the wishes of the Afghans. The second was that the Afghans themselves, in the existing circumstances, were as important as the Russians. Their friendship was the best available safeguard against an irruption from central Asia. The third was that the central Asian reservoir, now under Russian control, was not yet ready to spill over toward India.

Russia in fact turned her attention for the next twenty-five years to the Far East, where her activities culminated in the repulse of the Russo-Japanese War of 1904–5. The fourth was that distance (in the pre-air, preautomobile, and in that area prerailroad age) was still a ruling factor in military planning.

The next foreign crisis was brief and concerned Burma. Upper Burma was now in the hands of the crazy king Theebaw. France, who had established herself in Indo-China under Napoleon III, was seeking to extend her influence as part of the policy of seeking "compensation" overseas for the loss of Alsace-Lorraine to Germany in 1871. The signing of a treaty, the appointment of a consul, and the secret promise of arms aroused British suspicions and tilted the scale toward annexation. Upper Burma, or the kingdom of Ava, was annexed in 1885.

Lord Curzon's Tibetan adventure has already been mentioned in Chapter XXVIII. It may here be fitted into its context in world affairs. It comes as a kind of tailpiece to the long story of Anglo-Russian rivalry in the Near East and central Asia during the nineteenth century. The thirteenth Dalai Lama wished to resist a Chinese attempt to reassert authority in Tibet, part of a last spasm of energy by the expiring Manchu Ching dynasty. British policy at that time was to support the Manchus, a policy in the interest of which Britain had refrained from interference in Tibet. By the same token the Dalai Lama could hope for nothing from India, and he therefore looked toward Russia. This immediately set off a British reaction. The last clash had been in 1884 when the Russian occupation of Merv produced an attack of "Mervousness." This was followed by the Panjdeh incident. In 1894 Russia joined with France in the Dual Alliance, with whom British relations were strained, and in 1903 she was moving toward war with Britain's new ally, Japan. The expedition revealed how much Russian influence in Tibet had been exaggerated. Immediately afterward the Russo-Japanese War diverted Russian attention, and the diplomatic revolution in Europe altered the relations of the two great powers. Only eight years after the Dalai Lama had fled Lhasa from the British he was on his way to asylum in British India from the imperialism of the new China.

At the turn of the century both the old pattern of power politics in Europe and the pattern of Western imperialism in Asia were challenged. The one was the prelude to World War I and the other to the era of Asian resurgence. From 1871 until Bismarck's fall in 1890 Germany had been the leading power in Europe. With uncanny diplomatic skill Bismarck had prevented the formation of any hostile coalition, with unwonted moderation had refrained from exploiting his strength. Only in his later years did he demand "a place in the sun," which led to the acquisition of the German colonial empire. After his fall German policy grew both more erratic and more aggressive. Respect tempered with awe hardened into alarm. The process began which by 1908 had divided Europe into two rival diplomatic systems and virtually into two armed camps. France, looking for an ally against Germany, joined hands with a disgruntled Russia in 1894. Britain was alarmed by Kaiser William's project of creating a great fleet, by the German-Turkish alliance, and by the project of a Berlin-Baghdad railway, which was regarded as a threat to India. As a counterstroke to this latter move, she reinforced her position in the Persian Gulf in the form of a viceregal tour. The Arab states in the Gulf became virtually British protectorates. Feeling her diplomatic isolation, she allied with Japan in 1902, which prevented any other power coming to the help of Russia in her conflict with Japan. The real transformation, however, occurred in 1904 when Britain made up her long-standing differences with France. This still has relevance today, for not only did it determine the pattern of World War I, but its terms gave France a free hand in Morocco in return for a free hand for Britain in Egypt. The diplomatic revolution was completed in 1907 by the Anglo-Russian entente. Its underlying motive was the need for both parties for support against Germany; its form an agreement about disputed points. The principal problem was Persia, a difficulty solved by dividing the country into spheres of influence with a neutral zone in the middle. A *Punch* cartoon showed the British lion and the Russian bear regarding a Persian cat between them. "You can stroke the head, while I stroke the tail," said the lion to the bear. "And we can *both* stroke the back."

This act was one of the last examples of the old imperialism, when countries were bandied about as so many articles for sale before the nemesis of World War I and the deluge of Asian nationalism which followed it. The rise of Asian nationalism was the second significant change in the world situation which affected India. By the first, India was involved with one of the rival power groups and so in the coming World War. At the time few Indians realized the significance of these moves. It was to them an interesting game of chess played by Olympians. Their belief in British power was unshaken; British prestige remained undimmed. But the second movement was watched keenly and affected them deeply. Its influence began the mental revolution in the mind of the new India, which culminated with independence; it was a reorientation of thought which saw India as a nation among her equals (whatever her power status might be) instead of as a cloistered cultural garden or the hopeful satellite of an imperial sun. The anti-European Boxer movement in China affected India little. So far as it was regarded at all in India, it was considered to be an expiring effort of the old regime rather than an example of nationalism. But after this episode there came in turn the Japanese victory over Russia in 1904–5, the Young Turk revolution of 1908–9, the Persian nationalist movement of 1910, and the Chinese revolution in 1911. The most influential of these events was the Japanese victory, because it showed convincingly that Asians could outmatch Europeans in their most cherished field of war. Europe had chosen the scales of power as a standard of comparison and had fallen short. The Turkish and Persian revolutions added excitement to minds which had already been stirred, with the further stimulus that they were nearer home. We can perhaps sum up the effect of these events by saying that they encouraged the Tilak attitude of claiming rights, rather than the Gokhale attitude of seeking concessions. Sober-minded nationalists still believed the British position to be unshakable, but they were less sure of its indefinite continuance, and they felt more confidence within themselves.

We may conclude this chapter with some reference to the Indian communities overseas. Indians have always been active traders, and trading connections have existed beyond her shores since the earliest times. There was active intercourse with the ancient world, where traders and "gynosophists"—as the early Christian Fathers described yogis or ascetics—were familiar in cosmopolitan Alexandria. There were trading communities in the great cities of the Near East and strung down the east coast of Africa. To the east there were commercial connections with Malaya and Indonesia. During the early centuries of the Christian era there was the great cultural advance in southeast Asia, dealt with earlier.

The rise of the Arabs broke the connection with Europe, but trading communities were still to be found down the west-African coast when Vasco da Gama sailed up from the Cape of Good Hope. These bodies have continued up to this time; old mercantile groups form an important part of the large Indian population in East Africa today. But the British period saw the growth of a new kind of settlement. There was emigration for work instead of for trade, followed by settlement for subsistence rather than for commercial profit. The driving force on the Indian side was poverty, especially in south India, produced in the middle years of the nineteenth century by the effects of famine, and after 1870 by the pressure of the people on the land owing to the steadily increasing population. This largely explains why most of the emigrants were of the southern Telugu and Tamil races, though an important element also came from Gujarat in the west, with its traditional connection with East Af-

rica. On the British side the attractive force was the effects of the abolition of slavery throughout the empire in 1833. Planter communities
found themselves short of labor and began to demand the import of a
fresh labor supply to take the place left by the slaves. Planter pressure in
London and official caution in India produced the indenture system,
whereby men went abroad on seven-year contracts with the option of
settlement or repatriation at the end of it. By the end of World War I
the indenture system had ended everywhere. But it left behind it Indian
communities which now number about three and one-half million. In
many cases the time-expired indentured laborer stayed on because he
had lost his links with home, or had only poverty to look forward to
there, while in his new home he could subsist and raise himself by his
exertions. In this way the labor colonies have grown into complete communities with middle, professional, and upper classes. These communities are to be found in the New World in numbers in Trinidad and British
Guiana; in Africa in East and South Africa; in Asia in Burma, Ceylon,
Malaya; in Mauritius in the Indian Ocean; and in Fiji in the Pacific. In
British Guiana they are the strongest group, and everywhere else, except
in race-conscious South Africa, they are influential. And it was South
Africa which trained Mahatma Gandhi for the work which lay before
him.

CHAPTER XXXI

World War I in India: The Great Divide

The outbreak of World War I formed for India a dividing line between the old and new worlds. It was a watershed of ideals and attitudes. Before 1914 the emphasis was upon past tradition. Despite new ideas like nationalism and new movements like the Congress, despite the intrusion of Western thought, language, and techniques, India's glory lay mainly in the past. The Hindu system still retained its social and religious hold over the vast majority of the population. Politically, the British *raj* was still largely regarded as an umbrella protecting the traditional ways of life from the scorching rays of change. Its pomp and panoply continued undimmed, its prestige was largely unimpaired. The new movements just described seemed so far to be eddies on the surface rather than deep-moving currents. They were subordinate to the general scene. After the war all this was changed. Though the old systems remained, though the political structure of the Indian empire survived unimpaired, India as a whole was looking forward rather than back. Both in the political and social fields people were concerned with the shape of things to come rather than the glories of the past. India was on the march. The war's most important effect on India was a mental revolution, after which independence became merely a question of when and how. So marked and sudden was it that Europeans who had been absent for only a year or two on war service found themselves out of date on their return, while others who had remained in the country were bewildered by the transformation of the scene before their eyes.

We may first note briefly the facts of the war as they affected India, and then the nature of mental revolution which they brought about and the political manifestations in which it expressed itself. India, being a dependent constituent of the British Empire, found itself automatically at war at midnight on August 4, 1914. There followed such a scene of enthusiasm as should have warmed the heart of any government. When the legislature met in November, nonofficial members vied with each other in expressions of loyalty and themselves suggested that India should bear a share of the cost of the operation in Europe. The Indian princes, so suspicious of the British a century earlier, were loud in their expressions of loyalty and clamored for permission to lead their troops to the front. All their Imperial Service contingents [1] were offered for service overseas. This outburst was an index both of the prestige of the government and the esteem in which it was held at the time. It could have been made the basis of a forward leap amid popular acclamation, which might have made the existing authoritarian regime more popular than ever. If the government in the spirit of Akbar had taken both princes and people into partnership, there might have developed a government in the style of Bismarck's German Empire, Britain playing the part of Prussia and providing a directing policy to be administered by Indian hands. Here was perhaps the last chance for the creative renewal of the old regime. This did not happen for several reasons. In the first place the British lacked imagination. No one saw the possibilities of exploiting this enthusiasm for creative change, or realized how easily such emotion if neglected or spurned could turn to bitterness and hate. For the most part, officialdom took these expressions as a natural tribute to their integrity and benevolence; when the inevitable reaction occurred they were surprised, hurt, and indignant. The only concrete response was a call for recruits to fight overseas. In the second place, the governments of both India and Britain were too engrossed with the war crisis, which after all was the biggest Britain had encountered since the time of Napoleon a century before, to pay attention to political questions. They expected a short war. The easy and fatal course was taken of postponing every political issue until after the war. In Britain itself this was done in the case of Irish Home Rule, just enacted after many years of bitter struggle. The results were the Irish rebellion of 1916, the Sinn Fein campaign, and the separation of Eire from the Commonwealth. In the case of India, Prime Minister Asquith said in November 1914 that "henceforth Indian questions would have to be approached from a different angle of vision." But no positive proposals were made for nearly three years and then they were to be "after the war." But "Time, the old gypsy man," would not stand still. Amritsar and Gandhi's nonco-operation came before the Montagu-Chelmsford reforms. In the third place, there was an inner contradiction between the aspirations of the princes and middle class so that they could not both be satisfied at the same time. The princes believed in authority and accepted overlordship provided it was strong and not too interfering. They would move forward on lines of authority and enlightened despotism (enlightenment being a very flexible concept). But the middle class were democratic in outlook. They looked forward to increasing association with the British, not only as executants, but also as framers of policy in a representative capacity. Indianized enlightened despotism would not satisfy them for long, while any move toward democratic government (as the event proved) would frighten the princes. Only a Bismarck at that time could have smothered Indian desire for democratic government with the pillows of individual authority and nationalist fulfillment. Bismarck stifled German liberalism with nationalist glory, but in the Indian case the British could hardly do this without stifling themselves in the process. But there was no British Bismarck at the time. The tide was not taken at the flood. The moment passed, to be succeeded by years of misunderstanding and discord.

Once the crisis of the Marne campaign was passed, the Indian army found itself under increasing demand for service overseas. It had been designed by Kitchener for the defense of India, and this change of purpose brought about strains which led to scandals. There was a breakdown in Iraq, or Mesopotamia as it was then called, which led to the resignation of the Secretary of State for India in 1917. But the net result was a great expansion in numbers, a development in technique, and the gaining of experience in widely separated fields. The war record of the army was most distinguished. In the autumn of 1914 an army corps was dispatched to France to fill a gap until "Kitchener's army" could take the field. Only fifty-seven years earlier the obligation to serve overseas had been one of the military grievances leading to the mutiny. When Turkey joined the Central Powers in October 1914, Indian troops garrisoned the Suez Canal and repulsed a Turkish attack. Indian troops fought through the long campaigns of Macedonia and German East Africa. Above all, they played a large part in the Iraq campaign leading to the capture of Baghdad in 1917. In this way they helped to found the present state of Iraq. They were in the allied army which took Jerusalem in 1917 and swept to Damascus, Aleppo, and victory the next year. All this involved a great effort in India itself. In all some 800,000 men were recruited to the fighting forces, together with some 400,000 noncombatants. This resulted in a great expansion in the military machine, a greater mixture of classes, and a stronger feeling of self-confidence all around. If Indian loyalty was so great that at one time Britain could leave only 15,000 British troops in the country without untoward incident, Indian self-confidence grew when the magnitude of their effort and the extent to which it depended upon Indians themselves were realized.

The war had other effects upon Indian life besides the military. In the administrative sphere, the unwise decision to allow British civilian officers to serve in the forces deprived the government of some of its best personnel at a time of crisis. Many of them never returned, and those who did found themselves in a strange new mental world to which it was difficult to adapt themselves. Thus, when times grew difficult toward the end of the war, the government had only an aging and wearied cadre of officers to rely upon. In the economic sphere the first effect was one of stimulus, as supplies were sought for the new armies and for the allied forces in the Near East and Africa. The industrial development of modern India owes a good deal to the demands of World War I. But increasing demands and expenditure set in motion a rise of prices, a sure means of turning enthusiasm into discontent. When the submarine war intensified in 1917, India exported much grain to help Britain stave off starvation. There is little doubt that this was overdone and gave a further fillip to rising prices. In 1918, when the war drew to its final crisis, a further effort was made. Recruiting was pushed to the point of coercion in the Panjab, supplies were poured overseas, and prices were allowed to soar. The British put up with greater inconveniences in a more cheerful spirit. But they were fighting for their existence and had the glory of national victory to look forward to. To India the war was an external affliction. As a people they found little thrill in conflict and little glory in victory. To cheer on their rulers to victory was pleasant; to extricate them from defeat and help them through arduous struggle and great sacrifice was much less exciting. It is therefore not surprising that at the end of the war India as a country was not only exhausted and war-weary like Britain, but sour, discontented, and resentful as well. The question, to what end? asked persistently enough in the West, was in the East even more difficult to answer. To these economic ills we must add one more, the scourge of influenza which swept across India in 1918 with a toll of five million deaths—more than all the deaths in action during the whole war in Europe.

Apart from any other factors these developments would have made the course of any government of India in 1919 difficult and perilous. But there was another factor of prime importance. It was the mental revolution which has already been referred to. We have traced its be-

ginnings in the early years of the century under the influence of the
Russo-Japanese War and Asian national movements; but now it became a major phenomenon. The attitude of India toward Europe and
its peoples was altered radically and permanently. No longer were
they seen as the possessors of a culture which was morally as well as
technically superior to their own. Their moral prestige vanished in conflict, and they were now regarded at best as more powerful, the possessors of useful machines and processes, and the inventors of some
useful institutions such as British law and democratic machinery. Previously it was thought that Europeans in the main held together like
the members of some loose confederacy. Now it was seen that they
were as divided as themselves. The historic atrocities of Afghans,
Marathas, and Pindaris were matched by the reported behavior of the
Germans and the stories brought back by their own people overseas.
Europeans, it was realized, could lose control of themselves as much
as Indians; civilization everywhere was only skin deep. The war in
Europe came to be regarded as a suicidal strife of Western civilization;
thus, as the war proceeded, enthusiasm for the allied cause turned to
disgust at the general behavior. Europe and Europeans were still respected and admired for their qualities and achievements, but the respect was, as it were, on the level, and the admiration was for the
things done and the characters of the doers rather than for the former
Olympianism. The first war casualty in India was the idol of Western
superiority.

But this was only the first stage in the process. The war itself, as it
continued, shook faith in the whole structure of Western superiority.
Then came two great events. The first was the Russian Revolution of
1917, beginning as a hopeful liberal movement against the greatest of
the surviving despotisms. In the public eye Russia was linked as the
twin great power with Britain. If despotism could fall in its citadel,
why not in India where it had only a foreign government to support it?
The Russian disavowal of imperialism was specious and tempting. The
second event was American intervention in the war in 1917, which led
on to President Wilson's enunciation of his Fourteen Points. National
freedom and self-determination of peoples were magic words to a war-
weary and disillusioned people. As the war drew to a close Wilson
seemed to bestride the world like a colossus, and it was clear that
Europe hung upon his words, even if unwillingly. Perhaps, after all,
light would come from the West, was the thought in Indian minds. But
it would not be the light of the old paternal-imperial *raj*. If the course
of the war disillusioned Indians about Western superiority, these two

events emboldened them to demand self-government in the name of fundamental principles accepted by the Allied Powers. The new classes, as it were, went over from the Gokhale attitude of seeking concessions to the Tilak attitude of demanding rights.

Before considering the British side of this development, we must note the war's effect upon the Muslims. Upon the small Westernized group, among whom we may already discern the figure of Muhammad Ali Jinnah, the effect was much like that on the Hindus. The feeling was one of release from Western material and moral superiority. Upon the masses and their traditionalist leaders the effect was quite as profound, but also quite different. The Muslim "man in the mosque" saw the Sultan of Turkey, whom he accepted as the spiritual and temporal leader of the whole Muslim community, going forth to war against the British and meeting with defeat and finally disaster. He saw the Turkish empire dismembered and even the homelands of Asia Minor threatened by the Treaty of Sèvres in 1920. It was a disaster to him because he regarded Turkey as the sword of Islam; a belief in the secular arm is an essential part of the Muslim faith. It was no comfort to him that the Grand Sherif of Mecca, a descendant of the Prophet, protected the holy places as an independent Arab prince. To the Indian Muslim the Arabs were rebels against the Turkish Khalifa and their princes stooges of the infidel. The war in its Turkish aspect was therefore a strain on his loyalty. The Muslim masses were uneasy but inarticulate; their traditionalist leaders were both alarmed and determined. It was no accident that the most active leaders among the Muslims in the immediate postwar years were *maulvis* or men of religion.[2]

We have already seen that the British, in the person of Prime Minister Asquith, recognized in 1914 that changes must come after the war. This feeling deepened as the war proceeded and was not confined to the Liberal party. Before his resignation from the India office in 1917 Austen Chamberlain, one of the principal Conservative leaders, had been working on the declaration which was announced in Parliament on August 20 of that year by his successor, the Liberal Edwin Montagu. The declaration itself was agreed to and partly drafted by Lord Curzon, who had recently joined the coalition war ministry. This document, which was the starting point of the British policy toward self-government for the final thirty years of British rule, read as follows:

The policy of H.M. government, with which the Government of India are in complete accord, is that of the increasing association of Indians in every branch of the administration, and the gradual development of self-governing

institutions, with a view to the progressive realisation of responsible government in India as an integral part of the Empire.

With Indians demanding political rights and the British conceding
ultimate self-government, it may be asked, what was left to fight about?
In the ultimate sense there was very little, and this was the reason for
the slight air of unreality which persisted through the government-
Congress conflicts and could be felt in the bitterest denunciations of
Congress leaders. Their thunders were always more expressive of an-
noyance and exasperation than of hate. Gandhi spoke of "the satanic
government" with a twinkle in his eye. This lack of ultimate conflict explains why anti-British feeling so quickly vanished on the announcement
of the handover of power. But in the immediate future there was always
the question of the next step; there was always the question of face
which brought with it the question of sincerity or bona fides. Did the
British mean what they said? Here the differences were sometimes dangerously wide, and it is in this area that we must look for the essential
causes of the various conflicts between Congress and government.

The change of attitude in Britain toward India was genuine, though
there were to be many misgivings and hesitations which appeared as
attempts to whittle down or explain away the Montagu declaration
of 1917. Outright opponents or "diehards" were numerous and vocal,
especially in the House of Lords. Not until the 1930's were both major
parties convinced that self-government must not only be accepted but
worked and planned for. But this degree of flexibility was, perhaps
understandably, not to be found in the Indian administration. Its members, especially the senior ones and those therefore least in touch with
new currents of opinion, thought that they knew. They lived in a
mental world of conquest, pacification, communal tension, and paternalism. Their knowledge of what had been seemed to invalidate the proposals of what should be. They were therefore unresponsive to the
new secretary of state, Montagu, when he toured India in 1917–18.[3]
They had in the new viceroy, Lord Chelmsford (1916–21), a man who,
while sincerely believing in the new policy, lacked the flexibility for
difficult situations or the ability to impose his policy upon his subordinates. This provided, on the British side, a major cause for the first
great breach with the Congress.

At the outbreak of war in 1914 the Congress was still a middle class
body of Westernized professionals with some commercial and industrial
backing, and it was firmly under the control of Gokhale and the Moderates. The only cloud was the release of Tilak (June 14, 1914) from

his six years' imprisonment. Within two and one-half years he was the master of Congress and the director of a new dynamic policy. It was not Tilak's release in itself which was fatal to the Moderates, but the war circumstances which played into his hands. The Moderate policy was (like the Irish Home Rule) to wait until the end of the war. Tilak (like the Sinn Feiners) knew that people cannot live long on hopes, and easily become impatient. The enthusiasm for the Allied cause so marked at the outbreak of war soon subsided, all the more quickly for the almost total failure of the government to take advantage of it. It was replaced by a feeling of soreness and growing expectancy. Tilak's first care was to re-enter Congress, which he did by the end of 1915. He disarmed government by supporting the war effort and disavowing violence as a means of attaining self-government. He then launched his Home Rule League to demand the grant of self-government after the war. A few months later, in September 1916, Mrs. Besant, the Theosophical leader, formed a similar league in Madras. At the end of 1915 Gokhale had died at the age of forty-nine. The support given to the two leagues was a measure of the growing self-consciousness and restlessness of the middle classes. Concessions and "boons" were no longer felt to meet the case. Tilak's talk of "rights" and action struck responsive chords in the hearts of more and more. At the end of 1916 he captured the Congress at its Lucknow session and won the support of the Muslims as well. This was done by means of the "Lucknow Pact" with the Muslim League, which conceded separate electorates. It was a Muslim contention that joint electorates (constituencies in which Hindus and Muslims were on the same electoral roll) would be unfair to them, because on any property qualification the number of Muslim electors would be small. Muslim fears of being swamped by Hindu votes in democratic elections being thus calmed, their fears for Turkey and the caliphate prompted them to ally with Congress to press the government. This act of Tilak's marks his emergence to the larger leadership when his judgment matched his ability. It laid the foundation for the great antigovernment movement led by Gandhi in the next few years.

Tilak welcomed the Montagu declaration of 1917, though of course asking for more. The Montagu-Chelmsford Report, which appeared in the spring of 1918, seemed to many to confirm the hopes aroused by the declaration. Its proposals were much more radical than any that would have been dreamed of before 1914. A great extension of the franchise, popular representation, and ministerial responsibility were all to be found there. Tilak pressed for full provincial autonomy, but had no thought of an antigovernment movement. But events were now to outrun Tilak himself. The year 1918 was one of growing strain and rising political hopes in India. There was more social discontent as the result of war conditions and greater political expectancy than since the outbreak of war. Any injudicious action might precipitate a crisis of emotion. The action came from government, moved by its nervousness of terrorism. This aftermath of the Bengal partition had largely died down before 1914, but there was a recrudescence during the war, especially in the Panjab, where Har Dayal looked for German help.[4] Early in 1918, almost simultaneously with the publication of the Montagu-Chelmsford Report, a committee presided over by Justice Rowlatt proposed to combat subversive activity by giving judges power to try political cases without juries and giving provincial governments power to intern suspects without trial.[5] Whereas it took years to implement Montagu's report, it took the government only months to act on Rowlatt's, a fact which a now inflamed Indian opinion did not fail to notice. The Rowlatt bills, as they came to be called, were seen as a slur on Indian responsibility and as a reflection on the sincerity of declared British intentions. When they were passed, early in 1919, against the vote of every Indian nonofficial member of the Imperial Legislative Council, there was widespread indignation. The government's judgment in the matter may be gauged from the fact that the powers conferred were never in fact used.

At this moment a new figure stepped into the center of the stage. Tilak had gone to London, in the tradition of Naoroji and the older congressmen, to plead the case for provincial self-government before the new Parliament, which would consider the new Government of India bill. He did not return until October 1919. His mission was not fruitless, for he impressed all with his ability and convinced the British governing class that the word "extremist" in current Indian parlance was a very relative term, with a meaning not far removed from "opponent." Finally, finding the Liberal party unresponsive, he established a contact with the growing Labor party, which was to be of incalculable importance in the future. But this work at the moment proved to be a bypath of Indian politics, and another took the lead in the crisis which now arose. He was M. K. Gandhi, a lawyer aged forty-nine, recently returned from South Africa and an avowed disciple of the late Gokhale. Gandhi saw a moral issue in the Rowlatt Acts (the first of a long series). He launched a movement of protest with public meetings and hartals.[6] In the Panjab, already disturbed by the short-lived third Afghan war, this passed into violence which culminated in the mob murder of four

Europeans at Amritsar on April 10. On April 13 a prohibited meeting of about 10,000 people in a large enclosed space known as the Jallianwallah Bagh was broken up without warning by a body of troops under General Dyer. The official estimate of casualties was 379 killed and over 1,200 wounded. This was followed up by the proclamation of martial law, punitive measures, and humiliating orders.[7] Dyer thought that he was saving the Panjab for Britain. In fact he nearly lost India not only to Britain, but to the West altogether.

CHAPTER XXXII

Nonco-operation and Reform

"The shadow of Amritsar," said the Duke of Connaught when inaugurating the new legislatures in 1921, "lengthened over the fair face of India." Its effect was one of delayed action, like a time bomb or shock after an accident. At first the Panjab was cowed into quiescence, and men praised the strong men who had saved India from revolution. General Dyer went off to the Afghan war with the Panjab governor's praises ringing in his ears. It was only gradually that the facts, and still more their implications, leaked out in India itself, and it was not till the autumn that they aroused serious concern in Britain. Those months were the summer of the peace treaty, with its fevered effort to forget the war in pleasure, its short-lived, unhealthy prosperity, its neurotic narcissism. No one wanted to face a fresh crisis anywhere. In the autumn liberal opinion (still strong in Britain) bestirred itself, and a commission of four Indians and four Europeans, presided over by a judge, Lord Hunter, was appointed. Amritsar became a subject of discussion and soon an issue of acute dissension among the British themselves, and between them and the Indians. Briefly the issue was, had the Indian empire been saved by an act of terrorism and was terrorism justified to maintain the *raj?* Behind this came the deeper question, was an Indian life of equal value to a European one? Was there, in short, one standard or two for the two races? The division was not wholly on party lines, for there were many imperialists who believed in the sacredness of all individual life as much as in the imperial mission of uplift. To these people Amritsar was a ghastly mistake. There were also left-wing people who did not believe in racial equality. The controversy, in fact, brought to the forefront the very issue of racial equality which the government of India for many years had tried to avoid. The inquiry brought the issue to a focus, because General Dyer gloried in his deed. "If more troops had been present," he said in evidence,[1] "the effect would have been greater in proportion. It was no longer a question of merely dispersing the crowd, but one of producing a sufficient moral effect from a military point of view, not only on those who were present, but more specially throughout the Panjab."

It was this attitude, which found much support from British opinion both in India and Britain, which for Indian opinion turned Amritsar from being a tragic misjudgment of rattled authority into a political issue of the first magnitude. It was not the casualties but their justification which was crucial. India did not rise in flames on the first news. The Panjab had always been regarded by the rest of India as a place of violence, where Afghans rode and Pathans raided, a place from which bloodshed could be expected. But as knowledge spread of the facts, with their racial aftermath, and as justifications appeared in the British-owned press and in Britain, regret and concern turned to anger, resentment, and fear. Tilak returned to India in October 1919, still intending to work the reforms under the slogan of "responsive co-operation." This would have meant in fact carrying militancy into ministerial office, and it went too far for Gandhi, who still wished to accept the reforms without reservation. The Amritsar Congress in December compromised by declaring India fit for self-government, the proposed reforms "inadequate, unsatisfactory and disappointing," and then proposing to implement them.

In the next four months the controversy went on, and bit deeper into the issue. In those months, by one of those mysterious processes to which public opinion is sometimes subject, opinion swung from Tilak to Gandhi. The scepter of leadership glided almost imperceptibly from the rationalist and realist veteran to the emotional and mystical lawyer. While Tilak had been arguing with politicians in London, Gandhi had led hartals against the Rowlatt Acts; though they had ended in disaster he had nevertheless caught the popular imagination. India was now tense with emotion, and Gandhi was a man of feeling. He had an eerie sense of the working of the public mind; he would implement a policy by proclaiming it as a gospel, whereas Tilak tried to realize an ideal by defining it as a policy. So the rationalist gave place to the visionary and the Gandhian reign of twenty-eight years began.

The turning point came in the spring of 1920. The Hunter Committee's report showed that it had divided on racial lines. Though the government of India had disavowed Dyer's view of the use of force, its disciplinary action was not thought to be strong enough. Above all, Indian opinion was shocked by the support given to Dyer by a minority in the Commons and a large majority in the Lords which reached its climax in a heavily subscribed fund to mark appreciation of his services. Gandhi's attitude changed from that of unconditional co-operation to the view that "co-operation in any shape or form with this satanic government is sinful." In one sentence he appealed to the Hindu sense of moral superiority, to the always latent xenophobic feeling, and struck below the belt of the British public conscience on the tender spot of self-righteousness. He elevated Hindu feelings of superiority, stirred their resentments, and made the British feel profoundly uncomfortable even while he exasperated them. He was to do this again and again. It was the Gandhian way.

At the same time the terms of what was to become the abortive Treaty of Sèvres [2] with Turkey were published. Indignant Muslims formed a Khilafat committee, and Gandhi found them as ready for conflict as the Hindus. A special Congress in the summer repudiated the reforms, brushing aside the Tilak party's plea for "responsive co-operation" and entry into the councils if only to wreck them. It adopted Gandhi's program and left him in supreme command. There followed the great Gandhian movement. Its principle was nonco-operation with evil; its weapon resignation from government office, an exodus from schools and colleges, and boycott of the forthcoming elections to the new councils. Methods were to be scrupulously nonviolent, for this was to be a moral even more than a political protest. The calculation was that obedience to instructions would bring the whole machine of government to a standstill. So indeed it would, but the instructions were not in fact implemented. A few distinguished men like Rabindranath Tagore renounced their British titles. Fewer resigned their offices; the great mass of government employees remained at their posts. There was a large but temporary exodus from schools and colleges. The army and the police were untouched. Congress boycotted the election, but one-third of the electorate went to the polls. The movement really foundered on the unwillingness of government employees to risk their jobs and prospects. Nevertheless there were many months of tense excitement and uncertainty when India seemed to be on the verge of a general upheaval. The government was seriously alarmed as well as sorely perplexed by Gandhi's methods. In April 1921 the term of the mediocre and worried Chelmsford ended. He was replaced by Lord Reading, the Lord Chief Justice, who as Sir Rufus Isaacs had been one of the most brilliant of the young Liberal lawyers, a personal friend of Prime Minister Lloyd George, and now carrying the prestige of a successful embassy to the United States. He held long conversations with Mr. Gandhi, now acclaimed a Mahatma or "great soul," and puzzled the administration by his apparent reluctance to act. It began to be said that he was better at arguing cases and seeing issues than taking decisions. He was, in fact, no fire-eaters' friend;

it was fortunate that he had the insight to know when to do nothing and the strength of will to sustain his knowledge. In fact Reading divined the inner weakness of the apparently imposing Gandhian coalition. The middle classes were not prepared for extreme personal sacrifice; they would rather be in the new legislatures than in prison or the wilderness. The people's emotions were stirred by economic discontents and personal devotion to one whom they already regarded as a saint. As economic prospects improved, their enthusiasm would wane. The tenseness of the atmosphere encouraged outbreaks by subversive forces, each one of which tended to discredit the nonviolent movement. The Muslims were intent on their own Khilafat grievances and their fraternalism would wilt with the decline of their cause in Turkey.

So the event proved. When no *swaraj* had appeared by the end of 1921, a year after Gandhi's prophecy, enthusiasm was visibly on the wane. The new system got under way, making those outside it feel more and more isolated. Outbreaks of violence occurred such as those accompanying the planned boycott of the Prince of Wales on his visit in the fall of 1921. A rising of the fanatical Muslim Moplahs [3] in Malabar in August 1921 alarmed all moderate opinion and drove the first wedge between Hindu and Muslim collaboration. On the Muslim side, the revelation [4] that the government of India was championing their cause, followed by the resurgence of Turkey, did much to reassure religious sentiment, while Ataturk's later abolition of the caliphate (1924) cut the ground altogether from beneath the feet of the Khilafat movement. In February 1922 the Chauri-Chaura outrage led Gandhi to call off his contemplated mass-civil-disobedience movement. Shortly afterward Gandhi was arrested and sentenced to six years' imprisonment for incitement. The country acquiesced; mass nonco-operation collapsed. When Gandhi was released less than two years later, calm had succeeded the storm, the torpor of reaction to the fever of nationalist crusading. Reading had divined truly; he sat still and the coalition dissolved like a summer thundercloud.

Though the collapse was eventually so complete that some were able to doubt whether there had ever been any substance in the movement apart from war weariness and hurt feelings, the importance of the movement should not be underestimated. It completed that psychological transformation in the minds of the Westernized classes which the war had begun. Indians no longer saw themselves as living in a world apart, treasuring a tradition and culture denied to outsiders and only cautiously feeling their way toward coming to terms with the all-powerful Western world. They now saw themselves as equals in every respect, and any distinction made they saw as an outrage rather than as a price for their sacred "apartness." The war stirred them to demand their rights; Amritsar and its aftermath they regarded as a trampling on their rights; the nonco-operation movement as a vindication of their rights. The net result of the movement in Indian minds was a vindication of the national dignity; in other words we may say that India had thrown off for good the old colonialist mentality. Indian leaders were now in thought the equals of the British, though not yet, of course, in material power. In tactics they were often to prove superior. A second result, in the political field, was to establish the Congress as an important factor in the Indian political field. The Curzonian idea of "assisting Congress to a peaceful demise" had gone for good. British opinion would not yet admit that it was the dominant political force in India, but the leaders of both parties now realized that it was a power to reckon with. From this time it is possible to regard Indians and British in the political sphere as two negotiating parties rather than of one as the suppliant of the other. It was fortunate that both sides were basically agreed on the goal of their efforts, and were ready, in general, to negotiate with each other about the steps to its achievement. Otherwise India would have marched straight toward a violent revolution.

 Behind the struggle just considered, constitutional changes were steadily proceeding, and there is no doubt that the actual working of the new constitution was one of the factors in the collapse of the antigovernment campaign; for from the moment the new system started to work it was no longer possible to say "we have been denied our rights," but only "we have not been given enough" or "what we have been given is a sham." But both these assertions were disputable, so that the mere existence of the reforms, with their prospects of office and influence so attractive to politicians, tended to undermine the unanimity of the opposition. The first stages in the process were swift. Montagu toured India in the cold weather of 1917–18 and published his report with Chelmsford in April 1918. It has become a historic state paper under the name of the Montagu-Chelmsford Report. For convenience we shall, from now on, call it and the constitutional changes which followed, the Montford Report and the Montford reforms. There was then a delay, for during the summer World War I reached its crisis, and at its end Parliament was dissolved. The year 1919 was occupied by parliamentary committees, drafting legislation, and debates in both Houses; the India bill became law at the end of the year. On the whole this was quick work, but there was vexatious delay while the cumbrous machinery of the Indian government turned to the unfamiliar tasks of constitutional change and democratic elections. Thus it was not until February 9, 1921, that the Duke of Connaught (uncle of the then King George V and the only surviving son of Queen Victoria) inaugurated the new system in Delhi.

In the words of the duke, "The principle of autocracy has been abandoned." The new system was a reasoned attempt to implement the declaration of August 20, 1917, which envisaged "the gradual development of self-governing institutions with a view to the progressive realisation of responsible government in India as an integral part of the British Empire." Its principles may be briefly summed up as advance toward self-government by stages, control by Parliament of those stages, and a first step in the form of an enlarged legislature at the center, with the introduction of ministerial responsibility in the provinces in the form known as "dyarchy." We will consider each in turn.

The control by Parliament, as representing the British responsibility for India, was explicitly retained in the preamble of the Act. This was inevitable in the circumstances, but there was a very important addition. It was a provision that there should be a parliamentary inquiry every ten years to consider progress made and advise on the next steps. This was a reversion to the great public inquests on Indian affairs which took place in the Company's time before each renewal of its charter. It meant that Indian affairs would again attract general attention at least once in ten years. Only one such inquiry took place, but this proved of great and perhaps decisive importance for India.

The framework of government in Britain with the Secretary of State for India as a member of the cabinet, responsible to Parliament for Indian affairs, remained the same. But in India there were great changes. In the central executive itself there was no vital change. The viceroy and his council remained responsible to the London cabinet and not to an Indian parliament; he still retained his overriding powers over his council, so that he was (apart from his subordination to London) more like an American President on a five-year term than a British prime minister. But his council was enlarged to six besides the viceroy and the commander in chief, and a convention established that three of the six should be Indian. This meant that Indians were now well established within the sanctum of power, and some distinguished ones who held office from time to time exercised considerable influence. The old Imperial Legislative Council with 60 members and an official majority was replaced by a bicameral legislature. The Legislative Assembly of 146 members had 106 members elected directly on a property franchise from general and Muslim special constituencies. It sat for three years only. A Council of State of 61 members, elected for five years on a restricted franchise, was added. These bodies had the usual legislative and deliberative powers of parliamentary assemblies except that the government was not dependent on a majority vote. Their position resembled that of the Imperial German Reichstag before 1918 or the Japanese lower house before 1945.

We pass to the provinces, where the changes were much greater. There was first a measure of devolution. It was intended to give them greater independence as the main scene of the new constitutional experiment; it proved in practice to be the first step toward federation. Financially, a division was made in the heads of revenue; irrigation, excise, land tax, and stamp receipts going to the provinces.[5] It was thus possible for the new provincial governments to plan financially for their new policies. The same kind of division was made in the spheres of legislation, the center retaining residuary power.

The mainspring of the provincial arrangements was the principle of dyarchy or double government. The head of the administration was the governor, but his executive was divided between councilors (who were officials), responsible to him only, and ministers who were responsible to the provincial legislative councils as well as to the governor. This division was carried into the realm of administration also, in order to give the new ministers a sphere of action where a steady policy could be pursued. These subjects were called "Reserved" and "Transferred." The Reserved subjects remained under the control of the governor and his councilors and covered land-revenue administration, justice, the police, labor matters, and irrigation. They were often referred to as law-and-order subjects. The Transferred subjects, which were controlled by the ministers responsible to the councils, were local self-government, education, public health, public works, agriculture, and co-operative societies. They were often referred to as "nation-building" subjects. There was thus a division of control between ministers responsible to the new councils and officials responsible to the governor. The two branches of the executive were encouraged to sit together and in fact usually did so. In some provinces (like Madras and the Panjab) this tendency was strengthened by the habit of appointing a minister of reputation to a term as an executive councilor. In appearance the minister was worse off than the councilor, for he could lose office both by adverse vote of the council and by dismissal by the governor. In practice this second event rarely happened, for the governor had either to find a successor supported by a council majority, which was not easy, or to see the new system break down. It was a point of honor, or perhaps of duty, to work the system if at all possible, so that governors were restrained from abrupt dismissals by the thought of the discredit involved in a ministerial hiatus. Better the politician I have, was the general attitude, than the agitation which would follow his departure.

But there were in fact gaps in the ministerial ranks, caused usually by Congress as part of its political tactics. The possibility of a breakdown was provided for by the provision of special or "reserved" powers. The governors could take over the administration of the transferred departments if they could find no ministers backed by a majority of their legislative councils. They also had reserve legislative powers. They could pass bills over the heads of the legislature, if they were certified to be necessary for the safety and tranquility of India, and could authorize expenditure in the same way. This was known as the power of certification. The viceroy had the same powers at the center, and both he and the governors were able in emergency to legislate by ordinances valid for six months.

The provincial picture was completed by the enlarged legislative councils. In all of them at least 70 per cent of the membership was nonofficial, and in certain provinces like Bengal and the United Provinces, where the landlord element was strong, second chambers were added. The largest councils were those of Bengal, with 139 members, Madras with 127, and Bombay with 111. In all there were, excluding Burma, which was separated from India in 1935, eight governor's provinces with councils. To these the North-West Frontier Province was added in 1932, and Orissa and Sind in 1935, giving a final total of eleven. Apart from anything else, the councils provided, over the next twenty-six years, an effective school of public life. It was their existence, together with the background of general Western education and Indian employment in the services, which provided India with the "know-how" of government when independence came, and saved her from the embarrassments and troubles which beset Indonesia in a similar situation.

The councils were filled by the votes of the new electorate. The general rule was a property qualification, reckoned on the payment of land tax in the country and income tax in the towns. It was arranged so as to give over 5,000,000 voters for the central Legislative Assembly and a dignified 17,000 for the Council of State. Shortly after the reforms began, women received the vote on the same terms as men. In practice their votes were few, for few possessed independent property, but the change enabled women to sit in the councils, thus starting a practice which has become a distinctive feature of Indian public life. There were in addition certain special qualifications for special constituencies, such as a university degree or membership in a chamber of commerce. Constituencies were divided into "general" and "special," the special representing groups of special influence. A more important distinction, however, was in the general constituencies themselves. Here the communal principle, first admitted in 1909, was reluctantly but widely extended. The center and each province had a quota of Muslim constituencies, in which all the Muslim electors of the area were placed. In the Panjab the Sikhs also had their own constituencies, and Indian Christians had theirs in Madras. The remaining constituencies contained all other voters, the great majority being, of course, Hindu. This measure went against the grain with Montagu, but was virtually forced upon the promoters of the bill by the pressure of Muslim and other minority opinion. Nevertheless it struck a discordant and somewhat sinister note of division and proved a presage of greater evils to come.

The Montford reforms were attacked on all sides. Right-wing British opinion considered that they undermined the *raj* and gave authority to irresponsibility. Congressmen loudly proclaimed that they were a sham and not worth trying to work, and soon they were joined by some who had worked them for a time and acquired some grievance while so doing. Specially large targets were the reserved powers of the viceroy and governors, the lack of any ministerial responsibility at the center, and the communal provisions. There is no doubt that the reforms were full of defects and difficulties. But now that they have passed into history we can see them in truer perspective. Time has dimmed many of the censures, while leaving others in sharper relief. The reserve powers, for example, are seen to have been perhaps only an excessive dose of a necessary medicine; many of them were retained by the critics themselves in the constitution of 1949 on the plea of the necessity of a strong executive. Looking back after thirty years, we may pick out certain special points of weakness. One was the financial provisions. The central finances were flexible, but the provincial ones were not, so that ministers often in fact found themselves without the means of carrying out cherished measures such as the extension of education. They tended, very naturally, to suspect the reserved half, who controlled the revenue, of starving them of funds. Then there was the question of responsibility. The more closely the ministers were identified with the governors and councilors, the more they were liable to lose the confidence of their supporters. Yet such co-operation was necessary if anything was to be done. On the British side, every assertion of authority in the interests of law and order increased their unpopularity while any constructive measure went to the credit of the minister. It has further to be noticed that the provincial reforms were on the parliamentary plan of ministerial responsibility toward elected councils. This system presupposes a party system to provide the ministers. In India the major Congress party would not play. Only in Madras and the Panjab were local parties strong enough to take office, and there the reforms worked better than anywhere else. Elsewhere, there was a tendency for members to split into pressure and personal groups and for governors to construct *ad hoc* coalitions which did nothing but dissolve into fresh patterns. The reforms certainly suffered from lack of Congress co-operation as well as from excessive restriction and division of authority.

When all this is said the fact remains that the reforms proved to be a solid and substantial achievement. They were an essential milestone on the road to self-government. Without them Indian political progress would have been belated, erratic, and probably revolutionary. They gave, by and large, enough inducement to enough people to work them, and enough scope to provide experience and incentives for the future. Whenever there were determined leaders backed by coherent parties, solid results could be achieved. Thus the Justice party of Madras was able to reform the administration of the wealthy south-Indian temples; and the Unionist party in the Panjab, led by Sir Fazl-i-Husain and Chaudhri Chothu Ram, to extend education and protect the cultivator. Though tensions and frustrations could not be avoided, the new system went far enough and worked well enough to make further advance inevitable. This was its essential justification. It started a constitutional clock which would not stop. The present Indian government is the heir of Montagu as well as of Gandhi.

CHAPTER XXXIII

Mahatma

For nearly thirty years Congress was dominated by Gandhi, and India influenced more by him than by any other single man. It is not too much to say that the destiny of India was modified and the world itself influenced by this single personality. An unimpressive figure with a reedy voice, an ingratiating manner, and an astute expression concealed a character of great charm and baffling complexity. Gandhi was one of those men who concealed thought in the volume of his speech and meaning in a wealth of explanation. He was always explaining himself and was never understood. He convinced those whose attention was caught by one facet or other of his character in turn that he was a fanatic, a visionary, a consummate tactician, a saint, a prophet, or a trickster. To this day he remains an enigma; the only fact of which we can be quite certain is the magnitude of his influence upon the people and events of his time and afterward.

Mohandas Karamchand Gandhi was born in 1869 in Porbandar, a port in the Kathiawar Peninsula of western India and the capital of a small Hindu state. His father was the hereditary dewan or prime minister of the state, and the young Gandhi thus had a hereditary connection with politics, though authoritarian ones, and state service. Unlike so many of the leaders of the new India, Gandhi was not a Brahmin. He came from the Vaishya or merchant caste, popularly known as banya in the north, which in Kathiawar and Gujarat had close connections with the dissenting Hindu sect of the Jains. In the Jain religion nonviolence to every sentient being is an article of faith, so that we can at once see one origin of the later Gandhi's characteristic doctrine. As a youth he was sent to London to study, and duly qualified as a barrister-at-law. His departure and return provoked a crisis in his community, one half considering that he had lost caste by crossing the ocean to unholy regions. While in London he came into touch with liberal and

Christian ideas and the then novel teachings of Tolstoi about nonco-operation with evil and violence. For a time he practiced law in India, and then proceeded to South Africa, where the new Indian community formed by the immigration of indentured labor to Natal provided op-portunities to a young professional willing to live abroad. He stayed in South Africa until he was forty-six, and it was here that he matured in thought and character. He raised his family, conducted dietetic ex-periments, to his family's discomfort and occasional dismay, and de-veloped his philosophy from a mixture of Hindu, Christian, and general humanitarian ideas. He proved a Moses to his own people, applying conciliation to their disputes, often to his own hurt, and providing leadership when racial feeling grew and the new Union government acted like a Pharaoh that knew not Israel. In the South African war he led a corps of stretcher-bearers on the battlefield and won praise for his courage. In 1912–13 he disciplined and led his people in a passive-resistance movement against discriminatory race legislation. His method of conflict without violence and resistance without hate caught the imagination of another great man, General Smuts, and led to the conclusion of the Smuts-Gandhi agreement. It was in the reflected glory of this achievement that the now mature Gandhi returned to India at the beginning of 1915. He went to his guru, G. K. Gokhale, at the headquarters of his Servants of India Society in Poona. Gokhale advised him to watch and learn for a year before venturing into speech or action. Before the year was out Gokhale was dead.

Gandhi tried out his nonviolent technique on several limited issues before the challenge of the Rowlatt bills came along. From the fore-going it will be seen that his methods were no dramatic surprise, nor was the man a brilliant youth who flashed on a startled India like a comet. It was not a case of new men and new methods so much as tried methods by tried men in a new sphere. Gandhi's main obstacle was the prejudice expressed in a South African version of the query, "Can any good thing come out of Nazareth?" For Gandhi's secrets we must go to his South African, British, and Porbandar days.

Between 1916 and 1920 Gandhi climbed to the leadership of Con-gress over the live body of Tilak, all the time protesting his admiration for the older man. The process was so characteristic that it is worth a moment's consideration. In 1916 Tilak, at the height of his reputation, captured Congress and seemed to have united a new realism and cau-tion with his old fighting spirit. Just over three years later his policy of co-operation on terms was set aside in favor of Gandhi's all-out non-co-operation. Why were the people so fickle? The change symbolized a radical transformation in the whole Congress outlook. Tilak was a man of the middle class advocating the more advanced of two policies. He was a Brahmin and an aristocrat (in the Hindu sense). He appealed to the people, but as a superior to his dependents, not as an equal and one of themselves. He played upon racial pride and orthodox feeling; he postponed social reform until "after independence." Though homely and familiar in manner, he was remote and Olympian in popular conception. He and his class called for obedience from the people rather than co-operation. There was as yet, except in the matter of traditional beliefs, no organic union between people and the middle class. Gandhi, on the other hand, was by origin one of the people. The *vaishya* was third in the table of the four Hindu caste divisions, denied the respect given to both warrior and priest. Though brought up in the middle class and given a Western training, he had identified himself with the poor and the underdog from his early South African days. In his sanitary campaigns he would clean latrines himself, a duty thrust by Hindu society upon untouchables without the pale of respectable society. A man of the new class, he came and lived among the people on their own terms. Early in 1921 he discarded his Western clothes in favor not of the ascetic's saffron robe, but of the peasant's homespun loincloth and dhoti. While Tilak was to the people a Brahmin calling for respect and a politician immersed in strategy, Gandhi was something more than a Brahmin, a holy man, and something more than a realist—a prophet who appealed to moral principles which as Hindus they understood. Gandhi made himself poor like a peasant, and the people made him holy like a saint or guru. This subtle exchange was ratified by the popular accord to him of the title *Mahatma* or great soul. We may add that Gandhi had a far greater understanding of popular psychology, both Indian and British, than Tilak. He knew instinctively the moments and the issues which would both stir his own people and embarrass the British most.

We have now arrived at one of the essential reasons for Gandhi's hold on the country. He was a hyphen connecting the middle classes and the people which transferred energy from each to the other. It was he, and almost he alone, who converted Indian nationalism from a middle class movement to a mass emotion embracing all classes. His magic was identification with the people, a deep understanding, tactical skill, and an appeal to moral idealism as understood both by his own people and the British. His first link with the people was the voluntary poverty which has already been mentioned. It was popular and secular and quite un-Brahminical. Gandhi gave himself to the people instead of expecting them to make offerings to him. They repaid him with the greater devotion. Next came his vegetarianism, which accorded with general caste feelings of propriety. Then there was his campaign in favor of *swadeshi* or homemade goods, of *khaddar* or handspun cotton cloth, and of hand spinning. The *charkha* or hand-spinning machine, whose emblem now adorns the national flag, was his chosen symbol. His crusade on behalf of the untouchables, whom he called *Harijans* or Sons of God, was by no means approved by many villagers, who stood to lose by their emancipation. But it emphasized the brotherhood and dignity of man and so tended to raise the caste peasant's status in his own eyes and that of the world. And it automatically made Gandhi the champion of fifty million people for whom Hinduism had hitherto found no place. His nonviolence struck a responsive chord, for the principle runs deep in Hindu religion, though we should be very unwise to suppose that popular Hinduism is a nonviolent religion. Gandhi's religious language and habits were all calculated to appeal to the best in popular religion and the most familiar in popular life. He studied both Gita and Bible; he loved devotional songs, including Christian hymns; he held prayer meetings wherever he went; he lived in an *ashram* or religious retreat; he believed in and practiced fasts for self-purification and penance; he practiced silence on one day a week. In many ways he resembled a *bhakti* saint of the past who carried religion to the people while practicing devotion to his Lord. When it came to action, he could translate, with unerring insight, modern techniques into Hindu idioms. Resistance to government was nonco-operation with evil, a one-day political strike was a hartal or a moral protest, passive resistance was *satyagraha* or a campaign for truth. When he wanted to arouse feeling against the government, he attacked the salt tax, the one tax which every peasant resented, and recommended its illegal manufacture. All the devices of modern political tactics were translated into terms with a flavor of righteousness understood by the common man.

It might be thought that such behavior might separate Gandhi fatally from the politically conscious middle classes. Many of them disliked it and comparatively few followed him in those ways wholeheartedly. They constantly grated on a Westernized intellectual like Nehru. But though many of the middle classes did not like Harijans and prayer meetings and Gita classes—and hand spinning as a test of Congress membership—they put up with them. For one thing, however sophisticated many professed to be, they still had a lingering or "under-the-counter" belief in the virtue of fasting, of meditation, and of the basic Hindu beliefs. On the conscious level they knew that they could not do without him, for no one could both conjure and control the people as he did. Then, again, in the contest with government there was no shrewder tactician. Gandhi was the only man who knew when and how to arouse the masses. He also knew better than anyone else how to make the British feel uncomfortable by attacking them in the name of their own principles. The British civilian needs a good conscience, as the British soldier needs a full stomach, in order to stand up to his foes. Finally, Gandhi was no socialist. The propertied classes felt safe in his hands as well as pleasantly and not too rigorously Hindu. Henry IV of France said that Paris was worth a mass; thousands of congressmen felt in the thirties that independence was well worth a fast and a spinning wheel.

This half-naked little man, with his cheerfulness and infectious smile, his lofty idealism and his lawyer-like cunning, remains an enigma in his thought as well as in his life. Was he a near Messiah as many Christians as well as Hindus thought, or was he in fact all shifts and shuffles? The man of insight to lay bare his soul has not yet arisen and we can only hazard a few guesses. One has first to decide the question of inner sincerity of soul. If we grant this, as I think we must, we can proceed to consider the efficacy of his ideas. From this stage we can proceed to his most characteristic doctrine, nonviolence or ahimsa, and *satyagraha,* "soul force" or more literally "truth force." These Sanskrit terms cannot be exactly rendered, for they carry with them religious and philosophic overtones which are lost in translation. Ahimsa, nonviolence, may be said to spring from the inner principle of *satyagraha.* Gandhi conceived of nonviolence at several levels, and this "tier" system of thought has been fertile of confusion and misunderstanding. At the lowest or ground level, as it were, it was frankly a political tactic. Violence for freedom would put back *swaraj,* stiffen British resistance by putting them on ground where they felt sure of themselves, and alienate world opinion. Those who could not practice nonviolence from conviction of its inner truth were asked to do so because it worked and gave results. They should believe "for the very work's sake." There was a great deal of this nonviolence from expediency. The next aspect of nonviolence was its use as a moral method. It was a better method of achieving a good end than physical force; this view was echoed in Hindu traditional hartals and compulsive fasts such as sitting *dharna.*[1] At the third and highest level of Gandhi's thought, nonviolence was an inner spiritual principle. It meant the appeal of soul to soul in spirit; it aimed at the inner conversion of an opponent by the power of love and suffering. It was this concept which was behind Gandhi's fasts and which increasingly animated him as the years went by. It was the creed of his personal followers or *satyagrahis*. It was vital enough to transform the outlook of many who came to criticize and to impress opponents like Irwin and other Englishmen.

The second of Gandhi's principles was *swadeshi* or self-sufficiency. He believed in a rural self-sufficient society which lived simply on the land, supplying its own needs by means of village handicrafts. He sought to promote this end by encouraging hand spinning and weaving, by discouraging foreign imports and by the practice of the simple life. There was no real place for modern industry or the machine age in this ideal. Gandhi, however, was realist enough to take advantage of things as they were. He would accept most affably the offerings of the Indian mill-owners, while explaining that they would be used to make their existence superfluous.

These ideas came from Hindu sources, with perhaps some reinforcement from groups like the Quakers and seers like Tolstoi. Gandhi's nationalism was a definitely foreign product. It was deep and strong, embracing not only all castes but Muslims and other non-Hindus as well. This was one issue on which he parted company with the orthodox; it was because of his attitude toward the Muslims that he was struck down at the end by a militant Hindu fanatic. Along with nationalism went his acceptance of democracy, with its belief in the basically equal value of every man. He campaigned against caste restrictions though not against caste distinctions. Above all he championed the untouchables. The orthodox never forgave him for this. He was by no means consistent in applying the principle, and in particular seemed to adhere to traditional restrictions in the case of his wife which he gave up in the case of other women.

Finally, and perhaps most important of all, Gandhi insisted on personal service of others as an essential requirement of the good life. Tilak had interpreted the Gita as demanding practical action in the world even after truth had been attained. Gandhi interpreted Tilak as meaning by "action" personal service to others. He reinforced this from the Sermon on the Mount, which he was never tired of reading and quoting. Hindu religion on the whole has stressed contemplation rather than action, as the West has stressed action rather than contemplation; self-realization has been more important than service. Gandhi's example, itself influenced by missionary endeavor, has done more than any other single influence to promote social service and welfare, to naturalize in modern Hindu soil the notion that man *is* his brother's keeper. This may prove in the future to be a vital step in the reorientation of Hinduism as an activist ethical creed.

It is still too early to assess with confidence Gandhi's contribution in the fields of Indian ethics and life and the larger realm of the integration of Eastern and Western thought. But we can appraise his influence on India's political development. One thing is clear: the gadfly of the British imperialists in the twenties and thirties was in reality their greatest friend. It was his influence which primarily kept India peaceful during those years of unavoidable tension. Under other leaders she might easily have slipped into a large-scale terrorist movement or exploded in a violent outbreak which could only have led to widespread repression, delayed independence, and left a legacy of bitterness. The whole relationship of India with the West would have been placed in jeopardy. Gandhi evolved a method of nonviolent revolution which in fact largely succeeded in maintaining the good will between the combatants which he preached. Expressed in a paradox, Gandhi's method was to contrive to be constitutionally unconstitutional. Surprisingly little ill will survived even among those who, like Nehru, suffered several terms of imprisonment. In the larger view, Gandhi's influence in restraining his more ardent followers and keeping the party clear of the real terrorists was as important as the skill and ingenuity with which he perplexed the British.

Gandhi's second achievement was in making the Congress a truly national instrument, a political microcosm of the national life. As a result of his tactics and attitudes at various times, it became identified with most of the progressive movements in the country. The Congress had its own mass education program. By means of its anti-government campaigns and by admittance to leadership of people like Mrs. Sarojini Naidu, it became closely identified with the movement for women's liberation. Gandhi's crusade for the Harijans was in the Congress sense unofficial but the Mahatma's prestige effectively linked it with Congress in the public mind. Concern for the new industrial worker was expressed in Congress-sponsored trade unions and the Congress-socialist group while the peasant had his *Kisan sabhas*. Even art, with the revivalism of the Bengal school of painting, had a nationalist tinge.

Gandhi's third contribution was the firm introduction of moral values into politics. The early congressmen had been liberals of the Gladstonian brand; some like Gokhale were rationalists as well. Many were high-minded and earnest men, but their creeds were unknown to the masses and, if they could have been communicated, would have been unintelligible. As the Congress following widened it tended to become more cynical, leaving the old values behind and receiving in return the single concept of nationalism. In this sphere, as in that of tactics, Gandhi provided the necessary hyphen. He translated his moral ideas into popular terms and so made the whole political movement seem more of a pilgrimage than a war. He attracted high-minded followers to himself, and so raised the whole tone of public life. Gandhism as a creed is now confined to a dedicated few, but Gandhi's influence is one of the factors which distinguishes Indian public life from that of other Asian countries and has given India a unique position in the present international community. Gandhi could secure acquiescence from men like Nehru even when he could not convince them and could extort admiration and devotion even when he exasperated. Though he was an extraordinary mixture, we may conclude by asserting that his essential integrity is attested by two facts. He knowingly provoked Brahmin orthodoxy by his untouchable or Harijan campaign, and he knowingly provoked Hindu fanaticism by his stand for the Muslims of Delhi after the postindependence riots. Gandhi died for his faith, and in dying he created a nation.

CHAPTER XXXIV

The Twenties

When the Duke of Connaught inaugurated the reforms in February, 1921, nonco-operation was at its height. Mahatma Gandhi described this new system, which he had proposed to accept without conditions fifteen months earlier, as "a whited sepulchre." Feeling was intense; in some cases (as in Delhi) illiterate candidates were put up for the legislature and elected in derision. Nevertheless one-third of the electorate voted (about half the usual voting strength, as subsequent experience has shown) and enough able men were elected for ministries to be formed. The start was inauspicious but a start had been made.

History has shown that this was the moment when India crossed the Rubicon from authoritarianism to democracy. For there was to be no going back, only successive and lengthening strides toward freedom and popular government. The decade of the process in the twenties falls naturally into three sections. The first we may term the Liberal prelude, the second the Swarajist era, and the third the Simon boycott. During the first period the government of India had to work with Liberal ministries in India while facing right-wing criticism in Britain and Congress nonco-operation. It was fortunate for the experiment that Liberal influence was still considerable in the Lloyd George coalition and in Britain and was represented by Viceroy Lord Reading in India. Those in supreme authority wanted the experiment to succeed and were prepared to take risks on its behalf. While nonco-operation reached its emotional peak with threats of a no-tax movement and disintegrated after the arrest of Mahatma Gandhi, the new system gradually gathered confidence. At the center there was a new awareness of public feeling and a new desire to meet its wishes. There was a new sense of the dignity of India together with a reduction of pressure from London. The British official had often championed Indian interests against British commercial ones in the past, and now Whitehall no longer overrode him. The supreme government's first acts were to repeal the Press Act of 1910 and the Rowlatt Acts of 1919, which had never in fact been used. A new commission on the higher services was appointed which proposed a fifty-fifty Indo-British membership. Its achievement well before independence meant that the new Indian government found itself with a highly trained, efficient, and loyal service with which to run the country. The vexed question of the examination venue was settled by holding (from 1923) simultaneous annual examinations in Delhi and London. The Indianization of the officer cadre of the Indian army was begun which provided the new India with a core of experienced men to build up the new national army after 1947.

In the economic sphere, a convention of Fiscal Autonomy was established in 1923. By this arrangement the Indian government's right to arrange its own economic affairs and impose its own duties was recognized. The only exception was the continued inclusion of India in the British system of imperial preference. A commission followed to work out details. One result was the suspension in 1925 (followed by abolition) of the hated cotton excise, always regarded as a surrender to Lancashire. Another, and much more important one, was the setting up of a Tariff Board (1923). With the help of this body a policy of planned protection was developed. Customs became an instrument of economic policy and a flexible revenue producer. Young industries were fostered by protective duties and old ones protected in moments of stress. This system proved its worth in the great depression by saving the old cotton industry from Japanese competition and the young steel industry from extinction. Later, in the thirties, it fostered the rapid growth of the sugar and aluminum industries. This one measure of fiscal autonomy alone was enough to show that there was something much more than a corpse in the Mahatma's whited sepulcher. These economic changes were accompanied by social measures for controlling conditions in factories and mines and for securing workmen's compensation. On the reverse side, there was the doubling of the salt tax as part of the plan to balance the finances. However necessary it was to raise more revenue, this was the worst possible way of doing it from the political viewpoint. The salt tax was a poor-man's commodity tax, and its increase was at once felt throughout the country. The resentment which this measure aroused in the masses outweighed the satisfaction which others had produced in the classes; it was the one big blunder of Lord Reading's administration.

In the international field India was recognized as a separate political entity. She became, along with the then British Dominions, a foundation member of the new League of Nations with separate representation and vote in the Assembly. Her position was indeed remarkable, for this diplomatic status was combined with continued dependence on London on major issues. The Dominions went their own way from the first, leaving the Indian government representatives to be mocked as shadow players by congressmen. But while they certainly lacked real independence, they were able to make their influence felt in a number of ways, such as participation in the International Labour Office. The whole episode gave India a preindependence international standing and provided both public men and officials with valuable diplomatic experience.

In the provinces achievement was less obvious or uniform. Most of the ministries worked in the shadow of the extra-Parliamentary Congress opposition. Some were frustrated by financial difficulties or crippled by faction. But where there were coherent parties supporting stable ministries, as in Madras and the Panjab, good results were achieved. On the whole, despite the admitted defects of the new constitution and the difficulties of the situation, it is now clear that a measurable degree of success was achieved.

The confirmation of this success is to be found in the developments within Congress itself. By the end of 1921 it was clear that Congress had neither prevented the reforms from functioning nor had it killed them with derision. It had either to accept defeat or proceed to a further degree of opposition. The latter was the course proposed, in the shape of a no-tax campaign, but Gandhi withdrew it (to the dismay, not for the last time, of his left wing) after the Chauri-Chaura outrage and was shortly after arrested without any great public reaction. There followed a popular deadlock. It was clear that the middle class [1] was unwilling to support the antigovernment campaign further while the popular leaders were determined to continue. Cries for advance met with less and less response and gradually died away. There followed a general stock-taking and heart-searching. With Gandhi's presence withdrawn and his magic for the moment discredited, there emerged three trends of opinion. There were the devotees of Gandhi himself who clung to nonco-operation and called themselves No-Changers. There were those who felt that the councils could only be overthrown from within and that therefore nonco-operation should be combined with council entry, and there were those who reverted to the Tilak line of "responsive co-operation" or acceptance of office on terms. Disillusion, as usual, produced division. The rebels were led by C. R. Das, the last of the great Bengali leaders,[2] and Pundit Motilal Nehru, leader of the Allahabad bar and father of the present prime minister. The No-Changers were adamant in opposition, but the rest united on a formula of council entry for the purpose of wrecking the constitution from within. For this purpose a Congress Parliamentary party was formed called the Swaraj party, and the elections of 1923 were contested. Gandhi, on his release in 1924, neither approved nor hindered. He retired to his ashram at Sabarmati in Gujarat, where he pursued his social campaign and waited on events. The political transformation was completed by the virtual defection of the Muslims from the Congress cause. The Turkish leader Ataturk's abolition of the Caliphate in 1924 dealt a staggering blow to the Khilafatists in India. They were much put out of countenance. Bereft of its religious cause, the bulk of the community fell back into apathy. Fears of Hindu domination revived and found vent in ugly communal riots in 1924. The Hindu-Muslim honeymoon was over, and proceedings for a judicial separation were about to commence.

In this atmosphere of disillusionment and recrimination the Swarajist party dominated the political scene for the next five years. Motilal Nehru was its unquestioned leader. In those years he ranked second to Gandhiji in popular estimation. His loud voice and overbearing manner veiled a powerful and lovable personality. He exacted a salutary discipline from his followers and raised the whole tone of public life by the dignity of his presence and the weight of his contributions. He was an aristocrat to his finger tips, and it sometimes seemed that he would be more at home in Akbar's durbar or on the throne itself than in a democratic assembly. His presence in the Assembly was a standing reproach to a system which could find no better place for him than as leader of a nonco-operating opposition. His rubicund countenance, his leonine head, and his authoritative manner were the first things that struck the observer on entering the Legislative Assembly in 1924.[3]

In the 1924 elections the Swarajists achieved striking but not decisive success. In the Central Assembly they held 44 seats out of 146. They could not dominate the house or bring business to a standstill, but they at once became the major opposition group, and with the help of M. A. Jinnah's [4] Independent party they could defeat the government. The government's desire to avoid this so far as possible led to negotiations, compromises, and concessions. In the provinces their success was greater. In Bengal, Behar, the United Provinces, the Central Provinces, and Bombay they were able to prevent the formation of ministries and so secure the suspension of the reforms. At first it looked as though they were within striking distance of bringing the whole experiment in popular government to a standstill. But the situation was not so favorable as it seemed, and adverse factors soon became apparent. Council-wrecking from within was conceived as a reaction against the negation of noncooperation which had patently failed. But council-wrecking was itself negative; the more successful it was, the less was seen to be accomplished. The administration continued unshaken. The middle class wanted a share in this administration, not merely empty, if heroic, gestures. It had already seen enough of the reforms to realize that they had some practical value. Refusal of office after obtaining a majority therefore seemed to it to be a fresh dose of negation when it wanted positive action. A fresh feeling of frustration arose, and this time the Swarajists were the sufferers. On the one hand, Swarajist members grew discontented at having the fruits of office placed within their grasp, so to speak, and then being forbidden to taste them. This discontent led to a steady leakage of individuals, and in western India to a Responsivist revolt which restored ministerial office to the Central Provinces. On the other hand the "No-Changers" attacked the Swarajists' program as a failure and advocated a return to uncompromising opposition. But this was unwelcome to the political public too. The consequence was a general sense of malaise and a search for some new portent which might provide a new sense of direction. Outside the Congress ranks Hindu-Muslim relations continued to worsen. Mahatma Gandhi sat at his spinning wheel in his ashram exhorting Brahmins to open their temples and villagers their wells to the untouchables. He was biding his time.

The way out of this impasse was provided, all unwittingly, by the British government. The years 1924–26 offered a golden opportunity for some forward imaginative move which would rally an uncertain and hesitant middle class behind it. But Lord Reading, who had the legal acumen to divine the weakness in a hostile coalition, lacked the creative imagination to initiate a constructive movement. His only action was to appoint a committee to inquire into the working of the reforms, which was more productive of controversy than of results. His final act of abolishing the cotton excise was so overdue that it passed almost unnoticed. The initiative thus passed to Britain itself. The Conservatives were now securely in power and were to remain so, apart from the brief Labor interlude of 1929–31, until the World War II crisis. They had accepted the reforms as a party but without the faith of the Liberals or the desire of the Labor party to extend them. They recognized that the Congress was the principal political party in the country and a substantial political force. But they would not admit it to be either a dominant or a growing power with which a settlement would have to be made one day. They could point to the Congress divisions, and many argued, with some reason, that it was as likely to break up as to gather strength.[5] With our present hindsight we can see that these views overlooked the imponderables of national sentiment and Mahatma Gandhi. But there were many, at that time, in London, who underrated the former and misunderstood the influence of the latter. He was a unique and to many a bizarre world figure; could he really be taken seriously as a statesman? Had not his campaign "gone up like a rocket and come down like a stick"? Were not spinning and philanthropy his natural bent and future destiny? Those sharing these views were disinclined to any positive action and tended, in the style of Curzon in 1900, to look for the breakup of Congress rather than its revival.

But the party also contained a more enlightened wing. On Indian matters, Prime Minister Baldwin, with his brooding meditations leading to occasional insight, belonged to this group. In 1926 he sent Edward Wood (created Lord Irwin), grandson of Sir Charles Wood of the Mutiny period, to succeed Lord Reading. Irwin was forty-five, a member of the cabinet, a capable and imaginative man, already known for his integrity and moral earnestness. Baldwin explained the appointment by saying that he was sending the best man he had, because India deserved the best. It was one of the wisest of his actions. Irwin soon became aware of the need to provide a lead to break the impasse in which public opinion found itself. His first move was to call for an effort to restore communal harmony. But this, though acclaimed as noble, was ignored as impractical. In 1927 it was determined to give a lead in the political sphere. The statutory inquiry into the working of the reforms was due not later than 1929. Why not expedite the date and thus both make a gesture to Indian aspirations and forestall the possible appointment of a commission by a Labor government after the elections of 1929? In Britain the practice is for one government, broadly speaking, to accept its predecessor's actions. There were many Conservatives who thought that it would be much better to implement one's own commission's report than to have to work a Labor government's more radical implementation of its own commission's report, or worse still, to tone down or reject such a report.

This was the origin of the Simon Commission, which was appointed in November 1927 and immediately transformed the whole situation. The commission was appointed by the Crown from the members of the two houses of Parliament, to report, under the terms of the 1919 Act, on the working of the reforms and to make proposals for the future. Its chairman and dominant member was Sir John Simon, an eminent Liberal lawyer;[6] the only other member of interest was C. R. Attlee, then a young and unknown Labor M.P. In fact Simon, with his immense talent and industry, dominated the group and the report was virtually his own. The report became a classic state paper, the first volume having permanent value as a luminous description of the Indian constitution and administration as it stood in 1927, with a lucid historical introduction.

The commission's appointment produced an immediate outcry in India on the ground that it had no Indian members, that the fate of a great country was being decided over the heads of its representatives and that it was therefore a national insult. Irwin was as surprised by this outburst as was the British cabinet. It was his first major lesson in the working of Indian political psychology; his mind however was sensitive and quick to learn and we can therefore regard this episode as beginning the preparation for the part he was later to play as a conciliator. For the present nothing further could be done. The commission was taken as the sign for which Indian political opinion had been waiting. But it was not the sign the British had hoped, for it gave the signal to unite against the government. An intended gesture of good will became a rallying cry for freedom.

From this moment there was a steady crescendo of political feeling, until it culminated in a second great onslaught on the government. That this climax was reached from the depth of apathy into which people had sunk was due almost entirely to the tactical genius of Mahatma Gandhi. That constructive results and greater understanding came out of the conflict was due principally to the patience and insight of Lord Irwin. The commission's appointment drew all parties together except some Liberals and the Muslims, who were, however, divided among themselves. Here was a rallying cry which could bring together No-Changer, Responsivist, and Swarajist. The commission was boycotted and greeted with black flags and demonstrations wherever it went. By a device of associated committees from provincial legislatures, the commission was able to get into touch with many politicians, and enough evidence was received to make its report factually authoritative. But its movements through India during successive cold seasons were a godsend to Congress in that they provided a peripatetic irritant on which the Gandhian tactics could work. The next move was to devise a counterblast.

At its Madras session in December 1927 the Congress not only called for the boycott of the Simon Commission but also, at the instance of the young Jawaharlal Nehru and to the disquiet of Gandhi, passed a resolution stating that "The Congress declares the goal of the Indian people to be complete national independence." In substance this statement was only an English version of the political goal declared by Congress in 1920 at Gandhi's insistence to be *swaraj* or self-rule. But the English words had great precision, and, such was the psychology of the day, seemed to many Indian minds to be more definite and authoritative. In particular they were felt to go beyond the words "Dominion Status," which, though they had already received their classic definition by Lord Balfour (in 1926), were still a subject of discussion and had not yet been legally clarified in the enactment of the Statute of Westminster in 1931. The resolution was a calculated defiance in reply to an adjudged insult. It was also important in that it marked the entry of the young Jawaharlal Nehru into high politics on his return from a sojourn in Europe. He and the equally ardent Subash Chandra Bose of Calcutta quickly became the darlings of the politically minded youth and the radical wing of the party.

The next step was the organization of the boycott already mentioned, which had achieved much success. But something constructive was needed if indignation was to harden into a coherent opposition. The taunt of men like Lord Birkenhead was that Indians could not unite in action or agree on constructive proposals. The general indignation among the political classes made it possible to assemble an all-parties conference which set up a committee to draft an agreed constitution. Its chairman was Pundit Motilal Nehru, and it produced its proposals, known as the Nehru Report, during 1928. This was an able document, the work mainly of Motilal himself and the Liberal lawyer Sapru. It was a landmark in showing how mature Indian politicians had become, how far they had progressed from the art of agitation to the science of constructive thought. The report proposed complete self-government, but in the context of the time it was notable for two things. It accepted Dominion status instead of assuming extra-Commonwealth independence, and it ruled out separate communal electorates. The first proposal was a compromise in order to carry Liberals and minorities with the Congress. In this it succeeded, but only at the price of a storm within the Congress ranks themselves. The second was a device to keep Hindus of every shade together, which succeeded at the price of offending the Muslims. Their ablest leader, Jinnah, left the conference. Many Muslims felt that their suspicions of Congress *bona fides* were confirmed, and in the event they remained aloof as a body from the antigovernment movement which followed. This was one of the turning points in modern Hindu-Muslim relations. The report revealed both the statesmanlike qualities of the national leaders and the difficulties with which they had to contend.

Popular agitation and appeals to emotion inevitably strengthened left-wing sentiments. It was therefore not surprising that the young radicals, Nehru and Bose, should find themselves strong enough to challenge the veteran sponsors of the Nehru Report at the Calcutta Congress session in December 1928. Gandhi had much ado to prevent an open split. The result was a characteristic compromise. The Nehru Report with its goal of Dominion status was accepted for one year, with the proviso that if Dominion status was not granted by the end of 1929 resort should be had to mass civil disobedience. There was to be a year's breathing space.

There is no doubt that by this time the younger wing of Congress followers had been roused and were anxious for a conflict. They were helped by the Bardoli campaign, where a Gujarati lawyer, Vallabhbhai Patel, first attained prominence by leading peasants in a no-rent campaign as a protest against overassessment. There was also wide indignation with police handling of boycott incidents, in one of which the elderly Panjabi leader Lajpat Rai received injuries from which he died. But the middle class in general was unmoved. It sympathized entirely with the Congress cause, but it had no wish for direct action. The year 1929 began like a sultry summer's morning with gathering thunderclouds on the horizon.

CHAPTER XXXV

The National Struggle, 1929-34

During the spring and summer of 1929 India watched and waited. The first puff of the wind of action came from Britain itself. The general election of May returned a Labor government to power with Liberal support. The new prime minister, Ramsay Macdonald, was a known friend of Indian aspirations, and many Labor members were in close sympathy with Congress leaders. But Labor had not an altogether free hand, since it depended for its majority on sixty Liberal members who were, with their leader Lloyd George, notably more cautious. During the summer the viceroy, Lord Irwin, took leave in Britain for consultations with the new government. He had traveled far since he acquiesced in the appointment of the all-white Simon Commission. He was now convinced that Congress was a force to be reckoned with, with which a settlement would eventually have to be made. The National movement was real and growing, and therefore repression was no real answer. The Mahatma was neither a harmless eccentric nor a trickster, but a man of magnetism with a compelling moral force who could rouse Indians. He could release the springs of incalculable forces as no one else could. Yet he was a man of peace. Why not settle with Congress early rather than late and deal with a man who seemed providentially provided to save India from violent revolution? Irwin was a deeply religious man, and Gandhi's moral approach to politics made a deep impression upon him. He was yet to show the resolution and skill which was to turn this dream of *rapprochement* into a reality.

During the summer Irwin reached agreement with the Labor leaders and with his party leader Baldwin, who on Indian matters spoke for the more liberal wing of the Tories. These men recognized that the Congress was now a major factor in Indian affairs. There remained an important section of Conservative opinion and some rightist Liberals who still regarded Congress as a doctrinaire middle-class club and Mahatma Gandhi as a slightly bogus popular agitator. The events of the next few years were to give them an importance disproportionate to their numbers. Irwin returned to Delhi with a declaration which was to provide a center for the Indian political whirlpool for the next few years. It was released on October 31, and a section ran as follows: "I am authorised by His Majesty's Government to state clearly that in their judgement it is implicit in the declaration of 1917 that the natural issue of India's constitutional progress, as there contemplated, is the attainment of Dominion Status." The statement also proposed a round-table conference between the British government and representatives of Indian opinion to consider the next step after the publication of the Simon Report. This declaration marked a major step forward on the British side. The definition of Dominion Status as the goal of constitutional development brushed aside a tangle of controversy which had collected, like cobwebs in a neglected barn, about the original Montagu declaration. The words then used were, "the gradual development of self-governing institutions, with a view to the progressive realisation of responsible government in India as an integral part of the Empire." The words Dominion Status had not been mentioned; at that time they meant no more than internal autonomy with responsible government. But in the twenties the term had acquired significance, with an accepted meaning of independence from the time of the Imperial Conference of 1926. The exact words used were as follows: [1] "They are autonomous Communities within the British Empire, equal in status, in no way subordinate one to another in any aspect of their domestic or external affairs, though united by a common allegiance to the Crown, and freely associated as members of the British Commonwealth of Nations." "They" referred "to the group of self-governing communities composed of Great Britain and the Dominions." Britain and the Dominions were thus recognized as equal members of a voluntary association. Independence existed in all but name and only awaited legal definition by the Statute of Westminster in 1931. The new position, which Canada had taken a leading part in securing, was recognized in constitutional parlance by the use of the word "Commonwealth" to denote Britain and the Dominions as a group of free nations, and the word "Empire" for colonies and dependent territories. Irwin's declaration thus aimed Indian constitutional development clearly toward the goal of substantive independence. Doubts about the meaning of the 1917 declaration, which were natural enough in the circumstances, were cleared up, and suggestions that "responsible government in India" meant something different from and less than Dominion Status, which had aroused much suspicion in India, were set aside. The only cavil that could now be made was whether a Dominion could constitutionally leave the Commonwealth without the consent of Britain.

The first part of Irwin's declaration thus cleared the air in the realm of constitutional ends. The second part provided a new starting point in the more urgent sphere of means. Since Swarajist days the Congress had demanded a round-table conference with Britain, on the ground that India had a right to determine her own future. She must be mistress of her fate. One reason for the obloquy heaped on the Simon Commission was that both its appointment and composition seemed to deny that right. The declaration explicitly accepted the right of Indians to participate in deciding their own future, and there was never any going back on this. Thus in two fundamental respects the Congress demands had been conceded. Henceforward all controversy ranged round the means to attain the end. What was to be the pace of advance, what was to be the framework of self-government, who were to be the representatives of India? The Congress, from this time on, claimed to be the sole representative of the Indian people, a claim which many (including the Muslims) thought to be totalitarian. But all these controversies were essentially secondary rather than primary. That is why the bitterness and suspicion which they aroused fell away so rapidly once the Congress and British lines of development met in 1947.

Irwin's declaration went further than many Indians had believed possible in the circumstances. Gandhi and the Congress right wing at first wished to accept it. There was a brief moment of eager expectation in the country. But the leaders now reaped the fruits of arousing popular emotion and giving popular agitation its head. The left wing, led by the young Nehru, were able to include conditions which they knew could not be accepted by the viceroy. The key condition was that the conference should meet to draw up a Dominion constitution instead of merely considering the next step. Such a condition was impossible of acceptance by the Labor government, with its dependence on the lagging Liberals. The declaration had already been severely attacked in Conservative die-hard circles. It led to the defection of Churchill from Baldwin's leadership; if it had been pushed any further, Baldwin himself would have fallen. These things were not unknown to the Congress leaders, but Gandhi preferred a break with the government rather than with his own left wing. The time has not yet come to say finally whether he was right or wrong. Perhaps this tactic was the only way not merely to prevent a split in the Congress ranks, but to prevent the left wing from drifting into violence. In any case it is Gandhi and his lieutenants who must take the responsibility for the conflict that followed.

In the absence of a further government gesture the Lahore Congress in December opted for mass civil disobedience. Inevitably, full powers were given to Gandhi, who for the next two years was virtually the Congress dictator. The left wing and ardent youth were delighted at the prospect of battle, even if nonviolent; the general middle class, which had been greatly impressed by Irwin's character as well as by his gestures, was markedly reluctant. It wanted advance, but it wanted peace also. Irwin offered both, Gandhi ordered the former. They respected Irwin, but they revered Gandhi; eventually they preferred the Mahatma to the churchman. But the inner struggle was severe, and no one should suppose that the decision was easy or the conclusion foregone. India as a whole was not seething with discontent, but hoping wistfully for harmonious development.

Thus from the beginning of 1930 it was clear that there must be a further all-out conflict between government and Congress. The Congress aim, as previously, was so to paralyze government activity as to compel it to concede the declared goal of both parties—Dominion Status, with a round-table conference to determine its form. The methods were in the hands of Gandhi. His assets were a party far stronger and more disciplined than ten years before, with an inner core of his own *satyagrahis,* and a political public, which, if reluctant to move, was more ready to follow and to sympathize than in 1920. There was also mounting economic discontent with the onset of the great depression. On the government's side, which, if it lacked the dynamic personality of a Montagu, had a far more flexible leader in India itself than the mandarinate of Chelmsford's time, were the assets of a positive and far-reaching program, the general reluctance for an open conflict, and the disinclination of the Muslims to take sides. The course of the conflict turned on the efforts of the Congress to rouse the country and the attempt of the government to implement its own program of a round-table conference with limited aims.

Gandhi acted with characteristic simplicity and genius. He first created suspense by doing nothing and dropping hints of future action. He retired to his ashram and surrounded himself with an aura of holiness. He then announced defiance of the salt laws on the ground that the salt tax was iniquitous. The means was to be the illegal manufacture of salt, along with peaceful demonstrations. At one stroke the whole peasant mass was touched, for they were the people intimately affected by it. The middle class, many of whom were hardly aware that such a thing existed, had in many cases heard of the French *gabelle* as a prerevolutionary grievance and a wicked burden on the peasantry. Here were classes and

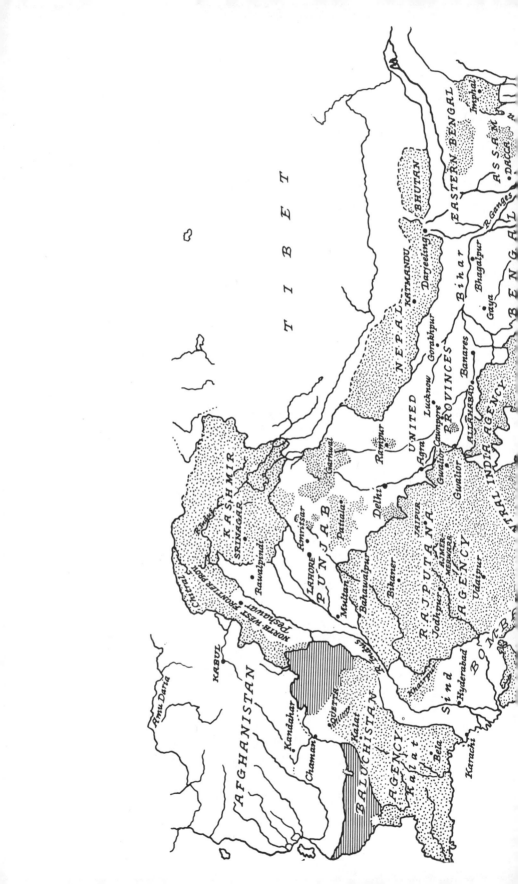

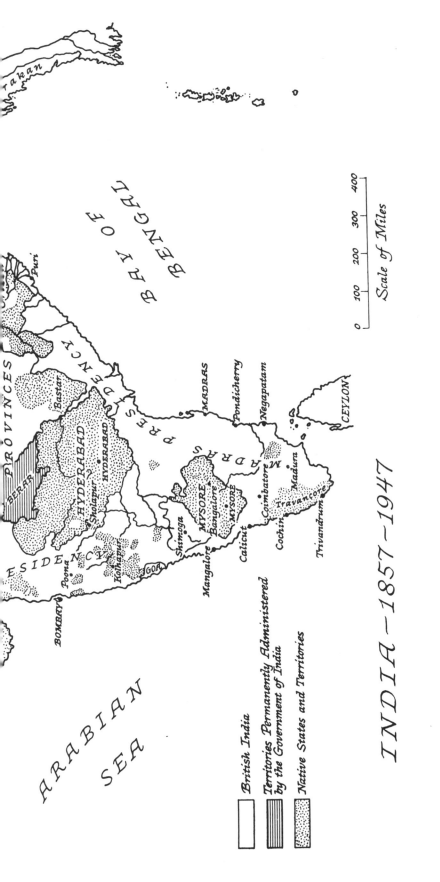

INDIA — 1857–1947

British India

Territories Permanently Administered
by the Government of India

Native States and Territories

Scale of Miles

0   100   200   300   400

masses united by a single and simple self-justifying slogan. Inedible and illicit lumps of salt became the sacrament of the national struggle. Gandhi's next problem was to arouse the people. This he did by the simplest but most effective publicity of the twentieth century. He *walked* from his ashram at Sabarmati to the sea at Dandi, and solemnly made salt on the seashore. Due notice was given to government of every move. At first the government did nothing, to the distress of the old-time officials; [2] the movement flagged and Gandhi seemed nonplused. But he had calculated correctly. Bombay took up the cause with enthusiasm; soon the proceedings were so tumultuous that government action became inevitable. Arrests, demonstrations, and more arrests followed. When Gandhi was taken into protective custody on May 5, the antigovernment movement was in full swing. Gandhi had won the first round. By the end of June some sixty thousand were in prison, mostly for symbolic defiance of the law and for a six-month period. Fresh arrests nearly balanced releases until the end of the year.

The second round concerned the Round Table Conference. Would the Liberals and Muslims attend in the tense and emotional atmosphere of a nationwide conflict? The situation was complicated by a frontier rising, which revealed some unreliability among the troops, and the publication of the Simon Report, whose concrete suggestions stopped short at provincial autonomy. However, the frontier episode alarmed the Liberals as much as the government, and the effect of the Simon Report was countered by a government proposal which included responsibility at the center. Early in July, in a speech to the Assembly, Irwin secured Liberal, Muslim, and princely participation in the conference. The Congress viewpoint found spokesmen through Hindu communal representatives. The Congress boycott was therefore virtually broken. The conference opened in the autumn. The second round had gone to Irwin. The third round centered in the conference itself. There was a dramatic development when the princes, led by Bikanir, declared themselves ready to enter a federation which would involve some limitation of their sovereign powers. In return, the British government agreed to the principle of ministerial responsibility at the center. The conference had been held; it had registered a positive advance and had produced an augury of a United India. This round went to Prime Minister Ramsay Macdonald.

It was now clear that the Congress effort was flagging. The Congress leaders were released, and on February 17 Gandhi started talks with the viceroy which lasted until March 4. He publicized these with the same flair as he did his march to Dandi, with daily walks up the processional Kingsway to the Viceroy's House. The result was the Gandhi-Irwin truce, in which the Congress left wing was set aside as firmly as the right wing had been eighteen months before. The terms were an ending of civil disobedience, the release of political prisoners (except those convicted of violence) and Congress representation at the second session of the Round Table Conference. The Congress session at Karachi ratified the truce, though not without left-wing protest, and Gandhi was appointed the sole Congress delegate to the conference. This round we may call a draw, though proponents of both sides complained that they had been tricked.

The truce at the time seemed to be a resounding achievement, rich with hope for the future. Moral values after all did count in politics; moral gestures could evoke a moral response. But all this was soon forgotten in the sorry sequel of misunderstanding, miscalculation, and frustration. We will carry the story to its end before trying to assess its significance. From the moment that the Congress agreed to be represented in the Round Table Conference and appointed Gandhi its sole representative, political attention turned to London. But the position in India was far from easy. On both sides there were embittered men (advocates of the "firm hand" or the "knockout blow" on the government side and of "no surrender" on the other) who thought that they had been let down by the settlement and took no great pains to work it. There were ticklish problems connected with evictions from landholdings and there was a background of agrarian discontent due to the economic depression. Officials could point to a revival of terrorism in the Panjab as an excuse for "firmness," and Congress leaders to peasant sufferings as a reason for intransigence. Both the presiding deities of the truce had departed, and there was no one to take their place. The new viceroy was the aging, reputed Liberal Lord Willingdon who had clashed with Gandhi when governor of Bombay and disliked and feared him. In these circumstances the Indian position drifted steadily toward a fresh conflict through 1931.

But the decisive theater was in London. Before the conference could meet,[3] the gathering economic depression had produced a financial crisis, which broke the Labor government in August. It was not until Britain had gone off the gold standard and a general election had given the "National Government" an overwhelming majority that Indian affairs could be seriously considered. Though Ramsay Macdonald was still prime minister, his government was now predominantly Conservative, with the able Conservative Sir Samuel Hoare as the new secretary of state. The new government did not disown the work of its predecessor. But there was a new tone in its attitude, a greater reluctance to bargain, a certain readiness "to say the last word," an added emphasis of Indian divisions and on minority rights. The Mahatma on his side did little beyond making a few general speeches, failing to carry on private negotiations with the British leaders and offending the Muslims on electoral matters. The various groups fell to playing for their own hand, and presented London with the unedifying spectacle of failing to agree on a scheme of electoral representation by a margin of one seat. The session broke up in December with nothing further achieved than a promise of some ministerial responsibility at the center.

The Congress was faced with the dilemma of eating its words or renewing its campaign. The left wing was now in control and had no doubt of the answer. But the government was now determined on repression, and people were weary of the struggle. The result was the renewal of the campaign, with its foregone conclusion of collapse and disillusionment. Within three weeks of his return to India, Gandhi was back in detention. The government struck hard, with wholesale arrests. The campaign blazed up for a few months, like the dying embers of a fire, into a shower of arrests, and then went dead. The number of political prisoners rose above 34,000 in April but sank below the 5,000 mark by July. A pretense of action was kept up for a time, but in 1934 it was formally abandoned.[4] Superficially, it seemed that the government had beaten Congress to the ground.

Meanwhile the British government pursued its course of constitutional reform in the happy belief that the Congress was being shattered in India. A communal award on electoral seats was made in 1932 by Ramsay Macdonald. This was repudiated by Gandhi because it placed the untouchables as a group outside the Hindu fold. To secure their inclusion he was ready to give them more seats and to fast unto death if need be. After agonizing discussions and under intolerable pressure the untouchable leader Ambedkar at length surrendered. Gandhi's life was saved, but Ambedkar always considered that he had betrayed his own cause. For were not the Hindus the people who had branded his brethren as untouchables? Was this not a further subtle move in the long history of Brahminical oppression? Gandhi on the other hand believed that only by keeping the untouchables within the Hindu fold could the Hindu conscience be aroused to remove their stigma. Bureaucracy made its own contribution to the problem by officially describing the untouchables as "Scheduled Castes." A third session of the Round Table Conference was but a ghost of its predecessors, attended by only forty-six delegates. The real field of action was in Parliament. Here the government faced a strengthened "diehard" opposition led by Winston Churchill, in revolt against the Conservative leadership and in militant mood. The discussions were so prolonged that the passing of the India Bill was delayed up to two years. It finally became law on August 4, 1935, nearly eight years after the appointment of the Simon Commission.

In judging the civil disobedience movement and its aftermath, it is almost fatally easy to apply hindsight to each stage. It is also easy to see the various processes in isolation and to forget that what was happening in one of the two countries, Britain and India, had a continuous effect upon what happened in the other. Thus an assessment of the revived civil disobedience movement in India from 1932–34 would be incomplete without taking into account the progress of the India Bill in London. We may take as a starting point the assumption that both sides made mistakes and misjudgments and that some sort of conflict was probably inevitable. The Congress (or an influential part of it) was not aware of the continuing government strength, and the government underestimated the growing power of the Congress. The Congress claimed to be the voice of all India (symbolized by Gandhi's appointment as sole representative to the second session of the Round Table Conference); many of its leaders hypnotized themselves into the belief that this was actually so. But in fact it was not the case in 1930, and still less so in 1932. The price of this miscalculation was near extinction in the years 1933–35. The government officials in 1929–30 thought that they could separate a militant Congress from a peaceful country and so bypass the former. We have Lord Irwin's words for their surprise and the extent of their miscalculation.[5] Again, from 1932–35 Hoare and Willingdon seemed to think that the Congress could be permanently broken by sharp repression. The Congress organization was severely injured, it is true, but a fund of bitterness was left behind which gravely added to the difficulties of a final settlement after World War II.

Going back to the beginning of the struggle, we may regret that Gandhi thought it necessary to yield to the left wing in rejecting the Dominion Status declaration and the Round Table offer. On the other hand, he may have preferred a peaceful conflict with the government by a united Congress to the splitting off of an action group led by S. C. Bose and the young Nehru which might have turned to violence. The government, on its side, would not have admitted the strength of Congress without a trial of wills. The Gandhi-Irwin truce was a moment of insight, when both sides recognized the limits of their power and the underlying good will which united them. For all the bleak aftermath of the truce, Indo-British political relationships were never quite the same again. For the first time the British leader in India had talked man to man to the Indian leader without pomp, reservations, or unreality. In those last few weeks of his rule Irwin conveyed a sense of sincere purpose to the Indian leaders which was never wholly erased. For the first time since 1920 they began to believe that the British, or some of them, at bottom meant what they said. This feeling lived on through the hostility of the Willingdon period and the frustrations of World War II to make possible a final settlement in amity. The final tour de force of Mountbatten would not have been possible without it. Without it, India might well have left the Commonwealth for the orbit of China.

The years 1932–35 saw further miscalculations on both sides. For the government there was the belief that the national organization could be broken by strong action, and for the Congress the idea that a war-weary public could be induced to continue a struggle indefinitely. The harm done by the government attitude to the cause of understanding was great. But we must remember that in Britain the Government of India Act was taking shape. This act would probably not have gone so far as it did without the Congress movement as a stimulus to outbid its demands. Once passed, it became a point of no return for British and Indians alike. It could always be said of the Montford constitution that it was an experiment which could be revoked as well as extended. The 1935 act made it clear that progress could only be in one direction— toward self-government. On the Indian side it determined once for all that the new India's political institutions should follow a Western pattern. The new constitution was too far-reaching and too convenient to be scrapped without a major upheaval, for which the Indian leaders were not prepared. Now habit and custom, the strongest of all Indian forces, have come to its support.

Looking back at the struggle as a whole, we can now see that it had far more than a purely political significance. It not only stimulated the still far from robust all-India consciousness of the average Indian but had important social consequences as well. The swelling popular national emotion beat against some of the traditional social obstacles to unity. In part this was by Gandhi's design, but in part it was spontaneous. The movement provided a turning point in the emergence of women from their traditional seclusion. Hitherto only a few highly Westernized women like Mrs. Besant (who was English) and Mrs. Naidu had taken part in public life. Now they came forth in thousands, and they never went in again. Especially in western India, women marched in processions of protest, organized pickets outside cloth and spirit shops, addressed public meetings, and offered *satyagraha*. The movement spread to the conservative north, where the local leader of the Delhi Congress for some months was a woman. The aftermath was seen in greatly increased participation by women in public life at local, provincial, and national levels and in the rapid development of women's schools and colleges.

A second result was a blow at the stricter caste restrictions in general and against the stigma of untouchability in particular. Men and women could not co-operate in mass political action and go to prison in thousands without breaking some caste customs. Each rule thus disregarded in name of patriotism ceased to be an essential for the future. To that extent the working of the whole system was eased, and the structure was undermined by the acceptance of ideas which contradicted it. Gandhi's Harijan movement was in theory unofficial. But his status as a national hero gave it a new prominence of which he did not forget to take advantage. National brotherhood and untouchability did not mix. The Mahatma's "fast to death" in 1932 on the untouchables' account made their cause a national issue. Though Ambedkar thought he had been betrayed, there is no doubt that the untouchables' cause gained greatly in the short run through association with the national movement. It was a major defeat for orthodox Brahmin opinion in the Congress. The abolition of untouchability was now part of the Congress creed. The fruit of this action was the formal abolition of untouchability by Article 17 of the Constitution of 1950.

The India of 1935, for all the apparent eclipse of Congress at that time, was much more a nation, in the Western sense of a united people, than she had been at the beginning of 1930.

CHAPTER XXXVI

The 1935 Act, Theory and Practice

Unlike the Montford reforms of 1921 or anything that was done after World War II, the Government of India Act of 1935 was enacted from strength. It could be said that after both world wars Britain was too enfeebled to take an uncompromising stand. But in the thirties she had recovered from World War I, was emerging from the Great Depression, and had just defeated the strongest frontal attack on the Indian government's authority since the Mutiny. There was no compelling force dictating concession or constitutional advance. What was done was done through conviction and might be said to represent a minimum rather than a maximum. That was why there was an air of solidity about the Act, and why its major features proved to be so fruitful in the future. It was generally realized that there could be no going back on it.

The Act was the constructive half of the dual policy of suppression of Congress defiance and advance toward self-government. It was meticulously drawn up and represented, in effect, a draft constitution for an Indian Dominion. It was made easy to fill in gaps later; old features which were left, such as the office of secretary of state, could be lopped off without difficulty, and provision was made for a measure of change within the constitution. The London connection began to assume the appearance of a legal umbilical cord which could be snipped at the right moment.

This result was achieved by a large extension of the existing features of the Montford constitution and by the introduction of certain vital new principles. The existing features which were extended were representation, dyarchy, ministerial responsibility, provincial autonomy, communal representation, and safeguards. A word may be said about each. Representation, first introduced under a pseudonym in 1892, received a large extension, both in the number and character of the representatives and in the voters who elected them. The central and provincial assemblies were all greatly enlarged, and second chambers were provided for six out of eleven provinces. The provincial property qualification was lowered to include thirty million voters of both sexes, which was five times the previous number and about one-sixth of the number under universal adult franchise. Dyarchy, the division of executive responsibility between responsible ministers and authoritarian councilors, was abolished in the provinces but extended to the center. Ministerial responsibility, which began in 1921 with dyarchy, now covered the whole provincial executive field and was extended to the center as well. Communal representation, a vintage of the 1909 reforms, ran right through the constitution, both in the legislatures and the public services. There were separate constituencies for Muslims and other major communities; there were reserved seats for the untouchables or "Scheduled Castes," as they were now called, and for other special interests. Finally safeguards, including reserve powers for governors, often thought of as a reactionary feature of the Montford era, were extended. Both the governor general and the governors could "certify" bills to make them law over the head of the legislatures and could promulgate ordinances with the force of law for six months. The governors had special powers to administer provinces in the event of a constitutional breakdown.

There were a number of administrative changes, representing an extension of a previous tendency, which may here be noted. The tendency was to approximate provincial boundaries to regional sentiment. It began with the arrangements of 1911 and reached its limit in the reorganization of state boundaries in 1956. In this process 1935 was an important landmark. Burma was finally separated from India with a constitution of its own. The North-West Frontier Province had already been given governor's status in 1932. Orissa and Sind (both one-time Mughal provinces) now became separate provinces. There were thus eleven full provinces in the last twelve years of British rule.

The novel features of the constitution were the introduction of the federal principle, with its corollary of provincial autonomy, the establishment of full responsible government in the provinces and of dyarchy at the center. The application of the federal principle had two aspects. It first gave the British Indian provinces a large measure of freedom to work out their own policies and decide their own fate. It next made it possible to bring the princes into the general constitutional pattern. Hitherto they had been a problem, for they owed allegiance directly to the Crown and did not fit into the development going on in British India. The most that could be done was to encourage the greater princes to promote parallel developments in their own states. The federal idea which the princes accepted in principle in 1930, offered a bridge by which they could enter the promised land of a united independent India. They were to surrender to the center powers over foreign affairs, defense, and communications, and in return to nominate one-third of the members of the lower central legislative assembly and two-fifths of the upper chamber. Entry into the federation was to be a voluntary act, and the federal legislature would start to function when one-half of the states reckoned by population had joined. Though the existence of the federal legislature was made dependent upon the princes' adhesion, the federal principle in general was applied at once to the provinces. Legislative powers were divided into central, provincial, and concurrent, with residuary power with the governor general. The three lists, however, were exhaustive, so that the residuary question was academic rather than actual. A Federal Reserve Bank and a Federal Court were set up. The latter was presided over by Sir Maurice Gwyer, one of the chief draftsmen of the Act in Britain and later an adviser on the constitution of 1950.

The federal proposals promised a constitution designed for the great diversity of Indian political institutions. The establishment of full responsible government in the provinces opened a real field of power for popular leaders. The ministries were to be headed by chief ministers responsible to the provincial assemblies, and governors were enjoined only to interfere or use their reserve powers in cases of dire necessity. Though this increase of authority might be described as merely adding two and two to make four, in fact the four arrived at proved to be far greater than two plus two. In the center there was to be dyarchy, with ministers for all subjects except defense and foreign affairs. There were considerable financial reservations which made this change less radical than it looked on paper. Nevertheless it was substantial, and the only further change that could be made was to full self-government.

In Britain the Secretary of State for India and his council were retained, but his powers were much reduced.

The view has been put forward that this Act was not only bulky in form but radical in nature and momentous in its consequences. This is not to say that it was without defects. They were important and had momentous consequences too. First among them was the nature of the federal tie between the princes and the Union. By the arrangements made, the six hundred princedoms were kept in being with all their anomalies of size, status, and institutions. Their direct relationship with the Crown was preserved, making change or amalgamation a matter of treaty rights, and the minimum of power was surrendered to the federal center. At the center itself they were given heavy weightage in both houses of the legislature, a weightage which was the heavier because the princes had the right of nominating all their representatives.[1] These provisions would have made it difficult to develop the strong center which India's development required. A major internal revolution would have been needed to assimilate "Indian India" into modern India, and it would have been almost impossible to carry through such a measure constitutionally in view of the position they were given in the central legislature. In the circumstances, India has cause for thankfulness that the princes were too stupid to see the advantages of the scheme from their point of view and failed in the event to join the federation. Apart from this major weakness, the federal structure was itself defective. The emphasis was on provincial autonomy, which would have made for a weak and perhaps divided India. The popular central legislature was elected indirectly by the provincial assemblies, which again tended to detract from its importance. By a curious anomaly, the British Indian members of the upper house were to be elected directly (on a restricted franchise), but the effect of this was nullified by the stranglehold possessed by the nominated princely representatives. We can sum up the position by saying that the federal structure was boldly conceived and skillfully worked out, but that the balance of political forces within it was such that the federal government would have been weak. It was calculated to maintain the *status quo* rather than to release dynamic and creative forces.

A second weakness, though it was little noticed at the time by friend or foe, was the failure to recognize the plural nature of Indian society. There was communal representation, it is true, and special measures for the "Scheduled Castes." But there was no realization of the fact that India contained separate cultures as well as regions and communities, and that these cultures must find constitutional recognition if the state were to be healthy. It was not realized that the Muslim and Sikh held sectors of their communal life sacred, sectors in which they would accept no dictation from an outside authority. The attempt was made to fit the mantle of a unitary state upon the body of a plural society, and the result was stresses and strains. The allegiance of these lesser bodies was necessarily partial and conditional to a state claiming authority as complete as the Parliament in Britain. Herein lay one of the causes of Pakistan. It was this basic defect which underlay the arrangements for "minorities." They were all given safeguards of various kinds and special representation, but none of them was given a palpable share of power. Could a body of about ninety-million Muslims be seriously regarded as just a minority, even though the caste Hindus were more than twice as numerous? The more the minorities were given treatment in relation to their numbers, the more conscious they became of the fact that they were minorities. And in democracies majorities rule.

The new constitution was presented to the country by a new viceroy, Lord Linlithgow, a rising Conservative, who had gained knowledge of its problems by acting as chairman of an agricultural commission. He was tall and severe in expression; earnest, hardworking, and sincere in character; and a capable administrator. He had every desire to make a success of the new regime. But he lacked large imagination and the ability to handle people with skill. In consequence, although he ruled longer than any of the viceregal series since 1858,[2] he gathered respect rather than affection or admiration. His aloofness, his lack of magnetism, his desire and inability to attract a following made of him one of those Olympians who is always looking down for support rather than one to whom people look upward for leadership. Though care was taken in his appointment, Britain had again failed to find a man equal to the demands of the age.

Lord Linlithgow arrived in April 1936; the new constitution was inaugurated just a year later. That is to say, the federal structure was set up so far as it affected British India, and the new provincial constitutions came into being. But the old central legislature and executive continued to exist, awaiting the adherence of the princes to federation. Congress now came out of the shadows, and at once it was seen that it remained the strongest political force in the country. As in the period 1922–25 no alternative grouping or party had emerged; during the Willingdon years there had been a suspension rather than a reorientation of politics. Congress could be suppressed but not extinguished. Congress had immediately to decide its attitude to the new regime, and it became clear that the political success of the constitution would largely hinge on its attitude. First it decided to contest the elections and then, when it had secured clear majorities in five out of the eleven provinces, with virtual control of two more,[3] to accept provincial office. At the center it was the largest party which could always give the government anxiety.

But these decisions hid turmoil within the party ranks, to which attention should now be turned. There was in fact now a well-defined left wing in the Congress, which in the late thirties very nearly secured control of the party. This decade was the period of the Great Depression and the emergence from it of America and Europe. Poverty and bleak prospects sharpened class divisions and bred bitterness, radical proposals, and a spirit of violence. While the United States was trying out the New Deal, British youth was passing "no war" resolutions and flirting with communism. In Europe the Nazis suppressed both communism and democracy and lauded violence as a virtue. It was the age of Hitler's violence, Stalin's purges, and Mussolini's attack on Abyssinia. India was not unaffected by these currents of thought and action, because she too suffered from the Depression and she too had suffered a major political upheaval. The result was an accession of strength to the left-wing elements of Indian life, a strength compounded of impatience with the results of Gandhi's tactics, bitterness at the Congress defeat, and the attribution to the British of responsibility for Indian economic ills. The emergence of this kind of left wing can be dated back to Nehru's return from Europe in 1927 and his sponsoring of the independence resolution at the Madras Congress at the end of that year. He was attracted to socialism and impressed by Russia though critical of communism. He and the brilliant young Bengali Subash Chandra Bose were the two *"enfants terribles"* of the Congress. Gandhi, with uncanny prescience, selected Nehru rather than Bose and determined to disarm him by promoting him. In 1930 he was elected president of Congress for the first time, at the age of forty. The events of the next few years tended to swell the numbers of the left wing. Gandhi found himself faced with a prolonged challenge to his Congress leadership, for if the left wing got control there would before long be an unconsidered challenge to government which might easily lead to a large-scale resort to tactics of violence. Gandhi's problem was to avert what in his opinion would be a disastrous development.

The left-wing movement as it developed in the thirties was a fork with three prongs. There were the violent revolutionaries who reappeared in the Panjab and later in Bengal. They enjoyed limited support, but they would have gained great strength from any breakup of Congress. Then there were the Communists. The government advertised their existence by arrests in 1929 and the staging of the Meerut Conspiracy Trial.[4] Through the thirties the Communists attracted, under the gifted leadership of M. N. Roy, the dispossessed in the cities and an increasing number of idealistic young middle-class people who were appalled by the poverty of the country and repelled by the apparent indifference of the average congressman. Many recruits came from the ranks of the "England-returned," who suddenly saw the fact of Indian poverty in a fresh perspective, together with the immense contrast between poverty and wealth. Here again was a waiting beneficiary of Congress dissensions. To Gandhi's mind the violence of the revolutionary and the class war of the Communist were equally distasteful and disastrous. If they were not to grow dangerously strong he had to keep the third prong of the movement firmly attached to the Congress. His plan seems to have been to divide the left-wing leadership by attaching Nehru to himself. Why did he choose Nehru rather than Bose, a choice to which he adhered with tenacity and suppleness? The answer lies, it may be suggested, in Gandhi's estimate of character. The young Nehru had great potential influence as the son of the stalwart up-country leader Motilal, while Bose came from the always rather apart Bengal. In addition, Nehru was more tractable. He was ardent and bitter at the time, but he was also idealistic and a humanist. He was also singularly susceptible to personal influence. His idealism and talent for discipleship made him respond to the Gandhian magic wand, even while his reason rebelled time and again against Gandhian logic. Above all, in the last resort he placed unity above ideology. He would denounce moderate courses and then withdraw in the interests of unity or submit to face-saving compromises devised by the Mahatma. A signal example of this trait occurred in 1936 when Nehru, elected president of Congress for the second time as a Gandhian device to induce moderation, alarmed the right wing so much by his advocacy of socialism that it resigned from the Working Committee in a body. Nehru offered to resign also, but withdrew at Gandhi's behest. Bose, on the other hand, was not under Gandhi's spell. He was a convinced socialist, desired a conflict with the government, and showed some sympathy with the authoritarian methods of the dictators. Nehru could be charmed into co-operation against his own judgment. Bose could only be restrained.

For as long as possible Gandhi avoided making a decision. His way of dealing with left-wing resurgence was to promote the leaders to positions beyond the strength of their support so that they had either to moderate their line or discredit themselves. Nehru was elected president of Congress in 1936 and re-elected in 1937, and went through the experience of a right-wing revolt to which he yielded with more or less grace. Bose followed him as president in 1938. In Gandhi's view this was enough, and the veteran moderate Sittaramaya was proposed for election in 1939. But the left wing in the All-India Congress Committee got out of hand and re-elected Bose. Gandhi was the adamant and within two months of the Tripuri session of Congress had forced his resignation. A moderate and Gandhian stalwart, Rajendra Prasad from Behar (later president of the Republic), took his place. Bose never recovered his position in the Congress, and with him Bengal. For a time he promoted a Forward Bloc within Congress. He then resigned altogether and in 1941 slipped away to the Axis camp, whence he hoped to return as India's savior-dictator. Of the three challenges to the Congress leadership, Bose's was the most severe. Ideologically he represented the dictator or national socialist principle, a principle which in the thirties drew support from feelings of disgust with things as they were and impatience with the slow-moving national leadership. Thus Congress continued, though not without stress, its constitutional middle-of-the-way course. The measure of Gandhi's success was that he had retained Nehru in the leadership and with him the bulk of the left-wing elements outside Bengal.

The Congress had now to decide its attitude toward the new constitution. The decision, acquiesced in with much misgiving by Nehru, was to work the provincial part, which meant taking office and forming ministries. The Swaraj party was in effect revived, providing a vigorous opposition at the center and controlling ministries in eight of the eleven provinces. Central control over the ministers was exercised by the "High Command," which did not hesitate to discipline those who were too independent of the party line.[5] On the whole this two-year honeymoon from 1937–39, or perhaps we should say somewhat guarded association, was of great advantage to the country. Responsible congressmen came to appreciate the worth and loyalty of the civil services in both their Indian and British members. This proved of the greatest value when they had to rule the country under most difficult circumstances. British officials on their side learned to appreciate many whom they had formerly regarded as "agitators." This new perspective made the postwar negotiations easier. Further, the Congress leaders, with full provincial responsibility, gained invaluable administrative experience. It is one thing to devise policies and another to carry them out amid the crosscurrents of public opinion and the tensions of rival interests. Congress was already accustomed to the first; it now acquired the know-how of the second.

The years 1937–39 were notable for a great success, a great failure, and a great mistake. The success was the Congress ministries, for which both government and Congress must share the credit. The failure was the inability of the government to persuade the princes to join the Federation. The viceroy was active and persuasive. But the princes had lost their enthusiasm of the first Round Table Conference. They were rent with jealousies among themselves; the more they saw of Congress with its democratic implications the less they liked it; they preferred dealing with the British direct (who were at least the devil they knew) to a viceroy inevitably influenced by nationalist ministers at the center. The British seemed well established; they should be good for a number of years yet. So they held out for better terms either in the hope of being better placed in the eventual setup, or with the more purblind desire of enjoying their full prerogatives a little longer. The viceroy, on his side, refrained from putting such pressure on the princes as would have compelled them to come in. There was in him a vein of scrupulosity which at times inhibited action. It appeared in 1943 when he failed to intervene in time in the Bengal famine for fear of wounding provincial susceptibilities. Thus from the princes' point of view the last opportunity of saving their order by integrating it with a conservative federation was lost. Having let down the British over federation as they had previously let down the Congress over democracy and nationalism, they found themselves friendless after World War II. They had no popular backing, and they were snuffed out like so many candles. Great as this failure was, however, India may perhaps be grateful for the princes' folly. It was the princes' failure to co-operate which prevented the federal center from coming into being. This fact enabled the Congress to take over complete power in 1947 and to set up a strong center. Without a strong center the development of modern India would not have been possible; with the princes there could not have been a strong center.

The great mistake was the Congress attitude toward the Muslims. Gandhi and the Congress leadership maintained that the Congress represented all Indians. There was therefore no need for Muslim political parties. The Congress had a Muslim wing whose most distinguished leader was Maulana Abul Kalam Azad, but the majority of Muslims remained outside. After the collapse of the Khilafat movement in 1924, they remained for some years divided. But they were increasingly suspicious of the Congress as a potential Hindu government. They stood aloof from the civil disobedience movements. With the passing of the 1935 Act, Muhammad Ali Jinnah, a Bombay lawyer and one-time nationalist, secured control of the main Muslim organization, the Muslim League. He fought the elections on a program of co-operation with Congress on a coalition basis. But the Congress, flushed with victory, would have no coalitions, and in provinces like the United Provinces would only admit Muslims to office who joined the party or came in as individuals. The League had not done very well, and it may have seemed good tactics to smother it before it gathered strength. This decision was a bitter blow to Jinnah, meaning, as it did, his virtual exclusion from national politics. His choice was submission to Congress or pursuit of a communal line. Not unnaturally, he chose the latter. From the classes he went to the masses with the cry of Islam in danger. Hinduizing tendencies of the ministries were played up, alleged slights and discriminations magnified. The magic worked. The present writer can testify to the changed atmosphere which greeted him on a return to Delhi in 1939 after an absence of two years. Pakistan was in the air. When the ministers resigned there was mutual regret on government and Congress sides. But Jinnah proclaimed a Day of Thanksgiving at relief from Hindu tyranny. More significant than the day itself was the fact that it was widely observed.

CHAPTER XXXVII

World War II

In the midst of these constitutional experiments, when Congress and government seemed to be growing toward one another, came the outbreak of World War II in September 1939. India was far more prepared for this event than for the outbreak of World War I, because she was in much closer touch with world opinion than previously, and the war had been expected in Europe for months. She now also had her own Cassandra, warning her of the future, in the person of Jawaharlal Nehru. The realistic attitude of India toward World War II was a measure of her progress toward adult national status in the previous twenty-five years.

Nationalist opinion in India during the thirties had been generally hostile to the dictatorships of Hitler, Mussolini, and Stalin. The British government had been widely criticized for its appeasement policy and especially for the Munich settlement, with its sacrifice of Czechoslovakia. The stand made after the Nazi occupation of Prague in March 1939 was therefore generally welcomed. But when war actually came, the attitude of the country was markedly detached. The Indian public was now (as it had not been in 1914) an independent entity in its own mind. It judged issues for itself without reference to British reactions. In this case it generally sympathized with the Allied stand against the Nazis. But its attitude remained detached for two reasons. One was the absorption of the country generally in its own concerns. Europe was still far off; Gandhi's latest fast or Subhas Bose being carried to a Congress meeting on a stretcher was more exciting to the average man than the tragic fate of a small and distant country. The other reason was India's dependent status. The manner of India's entering the war emphasized this continuing constitutional fact. The left wing considered the war an imperialist one and was strengthened in its view during the months of "phony war." The public in general considered it a war of interest indeed, but not yet its business. It was Britain's war, and let Britain get on with it. When Hitler invaded Norway,

Holland, and Belgium in the spring of 1940, and this was followed in quick succession by the evacuation of Dunkirk, the fall of France, and the Battle of Britain, Indian opinion was temporarily staggered. It was shocked by the dire peril of Britain, with the possibility of its collapse, and Nazi threats. The *spirit* of the British at this time deeply impressed them. From this period arose a dual attitude toward the war which persisted to the end. The politically minded were not prepared to help positively because of their dependent status; at the same time they did not wish to hinder a cause which they considered should have been their own. This attitude was one element in the feeling of almost agonizing frustration which oppressed Indians at this time—the vexation at being prevented from entering into a heritage by a government which agreed in principle with the entry.

The main facts of the war in relation to India may here be summarized before proceeding to consider its political effects. The first phase lasted through the period of the "phony" war until the fall of France in June 1940. During this period life went much as usual; army headquarters did not even think it necessary to alter the practice of allowing officers to attend the afternoon session in their offices in civilian clothes. The view taken was a simple syllogism. Only a mechanized army would be of use in the war; the Indian army was not mechanized; therefore very little could be done. All that was thought necessary was some expansion, with a capital outlay of about sixteen million dollars on ordnance factories recommended by the prewar Chatfield Committee.

The second phase began in the summer of 1940 and lasted until Pearl Harbor eighteen months later. During this period India, along with Australia, became a supply center for the Middle Eastern theater. An Eastern Group Supply Council was set up, with India as its principal member. In the first year of its work India supplied 60 per cent of the council's demands and later 75 per cent. All this development was under the general direction of the viceroy, who must be given credit for much farsighted and clearheaded planning. This preoccupation must be remembered when we come to deal with the political aspects of the war period. The demands of the council acted as a great stimulus to industry. Besides the old established cotton and jute industries there was a large expansion of heavy industry and an extension to other fields as well. The steel works of Tata (then the largest single plant both in Asia and the British Commonwealth) of the Bengal Steel Corporation and the Kumardhuti Groups were further extended. The cement industry was greatly expanded and an aluminum industry created on the strength of India's large bauxite deposits. Parallel with supply came the expansion of the armed forces. In 1939 the

WORLD WAR II
397

regular Indian army had a strength of 175,000 men. It was efficient and high-spirited, but it was not mechanized. It was still officered largely by Englishmen. From mid-1940 its numbers were increased until some two million men or 2 per cent of the adult population were under arms. Along with the army went a much smaller but still highly significant build-up of the Indian navy. In the later stages an Indian air force was created which worked beside Americans and British on the Eastern front.

The third phase, which began at Pearl Harbor, brought the war to India's doorstep. The Indian public had hardly grasped the fact that the Allies must win the war with America's entry before it was stunned by the fall of Singapore with thousands of Indian troops and the Japanese overrunning of Burma. Henceforward the war was an intimate domestic matter which affected the lives of everyone. Indian attention was diverted from the Middle East to Assam and Burma. The task was to save India itself from invasion and then to recover Burma. Indian efforts were devoted to supplying the forces, Indian, American, and British, which were holding the Eastern frontier.

The war thus brought a mounting impact upon the life of the country. In the first phase it was little more than a talking point. In the second phase there was a great deal of activity which spread in ever-widening circles across the life of the country. But it was still an activity largely external to the popular mind. The third radically affected everyone, his mind as well as his fortune. First among these effects may be placed the expansion of the armed forces. Though only a small proportion of the total went abroad, all were uprooted from their village homes, subjected to discipline and strange habits, and in many cases taught trades and modern techniques. This in itself was a major jolt to a tradition-bound society. There were large openings for the middle classes in the officer cadres and in the enlarged bureaucracy which increased their sense of responsibility and self-respect. And there was the actual record of the army, which gave the whole country a feeling of international pride and status. The next effect was the industrial expansion which has already been touched upon. Here again the middle classes found many openings in the managerial ranks and as technicians. Responsibility, status, and "know-how" were conferred on many thousands by these developments. Indians not only saw that these things could be done or that they were being done as in World War I; they were doing them themselves. There were enough Indian officers to take over all the armed forces at independence, and enough executives and technicians to control India's commercial and industrial life.

A further effect of the war was the stimulation of social change. The

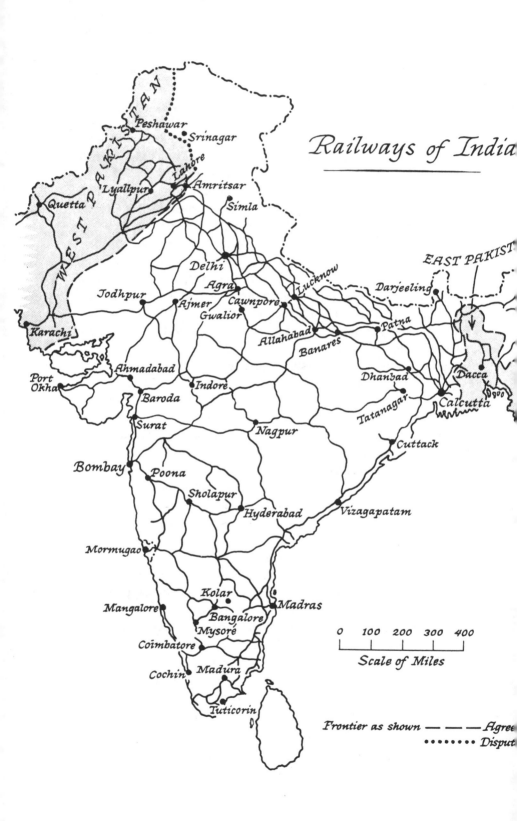

Railways of India

gathering together of large masses of men was one such stimulus, with its disturbance of custom, its pooling of ideas, its enlargement of horizons. The army continued to observe basic caste distinctions of food and touch, but the air force and the navy cast them aside and presented themselves to the world as streamlined, homogeneous units. The social emergence of women found further encouragement in the demand for work. The British sent some of their women's units to India and formed auxiliary women's units for the Indian forces. Then there were the openings provided in government and private offices. Education and the professions offered more openings, so that it became common to find both members of a middle-class couple engaged in public activity. Again industrial expansion moved thousands into new environments, often in temporary quarters where old habits provided no precedents. This especially benefited the "untouchables," both by making old distinctions difficult to maintain and by providing them with fresh opportunities in new conditions.

The economic effects of the war were wide-reaching. There was the expansion of industry already mentioned. From early 1943 there was a rapid price rise, which produced inflationary conditions by the end of the war. One unexpected result of this was to reduce the chronic indebtedness of the peasants, at least temporarily. Their cash receipts rose, and debts to the village moneylenders diminished in proportion. But those raising cash crops such as sugar, jute, and cotton soon found themselves overtaken by the price spiral in food. An unwelcome development was the acute embarrassment of the middle class. Just as it seemed to be entering a world of larger opportunity and solving its unemployment problem, it was overtaken by a decline in the real value of its earnings. Prices rose faster than manual wages and much faster than "white-collar" salaries. In Delhi, for example, it may be said that in the second half of the war commodity prices rose to about three times their prewar level; domestic servants' wages rose about twice, but the clerk or salaried worker had to be content with bonuses or cost-of-living allowances. This price rise was caused partly by the shortage of essential commodities owing to the spread of the war to the East. For example, shipping shortages tended to cause war supplies to monopolize imports, while the loss of southeast Asia removed a great area of supply. The other cause was the spending of large sums on military works by Britain and America. The expansive activities of the Indian government were largely financed by credit. Then came the build-up of the South-East Asia Command (SEAC) and the supply of the forces on the Assam-Burma front. Large sums of money were injected into the country to pay, for example, for the great airfields on the Eastern front, the foreign personnel in the country, and all their immense military impedimenta. This money found its way into Indian hands which could find nothing to spend it on.

There were two more effects of the war, which were interrelated—the transport crisis and the Bengal famine. Indian transport depended on the railways. Their essential pattern was a line along the northern plain to Peshawar with a strategic lateral line to Karachi port in Sind. Apart from this feature the pattern essentially revolved around the great ports of Calcutta, Bombay, and Madras, with connecting links between them. It was not until 1928 that Delhi was directly linked with Madras by a line through the interior. These lines were intended to facilitate exports and imports by providing feeders between the ports and the hinterland. Food shortages were dealt with by sea transport. For example, the rice shortage in Malabar (the spice country) was first supplied by sea from Bengal, and then, as the Bengal supplies diminished, by import from Burma. Famine conditions were combated by large-scale import from overseas. The war dislocated the railway system by imposing (from early 1943) a huge west-east traffic from Bombay to the Eastern front. The strain on Bombay was intolerable, and was made worse by the explosion of an ammunition ship in its harbor. Upon this strain was added an extra burden on the north-south line of communications, to carry a redistribution of internal supplies on account of the loss of those overseas. Thus, while the railways were struggling to keep the Eastern front supplied in a remote part of the country, the Indian government had also to meet a food shortage. Burma and Siam had been India's reserve depots for rice. With the loss of Burma there was an overall shortage of rice of about 5 per cent. The proportion seems small, but with the price situation and the knowledge that no overseas sources were available, it was enough to start hoarding and profiteering. Bengal had not only to supply itself but to help the permanent rice deficit areas of the south. And all foodstuffs had now to be moved by rail in an already congested transport system. In these circumstances there occurred the Bengal famine of 1943. There was a genuine but not catastrophic shortage. The Bengal government applied controls too late and too feebly. Peasants were gulled into selling their crops at fancy prices and then found themselves with nothing but rupees to eat. They poured into Calcutta, where they died in the streets, a terrible commentary on human folly and greed. The central government sent wheat from the Panjab, much of which never reached its destination. It interfered too late because of Linlithgow's scruples about provincial autonomy; he must bear a heavy responsibility for the suffering that followed. Not until Lord Wavell's arrival in October 1943 did the viceroy visit Calcutta, impose food rationing on all the great Indian cities, and detail the British forces to relieve the famine-stricken. Never was the British army better pleased in India or more popular with the people.

Something of the army's fighting record should now be noted, for it constituted a vivid fact in the Indian consciousness. Indian troops were in the Middle East from the beginning. They came into their own with Italy's entry into the war in June 1940. They took part in Wavell's campaigns in North Africa and the Abyssinian campaign. They continued under Auchinleck and had a hand in the Syrian and Iraqi campaigns. The Fourth and Seventh Divisions achieved enduring fame and came to be regarded as crack troops. After the entry of Japan into the war, Indian troops were mainly concerned with the defense of India. After the difficult days of the retreat from Malaya and Burma, they covered themselves with glory in the heroic defense of Kohima (on the Assam border). Thereafter they took a major part in the march into Burma and were poised for the attack on Malaya and Indonesia when the war ended.

It is against this background that we have to view the political maneuvers which continued throughout the war years. We see a country which was generally sympathetic to the purpose of the war but was generally out of sympathy with the government in charge. We see a government trying to postpone rather than avert the political issue. The country wanted freedom before victory, the government victory before freedom. It was a study in cross-purposes and of the gradations of frustration. But it was more than this, for it was not merely a question of people versus the government. There was a power triangle whose existence was even more responsible than government tactics for the delays which occurred. This triangle was made up of the government itself, the Hindus who politically were represented by the Congress, and the Muslims. By the end of the war it could be said that their political representative was the Muslim League. At the outset this could well be disputed, but the fact remains that the Muslims as a whole were a separate political factor. A peaceful settlement of the Indian problem required an understanding among all three groups. It soon became clear that any two of them could only agree at the expense of the third and at the price of civil war. In the early days tension was caused by the British reluctance to move before the end of the war; later it mounted because of the British endeavor to get a settlement acceptable to both the other two.

The first move was the resignation of the Congress ministries. Lord Linlithgow acted according to the constitution in declaring India at war with Germany from September 3, 1939, but his manner of doing it emphasized India's dependent status. Co-operation was called for, with constitutional advances "after the war." The authorities had assumed their favorite wartime constitutional stance. National danger was the great excuse for doing nothing. After the usual tug of war between right and left wings, the Congress ministries were ordered to resign by the High Command on the ground that they could have nothing to do with waging a war thrust upon India. In the Congress view it was an imperialist war so far as India was concerned, though Indians might sympathize with one side more than another. The Muslim League retorted with a Day of Thanksgiving for relief from Congress tyranny. The undoubted success of this occasion showed that anti-Congress feeling among Muslims was stronger than Congress leaders were willing to admit. A political storm cone had been hoisted in the national sky, and its color was green. The Congress ministers in general departed from the seats of British power amid mutual expressions of regret. They had won the respect of the British and in their turn had come to know them better. They had done much useful, constructive work and had gained valuable experience. The wisdom of their departure is still a subject of dispute. Mr. V. P. Menon, a close observer with intimate inside knowledge, thinks it the first of the cardinal mistakes which led to the formation of Pakistan. The viceroy, he thinks, was inclined to encourage the Muslim League as a makeweight to Congress which gave Jinnah's still far from secure position a valuable boost. The Congress also lost all that influence which comes from being in office instead of out. Of these two factors, the second was more important. The strength of the League in the last resort was a matter of Muslim sentiment, which was related to fear of Hindu domination. This basic sentiment was not dependent upon government patronage; in fact the Congress resignations tended to reduce popular Muslim fears rather than increase them. By its retirement from office, on the other hand, the Congress lost an important bargaining position at a moment when bargaining was to be the order of the day. Congress could have progressed faster if it had had the threat of resignation in reserve instead of only the threat of civil disobedience. Such a threat in wartime aroused maximum British resistance. Gandhi was the only man who could implement it, and it was known he would not go beyond a certain point in such a situation.

It must be remembered that, after the overthrow of Poland, September 1939, there were six months of "phony war" when nothing happened. The "appeasers" were still in power in Britain, and abroad there was widespread talk of compromise. With the blitz of April 1940 leading to Dunkirk and the fall of France, the situation was transformed. The Indian public caught its breath in wonder and anxiety. There was first satisfaction at British reverses, then anxiety, then consternation at the apparently imminent fall of Britain. In June there were a few days of panic when rupees went underground and dacoits appeared. King George was said to be sailing up the Jumna to take refuge in Agra Fort. This mood changed to admiration when Churchill defied the Nazis and carried the people with him. Even though he was regarded as their sworn adversary, "the ranks of Tuscany could scarce forbear to cheer." In these circumstances it was very difficult to mount a national movement against the government.

From this time the main actors on the political stage were Lord Linlithgow for the British, Mahatma Gandhi and Jawaharlal Nehru (representing the left wing) for the Congress, and Jinnah for the Muslims. In Linlithgow the British had a man of integrity, capacity, and good will, but one lacking in the art of managing men. His geniality was so forced as to seem painful, his smile would make children cry. Bismarck called the great Lord Salisbury a lath painted to look like iron; Linlithgow was a ramrod trying to act like a lath. Nehru was always for action, usually against the government, but he was also anxious to join in the fight against Nazism; he did not believe in nonviolence as an ultimate principle, but he was also determined never to part from his Mahatma mentor. Jinnah, the polished Westerner who was playing on traditional Muslim mass emotions, furbished the rapier of obstructive tactics while he waited in the wings, conscious that neither side could get its way without him.

From July 1940 to December 1941 there was deadlock tempered by sympathy for the Allied cause. The public watched Britain standing alone for a year with a fascinated gaze, and then Russia reeling under the Nazi attack, until Pearl Harbor at one stroke brought the war to India's doorstep and decided its issue by bringing America in. Just before the Battle of Britain the government made its August (1940) offer of an Indianized executive council at once and an Indian constituent assembly *after* the war to draw up a new constitution with due regard for minority rights. The proposed constituent assembly was an advance, virtually handing Indian fate to Indians themselves. But Congress insisted on independence at once and on recognition of itself as the sole representative of the Indian people. It also regarded the mention of "minority rights" as a concession to the Muslim League, which had declared for Pakistan, or an independent Muslim homeland, in the previous spring. With the Battle of Britain safely won and British survival assured, Gandhi was authorized to start a civil disobedience movement. Never was a revolutionary movement more carefully conducted on nonrevolutionary lines. Gandhi organized "individual civil disobedience," which consisted of the commission of symbolic illegal acts by selected individuals. The first *satyagrahi* was Vinoba Bhave, later famous as Gandhi's spiritual heir. By May 1941 some 14,000 were in prison, mostly on short terms, throughout the subcontinent.[1] Thereafter the numbers dwindled away. The whole operation was a gesture rather than a campaign, a symbolic ritual rather than a deliberate defiance.

With Pearl Harbor and the rapid loss of Malaya, Singapore, and Burma came a dramatic change. There was greater disposition to co-operate among congressmen and greater inclination to act on the part of the British. All congressmen were released, and a member of the War Cabinet, the left-wing Socialist and lawyer Sir Stafford Cripps, was sent to India with a new and radical offer. The main lines of the proposals were as follows. An Indian Union with Dominion (independent) status was to be set up immediately after the war. Its constitution would be decided by a constituent assembly elected by the various provincial legislatures. The result of its deliberations would be embodied in a treaty with Britain on the lines of those with Scotland in 1707 and Eire in 1922. Freedom to draw up the constitution would include the right of secession from the Commonwealth. The Indian states would be free to join the Union, and provinces could contract out if they wished. Finally, an interim government of party leaders would be formed which, though in form merely the executive council of the viceroy, would be treated as a responsible cabinet so far as possible.

These proposals created great excitement, and for a time hopes were high.[2] But the old suspicion of "after the war" revived, and disputes arose over the precise powers of the new council, particularly with regard to defense. Nehru and Rajagopalachari were for acceptance, but the final word was spoken by Gandhi, who traveled to Delhi to urge rejection. He was said to have described the offer as a "blank cheque on a failing bank." After such hopes, the pang of disappointment at rejection was the keener.[3] Cripps himself was nettled; there were angry exchanges and a feeling of soreness all round. Gandhi's reasons can only be surmised. But it may be suggested that he was unimpressed by an offer coming from such obvious weakness. On present form, would not the Japanese invade India at the end of the monsoon (October), and what could stop them? Why commit oneself to an apparently falling power? From another angle he could argue that the British had conceded all but full control to Congress. If pushed a little further by the Japanese menace, might not they concede full control? Then the Pakistan issue, on which Gandhi felt deeply, would be settled on Congress terms. Finally, Gandhi had no enthusiasm for heroic struggles against invaders, especially if unsuccessful. Heroism should be reserved for nonviolent ventures.

Whatever the workings of the Mahatma's mind, there is no doubt that his was the decisive voice in rejection. There was anguish in the Congress camp as well as with the British. Rajaji left the Working Committee, and Nehru came near to the breaking point with Gandhi. It was his supreme test in discipleship, a test so severe that he welcomed his subsequent arrest as a release from intolerable tension. There seems no doubt that the decison was a mistake. It precipitated the Congress revolt, which only created bitterness. It kept the congressmen out of government, in which they would almost certainly have occupied a key position. By the end of the war their situation would have been commanding. It left the field open to the Muslim League, which proceeded to occupy the key position which should have belonged to Congress.

Matters now mounted quickly to a crisis. Congress, under Gandhi's guidance, declared for nonviolent resistance to the Japanese. A few weeks later Gandhi coined one of the his magic phrases in the slogan "Quit India." The Japanese were indeed to be resisted, but the British must first quit India to remove any show of provocation to them. Congress sincerity was to be demonstrated by the offer of bases in India to Allied Powers. The sanction behind this demand was mass civil disobedience. The new slogan gathered, in one rush of feeling, all the discontents and resentments existing in the country at a time of great strain and tension. It was this upsurge of feeling which enabled Gandhi to carry his policy in the Working Committee in what was perhaps the hardest fight of his life. The resolution was put to the All-India Committee on August 7; it included sanction for a mass civil-disobedience campaign to enforce it. "After all," said the Mahatma, "this is open rebellion." It looked as though the peak of the crisis were coming in October, prepared with all Gandhi's uncanny skill. At this point the government struck hard. The whole Congress was declared an illegal organization. There followed a short but sharp outbreak of violence which caused widespread dislocation, especially in Uttar Pradesh, Behar, and Bengal. Official figures reckoned over 1,000 killed and 3,000 injured by the end of the year, while more than 60,000 were arrested. The government described it as the Congress Rebellion and tried to connect Congress leaders with it; Congress ascribed the violence to the intolerable strain imposed by government intransigence on popular feeling. In fact the outbreak reflected with equal gravity upon government and Congress. To both it was a warning that violence, which might take matters out of the hands of both, lay just around the corner if the deadlock were not soon broken by rational means.

For the moment the government triumphed. Early in 1943 Gandhi fasted for twenty-one days. But the viceroy resisted great pressure for his release, and he did not repeat the experiment. During 1943 the Allied fortunes steadily improved, and in the fall the new viceroy Wavell's firm handling of the Bengal famine and the general food crisis gave the government fresh confidence and prestige. It was generally felt that India was in the hands of a soldier who was both firm and humane; there was nothing to be done until the end of the war. The familiar process of approaches to government by Congress splinter groups began. The Muslim League continued to win by-elections until it had twenty-five members in the Assembly. The government caravan marched on.

CHAPTER XXXVIII

The Transfer of Power

When Germany surrendered in May 1945 the war was generally thought in Britain to be nearly over. But for India it was still in full swing. Burma had just been recovered; an attack on the Japanese in Malaya and Indonesia was impending; the great assault on Japan had yet to come. The war effort had been mounting in a steady crescendo since 1942 and had now reached its peak. In outward appearance the government was stronger than at any time since the fall of France.

But in fact appearances were deceptive. Though some Congress leaders were putting out feelers for a *détente* with the government and a Congress group had reappeared in the Assembly, it was clear to any careful observer that there was a great underground reservoir of national feeling awaiting a release of war pressure in order to come to the surface. The reservoir contained many currents which together gave it great potential force. Once again the government had succeeded in defeating an overt movement against its authority without deflecting the current of opinion behind it. Men argued that Gandhi had made a tactical mistake in defying the government in 1942, but there was no deviation from the general objective. Desire did but wait on opportunity. Components in this volume of feeling were many. Resentment at the crushing of the 1942 movement was one of the lesser of these. The sense of frustration at the prolonged deadlock was more obvious but rather superficial. Most important was a general awareness of nationality and national dignity. This awareness had been fostered by the large-scale war activities with their new industrial and administrative departures, and by the training of many thousands in new techniques and responsibilities. The Indian public felt itself a corporate unit and felt itself adult. Independence had been an ideal, a desideratum to be worked for; now it was an axiom of public life, to be implemented as soon as possible. India was already independent in spirit. Finally there was the suspicion, nourished on years of deadlock, that the British would somehow wriggle out of their declared obligations.

On their side, the British leaders were aware that their position was not nearly so strong as it looked. They knew that the national movement had been dammed up, but not deflected from its course. They knew also that Britain's weakest moment was not during a war, when she had her back to the wall, but after a war when the torpor of war-weariness dulled the appetite for power. The British public would not stand for a large-scale effort of repression just after emerging from a six-year life-and-death struggle. But they had, it was thought, the year during which the Japanese war was expected to last in which to negotiate from power. That was why the Churchill Conservative "Caretaker" government itself opened negotiations with the Congress within a few weeks of the German surrender.[1]

There was a third element in the situation, the third side in the power triangle of the later phase of British India. This was the Muslims, now organized in the Muslim League nearly as effectively as the Hindus in the Congress, and controlled by Jinnah even more completely than Gandhi controlled Congress. The League was committed to the concept of Pakistan or an independent Muslim homeland, and played a decisive role in the events of the next two years. It had been founded in 1906, but except for a few years it had never approached the Congress in standing and was usually weak and divided. Only ten years earlier, when Jinnah took control, it was a small body, rent with divisions and recriminations and capable of little more than angry expostulations. How did it come to achieve such a commanding position in so short a time?

While every credit must be given to Jinnah's leadership, it is clear that one man could no more create Pakistan without a volume of popular support than Churchill could have saved Britain in 1940 without an upsurge of popular feeling to sustain him. For the roots of the Pakistan movement we must go back to the fall of the Mughal empire in the eighteenth century. For over five hundred years the Muslims had been an imperial race, and in that time they had become a quarter of the population. They were dominant in Sind, Northwest India, the western Panjab, and eastern Bengal, and they formed important pockets in northern India. Elsewhere they were scattered groups, either engaged in trade (as in Gujarat) or clustering around warrior Muslim dynasties. They had developed a large upper class of officials, soldiers, and landholders and a proletariat made up of camp followers, converts, and the descendants of mixed marriages.[2] But the middle class was small because its functions were performed efficiently and willingly by the indigenous Hindus.

The Muslim faith sustained these people, and the Muslim empire united them in a common purpose. When the Muslim dominion passed they found themselves at once impoverished, divided, and directionless. They were impoverished because the upper class lost the fruits of office and there was no middle class to take its place; they were divided because there was no longer a secular purpose to divert Sunni, Shia, and Ismaili sects from their religious differences; they were directionless because the Muslim empire, an essential part of the Muslim way of life, had collapsed irretrievably. Many took to brooding on the past and a withdrawal from life; as a whole the community lost faith in itself. Others turned to religion for inward renewal since the state had failed them. The lead in this direction was taken by Shah Waliullah of Delhi (1703–62), who preached inner renewal as the way of revival. This meant an emphasis on the Islamic religion and a separation from Hinduism. A symbol of this process was the translation of the Koran into Persian and Urdu, the language of the Muslim man in the street. One such movement [3] took a violent form leading to a holy war against the Sikhs and conspiracy against the British. Others promoted peaceful renewal. All harked back to tradition and all called for separation from both the West and the Hindus.

As the Hindus took up Western education, acquired Western techniques, and exploited new commercial opportunities, the Muslims fell further and further behind. It was Sir Sayyid Ahmad Khan (1817–98), sprung from an old Mughal official family, who broke this spell. Like Ram Mohan Roy with the Hindus, he preached the duty of renewal by borrowing from the West. He too appealed to the principle of reason and emphasized the underlying ethical and philosophical connections between East and West. His monument was the Aligarh College,[4] founded in 1875 to provide Western education in a Muslim atmosphere. His special contribution to the movement for Western understanding was the study of science. Thus the Sayyid sought to bring Islam in India into line with modern thought and progress. But there was no thought of union with the Hindus. They were still a heathen body tainted with idolatry and superstition. Toleration was matched with aloofness in his thought, coexistence with separateness. He preached co-operation with the British to avoid eclipse and absorption by the Hindus. When the Congress was founded in 1885, he advised Muslims to hold back on the ground that in an independent India the majority would rule, and the Hindus outnumbered the Muslims by three to one.

Here, then, was one plank in the Pakistan program—separateness from the Hindus. Fear of Hindu domination grew steadily as the movement for self-government progressed. It took the form of calls for safeguards, which were provided by the separate Muslim constituencies in the Acts of 1909, 1919, and 1935. This general tendency was interrupted for a time, but not reversed, when fears for the Turkish caliphate induced co-operation with the Congress between 1916 and 1924. But more than fear was needed to provide a dynamic movement for separation. The further vision was supplied by the Panjabi poet, Sir Muhammad Iqbal (1876–1938). He conceived of Islam as a creed of dynamic struggle along Nietzschean lines which would enable man to control the new forces of science instead of becoming the victim of materialism. He was also the first to conceive of a Muslim homeland in India where this dynamic faith could be practiced without hindrance.[5]

Sayyid Ahmad Khan proclaimed the separateness of Muslims and reconciled them to the West. Iqbal gave them a dynamic faith and a sense of mission. Once more they looked forward. But the further they looked, the more widely the path diverged from their fellow Indians. Then came Muhammad Ali Jinnah (1876–1948) to provide political form to this movement of life and spirit. Ahmad was the philosopher, Iqbal the prophet, and Jinnah the statesman-creator of Pakistan. A lawyer from western India of impeccable Western dress and taste, the young Jinnah began as a Muslim Nationalist supporter of Congress. He was disillusioned by Gandhi's nonco-operation campaigns, but as late as 1937 he contemplated co-operation with the Congress in coalition ministries. It was only when the Congress leaders made it clear that for them co-operation meant absorption that his opposition became unrelenting. From then onward he was implacable. He saw no choice for Muslims between absorption into Hinduism or separation. Therefore separation it had to be. He adopted the Pakistan concept in 1940 and pursued his goal with remorseless logic and flawless skill. By 1945 no Indian settlement was possible without Jinnah's consent.

This maker of a nation was slight in build and precise in manner. He was the reverse of a demagogue or a fanatic, yet he could fan fanaticism and arouse popular passion. He was so little in touch with his own culture that he could not speak Urdu. He despised the mob and hated disorder. His disdain for the people whom he led and the implicit devotion with which they repaid him remind one of the Protestant Parnell leading the Catholic Irish toward Home Rule. In both cases there was a formal manner and icy aloofness; in Jinnah there was also a fund of cold logic, a quietude of manner, and a Western sartorial elegance which suggested anything rather than the fiery conviction of a prophet. But behind this daunting and uninspiring façade lay keen ambition, pride of achievement, an iron will, and a certain icy passion. Most men in anger are heated and confused; Jinnah was colder and clearer than ever. Such men are formidable when aroused because they are implacable and remorseless. From the day that the Congress broke faith with the League (as he considered) after the elections of 1937, his political passion was continuous. And it was remorseless against the Muslim Nationalists, whom he regarded as traitors and whose leader had penned the fatal message.⁶ This was the man who controlled the Muslims even more fully than Gandhi controlled the Congress. In both cases there were dissenting minorities and in both cases they were powerless.

In 1945 Indian fate hinged upon the reactions of three men, Gandhi, Nehru, and Jinnah. They were a strikingly contrasted trio. Gandhi was now a unique figure of wizened and almost uncouth appearance, a cheerful pauper-saint whose smile disarmed with humor and whose words bemused with good will and double meaning; there was Nehru, handsome, ardent, fascinating, sensitive, and mercurial, an intellectual moving with anguish amid scenes of passion. To many he was a Westerner playing at Indian patriotism, to others a patriot dogged with a Western heritage. Here was a soul in travail, whose impulses were often read as signs of weakness and whose outbursts were interpreted as indications of lack of depth; a Hamlet murmuring

> The times are out of joint, O cursed spite
> That I was ever born to put them right.

And there was the third figure already described, the master of the negative, the abettor of fanaticism in the clothes of Bond Street, the soft-spoken dispenser of doom to millions. No three could be more unlike, yet each honored in his own way his appointment with destiny.

On the British side there were no such arresting personalities until the arrival of Mountbatten, and he blazed like a comet rather than shone like a star. It was perhaps well that this was so, for otherwise an ordered withdrawal might have become a fighting retreat or even an attempted comeback, and these could only have had disastrous consequences. In the circumstances the slow reflectiveness of a Wavell and the matter-of-factness of an Attlee were more useful than the pugnacity of a Churchill. Lord Wavell, after winning military glory in North Africa and commanding in India, had been appointed to succeed Lord Linlithgow in 1943 as a wartime measure. He had done well in dealing with the Bengal famine, in instilling a sense of order and justice in the administration, and in restoring confidence. Now he had to deal with the wholly different problem of handing power to a group of critical and mutually suspicious politicians. Wavell's was a reserved and reflective nature. Sensitively aware in spirit and a poet in his own right, he was slow in manner and laconic in speech; he undid in long silences much of the good his spoken wisdom had begun. Though possessed of insight and good will and sincerely anxious to find an agreed Congress-League formula for the transfer of power, he found it difficult to cope with the agility of the political mind. He won esteem but not agreement or gratitude. He came to appear like a mastodon beset by the shafts of quick-moving enemies; the most honorable of men, he had to suffer charges of ill faith.

The first scene of the final drama of British rule opened at Simla in June 1945. In essence this was an attempt by the then Conservative government to arrange for a transfer of power on its own terms. The British could still speak from power because the Japanese war was expected to last another year and the country was full of troops and the government was full of confidence. The party leaders, including the released congressmen, were summoned to Simla where, in the cool mountain air and the shade of the deodars, the Cripps proposals of 1942 were revived. There was to be a national administration to carry on the Japanese war and a constituent assembly to draw up a constitution at its end. The crucial question was the composition of the viceroy's cabinet. The Congress claimed to represent all India and so to be free to appoint Muslims to any of their allotted seats. The League, on the other hand, claimed to be the sole representative of Muslims and so to have the sole right of their nomination. Jinnah refused to sit with any Nationalist or Congress Muslim, and the Congress insisted on nominating one. So the talks, which began hopefully as such talks usually do, ended with increased bitterness and frustration. The Congress on its part was not willing to surrender its all-India status; its leaders still doubted the reality of Jinnah's power and hoped to be able to smother the Muslim separatist movement as they had tried to smother the Congress-League coalition movement in the United Provinces eight years before. The League at that stage could not afford to give any ground on its claims. As the Congress hoped to convince the British that the League was unimportant, the League had to convince them that it was indispensable. The British at this stage were neither ready to agree to Pakistan, which they regarded as a counsel of despair, or to throwing overboard Muslim minority rights, which they thought would be a breach of their pledges. They thought they had a year of power in which to bring the two parties together, but in fact they only had a few weeks.

The next phase was ushered in by two unexpected events. The first was the result of the British general election at the end of July. It returned a large Labor majority, to the surprise of the Labor leaders themselves. The six-year regime of the Labor government under Attlee commenced. The second event was the surrender of Japan on August 14 after the dropping of the first two atom bombs. The Labor party had long been pledged to the grant of self-government for India. The large majority it had received meant that the country was in no mood for further sacrifices or adventures. Not only would the declared policy of handing over power be supported, but any large measures to cope with an emergency might be resented. The British freedom of maneuver was reduced; the postwar drainage of popular will power had commenced. The second event meant that there was no longer any international reason for keeping large forces, either American or British, in India. Their numbers were rapidly reduced, and along with them the British means of physical control. At the same time the ending of the war and the withdrawal of troops removed two restraints on the actions of the Indian parties. From being an umpire with power to enforce the rules, the British position became more and more that of a go-between trying to reconcile two independent parties. The doubt as to the exact extent of their waning strength at any given moment added one more uncertainty to an already confused situation.

The purpose of the Simla conference was to find an Indian government to finish the Japanese war. That war having now ended, the next step logically was to call a constituent assembly. The British were uncommitted, because the repeated offers of an assembly had always been attached to wartime strings which the parties had rejected. A Conservative administration might have been tempted to look back, to impose conditions which would not have affected the final result but would have caused delay and much ill-feeling with perhaps disastrous consequences. It was fortunate for Indo-British relations at this juncture that a strong Labor government was in office. But it was inexperienced, it was beset with postwar difficulties, and it allowed delay to occur. The first decision was to test the strength of the parties by holding general elections at both provincial and all-India levels. The deliberation of the government machine was such that the results were not complete until the spring of 1946. They showed that the League dominated the Muslim part of India as completely as the Congress did the Hindu. In particular the powerful Unionist party in the Panjab, a coalition of rural Muslims and Hindu Jats, was heavily defeated. The premier, Sir Khizr Hayat Khan Tiwana, could only continue in office with the support of the Sikhs and the Congress, representing the urban Hindus. In fact he was keeping the League at bay with the help of a constitutional technicality, for under the Communal Award the Muslims in the Panjab received fewer seats than their numbers entitled them to, in return for a larger proportion elsewhere. The fact was that the Panjab Muslims as a body had gone over to the League. They felt themselves cheated of office. This situation explains the steadily mounting tension in the Panjab throughout 1946 and the explosion which followed in 1947. Only in the Frontier Province did the pro-Congress "Red Shirt" government of Dr. Khan Sahib maintain itself. But here the vote was more an expression of sentiment in favor of independence or "Pukhtunistan" [7] than of Congress or Hindu rule. It was anti-British and anti-Pakistan but not pro-Congress.

These results showed the two main parties in greater relief than ever. It was India's misfortune that they were not just office-seeking organizations, but bodies dominated by cultural religious forces. The Congress was avowedly an all-Indian and secular body; many congressmen were genuine secular nationalists, but the weight of Hindu feeling behind them was too great for them to be able to convince the Muslims of their case. The League was triumphant, and less inclined to compromise than ever. The Congress was impressed, but unwilling to believe that the League leaders really meant what they said or that their supporters would follow them. For the former doubt they had much excuse so long as they did not realize that Jinnah was an exception to the general rule in this as in other ways. From the latter error they should have been saved by a knowledge of history, but the lessons of history were something they suspected to be of British manufacture. The British Labor leaders, on their part, now conceded the reality of the League's strength, although their previous affiliations had been with Congress.[8] Meanwhile tension, with neither war to inhibit it nor large forces to control it, was steadily mounting. The brief mutiny of the Indian navy in February 1946 along with "strikes" at air force bases, though smothered with the help of alarmed Congress leaders themselves, showed how thin the crust of British power was becoming. The trial of certain "national army" officers (who had worked under S. C. Bose with the Japanese in Burma) further irritated highly wrought nationalist nerves.

London now took action and dispatched a cabinet mission to India. Its members were the leader, Lord Pethwick-Lawrence, Sir Stafford Cripps, and A. V. Alexander. It was generally known as the Cripps Mission because of the activity of its ingenious second member. After fruitless efforts at mediation between the parties it put forward its own plan in May. The essence of the plan was to retain Indian unity while giving reasonable satisfaction to Muslim demands. This could only be done by according them some sort of regional autonomy, a sort of Pakistan *in parvo*. Accordingly two plans were put forward. The first, or long-term, plan provided for a federal union of British Indian provinces to which the Indian princely states could later accede. The federal powers were to cover defense, foreign affairs, and communications. They were in fact a minimum, and amounted to a concession to the League, because they correspondingly increased the powers of the federal units. In addition there could be subordinate unions between individual provinces which would make possible a Muslim state within a state in northwest India with the union of Sind, the Frontier Province, and the Panjab. On this basis a constituent assembly would be summoned to draw up a constitution. The second plan was for an interim national government. At first both sides accepted the long-term plan, but they soon fell to wrangling on the short-term. Equal representation of Muslims and caste Hindus was proposed; the negotiations broke down on League insistence on the appointment of all five Muslims and Congress insistence on the right to appoint a Muslim. Behind these charges and countercharges lay the Congress belief that it substantially represented all India. The only way for the League to break this down was to make difficulties for the Congress. The British could only argue and persuade; they could no longer command.

The prolonged conference seemed to have been completely sterile. But in fact the situation had altered in several ways. The close contact between the British and Congress leaders convinced the latter that the British really meant to withdraw. Thereafter, while the bitterness of controversy continued, the underlying suspicion of the British decreased. Anglo-Congress relations improved. Contrariwise, Anglo-League relations became more difficult, because Jinnah suspected a British deal with the Congress. The effect of this was to bring Jinnah to the brink of direct action. Once this Rubicon had been crossed there would be no alternative to partition or a bloody civil war or both.

The two parties, like boxers, were now circling each other searching for weak spots. The worried umpire, who wanted them to shake hands, was beginning to lose control of the situation. Jinnah accused the viceroy of breach of faith in the matter of the interpretation of paragraph 8 of the mission's statement of June 16.[9] This paragraph implied that the viceroy would proceed to form a government with any party which accepted the proposed arrangements. The Congress having refused to cooperate, the League accepted, thus posing an impossible situation. When the viceroy postponed the implementation of this paragraph, Jinnah declared for "direct action" to achieve Pakistan, alleging an Anglo-Congress plot and fixed August 16 as the day of preliminary protest meetings and speeches. In Calcutta this started riots lasting four days and known as the "Great Calcutta Killing." [10] The League government of Bengal was helpless, and British troops had to restore order. No communal riot in British Indian history had ever reached such dimensions. It was in fact the beginning of civil war in an odious and horrible form. This was emphasized by the extension of the massacres over eastern and northern India. In Calcutta the Muslims had been the aggressors; in Behar the Hindus set on the Muslims. In East Bengal and the United Provinces there were further outbreaks. Everywhere the pattern was the same; the contestants were frenzied with passion, atrocious in their actions, and fiendish in their cruelties. These fearful events marked the real end of united British India; henceforward it was merely a question of how long it would take the leaders of all parties to recognize the stark facts, and how great the cost would be before that recognition came. Jinnah must bear the responsibility for Direct Action Day in Calcutta and all that flowed from it.

From this moment, the constitutional discussions were accompanied by the rolling overtones of violence. It needed another explosion in the Panjab early in 1947 to convert the remaining Congress leaders to the necessity of compromise. Only Gandhi stood out in the end, a lone apostle of nonviolence opposing the one course which could stop it. The remaining steps can now be quickly surveyed. On August 24, 1946, the Congress, afraid that it might again miss the political bus, agreed to join the interim government. In October Jinnah, drawn by the magnets of suspicion and fear of isolation, sent in his League lieutenants. The way now seemed clear for the Constituent Assembly, which met in December. But the League members declined to attend, and a further deadlock ensued. In fact the position was farcical, for two parties were now being asked to draw up a constitution on lines which one disliked and the other was determined not to accept. There were fruitless flittings to London until February 20, 1947, when what proved to be decisive action was taken. The Attlee government announced that the British would withdraw not later than June 1948, and replaced Wavell by Lord Mountbatten as its agent for the final phase. Much sympathy was felt for the old soldier who had borne the heat of the day. But he was tired and bemused by political acrobatics; it was time for a new personality. Mountbatten was younger, full of vigor and dynamism, with an aura of royalty, with a forward-looking optimism. He and his wife infused a new spirit into Indo-British relations from the moment of their landing. Most fortunate of all, they captured the imagination and affection of Nehru from the start.

The Mountbattens arrived in March. It was not a moment too soon. The fall of the Khizr ministry in the Panjab had plunged India's martial province into a virtual civil war, and the whole country trembled on the brink of anarchy. Mountbatten soon convinced himself that Pakistan was inevitable and that the pace must be even quicker than London anticipated. The British could now scarcely keep the two parties from each other's throats, let alone impose their will on them. On June 3 Mountbatten announced a plan for partition and British withdrawal on August 14 following. Under these shock tactics the last Congress opponents gave way, and the plan was accepted by the Congress, the League, and the Sikhs. The specters of civil war and anarchy had at last convinced all but Gandhi that partition must be accepted. Jinnah had won the day. Thereafter with unrelenting drive and consummate skill Mountbatten hustled both sides through the final stages.

The main lines of the settlement were as follows. The new state of Pakistan was recognized, with two wings in northwest India and eastern Bengal. The decisions for this purpose were taken by the Provincial assemblies voting, where the divisions were sharp, by community majority areas. In this way the Panjab and Bengal were both divided between India and Pakistan. Sind opted for Pakistan. The fate of the Frontier Province was decided by a plebiscite, as was that of the district of Sylhet in Assam. The detailed boundary in disputed areas was to be drawn by a commission presided over by the British judge Radcliffe. There was to be a division of assets between the states, and government servants could opt for either. Finally, the princely states were released from their allegiance to the Crown and strongly urged to join one or another state. The whole settlement was ratified in legal form by an Act of Parliament which conferred Dominion status on both countries as from August 14, 1947. Mountbatten was the first governor general of independent India, and Jinnah of Pakistan.

Was partition inevitable? In my opinion it was so as soon as Jinnah resorted to direct action in 1946, for the only alternatives then were the frightful excesses of civil commotion and anarchy. But the die was probably cast much earlier, when the Congress failed to realize the new strength of the League in 1945 or to take office under the Cripps proposals of 1942. The Simla talks in 1945 were probably the last chance of getting the League to accept something short of full Pakistan; the Cripps offer of 1942 the last chance for the Congress to smother the League before it became a formidable mass movement. But there is another point to remember before too much regret is felt for the lost unity of India. The federal provisions of the Cripps and later proposals so reduced the powers of the central government that it is very doubtful if the great developments of Nehru's India would have been possible under them. It is probable that the center would have been weak, and political energy spent by the communities in jostling for position instead of reorganizing the country. Industrial development would have waited on party tactics, and five-year plans on political polemics. Only a joint directorate of the two parties could have achieved the kind of development which has actually occurred, and of this there was never any sign. However much partition may be regretted in principle, it was perhaps necessary, on this account, in the larger interests of the country.

CHAPTER XXXIX

Independence and Consolidation

On the night of August 14, the eve of independence, Nehru, with his fine sense of the dramatic, addressed the following words to the tense Constituent Assembly:

"Long years ago we made a tryst with destiny and now the time comes when we shall redeem our pledge, not wholly or in full measure, but very substantially. At the stroke of the midnight hour, when the world sleeps, India will awake to life and freedom. A moment comes, which comes but rarely in history, when we step out from the old to the new, when an age ends and when the soul of a nation, long suppressed,, finds utterance. It is fitting that at this solemn moment we take the pledge of dedication to the service of India and her people and to the still larger cause of humanity."

These were noble words from a dedicated leader. There can have been few nations which set out on their course with finer ideals or more exalted leadership. How far have these words been realized in fact in the years which have supervened? Here the reader must be cautioned and perhaps disappointed. It is too early yet to give any but the most provisional of answers to this question. Our proximity to the tossing waves of events since 1947 is far too close for an appraisal of the deeper currents and the underlying groundswell. One cannot measure Atlantic currents and storm patterns from a rowboat close to the shore. All that can therefore be attempted is a broad and general survey of the next ten years, picking out what seem to be salient points and significant trends, matching the gems of personalities to the settings of events, aware all the time that developments of fundamental importance may have been missed, or the pivotal nature of some events misconstrued. In the same way the answers to all the contemporary questions which crowd into the mind can only be provisional and tentative. Will India go Communist? Will she strengthen or weaken her links with the West? Will traditional Hinduism revive or wither away or form new patterns with Western influences? What will be India's relationship to China and her position in Asia?

Granted the provisional nature of all assessments post-1947, some such survey must be attempted if the historian is not to abandon all attempts to interpret the present in the light of the past and to make of history a portentous compendium of wisdom after the event. It is in this spirit that a survey of the first ten years of independent India, which can be described with a greater measure of truth than that attached to most slogans as "Nehru's India," will be attempted.

At first the omens were auspicious. On August 15 Lord Mountbatten was sworn in as the first governor general of the new India at the invitation of both Congress and the Constituent Assembly. In his speech he hailed Gandhi, Patel, and Nehru, "under whose able guidance, assisted by the colleagues he has selected and with the loyal co-operation of the people, India will now attain a position of strength and influence and take her rightful place in the comity of nations." This may be called a death-bed repentance; it was certainly repentance with a will. Rajendra Prasad, the president of the Constituent Assembly, said in his reply: "While our achievement is in no small measure due to our own sufferings and sacrifices, it is also the result of world forces and events and, last though not least, it is the consummation and fulfilment of the historic tradition and democratic ideals of the British race. . . . The period of domination of Britain over India ends today and our relationship with Britain is henceforward going to rest on a basis of equality, of mutual goodwill and mutual profit." Both Nehru and the Congress leaders and the Mountbattens were acclaimed by happy crowds and almost mobbed with affection. The scenes were more like those of the popular *diwali* night in northern Indian than a great state occasion. The British, who will now (except for stray references) disappear from this narrative, found themselves suddenly popular after the tense relations of the previous few years. They had been fortunate to escape armed clashes with Indian nationalism, thanks, largely, as has already been pointed out, to Gandhi. But more than this is needed in explanation. Perhaps it was the reaction of a friendly people when they discovered that their deep-rooted conviction that the British would somehow or other wriggle out of the commitment to hand over power was mistaken after all. It followed that many hard words had not been altogether needed. The pendulum swung back across the line of correctness to friendship. Whatever the cause, it was a generous reaction and it has continued. At the time of Suez they were severely chided, but it was the scolding of a friend who had gone astray, not the reproach of an enemy.

The very next day the clouds began to gather, and the new India was presented with its first crisis, that of the Panjab massacres. Let us here note the group in whose hands the country now lay. The government at this time was essentially a triumvirate. There was Mahatma Gandhi, the father of the nation, now nearly seventy-eight years of age. He held no office, had disassociated himself from partition, and was far away in Bengal on Independence Day. His cherished dream of a united India had been shattered, in part by his own friends. He was in some ways a disappointed man. Yet his word still carried power with the millions and authority with Nehru, who had only broken away on partition under the compulsion of what he believed to be dire necessity. The second figure was Nehru himself, who represented the idealism and social aspirations of Congress. To the middle class he was the architect of victory, and he had a large following in the masses of north India. Could he sustain his idealism and stand without Gandhi? The third was Vallabhbhai Patel, known affectionately as "Sirdar" or commander for his leadership of the Bardoli peasants in a campaign against land-tax assessment increases. A tough, realistic, and combative Gujarati, he represented the Congress right wing, the industrialist mill owners, financiers, and moneyed men generally. He also controlled the Congress party machine, which he worked in a forthright, down-to-earth manner. He was seventy-two. In the wings, as it were, was Mountbatten, now formally nothing more than a constitutional observer, but able, through his close relations with Nehru and the esteem in which he was generally held, to exercise an important moderating influence.[1] Within a year Gandhi's death and Mountbatten's departure reduced this arrangement to a duumvirate of Nehru and Patel. It was not an easy relationship because of the contrasting personalities of the two men and their dissimilar ideals. Nehru leaned to the left and Gandhian ideals; to Patel nonviolence had never been more than a political tactic, and he inclined to the Hindu right and big business. Patel, with the control of the party machine, could perhaps have ousted Nehru at this time. But he was a patriot and a realist as well as a man of ambition with a contempt for doctrinaires. He was in his seventies and had a heart condition. His position had also been shaken by the repercussions of Gandhi's murder, because he had been a chief obstacle to Gandhi's policy of Muslim reconciliation. Though relations were often difficult between the two, and deteriorated just before the end, Patel seems to have decided to keep the peace in the larger interests of national unity. It must have seemed to him a decision to his own hurt, and it earns our respect. The man of ambition apparently sacrificed himself to the man of dreams. He concentrated on the integration of the Indian states, where he had virtually a free hand. He had completed this task before he died in December 1950.

From that time Nehru has been supreme both within the Congress party and the state at large. As the years passed and Congress showed increasing signs of staleness and strain, it became increasingly clear that Congress had more need for Nehru than Nehru of Congress. Nehru found himself armed, for party purposes, with an infallible weapon, the threat of resignation. The only serious threat from within came in 1951 from the Congress president Purshottamdas Tandon, who had been elected with Patel's help the previous year. In some ways he was Patel's lesser and eccentric successor, representing broadly the orthodox Hindu and socially conservative elements in Congress.[2] A sharp crisis on the eve of the general election hinged on Tandon's attempt to dictate to the prime minister and his retort of resignation from the Working Committee. This proved decisive. Tandon disappeared. Nehru became president of Congress as well as prime minister, holding the office until 1954 and passing it on to his own nominee.[3] Since then he has been, in Michael Brecher's words, not only prime minister but the superpresident of the party, as Gandhi was.

The new government had first to find its feet. It was beset with problems, but it was not prepared for the crises which immediately befell and nearly overwhelmed it. These were the massacres and migrations which occurred on both the eastern and western borders but especially in the Panjab. In that province a suppressed civil war had been raging ever since the fall of the Khizr ministry among Hindus, Sikhs, and Muslims, centering mainly in the Muslim city of Lahore and the Sikh city of Amritsar. Possible trouble was foreseen, and a boundary force of 50,000 Indian troops under General Rees constituted. Pakistan accepted the Radcliffe boundary award, though it was little to her liking. But the people saw only the fact of partition. Above all the militant Sikhs saw their community divided into two, in each new province a minority. It mattered not at all to them that they would be divided by any conceivable Indo-Pakistan frontier. They saw red and brandished their swords. Sikhs (as all acquainted with them know) fight as well and willingly in bad or hopeless causes as in good ones. From the day of independence the Panjab was in turmoil. Broadly speaking, Sikhs and Hindu Jats fell on the Muslims of the east Panjab and Muslims on the Sikhs and Hindus of the west Panjab. Communal fury mounted to frenzy and was fed on reports of what the other side had done elsewhere. Whole villages were exterminated and trainloads of migrants butchered as they huddled in the coaches. The administration was paralyzed, and the Boundary Force was helpless because its sympathies were too sharply divided. Soon the massacres resolved into two lines of migration which piled up into convoys 30,000 to 40,000 strong. As refugees arrived in Delhi at the end of August, the same frenzy overtook the capital. For some days the very existence of the government was in question. Restoration of order in Delhi was the turning of the tide; control of the Panjab was recovered and the great migration finally reduced to order. By the end of the year the main movements were over, leaving each state with a formidable problem of rehabilitation. By mid-1948 it is estimated that five and one-half million refugees had been moved *each way* between West Pakistan and the western border of India, with another million and one-quarter moving from East Pakistan into West Bengal. Later, 400,000 Hindus left Sind in Pakistan for India. The exact number of casualties is unknown, but the dead are thought to have approached the million mark. The horrors of the episode and the size of the migrations embittered the relations of the two countries and left a deep scar on the consciousness of both.

It is best not to attempt to assign responsibility for the actual outbreak, for the evidence is too confused and the shades of guilt too fine. The element of conspiracy was not absent, but that of spontaneity was much larger. The Boundary Commission's report was the flashpoint of an explosion for whose ingredients every party must take its share of responsibility. We may ask, however, why the danger was not more clearly foreseen and why more effective shock absorbers, as it were, were not provided in advance. It seems certain in the light of hindsight that an outbreak of violence was inevitable; could the holocaust that followed have been prevented? The key to this problem lies in the Boundary Force. If Lord Mountbatten had realized more clearly the do-or-die nature of the Sikhs, its 50,000 men might have been augmented. But the trouble with the force was that it was too emotionally committed to perform its functions. A larger force might have meant a greater fiasco. A force composed exclusively of South Indians (the Madras regiment was most effective in Delhi) and Gurkhas might have been too small for the immense task. The only other alternative was the use of British troops. Instead of being withdrawn to the ports for shipment to Britain, they could have been concentrated in the boundary area and withdrawn via Karachi and Bombay after the initial tension had eased. They had been popular in relieving the Bengal famine, and they had quelled the Calcutta killings after Direct Action Day. They were known to be impartial (the *sine qua non* of dealing with civil disturbances) if only because they did not clearly know the difference between two sets of rioters. But they were not used, partly on account of the general optimism for which all parties must take responsibility, and partly for reasons of national prestige on the part of the two new countries. But prestige alone cannot excuse the loss of nearly a million lives. The question remains, should not the British government have insisted on policing the boundary for six months after partition on the strength of its knowledge of conditions and in the name of humanity? The question cannot be answered yet. But this and related ones must continue to be asked, for it can never be admitted that the massacres were a small thing nor can any of those concerned be allowed to shuffle off the responsibility into the airy realm of abstractions.[4]

Whatever may be said about the cause of the emergency, there is no doubt that the government of India was resilient and resourceful in dealing with it. It emerged stronger from the ordeal, but it had still to deal with the troubled aftermath. There was the great refugee tide, which had surged as far as Delhi, carrying bitterness and anti-Muslim feeling with it. The refugees filled the great enclosures of the old historic monuments. They crowded the streets and pavements. They took over many mosques in the old city. No one at first had the means or the will to eject them. Anti-Muslim feeling ran high, and the remaining Muslim minority was in grave danger. This was Gandhi's noblest hour. He came up from the troubled areas of Bengal, where he was described by Mountbatten as more valuable alone than the whole boundary force in the Panjab, and spent the last weeks of his life in persuading, soothing, exhorting, and commanding in the cause of communal harmony. Some inner force seemed to drive him on. He clashed sharply with Patel and wrestled with him on the very afternoon of his murder. By moral suasion and by a fast he secured the evacuation of the mosques and the payment of pledged cash balances to Pakistan.[5] Just after 5 P.M. on January 30, while walking toward his daily prayer meeting, he was shot by a Hindu fanatic. The manner and circumstances of his death transformed the situation. The Mahatma was even more powerful in death than in life. The policy of revenge was abandoned. The Hindu extremists were discredited. A shadow fell over the reputation of the Sirdar. The danger of bitterness boiling over into anti-Muslim pogroms was averted.

The next problem which faced the new government was that of the Indian princes. Since 1818 the British had claimed paramount power over all of them and had repressed even the nizam of Hyderabad's claim to independent status. Before the Mutiny they were generally regarded as archaic survivals, chiefly useful as saving administrative expense. At one time, as we have noted, it was thought they would all be eventually absorbed. After the Mutiny they were cherished as "breakwaters in the storm." They were encouraged to develop as "enlightened despots" by such means as Western education, social patronage, and modern administrative training. Some actually did so,[6] but many lagged behind. The new policy of Indian self-government after World War I dealt the princely order a blow from which it never recovered. The princes feared the Congress as a democratic threat to their power and existence more than the British as overlords. They were unwilling to turn themselves into constitutional sovereigns as the British wished, and the British were unwilling to compel them. Federation seemed to open the way for their integration in a united India, but at the last moment they drew back. They thus alienated both the Congress (by clinging to despotism) and the British (by withdrawing from federation). Thus after the war they found themselves isolated, and in 1947 face to face with the triumphant Congress.

The princes were suspicious of each other as well as of Congress, and proved themselves, after twenty-five years of effort, quite incapable of united action. But the magnitude of the problem of their integration in the new India should not be underestimated. They numbered more than 500,[7] and the mere problem of dealing with so many authorities at once was considerable. They covered one-quarter of the area of British India, scattered about as the result of historical accident rather than geographic convenience. Their people numbered more than one-fifth of the total population of undivided India. Although the average population of a state was only about 150,000, there were a number which were large enough to form focal points of power in a divided India. One hundred and nine states were important enough to have individual representation in the British-sponsored Chamber of Princes set up in 1921. Many of these were small, but there were twenty or thirty of significance. The largest was Hyderabad, covering 32,000 square miles in South India and having over sixteen million inhabitants. Among other states of substance may be mentioned Jammu and Kashmir in the north, Jaipur and Jodhpur in Rajasthan, Gwalior, Indore, and Baroda in west and central India, Mysore and Travancore in the south. Hyderabad itself was a dynastic museum piece, being a fragment of the Mughal empire whose governors had made themselves hereditary in the eighteenth century and had come to terms with the British before they had been overthrown by other Indian powers. Others were dynastic creations like Indore and Gwalior whose founders had been Maratha generals. Others, like the Rajput states, represented feudal traditions and might have some real hold on at any rate a proportion of their people. No one really knew, in the case of the larger states, where tradition stopped short and real popular support began. It was therefore a serious matter for the new India to be faced with this array of independent critics at the outset of its career.

The British action on withdrawal was to release all the princes from allegiance to the Crown and to recommend that they join one or another of the two emergent states, due regard being paid to the principle of physical propinquity. It was considered that it would be a breach of treaty obligations to hand them over directly to the two new countries, since the British had not only recognized their existence but guaranteed it in the documents handed to them after the Mutiny. It was thought that pressure and a dawning apprehension of the obvious would virtually solve the problem. In India the task of integration was handed to Sirdar Vallabhbhai Patel, who had contacts and sympathetic relations with some of them. Patel liked tradition and the principle of authority; in the national struggle, he found them useful as areas free from direct British control. But he was above all a realist, who was determined to allow nothing to stand in the way of national unity or to weaken the new central government. There followed one of the most efficient integrating movements of modern times. At times it was ruthless, but the whole process was made palatable and almost agreeable by the suave skill of the States Department secretary, V. P. Menon. He was the velvet glove on the mailed fist. He could explain the pleasures of extinction so convincingly that in the end, apart from Kashmir, only the state of Hyderabad presented a real problem. Broadly speaking, the plan was to attach states to existing provinces, now called states, or to join several together to form new state units. These new units were given democratic patterns of government, former rulers being allowed to linger on as constitutional heads under the title of *Rajpramukh*.[8] Only Hyderabad, Mysore, Travancore (with Cochin), and Kashmir retained their former identity. The personal problem was solved by giving the former princes personal privileges and guaranteed pensions free of income tax. Since for generations most of them had thought more about these matters than the business of governing, they showed a surprising degree of acquiescence. Not the least surprising thing about the princes' tenure of power was their manner of quitting it. The descendants of hardy adventurers from the north or battle-scarred Rajput warriors meekly effaced themselves for a handful of silver and a few baubles. They had, in fact, no support apart from their nobles. The middle class and the people at large were indifferent; the new national sentiment had passed them by.

The difficult cases were Kashmir, Hyderabad, and Junagadh. Kashmir we shall refer to in dealing with relations with Pakistan. Junagadh was a small state with 670,000 inhabitants on the coast of Kathiawar, the majority of whose people were Hindu but whose prince was a Muslim. It was entirely surrounded by Indian territory. After some hesitation the prince acceded to Pakistan. After a further interval India occupied the state and held a plebiscite which declared for union. This was a unilateral act for which there would seem to be no justification in international law. On the other hand there is no reason to doubt the genuineness of the popular verdict. The case was so small and the non-juridical considerations so strong that even Pakistan contented itself with indignant protests. A slight embarrassment came to India later in the parallel case of Kashmir (the ruler being of differing community from the majority of the people) when she persistently refused to implement proposals for administering the very medicine already meted out to Junagadh. Hyderabad was a different matter. The Nizam realized that he could not stand aloof from India, but wished to secure recognition of the independent status he had always claimed from the British. India urged that she was a single entity and the new government the natural successor of the British. The size of the country and its vital position astride the north-south routes made the position critical. But Hyderabad's position as a prospective independent power was hopeless because it was completely surrounded by Indian territory and four-fifths of its inhabitants were Hindu. After a preliminary skirmish there was a standstill agreement for a year. Both sides proceeded to put pressure on each other, the Congress by organizing subversive activities from Madras, the Muslims by organizing a body of semimilitary fanatics called Razakars. The Communists took advantage of the situation to get control of two districts. Before the standstill year was up the negotiations broke down and Indian troops marched in "to restore order." The move was officially described as "a police action," but the fact remained that one state authority was replaced by another state authority. The legal aspects of the question will provide matter for discussion for many years, but need not detain us here. It may be summarily remarked that India was juridically wrong, practically impatient, but politically right. Hyderabad had to be in some way linked with India, though Patel's way may not have been the best one. Throughout, the Nizam cut a pitiable figure whose vacillations were the principal cause of his own misfortunes. Morally it is difficult to have strong feelings. The government was a minority one, and any virtues it possessed were mainly the result of pressure and interference from outside. The Nizam disappeared into his palace unlamented and unrespected.

The next task of the government was the drafting of a constitution. India took over the Government of India Act of 1935 with the new powers conferred by the Independence Act of 1947. She had a Constituent Assembly in being, elected by the old provincial legislatures. This was something to go on with, but clearly no time could be lost in drawing up a constitution in spite of the many preoccupations of the new government. The work was carried out by the existing Constituent Assembly, in which the Congress had an overwhelming majority. It must on the whole be pronounced a signal success. The smoothness of the process owed much to Nehru's willingness to listen to others beside congressmen and give weight to all constructive suggestions. The Act of 1935 provided a convenient framework, long passages from it being in fact incorporated in the new document. The principal draftsman of that Act, Sir Maurice Gwyer, now vice-chancellor of Delhi University, was active in discussions behind the scenes. In general the British pattern of parliamentary democracy was followed, whose essence is the collective responsibility of ministers to a popularly elected legislature. But there was no mere imitation. The constitution as it now stands is an original construction working on materials mainly of Western provenance. Besides the British concept of parliamentary government, the idea of fundamental rights, with which the constitution is prefaced, was borrowed from the United States. So were certain presidential powers, though the president in general is more a constitutional sovereign than a chief executive. The Federal Supreme Court, to safeguard the constitution, is also an American loan, although this had already been made by the British in 1935. From Eire came the idea of constitutional directives or goals of endeavor, and from Canada ideas about federation.

Regarding the federal structure it may be noted that a strong center was provided. The powers solely lodged with the center were more extensive than those proposed by the Cabinet Mission of 1946. They included sole control of defense, foreign affairs, railways, ports, and currency. The states' need of financial grants from the center provided an important lever for influence. In addition to separate lists of legislative powers, there was a concurrent list in which the center could override the states and a reservation of residuary powers to the center. Finally, the president had extensive powers of intervention in certain conditions and could take over the whole state administration in case of emergency. This has in fact been done more than once. [9] It is this strong center, which could not have been achieved without the creation of Pakistan, which has made the rapid progress of India since 1947 possible. In the provinces the same pattern of parliamentary government, which had already been working to an extent for twenty-five years, was followed. The constitution was rounded off by universal adult suffrage, which gave to India, with one hundred and seventy-five million voters, the largest electorate in the world, of whom the majority were illiterate. The constitution-makers could not be said to lack either courage or vision. The central legislature has two houses, the Lok Sabha (Council of the People), representing the people as a whole and elected by universal suffrage, and the Rajya Sabha (Council of the States), indirectly elected and representing the States of the Union.

Parliamentary responsible government and universal adult suffrage were thus two key features of the new constitution. Another was the use of the federal principle, not so much to weaken the central authority or preserve local liberties as to integrate the old with the new India. Only time can show whether Indian federalism will turn out to be a generous form of local government or the crack into which the wedge of separatism can enter to cause dissolution. Further features are the independence of the law courts and their role as the guardians of the constitution. So far they have been both fearless and effective in discharging this duty, and their prestige stands high. The procedure for amending the constitution is an interesting compromise between the British idea of a sovereign parliament which can do anything, and the idea of special constitutional law which can only be changed by a special and often difficult process. In India there is an elaborate written constitution, but it can be changed by a comparatively simple procedure.[10] Finally we may note the strongly Western tinge of the constitution. Its fundamental rights of the citizen, its directives of policy, its political machinery are all of Western provenance, and they assume Western political and ethical principles. The only Indian institution mentioned with approval is the *panchayat* or village committee; on the other hand "untouchability" is abolished by Article 17, and caste distinctions are ignored (Articles 15 [2] and 16 [2]). It is difficult to realize that these provisions were drawn up in a land where the Laws of Manu were composed and still have some measure of observance.

With independence achieved and the attendant convulsions of partition survived, with the refugees in the main resettled and life restored to normal, with the princely states integrated and a strong central government and democratic constitution established, the new India had passed the first critical milestone in her career. Jawaharlal Nehru was now firmly in the saddle. Whither would he lead India?

CHAPTER XL

Nehru's India

Nehru

The sixth decade of the twentieth century in India can properly be described as the period of Nehru's India. In 1950 Patel, his last rival for or cosharer in power, died. Henceforward his prestige and personal ascendancy were such that he dominated the whole Indian scene. Whatever the final judgment on him may be, his memory will linger in the popular mind like that of Akbar or Aurangzeb. He came to be looked up to as the fount of all authority, the impulse of all action, and the source of all inspiration within the country. He was tireless in speech and ubiquitous in movement. Like Queen Elizabeth I on her travels from manor to manor, Nehru became a living figure to the people. While she had her thousands of viewers, he, with the help of the automobile, the plane, and the radio, had his millions. He was the visible *mah-bap*—"father-mother"—of the Indian nation.

Pandit Jawaharlal Nehru was born at Allahabad, where the Jumna joins the sacred Ganges, in November 1889. His family were Kashmiri Brahmins, who are considered the most purely Aryan of the whole Brahminical stock.[1] An ancestor, who was a Persian poet in Kashmir in the early eighteenth century, migrated to the court of Farrukhsiyar. He was given a grant of land on a canal bank, whence his family (whose subcaste name was Kaul) adopted the surname of Nehru.[2] Members of the family held office under the Mughals and the British after them. His father Motilal was an interesting case of the metamorphosis of the old official family into the new middle class. He took up the new legal profession which grew up around the British law courts. He achieved notable success and became a leading advocate in the Allahabad high court. Like many of his time, he adopted the Western externals of life along with Western legal and political notions while maintaining Hindu tradition within his home. There his wife remained secluded, but both his son and daughter received a modern education.

The young Nehru went to Harrow School and then to Trinity College, Cambridge. He was called to the bar and returned to India before World War I, apparently a Westernized, sophisticated, and not very effective youth. His father's towering personality overshadowed him. It was World War I and its aftermath which transformed him. Official heavy-handedness after the war stung his sensitive nature; Gandhi's teaching and concern for the poor aroused his idealism. The nonco-operation movement turned him to the *kisans* or peasants; moving among the poverty-stricken masses aroused his latent passion for social justice. Nehru's socialism came from this source rather than from Russia. The peasant masses acted as the positive pole to his negative; the spark of inspiration ran between to give him a new confidence. The fastidious Nehru drew continued inspiration from mass contacts which he never received from the classes. This fact is one of the secrets of his hold over the people at large, which only fell short of that of Gandhi. His magic was wholly different from Gandhi's, but it was magic neverthe-less.

In the twenties Nehru traveled extensively in Europe, including a visit to Russia. It was during this time (while his father led the Swaraj party) that he acquired his interest in and knowledge of international affairs. His views were generally left-wing, but in Russia his impression of the Soviet experiment was counterbalanced by shock at the consequences of authoritarian measures. He returned to India ardent and eager, a na-tionalist, a socialist, insistent on action, and impatient with the senior leadership, but out of love with communism. At the Madras session of Congress (December 1927) he moved a resolution declaring the goal of Congress to be "complete national independence." From this mo-ment he became a leader of the left and the darling of the younger gen-eration. His only rival was the equally youthful and fiery Subhas Chandra Bose. It was at this time that Nehru's future was settled by the perspicacity of the Mahatma. He saw in him a man who could keep the younger generation within Congress and wean it from violence. He knew that Jawaharlal not only shared its impatience, like Bose, but would also in the last resort listen to the counsels of his elders. In two of his biggest battles Gandhi forced Nehru into the Congress presidency over the head of Patel in 1929, and ten years later steam-rollered Subhas Bose out of the Congress altogether. During the years down to 1945 Nehru's impatience again and again led him into conflict with his mentor, but always in the end he fell into line. During the war he graduated from the status of the champion of youth and the Mahatma's favorite son to that of the inner ring of leadership and the recognized heir-apparent. By 1946 there was no question that he, and no other, would be the Congress choice for the vice-presidency of the Executive Council, and the next year India's first prime minister.

When Nehru took over power there was no doubt of his brilliance, his idealism, or his dedication. But there were doubts, in the minds of many who had watched his career, as to his staying power, his ability to impose his will on others and manage his colleagues and the party machine. Might he not prove too mercurial to last and too high-minded to deal with party managers? There was a streak of vacillation and dependence in his character, which suggested that he might prove to be one of those second-in-commands who falter when they come to the supreme position. Was he one of those talkers like Kerensky who mistakes volubility for action? In early life he had leaned on his father; then it was the Mahatma right up to his dying day. Convictions seemed often to have been sacrificed for unity, and personal loyalty viewed as a comfortable way of escape from political dilemmas. In fact these questionings overlooked another quality of Nehru's which proved of fundamental importance. It was a strain of realism beneath his idealism. What was thought to be undue dependence on the Mahatma's will became a calculated deference in the interests of Congress unity. This was conspicuous in 1942. The proof of this distinction between deference and dependence is to be found in Nehru's disregard of Gandhi's views in the vital decision of accepting partition. The believers in his alleged "innocence" failed to notice the uncanny and perhaps unconscious skill with which he got the better of Bose in the race for the left-wing lead and managed to retain his popularity with the left while co-operating with the senior rightist leadership. His dealings as prime minister with Patel and Tandon, which surprised many at the time, were only further examples of this quality. After all, for all his professed secularism, he still had the hereditary skill of the Brahmin.

With the reasons for Nehru's ascendancy explained, its consequences have now to be noted. His hold on the country was so great that, apart from the Communists, the most effective opposition came from covert obstruction within the party. The non-Congress groups were powerless; no congressman after the disappearance of Kripalani and the fall of Tandon dared openly to oppose his policies. Nehru's personal views therefore became of national importance and were reflected in Indian policy at every turn. His views reflected his complex personality. First, he was a Westerner by temperament and taste as well as by education. Next, he was an ardent nationalist, a creed into which he poured the emotional devotion of a personal religion. In keeping with these views, he was a convinced democrat who was prepared to go further in this direction than many of his colleagues. Further than this, he was a socialist; he toyed with but never adopted Marxism. For him personal dignity and individual freedom were more important than the mass, persuasion more important than compulsion. He saw Indian development as a gigantic experiment in national regeneration on the democratic as opposed to the authoritarian plan. All these views were derived from the West, and raise the question of his attitude toward Indian tradition. Here he was uncompromisingly secularist. He gloried in the name of Indian but would not accept the title of Hindu. He was against priest-craft of all kinds and Brahmin dominance in particular. He regarded the Brahminical supremacy as a major cause of Indian decline and was as stern a critic of untouchability as Gandhi himself. The drive toward equal rights for men and women, toward social justice and the leveling of caste since partition had its source in Nehru himself.

In international affairs Nehru enjoyed even more freedom than at home. There was an equal absence of open criticism (until the Hungarian crisis of 1956) and less concealed opposition. There were fewer vested interests involved, and in the eyes of all he was the man who knew. Here a dominant motive was anticolonialism, with a natural bias toward the Western powers, the wrecks of whose empires still littered Asia in 1947. This sensitivity made him react more vigorously to what he considered to be British backsliding at Suez than to Russian behavior in Hungary. It explains his suspicions of the United States (as linked with the colonialist West) and slowness to see the same force at work in China. Apart from this basic outlook Nehru was in principle a good internationalist, and this was reflected by the part played by India at U.N.O. His policy of neutralism was also a personal one, but it arose more from calculation than principle or feeling.

Rarely has so complex a personality been permitted so great a latitude of action on the stages of national and world affairs. An aristocrat to his fingertips and a Westerner by taste and conviction, he was the champion of Eastern democracy. It is no wonder that inconsistencies have been observed and misunderstandings have occurred. But in one thing he did not succeed—in working on a level with his colleagues. He was a dictator in spite of himself. He was his own foreign minister not because India lacked talent, but because he lacked confidence

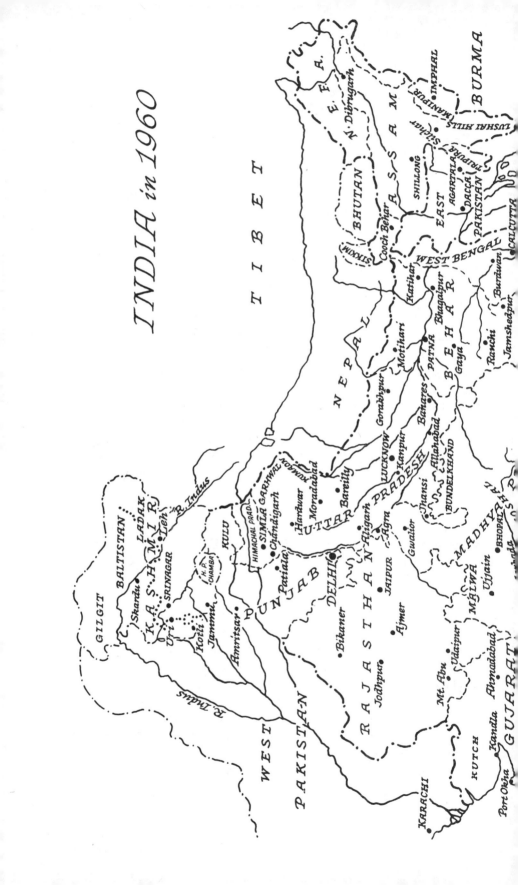

INDIA in 1960

ARABIAN SEA

BAY OF BENGAL

Scale of Miles

0   100   200   300   400

ANDAMAN ISLANDS

DAMAN

BOMBAY
Poona

MAHARASHTRA

Aurangabad
MARATHWADA

Adilabad

Warangal

HYDERABAD

Rajahmundry

TELINGANA

Guntur

Vizianagram
Vizagapatam

BHUBANESWAR

Puri

ORISSA

ANDHRA PRADESH

Nellore

MADRAS

Ratnagiri

(GOA)

Chitaldrug

Raichur

MYSORE

Bangalore

Salem

Tanjore

Madura

Mangalore

Calicut

Cochin

KERALA

TRIVANDRUM

Tuticorin

CEYLON

in others. His equals in the government died or retired; his juniors remained lieutenants or agents. It seemed that Nehru could do everything except work with an equal or train a successor.

Internal Policy

How did Nehru maintain himself in power, so that he became not only a Nestor among prime ministers but a being apart in India itself? That white-clad figure with the white Gandhi cotton cap tilted at an angle and the silver-topped cane twirling in his fingers could freeze the highest official with a word or a glance or charm audiences of half a million at will. He had, of course, the double asset of being the only surviving founding father of the republic and of being the favored son of Mahatma Gandhi. With the Indian capacity for veneration, this put him on the threshold of the gods already. As he grew older, he acquired the prestige which India attaches to age. But something more is required to account for this apparently effortless supremacy. Men in India as elsewhere enjoy power, and many would not willingly have remained in the shadows for so long. The Nehru supremacy was not in fact so effortless as it appeared to the outside world, and it is worth trying to analyze some of its constituents.

Nehru first had to deal with his own party, in which, in spite of its nationalist and democratic principles, the advocates of social reaction and free-for-all capitalism have always been strong. Nationalism was a political umbrella which sheltered all kinds of views and interests during the struggle for freedom. After independence these elements found a leader in Patel and later in Tandon. We have already seen how Nehru dealt with these two. In effect he used his prestige as a national hero to smother conservative sentiment and set the general desire to see India stand well in the world against the sectional desire to revert to old ways in the social and economic spheres. Nehru, it was felt, was the man who could satisfy the general craving for equal recognition in the larger world and therefore Nehru it must be. The right wing in Indian public life was overshadowed but not extinguished. The emergence of the Swatantra party, led by the veteran Rajagopalachari, and of the Jan Sangh party, were signs of its continued existence. The opposition from the right being thus accounted for, there remains to be considered that from the left. Prakash Narayan, the rather nebulous hope of many forward-looking people, left the Congress because it was not socialist enough. So did the astringent though dedicated Acharya Kripalani. The Praja Socialist party hoped to become the regular opposition and heir apparent to Nerhu's policies. But it was never able to overcome Nehru's *mystique* as national hero and his vehement assertions that he was a socialist. If you want to go socialist, argued many, why not support Nehru, who may produce *some* of the goods, while others have no power to produce anything? So at the first general election they found themselves outdistanced by the Communists.

The Communists became the effective opposition not only because they were well organized and financed, but because they were the only group that had an effective alternative policy to that of Nehru. They stood for attacking the problem of poverty by the quick and drastic method of dictatorship as opposed to the slow methods of democracy; they stood for alignment with the East rather than the West. Their great strength was the vast sea of India's poverty; their weakness their unpopular foreign associations and their taint of irreligion. They were overthrown in Kerala with the help of religious interests. They gained credit while the communist reorganization of China seemed to be proceeding both smoothly and quickly. But they lost more ground than they had gained on the Chinese seizure of Tibet. Here again religious sentiment played its part. Many who would not lift a finger to aid the Tibetans were shocked when the Dalai Lama fled to India.

We have said that Nehru became something of a dictator in spite of himself. Something of the same kind happened to the parliamentary system. It was intended to be worked by a two-party system, alternating in power; it became something like the durbar hall of the reigning Mughal. Nehru himself remained a democrat and observed meticulously parliamentary forms. No one was more ready to resign than he, if only the Lok Sabha would pass a vote of no confidence. He allowed free speech and treated the opposition with respect. But his overwhelming ascendancy within Congress, the great majority of Congress in Parliament, and the divided nature of the opposition groups made the whole parliamentary routine unreal. His very magnanimity in including non-congressmen in the administration served to underline the fact. The tradition of Indian government has not been mere autocracy, but authority taking the advice of notables and people through public and private assemblies. So it was with Nehru. Parliament may be likened to the public audiences of the Mughal emperors, attended both by the public and high officers, where petitions were presented, ambassadors received, and public business transacted. The cabinet chamber corresponded to the Hall of Private Audience where the leading officers were consulted on policy. The special confidants of the prime minister, like Krishna Menon, may be likened to the *Lal Purdaris* or those who had the privilege of passing the red curtain to the private imperial quarters. Nehru listened to opinions expressed in Parliament and discussed policy with his colleagues but took all major decisions himself. The governmental machine visibly slowed down when he was absent from Delhi. From 1947 to 1960 the only serious parliamentary opposition on internal matters came from orthodox Congress quarters in the matter of social legislation. There was no serious criticism of foreign policy until the Hungarian revolt of 1956.

Nehru was a man in a hurry. He wanted to create a modern and prosperous India in his own lifetime. He was faced with the two giants of poverty and increasing population. Under the British, the population increased from about one hundred and thirty to four hundred millions between 1800 and 1947. From the ending of the influenza epidemic about 1920, it has been increasing at the rate of between three and five millions a year. In that time the British fed the extra mouths, ended starvation by famine, created a prosperous middle class, but left the major problem untouched. The new government had therefore to face the immense task of both keeping pace with the growing population and raising the standard of living. Though Nehru himself was conscious of the problem, little was done about population control, and we can therefore concentrate on the standard of living. A first step was the nature of the economy to be planned. Nehru soon realized that he could not introduce socialism at a stroke without risking initial disaster. A compromise was reached by which the national economy was divided into public and private sectors. Broadly speaking, established industries were left in the private sector, while public utilities, great new projects like the three steel plants, irrigation and power plans, were in the public one. The next step, taken in 1950, was to set up a Planning Commission. It was from this moment that Indian planning may be said to have become a coherent whole. With its help the government decided that the development of industry was the key to the raising of the standard of living and devised three successive five-year plans. The first plan was aided by the Colombo plan of 1950, a co-operative Commonwealth plan to help development in Commonwealth countries. The first five-year plan, launched in 1951, placed special emphasis on agricultural production in order to reduce India's dependence on foreign supplies. This part of the program was an outstanding success, production increasing about 25 per cent. Along with this went great power and irrigation projects such as the Damodar Valley scheme and the Hirakud dam project. Three new steel plants, sponsored respectively by the United States, Britain, and Russia, were started, while the private sector made a substantial if less spectacular contribution. It was claimed that the national income rose 18 per cent as a result. Encouraged by this success and perhaps spurred on by the sight of Chinese activity, a second and far more ambitious five-year plan was launched in 1956. Largely inspired by Professor Mahalanobis, it hoped to achieve large-scale industrialization and by this means to increase employment, to reduce inequalities of wealth, and to increase the national income by 25 per cent. The cost was to be nearly twice that of the first plan, some twelve billion dollars in the public and six billion dollars in the private sector. This involved the raising of six billion dollars outside the country, and for a time India ran into foreign exchange difficulties. Thanks to outside help, not least from the United States, India was able largely to overcome the added difficulties of unfavorable seasons and an adverse turn in the terms of trade. The plan was scheduled for completion by 1961, with some trimming and reduction of targets, and the third five-year plan was launched on a still more ambitious scale. It was hoped to increase the national income by 5 per cent a year, to make India self-sufficing in the matter of food, to expand industry further, and in particular to establish a machine-tool industry which could make India industrially self-sufficient in ten years time. The total investment was about twenty-three and one-half billion dollars, of which more than seven billion dollars was needed in foreign exchange.

This was Nehru's bid to solve the problem of Indian poverty. He made an equally strenuous though far less publicized effort to solve the social problem. Untouchability was declared to be abolished by the Constitution (Section 17) and caste restrictions to have no legal force. There was no vocal opposition on these points, though much continuing covert obstruction. But the great fabric of Hindu law remained, with its semisacred sanction, its subjection of women, and its stark contradiction of the modern rights of man. Nehru hoped to pass the Hindu Code Bill, largely drafted by his "untouchable" law minister, Dr. Ambedkar, in a single session after the passing of the constitution in 1949. But orthodox elements held up progress to such an extent that the two vital laws dealing with Hindu marriage and Hindu succession were not passed until 1955 and 1956. The whole process is not yet complete. The most important measures have been the Hindu Succession Act (1956) and the Hindu Marriage Act (1955). The former in general gives equal rights to men and women (including widows) in the matter of inheritance and the holding of property. In both these spheres women's rights were previously severely limited. The Hindu Marriage Act by making bigamy and polygamy criminal offenses provides a legal basis for monogamy— for the general practice in recent years has been by no means universally so, and in the past had large exceptions. Divorce was introduced into Hindu law for the first time, with provision for alimony and maintenance. The Hindu Adoption and Maintenance Act has also provided for maintenance of widows and separated wives. The influence of orthodoxy can be seen here in the provision (Section 25) that the dependent loses the claim to maintenance on conversion to another religion. The revision of the Hindu Code is even yet not complete. Who can say how it will affect the texture of Hindu society in time? It may turn out to have been Nehru's most important achievement. But for the present all that can be said is that it seems to have provided, in some measure at least, the legal basis in personal law for that active participation in public life which public opinion and advancing education had already begun to give the women of India.

The prime minister was forced to deal with another problem about which he cared less and was certainly less successful. It was the problem of language, which linked itself with that of states reorganization. The Congress originally articulated itself in a number of linguistic regions, whereas the British-Indian provinces were units built up for reasons of political circumstance and administrative convenience. From 1920 the Congress included a provincial reorganization on a linguistic basis in its declared policy. The new government was therefore faced with a commitment on the subject, and in addition Hindi was adopted as the national language alongside English. Nehru was not enthusiastic for either proposal. His own family linguistic background was that of Urdu or Hindustani, and he suspected the orthodox pundits of wanting to twist Hindi (akin to Sanskrit) to their purposes. He was also aware of its unpopularity in the Dravidian south. He had come to be a firm believer in a strong central government as necessary for rapid development; he feared that linguistic provinces, by providing regional governments with a strong emotional backing, might enable them to obstruct and oppose the center and in time withdraw talent from the center to the constituent states. The fate of the Mughal empire, with which his family had a long connection (memories are long in India), was not far from his thoughts.

In fact the two issues affected each other. The drive to make Hindi the national language offended the non-Hindi speaking areas, and opposition to it tended to strengthen the demand for local units of administration where a local language could be used for state business. If you will force Hindi on us for national purposes, ran the argument, then you should let us use our own language in our own state. It is significant that the first big movement for a linguistic state came from a Dravidian

language region (Andhra). The first stage in the process of reorganization was the integration of the Indian princely states with the rest of India. This, the work of Sardar Patel, was virtually completed by the "police action" against Hyderabad in 1948. From this time the government,
absorbed in reconstruction and development, wished to delay further
action, but its hand was forced by a number of pressure groups which
each thought redistribution might favor its interests. It was popular sentiment which proved decisive. In 1952 there was an agitation for an
Andhra state, which led to the death by hunger strike of Shri Potti Srir-
amulu. This Gandhian tactic prevailed with Nehru, and the Telugu-
speaking state of Andhra was taken from Madras and established on
October 1, 1953. The breach once made in the administrative dam, the
flood could not be stopped. In December 1953 a States Reorganization
Commission was set up, with Sardar K. M. Panikkar as its most active
member. It reported in 1955, and there followed a radical reorganization
in the following year. The south was divided into four states on linguistic
principles. Hyderabad disappeared. Uttar Pradesh remained one state,
in spite of its size, on the same principle. The only large exception was
the union of Gujaratis and Marathas in Bombay state. But this did not
last. Public feeling was too strong and Mr. Nehru not adroit enough.
Much agitation and some violence ended in division into Marathi-speak-
ing Maharashtra (with Bombay), and Gujarati-speaking Gujarat. It remains to be seen whether this development, though according with Congress ideology, may not in the long run undermine the authority of the
central government. As a postscript it may be added that the Sikhs were
given their long-desired Sikh *subah* of the Punjab in November 1966 by
Nehru's daughter. The Hindus retained the eastern half of the old state
under the name of Haryana.

Foreign Affairs

In foreign affairs Nehru had practically a free hand for many years.
The general desire was that India should play a full part in world affairs
and gain recognition on equal terms with the Western powers, including
Russia. This desire for satisfaction to the Indian sense of self-respect,
went with a large measure of ignorance of world affairs themselves.
Nehru had been the party's expert on international affairs since the thirties, when everyone else had been absorbed in the struggle for freedom.
The party's mentor now became its foreign director. The country was
content for him to shape policy as he would until ripening knowledge
began to breed real feeling.

The first issue was India's relationship with the British Commonwealth. Nehru here had to deal not so much with a residue of anti-British bitterness (although it existed) as with the feeling that the connection with the British monarchy implied some sort of continued subordination and that this was incompatible with Indian national dignity. On the other hand was the desire to maintain the commercial and cultural links with Britain, whose strength was realized more fully now that the political issue had been removed. For the final burial of this issue credit was shared between Lord and Lady Mountbatten, Nehru himself, who was on terms of close friendship with them, and the London Labor cabinet of Clement Attlee, who suffered from no backward glances at the past. The problem was therefore one of feeling rather than of interest; how to make the people of India feel free as well as be free. The solution was the proclamation of a republic on January 26, 1950, while retaining membership in the Commonwealth. In this way Nehru met the demands of sentiment and also began a new phase in the evolution of the Commonwealth. The visit of the Queen to India in 1961 at Indian invitation may be said to have set the seal on this development.

India's nearest neighbor is Pakistan. Their relationships are so intimate and particular that they require treatment outside the range of foreign policy in general. From the outset, relations were bedeviled by the Panjab massacres and the Panjab and East Pakistan migrations, coming on top of the mutual recriminations and suspicions of the previous few years. Then, in October 1947, came the tribal incursion into Kashmir and its accession to India. Fighting flared up for a time in 1948, to be followed by a truce arranged by the United Nations. During the tension canal water was denied to Pakistan for about three weeks from head works under Indian control. From that time relations have never been normal. There have been three principal issues between India and Pakistan: Kashmir itself, the disposal of refugee properties, and the control of canal waters. The property question arose from the migrations, and the settlement depended upon feeling on the other two issues. The Kashmir issue can be oversimplified by saying that while Pakistan invoked the principle of self-determination, India stood on the legal ground of the ruler's accession to India and insisted that the tribal incursion was an act of Pakistani aggression. United Nations' attempts at mediation broke down upon Indian failure to agree to the terms for the plebiscite which she had accepted in principle. There the position still stands, and we are left asking the reason for the Indian attitude, maintained as it has been at great cost in prestige, resources, and freedom of diplomatic maneuver. The fact of Nehru's Kashmiri descent may be dismissed as a serious factor in his stand. The strategical argument perhaps carried more weight but was not decisive. A stronger argument advanced was that the cession of Kashmir under plebiscite might set off a Hindu reaction in India which might lead to the genocide of the remaining fifty million Indian Muslims. But perhaps the decisive consideration in Nehru's mind was the thought that the voluntary association of a Muslim country with India was a decisive justification for his cherished ideal of an Indian secular state. If Kashmir were given up, the Hindu reaction in India might grow to the point where it could no longer be resisted.

Relations deteriorated when Pakistan accepted American bases and military aid because India did not believe assurances that these were meant only for defense against the Iron Curtain. But after the advent to power in Pakistan of General Ayub Khan in 1958 relations improved. The refugee property question was first settled, and in September 1960 the canal water problem was solved by a Water Treaty which Nehru signed on September 19. The water problem was in fact the more dangerous of the two, for its use was a matter of life or death. Briefly, the problem was that India controlled the headwaters of canals which fertilized the Pakistan Panjab. In addition she intended to use the waters of the Sutlej for great irrigation works in northern Rajasthan. It was then agreed that India should have the waters of the three eastern rivers, the Sutlej, Beas, and Ravi; while Pakistan has those of the three western ones, the Indus, Jhelum, and Chenab. With the active help of the World Bank a scheme was worked out by which crosscanals were to be built so that Pakistani canals could be entirely fed from the three western rivers. The cost of $1,000,000,000 was financed through the World Bank, the United States contributing $177,000,000 in grants and $70,000,000 in loans, Britain $58,000,000 in grants. For this major achievement Nehru's patience and prescience must be given full credit.

In foreign affairs proper, Nehru's first concern was to round off the territories of the new state. Hyderabad was absorbed in 1948 and the French possessions soon after. Only the Portuguese clung to Goa. A democratic regime was sponsored in Nepal, which, however, has proved unstable. These measures caused some to fear a revival of the Mauryan imperialism of the third century B.C., but time has shown them in the perspective of a rounding-off process and a precautionary measure against Chinese penetration of the Himalayas.

Nehru next marched on the world stage as a good internationalist, believing in self-determination, co-operation, and conciliation. His force of character made up for his lack of armed force; in spite of the handicap of the Kashmir controversy he impressed an Indian point of view on the world by sheer weight of personality. His first line was anticolonialism. His attitude helped the Dutch handover in Indonesia and the French withdrawal from southeast Asia. His last blast on the trumpet of anti-colonialism and anti-imperialism was at Suez in 1956. India was prominent as a conciliator in Korea in 1950, and her services were increasingly utilized for plebiscites and other international duties, as in the Sudan and later the Congo.

For a time Nehru toyed with the will-o'-the-wisp of "Asianism," the idea that there was an underlying unity of spirit in all Asia as distinct from the rest of the world. The idea was assiduously put about by the Congress "ideas" man, K. M. Panikkar; it served well enough while colonialism in Asia was still an issue, but with that settled its inner contradictions became apparent. China never much relished being linked with India in any but an anti-Western sense, and later India had doubts about being linked with China.

But it was Nehru's policy of "neutralism" and "nonalignment" which caught the imagination and aroused the controversy of the world. The policy sprang from Nehru's conviction that in the conditions of the atomic age a third world war would be disastrous for all. India would inevitably be drawn in, and all the work of national regeneration would be lost. This position did not imply any particular love for Russia and the Communist system. Mr. Nehru was a convinced democrat as well as a socialist. He found the Russian system of the thirties drastic and repugnant, and he dealt severely with subversive Communist activities. But on the other hand the West, in his view, was deeply involved with colonialism. Britain had perhaps repented, but she had also grown weaker; the two aspects might be connected. America stood for freedom for everyone and everything, including the dollar, and he feared the dollar more than any American government. All these considerations weighed in the adoption and pursuance of "neutralism."

With these views Nehru's first tactic was to lead the anticolonialist camp. This policy reached its peak at the Bandung Conference of Afro-Asian states in 1955. The next move was to cultivate relations with both sides and to spread the idea of "nonalignment." The larger the number of uncommitted nations, he calculated, the less likely were the two great power blocs to go to war. This did not suit the policy of the United States; hence a certain tension in the relations between the two. Nehru opposed both SEATO and the Baghdad Pact. Pakistan's adherence to the latter was a shock because it broke the line of uncommitted states running from the Atlantic to the Pacific. Later the rapid growth in the number of African states gave new life to the noncommittal concept. Nehru's leadership of the neutral "five" at the U.N. Assembly of 1960 was in direct line with this policy.

The next step was the cultivation of relations with both sides. India remained within the Commonwealth, and Nehru visited the United States. After the death of Stalin, he visited Moscow in 1955. The erection of the three new steel plants in India were allotted respectively to the United States, Britain, and Russia. More disturbing from the Western point of view was the return visit of the Russian leaders Bulganin and Khrushchev to Delhi at the end of 1955. The new Chinese regime was recognized at once. There were visits to and from China, one fruit of which was the *Panch Shila* or five principles of coexistence and nonaggression. Briefly these were mutual respect for sovereignty, nonaggression, internal non-interference, mutual recognition of equality and development, and peaceful coexistence.

These tactics perhaps achieved their greatest success about 1956 with a curious triangular relationship among India, Russia, and China. Nehru saw in China a bridge between Russia and the West. China would mediate between Russia and India, India would interpret the Communist world to Britain, and Britain interpret to the United States. Indian cordiality with China seemed to bring a noticeable thaw in the Russian attitude. It looked at one time as though each state was courting India for fear that the other might make a separate deal with her.

The year 1956 can be taken as the peak of Nehru's reign. He had eliminated his Congress rivals; he had recovered from the strains of partition and the migrations; he had integrated the princely states with scarcely a ripple of protest and was in the process of reshaping the Indian state system on a linguistic basis; within Congress his primacy was unchallenged and the opposition groups outside were divided and factional. Education, specially higher, had burgeoned out; the progress of agriculture was considerable and of industrial expansion spectacular. At 66 he retained his vigor and resilience and seemed to have many years of relatively unhindered rule before him. Abroad his position also seemed enviable. India's neighbor Pakistan was floundering towards a military dictatorship and unable to renew her bid for Kashmir. Pakistan's approach to the United States and membership in SEATO were signs of weakness rather than of strength. Nehru had avoided involvement with either group of great powers, while taking economic help from both. He was the virtual leader of a group of neutral or non-aligned states and was increasingly looked to for guidance. He was holding a balance, not only between America and Russia, but also between Russia and China. His feat of diplomatic juggling at that time seemed remarkable.

But was he really as strong as he looked? Here one must resist the temptation to label as a dictator anyone who achieves large legal powers or faces little overt opposition. Nehru enjoyed both these advantages and had as well the halo of a founding father round his head. But he suffered from two important handicaps. One was the covert opposition from within the ranks of Congress itself, and the other factionalism within Congress. There was a hard core of orthodox Hindu sentiment opposed to his social policies of Hindu legal reform and Harijan uplift. Their formal representation was the Jan Sangh party,[3] but their real power lay within Congress. While Jan Sangh members could seize upon any incident, such as the Dalai Lama's flight, to promote Hindu feeling, orthodox-minded Congressmen could obstruct from within the party the execution of measures they disapproved but dared not openly oppose. In this way Hindu law reform was delayed, compulsory universal elementary education held up, birth control measures slowed down, and much socialist legislation postponed. Like the apparently all-powerful Mughal emperor, with whom he was often compared, Nehru had always to be thinking how much of his program Congress supporters would actually stand. In the All-India Congress Committee factionalism could be scotched by authority, but in the States its emergence could not be prevented. Congress had risen as a power-seeking body acting as a spearhead against a foreign domination. The foreigner removed, it was inevitable that the varied components of local Congress parties should drift apart, wanting more power than they could achieve in competition with their rivals. Factionalism led to the suspension of parliamentary government in a number of states, to the fall of Partab Singh Kairon, the vigorous Chief Minister of the Panjab, and to the four-year chief ministership of Mrs. Sucheta Kripalani in Uttar Pradesh as a means of getting two rival groups to work together under a third party. With these deterrents around him Nehru was less free than he appeared, though of course he was still a powerful figure.

From about 1956 Nehru was increasingly hampered by these factors. The Jan Sangh party had been founded in 1949 by Shyam Prasad Mukherjee as a successor to the ineffective Mahasabha and the tainted R.S.S.[4] Though poorly represented in the Lok Sabha, it played cleverly on Hindu and national feelings whenever an issue arose, and thereby influenced the Congress members themselves. Kashmir, Tibet and the Dalai Lama, Goa, and the Indo-China border were some of the occasions for these tactics. Then in 1959 the Swatantra party, numbering among its leaders the veteran Rajaji of Madras, K. M. Munshi and M. Masani of Bombay, was founded. It was also conservative, less theological in tone than the Jan Sangh, and more closely linked with Indian big business and capitalism. Though also making a poor showing in elections (except in Gujarat), the distinction of its leaders gave it influence, rather in the style of Liberal leaders of a former day like Sir Tej Bahadur Sapru, out of proportion to its members. The Swatantra party opposed most of Nehru's internal policies and, like the Jan Sangh, advocated a forward policy abroad.

Within the Congress party itself, there was a widening gap between the official socializing party program and the desires of Congressmen. Office rather than renewal was the conscious goal of many, and since one group (with caste or occupational affiliations) could only obtain powers at the expense of another, the factionalism which distressed outside observers steadily grew. Its symptoms were personal recriminations, a preoccupation with places and perquisites rather than measures, and an epidemic of floor-crossing and assembly postponements. This was reflected in the elections of 1962, in which, though the Congress retained its large majority in the Lok Sabha, its percentage of votes cast declined from 48 to 45 and its position in the states was eroded. The lack of Congress achievement or dynamic appeal made Nehru more inclined towards advocates of extreme courses like Krishna Menon, now his Defence Minister. It would seem that the need to restore Congress glamor before the 1962 election was at least one motive for his sanctioning the occupation of Goa in the fall of 1961. In 1963 Nehru tried to infuse new life into the Congress party by the self-denying call which came to be known as the Kamaraj plan, from the Premier of Madras (1954–63) who was its proponent. Six union ministers and six state premiers retired, ostensibly to strengthen and purify the Congress organization. Kamaraj himself became the President of Congress. But apart from placing an experienced operator in charge of the party machine, not much change was visible. There was little rejuvenation and it was whispered that advantage had been taken by the Prime Minister to part with some of his less congenial colleagues.

While the political world felt itself puzzled and frustrated, it seemed that the great Nehruan effort to modernize the country and raise its standard of living was grinding to a halt. The first five-year plans had produced a greater increase in the gross national product than the increase of population. There was a steady increase in per capita income. Further, the establishment of new industries like the steel and motoring plants had not only provided more jobs, but given a sense of progress even to those who did not directly benefit. But with the third five-year plan, the most ambitious of all, there came a change. People felt the burdens more than they enjoyed the results. A sense of general even if sometimes vicarious participation, was replaced by a sense of exclusion. The growth of national income declined from 4.3% per annum in the second plan to 3 per cent against a planned 7 per cent, while per capita income, which had risen 8.2 per cent under the first plan and 9.5 per cent during the second plan, remained static in the years 1961–64. The reason for this was partly a failure to increase food production but mainly the unexpectedly rapid rise of the population. In the third plan there was a 1 per cent instead of 5 per cent annual increase of agricultural production. Food production declined from 81 million tons in 1961–62 to 79.4 million tons in 1963–64, compared with the third plan target of 100 million tons. This failure made India the less able to deal with the population explosion. A Planning Committee estimate of 408 million for 1961 became a census figure of 439 million with a growth rate of 12 million a year. By 1965 it was feared India would reach 500 million by 1970, and in fact this figure was passed before then. With virtually static food production, soaring population, and halting industrial production, it seemed that India was beginning to move backward rather than forward. Voices were raised to criticize heavy industrialization, to advocate birth control, and increased food production. There was bewilderment and concern, the planners puzzled and bemused, the politicians fearful, defensive, and recriminatory. There was no consensus about what to do next; men were looking for a scapegoat rather than a savior.[5]

If we now return to the field of foreign relations we find Nehru, about the year 1956, at the peak of his fame. Pakistan was contained, nonalignment had been successfully asserted. John Foster Dulles's efforts to cajole or compel India's entry into the American anti-communist orbit had been repulsed, and India was herself balancing between Russia and China. But this position was not as stable as it looked. It was a brilliant balancing trick, but a trick of balance all the same. Change the content of the balls and the performer will be in difficulties. And this is what in fact happened. The first change was the gradual realization of the implications of the hydrogen bomb. The first atomic bombs were seen essentially as a great escalation in the means of destruction. They might be used and it was worth following Nehru's lead to avoid this (They nearly were used against North Korea in 1951). But the hydrogen bomb was gradually seen as destructive to the point of inhibition. For all but the greatest conflict the bomb was out; as fear of the bomb declined the necessity of non-alignment grew less. This was underlined in 1960 by the death of Dulles, the apostle of anti-communism and the advocate of the bomb. "Agonizing re-appraisals" were out; cautious re-deployments possible.

The second change occurred in China. That country's honeymoon with Russia ended when Khrushchev withdrew his Russian aid teams. Coolness gradually turned to hostility, and this upset Nehru's balancing arrangements. Further, the policy of internal reorganization passed into one of Chinese assertion. In Chinese eyes this assertion was not aggression but the re-assertion of age-old claims on surrounding terri-tories. For India such a development was bound to be a matter of deep concern because of its long frontier adjoining the Chinese world. For centuries China had claimed control over Sinkiang, suzerainty over Tibet, and a vaguer overlordship in Nepal and Burma. Both the Ching dynasty and Chang Kai-shek, in their respective last years of power, had asserted these claims.

The first overt sign of this changing international climate came in 1956 when the Anglo-French Suez adventure and the Hungarian revolt occurred almost at the same time. Suez aroused Nehru's anti-colonialist feelings and he was unsparing in denunciation. But Hungary aroused different feelings; he was reluctant to see the Russians as aggressors and suspicious of Imre Nagy and his followers as reactionaries. The rejec-tion, when it came, was belated and halting in comparison to his Suez stand. He lost credit in the West—with Britain over Suez and with the United States over Hungary. In 1961 came the unilateral occupation of Portuguese Goa. The Portuguese presence was archaic and a provo-cation, and the Portuguese attitude stiff-necked. But it was a defiance of international law of which Nehru was a champion. So un-Nehruan was it that one is tempted to look for expedient explanations like the need for a Congress trophy in the forthcoming elections. As it was, Indian international prestige was injured, with diplomats saying, not without some self-satisfaction, "Et tu, Brute?"

But it was China which proved too much for Nehru. Free India in 1947 inherited a formidable frontier problem from the British. The cre-ation of Pakistan removed the accepted Durand line on the west, shortly to substitute an unstable truce line in Kashmir, devised by the United Nations after the shortlived war of 1947–48. Then there was the long frontier with China, stretching from the Karakorams to Burma with a gap provided by independent Nepal. No hard agreements defined this frontier. It had three sections, but for practical purposes we can con-centrate on two. The first was in the northwest where the frontier ran with Ladakh from Chinese Tibet to Sinkiang; the second was the stretch from Sikkim to Burma covered by the North East Frontier Agency (NEFA). The first area was one of desolation, in which the Aksi Chin plateau was the most important. Yet it was to be one of the two causes of combat. In the British period the nearest approach to a defined frontier, and this a matter of map drawing rather than personal investigation, was the British proposal to China in 1899 giving most of the Aksi Chin to China. But the Chinese never replied to this demarche. On British maps the line tended to oscillate according to current British estimates of Russian threats or Chinese friendliness. In the eastern sector British action had varied according to their estimated need for thwarting Russian designs on Tibet. In the early twentieth century their line was the foothills north of the Brahmaputra in Assam. The Chinese occupation of Lhasa in 1910, a last attempt to assert authority over Tibet, led the British to move the line northwards into the foothills, all non-Tibetan except Tawang, covering the area now known as NEFA. The Manchu collapse in 1912 provided an opportunity for a settlement with the Tibetans and there followed the Simla conference of 1913–14 between the British, the Tibetans, and the Chinese. The upshot was the McMahon line, which gave the NEFA area to the British, including the Tibetan district of Tawang. The Tibetans accepted this line, but the Chinese did no more than initial the agreement. The least satisfactory part for the Tibetans was the Tawang cession, but the British never administered the northern part of the district which the Indians only entered in 1951.

These matters began to impinge on India with the establishment of the Mao regime in China in 1949. China had two problems: the reassertion of authority in the outlying province of Sinkiang, and the establishment of authority over Tibet, long claimed but rarely exercised. China's recipe for Sinkiang was the building of an all-weather motor road from Tibet, which ran across the Aksi Chin plateau. This was started in the early 1950's, but was not officially noticed by India until 1957. For Tibet it was hoped to persuade the Dalai Lama and his advisers to accept Chinese advice and a policy of social reconstruction. Nehru at first ignored the Aksi Chin road (if he knew of its existence). He recognized Chinese suzerainty over Tibet (a British legacy) and advised the young Dalai Lama to co-operate with them. He was cultivating good relations with China expressed in the *Panch Shila* (five principles) of 1954.

The change came in 1959 when a revolt in Tibet led to the Dalai Lama's flight to India and the granting of asylum to him there. The

Chinese objected, but more serious was the reaction of Indian public opinion. The Dalai Lama was the head of an unorthodox Buddhist sect, but Hindus looked on him as an *avatar,* a divine incarnation, a holy man, a Hindu by ritual descent if not by profession. A flame of feeling swept the country, fanned certainly by the communal parties, but going far beyond the normal limits of their influence. Nehru was no longer a free agent.

The rest of the story can be soon told. The Aksi Chin road now came to light and what might have been quietly bargained away by an imperialist power whose public cared little for a remote outpost, became sacred soil (even if it was only rock) to a newly emancipated and self-conscious nation. Through the tortuous negotiations which followed Nehru held both to the advanced British Aksi Chin line (instead of the 1899 one) and to the full McMahon line in the east. Each exchange of notes added fuel to the flames of public indignation and reduced Nehru's freedom of action. Then he was persuaded that India should advance beyond the McMahon line in Tawang to the Chag La range. He was led on by faulty intelligence and, it is said, by the promptings of his Defence Minister, Krishna Menon, to believe that no serious Chinese resistance need be apprehended. So the order to advance was given in October 1962 to troops badly led, clothed, munitioned, and informed. Then the blow fell. By November 20 the district town of Tezpur was being evacuated and the way seemed open to the plains and even Calcutta. On November 21 the Chinese announced a unilateral cease-fire and withdrawal from NEFA. A further blow to Indian prestige was the Chinese return of prisoners with their arms.

In the alarm of defeat Nehru had called for aid from the West. America and Britain responded enthusiastically, but added fresh pressure for a settlement in Kashmir. Nehru soon recovered his outward poise. The appeals to village women to offer their jewels, the drillings of young men quietly ceased, foreign aid slowed down and ended. The Kashmir issue was stalled and then buried again. A few months later, the Prime Minister could still shuffle Congress ministers and ministries with his accustomed skill. But inwardly he was a broken man, surveying a scene of unfulfilled dreams, wrecked hopes, and frustrated ambitions. The new India seemed to be breaking in his hand, and at the touch of the Chinese. In the spring came his last move in releasing Sheikh Abdullah and sending him to Pakistan in a new hope of a negotiated Kashmir settlement. But before much could be done he died suddenly on May 27, 1964.

In seeking to evaluate Nehru's reign one must avoid the extremes of adulation, which beset him during his first years of power, and of condemnation which echoed around and beyond his funeral pyre. It is true that what seemed to start as a triumphal march seemed to end in the tragedy of nemesis. But if the heights were not all scaled, the depths were not plumbed either. All was not lost and some very tangible things were gained. Surveying Nehru's work we find an air of half-achievement. In politics we have a western democratic machine without a party system to work it. There had been great industrial expansion but the economy had not "got off the ground" in an economic sense, unemployment had not been cured and the standard of living remained low. A large middle class had been created but the gulf between it and the masses remained deep. Higher education had expanded but primary education had lagged. Universal education only existed in some cities. Social progress had been achieved in the reform of the Hindu Code, but the forces of reaction remained strong. The population had grown much faster than expected with little done to restrain it. This one factor threatened to counterbalance all the other achievements together. Internationally, India had lost the halo of moral authority bequeathed by Gandhi.

Yet all was not lost. The giant was wounded but was still a giant. I think Nehru's greatest achievement was in the social sphere because his reforms may here have influenced Indian life most deeply. For the rest, he set India on the way to full membership of the developing world community, politically, industrially, educationally, culturally. He gave her a sense of purpose for the future as well as pride in her past, and he laid foundations, whatever faults there may have been in the superstructure which he added, upon which his succssors have been able to build securely. At his death he was widely regarded as a fallen idol. We can now see him as a bruised and limping giant who had completed half the great causeway to the future to which he had set his hand.

CHAPTER XLI

Contemporary India

This chapter seeks to cover the years from the death of Nehru to the end of 1971, years which have seen an apparently striking reversal of Indian fortunes. But before embarking on this final survey, a word must be said about the nature of contemporary history, of which this is India's most contemporary portion. Contemporary history is necessary and desirable, for we all need interpretations of the immediate past, even if provisional ones, which may gather insights for the future. But the limitations of this class of history should also be recognized. Narrative must depend largely on public statements; the external record cannot usually be backed by the knowledge of the internal why and wherefore of decision and actions. Analysis has incomplete data so that its conclusions must be tentative. Above all, the attainment of perspective and proportion is a problem. Is the event which fills the headlines today the one which will be marked as a turning point a hundred years hence? What looms large close in time may seem small in time's perspective. The waves of the sea rock those riding on it in a small boat, but the same waves from a height appear quite smooth and from a level distance little more than ripples. Having noticed these difficulties, let the importance of understanding the near present as well as the middle or remote past be again emphasized. In these seven years we may take as our guiding thread through the maze of current events, how has the transformation from the gloom of the years 1964–65 to the confidence of 1972 come about?

There had been many dire prophecies about the consequences of Nehru's death and much speculation about his successor. In fact, the succession was arranged very smoothly. The stroke suffered by Nehru at the beginning of 1964 had provided a warning sign, and before that it was clear that Nehru was making his own preparations. He refused to nominate a deputy Prime Minister saying that this would arouse such jealousy as to ensure his later rejection. But he used the Kamaraj plan

of 1963 to remove from the cabinet two powerful but uncongenial contenders, Morarji Desai and Sadashiv Kanoji Patil of Gujarat, and so
leave the field clearer. Lal Bahadur Shastri, who had been a willing
Kamaraj sacrifice, was soon brought back as Minister without portfolio
and his conciliatory talents were increasingly used. A notable case was
the affair of the Prophet Muhammad's hair, a sacred relic in Kashmir,
which was stolen. Shastri was in fact selected by the inner ring of Congress leaders,[1] headed by Kamaraj, then Congress President. Morarji
objected, but allowed himself to be overruled, making the election
formally unanimous. Morarji was rejected because of his right-wing
leanings. These would have been less than acceptable to the left wing
and would have made it difficult to hold the government to its middle-
of-the-road path, while his authoritarian temper made some fear dictatorship. Lal Bahadur Shastri was a dedicated Gandhian, who had
worked his way from a small-town background to the Home Ministry
of the central government, making a reputation in the jungle of Uttar
Pradesh factional politics for integrity, disinterestedness, conciliation,
and efficiency.

Mr. Shastri was a man of small stature with a somewhat ingratiating
manner, of kindly nature and gentle speech. But he was capable of
firmness, was efficient and hard-working, and in the rough and tumble
of Uttar Pradesh politics had shown himself a shrewd and sometimes
ruthless operator. He lived austerely and gave most of his salary away,
to the extent that his widow had to be given a special state pension on
his death. He had in him the makings either of a Gandhi-like charismatic
leader or of an introverted platitudinous Hindu saint. Office would
decide the choice. The new Prime Minister retained most of Nehru's
ministers, bringing in only three. These included Mrs. Indira Gandhi
and S. K. Patil of Gujarat. Shastri's cabinet was described as safe but
dull, struck in the low key which seemed to be part of his style. It may
be noted here that, while Mrs. Gandhi made no visible impact on the
Ministry of Information, to which she was appointed, she began at
once those journeys which made her a familiar figure all over India.
In the Tamil language riots, for example, it was she who visited Madras
and not the ex-Chief Minister Kamaraj, who tarried in adjacent Kerala.
To his undramatic and matter-of-fact style, Shastri added the device of
persuasion. Consensus was his prescription for holding Congress together and it was to be achieved by persuasion through unlimited discussion. The charismatic leader was to be replaced by a collective
moved by reason and public spirit and inspired by moral ideals.

The first result of this was an impression of indecisiveness. Successive subjects would come up, be discussed, and a decision delayed. Shastri hoped to wear down his colleagues by persistence and patience but he was denied the time and tranquillity needed for these tactics to work. The first crisis was a food shortage, stemming from the combined effects of a bad harvest and a growing population. Here he met the opposition of Chief Ministers. The proposed rationing of the chief cities was confined to Calcutta only and the pooling of food grains reduced to a limited release of rice from surplus states for one year. Before matters could go further the good harvest of 1965 shelved the problem without solving it. The next challenge was the Hindi crisis. Hindi was due to become the sole national language, a decision deeply feared and resented in the south, which wished to continue English as Hindi's twin. The day was greeted by riots in Madras (January–February 1965) and throughout the state, including ritual burnings in the Vietnam style, shootings, and many deaths. Only in March were amendments to the Official Languages Act of 1963 promised, safeguarding the continued use of English by those who desired it.

Then events moved to a field where they would not wait for a consensus. In April clashes occurred in the Rann of Kutch, the marshy area between India and Pakistan abutting on the Arabian Sea coast and irregularly washed by this sea. Indian troops were at first not conspicuously successful, a fact which may have encouraged the Pakistanis towards further action later. But Shastri refused to be pushed to the extremes of belligerence or surrender. The Indians stood their ground, agreed to an informal cease-fire on April 30, which was formalized on June 30, and arranged for a final demarcation of the boundary by arbitration. The Rann of Kutch occupies nine thousand square miles of barren land inundated during the monsoon season except for a few hillocks. Pakistan claimed that the Rann was an arm of the sea, so that the frontier should run through the center. India stood on the old provincial border between Sind and the Kathiawar states, which in her view was now the international boundary.

Shastri emerged from this incident with heightened prestige. The man of soft words and conciliation could also say 'no' with firmness. A greater test soon followed. In August, Pakistani infiltrations into Kashmir occurred. They did not produce the hoped-for Kashmir rising and the Indians seized the strategic Haji Pir pass of entry in reply. At the end of the month, the Pakistanis launched an armored column towards Aknur, whose capture would have cut off the supply route from Jammu to Srinagar in the Vale of Kashmir. This was open war; there were appeals to the Security Council and within a few days there was an Indian thrust across the international frontier towards Lahore. Pakistan contended that this was an act of war, her previous actions in Kashmir being merely a continuation of a domestic dispute over the control of the country. India replied that the Pakistani incursions were acts of war, inasmuch as they were infringements of the United Nations cease-fire line of July 29, 1949, and further, that the Kashmir frontier crossed near Aknur was a juristically valid international line. Therefore her Lahore thrust was a justifiable defensive measure. Thus each side convinced itself that the other was the aggressor. There followed a confused struggle in which neither side gained much visible advantage. Pakistani pressure on Aknur ceased, but Lahore did not fall. Amid a welter of claims, it seems that the Indian Centurion tanks did better than Pakistan's Pattons, though whether this was due to superior construction or more skilful handling is not clear. A smaller Pakistan air force appeared to have held its own. On both sides there seem to have been supply and repair difficulties. The United Nations was active in mediating efforts, which were supported by the efforts of Britain, the United States and Russia. China condemned India but took no overt action. The upshot was a "cease-fire" on September 22, arranged by the Security Council. Interest now centered on efforts to secure the Council's goal of a return to the positions of August 5 (before the big infiltrations into Kashmir began). This led to the Tashkent conference (January 4–10, 1966) at which Mr. Kosygin, the Russian Prime Minister, acted as the honest broker. The Tashkent Declaration of January 10 provided for a return on both sides to the positions of August 5, undertook the settlement of future disputes by peaceful means, and arranged for high level discussions on outstanding questions. Initial relief was followed by rising resentment at withdrawal without a no-war pact, and at the return of the Haji Pir pass without a renunciation of guerrilla activity in Kashmir. Shastri would have had to fight hard for his agreement, but before this could be put to the test came the news of his sudden death in the early morning of January 11.

Shastri had repeated, on a much larger stage, his blend of conciliatory firmness. Before Tashkent he was being hailed as the leader India was seeking, as the spiritual as well as the legal heir of Nehru. It is possible that the prestige thus acquired, provided he weathered the initial storm of criticism over the Tashkent terms, might have enabled him to turn "consensus" into a workable weapon and in time have elevated him to the position of a more practical if lesser Gandhi. Moral conviction and personal integrity still have magnetic force in India. But this we shall never know and the spiritual premiership of Lal Bahadur Shastri remains one of the intriguing might-have-beens of history.

The second succession to the premiership went nearly as smoothly as the first. The basic reason was the Syndicate's aversion to Morarji Desai, and the fact that Mrs. Gandhi was the only candidate who could certainly defeat him. The claims of Messrs. Chavan, Nanda, and Jagjivan Ram faded before this conviction, and the advantages of her name, her connection with Uttar Pradesh, the "heart" and largest state in the Union, and her wide popularity in view of the coming general election. This time Morarji would not give way and Mrs. Gandhi was elected leader of the party by 355 to 169 votes. She was sworn in as Prime Minister on January 24, 1966.[2]

On the threshold of the Gandhi premiership it is appropriate to look at the Congress party as it then stood. The party had grown up as the voice of nationalist India, which with Mahatma Gandhi seemed to become the voice of India itself. Apart from some fissiparous tendencies in the thirties, it broadly maintained this role to independence. Gandhi himself expected the Congress to break up, on the ground that it had done its work. Its organization, its prestige, its leadership by Gandhi's chosen heir, combined to keep it in being as the dominant political force in the country. But a subtle change did take place in its character. It ceased to be the umbrella over national sentiment, for this now pervaded the whole country. Instead, it gradually developed into a center party, holding together a major spectrum of political opinion, and flanked on each side by peripheral groups. Both those who looked for a two-party system on the British model and those who expected a multi-party pattern to appear were disappointed. They fell back on the explanation that Nehru's charismatic leadership, the aura of a founding father, had concealed real differences. All would change at his death. But would it?

There was something to be said for the concealment of differences. These differences found open expression in the peripheral parties and these, it was thought, would grow as soon as Congress lost its personal magic. These parties were both to the right and left. On the right the Mahasabha and its offshoot the R.S.S. had lost credit with Gandhi's murder. In 1949 Shyam Presad Mukherjee replaced it with the Jan Sangh, which became influential in Uttar Pradesh, Madhya Pradesh, and Rajasthan. The Jan Sangh stood for traditional ideas and Hindu self-assertion but was better organized and more aware of modern problems than its predecessor. The Jan Sangh was matched with the Swa-

tantra party founded in 1959 with whom the veteran C. Rajagopalachari, Kanaiyalal Maneklal Munshi, and Minou Rustam Masani were
associated. With traces of Gandhism and Hindu communalism it was
essentially a right-wing economic party, concerned with the maintenance
of capitalism and roused by the Nehruite Congress's leanings towards
socialism. On the left were the Socialist parties, of which the Praja Socialist party (1953) and the S.S.P. were the chief, and the Communist
Party with its Maoist and Trotskyite splinters. Finally there were the
regional parties in Orissa, Madras (the D.M.K.),[3] and the Panjab (the
Akali Dal Sikhs). These expressed regional or community patriotisms as
distinct from all-India nationalism.

Nehru had provided the motive force in Congress, and his leanings
were to the left. But from his left-wing days in the thirties, he had always placed much emphasis on party unity and been willing to make
sacrifices for it. So his course had been a left-of-center one. His policies
had included secularism and social reform in the social sphere, but not
pressed too far, a controlled and planned economy with growth organized by state enterprises in the economic field. There were public and
private economic sectors, with emphasis on the public. In his last years
he was unable to keep up his leftward pressure, so that the question
was now wide open; would Congress with ineffective leadership split
into its component ideological parts, or would it rally under a new
leader and swing to the right or left? Shastri's answer was to create a
consensus of both right and left but he did not have time to carry the
experiment far. Morarji Desai would have carried the Congress right-
wards. What would Indira do?

Mrs. Gandhi was not a prisoner of the Syndicate, but she certainly
owed her election to them, and specially to Kamaraj. The Syndicate
were themselves, except perhaps Patil, middle-of-the-roaders; their
weakness was that they were more concerned with the possession and
manipulation of power than its direction. They saw in Mrs. Gandhi the
best available election agent. Mrs. Gandhi leaned to the left along the
lines of her father's socialism. She had links with leftists like Menon
but she was also as conscious as her father of the need to retain overall
unity. The appointment could therefore only be called provisional since
the future direction of the party remained wide open.

During 1966, India continued on her uneasy way. Though heartened
by the repulse of the Pakistanis from Kashmir, there was disappointment at the struggle's indecisive outcome and there was continued apprehension about China. At home the problems remained. The one positive action was a drastic devaluation of the rupee. Events and people

waited on the elections. When they came, in early 1967, they seemed to mark the beginning of the end of the Congress reign. In the Lok Sabha, Congress had its overall majority cut to less than fifty; and its share of the vote declined from 44.7 per cent to 41 per cent. In the country it lost control of eight out of sixteen states. The Jan Sangh and the Swatantra parties made large gains on the right, and the Communist parties on the left. In Madras the separatist D.M.K. swept the board, with 138 out of 234 seats in the state assembly. But the opposition was still fragmented. There was little sign of a viable coalition against Congress at the center; in the states only the D.M.K. had an overall non-Congress majority. Elsewhere coalitions were inevitable.

It seemed that the trend was towards a multi-party system, perhaps helped by a Congress split. The former prediction was damped, however, by a spate of defections and floor crossings which now affected the assemblies. In too many parties, office seemed more important than policy. With its greater cohesion and prestige the Congress began to win back some of its lost ground. There remained the second prediction, which was now to be put to the test.

The Congress government continued its uneasy course, in a situation brightened only by signs of a scientific and economic break-through. Mrs. Gandhi was re-elected to the premiership and this time compounded with Morarji by admitting him as Deputy-Premier and Finance Minister. She managed him deftly but could hardly have been happy with his financial outlook. Both sides of the partnership were uneasy, but it was not until the spring of 1969 that two events set off the long expected crisis. During this time she built up her national image with tours abroad and at home, and by appearing as a conciliator between the rival wings. In the spring the right-wing Mr. Nijalingappa was elected the next President of Congress at the behest of the Syndicate and to Mrs. Gandhi's evident distaste. Then in May came the sudden death of the much respected President Zakir Husain. Here was an issue of the first importance. It was widely thought that the next general election would see the end of the Congress majority. In such a circumstance the President's reserve powers would become of great importance. A stable government could enforce its advice on their use as provided by the constitution, but in a climate of shifting coalitions and uncertain majorities the President would have much greater freedom and might become a sought-for prop to a weak administration. His duty of finding a Prime Minister with a majority in these conditions would also enhance his power. The spectre of Paul von Hindenburg, the President of the Weimar Republic who practically ruled Germany in the last pre-Nazi years, sprang to mind. The Syndicate adopted Sanjiva Reddy, speaker of the Lok Sabha, a known right-wing critic of Mrs. Gandhi, in preference to Varahagiri Venkata Giri, the Vice-President and a veteran and distinguished Congressman of left-wing sympathies. It seems that Mrs. Gandhi decided that she was in danger of virtual political imprisonment rather than mere restraint and was crudely threatened by the Congress president with dismissal after the 1972 elections. Then the lightning flashed. She demanded the nationalization of the banks, a long unfulfilled item in the Congress program. At a stroke this threw the Syndicate into confusion and gave her a popular backing. Having secured support for this move from the Bangalore Congress, she relieved Desai of the Finance Ministry while offering to retain him as Deputy Premier. And when Giri decided to stand for the Presidency on his own, she lent her support and secured his election. The party managers were nonplussed, outraged, and outmaneuvered. They had only tactics and control of the party machine with which to oppose popular action and national popularity. They found that the machine would not work without a popular animating figure or cause. They found the tactics in which they thought they excelled thrown back on themselves by a suddenly revealed mistress of the art.

The final breach between the two wings of Congress came in November 1969. The right wing secured the control of the Working Committee of Congress by one vote but Mrs. Gandhi retained two thirds of the Congress parliamentary party, and with left-wing tacit support, was assured of a parliamentary majority. She was restricted in action but free of the Congress opposition. The two wings now held separate party meetings from which verbal salvos were hurled. They were respectively known as Congress (R)—ruling, and Congress (O)—organization. Thus matters remained through 1970, each side looking warily for an opening. The success of Congress (R) in the Kerala elections encouraged Mrs. Gandhi to draw out another party plank, the ending of the former ruling Princes' pensions and privileges. This required a constitutional amendment which the opposition were just able to prevent. This success was their ruin for it gave Mrs. Gandhi the cue to call a general election a year before the statutory limit of Parliament. The opposition now sought alliances with the right-wing Jan Sangh and Swatantra parties while the left-wing groups, viewing a left-looking Congress with some alarm as well as pleasure, approached the Prime Minister. The electoral argument was that national issues were now so well understood that they overrode local issues and machine-party loyalties. This calculation proved correct. In her own way Mrs. Gandhi was following Mao in disciplining her own party.

The election victory surprised everyone by its magnitude. Congress (R) with 353 seats had an overall majority of 165; Congress (O) became a splinter group of about 23. In the states the story was similar, only the D.M.K. holding out in Tamil Nad, and the leftist parties in West Bengal, despite Congress inroads. We may sum up the result by saying that Indira Gandhi emerged as a national figure, with both a defined attitude and policy and massive popular support. The Indian love and need for hero-worshiping now found a picturesque and satisfying focus for their devotion. Next, the Congress had been given a leftward twist, restoring the long-faded image of secularism, gradual socialism, planned economy, and social reform. Thirdly, the expected fragmentation of Indian politics had vanished. Instead the old center idea with its peripheral groups had been restored, only this time was leaning leftwards. It was perhaps significant that the right-wing parties lost 7½ per cent of their vote between them, while the left-wing ones held their own. It remains to be seen whether the leftward momentum will be maintained, or whether there will be a gradual swing back to a central position.

Another side to the contemporary Indian situation, which tends to be overlooked in the drama of these and other recent events, has been the recent upsurge in the economic situation. Mention has been made of the drastic devaluation of the rupee in 1966. Painful as it was internally, it did enable Indian exports to gain much lost ground. In 1969 the fourth five-year plan, held up for some four years, was presented to Parliament, showing a total outlay of 243,980 million rupees, of which the public sector would take 143,980 million rupees, all but 21,000 million rupees being investment. The two chief targets in the public sector were organized industries and communications. The plan was launched, after revision, in 1970. This was an important step forward. Alongside the drive for production, the drive for population control seemed to be making progress. Figures released by the Government of India at the end of 1970 showed an estimated increase in the number of births prevented rising from around 100,000 in 1964 to 1,417,000 in 1969 and to an estimated 10.8 millions in 1973–74. Then there was the Green Revolution. Briefly, total food production which was 74.2 million tons in 1966–67 reached 95.6 million tons in the following year, passing the previous record by 6 million tons. It has now passed the 100 million ton mark. This dramatic result has been attained by a combination of four factors. The first is the proper use of the Indian soil, which a leading authority has said is probably the best in the world. The second is the introduction of new strains of wheat and rice, and the third the liberal use of fertilizers, which India is now both importing and producing in large new fertilizer plants. A fourth is the policy of sinking tube wells in the unirrigated eighty per cent of Indian cultivable soil. It is reckoned that while production has doubled in twenty years, it takes twenty-eight years for the population to follow suit. Therefore, in a measurable time the problem of scarcity should transmute into a problem of finding the means to buy the available food. Wheat has done better than rice, irrigated lands than unirrigated. But the fact remains that the specter of famine has been exorcised, if only for a time, and the problem of shortage turned into one of storage.

We now come to the final phase, to what may be called the stop-press of contemporary history, the East Pakistan or Bangladesh episode. Here full documentation is necessarily lacking and there must therefore be reliance on newspaper reports and verbal appraisals. However, the main lines seem sufficiently clear for a narrative to be constructed.

It was the middle of March 1971 when the great electoral victory of Mrs. Gandhi and the Congress (R) was announced. There seemed for once, to be a clear field for positive action. But only ten days later, on March 25, President Yahya Khan of Pakistan began his punitive action in East Pakistan, leading to heavy fighting, disorder, massacres, and the arrest of Sheikh Mujibur Rahman, the East Pakistani leader. Hitherto prospects had seemed good, for Yahya had kept his promise to hold elections in the autumn of 1970. Sheikh Mujib had swept East Pakistan while Zulfikar Ali Bhutto had won a substantial victory in the West. It seemed that it was for these two to make a deal about the Constituent Assembly and this was what President Yahya in his visit to Dacca was thought to be promoting. Therefore the shock of the breach was the greater for being unexpected.

At first the Indian attitude was one of observation, though there was some inevitable outpouring of public sympathy for the Bengalis. The arrival of the first refugees followed a familiar pattern, and it was not thought at worst, as this trickle became a stream, that it would exceed the million mark, about the number of Muslim Biharis said to have migrated to East Pakistan in the post-partition migration of 1950. But the stream grew to a river and then to a flood, so that by the end of August the refugees were reckoned to number over nine million. Of these, it was said that about two million were Muslims and seven million Hindus. Pakistan itself admitted to two million, which moved unsympathetic observers to suggest that they perhaps did not count Hindus. The eventual figure must have been between nine and ten million out of an East Pakistan population (estimated) of seventy-five million.

The refugee phenomenon was, in Indian eyes, the central fact of the situation, inevitably involving India in what began as an internal Pakistani crisis. The refugees had to be sheltered, fed, and protected from epidemics, an immense task which it is generally agreed was efficiently and humanely performed. The refugees, as has been noted, were Hindu by a large majority, coming from the Hindu rural minority of about ten million within East Pakistan. Here was a challenge to militant Hindu opinion and an opportunity for extremists to beat the communal drum with a patriotic cover. The refugees had to be paid for by a country scarcely emerging from an economic crisis. One reliable estimate [4] of cost was at least 2.5 million dollars a day or over 900 million dollars a year. If the refugees did not eventually return, what was to become of them? Their continued presence in West Bengal and Assam would overwhelm those states' economies, and no other state was willing, or probably able, to absorb them. To keep them in camps in the Middle Eastern style would be to court economic disaster as well as human catastrophe. On the other hand the short answer of war, or the taking of enough territory to resettle the refugees, which meant the same thing, might raise more problems than it solved.

The Indian answer was to soothe Indian public opinion by cautious expressions of sympathy, to seek financial aid from the international agencies while publicizing the magnitude of the problem and prospective burden, and to call on the super and western powers for intervention to compel a political settlement. To this end, Mrs. Gandhi undertook a tour to the West and America, asking for intervention. The international balance was delicately poised: for some time America and Russia had tacitly agreed that India should not become "too independent and a center of regional power in Southern Asia." Therefore Pakistan must be supported but not too much. Chinese support for Pakistan inclined Russia towards India but again not irrevocably. From July there were two developments. President Nixon's initiative towards China (the Kissinger journey) pushed Russia towards India. On August 9, a long considered treaty between the two countries was announced. No military aid was promised but the pact meant supplies, diplomatic support, and a veto on outside interference. At the same time, Indian support for Bangladesh guerrillas, known as the Mukhti Fauj (Freedom Army) or Mukhti Bahini (Freedom Brothers), was stepped up. It was the beginning of Indian self-help in the absence of international diplomatic or financial aid. The guerrillas were first sheltered, then trained and armed, and finally supported from the border.

From then until December this technique was gradually extended until not only was Indian artillery firing across the border in support of the guerrillas, but Indian troops were making short incursions. It was reminiscent of President Roosevelt's policy towards Japan in the summer and fall of 1941. On December 8 came the Pakistan counterpart to Pearl Harbor in the form of a surprise strike against the western Indian airfields. It was a failure, but like the Egyptian closure of the Gulf of Aqaba in 1966, an irreversible action. Then the lightning struck again; in twelve days Dacca was captured with ninety thousand Pakistani troops and the state of Bangladesh was born.

Indira Gandhi had triumphed and India had recovered the confidence lost more than seven years before in the Himalayan snows. To observers it seemed that for the second time she had showed Bismarckian skill in dividing her opponents so that in the moment of crisis they found themselves isolated. China showed clearly that she had no intention of intervening so long as West Pakistan was untouched; the American government displayed a chagrin which was irritating to the Indians without being helpful to the Pakistanis.

At this point, on the threshold of a new period, whose course is bound to be difficult and outcome uncertain, we take leave of India. India has secured the return of the refugees and Mrs. Gandhi has conferred with Mr. Bhutto in Simla (June 1972). India has now to thread her way through the maze of world power politics. She knows that China will resent the supposed spread of Russian influence in Bangladesh, an area the Chinese consider within their sphere of interest. She knows that the United States government dislikes the dismemberment of Pakistan and what it regards as the spread of Russian influence through the sub-continent. She does not know, in view of the current Russo-American negotiations, just how far Russia will be willing to support her. Against this she has new-found confidence, and as is believed, skilled leadership. We may conclude by quoting the words of Mrs. Gandhi herself at a recent mass meeting in New Delhi. "I do not know whether I will be there, whether you will be there, or whether many of us will be there to see. But I am sure the generations to come will see India a great nation shining on the world map . . . not for her military might but for policies of peace, progress, and friendship." [5]

CHAPTER XLII

Concluding Reflections

As we contemplate the long procession of Indian history it may at first sight seem little more than an unending procession, with the elephants of state and umbrellas of authority appearing at intervals, interspersed with trains of attendants and disturbed by the brawls of contending factions. An Amurath to Amurath succeeded, it would seem, with intervals of anarchy while one dynasty replaced another. Or it can be seen as a series of invasions, each adding some new element to the population, whose rule is displaced in turn by the next arrivals. Professor A. L. Basham, in a recent inaugural lecture, could see no thread of meaning running through the four and one-half thousand years of which we have some knowledge. The dynastic and racial view was given its classical form by Mountstuart Elphinstone in his *History*, which ran through nine editions from 1841 to 1909. The Indian historian is inclined to see Indian history as a splendid Hindu creative cultural achievement leading to a golden age in the fourth and fifth centuries A.D., followed by the humiliation of Muslim conquest and domination, the British episode, and the glorious renaissance and revival in the last and present centuries. The Pakistani may see Indian history as a great Muslim creative achievement superimposed upon a corrupt pagan society and culminating in the Mughal period and the reign of Aurangzeb. The British were the darkeners of the light, the precursors of the greater degradation of the modern Indian infidel state. British historians in the past have tended to see Muslim rule as a preface to their own, and their own as a restoration of ordered life in a decayed society and the introduction of fresh light from the West, and more particularly the Western isles.

Looked at from this level, it is indeed difficult to discern much trace of progress or detect a continuing thread of inner meaning. Indian history would seem to be a broken country in the world of time, with ups and downs but few vistas and no through routes, or like a continuous movie reel alternating between Wild West scenes of action and Manhattan shots of luxury and repose. Neither politics nor war provides a key to the meaning of Indian history.

But if we turn our attention to the society and culture of India we find at once a very different picture. We shall not indeed find a steady progression as was required by the optimistic historians of the nineteenth century, but we shall find a process of constant modification and development which gives meaning and significance to the whole outer drama of action and pageantry. We shall indeed find many different interpretations. Some Hindus consider that the *Vedas* contain all that man needs to or should know and that the Vedic way of life is the path appointed by the gods for mankind. All later additions and subtractions are so many desecrations of the way of the gods. A school of "development" holds that the Aryan culture was the founding charter, as it were, of Indian life, to which have been assimilated various accretions and foreign importations. The Indian genius has been to add fresh gems to the jewel in the lotus to make an ever more dazzling display. A more daring modern view is that the Indian genius is primarily that of assimilation. Influences of all kinds (including the Vedic) are received and blended with deft touches into a harmonious whole. No other culture can do it as India does it; Western influences are at this moment undergoing the same process.

Without going to this length, we may take as our starting point an Indian way of life and view of life. India has developed and presented both to the world and is at this moment continuing the process. It is by this method that we may hope to understand something of India and also something of the Indian contribution to the coming world culture and world view. In parantheses we may note another popular way of regarding India—the economic. India is seen as a seat of trade with the West or as a field for Western technical enterprise. Interesting as such studies may be, they obviously touch only a part of Indian life and can explain only a fraction of its meaning. It is rather like trying to judge the nature of a redwood by measuring its topmost branches. We start our survey, then, with the earliest society of which we have any knowledge. The earliest known society is not the Aryan of the second millennium B.C. but the Harappan of Sind and the Panjab in the third and second millennia B.C. What went before we do not know. This society broke down, but we now know that it profoundly influenced the Aryans who succeeded it. It was contact between the two and between the Indo-Aryans and primitive tribes which produced the most original and powerful of Indian institutions, caste. A comparison between the Indian of Epic and Vedic times (roughly 1500 and 1000 B.C.) shows how deeply the older society, even with our imperfect knowledge of it, influenced the younger.

From this time we have a pattern set. A view or philosophy of life followed the way of life or social institutions. The great monistic philosophy of the *Upanishads* was built up over a thousand years to 500 A.D. The pattern and the view of life were challenged and modified by a series of influences both internal and external. Within, there were the Jains and other sects now forgotten, and above all the Buddha, whose influence extended across central Asia through China to Japan and has been profound for two and one-half millennia. Without, first came the Persians with their doctrines of light and the duality of good and evil, and their imperial ideas, which bore fruit in the bureaucratic Mauryan empire of the third century B.C. After them came a succession of peoples, the volatile Greeks of Alexander and the Indo-Greek kingdoms, of trade, literature, and philosophy; the Pahlavas, Sakas, and Kushans. As separate races these peoples have all been absorbed in the ocean of Indian life, but they have each made a contribution to the quality of the water. We do not know enough of Greek contacts to say with any certainty which ideas passed from one to the other; but we do know that the impact was such that the Arab philosopher Alberuni commented on it in the eleventh century A.D. The Pahlavas, Sakas, and Kushans all contributed to the racial mixtures of the north and west of India.

The Huns and associated invaders of the fifth and sixth centuries A.D. contributed to India many of the Rajput clans that today seem so ancient as well as a number of other communities in northern India. The invaders provided the physical material, but it was Indian culture which molded them into Indian communities with special characteristics of their own. Without them, the India of the last ten centuries would have been quite different. With the coming of the Turks and the Afghans from the eleventh and twelfth centuries onward, both racial and ideological elements were added. The racial characteristics of the northwest (now West Pakistan and the Indian Panjab) were materially affected. The new religion and ideology of Islam were imported and a new cultural influence from Persia introduced. Islam and Hinduism being culturally on a level and in many ways antipathetic both in their ideas and customs, the tension was considerable and lasted for centuries. Some may think that it was only at partition that India finally worked Islam out of the system, by the purgatives of massacre and migration. But this is not so. A great deal of Islamic influence has remained within the Indian body social, some of it as a sort of antibody against Muslim infection or, to use a psychological term, as a defense mechanism, some of it an almost subconscious borrowing (as Brahmins once borrowed from the Buddhists) and some of it a self-conscious attempt at reconciliation and understanding. In the antibody class can be cited such examples as the tightening of caste rules, increased social segregation, and emphasis on cow protection. In the realm of borrowing we have such things as the emphasis on sin, guilt, and forgiveness to be found in the bhakti cults of devotion, and the movement toward theism and monotheism in Hindu thought in general. Many movements exemplified the conscious attempt at understanding between the two from the cult of the Emperor Akbar in the sixteenth century to the teachings of the weaver-poet-saint Kabir of Banaras in the fifteenth. The body which borrowed most heavily from Islam is the one which is now the most antipathetic—the Sikhs. Let no one suppose that the influence of Islam in India departed with the Pakistanis.

Much more pervasive because less militant was the influence of the Persian culture which the Turks brought with them. It was used by the Mughals from the sixteenth to the eighteenth centuries to create almost a new Indian civilization. The "charm" of Persian culture captivated the Indian aristocracy, Hindu as well as Muslim, throughout India. Persian political and administrative concepts, Persian manners and costumes took root through the subcontinent. It acquired its own intellectuals, and it created its own language of Urdu, the mother tongue of the first Indian prime minister. Its spell is not quite broken today. Persian influence on Indian life and thought has been profound; but for the hard core of Brahmin ideology and caste custom it might have transformed Indian civilization altogether. Even the Maratha chiefs acquired a veneer of Persian manners.

Into this general pattern we can now see the British period of Indian history falling quite naturally. Politically it witnessed the rise and decline of one more foreign dominion. Like all other foreign dominions, it had its special features and oddities, its virtues and failings, but basically in this aspect it was in line with all the rest. Physically the contribution has been small, and in a comparable time will be as difficult to trace as that of the Kushans or the Mughals themselves. But the British influence as a whole was much greater than this, for they brought with them a religion and an ideology of their own, together with a whole set of material techniques. If the British influence had been limited to this it would have left a post-British India different from the pre-British one, just as post-Mughal India differed from the pre-Mughal. But it would have lacked the dynamic quality of present-day India. India would have been ready only for another set of external influences. The difference between the effect of the two sets of influences is to be found in the difference between the two cultures and their affiliations. India borrowed *modes* of thought and taste from Persia; she borrowed ideas from Britain. Persian culture was affiliated with the Islamic world; the deeper one probed, the more firmly one struck a substratum of Islamic ideas already known and rejected. British "culture" and ideas and the British way of life itself were affiliated with the relatively new and strange civilization of the West. The further one probed, the further one penetrated into a new world of universal ideas and material developments springing from them. The Portuguese had introduced the world of Renaissance and Counter-Reformation Europe to India without any very visible effect. The elements of that age in Europe repelled as well as attracted, and lacked the revolutionary force of the next age. It was the Europe of the eighteenth and nineteenth centuries, of general ideas, of the ideas of progress and the rights of man, of scientific discovery and mechanical invention, of dynamism and restless change, which was to move India. Persian influence charmed and fascinated; modern Western influence transforms and revolutionizes. The role of the British as rulers in India was to be that of the harbingers of the modern West.

If the British period is viewed in this light, if it is placed in the whole perspective of Indian history, it will be seen that it is this aspect which provides the key for its understanding, which gives it ultimate significance for India. Of course there was colonialism, of course there was imperialism, of course there was exploitation. These three elements were certainly present, but the important point is that they were not the only or the dominant elements from the angle of Indian development. A regime which was exclusively colonialist or imperialist would have left an India exhausted or resentful or both. Instead of this we have seen an India full of life, energy, and hope, carrying on in many respects with remarkable continuity from the old regime and showing no less remarkable good will to the members of the old ruling race. Clearly there is something in addition to oppression which the British name and regime conjure up in the Indian mind.

What then are the things of value which India absorbed during the British period—say from 1757 to 1947? It is the writer's contention that these were patterns of life, philosophies, and techniques which essentially belonged to the West as a whole and for which the British in effect acted as importing agents. The goods came from the West, but sometimes they were wrapped in the Union Jack. In some cases, of course, it was more than this, for every nation gives a national shape to the most universal of cultural goods. Western influence in North Africa, for example, has taken a French form, while in Japan in the Meiji era it often had a German one. Shakespeare would not have been so popular as he is in India today if French had been the language medium for communication with the West. Cycling instead of cricket might have been a modern India national sport. But in general, with due allowance for national idiosyncrasies, what Britain did was to import ideas, values, and inventions from the West and add them to the rich mixture of Indian life. It was for India to survey and consider, to select or reject, to absorb and assimilate.

Some features of this contribution may now be noted. Politically, the first contribution was a sense of order and regulation. The British derived this sense from the Roman West, and it served to strengthen the same sense implanted by the Mughals, who derived their feeling for it from Persia. The sense of rule found expression in a great fabric of law, which has been taken over entire by the new India. But beneath rules and the administrators' *expertise* come ideas; ideas are the solvents and creators of societies. Here we find the fundamental concept of the individual, which, rooted in Graeco-Judaic soil, has flowered in the democratic concept of the rights of man and the ethical concept of the Sermon on the Mount. Every individual is a person of equal worth in the eyes of God and society and entitled to an equal chance in the community. Everyone is his brother's keeper; none can shirk responsibility for the plight of others. These ideas were revolutionary to the orthodox Hindu society of the last century. They found expression in British India through the educational system and the activities of missionaries; they took form in the concept of civil liberty which put Brahmin and untouchable, raja, nawab, and peasant on an equal level before the law, and in humanitarian movements and measures of uplift like the famine and irrigation schemes. They were the justification of the whole movement for self-government in the latter years of the British period. Nor must we forget nationalism. Every Englishman carried with him abroad the virus of paternalism and the virus of nationalism; it was paternalism which developed in himself and nationalism which infected others.

Apart from these moral and personal ideas and their practical outcome there were the abstract ideas of the West, with their expression in scientific study, in mechanical invention, and in industrial techniques. Western science has its own philosophy, resting on reason, objective observation, and knowledge of the processes of nature. The whole conspectus of the scientific outlook was similarly transported to India and spread through the medium of educational institutions and governmental agencies. Its practical consequences were seen in the public works of Dalhousie, the railways and canals of the later nineteenth century, the cotton and jute mills, and the Tata steelworks. For good or ill the scientific attitude toward life and the industrialists' vision of plenty flowing from mass production were taken to India.

If these are some of the things which the West sent to India through their British agents, we may now ask, how far have they been accepted by Indians and absorbed into their own system? Acceptance of a gift is not the same thing as its reception; and when the article is brought by a foreign ruler, there might seem in Eastern eyes a good reason for its rejection in that fact alone. In judging the Indian attitude toward these Western cultural imports we have two valuable criteria. They are the policies and attitudes of the Indian National Congress from its foundation in 1885 to independence in 1947, and the measures of the new government since then. Whither is independent India heading? In the first case we notice that the Congress based its whole case for self-government on the Western concepts of nationalism and individual rights. The Congress movement sprang from the middle class, and the middle class accepted broadly the Western gospel. The merchants went in for industrialism. The academic accepted Western science, the philanthropists human rights. Then came Gandhi. He married the middle class to the people; in so doing he carried nationalism to the masses. But his supreme achievement was perhaps to innoculate the Hindu social body with the idea of human rights and mutual moral obligations. His methods were his own life of simplicity and sacrifice on the one hand and the great Untouchable campaign on the other. He died extending the principle to Muslims at a critical moment. Thanks to him it may be said that the modern Hindu Indian would now agree that he *is* his brother's keeper and not merely his brother caste-fellow's keeper. In the second case of the new government's policies, we have already noted in chapters XXXIX and XL, the way in which the Nehru government made many of these Western imports the mainspring of its actions.

Enough has been said to show that, while the assimilation of Western ideas by India has certainly not been completed, it has equally certainly commenced. The end is not and could not be yet in so large a process, nor is it for us to speculate with any confidence on the end product. But India has not spurned the foreign banquet even after the withdrawal of the foreign purveyors and waiters. What then of the future? We can say with certainty that this great process will go on, whether in outward political form India is "democratic" or "communist," "authoritarian" or "liberal." We can also believe that as India becomes more akin to the West in some respects and so more intelligible to it, she will radiate to the world with increasing power the light within her own soul which once took such forms as the teachings of the Buddha and the *Bhagavad Gita* or "Song of the Lord." This tendency became visible with the portent of Swami Vivekananda at the World Congress of Religions at Chicago in 1893. Greater than the swami was Mahatma Gandhi, with his universal ethic of nonviolence. On the material plane, it may be suggested that India will contribute to the world culture of the future the concept of simplicity with efficiency which is a feature of many of her traditional devices. In another sphere there is the sense of the oneness of all creation, animal, vegetable, and mineral, an awareness toward which scientists are laboriously working but which in Indian minds is inherent and taken for granted. There is also an awareness of the spirit behind all life, which may not in the past indeed have had much visible or practical effect but which in combination with the more positive ethic India is absorbing from the West has tremendous potentiality. And then there is the Gandhian ethic of ahimsa or the way of gentleness, which has already made an impact on the West as a personal code through Gandhi himself and has been brought to the international sphere by Nehru. India will not lead the world in science, in industry, or luxury living, but she may well make invaluable contributions to mankind's understanding of itself and the human art of living.

Returning from more distant time to the immediate future, we may note in conclusion the clamant questions which demand immediate solution. In the international sphere it is the problem of peace, for which Nehru prescribed noninvolvement and the cultivation of neutral blocs. A little thought will show how essentially this fits in with the Gandhian outlook and what a departure it is from the old assumptions of power politics. At home there are the huge linked problems of poverty and population. If population increase is not checked poverty cannot be greatly alleviated; if this is not done there is bound to be suffering and violence before long and probably a change of regime. In the Himalayan setting of these problems, such questions as unemployment and the completion of industrialization are comparatively simple. Finally there is the social reintegration of the Indian people to express the absorption of the new ideas. The ideas will go on working, the yeast will heave and germinate; but unless it is guided its workings will produce much suffering and upheaval. In the past, light came from the East; in the future it will come again. But this time it will be a rainbow ray through a prism, one face of which was made in the West.

NOTES

NOTES TO CHAPTER I

1. They are the *Rig, Sama, Yajur,* and *Atharvaveda.* The *Samaveda* is a hymn book for sacrifices copied from the *Rigveda* except for 75 stanzas; the *Yajurveda* is also largely drawn from the *Rigveda;* the *Atharvaveda* is largely a collection of spells, which, though very ancient, are also very obscure.
2. Book VII, No. 77, *Hindu Scriptures,* ed. N. Macnicol (1938).
3. Sir E. Arnold rendered it "The Song Celestial" when he transposed it into English verse.
4. The Dasehra covers the first ten days of the waxing moon in late September or early October. The *diwali* night is the dark night following about nineteen days later.
5. About a tenth of the text is found in the *Mahabharata.*

NOTES TO CHAPTER II

1. See S. Radhakrishnan, *The Hindu View of Life.*
2. See K. M. Panikkar, *Hinduism at the Crossroads.*
3. The English word is derived from the Portuguese *casta* meaning race or species. There is no specific Indian word for caste as an institution. The Sanskrit term for a caste is *varna* which has become in modern Hindustani *zat.*
4. There is no exact translation of *dharma,* which includes overtones not implied in the English words.
5. Thus Professor J. H. Hutton calls them "the exterior castes."
6. E. Senart, *Les Castes dans l'Inde* (Paris, 1896, etc.).
7. Sir H. Risley, *The People of India* (London, 1908, etc.).
8. A. M. Hocart, *Caste, a Comparative Study* (1950).
9. J. H. Hutton, *Caste in India* (Cambridge, 1946).
10. E.g., scavenging, tanning, leatherworking.

NOTES TO CHAPTER III

1. Literally, "old writings." They are mainly legendary and marvelous, but may be said to contain hints of historic fact.
2. In the foothills near the modern Rawalpindi, capital of Pakistan.
3. Altogether some thirty "edicts" have been discovered with several miscellaneous inscriptions.
4. Romila Thapar, *Asoka and the Decline of the Mauryas* (Oxford, 1960).

NOTES TO CHAPTER IV

1. The traditional dates are 600–527 B.C.
2. They celebrated the twenty-five hundredth anniversary of his death (543 B.C.) in 1957.
3. Quoted by R. K. Mokerji, *Men and Thought in Ancient India* (1924), p. 51.
4. The Buddhist virtues as portrayed in the *Dhammapada* may be described as a paler version of the Sermon on the Mount, e.g., "Never shall hatred cease by hating; by not hating shall it cease."
5. Sarojini Naidu, "The Golden Threshold," quoted from the *Oxford Book of Mystical Verse* (London, 1917), pp. 611–12.
6. So called from the site of its first discovery.
7. From Shiva, the third member of the Hindu trinity. The great temple of Angkor in Cambodia was erected to this god.

NOTES TO CHAPTER V

1. W. W. Tarn and A. K. Narain.
2. It should be made clear that hardly one of the above statements is undisputed. In this summary I have been guided by what seems to be the general consensus of learned opinion, which has a substratum of agreement. For example there is disagreement as to who marched to Pataliputra, but agreement that the march took place.
3. *Alberuni's India,* ed. E. C. Sachau (London, 1914), p. 23.
4. At Bhilsa, near Bhopal in central India.
5. Yavana was the Indian term for Greeks, from Greek Ionia. It was often used loosely of foreigners in general, but in the context of south Indian trade the term could only refer to Greeks, Romans, or Arabs.
6. The Syrian Christians today in their various branches number over a million souls.
7. The word "Saka," like the word "Yavana," was often used loosely for any kind of foreigner. But this very fact suggests that these people must first have made a deep impression on the Indian mind.

NOTES TO CHAPTER VIII

1. There were sieges in 668–75 and 717.
2. The word "Mussulman" is a corruption of Muslim. Muslims are incorrectly called Muhammadans on the Christian analogy. They do not worship Muhammad as divine, as Christians do Christ. Strictly they are not followers of Muhammad but of God.
3. The Muslim state of Bhopal was ruled by begums or princesses during much of the last century. The Mughal princesses Jahanara and Roshanara were great ladies of cultivation who played an active part in politics from "behind the purdah." All these, it may be noted, were of Turkish race.

4. The last occasion on any scale before independence was at the time of the Moplah rebellion in 1921.
5. E.g., the shrines of Nizam-ad-din and Qutab Sahib at Delhi, or Salim Shah Chishti at Ajmir.
6. The Christians of India as a community were confined to Malabar.

NOTES TO CHAPTER IX

1. E.g., the Janissaries of Turkey and the Mamelukes of Egypt.
2. The shadow of the Mongol menace may still be felt when looking at the frowning walls of Tughluqabad near Delhi.
3. Known in literature generally as Tamerlane, and in Marlowe's famous play as Tamburlaine. The suffix "lane" stands for "i-lang," "lame."
4. They were really Chagatai Turks.
5. Palam is the site of the New Delhi airport. The Shah Alam referred to reigned from 1444–51.
6. So called from the family name of the dynasty, which claimed descent from Bahman, the Artaxerxes of the Bible.

NOTES TO CHAPTER X

1. Daulat's fickleness provided an occasion for the exercise of Babur's humor. After his defection and capture, he was brought, by Babur's command, into his presence with *two* swords hanging round his neck, one for Babur and one for Ibrahim.
2. Babur's *Memoirs*, trans. J. Leyden and W. Erskine, ed. L. King (Oxford, 1921), II, p. 241.

NOTES TO CHAPTER XII

1. Ed. S. N. Sen, *Indian Travels of Thevenot and Carreri*, pp. 220–21. New Delhi: Indian Records Series, 1949. The spelling has been modernized.

NOTES TO CHAPTER XIII

1. Brit. Mus. Add MS. 6,588, f. 55b, quoted, Ibn Hasan, *Central Structure of the Mughal Empire* (1936), p. 360.
2. The Persian suffix *dar* indicates the holder or doer of a thing.
3. Blochmann and Jarrett, *Ain-i-Akbari*, Vol. I, p. 535.
4. W. E. Moreland, *India at the Death of Akbar*, p. 69.
5. *Ibid.*, p. 70.
6. F. Bernier, *Travels in the Mogul Empire*, tr. by A. Constable (2d ed.; Oxford, 1916), p. 264.
7. A. H. Lloyd, in *Transactions of International Numismatic Congress* (1936), pp. 426–38.
8. W. E. Moreland, *From Akbar to Aurangzeb*, pp. 57–58; and *India at the Death of Akbar*, pp. 227–39—a careful analysis.
9. W. E. Moreland, *India at the Death of Akbar*, p. 68.

10. Estimates of the cost of the Taj vary. A likely figure is about £4,000,000 or 400 lacs of rupees. This would be about $12,000,000 at the present rate of exchange. A better comparison would be to say that the cost equaled about four years' revenue during James I's England or one-sixth of the annual revenue of Shah Jahan himself.

NOTES TO CHAPTER XIV

1. R. C. Whiteway, *Rise of the Portuguese Power in India, 1497–1550,* pp. 7–8.
2. E.g., Francesco Pelsaert's *Remonstrantie,* translated by W. H. Moreland under the name of *Jehangir's India* (London, 1925).
3. See W. Foster, *England's Quest of Eastern Trade* (London, 1933).
4. In 1595 and 1598.
5. Spear, T. G. P., *The Nabobs* (Oxford, 1932), p. 21. The information is to be found in H. D. Love, *Vestiges of Old Madras* (London, 1913), II, pp. 110–11.
6. They required a separate servant for maintenance.

NOTES TO CHAPTER XV

1. Sivaji, when giving the customary ceremonial embrace, clawed him with a steel weapon known as "the tiger's claw." The incident is important for it has been a cause of lasting resentment between Muslims and Marathas. Certain Maratha patriots, including Tilak, gloried in it.
2. Malik Amber's of Ahmadnagar.
3. They provided their own horses and arms and lived on plunder. They were called *Pendharas,* later corrupted to Pindaris.
4. In 1526 when Babur defeated Sultan Ibrahim Lodi and in 1556 when Akbar and Bhairam Khan defeated Hemu. It was thus at Panipat that the Mughal Empire began, was restored, and finally dissolved.

NOTES TO CHAPTER XVI

1. A corruption of the plural form of *Naib,* Arabic for deputy. The plural form was used for the deputies of high offices, and then, by association, came to be used as a title of honor in itself.
2. From *Sipahi,* a soldier (Persian).

NOTES TO CHAPTER XVII

1. The title was Sabat Jang, "the tried in battle." By this title Clive was known in the contemporary Indian histories.

NOTES TO CHAPTER XVIII

1. See p. 208.

NOTES TO CHAPTER XIX

1. C. H. Philips, ed., *The Correspondence of David Scott etc. 1787–1805* (2 vols.; London, 1951).
2. Sir J. Malcolm, *Memoir of Central India*, Vol. 1, pp. 430–31.
3. He came to India as Earl of Moira. He received the title of Marquess of Hastings as a result of his successes.

NOTES TO CHAPTER XX

1. W. Hamilton, *Description of Hindustan and the Adjacent Countries* (2 vols.; London, 1820), p. xxxvii. In the totals given Sindia has been treated as an ally and Cabul (Afghanistan) omitted. The independent states were Lahore (the Sikhs in the Panjab), Sind, and Nepal.
2. S. P. Sen, *The French in India, 1763–1816* (Calcutta, 1958), pp. 305–6.
3. The interested reader may consult Sir J. Malcolm, *Memoir of Central India* (2 vols.; London, 1832), or M. Elphinstone, *Report on Territories Recently Acquired from the Peshwa* (London, 1822).
4. See W. Adam, *Reports on the State of Education in Bengal* (1835 and 1838), ed. by A. Basu (Calcutta, 1941).
5. See Meadows Taylor, *Confessions of a Thug*, ed. C. W. Stuart (Oxford, 1916).
6. See E. Thompson, *Suttee* (London, 1938).

NOTES TO CHAPTER XXI

1. For a rather idealized account of him see P. Woodruffe, *The Men Who Ruled India* (2 vols.; London, 1953–54).
2. For a full description see B. H. Baden-Powell, *Land Systems of British India* (3 vols.; Oxford, 1892).
3. From *mahal*, a term for a subdistrict or estate—to be distinguished from *mahal*, Persian, a palace.

NOTES TO CHAPTER XXII

1. Modern Karachi, the capital of Pakistan, was occupied in 1839 and owes its development to this event.
2. In 1820 the area of the Lahore state was estimated at fifty thousand square miles and its population at three million. In 1951 the first Pakistan census gave to the West Panjab, roughly equivalent to the Sikh kingdom, an area of fifty-three thousand square miles and a population of nearly nineteen million.
3. The modern Sikh normally wears a miniature dagger in his turban; but in the troubles of 1947 the full-sized sword was very much in evidence.
4. From the Sanskrit meaning "timeless." *Akalis* therefore means "worshipers of the Timeless One."

NOTES TO CHAPTER XXIII

1. To the House of Commons, July 10, 1833.
2. A *lakh* (lac) or 100,000 rupees, or £ 10,000.
3. Regulation XVII of 1829.
4. Shakespeare, *Richard II,* Act II, scene i.

NOTES TO CHAPTER XXIV

1. "Vengeance," that is, in the sense of "to the limit," not of taking revenge.
2. Now the Engineering University at Roorkee, Uttar Pradesh.
3. These were at Calcutta, Bombay, and Madras. They were organized on the model of London University and were opened in 1857.
4. Oudh—area 23,000 sq. miles, population about 5,000,000. A. Campbell, *Modern India* [London, 1853], p. 150.
5. Bishop R. Heber, *Narrative of a Journey* . . . (3d ed.; London, 1828), II, p. 90.
6. Nagpur—area 76,000 sq. miles, population about 4,500,000 (Campbell, p. 151).
7. He died of wounds on July 4, 1857.

NOTES TO CHAPTER XXV

1. They were James Wilson and Samuel Laing.
2. In 1863 the figures were Indians, 140,000; Europeans, 65,000. Before 1857 they were Indians, 238,000; Europeans, 45,000.
3. It is interesting to note that the word "loot" is derived directly from the Hindustani *lut.* The loan took place at the time of British contact with Marathas and Pindaris.
4. The standard Indian railroad gauge is 5′6″, compared with 4′8½″ on American and British railroads. In addition, the meter gauge was used for lines with lighter traffic, and a narrow gauge in the hills and a few other places.
5. The upper and lower Ganges canals with their distributaries have a length of 8,000 miles.
6. The "five rivers" of the Panjab are the Jhelum, Chenab, Beas, Ravi, and Sutlej, which all find their way into the Indus.
7. In recent years British production has been about 200,000,000 tons a year.
8. Reckoning by weight. See V. Anstey, *Economic Development of India* (ed. 1949), p. 262, note 2.

NOTES TO CHAPTER XXVI

1. E.g., the Hunter Commission of 1882, Curzon's Calcutta University Commission of 1903, the Sadler Commission of 1919.
2. The Black age—the third and worst of Indian cosmology.
3. Founder of the Scottish Churches College, Calcutta.

4. Lived about 1770–1833.
5. Now the Government Presidency College.
6. The Tagore family for three generations were pillars of this body—the entrepreneur Dwarkenath, the sage Devendranath, and the poet Radindranath.
7. Dayananda lived from 1824–83.
8. Lived from 1834–86.
9. Lived from 1862–1902.
10. Miss Margaret Noble, who died in 1911.
11. The Muslim revival and Sayyid Ahmad Khan are more fully dealt with in the chapter on the rise of Pakistan. The name Sayyid is applied to a descendant of the Prophet Muhammad.

NOTES TO CHAPTER XXVII

1. Sir B. N. Mittra, member of the Executive Council in 1924, is an example.
2. The first was appointed in Calcutta in 1870.
3. So called because they were appointed directly in India and did not hold "covenants" from the Secretary of State in London.
4. The popularity of Tod's *Annals* may be judged from the fact that while its actual English editions were dated 1829–32, 1914, and 1920, there were seven Indian reprints between 1873 and 1912 designed entirely to meet the demand of Indian readers of the new middle classes.
5. It was very difficult for Indians to sit in London at the specified age.

NOTES TO CHAPTER XXVIII

1. See D. V. Tahmankar, *Lokamanya Tilak* (London, 1956).
2. Until World War I, when the import duty was raised to 7 per cent.
3. For a discussion see V. Anstey, *Economic Development of India.*
4. Hazara, Kohat, Peshawar, Bannu, Dera Ismail Khan.
5. For fuller treatment see Chapter XXX, "India in World Affairs, 1858–1914."
6. This institute was destroyed in the 1934 earthquake in Behar. It was then transferred to New Delhi under the name of the New Pusa Institute.

NOTES TO CHAPTER XXIX

1. In Hindustani, *vilayat,* or the metropolitan province. This was corrupted to "blighty" by the British soldier and used for "home" in World War I by the British troops in France.
2. The existence of the American species of the genus was not yet appreciated.
3. According to the account by his centenary apologist D. V. Tahmankar, *Lokamanya Tilak* (1956), pp. 145–46.

4. As distinct from the provinces of lieutenant governors and chief commissioners. The change appealed to the Indian sense of caste and hierarchy.

NOTES TO CHAPTER XXX

1. It was absorbed in 1881.
2. Son of the historical novelist Edward Bulwer-Lytton, and a poet in his own right.
3. At the existing rate of exchange this sum equaled £60,000, or $180,-000 at the *present* rate of exchange.

NOTES TO CHAPTER XXXI

1. Bodies of Western-trained men with Indian officers.
2. A *maulvi* or *mullah* is a man learned in Muslim law, which is both civil and ecclesiastical. In the absence of a priesthood or religious hierarchy this class provides the religious leadership in Islam.
3. For Montagu's opinion of the Indian administration, see E. S. Montagu, *An Indian Diary* (London, 1930).
4. He eventually settled down in California.
5. This power was allowed to the supreme government only by Regulation III of 1818.
6. A hartal is a cessation of all activity for a specific period, usually a day, in protest against some action (usually of government). It is a kind of one-day strike, but the idea is rooted in Indian tradition and has vague religious associations in the Indian mind.
7. E.g., public floggings and a crawling order.

NOTES TO CHAPTER XXXII

1. Report of the Hunter Committee, 1920.
2. The treaty sparked off the rising of Ataturk (Mustafa Kemal Pasha) in Asia Minor. He defeated the Greeks as allied agents in 1922 and concluded a fresh treaty of Lausanne in 1923. This laid the diplomatic foundation of modern Turkey.
3. They were Muslims descended from Arab traders on the southwest coast of India, noted for their belligerence and fanaticism.
4. This "leak" lead to the resignation of Mr. Montagu.
5. The center retained customs, income-tax, posts, salt, and railways receipts.

NOTES TO CHAPTER XXXIII

1. Sitting *dharna* was the practice of fasting on the doorstep of one who has wronged you until the wrong is righted. Death as a result of this process placed a curse on the wrongdoer. It was forbidden by law in British India but still occasionally practiced.

NOTES TO CHAPTER XXXIV

1. This word or the term "political class" is used instead of the word "public," which may be misleading. The only articulate "public" at this time was the middle class.
2. He died in 1925.
3. The author went to Delhi early in 1924. From this point in the book until 1945 there is an element of personal experience and reminiscence in the narrative. The sight of Motilal addressing the Assembly was one of his first Indian experiences.
4. He was a member of Congress until nonco-operation days.
5. If Lord Birkenhead's tentative correspondence with C. R. Das in 1924–25 had come to anything, it would have increased Congress divisions.
6. He was later Foreign Secretary, Home Secretary, Chancellor of the Exchequer, and Lord Chancellor in successive governments from 1931–45.

NOTES TO CHAPTER XXXV

1. Report of the Inter-Imperial Relations Committee, Imperial Conference, 1926, Section 1, "The Status of Great Britain and the Dominions."
2. See S. Gopal, *Lord Irwin.*
3. On September 7, 1931.
4. It virtually ended with the beginning of the Gandhian fast on May 8, 1933.
5. Irwin wrote in June 1930, "I certainly am [myself]—and we should delude ourselves if we sought to underrate it." Quoted by M. Brecher in *Nehru* (1959), p. 153. His source was the National Archives of India, used by permission of the Ministry of Home Affairs, Government of India.

NOTES TO CHAPTER XXXVI

1. One-third in the lower house and two-fifths in the upper.
2. Seven and one-half years.
3. In Bombay with the support of Hindu sympathizers and in the Frontier Province with the "Red Shirts."
4. Thirty-two trade unionists were arrested. The trial lasted for three and one-half years.
5. Dr. Khare, chief minister of the Central Provinces, was replaced in 1938 by Pundit Shukla.

NOTES TO CHAPTER XXXVII

1. About one in 28,500 of the population, or .0035 per cent.
2. The author was present at the Press Conference at which the proposals were explained.

3. See M. Brecher, *Nehru* (1959), pp. 277–82.

NOTES TO CHAPTER XXXVIII

1. The "Caretaker" government was formed on the breakup of the coalition government in May 1945 and existed until the results of the general election were known in July.
2. E.g., in East Bengal the whole countryside turned Muslim; in Malabar the Arab traders formed a community by intermarriage with Hindus.
3. The Wahabi—so called from the puritan Arab movement of the same name whose leaders now rule Saudi Arabia.
4. In 1920 it became the Aligarh Muslim University.
5. In 1933 the visionary Rahmat Ali coined the portmanteau word Pakistan: P for Panjab, A for Afghans (Pathans), K for Kashmir, S for Sind; *stan* is Persian for country. By a happy chance *pak* means pure in Persian-Urdu, so the whole word denoted "Land of the Pure." The word was first used in his pamphlet, *Now or Never* (1933).
6. Maulana Abul Kalam Azad.
7. Pukhtunistan is the land of the Pathans or Pushtu speakers. The word represents the aspiration of some Pathans to have a hill-state independent of both Pakistan and Afghanistan.
8. E.g., Cripps was a friend of Nehru, and Lord Pethwick-Lawrence was close to Gandhi.
9. The text of para. 8 is as follows: "In the event of the two major parties or either of them proving unwilling to join in the setting up of a Coalition Government on the above lines, it is the intention of the Viceroy to proceed with the formation of an Interim Government which will be as representative as possible of those willing to accept the Statement of May 16th." This incident still needs full elucidation. It is by no means certain that Jinnah was not disingenuous in his conduct. See E. W. R. Lumby, *Transfer of Power in India,* pp. 99–105.
10. The official estimates of casualties were 4,000 killed and 10,000 injured.

NOTES TO CHAPTER XXXIX

1. E.g., in states, Pakistani, and personal affairs and during the Panjab-Delhi disturbances. In the Delhi disturbances he was *sent for* from Simla by Patel with Nehru's agreement. K. P. Menon, *Transfer of Power in India,* pp. 423–24.
2. Tandon and his group had been holding up the measure of social reform known as the Hindu Code Bill.
3. U. N. Dhebar.
4. For the author's fuller views on the question of responsibility see his review article, "Britain's Transfer of Power in India," in *Pacific Affairs,* Vol. XXXI, no. 2 (June 1958), pp. 173–80.
5. For the moving final scenes see M. Brecher, *Nehru,* pp. 381–88.
6. E.g., Baroda, Mysore, Travancore, Gwalior.
7. The exact number depends on a rather fine distinction between estates and states. The usually accepted number is 562.

8. E.g., Rajasthan, Travancore, Vindhya Pradesh.
9. E.g., in the cases of the Panjab (India) and Kerala.
10. See Cl. 368 of the constitution. For most purposes a bare majority of the membership of each house and a two-thirds majority of those present and voting is required.

NOTES TO CHAPTER XL

1. There are about twenty-five million Brahmins in India; or one in fourteen of the population.
2. *Nahr* denotes "canal" in Persian. Hence *Nehru*—the person associated with a canal.
3. See Chapter XLI (pp. 457–58) and Glossary.
4. *Rashtrya Swayamsevak Sangh,* alleged to have been implicated in Gandhi's assassination.
5. See D. V. Rangnekar, *The Crisis of Confidence,* in *The World Today,* Vol. 21, no. 2, Feb. 1965, London.

NOTES TO CHAPTER XLI

1. Popularly known as "The Syndicate".
2. For the successions and the Shastri regime, see M. Brecher, *Succession in India* (London, 1966).
3. Dravida Munetra Kazagham.
4. *The World Today* (Chatham House, London), Vol. 27, no. 9, Sept. 1971, p. 375.
5. *India News* (London), Vol. 25, no. 7, 19 Feb. 1972, p. 1.

SUGGESTED READINGS

The following readings are intended for readers who wish to pursue further studies, either in general or in particular topics. The references are mainly to printed works and, in the later portion, to government and other reports. These references will in turn lead on the inquiring student to the further sources of the subjects concerned.

GENERAL

The best-known standard history is the *Cambridge History of India* in six volumes. Five volumes were published between 1922 and 1932. Volume II, covering the first ten centuries of the Christian era, is being prepared by Professor A. L. Basham of London. There is a supplementary volume on the Indus civilization (1953) by Sir Mortimer-Wheeler. The volumes vary in merit. The best is the first. Vols. III and IV adopt the style of the Muslim chronicles they rest upon and Vols. V and VI are almost exclusively political and administrative. But all are weighty and equipped with extensive bibliographies. In India the Bharatiya Vidya Bhavan is publishing the *History and Culture of the Indian People* in 10 volumes. The work is directed by Dr. K. M. Munshi, and the general editor is the veteran scholar Dr. R. C. Mazumdar. Special attention is paid to social and cultural aspects, and the six volumes so far published reveal the high standard of modern Indian historical scholarship. These are the *Vedic Age* (1951), *The Age of Imperial Unity* (600 B.C.–300 A.D.) (1951), *The Classical Age* (320–750 A.D.) (1954), *The Age of Imperial Kanauj* (750–1000 A.D.) (1955), *The Struggle for Empire* (750–1200 A.D.) (1957), and *The Delhi Sultanate* (1960). The set is now nearly complete.

Of the many single-volume histories the following may be mentioned. The standard was set by Mountstuart Elphinstone's *History of India*, which was first published in 1841 and achieved a reprint of the ninth edition (London) in 1911. The Muslim section was based on the standard Muslim historians and set the dynastic framework of Indian history which has survived until recently. The best-known recent single-volume work is the *Oxford History of India*, originally written by Vincent Smith (1919). The third edition (1958) has been edited and the British section rewritten by Percival Spear. The Indian scholars R. C. Mazumdar, H. C. Raychandhuri, and K. K. Datta published an *Advanced History of India* (London: Macmillan) in 1946. These two works may be said to represent modern British and Indian views of Indian history respectively, and they provide an interesting comparison. *The Cambridge Shorter History of India* (1934) is notable for an acute study of the British period by H. H. Dodwell. An original and challenging sketch is K. M. Panikkar's *Survey of Indian History*, first published in 1946. A more orthodox but well-written sketch representing an Indo-British liberal view is a *Short History of India* by W. H. Moreland and A. C. Chatterjee, first published in 1936 and now in its fourth edition. For a brief introduction the author's *India, Pakistan and the West* (3rd ed.; London, 1958) may be mentioned. As a companion to these works should be consulted the excellent compendium of source material *Sources of Indian Tradition* (New York, 1958). Its editor is Wm. Theodore de Bary and it is no. LVI of the Records of Civilization series (Columbia). For South India the learned Professor Nilakanta Sastri's *History of South India* (to 1563) (London, 1955) is authoritative.

In the realm of art mention may be made of Vincent Smith's *History of Fine Art in India and Ceylon* revised by K. de B. Codrington (Oxford, 1930) and of A. Coomaraswamy's *History of Indian and Indonesian Art* (London, 1927).

ANCIENT INDIA (CHS. I–VII)

For this period in general the first volume of the *Cambridge History of India* (edited by Professor Rapson) is of very high quality. The second volume, edited by A. L. Basham is likely to rival it. The first four volumes of the *History and Culture of the Indian People* are more recent and on a larger scale. The first volume is somewhat controversial; the others are all authoritative as well as learned. The best single-volume work is A. L. Basham's *The Wonder That Was India* (London, 1954) which skilfully combines political, cultural, and social elements to give a vivid picture of ancient Indian life and thought. An Indian work is Radhakumud Mookerji's *Hindu Civilisation* (London–New York, 1936), which takes the readers to the Mauryan empire. As an introduction E. J. Rapson's *Ancient India* (Cambridge, 1916) may be consulted. Outstanding among single-volume works are V. A. Smith's *Early History of India* (4th ed.; Oxford, 1924), K. A. Nilakanta Sastri's *History of India,* Part I (Madras, 1950), and H. C. Raychaudhuri's *Political History of Ancient India* (6th ed.; Calcutta, 1953).

On the cultural side G. T. Garratt (ed.), *The Legacy of India* (Oxford, 1937), can be warmly recommended. A. A. Macdonnell's *India's Past* (Oxford, 1927) is valuable on the linguistic side and the work of Coomaraswamy and Smith already mentioned for art. H. G. Rawlinson's *India, A Short Cultural History* (London, 1943) is a good introduction on the cultural side.

References for the individual chapters of this section should be read in conjunction with the foregoing list, which covers the whole of the ground and in some cases provides the best available printed sources.

I. THE EARLY CULTURES

For the prehistoric period the best work is that of Sir R. E. Mortimer-Wheeler, *The Indus Civilisation* (Cambridge, 1953), a supplementary volume to *The Cambridge History of India.* The author himself conducted some of the most striking excavations at Harappa. S. Piggott, *Prehistoric India* (London, 1950) gives an excellent general survey.

Works purporting to interpret the Harappan script should be viewed with caution. The most recent survey is B. & R. Allchin's *The Birth of Indian Civilisation* (London, 1968).

For the Vedic period, apart from general work, the reader may consult A. B. Keith, *Religion and Philosophy of the Vedas and Upanishads* (Cambridge, Mass., 1923).

There are many translations of Vedic and epic Indian literature, which are the main historical sources for these periods. A convenient and excellent compendium is N. Macnicol's (ed.) *Hindu Scriptures* (London, Everyman, 1938). The same Everyman series contains (London, 1917) R. C. Dutt's free verse rendering of the *Mahabharata and Ramayana*. There is a full translation of the *Mahabharata* by P. C. Roy in 11 vols. (Calcutta, 1919–33). The Vedic Hymns are translated in full by F. Max Muller and H. Oldenburg in *Sacred Books of the East,* vols. XXXII and XLVI (Oxford, 1891–96).

II. HINDUISM

Good introductions are by J. N. Farquhar, *A Primer of Hinduism* (London, 1912) and by L. S. S. O'Malley, *Popular Hinduism* (Oxford). Farquhar's *Crown of Hinduism* provides a description of Hinduism of 1900 from a liberal Christian point of view. For caste J. H. Hutton, *Caste in India* (Cambridge, 1946) and E. Senart (tr. Sir E. Denison Ross), *Caste in India* (London, 1930), should be consulted.

The standard translation of Manu's Laws is by G. Bühler in the *Sacred Books of the East*, vol. XXV (Oxford, 1886). Selected Upanishads are translated in Macnicol's work mentioned under the previous chapter, by F. Max Muller in vols. I and XV in the *Sacred Books of the East* (Oxford, 1879–82), and by R. A. Hume, *Thirteen Principal Upanishads* (Oxford, 1921). The *Bhagavad Gita* has had many translators. Two of the best are by C. D. Barnett in Macnicol's *Hindu Scriptures* mentioned above and by E. J. Thomas, *The Song of the Lord* (London, 1948), in the Wisdom of the East series. A text, translation, and interpretation are provided by F. Edgerton, 2 vols. (Cambridge, Mass., 1946).

For a study of modern problems see K. M. Panikkar's *Hindu Society at the Crossroads* (Bombay, 1955).

III. THE DAWN OF RECORDED HISTORY: ALEXANDER AND ASOKA

H. C. Raychaudhuri, in his *Political History of Ancient India,* has attempted a reconstruction of political history down to the time of the Buddha on the basis of Puranic King lists, etc. The *Age of the Nandas and Mauryas* (Banaras, 1952), edited by K. A. Nilakanta Sastri, takes the story down to the Mauryas. For Alexander's incursion Vincent Smith's *Ancient History of India* and the first volume of the *Cambridge History* are still good guides. The latest study is by Sir W. W. Tarn, *Alexander the Great,* 2 vols. (Cambridge, 1948). For Chandragupta, see R. K. Mookerji's *Chandragupta Maurya and His Times* (Madras, 1943). For Asoka, see R. K. Mookerji's *Asoka* (1928) or D. R.

Bhandarkar's work (1925) with the same title. An important new assessment is by Romila Thapar in *Asoka and the Decline of the Mauryas* (Oxford, 1960). The inscriptions are given in full in vol. 1 of Hultzsch's *Corpus Inscriptionum Indicarum* (Oxford, 1925). Selections are given in the books mentioned. *The Arthasastra* is translated by R. Shamasastry (3d ed.; Mysore, 1929). Beni Prasad's *The State in Ancient India* is also of value.

IV. JAINISM AND BUDDHISM

For *Jainism* see Mrs. S. Stevenson, *The Heart of Jainism* (Oxford, 1915). A valuable modern study is by A. L. Basham in the *History and Doctrines of the Ajivikas* (London, 1951).

Buddhism. R. K. Mookerji's sympathetic study in *Men and Thought of Ancient India* (London, 1926) may serve as an introduction. T. W. Rhys Davids' *Buddhism, Its History and Literature* (London, 1926) is perhaps the best general study. Sir C. Eliot, *Hinduism and Buddhism,* 3 vols. (London, 1922), may be further consulted. The *Dhammapada* is translated in the Wisdom of the East series and the charming Jataka stories (former incarnations of the Buddha) are translated by E. B. Cowell, *The Jatakas,* 3 vols. (2d ed.; London, 1957). F. L. Woodward in *Some Sayings of the Buddha* (Oxford: World's Classics, 1938), and H. C. Warren in *Buddhism in Translations,* have provided anthologies from the texts.

V. THE INVADERS

For the Greeks in India there is the daring and somewhat speculative work of Sir W. W. Tarn, *The Greeks in Bactria and India* (2d ed.; Cambridge, 1951). The balance is partly corrected by A. K. Narain in his very promising *Indo-Greeks* (Oxford, 1957).

For the Christians of S. India see Bishop L. W. Brown, *The Indian Christians of St. Thomas* (Cambridge, 1956), a study which is both sympathetic and critical.

For western contacts H. G. Rawlinson's *Intercourse Between India and the Western World* (Cambridge, 1916) and E. H. Warmington's *Commerce Between the Roman Empire and India* (Cambridge, 1928) are valuable.

For the Pahlavas, Sakas, and Kushans there are no set studies in English. J. E. Van Lohuizen de Leeuw has contributed a valuable study in art and chronology in her *The Scythian Period* (Leiden, 1949). Otherwise, the reader is advised to consult the general histories already listed, specially the *History and Culture of the Indian People,* vol. II, and *The Cambridge History of India,* vol. I.

VI. THE IMPERIAL AGE

Volume III of the *History and Culture of the Indian People, The Classical Age* (Bombay, 1954), largely the work of R. C. Majumdar, is the best single volume for this period. R. K. Mookerji's *Gupta Empire* (Allahabad, 1949) is also valuable. P. T. S. Iyengar covers the south in *The History of the Tamils* to 600 A.D. (Madras, 1929).

For literature A. B. Keith's *History of Sanskrit Literature* (Oxford, 1928) and the *Sanskrit Drama* (Oxford, 1924) may be recommended. For philosophy the standard works are Sir S. Radhakrishnan's *Indian Philosophy*, 2 vols. (London, 1923–27) and S. N. Das Gupta's *History of Indian Philosophy*, 4 vols. (Cambridge, 1923–49). For the arts see the works of Coomaraswamy and Smith already mentioned, with S. Kramrisch's *Indian Sculpture* (London, 1937) and A. H. Fox-Strangeway's *Music of Hindustan* (Oxford, 1914). The most accessible sources for Indian scientific achievement are the appendices of A. L. Basham's *The Wonder That Was India* and G. T. Garratt's (ed.) *Legacy of India* (Oxford, 1937).

For greater India the best general source is D. G. E. Hall's *History of South-East Asia* (London, 1955). The best monograph is G. Coédè's *Les États hindouises d'Indochine et d'Indonésie* (Paris, 1948) and in English H. G. Q. Wales, *The Making of Greater India* (London, 1931).

VII.   NEW PEOPLES: THE RAJPUT WORLD: SOUTH INDIA

For Harsha and Kanauj there is D. Devahuti's *Harsha* (Oxford, 1970) and R. S. Tripathi's *History of Kanauj* (Banares, 1937). The period is one of great perplexity and obscurity and no easy way through it can be recommended. The best single-volume treatment is the *Age of Imperial Kanauj*, vol. IV of *The History and Culture of the Indian People*. De la Vallée Poussin's *Dynasties et histoire* (Paris, 1935) deals with the earlier dynasties and H. C. Ray's *Dynastic History of Northern India*, 2 vols. (Calcutta, 1931–36), with the later ones. For South India see Nilakanta Sastri's *History of South India*, as before.

We still await a work which will draw together the sociological, linguistic, and literary threads with the political to provide a complete picture of the great transition in Indian culture.

For an account of Indian culture and religion about 1000 A.D. see Albiruni's great work (ed. and tr. E. C. Sachau), *Alberuni's India* (London, 1910, etc.).

THE MUSLIM PERIOD, 1191–1750

GENERAL

Volumes V and VI of the *History and Culture of the Indian People*, *The Struggle for Empire* (Bombay, 1957), and *The Delhi Sultanate* (Bombay, 1960) have appeared, and the series may continue to be used. The period is covered by vols. III and IV of the *Cambridge History of India;* though scholarly, they unfortunately follow in large measure (specially volume III) the annalistic style of their Persian sources. A distinguished though old work is M. Elphinstone's *History of India*, first published in 1841. A good modern general history is Ishwari Prasad's *History of Medieval India* (3rd ed., Allahabad, 1950).

For the later part of this period the sources are far more copious and concentrated than before, and they are also more easily available. A standard work is the *History of India as Told by Its Own Historians,* translated and edited by Sir H. M. Elliot and J. Dowson (London, 1866–77). It is in seven volumes and has been supplemented by S. H. Hodivala's learned commentary *Studies in Indo-Muslim History* (Bombay, 1939). For the Rajputs there is Tod's classic *Annals of Rajasthan* (2d ed.; Oxford), first published in 1829–32 and based on the Rajput bardic lore.

Of the general one volume histories of India, Panikkar's *Survey of Indian History* has original views and Mazumdar, Raychaudhuri and Datta's book is sound if unimaginative.

VIII. ISLAM IN INDIA

H. A. R. Gibb's *Mohammedanism* (London: Home University Library, 1949) provides a good introduction. For origins see Sir W. Muir, *Rise and Decline of the Caliphate* (Edinburgh, 1915) and the works of Philip Hitti. R. Levy deals with the sociological aspect in his learned *Social Structure of Islam* (Cambridge, 1957). For a sympathetic account of Islam see the work of the Indian Muslim, S. Amir Ali, *The Spirit of Islam*. There are numerous translations of the Koran, among which may be mentioned those of D. M. Sale, Rodwell (Everyman's Library), and Maulana Muhammad Ali.

For Islam in India the work of the American scholar Murray T. Titus, *Indian Islam* (London, 1930) at present holds the field. An account of popular Islam in the early nineteenth century is to be found in *Islam in India,* edited and translated by G. A. Herklots (new ed.; Oxford, 1921). For modern developments see W. C. Smith, *Modern Islam in India* (rev. ed.; London, 1946). I. H. Qureshi's *History of the Muslim Community in the Indo-Pakistan Sub-continent* (The Hague, 1962) is important. See also S. M. Ikram and Percival Spear (eds.), *The Cultural Heritage of Pakistan* (Karachi, 1955), Tara Chand, *Influence of Islam on Indian Culture* (Allahabad, 1952), Aziz Ahmad, *Studies in Islamic Culture in the Indian Environment* (Oxford, 1964). M. Mujeeb's *Indian Muslims* (London, 1967) is a most valuable new work.

IX. TURKS AND AFGHANS

Sources are meager until the sixteenth century. Extracts from the chief ones are given by Elliot and Dowson in their history. For a new appraisal of the historical value of some of them, see P. Hardy, *Historians of Medieval India* (London, 1960). For Mahmud of Ghazni see Mohd Nazim, *Life and Times of Sultan Mahmud of Ghazna* (Cambridge, 1931). For the Delhi sultanate and the Deccan kingdoms it is best to follow the general works referred to, but there are certain other works which may also be mentioned. I. H. Qureshi in his *Administration of the Delhi Sultanate* (Lahore, 1942, 1945) deals ably with the Turkish government. W. H. Moreland in the *Agrarian System of Muslim India* (Cambridge, 1929) covers the revenue system with equal authority. For South India Nilakanta Sastri's *South India* should again be used. Vijayanagar is dealt with in what has come to be a minor historical classic in a *Forgotten Empire* (*Vijayanagar*) (London, 1900), by R. Sewell. For a description of north India in the fourteenth century see

H. A. R. Gibb's selections from Ibn Batuta's travels, *Travels of Ibn Batuta* (London, 1929). A complete edition is on the way.

THE MUGHAL EMPIRE

X. BABUR AND THE MUGHALS

The best introduction is still L. F. Rushbrook-Williams' *An Empire-Builder of the Sixteenth Century* (Allahabad, 1918). W. Lane Poole's *Babar* in the Rulers of India series (London, 1898) is still useful. W. Erskine's *Babur and Homayun,* 2 vols. (London, 1852), is a standard work not yet superseded. Ishwari Prasad has made a new study of Homayun in his *Life and Times of Homayun* (London, 1955). For Sher Shah see K. Qanungo, *Sher Shah* (Calcutta, 1921). The Sur dynasty needs further study. .

The best authority on Babur is Babur himself. His classic autobiography is available in English as the *Memoirs of Babur* (Oxford, 1921), 2 vols.

XI. AKBAR

The standard work in English on Akbar remains V. Smith's *Akbar the Great Mogol* (Oxford, 1917). There is a factual study by Sir W. Haig in vol. IV of *The Cambridge History of India.* A new interpretation is urgently needed. L. Binyon's *Akbar* provides a penetrating character sketch. The economic conditions of Akbar's time are studied in W. E. Moreland's *India at the Death of Akbar* (London, 1920).

C. H. Payne's *Akbar and the Jesuits* (London, 1930), a translation of du Jarrie's *"Histoire,"* gives a first-hand picture of Akbar and his court. For general reference there is Abu'l Fazl's *Ain-i-Akbari,* a monumental survey of the empire and its institutions. The three volumes were translated by Blochmann and Jarrett (Calcutta, 1873–96). Vol. I has been revised by D. C. Phillott (1939) and vol. III by Sir J. Sarkar (1948).

XII. THE GREAT MUGHALS

A useful sketch for this and the next chapter is S. M. Edwardes and H. L. O. Garrett's *Mughal Rule in India* (London, 1930). Part I gives an outline of the history and Part II deals with institutions and the arts. For Jahangir see Beni Prasad, *History of Jahangir* (London, 1922). Sir T. Roe in *The Embassy of Sir T. Roe in India, 1615–19,* edited by Sir W. Foster (London, 1926), gives a vivid picture of north India, of the ways of the Mughal court, of Jahangir himself and of the young Shah Jahan. For Shah Jahan see B. P. Saksena, *Shah Jahan of Delhi* (Allahabad, 1932). For the war of succession the classic account is by F. Bernier in his work first published in Paris in 1670. It is available in English in the Oxford edition, *Travels in the Mugol Empire* (2d ed.; 1934), edited by A. Constable and V. A. Smith. There is a study of *Dara Shukoh* by K. R. Qanungo (2d ed.; Calcutta, 1952). Aurangzeb's reign is covered in Sir J. Sarkar's great work, *History of Aurangzeb,* 5 vols. (2d ed.; Calcutta, 1925). There is also a single volume edition. For the Rajput side see Tod in his *Annals of Rajasthan.*

XIII.   INDIA IN THE SEVENTEENTH CENTURY

The basic document for administration is the *Ain-i-Akbari* already mentioned. It also contains a description of current Hinduism (vol. III) which may be compared with the acute Frenchman Bernier's description from a European point of view. An introduction to Mughal administration is by Sir J. Sarkar, *Mughal Administration* (2d ed.; Calcutta, 1924). A scholarly work is that of Ibn Hasan, *The Central Structure of the Mughal Empire* (Oxford, 1936), and I. H. Qureshi's *Administration of the Mughul Empire* (Karachi, 1966) is authoritative. P. Saran has dealt with the provinces in his *Provincial Government of the Mughuls* (Allahabad, 1941). For the Marathas see S. N. Sen, *Administrative System of the Marathas* (2d ed.; Calcutta, 1925), and Sir J. Sarkar, *Sivaji* (2nd ed., Calcutta, 1929). W. E. Moreland deals with economic matters in his *India from Akbar to Aurangzeb* (London, 1923). See also Irfan Habibh's *Agrarian System of Mughal India* (London, 1963), an impressive work.

Sir E. Maclagan, *The Jesuits and the Great Mogol* (London, 1932) deals with Catholic missions. Descriptions of great ability of court and country are those of Bernier already mentioned and J. B. Tavernier, *Travels in India,* ed. by V. Ball and W. Crooke (2d ed.; Oxford, 1925). N. Manucci's *Storia da Mogor,* a vivid and gossipy account of life in Aurangzeb's India, has been brilliantly edited by W. Irvine, 4 vols. (London, 1907–8).

XIV.   EUROPEANS IN INDIA IN THE SIXTEENTH AND SEVENTEENTH CENTURIES

For the Portuguese see the scholarly account of R. S. Whiteway, *Rise of the Portuguese Power in India* (London, 1895). For Albuquerque see also E. Prestage, *The Portuguese Pioneers and Alfonso d'Albuquerque* (London, 1929 and 1933). There is a good survey by C. R. Boxer in *Portugal and Brazil* (Oxford, 1953), edited by H. W. Livermore and in his *Portuguese Seaborne Empire 1615–1825* (London, 1969). A readable account of the whole episode is to be found in vol. I of Sir W. W. Hunter's *History of British India,* 2 vols. (London, 1899). This, with the second volume, is still the best account of the early days of the English East India Company.

Good short accounts of the English, Dutch, and French companies in India are to be found in the *Cambridge History of India,* vol. V, Ch. I–IV. S. P. Sen, in his *French in India, First Establishment and Struggle* (Calcutta, 1947), has given an authoritative and elegant account of early French efforts. For a further bibliography see *Portugal and Brazil* and the *Cambridge History.*

XV.   INDIA, 1700–1750

Most British works are defective in treating this period, regarding it as the darkest hour which precedes the dawn. It is, in fact, a most important half-century, well worthy of serious study. The Mughal side of the picture has now been fully covered in two distinguished and scholarly works. These are W. Irvine's *Later Mughals,* 2 vols. (London and Calcutta, 1922), and Sir J. Sarkar's *Fall of the Mughal Empire,* completed in 1950 (Calcutta). The first work goes to 1739, the second continues it to 1803. The final Mughal phase (1803–57) is dealt with in T. G. P. Spear, *The Twilight of the Mughals* (Cambridge, 1951). The best single-volume description is still to be found in Elphinstone. A valuable and brilliant picture of the times is provided by Sayyid Ghulam Husain in his *Siyar-ul-Mutaqherin,* 3 vols., tr. Raymond (Calcutta, 1789), and 1 vol. tr. J. Briggs (London, 1832). For the Marathas see the works of S. N. Sen and J. Sarkar already referred to. See also Grant Duff's classic *History of the Marathas,* 3 vols. (London, 1826). There is a more modern work by C. A. Kincaid and D. B. Parasnis (2d ed.; Oxford, 1931).

THE BRITISH IN INDIA

GENERAL

There are numerous general works but many are now out-of-date. A generally fair-minded study is that of P. E. Roberts, *History of British India* (3d ed.; Oxford, 1952). The third edition of the *Oxford History of India* (Oxford, 1958) has a new British section covering half the book written by Percival Spear. This is now available separately as the *Oxford History of Modern India, 1740–1947* (Oxford, 1965). The imperialist point of view is well put by Sir A. Lyall in his *British Dominion in India* (3d ed.; London, 1894). The *Cambridge History of India* covers the period in vols. V and VI. Some of this work is excellent, but vol. VI overstresses the administrative and underestimates the national and cultural sides. The best Indian general work so far is Part III of the *History of India* by Majumdar, Raychaudhuri, and Datta. E. Thompson and G. T. Garratt's *Rise and Fulfilment of British Rule in India* (London, 1934) is original and stimulating.

A standard early work is that of James Mill, *History of British India* to 1805. It was continued to 1835 by H. H. Wilson and reached its fifth edition in 10 volumes in 1858.

For the cultural clash see *Modern India and the West,* ed. by L. S. S. O'Malley (Oxford, 1941). A valuable introductory sketch is *India* (London, 1949) by C. H. Philips.

For further works and original sources consult the full bibliographies of the *Cambridge History of India.* See also *History and Culture of the Indian People,* edited by R. C. Majumdar and A. D. Pusalker, vol. IX, part 1, *British Paramountcy and Indian Renaissance* (Bombay, 1963).

XVI. BRITISH AND FRENCH

Robert Orme, *History of the Military Transactions of the British Nation in Indostan,* 3 vols. (4th ed.; London, 1803), provides a classic and first-hand account. H. H. Dodwell's *Dupleix and Clive* (London, 1920) is an outstanding modern work, while the writings of both Dodwell and P. E. Roberts in the *Cambridge History* and Roberts'

History are authoritative. For the French A. Martineau, *Dupleix et l'Inde Française,* 4 vols. (Paris, 1920–28), is a standard work. For Indian India see J. Sarkar's work already mentioned.

XVII.   BENGAL

Robert Orme gives a near-contemporary account of Clive in Bengal while the *Siyar-ul-Mutaqherin* is invaluable on the Indian side. Dodwell's treatment of Clive in Bengal in his *Dupleix and Clive* is detailed and authoritative, and P. E. Roberts' work on this period is also valuable. The English background of corruption and intrigue can be studied in Lucy Sutherland's *East India Company in Eighteenth-century Politics* (Oxford, 1952). A good biography of Clive is by A. M. Davies, *Clive of Plassey* (London, 1939). Indian monographs are now beginning to appear of which those on *Mir Jafar* by A. C. Roy (1953) and *Mir Kasim* by N. L. Chatterji (1935) may be mentioned. On the economic side see N. K. Sinha, *Economic History of Bengal* (Calcutta, 1956), and Sir W. W. Hunter, *Annals of Rural Bengal* (London, 1871). For Siraj-ad-Daula see B. K. Gupta's *Sirajuddaulah and the East India Company* (The Hague, 1962).

XVIII.   THE COMPANY BAHADUR

An admirable study of the Company is Holden Furber's *John Company at Work* (Cambridge, Mass., 1948). The last stand of Mughal administration is described by A. M. Khan in *The Transition of Bengal, 1756–1775* (Cambridge, 1969), an able study of M. Reza Khan.

For Clive's second governorship see Dodwell in his *Dupleix and Clive.* Verelst is dealt with in N. L. Chatterji's *Verelst's Rule in India* (Allahabad, 1939). Warren Hastings' early reforms are described by M. E. Monckton-Jones in *Warren Hastings in Bengal* (Oxford, 1918). There is a weighty modern study of Hastings by Keith Feiling (Oxford, 1954) and a good biography by A. M. Davies (London, 1935), but he continues to draw controversy as iron attracts the lightning. P. E. Roberts is perhaps the best modern authority on Hastings, whom he admired with discrimination. For Cornwallis consult A. Aspinall, *Cornwallis in Bengal* (Manchester, 1931), and C. Ross (ed.), *The Cornwallis Correspondence,* 3 vols. (1859).

For Calcutta at this time see W. E. Busteed, *Echoes of Old Calcutta* (4th ed.; 1908), a charming book. For English social life H. H. Dodwell, *The Nabobs of Madras* (London, 1926), T. G. P. Spear, *The Nabobs* (Oxford, 1932), and W. Hickey, *Memoirs,* 4 vols. (London, 1933).

For the London background see Lucy Sutherland as before, and C. H. Philips, *The East India Company* (Manchester, 1940).

For constitutional matters Sir C. Ilbert, *The Government of India* (London, 1916), is authoritative.

XIX.   THE ROAD TO SUPREMACY

A general guide can be found in Mill's *History,* in P. E. Roberts'

History of British India and in the *Oxford History of India*. A fuller narrative is to be found in the *Cambridge History,* vol. V, with full bibliographies. There is a study of Wellesley by P. E. Roberts, *India under Wellesley* (London, 1929). Holden Furber has contributed two valuable studies, *Indian Governor-Generalship—The Private Record of Sir John Shore* (Cambridge, Mass., 1953) and *H. Dundas, 1st Viscount Melville* (1931). H. G. Keene, *Hindustan under the Freelances* (London, 1907), is of great interest. E. Thompson, in the *Making of the Indian Princes* (Oxford, 1943), catches the excitement of the British forward school of the time. For the final episode H. T. Prinsep, *History of the Political and Military Transactions in India During the Administration of the Marquess of Hastings,* 2 vols. (London, 1825), is a standard work.

XX. INDIA IN 1818

A good general description is by Bishop R. Heber, *Narrative of a Journey etc.,* 2 vols. (London, 1828), who toured in 1824–25. More detail may be found in the reports of the great "politicals" of the day. The best are Sir J. Malcolm, *A Memoir of C. India,* 2 vols. (London, 1832), M. Elphinstone, *Report on the Territories Recently Acquired from the Peshwa* (London, 1822), and R. Jenkins, *Report on the Territories of Nagpur* (1827). Tod deals with Rajasthan.

For the state of Hinduism see Abbé J. A. Dubois, *Hindu Manners and Customs* . . . (3rd ed.; Oxford, 1906), remembering that his knowledge was limited to the south, and the writings of Ram Mohan Roy; for popular Islam, G. A. Herklots, *Islam in India* (new ed.; Oxford, 1928), and for Thuggee, Sir W. H. Sleeman, *Report . . . on Thug Gangs,* . . . (Calcutta, 1840), and Meadows-Taylor, *Confessions of a Thug* (London, 1839, and Oxford, 1933).

XXI. THE NEW GOVERNMENT

There is a good summary of the administrative development in the *Montagu-Chelmsford Report,* vol. I (London, 1918), and a good pre-Mutiny study by J. W. Kaye, *The Administration of the East India Co.* (London, 1853). The administrative chapters of the *Cambridge History,* vols. V and VI, will take the reader into further detail with full bibliographies.

B. H. Baden-Powell produced a standard work on land systems, 3 vols. (1892), and there is a summary in one volume (1894). W. K. Firminger's edition of the *Fifth Report to the House of Commons 1812,* 3 vols. (1917) is also a standard work.

For the part played by the civil service see two well-written volumes by Philip Woodruff, the *Founders* and the *Guardians* (London, 1953–54).

For the attitude of local Indian officials to British control, in one part of India, see the striking study by R. E. Frykenberg, *The Guntur District, 1788–1848* (Oxford, 1965).

XXII.　THE COMPLETION OF DOMINION

Apart from the general authorities already cited the following are suggested. J. W. Kaye, *History of the War in Afghanistan,* 3 vols. (London, 1851), remains a standard authority. M. Elphinstone's *Account of the Kingdom of Cabaul* (London, 1815) makes a good starting point for the Afghans. Reference works are Sir P. Sykes, *History of Persia,* 2 vols. (London, 1920), and *History of Afghanistan,* 2 vols. (London, 1940).

For Nepal see P. Landon, *History of Nepal,* 2 vols. (London, 1928), and J. Pemble, *The Invasion of Nepal* (Oxford, 1971). For the Sikhs K. Singh's *The Sikhs* (London, 1953) is the best introduction. J. D. Cunningham, *History of the Sikhs* (new ed.; Oxford, 1918), is an accepted classic. The standard work on the Sikh religion is M. A. Macauliffe's *Sikh Religion,* 6 vols. (London, 1909). For origins see the important new work by W. H. McLeod, *Guru Nanak and the Sikh Religion* (Oxford, 1969). For Sind H. T. Lambrick's *Sir Charles Napier and Sind* (Oxford, 1952) is authoritative.

XXIII.　THE NEW POLICY

There is no full study of Bentinck yet. The reader may consult H. H. Wilson in vol. IX of Mill and Wilson's *History of India,* 10 vols. (5th ed.; London, 1858). K. S. Ballhatchet, in *Social Policy and Social Change in Western India, 1817–30* (London, 1957), deals with Elphinstone's contribution. E. Stokes, in his striking *English Utilitarians and India* (Oxford, 1959), traces the influence of Utilitarian ideas. The Evangelical influence can be studied in Sir R. Coupland's *Wilberforce* (2d ed.; London, 1945) and that of the missionaries in K. Ingham's *Reformers in India* (Cambridge, 1956). For reference there is K. S. Latourette's *History of the Expansion of Christianity,* 7 vols. (New York, 1938–45). For a general treatment see L. S. S. O'Malley's *India and the West* already mentioned. See also studies of Ram Mohan Roy by N. C. Ganguly (Calcutta, 1936) and Amal Home (Calcutta, 1933) and his *English Works,* ed. by K. Nag and D. Burman, 6 parts (Calcutta, 1945–51). See also S. D. Collett's *Life and Letters of Raja Ram Mohan Roy,* 3rd edition, ed. by D. K. Biswas and P. C. Ganguli (Calcutta, 1962), and "Class, Caste and Politics in Calcutta," by S. N. Mukherjee in *Elites in South Asia,* ed. by E. Leach and S. N. Mukherjee (Cambridge, 1970). The humanitarian approach can be studied in the works of Macaulay, especially his speeches and *Minute on Education;* see also C. E. Trevelyan's *Education of the People of India* (London, 1838).

XXIV.　DALHOUSIE AND THE MUTINY

For Dalhousie see the study by Sir W. W. Hunter (Oxford, 1905) in the *Rulers of India* series, the two-volume *Life* by Sir W. Lee Warner (London, 1904), and the *Private Letters of the Marquis of Dalhousie* (London, 1910), ed. by J. A. Baird. There is a two-volume study by

E. Arnold on *Dalhousie's Administration of British India* (London, 1861). For Canning see the study *Clemency Canning* (London, 1962) by M. Maclagan, using the Canning Papers.

For the Panjab see the *Lives* of John Lawrence by S. B. Smith, 2 vols. (3rd ed.; London, 1883) and of Henry Lawrence by J. L. Morrison (London, 1934). For the Indian states see Sir W. Lee Warner, *The Native States of India* (London, 1910).

A succinct account of the Mutiny is available in the *Cambridge History*, vol. V, with the usual bibliography. The best modern study is the judicious work of S. N. Sen, *1857* (Delhi, 1957). An exhaustive work is by J. W. Kaye and G. B. Malleson in 6 volumes (new ed.; London, 1897). E. Thompson's *Other Side of the Medal* (London, 1925) helps to correct perspective. Sir S. Ahmad Khan's *Causes of the Indian Revolt* (Benares, 1873) is an acute analysis by a contemporary Indian.

MODERN INDIA

XXV. THE NEW INDIA

For the modern period the reader should consult a most valuable documentary, *The Evolution of India and Pakistan, 1858–1947,* ed. by C. H. Philips (London, 1962). Three more volumes are planned covering the whole range of Indian history.

The *Cambridge History of India,* vol. VI, is good for administrative organization, specially Chap. XVIII on finance. The historical survey in Sir C. Ilbert's *Government of India* (London, 1922) is valuable for constitutional matters. *The History and Culture of the Indian People,* ed. by R. C. Majumdar, vols. IX and X (Bombay, 1963–   ), provides the standard Indian interpretation of the whole period to 1905.

For railways L. C. A. Knowles, *Economic Development of the British Overseas Empire* (London, 1924) is specially useful. For canals see D. G. Harris, *Irrigation in India* (London, 1923). For development generally Vera Anstey's *Economic Development of India* (3rd ed.; London, 1949) is a standard work. D. H. Buchanan in the *Development of Capitalist Enterprise in India* (New York, 1934) contributes a valuable American study, D. R. Gadgil's *The Industrial Evolution of India* (London, 1934) is an Indian one.

XXVI. THE MIND OF THE NEW INDIA

A useful general work for this subject is L. S. S. O'Malley's *Modern India and the West* already mentioned. For education C. E. Trevelyan's book mentioned above (Ch. XXIII) gives the reformers' views and expectations. A. Mayhew's *Education of India* (London, 1926) is a sober account of actual achievements.

For religious movements Devendranath Tagore's *Autobiography* (London, 1914) will be found interesting. The works of Romain Rolland and Sister Nivedita on Ramkrishna and Vivekananda are attractive and weighty. The *Lives* of Ram Mohan Roy mentioned earlier should also be consulted. The best work in English is J. N. Farquhar's

Modern Religious Movements in India (New York, 1918). The reader should not be deterred by an attack on theosophy in the center of the book. J. C. Smith deals with the Muslim side in his *Modern Islam in India* (London, 1946). For Muslims see also G. F. I. Graham, *Sir Syed Ahmad Khan* (1909). N. C. Chaudhuri, in describing his early life in Bengal, *The Diary of an Unknown Indian* (London, 1951), gives a brilliant and moving account of the thought processes involved.

XXVII. THE NEW CLASS AND THE NEW PARTY

A basic work is B. B. Misra's *The Indian Middle Classes* (London, 1961), supported by A. Seal's *The Emergence of Indian Nationalism* (Cambridge, 1968). Something can also be found in *Modern India and the West* and V. Chirol's *India* (London, 1926). Autobiographies of eminent Indians as yet are few: but S. N. Bannerjee's *A Nation in the Making* (London, 1925) is outstanding for the early days. A good sketch is by C. F. Andrews and A. Mukerji, *The Rise and Growth of Congress in India* (1938). The following are also useful: Sir H. Cotton, *New India* (London, 1885), Sir W. Wedderburn, *A. O. Hume* (London, 1913), H. P. Mody, *Sir Pheroseshah Mehta* (1927), and B. C. Pal, *Memories of My Life and Time* (1932).

For the foundation of Congress see P. Sitaramaya's *History of the National Congress,* 2 vols. (Allahabad, 1946).

XXVIII. NATIONALISTS AND GOVERNMENT, 1885–1905

A basic authority for Congress is P. Sitaramaya's book, but he is disappointingly brief in the early years. Andrews and Mukerji's book is useful here and so are the biographies mentioned under the last chapter. Bannerjee is specially useful for Bengal. The best guide to Congress is the reports of the sessions. British policy is ably surveyed by S. Gopal, *British Policy in India, 1858–1905* (Cambridge, 1965).

S. Gopal has written a thoughtful study on *The Viceroyalty of Lord Ripon* based on papers recently released for study (London, 1953) and Lord Ronaldshay devoted vol. II of his *Life of Lord Curzon* (London, 1928) to his viceroyalty. Lovat Fraser's *India under Curzon* (London, 1911) is a useful account of Curzon's measures.

The little work of H. H. Dodwell, *A Sketch of the History of India, 1858–1918* (London, 1925), contains much insight as well as authority and incisiveness.

XXIX. PORTENTS OF THE NEW INDIA

For Morley see J. Morley, *Recollections,* 2 vols. (London, 1917) and *Speeches on Indian Affairs* (London, 1909). For Minto see Mary, Countess of Minto, *India, Minto and Morley* (London, 1934), a valuable collection of papers. See also S. R. Wasti, *Lord Minto and the Indian Nationalist Movement* (Oxford, 1964), M. H. Das, *India under Morley and Minto* (London & New York, 1964), and S. Wolpert, *Morley and India, 1906–1910* (California, 1967). Hardinge's papers are now available for his viceroyalty, and we have his *My*

Indian Years (London, 1948). For the Congress side see S. N. Bannerjee, *A Nation in Making* (London, 1925), A. Besant, *How India Wrought for Freedom* (London, 1915), D. V. Tahmankar, *Lokmanya Tilak* (London, 1956), and P. Sitaramaya's work. See also S. Wolpert, *Tilak and Gokhale* (California, 1962).

The Act of 1909 is best dealt with by Sir Courtenay Ilbert.

XXX.   INDIA IN WORLD AFFAIRS, 1858–1914

There are chapters of high quality in the *Cambridge History,* vol. VI by H. H. Dodwell on Central Asia and G. E. Harvey on Burma. Bisheshwar Prasad is producing a four-volume history on *The Foundations of India's Foreign Policy.* Vol. I, so far the only one published (London, 1956), covers the years 1860–82. A. Lamb, has ably studied Indo-Chinese relations in *Britain and Chinese Central Asia* (London, 1960). C. N. Parkinson has dealt with Malaya in the *British in Malaya* (London, 1960). See also S. R. Mehrotra, *India and the Commonwealth* (London, 1965).

Afghanistan is covered by Dodwell's chapter, but contemporary fears can be judged from Sir H. Rawlinson's *England and Russia in the Far East* (London, 1878). For Afghan and Persian affairs see the works of Sir P. Sykes already mentioned. The Amir Abdurrahman's *Autobiography* in two volumes was published in 1900.

The northwest frontier is dealt with by C. C. Davies in his *Problem of the North-West Frontier* (Cambridge, 1932).

XXXI.   WORLD WAR I IN INDIA: THE GREAT DIVIDE

The reader will find a good picture of pre-1914 India from the official standpoint in *The India We Served* by Sir W. R. Lawrence (London, 1928). The same viewpoint through World War I (with a Panjab twist) is provided by Sir M. O'Dwyer's *India as I Knew It* (London, 1925). For India's part in the war the government publication, *India's Contribution to the Great War* (Calcutta, 1923), may be consulted. See also the independent *The Empire at War,* vol. V, by Sir C. Lucas, and Sir J. Willcock's *With the Indians in France* (London, 1920).

For internal affairs Hardinge's concise *My Indian Years* (1948) finds a vivid successor in E. S. Montagu's *An Indian Diary* (London, 1930). The nationalist side will be found in Sitaramaya's work already quoted, in A. Besant's *How India Wrought for Freedom* (London, 1915), in S. N. Bannerjee's work, and in Tilak's *Writings and Speeches* (Bombay, 1922). Good background works are J. Cumming's *Political India* (London, 1932) and Sir V. Chirol's *India* (London, 1926).

For the events leading up to Amritsar, and Amritsar itself, see the two government reports, *The Rowlatt Report* (London, 1918, Cmd. 9190) and *The Hunter Committee's Report* (London, 1920, Cmd. 681).

XXXII.   NONCO-OPERATION AND REFORM

Summaries of the nonco-operation period can be found in V. Chirol's *India* (London, 1926) and in *The History and Culture of the Indian People,* vol. XI, *The Struggle for Freedom.* S. N. Bannerjee in his *A Nation in Making* describes the scene from an Indian Liberal's point of view. D. V. Tahmankar in his *Lokomanya Tilak* deals with Tilak's part and his relations with Gandhi. For Gandhi himself reference should now be made to vol. II of his *Experiments with Truth.* Sitaramaya's *History of the Congress* is again vital. The early pages of M. Brecher's *Nehru* and Nehru's *Autobiography* are also useful. See also Judith M. Brown, *Gandhi in India, 1915–1922* (Cambridge, 1972), and S. D. Waley, *Edwin Montagu* (London, 1964).

For the reforms see first the *Montagu-Chelmsford Report* (London, 1918, Cmd. 9109) and read in conjunction Montagu's diary listed under the last chapter. The idea of dyarchy was expounded by L. Curtis in *Dyarchy* (London, 1920). A good summary of the new constitution was produced by E. A. Horne in *The Political System of British India* (London, 1922).

XXXIII.   MAHATMA

For Gandhi the basic works are his own *Autobiography, The Story of My Experiments with Truth,* first published at Ahmedabad in 1927, and D. G. Tendulkar's *Mahatma* in eight volumes (Bombay, 1952). The first important *Life* was a joint work by H. S. L. Polak, H. N. Brailsford, and Lord Pethwick-Lawrence (London, 1949). The first part by Polak, covering the South African period, is the best. Louis Fischer, who was in India during World War II, provides an American interpretation in his *Life* (New York, 1950) and another thoughtful study is by M. Bondurant, *The Conquest of Violence* (Princeton, N. J., 1959). C. F. Andrews provided useful summaries in *Mahatma Gandhi's Ideas* (London, 1929) and *Mahatma Gandhi at Work* (London, 1931). E. Morton's *The Women Behind Mahatma Gandhi* (London, 1954) deals with an important side of his character. For the full record we have *The Collected Works of Mahatma Gandhi,* now running into many volumes.

XXXIV.   THE TWENTIES

For the working of the new constitution a useful summary can be found in Sir J. Cumming's *Political India* already mentioned. J. Coatman in *Years of Destiny* (London, 1932) provides a commentary from the British angle, while Kerala Putra (K. M. Panikkar) gives an acute Indian criticism in the *Working of Dyarchy in India* (London, 1928). On the political side Sitaramaya's work is now basic. Jawaharlal Nehru's *Autobiography* throws sidelights from the standpoint of ardent youth. M. Brecher's *Nehru* is very valuable from the time of the appointment of the Simon Commission. President Rajendra Prasad's *Autobiography* (Bombay, 1957) and Maulana Abul Kalam Azad's *India Wins Freedom* (New York, 1960) begin to be important. For the non-Congress Panjab the work of Azim Husain on his father *Fazl-i-Husain* (London, 1946) is valuable. B. Chaturvedi and M. Sykes,

C. F. Andrews (London, 1949), is also useful.

Government reports to be noted are the *Muddiman Committee Report* on the working of the reforms (1925) and the *Agricultural (Linlithgow) Commission Report* (1928).

There is little original material from the London end, but the lives of Lord Reading and Lord Birkenhead may be consulted.

XXXV.   THE NATIONAL STRUGGLE, 1929–1934

First should be noticed certain state papers. These are the *Nehru Report* (1928), the Congress reply to the Simon Commission, the *Simon Commission Report* (London, 1930, Cmd. 3568–9), the *Report of the First Round Table Conference* (London, 1931), and the *Communal Award* (London, Cmd. 4147). Vol. I of Sir M. Gwyer and A. Appadorai's *Speeches and Documents on the Indian Constitution* (London, 1957) should also be consulted.

A good deal of personal testimony and work based on original material is also available. Examples are the works of Rajendra Prasad, Maulana Azad, and of Azim Husain on Fazl-i-Husain already mentioned. To these may be added Jawaharlal Nehru's *Autobiography,* now an important source, the memoirs of Lord Halifax, *Fullness of Days* (London, 1957), and Lord Templewood (Sir S. Hoare). Tendulkar provides original material for Gandhi; M. Brecher's *Nehru* is now an important source based on original material, as is S. Gopal's study of *Lord Irwin* (Oxford, 1957). For Patel see N. D. Parikh *Sardar Vallabhbhai Patel* (Ahmedabad, 1953). See also Lord Birkenhead's *Life of Lord Halifax* (London, 1965), which deals fully with his years in India.

For the Congress Sitaramaya may be used and the *Reports* of the annual sessions consulted (Allahabad, 1918–). The *Indian Annual Register,* ed. N. N. Mitra (Calcutta, 1920–47), is a useful work of reference. Sir R. Coupland, in vol. I of his *Constitutional Report,* provides a lucid summary of the period. M. R. Masani in his *Communist Party of India* (London, 1954), deals with that party's activities in the early thirties.

XXXVI.   THE 1935 ACT, THEORY AND PRACTICE

The 1935 Act is well summarized by Sir R. Coupland in vol. I of his *Report on the Constitutional Problem in India* (London, 1943). Extracts from the Act and related documentation will be found in vol. I of Gwyer and Appadorai's *Speeches and Documents* (1957). P. Eddy and F. H. Lawson published a legal commentary in *India's New Constitution* (London, 1935). The autobiographies and works on Nehru and Patel cited in the last chapter hold good for this one: see particularly M. Brecher's *Nehru* for the struggle between right and left wings in Congress during the thirties. The course of events may be followed in the *Indian Annual Register* and *Reports* of Congress sessions already mentioned. There is a valuable summary of the course of politics in 1936–42 in vol. II of Coupland's *Constitutional Report.*

M. H. Saiyed's *M. A. Jinnah* (Lahore, 1943) and H. Bolitho's *Jinnah* (London, 1954) are perhaps the best for the Muslim side. The former is tendentious, the latter an acute character study. A valuable commentary on the British position is by G. Wint, *The British in Asia* (2d ed.; London, 1955).

XXXVII. WORLD WAR II

An *Official History of the Indian Armed Forces During Second World War, 1939–45* is being prepared under the direction of Bisheshwar Prasad. Five volumes are now available (New York: Longmans, Green, 1960). G. W. Tyson, in *Indian Arms for Victory* (2d ed.; Allahabad, 1944), provides a useful summary.

The second volume of *The Coupland Report* goes up to the rebellion of 1942. It also contains the text of the Congress constitution as revised in 1939 (Appendix I) and the Congress Declaration of Fundamental Rights (Appendix V). The *Annual Register* continues until 1947. Brecher's *Nehru* has great authority for this period. The works dealing with Gandhi, Patel, Azad Prasad, and Jinnah are also important. The papers of the Cripps Mission of 1942 were published in *Lord Privy Seal's Mission, Statement and Draft Declaration* (London, 1942, Cmd. 6350). The Government of India published *Correspondence with Mr. Gandhi, Aug. 1942–April 1944* (Delhi, 1944). The government put its case about the 1942 disturbances in a pamphlet called the *Congress Revolt,* while the All-India Satyagraha Council replied with *Report on the August Struggle* (n.d., c. 1945). At the London end the *Life of R. S. Cripps* by C. A. Cooke (London, 1957) and the forthcoming concluding volume of L. S. S. Amery's *My Political Life* (London, 1953–) are important. See also Gwyer and Appadorai's *Speeches and Documents,* vol. II. Lord Linlithgow's record is defended by his son, Lord Glendevon, in *The Viceroy at Bay* (London, 1971).

XXXVIII. THE TRANSFER OF POWER

The most important official documents are the following: *Statement of Policy of H.M. Government* (1945, Cmd. 6652), *Statement by the Cabinet Mission and the Viceroy* (1946, Cmd. 6821), *Correspondence etc. Between the Cabinet Mission, Congress and League* (1946, Cmd. 6829), *Statement by the Mission* (1946, Cmd. 6835), dated 25 May.

These and other documents are to be found in vol. II of Gwyer and Appadorai's *Speeches and Documents.* An excellent summary of events is E. W. R. Lumby's *Transfer of Power in India* (London, 1954). The inner Congress history is best given by M. Brecher in his *Nehru* and a first-hand account of the Indo-British negotiations is by V. P. Menon in his *Transfer of Power in India* (Princeton, N.J., 1957). A. Campbell-Johnson provides a vivid account of the final stages in *Mission with Mountbatten* (London, 1951). A first-hand description of the Bengal riots is given by Sir F. Tuker in *While Memory Serves* (London, 1950).

Pakistan: I. H. Qureshi's *History of the Muslim Community in India*

(New York, 1961) is a learned background study. The cultural background is dealt with by S. M. Ikram and T. G. P. Spear (eds.), *Cultural Heritage of Pakistan* (Karachi, 1955). An informative though tendentious approach is by W. C. Smith, *Modern Islam in India* (London, 1946). For the modern movement see G. F. I. Graham, *Sir Syed Ahmad Khan* (London, 1909). W. W. Hunter has dealt with the position of the Muslims in the nineteenth century in his *Indian Mussulmans* (London, 1876). For Iqbal see *Secrets of the Self,* tr. R. A. Nicholson (London, 1920) and the *Reconstruction of Religious Thought in Islam* (London, 1934).

A. H. Alberuni in *Makers òf Pakistan* (Lahore, 1950) has contributed useful studies of prominent leaders. The books on Jinnah by Bolitho and Saiyad trace his build-up of the League. Finally there may be mentioned a dispassionate study by R. A. Symonds, *The Making of Pakistan* (London, 1950).

Recent Publications: Publication of a comprehensive series of selected documents is now proceeding. The series is entitled *The Transfer of Power 1942–1947,* ed. by N. Mansergh and E. W. R. Lumby. Three volumes have been published and several more are expected at roughly annual intervals. Those published are: I. *The Cripps Mission* (London, 1970); II. *"Quit India"* (London, 1971); III. *Reassertion of Authority* (London, 1971).

C. H. Philips and M. D. Wainwright have edited a series of papers entitled *The Partition of India, Policies and Perspectives, 1935–1947* (London, 1970). A distinguished work by an observer and sometime participant is H. V. Hodson's *The Great Divide* (London, 1969). Dr. I. H. Quereshi has written an account of the transfer from the Pakistani point of view in *The Struggle for Pakistan* (Karachi, 1965).

XXXIX. INDEPENDENCE AND CONSOLIDATION

There is a good general survey, specially on the economic side, by Sir P. J. Griffiths in *Modern India* (London, 1957). See also A. Gledhill, *The Republic of India* (London, 1951). For these years as a whole M. Brecher's *Nehru* is a primary authority.

The Partition massacres are described in an Indian government White Paper. The author's view on responsibility for them will be found in "Britain's Transfer of Power in India," *Pacific Affairs* (vol. XXXI, no. 2, June, 1958). A vivid picture of New Delhi at the time of the take-over and Gandhi's death is given by M. Bourke-White, *Interview with India* (London, 1950).

Patel's integration of the Indian princes is described by V. P. Menon, who carried it through, in the *Integration of the Indian States* (Princeton, N.J., 1956). For tension between Nehru, Patel, and Gandhi, Brecher's *Nehru,* Parikh's *Patel,* and Tendulkar's *Mahatma* should be consulted.

The text of the constitution is available in a Government of India publication with amendments up to 1956. For comment see G. N. Joshi's *The Constitution of India* (3rd ed.; London, 1954) and Sir Ivor

Jennings' *Some Characteristics of the Indian Constitution* (London, 1952). W. H. Morris-Jones in *Parliament in India* (London, 1957) has made a valuable study of the first few years of Indian parliamentarianism. The revised *Constitution of the Indian National Congress* (1953), with amendments up to 1957, has been published in Delhi.

An interesting account of the early years of the new state will be found in Chester Bowles, *Ambassador's Report* (New York, 1954).

Recent Publications: The following books may be recommended: G. Austin, *The Indian Constitution* (Oxford, 1966), a valuable study of the constitution-making process; and D. E. Smith, *India as a Secular State* (Princeton, 1967). There is a valuable general survey in a symposium edited by D. E. Smith, *South Asian Politics and Religion* (Princeton, 1966).

XL. NEHRU'S INDIA

On the subject of Nehru the reader should first consult Nehru himself in his autobiography, *Towards Freedom* (New York, 1941), *Glimpses of World History* (Allahabad, 1934–35), and *Discovery of India* (Calcutta, 1946). The standard work on Nehru, which is also a penetrating study, is Michael Brecher's *Nehru*. Frank Moraes in *Jawaharlal Nehru* (New York, 1956) did not have access to all Brecher's material, but his character analysis is acute and valuable as representing an Indian estimate.

For the recent years books are naturally scarce, but we are helped by the Government of India's continuance of the previous practice of holding enquiries on important issues and publishing reports as blue books. Other basic authorities are the official reports of debates in the *Lok* and *Rajya Sabhas* of the Indian Parliament and the *Reports* of the annual sessions of the Congress.

A good general survey up to 1957 is that of Sir P. J. Griffiths in his *Modern India* already cited.

The final steps in the integration of the old Indian states can be studied in the White Papers on Hyderabad (1948) and on the Indian States (1948 and 1950). For the organization of the federal states-system of India the *Report of the States Reorganisation Committee* (1955), of which Sardar K. M. Panikkar was a leading member, should be consulted. The linguistic aspect is dealt with in the Congress *Report of the Linguistic Provinces Committee* (1949). For the general language question see the government *Report of the Official Language Commission* (1957).

On the general elections there are two government reports (1955 and 1958) and an independent one by S. V. Kogekar and Richard L. Park (eds.) on the 1951–52 election (Bombay, 1956). For party politics see Myron Weiner's *Party Politics in India* (Princeton, N.J., 1957).

For the five-year plans see *Science and National Planning* (1958), an address by their intellectual parent P. C. Mahalanobis. Then there are the Planning Commission's two reports, the *First Five Year Plan* (1953) and the *Second Five Year Plan* (1956), and their statement *The New India* (New York, 1958).

It is much more difficult to find reliable information about social reform. There are government reports about the "scheduled castes." Taya Zinkin, an acute observer, gives valuable insight into social reform specially in the women's sphere in *Changing India* (London, 1958). The Ministry of Law in its pamphlets LD85, *The Law Relating to Hindu Marriages* (1956) and LD82, *The Law Relating to Hindu Succession* gives the gist of much recent legislation with regard to the "Hindu Code" or personal law.

With regard to Pakistan there is little written in India which is not polemical. R. A. Symonds, in the work already cited, gives an objective view of the early stages. Michael Brecher, *Struggle for Kashmir* (New York, 1953), and Josef Korbel in *Danger in Kashmir* (Princeton) have provided two objective external studies of the Kashmir problem.

In foreign affairs the publications of the Indian Council of World Affairs are of value. See K. P. Karunakaran, *India in World Affairs 1947–50* (Bombay, 1952) and *1950–53* (Bombay, 1958). For Communism in India the reader can find the Communist viewpoint expounded by R. Palme Dutt in *India Today* (London, 1940). In addition to M. R. Masani's book already mentioned G. D. Overstreet and Marshall Windmiller's *Communism in India* (Berkeley, Cal., 1959) should be consulted.

Recent Publications: For Kashmir see Sisir Gupta's *Kashmir, a Study in India-Pakistan Relations* (London, 1966), a very able pro-Indian study. A foil to this is G. W. Choudhry's *Pakistan's Relations with India, 1947–1966* (London, 1968). For relations with China three works may be mentioned: A. Lamb, *The McMahon Line*, 2 vols. (London and Toronto, 1966); A. Lamb, *The China-India Border: Origins of the Disputed Boundaries* (London, 1964); and N. Maxwell, *India's China War* (London, 1970). The first and third are detailed, the second concise and general. All are very able and all are considered controversial in different quarters.

For internal affairs H. L. Erdman deals with Indian conservatism in *The Swatantra Party and Indian Conservatism* (Cambridge, 1967), while Francine L. Frankel has written a study in *The Green Revolution* (Princeton, 1971). For the succession to Nehru and Shastri see M. Brecher's valuable study *Succession in India* (London and Toronto, 1966).

The following general works may also be mentioned. C. H. Heimsath has made a valuable general study of *Indian Nationalism and Hindu Social Reform* (Princeton, 1964). Gunnar Myrdal's three-volume *Enquiry into the Poverty of Nations* (London, 1968) has been much discussed. In the cultural field there is R. Lannoy's reflective and original work *The Speaking Tree: a Study of Indian Culture and Society* (London and New York, 1971). Finally, there is *Modern India: an Interpretative Anthology* (London and New York, 1971), an attractive collection edited by T. R. Metcalf.

AHIMSA *Literally* nonviolence. Used negatively by Mahatma Gandhi to describe his political tactics and positively to express his doctrine of moral or spiritual force as the dominant principle of life.

AKALI *Literally* followers of the Timeless One (*Akal*). Description of a class of armed devotees among the Sikhs. Today it is applied to a Sikh political organization.

AMIR *Literally* lord. Used as both name and title and to denote a member of the Mughal official nobility.

AVATAR Incarnation of a deity. Vishnu has had nine forms including Krishna and Rama, with a tenth to come.

BAHADUR *Literally* warrior or hero. Used as a name and title and as a general name for a prominent as well as a valiant person.

BEG A Turkish word for chief or leader. Used of Babur's followers.

BHAKTI Religious devotion to a deity. Such cults of Hindu deities are an important part of popular Hindu religion.

CHAUTH *Literally* one-fourth. The fourth part of the revenue claimed by Marathas when they overran but did not annex a district.

DACOIT Member of a robber gang.

DARSHAN *Literally* seeing. The beholding of saints, kings, and other distinguished persons was thought to confer merit.

DAR-UL-ISLAM *Literally* House of peace. A country ruled by Muslims.

DAR-UL-HARB *Literally* House of war. A non-Muslim country.

DASTAK A permit or passport. In early days of the Company the permit authorizing free transit of goods.

DHARMA Moral duty or virtue.

DHIMMI Non-Muslim under a Muslim government who paid a tax in return for protection.

DIWALI Hindu festival of lights commemorating Rama's homecoming after defeating Ravan and rescuing Sita. Held on the dark day of the moon in October.

DIWAN Court or tribunal. Title of the chief revenue officer of a state or province.

DIWANI Relating to the revenue administration.

DURBAR The court of a king or a man of rank. Also used as a synonym for government.

FARMAN A royal mandate or ordinance.

GURU Hindu religious teacher or spiritual guide.

HARTAL Suspension of work or business as a mark of indignation.

HEGIRA Flight of the Prophet Muhammad from Mecca in 622 A.D. from which the Muslim era is dated.

HOLI The Hindu spring festival in the month of March.

JAGIR Assignment of land and its rent on varying conditions.

JAGIRDAR   Holder of a *jagir*.

JAN SANGH   A conservative and pro-Hindu party founded in 1949 by Dr. Shyam Prasad Mukherjee in place of the then discredited Mahasabha party which he had formerly led.

JIZYA   A personal tax imposed on non-Muslims by Muslim law.

KALI   Name of one of the forms of the consort of the Hindu god Shiva, in her aspect of destruction.

KARMA   An act or acts, and so the law of the consequences of every act.

KAYASTH   A mixed caste in North India whose traditional occupation is clerical and accounting work. Its members have been closely connected with government administration.

KHALSA   *Literally* pure, sincere. Best known as the collective designation of the Sikh government and people. Also land with no intermediate tax collector between government and cultivator.

KHAN   *Literally* lord. A noble title in Muslim times. Now much used as an adjunct of Muslim names.

KHAS   Select, private, privileged.

KHATTRI   A *Kayasth* of the Panjab.

KISAN   A peasant or cultivator, also known as a *ryot*.

LAC   One hundred thousand.

LOK SABHA   Council of the People, the popular chamber of the Central legislature under the constitution of 1950, elected by universal suffrage.

MAHALWARI   The revenue term used for the system by which estates or tracts of land are separately assessed for land revenue. The word distinguishes the system from the *zamindari* (settlement with a landlord) and the *ryotwari* (settlement with the individual cultivator) systems.

MANSABDAR   Holder of an official appointment or *mansab*. A member of the official Mughal nobility.

MANTRA   *Literally* a prayer. More specifically, forms of prayer used by Brahmin priests in Hindu religious ceremonies and often popularly regarded as having magical properties.

MAULVI   A master of Muslim law; a teacher, especially of Arabic.

MAYA   *Literally* illusion. The word is used in connection with the philosophic doctrine that external objects exist only in the imagination of the beholder.

MELA   An assemblage of all sizes with a fair and markets, usually connected with a religious festival.

MOFUSSIL   Colloquially used for country districts; the interior.

MOKSHA   Freedom in general, but especially freedom of the soul from rebirth.

NAWAB   *Plural* of *naib*, a deputy. Applied honorifically in late Mughal times to governors and then to men of high rank in general.

NIZAMAT   The administration of police and criminal law; the "law and order" sector of Mughal government.

NIZAM-UL-MULK   *Literally* administrator (or viceroy) of the country. The title of the ruler of Hyderabad state. The title was conferred by the Mughal emperor and retained by the Nizam after he had become independent of Delhi.

OMRAH   A collective word applied to the higher ranks of the Mughal official nobility.

PANCHAYAT   *Literally* a council of five persons. Term applied to the traditional village councils of rural India.

PANDIT   Title (feminine *pandita*) prefixed to members of the Brahmin caste.

PARGANA   A subdistrict, a number of which constitute a district or *sarkar*.

PESHWA   Originally the chief minister of the Maratha state. In the eighteenth century he became the head of the Maratha confederacy.

PUJA   Worship, adoration.

QAZI   A judge administering Muslim law. Under the British he advised in cases of Muslim law.

RAJ   Government or rule.

RAJYA SABHA   Council of the States, the upper chamber of the Central legislature, indirectly elected by the States' legislatures, and representing the federal principle.

RANI   *Feminine* of *raja*. A Hindu queen or princess.

RUMAL   A handkerchief or small cloth: used by the Thugs for strangling their victims.

RYOT   (Arabic *raiyat*) A cultivator. Cf. *Kisan*, its Hindi equivalent.

RYOTWARI   System of land revenue administration under which each cultivator's plot is separately measured and assessed.

SANNYASI   A Hindu who has renounced the world; a general term for a religious ascetic.

SAR-DESHMUKHI   A tenth of the revenues in addition to *chauth* or one quarter, exacted by Marathas from provinces which they plundered but did not annex.

SARKAR   An administrative district under the Mughals.

SIJDAH   Prostration customary in Muslim worship and exacted by Emperor Akbar from his nobles.

STUPA   A Buddhist shrine with a solid core usually containing sacred relics.

SUBADAR   Governor of a Mughal *suba* or province. Under the British, a subordinate Indian officer.

SWATANTRA PARTY   A right-wing party of property and industrial interests without the communal color of the Jan Sangh, formed in 1959 by C. Rajagopalachari of Madras, K. M. Munshi, and others. See H. L. Erdman's *The Swatantra Party and Indian Conservatism* (Cambridge, 1967).

THUGS   Ritual murderers who strangled travelers as a religious act, concealed their bodies, and appropriated their goods.

VARNA   *Literally* color in Sanskrit and thence used to denote caste.

ZAMINDAR   Landlord, or landholder. In Bengal *zamindars* were originally hereditary tax collectors. The British turned them into landlords, often great proprietors. In the northwest they were small freeholders.

INDEX